SACRAMENTUM MUNDI

VOLUME SIX: SCANDAL — ZIONISM

SACRAMENTUM MUNDI

An Encyclopedia of Theology

Edited by

Karl Rahner SJ, Münster
and
Juan Alfaro SJ, Rome
Alberto Bellini, Bergamo
Carlo Colombo, Venegono
Henri Crouzel SJ, Toulouse
Jean Cardinal Daniélou SJ, Paris
Adolf Darlap, Munich
Cornelius Ernst OP, Oxford
José Fondevilla SJ, Barcelona
Piet Fransen, Louvain
Fergus Kerr OP, Oxford
Piet Schoonenberg, Nijmegen
Kevin Smyth, Paris
† Gustave Weigel SJ, Woodstock

Published by Herder and Herder New York · Burns & Oates London · Palm Publishers
Montreal · Herder Freiburg · Éditions Desclée de Brouwer Bruges · Editorial Herder
Barcelona · Edizioni Morcelliana Brescia · Paul Brand Hilversum

SACRAMENTUM MUNDI

AN ENCYCLOPEDIA OF THEOLOGY

VOLUME SIX

SCANDAL

TO

ZIONISM

HERDER AND HERDER

1970
HERDER AND HERDER
232 Madison Avenue, New York, N.Y. 10016

BURNS & OATES LIMITED
25 Ashley Place, London S.W. 1

General Editor: Adolf Darlap

Library of Congress Catalog Card Number: 68–25987
First published in West Germany © 1970, Herder KG
Printed in West Germany by Herder

ABBREVIATIONS

The following list does not include biblical and other well-known abbreviations.
Whenever an author, not listed below, is cited in an article by name only, followed by page number(s), the reference is to a work listed in the bibliography at the end of the article.

AAS	*Acta Apostolicae Sedis* (1909 ff.)
ACW	J. Quasten and J. C. Plumpe, *Ancient Christian Writers* (1946 ff.)
Billerbeck	(H. L. Strack and) P. Billerbeck, *Kommentar zum Neuen Testament aus Talmud und Midrasch,* I–IV (1922–28; reprint, 1956), V: rabbinical index, ed. by J. Jeremias and K. Adolph (1956)
CBQ	*Catholic Biblical Quarterly* (1939 ff.)
Chalkedon	A. Grillmeier and H. Bacht, eds., *Das Konzil von Chalkedon, Geschichte und Gegenwart,* 3 vols. (1951–54; 2nd enlarged ed., 1962)
CIC	*Codex Iuris Canonici*
CIO	*Codex Iuris Canonici Orientalis* (Unless stated otherwise, the references are to the law relating to persons.)
Collectio Lacensis	*Collectio Lacensis: Acta et Decreta Sacrorum Conciliorum Recentiorum,* ed. by the Jesuits of Maria Laach, 7 vols. (1870–90)
CSEL	*Corpus Scriptorum Ecclesiasticorum Latinorum* (1866 ff.)
D	H. Denzinger, *Enchiridion Symbolorum, Definitionum et Declarationum de Rebus Fidei et Morum* (31st ed., 1957); see also *DS*
DB	F. Vigouroux, ed., *Dictionnaire de la Bible,* 5 vols. (1895–1912)
DBS	L. Pirot, ed., *Dictionnaire de la Bible, Supplément,* continued by A. Robert (1928 ff.)
DS	H. Denzinger and A. Schönmetzer, *Enchiridion Symbolorum, Definitionum et Declarationum de Rebus Fidei et Morum* (33rd ed., 1965); see also *D*
DSAM	M. Viller, ed., *Dictionnaire de Spiritualité ascétique et mystique. Doctrine et Histoire* (1932 ff.)
DTC	A. Vacant and E. Mangenot, eds., *Dictionnaire de théologie catholique,* continued by É. Amann, I–XV, *Table analytique* and *Tables générales,* XVI ff. (1903 ff.)

V

ABBREVIATIONS

Enchiridion Biblicum	*Enchiridion Biblicum. Documenta Ecclesiastica Sacram Scripturam Spectantia* (3rd ed., 1956)
ETL	*Ephemerides Theologicae Lovanienses* (1924 ff.)
GCS	*Die griechischen christlichen Schriftsteller der ersten drei Jahrhunderte* (1897 ff.)
Hennecke-Schneemelcher-Wilson	E. Hennecke, W. Schneemelcher and R. McL. Wilson, eds., *New Testament Apocrypha,* 2 vols. (1963–65)
HERE	J. Hastings, ed., *Encyclopedia of Religion and Ethics,* 12 vols. + index (1908–26; 2nd rev. ed., 1925–40)
JBL	*Journal of Biblical Literature* (1881 ff.)
JTS	*Journal of Theological Studies* (1899 ff.)
LTK	J. Höfer and K. Rahner, eds., *Lexikon für Theologie und Kirche,* 10 vols. + index (2nd rev. ed., 1957–67)
Mansi	J. D. Mansi, *Sacrorum Conciliorum Nova et Amplissima Collectio,* 31 vols. (1757–98); reprint and continuation ed. by L. Petit and J. B. Martin, 60 vols. (1899–1927)
NRT	*Nouvelle Revue Théologique* (1879 ff.)
NTS	*New Testament Studies* (1954 ff.)
PG	J.-P. Migne, ed., *Patrologia Graeca,* 161 vols. (1857 ff.)
PL	J.-P. Migne, ed., *Patrologia Latina,* 217 vols. + 4 index vols. (1844 ff.)
Pritchard	J. B. Pritchard, ed., *Ancient Near Eastern Texts relating to the Old Testament* (1950; 2nd revised and enlarged ed., 1955)
RGG	K. Galling, ed., *Die Religion in Geschichte und Gegenwart,* 6 vols. + index (3rd rev. ed., 1957–65)
RHE	*Revue d'histoire ecclésiastique* (1900 ff.)
RHPR	*Revue d'histoire et de philosophie religieuse* (1921 ff.)
RSPT	*Revue des sciences philosophiques et théologiques* (1907 ff.)
RSR	*Recherches de science religieuse* (1910 ff.)
RSV	Revised Standard Version of the Bible
TS	*Theological Studies* (1940 ff.)
TU	*Texte und Untersuchungen zur Geschichte der altchristlichen Literatur. Archiv für die griechisch-christlichen Schriftsteller der ersten drei Jahrhunderte,* hitherto 62 vols. in 5 series (1882 ff.)
TWNT	G. Kittel, ed., *Theologisches Wörterbuch zum Neuen Testament,* continued by G. Friedrich (1933 ff.); E. T.: *Theological Dictionary of the New Testament* (1964 ff.)
ZAW	*Zeitschrift für die alttestamentliche Wissenschaft* (1881 ff.)
ZKT	*Zeitschrift für Katholische Theologie* (1877 ff.)

S

(continued)

SCANDAL

1. *The notion of scandal.* a) *Functional definition.* The personal development of the individual, like the cultural evolution of groups, is affected both by endogenous impulses, like creative ideas and the force they generate, and by exegenous impact, such as example and scandal. So the development of spiritual existence and culture is hindered not only by innate incapacity or failure but also by faulty upbringing and education and by scandals. Scandal, then, plays an ambivalent psychological and social role which religion and morality must take into account.

We speak of scandal when people (or an individual) are so moved, wounded, and threatened in their personal attitudes and beliefs that their existence is seriously jeopardized and they adopt an emotional and defensive attitude towards this disruption of their normal life and thought — an attitude that may carry them beyond defence to reprisals. As contrasted with dialogue, scandal consciously given is a weapon of psychological warfare.

When this or that natural aspiration of a man is partially frustrated, the disturbance occurs on the periphery of his life and provokes his anger, whereas scandal always injures personal values that are necessary to the existence of a man or a society — it attacks their fundamental selfhood.

Again, anger relates only to particular interests bearing on the individual's convenience or well-being; but scandal relates to the essential spiritual values of society, extending beyond the purely psychological into the sociological sphere. The reason is that man is by nature as much a social being as an individual one, with the result that any threat to his very existence must have a social significance. Similarly, groups held together by a common attachment to particular personal values will be scandalized to the extent that attacks on the unifying values threaten the existence of the group.

Defining scandal in these functional terms, we can distinguish between genuine and spurious scandals. We have genuine scandal when the response to it is given in terms of corresponding value — when a religious offence calls forth a religious reply. The more keenly a high value is grasped, the deeper pure scandal can be. (Compare the scandal Peter caused Jesus.) On the other hand scandal is "impure" if the response is not given in terms of corresponding value — for example, if religion provokes aesthetic scandal. Supposing that mingled moral and religious scandal, even predominantly religious scandal, is felt at the moral but not properly religious failings of a priest, that too would be spurious scandal; and the same applies to resentment, which is not based on positive attachment to any value but is a purely negative rejection of value.

b) *Effects of scandal.* The distinction we have just made is of psychological and sociological importance, because by the nature of the case unsound values — like those connected with image-forming and ideology — make men prone to scandal, for those values are based on and reinforced by a lack of personal resolution.

Moreover, this susceptibility depends on unstable subjective and historical factors. We can only be scandalized at attacks upon values if those values are operative in concrete life. Now since the significance of

1

spiritual values in a given situation depends not only on their objective importance but also on the necessity for their concrete embodiment, susceptibility to scandal varies with changing spiritual and cultural circumstances.

Accordingly it may be very difficult to foresee the effect of an attack on existing values that are latent or repressed. Cultivated individuals and societies are less prone to scandal than primitives, having more adaptable and more effective defences so long as the roots of life are spared. Religion, essentially a conservative force because of its bond with the eternal, tends to become an isolated fortress of faith, with only defensive reactions. Moreover, scandals arising within its own spiritual world generally tend to disintegrate religion, whereas scandals from outside consolidate it, because the former tend to be spiritually assimilated, whereas the latter can hardly be mastered without self-sacrifice. The more authority a man has, the greater scandal he can give because of his spiritual power.

The good and bad effects of an offence that gives scandal can be correctly judged only by a realistic estimation of changing spiritual circumstances, and by noting the psychological and sociological laws of such scandal. Here the psychological problem is the role of scandal in striking the best balance between inner and outward directedness. Sociologically one must consider the effect of scandal on communication, isolation, or even hostility between groups.

c) *Distinctions.* As to method, we must first distinguish the scandal that a man gives *(scandalum activum)* from the scandal that he takes *(scandalum passivum).* It is a point relevant to moral theology that scandal may be intended directly or indirectly, and that the main reason for one's being scandalized may lie either in the mind or in the objective attack. Scandal directly willed becomes *scandalum diabolicum* if what one has in view is the actual corruption of another through the scandal given, not just the material sin of the other as is often the case with unchastity, for instance. Behaviour that gives scandal where such is not even indirectly intended, entails *scandalum mere acceptum.* If the person scandalized is highly impressionable, and has not the spiritual resources to assimilate the impulse in a manner appropriate to his stage of development, we speak of *scandalum pusillorum. Scandalum pharisaicum,* on the other hand, presupposes a one-sided inner-directed-

ness in the person scandalized which makes him impervious to the *stimuli* necessary for self-preservation and development.

2. *Scandalum in Scripture (religious scandal).* Scripture uses the term scandal in a specifically religious sense. Scandal blocks one's road to faith, or leads one astray from the faith. In NT usage σκάνδαλον is only an occasion of falling, which may or may not lead to a fall; σκανδαλίζω means causing the fall; and σκανδαλίζεσθαι the actual fall.

a) *The synoptics: the scandal of Jesus.* Scandal, being in the religious sphere, is seen in an eschatological framework. Thus Mt 24:10 speaks of a great scandal, i.e., apostasy in the last days, and Mt 13:41 says that those who have led others to sin and apostasy will be condemned to hellfire. Mt 18:7 (Luke 17:1) says that scandals must come (7b) but pronounces woes upon those who passively (7a) or actively (7c) have a hand in their coming. The actual coming of scandal is mentioned in the Lord's words to Peter, Mt 16:23. Here Peter becomes a kind of rock of offence for Jesus himself, whereas in verse 18 he was called the rock on which the Church will be built. For all the differences, Peter's role strikingly resembles that of Jesus: Jesus the foundation-stone (cf. 1 Cor 3:11 etc.), the rock of salvation (Rom 9:33b; 1 Pet 2:6), becomes a rock of offence to many (Rom 9:33a; 1 Pet 2:8). By scandal, Peter who is to protect the Church against the powers of hell, becomes a tool of Satan (cf. Mt 13:41). Scandal arises from the antagonism between God and man which stands out uncompromisingly here (cf. Mt 7:11; 15:19; 12:34): to think and desire merely human things is to resist God and his will.

The taking of scandal in the present is erring from faith in the message of God's kingdom — falling away from the gospel (Mt 13:20ff. and par.; Mk 4:17). Here Jesus becomes the great scandal. His work not only has power to awaken faith, it also has power to lead men astray from faith. This going astray because of Jesus (Mt 26:31, 33; 11:6 and parr.; Lk 7:23; Mt 13:57 and parr.; Mk 6:3) can become the counterpart of believing in him (Mk 14:27; 14:29; Mt 13:57; Mk 6:3). The Pharisees not only take personal offence because Jesus attacks them (Mt 15:8), they take grave religious offence at his preaching (Mt 15:12). Their blindness means unbelief and falling into the pit — eschatological ruin. The unexpectedness of Jesus' messianic way (Mt 11:6), his earthly origins (Mk 6:3), his attitude towards human tradition (Mt 15:3 ff.), his complete reinterpretation of the idea of purity (Mt 15:11), his independent attitude to the law (cf. Mk 2:23 ff.; 3:1 ff. and *passim*), become an occasion of scandal and at the same time of offence at his person, of aversion from him in unbelief.

Jesus knows that his words and deeds unavoidably occasion unbelief. Nevertheless his deliberate aim is to avert the eschatological apostasy from the faith. Such is the sense of the passage on scandalizing little ones (Mk 9:42 and parr.), and that about our members' scandalizing us (Mk 9:43–48; Mt 18:8 f.; 5:29 f.).

b) *Paul: the scandal of the cross.* Paul too knows that one must inevitably give scandal (Rom 9:33; cf. 1 Pet 2:6–8). Christ summoning us to faith is an offence to the unbeliever simply because he does not believe; just as the believer experiences Christ as honour (1 Pet 2:7 a) and righteousness (Rom 9:30), by believing. An essential part of the faith is overcoming the scandal of God in Christ. Paul sees the Jews as the eminent example of how offence at the gospel leads men to ruin. This point emerges very clearly in 1 Cor 1:23, where he contrasts the folly of the cross with the scandal of the Jews and the foolishness of the heathen which is only another kind of scandal. Gal 5:11 has in mind those who took offence at a gospel of grace that delivers men from the law.

The offence which the faith gives is not to be eliminated or even lessened by joining the cross with circumcision. Nor must high-flown eloquence seek to smooth over the scandal (1 Cor 1:17; 2:4).

On the other hand Paul knows of a scandal that must be avoided at all costs and that occurs in his churches because of differences in belief (1 Cor 8:11 ff.; 10:23 ff.; Rom 14:1 — 15:7). Though the Apostle personally shares the outlook of the strong as a pastor, he sides with the weak, like Jesus in his solicitude for "little ones".

c) *John: the overcoming of scandal by love.* He who does not love, says St. John, is blind and therefore vulnerable to scandal (1 Jn 2:10). Here faith and love are intimately connected. He who loves encounters no obstacle on the road to faith (Jn 6:61). Jesus' last discourses in St. John, as in the synoptics, are designed to guard against apostasy. But whereas the synoptics represent apostasy as inevitable even among the disciples, the Johannine Jesus wakens a hope that it may be avoided: "I have said all this to keep you from falling away" (Jn 16:1; cf. Jn 6:63).

3. *Tradition.* a) *The Fathers* so transform and secularize the NT idea of scandal that secondary points of view now dominate.

(i) The psychological (cf., for example, Mt 13:57; 15:12; 17:27): *Scandalum* is more and more equated with *offendiculum,* and then adopted in the Christian vernacular to mean an occasion of feelings like pride and envy, anger and indignation — something "scandalous".

(ii) The moral: (thus the Ambrosiaster's commentary on weakness in 2 Cor 11:29 as sexual temptation and seduction). The word comes to mean moral offence, bad example, seduction, and temptation, whether for the individual or as a "public scandal". "Religious" offence was a special form of scandal, acquiring the sense of "dogmatic" offence, religious error, and finally even heresy.

b) *Schoolmen: scandal and its immoral effects.* Hence scandal entered the systematic moral theology of the scholastics, especially St. Thomas's, as an external act which occasions one's neighbour to commit sin, and which one has no just cause for doing. The fact that an act is likely in given circumstances to become an occasion of sin for another makes it a duty of love to refrain from it unless we have a good moral reason. The sin consists in consciously exposing another to a fall which but for our act would not occur. Indirect scandal can be tolerated if the act concerned can be justified by a good end directly intended according to the principle of double effect (Aquinas, *Summa Theologica,* II/II, q. 43; *4 Sententiarum,* 35). The casuistry applied when giving scandal is under discussion always assumes a grave obligation to avoid giving scandal and then, to avoid immobilization, makes all sorts of distinctions so that reasons may be quickly seen to justify the actions in question.

In contrast to giving scandal, taking scandal is only a sin against the virtue we have violated by our own act, while its malice may even be diminished as by the circumstances. But all the malice in pharisaic scandal attaches to the person who takes offence.

c) *Criticism.* Against this traditional approach there is the serious objection that it narrows down the NT idea of scandal, especially the Pauline form. But the vigour of Christianity depends in no small measure on the undiminished scandal of the cross. Moreover, this interpretation of scandal by moral theologians does less than justice to the psychological, sociological, and moral functions of scandal. For inducing others to sin is not the sole function of scandal; it can also foster the personal and cultural development of individuals and groups, and therefore contribute to others' salvation, when scandal has a broadening effect, so that even what at first seemed undesirable impulses can be assimilated and profited by.

Neglecting this aspect of scandal in moral theology necessarily leads to a one-sided interiorization of ethics which multiplies prohibitions and warning signs. It obscures our view of our task which is to bring about the good within the concrete bounds of possibility.

4. *Ethics of scandal.* A responsible ethics of scandal that will correspond to its importance must work from the premise that scandal in the abstract is morally neutral. In the concrete it is desirable or undesirable according as it is necessary for the just maintenance of one's own spiritual existence, or helps to perfect another or the group, or not.

So that necessary and desirable scandal may not have bad effects, the value it is meant to further must be asserted as clearly as possible, in order that people may recognize its worth and be more prepared to accept it. Again, offence may be given on behalf of values only to the extent that these can be assimilated by the people "offended". So the scandalizer must really have the value at heart, not simply his own interests, and serve lovingly the good of others, even at the expense of his own just interests, unless he is bound to uphold them to safeguard his dignity as a human being.

In any case one should attempt to substitute dialogue for scandal, or at least to observe standards worthy of human beings so that tolerance may preside over any unavoidable spiritual conflict. Hence controversy should be carried on in a manner befitting the values at issue. Religious scandals must be met on religious ground, scientific scandals on scientific, and so forth. Keeping to these rules will not only forestall a disastrous extension of the conflict, but give more promise of a useful upshot of the controversy — even of mutual benefit. Personal confrontation will be less direct, coexistence and collaboration easier.

Scandalizers and scandalized, individuals and groups, must remember that over-sharp provocation and reaction usually produce the opposite effect to that intended, by the operation of psychological and sociological laws. Thus persecution of Christians strengthens a vigorous Church, and too great a scandal within the Church causes divisions (even heresy and schism). The greater a man's authority, the graver the responsibility he assumes in giving scandal. On the other hand, the weak must strive to do more than merely react to what is done to them.

Consciously exaggerating what seem to us abuses may have the disagreeable result of consolidating them, for the very fact that they scandalize us may commend them in the eyes of another — one need only mention the failure of spectacular campaigns against some bad films. Values, especially public ones, can only be appealed to if they are alive. Otherwise, from the functional point of view, the scandal is pharisaic.

Accordingly there is no ready answer to the question how far scandals are desirable in certain circumstances. Each case must be prudently decided on its own merits, striking a balance between boldness and caution, making allowances alike for scandal that is necessary and inescapable and scandal that must be avoided at all costs.

As to whether giving public scandal should be punishable at law, we must again consider the ambivalent character of public scandal, in relation to the common good. The utmost possible freedom of discussion must be ensured, and no campaigns should be allowed that would frustrate necessary or desirable communication. Therefore public authority must suppress feuds which gravely threaten the peace of society, since public insults, defamation, and the like call forth specially violent defensive reactions. Personal sentiments and beliefs, even from a morally neutral point of view, must be protected insofar as necessary to preserve the essential solidarity of a community. So it is fair to forbid blasphemy and scurrilous attacks — especially on religious belief — but not to the extent of interfering even with fierce objective controversy, which of course involves value judgments.

The suppression of public scandals arising out of social criticism or shocking works of art and literature is to be undertaken with hesitation, since such high values as social justice and art are jeopardized. Scandals involved in fashions and advertising, etc., can be suppressed without misgiving, so far as the common good and public decency require — for example, to protect youth, discourage crime, etc. What is appropriate in a given situation can only be determined *a posteriori* on the basis of a careful weighing of values.

To sum up, we may say that a due appreciation of scandal plays a most important role in making human relations fruitful, encouraging cultural progress, keeping the peace in society, and responsibly propagating acknowledged values, especially religion, so that the mission of the Church is involved.

See also *Value, Virtue, Temptation.*

BIBLIOGRAPHY. John Milton, *Areopagitica* (1644); J. H. Newman, *The Idea of a University* (1852); Lord Acton, *The History of Freedom* (1907); W. Schöllgen, *Soziologie und Ethik des Ärgernisses* (1931); N. Jung, "Scandale", *DTC,* XIV, cols. 1246–54; D. Wiest, *Precensorship of Books* (1953); A. Humbert, "Essai d'une théologie du scandale dans les synoptiques", *Biblica* 35 (1954), pp. 1–28; G. Kitson Clark, *The Kingdom of Free Men* (1957); G. Stählin, "σκάνδαλον", *TWNT,* VII, pp. 338–58; K. Rahner, *Free Speech in the Church* (1959); B. Häring, *The Law of Christ,* II: *Special Moral Theology* (1963).

Waldemar Molinski

SCEPTICISM

1. *Concept.* The term "scepticism" in its classical sense comes from σκέπτομαι, "to inspect". One may distinguish between total (radical, absolute) scepticism and partial (moderate, relative) scepticism, the latter appearing as religious, ethical, aesthetic, etc., scepticism; there is also methodical scepticism or methodical doubt.

2. *History.* A partial scepticism appears in the West as early as the pre-Socratic philosophers (Xenophanes, Parmenides) and was built up to one of its first high-points by the Sophists, as a criticism of the naive dogmatism of pre-Socratic philosophy. Gorgias denied that anything could be known or indeed communicated; Protagoras enunciated his principle that "man is the measure of all things" to stress the subjectivity of all knowledge. But this gave rise to a fruitful study of the art of persuasion by logic and rhetoric, which reached its methodical climax in Socrates and provided an answer to the Sophists in the metaphysics

of knowledge worked out by Plato and Aristotle. Then the only tenable position became the radical scepticism as maintained by Pyrrho of Elis: there is a counter to every argument, hence it is best to remain unmoved (ἀταραξία) and refrain from passing judgment (ἐποχή). Archesilaus put forward the probable (εὔλογον) as a practical guide. In the Middle Scepticism of late antiquity, Carneades took scepticism further and raised the question of the criterion of truth in general: every proof must go on *ad infinitum,* because no proposition can be proof of itself. This gave rise to the first theory of probability. Late Scepticism (Aenesidemus, Agrippa, Sextus Empiricus) returned to a more dogmatic form of argument, using ten instances to prove that all knowledge was impossible. The most important grounds adduced were the contradictions of the philosophers, the variability of sense-perception, the influence of temperament and environment. Conformity to the general practice and obedience to the impulse of the moment are recommended, rather than the riskiness of the search for truth.

In the early clash between philosophical scepticism and Christianity, the decisive question was whether there was a means of passing from scepticism to the certainty of faith, or could they exist legitimately together. Tertullian offered the choice between "Athens" and "Jerusalem": the Christian faith excludes all questioning doubts, a dialogue between the believer and the sceptic is meaningless. St. Augustine likewise denies *(Contra Academicos)* that questioning is its own justification, but tries to refute scepticism by philosophical arguments. The condition of the believer does not mean that his knowledge is perfect, but scepticism is excluded on principle. Where doubt could lead to despair, a scepticism which overcomes the mental attitude of indifference (ἀταραξία) takes on a dimension which disposes towards faith.

Scholasticism shows no traces of scepticism, and it is only in Scotism and in Occam that the tendency appears to use scepticism as an argument for the authority of revelation, against a dogmatizing type of philosophy. Montaigne takes up the Pyrrhonism of antiquity to reach a non-committal attitude which sets the mind free from dogmas and authorities. P. Charron, on the contrary, uses scepticism as an argument for the faith. The *cogito* with which Cartesianism seeks to retrieve all scepticism is questioned by B. Pascal and P. Bayle. The greatest influence was that of Hume, who questioned rational ethics and the principles by which causality could be known. Kant's Critique, on the contrary, was an endeavour to restore to knowledge a limited validity, but referred religious knowledge to its own postulates. Hegel included and went beyond scepticism, as a moment in the truth of the whole, while Kierkegaard reacted by exposing the existentiell components of doubt. In modern philosophy scepticism has been embodied in various trends: see *Positivism, Life-Philosophy, Existence* II and *Ideology*.

3. *Significance*. Scepticism is explicable as the contrary of dogmatism. Total scepticism is meaningless, because it must call its own statement in doubt and so become a dogmatism of doubt. Methodical doubt, on the other hand, is so much taken for granted that it has become synonymous with scientific method: scientific thought must always be critical, to avoid the charge of a naive dogmatism and to survive the probings of the intellect. Between methodical and radical scepticism there are degrees which cannot be dismissed at once as absurd. Such scepticism differs from indifferentism by the intensity of its thought; from agnosticism by its inexorable quest for truth; from make-belief by its seriousness.

There is a peculiar ambiguity about scepticism as a historical phenomenon. It can be a mark of decadence in a culture resigned to extinction, or again, an instrument of "Enlightenment". In the latter case it will be an ally in the conflict with tradition, and a method of verifying new experiences, so that it appears as a search for truth which continues to doubt as long as it has not found sure footing. Thus a partial scepticism can expose the ambivalence of certain situations, by questioning what is taken for granted and criticizing received axioms. Its justification is the fact that knowledge is conditioned by so many factors. It doubts the possibility of arriving at a secure knowledge of the truth, because the history of philosophy can be depicted as a series of insoluble contradictions. It takes offence at the logical impasse, that no proposition can be its own proof. In its quest for the evidence to which all premises may ultimately be reduced, it pushes the probative power of reason to its limits. It sees clearly how impossible it is for rational thought ever to be quite adequate to

the experience of reality, or it reduces human intellectual activity to a merely relative role in face of the absolute claim of supernatural revelation.

On this last point, the otherwise disparate entities of faith and scepticism converge, since the basic attitude of both is to challenge the ordinary assumption of the infallibility of science. A non-universal scepticism has a legitimate place in theology insofar as this claims to be a science, because the various enunciations of the faith effected by theology are subject to all the conditions by which knowledge is coloured and therefore need constant and critical investigation. Finally, faith itself must not be regarded as an unchallengeable possession taken under control once and for all. The early Christian experience of the tension set up by the two-fold presence of faith and doubt is already voiced in Mk 9:24, and Paul would have Christians test their own faith, as in 2 Cor 13:5. Even the philosophical scepticism which is of itself contrary to faith — provided it does not compound for agnosticism or take refuge in irrationalism — can go through the upheaval which turns doubt into despair, and so attain a new openness for faith.

See also *Dogmatism, Agnosticism, Faith, Philosophy*.

BIBLIOGRAPHY. R. Hönigswald, *Die Skepsis in Philosophie und Wissenschaft* (1914); P. Glenn, *Criteriology* (1933); W. Stegmüller, *Metaphysik, Wissenschaft, Skepsis* (1954); J. Pieper, *Belief and Faith* (1963); S. Coval, *Scepticism and the First Person* (1966); K. Jaspers, *Philosophical Faith and Revelation* (1967).

Werner Post

SCHISM

I. Concept of Schism. II. History of Schism. III. Eastern Schism. IV. Western Schism.

I. Concept of Schism

The word "schism" means "a deliberate separation from ecclesiastical communion; it is also the state of being separated, or the Christian group which is in such a state. The schismatic is one who causes schism, who favours or bears responsibility for it, or who simply adheres to it through conviction or in fact" (Y. Congar).

In classical Greek, σχίσμα means a crack

or tear. St. Paul uses it in a moral sense for differences of opinion or of inclination which endanger the peace and unity of the Church in a given place (1 Cor 1:10; 11:18; 12:25). From the earliest Christian times, the word was retained to express a breach of communion occasioned, or accompanied, by disagreements and manifested by a refusal of obedience to the legitimate authority of the bishop.

Heresy, which likewise involves breach of communion, was not at first clearly distinguished from schism. But custom, with the passage of time, reserved the term "schism" for breaches of communion provoked by personal conflict or mere refusal to obey. The word "heresy" was applied to breaches of communion caused by serious divergences in the understanding of the faith.

Schisms made their first appearance at a local Church level. However, the necessary solidarity of local Churches (obliged to safeguard both their unanimity in the confession of the faith and their good mutual relations) inspired canonical rulings which reserved the lifting of excommunication (the penalty for the crime of schism) to the bishop who first inflicted the censure. In the Roman Catholic Church, because of its progressive centralization to the advantage of the Roman See and the development of a monarchic form of ecclesiology of the universal Church, schism came to be defined mainly in terms of a breach of communion with the Pope. In those places (the Orthodox East) in which an ecclesiology based on the harmony of local Churches continued to prevail, the concept of schism underwent quite another evolution. History shows, indeed, that dissident sectors of a local Church often maintained undisputed communion with other local Churches.

The development of the notion of schism owed much to St. Cyprian and St. Augustine (controversy with the Donatists); it was greatly influenced by the Gregorian reform (11th century). The notion of schism, being correlative to the notion of the unity of the Church, advanced step by step as ecclesiology evolved. It took a long time before a theological treatise specifically on the Church made its appearance, although many of the elements necessary to it were to be found scattered in various other works: one would look for it in vain among the great scholastics. St. Thomas Aquinas studied schism less as a distinct phenomenon than as individuals or groups culpable of it or adhering to it. For

him it was a sin against the peace which is a fruit of love (*Summa Theologica,* II/II, q. 39).

Counter-Reformation theology profoundly modified the way in which the theological nature of schism was interpreted. Hitherto, as long as grave differences in the matter of faith were not involved and above all as long as rupture with legitimate authority left intact the sacramental, hierarchical organism of the Church (episcopate, priesthood of apostolic succession), schism appeared as prejudicial to the unity of the Church. But, while the position of the separated part was irregular, no one imagined that that portion was shut out from the mystery of the Church, the fundamental riches of which it continued to share (episcopate, sacraments). The drama of separation was conceived of as taking place *within* the Church, considered essentially as a *fellowship.* By defining the Church as a hierarchically constituted *society* under the supreme authority of the Bishop of Rome, and by identifying the Church purely and simply with the Roman Catholic Church, the Counter-Reformation made out schism to be a separation *from the Church* itself. This ecclesiology, evoked by the desire to reply to the denials of the Reformers, modified unconsciously the traditional attitude of the Church of the West towards the sister Churches of the East (Orthodox). In effect, it supplied a theological justification for a Roman policy of "the Catholic or united Eastern Churches", substituting the intention to convert and absorb for a plan of reunion.

The Second Vatican Council has recovered the traditional outlook by putting forward an *ecclesiology of fellowship* which, instead of emphasizing jurisdictional factors (which are, however, maintained), stresses the sacramental and spiritual elements: sacraments (baptism, orders, Eucharist), sanctifying grace, theological virtues, gifts of the Holy Spirit. Henceforward, the entire reality of the mystery of the Church is to be regarded as overflowing the borders of its full and sole legitimate realization under the species of the Roman Catholic Church. It is admitted that there are various degrees of participation in that reality. If it remains true, canonically speaking, that one is necessarily in the Roman Catholic Church or out of it, it is still more true to say, taking the mystery into account, that one is more or less of the Church. Hence the distinction (cf. *Lumen Gentium* and *Unitatis Redintegratio*) between *plenary communion* and *partial communion,* both with the Roman Catholic Church and with the Church as such. It follows that one must distinguish two meanings in schism: *canonically,* it is a breach of jurisdictional relations with the See of Rome; *theologically,* without excluding full participation in the mystery of the Church, it places an obstacle to the full and manifest realization of its unity — a realization and manifestation which require the unanimous profession of the faith, effective membership of a unique, hierarchical, sacramental organism, and the common celebration (reception) of the same sacraments, particularly the Eucharist, the internal bond and external sign *par excellence* of the unity of the Church.

The notion of schism so defined in respect of the Roman Catholic Church may be applied analogically to breaches of communion between different Churches and ecclesiastical communities separated from the Roman See. But in each of these confessions or denominations, schism is defined according to a given concept of the Church and of its unity. It is a key-concept, an object of study and discussion, in the complex debate of the ecumenical movement. From the Protestant point of view, the healing of schisms is sought by means of mutual agreement in regard to the practice of intercommunion (the Eucharist, and other acts of worship) which leaves untouched even outstanding differences concerning the content of the faith and the structure of the Church. On the other hand, the Churches which are described as being (broadly) "Catholic" in tendency (Orthodox, Old Catholics, Anglicans) cannot envisage the re-establishment of full sacramental communion until unanimity in faith and mutual harmony within a single, common, hierarchical, sacramental structure (episcopate of full apostolic succession) has been achieved.

From motives of charity, one nowadays avoids as far as possible using the term "schismatic" with reference to members of Churches and Christian communities which disagree with the Roman Catholic Church, all the more so if the people concerned have been born and received their religious formation in these communities. They cannot be held responsible for the state of division from us in which they live today. Besides, both parties must share responsibility for the creation of that division.

See also *Church* II, III, V, *Heresy, Ecumenism* I, IV.

BIBLIOGRAPHY. See bibliographies on *Church* V, *Ecumenism* IV; also: *Dictionnaire de Droit Canonique,* VII, cols. 886f.; Y. Congar, "Schisme", *DTC,* XIV, cols. 1286–1312; J. Szal, *The Communication of Catholics with Schismatics* (1948); G. Baum, *Progress and Perspectives* (1963); S. L. Greenslade, *Schism in the Early Church* (2nd ed., 1964); C. Maurer, "σχίζω, σχίσμα", *TWNT,* VII, pp. 959–65; P. Dias, *Vielfalt der Kirche in der Vielfalt der Jünger, Zeugen und Diener* (1968).

Christophe Dumont

II. History of Schism

1. *General.* The NT speaks of divisions in the local Churches in consequence of differences in the explanation and assimilation of the apostolic kerygma (1 Cor 11:9; Gal 5:19; Rom 16:17). They endanger the fellowship *(koinonia)* of the Church as established by Christ (one God, one Lord, one Spirit, 1 Cor 12:4–6; one gospel, 1 Cor 1:10–13; Gal 1:6–9; one baptism and one bread, 1 Cor 12:13; 10:17; Gal 3:27). Nothing is known of a division which led to a break with the whole Church. But the NT schism has the tendency to isolate men from the Church, which can be very rigid about divergencies in doctrine. In post-apostolic times, schism and heresy are treated as the great enemies of the early Christian Church. They are attributed to ambition, jealousy, indulgence in calumny and rebelliousness against superiors. In contrast to the ecclesiastical office and service of the whole community, for the building up of which all charisms and ministries are given, personalities and personal elements are stressed. Schism and heresy were not yet distinguished formally as clearly as they were later. But in most cases schism was combined with an error in the faith. The history of schism is therefore for the most part identical with the history of heresies. The basic considerations and references of the article on heresies are also valid here.

The whole history of the Church is marked by the rise of schismatic movements which developed their own Church order and formed rival Churches. In early Christian times there were, for instance, the schism of Marcion in the 2nd century (exaggerated Paulinism and an antinomianism exploiting the gospel against law); Gnosticism and Arianism (see articles on these), the millenarianism of Montanism, the rigorism of the Novatians (3rd century), the "Church of the Martyrs" of Bishop Meletius of Lycopolis, and in the wake of this the much more important Church of the Donatists, which rejected the imperial Church of Constantine (4th century). The Eastern Schism of the 11th century was heralded by the Acacian Schism of the 6th and the Photian Schism of the 10th century.

The slow process of the assimilation of Christianity by the Franks and the Germans and the priority given to the repulse of the Saracens, Normans and Hungarians left no room for the rise of sectarian movements on a large scale in the last part of the Carolingian era. Schisms arose in the great popular religious movements only in the 11th century. The most important was that of the Catharists, a movement under Eastern influences, which set up a counterpart to the Church in southern France, with its own hierarchy and system of dogma, the latter based on a dualism which included rejection of the Incarnation and was rigorously opposed to the doctrine of the Church. Down to the present, there are still communities of Waldenses in the Alpine valleys of Savoy and Piedmont going back to lay Churches set up as a consequence of the preaching of Valdes, whose rigorously ascetic programme was modelled on apostolic and evangelical poverty. These sects hardened into schism, but the Popes such as Innocent III succeeded in re-integrating into the Church the Humiliati of North Italy and other groups in South France who had been condemned as heretical. All these "Poor Men's" movements (see *Poverty* II), for which Gregory VII provided living-space by relying on them in his reform (against Nicolaites and Simoniacs; see *Reform* II C), criticized selfcentred ecclesiasticai institutions and the luxurious living of some of the clergy. These two defects obscured the testimony of the Church and launched recurring trends to reform in the late Middle Ages. In Wycliffe and Huss (see *Hussism*) they deviated into schism. The worldliness of the papacy and the cardinals was undoubtedly the main cause of the Great Western Schism, during which two and then even three contenders claimed the papacy. Contemporaries could not decide between them, and even later research has not cleared up the matter. The Reformation profited from the dynamism of lay religious movements. Its protest against distortions in the late medieval Church took the form of rejection of the whole medieval Church system with its combination of Church and State, papal centralism and a rigidly formalized scholasticism. Even the Church reinforced and regenerated by Trent was not spared divisions. In consequence of the general debility of faith and their own limited bases, these schisms remained confined to the local or national level (schism of Utrecht, 1724; schism of the Petite Église de la Vendée, which refused to recognize the concordat under Napoleon; schism of Gregorio Aglipay in the Philippines, 1902; schism of the Czech National Church, 1920). National sentiment had much to do with nearly all these schisms, engendered by resentment against the Roman Curia and established as organized Churches with the help of the State.

The following distinctions may be made between the vanished schisms and the dissenting groups such as Protestantism and Orthodoxy which still survive.

a) The ancient heresies and schisms questioned the right doctrine in decisive matters of the history of salvation (Trinity, soteriology, the place of Mary in the economy, the grace of God) and had a predominantly "particular" character. The present dissenters appear as "universal", that is, base themselves on a notion which colours their whole understanding of Christianity. Such global re-interpretations existed in earlier times, as in Gnosticism, the Bogomiles of the East and the Catharists. But here the specifically Christian element was perilously recessive, in contrast to the present-day dissidents, among whom the mystery of Christ is accepted unconditionally, at least on principle.

b) The Eastern Orthodox and the Protestants did not start by rejecting a specifically Christian doctrine, but as protests against a given historical condition of the Church: the political estrangement between East and West in the 11th century and the abuses of Church life in the widest sense in the 16th century.

c) In their internal structure, the dissident Churches today tend towards Catholicity and deliberate efforts are made to overcome the divisions.

d) Much more than the schismatic movements of earlier times, the great dissident Churches of today embody Christian values which indicate the work of the Holy Spirit (Vatican II, *Lumen Gentium,* art. 15).

2. Schism in the theology of history. A starting-point for an eschatological interpretation of schisms is provided by 1 Cor 11:19: "oportet haereses esse". This affirms the concrete historical inevitability of schism. Hence schism and the ecumenical movement which eliminates it are on the level of history, not on that of supratemporal dogma. The pilgrim Church is always subject to the law of sin and hence liable to divisions, of which the cause may be personalities, politics, social, theological or disciplinary matters. But the Church as a whole like all of its members has to uphold the gospel in its entirety. It must at times pay the price of division. Since the living truth in the universal Church is prior to the knowledge of faith in the individual members, the guardians of the faith appointed by the Church have the right and the duty to oppose one-sided views of the truth in individuals. Hence schism is not just a manifestation of the spirit of the world. It can result from a genuine conflict of duties.

There are two main lines of interpretation of the text of St. Paul. One understood *haereses* as tensions between groups through which the purity of faith of the orthodox stood out more clearly. This was the psychologizing interpretation of St. John Chrysostom, and it regarded the divisions mentioned by St. Paul as more or less accidental. But for St. Augustine, they had, on the contrary, significance in the history of salvation. The *haereses* were formal errors of doctrine, the *oportet* was a divine decree and a prophecy which had to be fulfilled. Without the heretics, we would go to sleep over Scripture without reading its message. We need to be goaded by the others to take up the word of Scripture and live by it. What is stressed here is less loyalty to the faith than the fullness of faith. St. Augustine's interpretation prevailed in the Western Church. The scholastic doctrine of the "permissive will" of God gave it a basis in speculative theology. The Reformation rediscovered Chrysostom's interpretation. But Calvinist theology linked up directly with St. Augustine and explained divisions as the necessary results of supramundane forces, directed by God's sovereign salvific will to the good end intended by him. In the controversies between the confessions the Pauline text was used by all sides, none of which allowed it to shake their confidence in their own title-deeds. Modern exegetes, particularly among Protestants, depart very widely from the strictness of the Augustinian interpretation and tend rather to that of Chrysostom.

The history of schism does not bring out only negative aspects. It also shows, retrospectively, that division contributes to the growth of the Church and possesses prophetic and charismatic qualities. The struggle against Gnosis helped to clarify the thought of the Great Church with regard to a number of important theological problems, and contributed directly or by reaction to the development of doctrine (the fixing of the canon of the NT, the doctrine of the Incarnation and of grace). The struggle against Arianism aided the theology of the Trinity to attain greater conceptual clarity. Donatism forced men to reflect on ecclesiology, a realm almost totally neglected by the classical Greek theology. The poverty movements of the Middle Ages, especially that of the Catharists, compelled Catholics to give a dogmatic statement on their understanding of the world and contributed to the realization of the *vita apostolica*. The Reformation of the 16th century gave the decisive impulse to Catholic reform at Trent (see *Reform* II D). But it must always be remembered that the Church, in its combat against heresy and schism, always ran the risk, and indeed succumbed to it, of allowing truths upheld by the dissident to fall into oblivion, and met true prophetic testimony with distrust.

Hence schism has a certain integrating force which comes out more and more strongly in the course of history and finally paves the way for the ending of the schism. Heresy and schism are essentially stresses laid upon partial truths or a forgotten aspect of ecclesiastical structures, and they are forces in history because of the one-sided truth which they embody in error. Divisions in faith and Church polity can well be detours on the way to the kingdom of God, when they lead to reforming and creative reflection on the Christian message, and when they act as prototypes of reform by developing elements which can again be integrated into the whole *communio*. Until this comes about, the division is punishment for the culpable failure of Christians to give due testimony in their common life of love and faith. In its divisions, Christianity is under the judgment of God. The final judgment is anticipated, as it were, in history (cf. Mt 24 and 25). But the wrath of God is a cloak for his grace which urges the confessions to the overcoming of the division.

There is a parallel to schism in the OT history of salvation, the division between Judah and Israel under the monarchy. Moses had confirmed the covenant of Sinai by offering the sacrifice of the twelve tribes on one altar, binding them together as one fellowship of kinship and life. Under David's rule the unity of the people of Israel was given an outward visible form. Basically the unity was religious, while the tribes had remained since Moses relatively independent of each other. After the death of Solomon the sociological unity broke up. Differences which had been latent for centuries, rooted in different spiritual traditions (tendency to charismatic theocracy in the North, institutionalization and juridical establishment of the dynastic monarchy in the South), hardened into schism. The occasion of the split was the excessive burdens which Solomon imposed on his people and the harshness with which his successor Rehoboam treated them. With charismatic authority the prophet Ahijah announced the rival kingship of Jeroboam in the North. The kingship in the people of Israel should have had both dynastic and charismatic character, but this unity, achieved under David, was lost. The division was only provisional. The two elements of the Israelite kingship were to be re-united again.

This division between Israel and Judah suggests a comparison with the great divisions in Christendom. The schism between East and West was long latent before the definitive break in the 11th century; in consequence of a chronic lack of *communio* the differences became hostilities. The reformers of the 16th century could build on centuries of anti-Roman resentment. Even in the subject-matter of the schism there are analogies: the charismatically-inclined Eastern Churches show extreme reserve towards Roman juridicalism, just as Protestantism manifests its fidelity to God in the line of prophetic obedience at the expense of institutions. More important than these parallels is the basic structure of this schism. In spite of political, human and historical differences, there is a spiritual solidarity. Israel and Judah both appeal to the Mosaic covenant, though with a difference of emphasis which seeks to justify the schism. Israel stresses the Mosaic element, Judah the Davidic. But both focus on the same centre. Then, the prophets raised up by God in the North are not prophets of the schism but fundamentally preachers of God's word. In spite of the division, which is not regarded as final, hope of ultimate reunion remains. But it only came when both kingdoms had fallen and when the chosen people had attained a new interiority in the Babylonian captivity, bringing with it a re-discovery of their common call.

See also the various articles on Church history.

BIBLIOGRAPHY. See bibliography on *Heresy* II; also: L. Salembier, *The Great Schism of the West* (1907); W. Bauer, *Rechtgläubigkeit und Ketzerei im ältesten Christentum* (1934); E. Käsemann, "Ketzer und Zeuge", *Zeitschrift für Theologie und Kirche* 48 (1951), pp. 292–311; S. L. Greenslade, *Schism in the Early Church* (1953); H. R. Williamson, *The Arrow and the Sword: An Essay in Detection* (1955); Y. Congar, *After Nine Hundred Years* (1959); id., "Considérations sur le schisme d'Israël dans la perspective des divisions chrétiennes", *Chrétiens en dialogue. Contributions catholiques à l'œcuménisme,* Unam Sanctam 50 (1964), pp. 185–210; C. Dawson, *Dividing Christianity* (1965); C. Argenti, H. Bruston, Y. Congar and P. Gouyon, *Le schisme: Sa signification théologique et spirituelle* (1967).

Victor Conzemius

III. Eastern Schism

Political events and policies did more to bring about the Eastern Schism than the dogmatic differences to which it is often attributed. The roots of the process must be sought in the political ideology of the early Christian Church. The first political philosophers of Christianity, Clement of Alexandria and Eusebius of Caesaraea, adapted the political outlook of Hellenism, the only system then in existence, to the doctrine of Christianity. The Christian Emperor was denied the divinity which had been attributed to him under the pagan system. Nonetheless, he was still regarded as the representative of God on earth, possessing all power in civil and religious matters.

The Christianized political philosophy of Hellenism was accepted by the whole Church as well as by the emperors. In consequence, the Christian emperors from Constantine on thought that their first duty was to provide for the well-being of the Church and to defend the true faith. On the part of the Church, the first result of accepting the Hellenistic political system in a Christianized form was that ecclesiastical structures and organization were adapted to the civil forms of the Roman Empire. The unity in which the Empire combined the peoples seemed to represent a prelude to the universality of the Church. The division of the Church into patriarchates and dioceses was co-ordinated with the regional division of the Empire into larger and smaller units. The Roman pontiff was all the more readily recognized as head of the Church because he resided in Rome, the capital and cultural centre of the Empire.

And the choice of Constantinople for the emperor's residence did not diminish the standing of the Roman pontiff in the Church. His position was acknowledged by the early councils, especially Chalcedon, and confirmed by the Emperor Justinian. The clear recognition of the special position of the Roman pontiff by virtue of his apostolic and Petrine character explains why the Roman pontiff himself affirmed this primacy relatively seldom. The elevation of Constantinople to second place in the Church hierarchy, by the Second Council of Constantinople in 581, was regarded as precedence in honour only. In the East, it was regarded as the logical consequence of adaptation to the political structure. Hence it was also accepted without demur by Damascus I. But when the Council of Chalcedon entrusted the Patriarch of Constantinople with jurisdiction over the whole of Asia Minor and Thrace, Leo I regarded this measure as a danger to the ecclesiastical primacy of Rome and refused to confirm the twenty-eighth canon of the Council. The canon was not inserted into the official collections of canons in the Eastern Church, but the Patriarch of Constantinople continued to govern the regions allotted to him by the Council and retained supreme rank in the Eastern Church.

Subsequently, Leo I and his successors stressed more strongly than their predecessors the apostolic character of the Roman primacy and their position as successors of St. Peter. But the Eastern Church was not greatly impressed by the appeal to the apostolic character of an episcopal see, since there were many sees founded directly or indirectly by apostles within its own territory.

But the Christian adaptation of the Hellenistic political system also had harmful effects on the development of the Church which were soon apparent. The emperors, taking advantage of their claim to be guardians of the true doctrine, often sought to subordinate purely ecclesiastical matters to their own political or personal interests. The bishops acknowledged the emperor's right to convoke councils, but maintained more or less successfully their ancestral right to define and explain the orthodox doctrine. The resulting tension between imperial and ecclesiastical power became particularly grave in the reign of the Emperor Constantius (337–50), who favoured Arianism, as also under the Emperor Anastasius I (491–518), who induced the Patriarch Acacius to favour monotheletism. Justinian, who ended the Acacian Schism in favour of Pope Hormisdas, reserved to himself the right to solve theological questions. But he was forced by the opposition of the bishops to declare solemnly in the Sixth Novella of 535 that "the greatest gift which God in his infinite goodness has conferred on mankind is the *sacerdotium* and the *imperium*". The spiritual power was to be competent in divine matters, the worldly in human affairs. Both powers were to be exercised with discretion and in harmonious co-operation, for the benefit of mankind. This novella was inserted into all the collections of canons in the East. This explains why all Eastern Churches always strove for harmonious relationships with the civil authority. The protest of Pope Gregory the Great against the assumption of the title "Ecumenical Patriarch" by the Patriarch of Constantinople led to hard feelings between East and West, which induced the Emperor Phocas to confirm once more the primacy of Rome in the Church, at the instigation of Boniface III (607). The sixth ecumenical council (680–1), at which monotheletism was condemned, was a triumph for Pope Agatho. When new differences had arisen between East and West after the condemnation of some Western customs in Eastern synods, the Emperor Justinian II smoothed matters out by re-affirming the primacy of Rome in the Church, on the occasion of the visit of Pope Constantine I to Constantinople. Throughout this whole period, the Popes acknowledged the political supremacy of the emperors, announced their election to the emperor's representative in Ravenna and requested the emperor's confirmation. Political events severed these ties of loyalty in the 8th century. The Popes had to use their militia to defend Rome and central Italy from the attacks of the Lombards who had established themselves in the North and were trying to extend their power over the rest of Italy. The emperors, menaced by the Persians, Arabs, Avars and Slavs, could not respond to the Popes' requests for military help. When in 752 the Lombard king, Aistulf, was at the gates of Rome, Pope Stephen II turned for help to the Frankish ruler Pepin. Pepin defeated Aistulf and bestowed the conquered Exarchate of Ravenna and the duchy of Rome on the Holy See. These events put a further strain on relations between the Popes and Constantinople. But as the liberated territory was still designated at least officially as an imperial province, no open breach occurred.

Even the iconoclast controversies did not really deepen the estrangement. The defenders of images turned to Rome for help, successfully. The Empress Irene, in a document put before the seventh ecumenical council (787), acknowledged the Pope as the First Priest, presiding over the Church on the throne of St. Peter.

The first major breach was caused by strictly political events. Pope Leo III (795–816), menaced by the Roman nobles, turned to Pepin's successor, Charlemagne, for help. Charlemagne not merely supported the Pope but brought Lombard rule in Italy to an end. To show his gratitude, the Pope crowned Charlemagne as emperor in Rome on Christmas Day, 800. This could only appear to the Byzantines as a revolt against the legitimate emperor in Constantinople. Charlemagne was well aware of this. He had not in fact foreseen the coronation. To legitimate the event and re-unite the ancient Roman Empire, he offered to marry the Empress Irene. When Irene was dethroned by Nicephorus I (802–11), war broke out, and was ended only in 812 when Emperor Michael I acknowledged Charlemagne as co-regent in the West. These events greatly influenced the subsequent development of the papacy and the relation between the Roman and the Eastern Church. The Popes, no longer politically dependent on the Eastern emperors, could now rely on the help of the Frankish emperors and could secure their position in the West without having to consider the special position of the Eastern Church. Pope Nicholas I (858–67), appealing to the declarations of Pope Gelasius I during the Acacian Schism (492–6), first eliminated all efforts at autonomy in major regions of the West by subjecting to his authority the Metropolitan of Ravenna and Hincmar of Rheims. The Pope also wished to extend his direct authority to take in the Eastern Church. The quarrel between the Patriarchs Ignatius and Photius seemed to offer a good occasion to do so. Ignatius, who had been appointed patriarch by the Empress Theodora without having been elected by the local synod, had come into conflict with the new regent Bardas after the deposition of Theodora, and on the advice of the bishops, who wished to avoid difficulties with the new government, had renounced the patriarchal dignity. The episcopal synod chose as his successor the layman Photius, president of the imperial chancellory (856). He was acknowledged as the legitimate patriarch by all the bishops, including the supporters of Ignatius. But soon a minority of the clergy refused him obedience and proclaimed Ignatius once more as patriarch. The move seems to have been based on political reasons, namely, the appointment of Theodora as regent. But the dissenters were condemned at a synod, and Photius announced his enthronement to the Pope, who then sent two legates to Constantinople to verify the facts. The legates were able to convince themselves of the legality of the election of Photius and along with the local synod (861) declared that Ignatius had no claim to the patriarchate. But the Abbot Theognostus, the leader of the opposition, succeeded in fleeing to Rome, where he delivered to the Pope an appeal against the sentence, supposedly written by Ignatius, but actually forged by the abbot. Ignatius himself had declared to the synod that he had not appealed to Rome and that he would not do so. Since Theognostus promised the Pope the full obedience of his party, while Photius, convinced of the justice of his claim, refused all further negotiations, Nicholas decided in favour of Theognostus, condemned the legates, excommunicated Photius and declared Ignatius to be the legitimate patriarch. When the Pope later sent missionaries to Bulgaria, which had been Christianized from Byzantium, Photius, along with the Emperor Michael III, convoked a synod of the Eastern Church (867) which protested against the Pope's violation of their rights in Constantinople and Bulgaria and called on the Western Emperor, Louis II, to depose Nicholas. But meanwhile Michael III had been murdered by his fellow-emperor Basil I, who then became emperor, and to win the favour of the Pope, deposed Photius and re-installed Ignatius. In Rome, all this was regarded as a confirmation of Pope Nicholas's policies towards the East. Hadrian II again condemned Photius and sent legates to a council (869–70) which ratified the Pope's decision. Photius was banished, but the majority of the bishops and clergy remained loyal to him.

These events occasioned the first great schism between Rome and the Eastern Churches. It was caused by political interests, and misunderstandings on both sides. But it lasted only a few years. Closer research into the documents has shown that Ignatius and Photius were reconciled and that Ignatius himself asked for legates from Rome at a new council which would bridge the misunderstanding. But the council took place only after the death of Ignatius (879–880), and was presided over by Photius, who had been once more installed as patriarch. The decrees of the council which had concemned Photius were set aside and union in the Byzantine Church and unity with Rome were reaffirmed. Thus the Eastern Church defended its autonomy in deciding matters proper to itself. From this point of view, Ignatius and Photius were in agreement. Hence the Pope did not succeed in undermining the autonomy of the Eastern Church.

The documentation of this controversy provides sufficient proof that the Roman primacy as such was not denied by the Eastern hierarchy, not even by Photius. The acts of the local synod held under Photius in 861 contain statements which indicate that the Eastern Church acknowledged the right of appeal to the Roman pontiff. And even the supporters of Photius appealed to the Pope against a decision of the Patriarch Ignatius.

But the reliance of the Popes on the Frankish rulers soon proved to be a greater danger to the freedom of the Church. Charlemagne and his successors developed a theory according to which the Christian king was not merely the civil ruler, but also a priest, like the priestly king Melchizedek. They claimed the right to intervene in Church matters, even in the election of the Popes. They were not impressed by the effort of certain clerics to prove to them, with the help of the forged "Donation of Constantine", that Constantine the Great, before the transfer of the imperial residence from Rome to Constantinople, had left the Pope in charge of Rome and all Italy. The Western emperors regarded Rome and Italy as part of their empire. Their efforts to gain control of the Byzantine provinces in southern Italy put a further strain on East-West relationships. Byzantium was ready to acknowledge the Popes elected by the Romans, but reacted sensitively to the growing interference of the Frankish rulers in papal elections and to the Frankish innovations introduced into Rome, especially the addition of *Filioque* to the Nicene Creed, which had come into the Frankish liturgy from Spain. For a long time, the Popes refused to acknowledge this addition to the Nicene Creed, to avoid disturbing the Easterns, who held that only a general council was competent to make such changes. Photius defended the procession of the Holy Spirit from the Father alone, but the question was not at the basis of his schism,

since Rome at the time had not yet accepted the addition to the Creed. But at the synod of 867, Photius and his bishops complained that the Frankish missionaries were disseminating the addition in Bulgaria. With the Frankish Popes, the custom came into Rome. Apparently Pope Sergius IV (1009–12) was the first to send, after his consecration, the confession of faith including the *Filioque* to the Byzantine patriarch, along with his notification of enthronement. Sergius II, Patriarch of Constantinople (999–1019), rejected the letter with the creed in question. It seems that from then on the name of the Roman pontiff was no longer inscribed on the Eastern diptychs. This unfriendly act illustrates the growing hostility, but it was not an overt declaration of schism.

More decisive still for the Western Church was the re-organization of Church government consequent to the introduction of the Frankish system of the "proprietary" or imperial ("king's own") Church, by which the authority of the Pope was restricted. According to the approach of Roman law, an organization or corporation was owner of a Church, foundation, bishopric or monastery. But according to Germanic custom, the ruler was the owner of the Church, and the revenues of monasteries or churches erected on his territory were his by right. This system of the proprietary church then spread rapidly throughout the West, and founders also claimed rights in the election of the administrators of churches and abbeys which they had founded and endowed. This system, combined with feudal law, placed the kings and rulers of the West in a very strong position, and the powers of the bishops and Popes were greatly weakened. Simony, marriage of priests and lay investiture followed, and contributed to the calamitous state of the Western Church in the 10th and 11th centuries.

One reaction to the situation was the monastic reform launched by the abbey of Cluny. Other movements for reform started in Lorraine and Burgundy. These reformers regarded as the root of all abuses the theocratic system introduced by the Franks, which made the king a priest and hence recognized his authority in the ecclesiastical as well as in the civil domain. To their mind, the salvation of the Church depended on the strengthening of papal power over kings and princes as well as bishops. But since they were ignorant of the very different development of the Eastern Church, where such abuses were unknown and priests were not obliged to celibacy, they also wished to extend their reforms to the Eastern Church.

The reform also gained foothold in Italy when the reforming Pope, Leo IX (1049–54), was elevated to the papacy by the Emperor Henry III (1039–56). He chose three helpers dedicated to reform: the monks Humbert and Hildebrand and Frederick, Archbishop of Lorraine. They helped him to establish the reform movement effectively in Italy. Leo was naturally anxious to strengthen his authority in the Latin Churches of South Italy, especially Apulia. But these regions were under Byzantine rule, and mostly belonged to the Greek rite. Michael Caerularius (1043–58), Patriarch of Constantinople, suspicious of the Latins, also wished to strengthen his authority in the Byzantine regions of South Italy, and hence followed with close attention all the activity of the reformers in this region. Becoming convinced that the interests of the Church were threatened in Italy, he decided upon a counter-attack. He ordered the Latin churches and religious institutes in Constantinople to go over to the Greek rite. His partisans closed the churches and monasteries which refused to comply. The brutality of this attack was certainly unjustified. At the same time, the patriarch asked the Archbishop of Achrida to warn Byzantine subjects in Italy against the activity of the Latins in the area. The archbishop sent a letter to the Latin Bishop of Trani in Apulia, criticizing some Latin customs in the liturgy and especially the Latin custom of using unleavened bread for the Eucharist. There was great agitation in Byzantine Apulia, and the situation was again rendered more difficult by political events.

The Normans, called in by some defecting Byzantine administrators, defeated the Greek army and established themselves as rulers in a large part of the province. From here they threatened other Byzantine possessions, and also the patrimony of the Popes. The Emperor Constantine IX appointed a Latin, Argyros, as supreme commander in Apulia (1051). The patriarch, who regarded Argyros as his personal enemy, tried unsuccessfully to prevent his being appointed. At the wish of the Emperor, Argyros offered the Pope a military alliance against the Normans, which the Pope accepted. But the allied troops were defeated by the Normans (1053) and the Pope was interned in Benevento for a year by his conquerors.

Meanwhile the Pope charged his helper, Cardinal Humbert of Silva Candida, to refute the accusations of Leo of Achrida against the Latins. Humbert composed a cutting treatise, in which he sharply condemned the customs of the Greek Church. But since in the meantime a new imperial embassy had appeared at the papal court, presenting a brief but polite letter from the patriarch, the Pope decided not to publish Humbert's treatise and to send three legates to Constantinople, Humbert, Frederick of Lorraine and the Bishop of Amalfi. They were to form a new alliance with the emperor against the Normans and to deliver to the patriarch a letter outlined by Humbert. But the patriarch refused to receive the legates, because the document denied him the title of Ecumenical Patriarch and second place in the ecclesiastical hierarchy, while also expressing doubts on the legitimacy of his elevation to the patriarchate.

Offended by this refusal, Humbert published his anti-Greek treatise, and accused the Greeks in a public debate of having struck out the *Filioque* from the Nicene Creed. But contrary to his expectations, his attacks had the effect of making the Greek clergy close their ranks round the patriarch. The emperor strove in vain to induce a more friendly attitude to the Latins in his clergy, since he was very anxious to conclude the alliance with the Pope. Embittered by the hostility of the patriarch and clergy, Humbert composed a bull in which he excommunicated the patriarch and condemned the customs of the Greek Church. He laid the bull on the altar of the Hagia Sophia and left the city with his retinue. The bull displays great ignorance of historical developments and of the ecclesiastical customs of the Greek Church. Its terms were highly offensive and repugnant to the Greeks. The emperor found himself compelled to have the bull rejected by the patriarch in a synod. The synod excommunicated the legates. It is ironical that the papal letter which was meant to restore mutual harmony ended with schism between Rome and the Eastern Churches.

The major responsibility for this situation is to be laid at the door of two men, Humbert with his tragic ignorance of the Greek Church, and the haughty Patriarch Caerularius with his anti-Latin prejudices. But since the patriarch condemned only the legates, not the Pope and the Western Church, there was no really complete schism. The legitimacy of the excommunication of the patriarch by Humbold can be questioned, as Pope Leo IX was already dead. But in any case, the sad events show how far the Western and Eastern Churches had drifted apart in the preceding centuries. Even in this last act, political rather than dogmatic reasons played the decisive role. The faithful in the Church knew nothing of the schismatic situation for a long time. In the following years, several attempts at reconciliation were undertaken by both sides. At the beginning, the idea of the Crusades led to hopes of reunion, but in the end caused only greater estrangement, especially in the broad masses of the people. The first schismatic action took place in Antioch when a Latin patriarch was appointed beside the Greek, after the capture of the city by the Crusaders.

Political theories were to a great extent to blame for the collapse of all efforts at reconciliation. The Greeks insisted on their Hellenistic viewpoint, which left little room for the Pope as head of the universal Church, while the Westerners developed the theory of the superiority of the spiritual over the temporal power. This theory, which was alien to the Eastern Church, coloured the development of the Western Church during the Middle Ages, after Gregory VII. Mutual distrust grew during the age of the Crusades and led to the capture and sack of Constantinople in 1204. When a Latin patriarch was installed in Constantinople, the schism was complete. This final act of the tragedy cast a shadow on all attempts at union in later times.

Theological questions, especially the *Filioque,* which had played a minor role at the start, were turned into battle-cries. But this should not conceal the fact that the main grounds of the Eastern Schism were not theological.

On 7 December 1965, the representatives of the Greek Orthodox and the Roman Church, Patriarch Athenagoras and the Patriarch of the West, the Bishop of Rome, Paul VI, made a common declaration on the mutual excommunications, which did not in fact end the schism, but which may be regarded as the groundwork of future reconciliation.

See also *Patriarchate, Reform* I, *Crusades, Pope.*

BIBLIOGRAPHY. J. Hergenröther, *Photius,* 3 vols. (1867–9); M. Norden, *Das Papstum und Byzantium* (1903); J. Gay, *L'Italie méridionale et l'empire byzantin, 867–1071* (1904); F. Chalandon, *Histoire de la domination normande en Italie et en Sicilie* (1907); A. Michel, *Humbert und Kerullarios,* 2 vols. (1924–30); L. Bréhier, *L'Église et l'Orient au Moyen-Age* (1928); E. Amann, "M. Cérulaire", *DTC,* X, cols. 1677–1703; M. Jugie, *Le schisme byzantin* (1941); F. Dvornik, *The Photian Schism* (1948); S. Runciman, G. Ostrogorsky and S. Greenslade, *Schism in the Early Church* (1953); V. Vinogradov, *Hauptursache des endgültigen Bruches ... in orthodoxer Schau* (1955); F. Dvornik, *The Idea of Apostolicity in Byzantium and the Legend of the Apostle Andrew* (1958); A. Michel, *Die Kaisermacht in der Ostkirche 843–1204* (1959); Y. Congar, *After Nine Hundred Years* (1959); A. H. H. Jones, *The Later Roman Empire* (1964); F. Dölger, *Byzanz und die europäische Staatenwelt* (1964); H.-G. Beck, "The Byzantine Church in the Age of Photius", in H. Jedin and J. Dolan, eds., *Handbook of Church History,* III (1969), pp. 174–93.

Francis Dvornik

IV. Western Schism

The period from 1378 to 1417 (or 1449) is known in Church history as the great Western Schism. It was essentially a schism in the papacy, involving the simultaneous claim to and actual exercise of supreme Church authority by two and later three Popes. The Church has never officially pronounced on the question which of the two (or three) papal successions was the legitimate one. Nor did the choice of the papal name of John XXIII by Angelo Roncalli on his election as supreme head of the Church on 28 October 1958 imply any authoritative settlement of this historical controversy. This did not even form any part of his intention.

1. *Outbreak of the Schism.* a) The Great Schism began with the contested elections of 1378. Gregory XI had died in Rome on 27 March 1378. A year earlier he had transferred the papal seat from Avignon back to the eternal city. Six of the cardinals had remained in Avignon. Only sixteen of the twenty-three cardinals participated in the papal election. Twelve of these were non-Italians (eleven French and one Spanish). The election took place amid scenes of tumult and the electors were exposed to outside pressure. Armed mobs invaded the conclave demanding a Roman or at least an Italian Pope. In great haste on 8 April 1378, the cardinals elected Bartolomeo Prignano, head of the papal chancellery, as supreme head of the Church. He had previously been proposed by various sides and was well-known to the electors, yet they did not dare to announce his name to the public. They

simply announced their choice of a Roman as Pope and took refuge in flight. On learning what had taken place, the Romans were mollified since the new Pope, Urban VI (1378–89), was an Italian. The cardinals returned and were present at his coronation and later at consistories. This continued for three months. Until recently it was possible to regard this tacit recognition as providing a subsequent legitimation of Urban's election, but recent research suggests that even this silent assent was accorded only "in a very incomplete fashion and under further persistent coercion" (K. A. Fink). A second argument used to challenge the legality of Urban's election was his mental incapacity. Certain indications point to his being mentally unbalanced, and according to the canonists indications of insanity affected the legality of an election. Complete certainty about the degree of mental instability as about the degree of intimidation is unattainable. All that can be said, therefore, in the present state of knowledge, is that the election of Urban VI was neither clearly valid nor clearly invalid.

b) The cardinals believed themselves justified in proceeding to a fresh papal election. Personal motives also played their part. Had Urban VI not treated these worldly cardinals in such an offensive manner, it is probable that a breach would not have occurred. But in fact the 12 non-Italian cardinals quitted Rome and, on 9 August 1378, in a declaration addressed to Christendom, they proclaimed the election of Urban VI invalid. On 20 September 1378, at Fondi, they elected a new Pope, Clement VII (1378–94). Even the Italian cardinals tacitly accepted this election and abandoned Urban. Clement VII took up residence at Avignon. Henceforth Christendom had two Popes. Which of them was the lawful successor of Peter? That is the important question. At the time it was impossible to answer it objectively. "If even contemporaries found themselves incapable of making up their minds, we too should be cautious and not pretend to know more than they knew." We can only endorse this judgment of the French scholar G. Mollat. Things were far more complicated than appears at first sight.

c) The immediate consequence of the double election was the division of Christendom into two opposing camps: the Roman obedience and the Avignon obedience. On the whole the Western countries adhered to the Avignon Pope, and the rest (Germans and Italians) to Rome. The schism extended into dioceses and the monastic orders. Practically the whole of Christendom was plunged into anxiety and uncertainty. A decision in earlier papal schisms had been assisted by the influence brought to bear by saints, as for example by Bernard of Clairvaux, who after the contested election of 1130 had helped to secure the recognition of Innocent II (1130–43), especially in France. But this time the most respected saints were divided between the two Popes. Catherine of Siena supported Urban VI, while St. Vincent Ferrer, the Spanish preacher of repentance, took the side of Clement VII.

2. *Attempts to heal the Schism*. At first responsibility for the schism was laid on the two Popes, but contemporaries soon abandoned this approach, concentrating their efforts instead on seeking ways and means to restore unity. These efforts provide the only rays of light in that confused period. The initiative came from the University of Paris. Broadly speaking, the solutions proposed by the Paris Faculty in 1394, following an enquiry, may be reduced to three: voluntary abdication *(via cessionis),* decision by a court of arbitration *(via compromissi),* and the calling of a General Council *(via concilii).* The first two ways involved an appeal to the good will of the Popes. But this solution, apparently the simplest, came to grief on the attitude of the Popes themselves. Clement VII had shown his hostility to the efforts at union. His successor Benedict XIII (1394–1417 or 1424) was so convinced of the legitimacy of his papal dignity that he rejected voluntary abdication as a profanation of the papacy. When in 1398 France withdrew from his obedience *(via subtractionis)* with the intention of forcing him to resign, he refused to be intimidated by this attempt at compulsion. France returned to Benedict's obedience in 1403.

The election of Gregory XII (1406–15) as the Roman Pope brought fresh hopes of restoring unity, since he was regarded as favourably disposed to union. Yet all efforts to bring the two Popes together for joint negotiations to reach agreement on abdication *(via discussionis)* proved fruitless. At this point thirteen cardinals from both camps took the decisive step, summoning a council to begin at Pisa on 21 March 1409. The Council was to depose the two Popes of dubious legitimacy and so clear the way for the election of one who would be universally acknowledged. The cardinals were able to find support for this course in the teaching of the canonists. A Pope who departed from the faith or who was guilty of immorality might be reprimanded by an institution and, if necessary, deposed. This was the task now undertaken by the Council of Pisa (1409). Most of the Christian countries were represented. By a duly ordered canonical process the two Popes were declared responsible for the continuing schism and deposed as notorious schismatics and heretics. The Council also elected a new Pope, Alexander V (1409–10). He was recognized by most of Christendom as rightful supreme head of the Church. In all probability the Pisan papal succession would have established itself as the legitimate one had not John XXIII (1410–15), the second in the line, undermined its credit. As it was, the other two Popes continued to maintain their position, even though their respective obediences had dwindled considerably.

3. *Restoration of unity by the Council of Constance.* While the Council of Pisa had pioneered the way for the healing of the breach, it was actually the Council of Constance (1414–18) which succeeded in restoring unity. Mainly on the insistence of King Sigismund, John XXIII had summoned this Council at the city on the Lake of Constance, hoping to carry the day with the help of his numerous Italian bishops. But the other nations opposed this, and succeeded in securing a change in the existing procedure. From 7 February 1415 the voting was no longer by individuals but by nations (Italian, French, German and English). This put an end to Italian preponderance. The position of John XXIII was still further shaken when he was attacked from his own ranks on the ground of his dubious morals. By his flight from Constance (March 1415) the Pisan Pope hoped to break up the Council, but it was saved by Sigismund who prevented it from dispersing and kept it in session. On the basis of the emergency decree *Haec Sancta* of 30 March 1415, the runaway Pope was deposed 29 May 1415. The greatest obstacle to the resignation of Gregory XII was thereby removed. The Council agreed to Gregory's condition, that it should let itself be re-convoked by him as Pope and on 4 July 1415, through his representatives, he renounced his papal title. Only the Avignon Pope, Benedict XIII, remained. Although Sigismund visited him in person, Benedict could not be persuaded

to resign. Instead, the king succeeded in persuading Aragon, Castille, Navarre and Scotland to abandon Benedict and won their support for the Council of Constance. A process against Benedict XIII was opened and he was deposed on 26 July 1417. The Apostolic See was now vacant. Martin V (1417–31) was chosen as the new Pope and in him the Church once more received a universally acknowledged head. The Western Schism was only finally healed in 1449 when Felix V, illegally elected by the Basle Synod in 1439, submitted to Nicholas V (1447–55).

4. *Ecclesiological significance of the Schism.* A sober recital of the main events of the Western Schism suffices to show that it brought the Church to a most serious crisis, in which it was in danger of breaking up. The seat of the crisis was the hierarchical summit. During the period when first two and then three Popes of dubious legitimacy reigned simultaneously, supreme authority devolved upon the college of bishops. In this way, formal unity was preserved, just as it is in the vacancy following the death of a Pope. The appalling danger lay in the fact that this state of affairs lasted forty years and flared up again from 1439 to 1449. Deliverance for the Church came through the conciliar (not "conciliarist") idea. A Council was the only viable means of restoring unity to the Church. The disputed decree *Haec Sancta* (superiority of the Council to the Pope) was "an emergency measure adopted in face of a quite definite and exceptional situation" (H. Jedin). It was only the Basle Synod which wished to make it a rule of faith. But the Council of Constance illustrates the fact "that an episcopalism sustained by the spirit of real collegiality and in solidarity with the Pope represents an essential extension and assurance of the primacy" (A. Franzen). Since the Second Vatican Council in particular it can be affirmed that the dangerous crisis of the Western Schism was overcome by the basic collegial structure of the Church.

See also *Episcopalism, Conciliarism, Cardinal.*

BIBLIOGRAPHY. See bibliography on *Conciliarism;* also: L. von Pastor, *History of the Popes,* I: *(1305–1447)* (1891); P. Hughes, *History of the Popes,* III: *(1274–1514)* (1947); J. Mundy and K. Woody, eds., *The Council of Constance. The Unification of the Church: Three Contemporary Accounts* (1961); A. Fliche and V. Martin, eds., *Histoire de l'Église,* XIV: *Le Grand Schisme de l'Occident,* by

E. Delaruelle and P. Ourliac (1962); N. Valis, *La France et le Grand Schisme de l'Occident,* 4 vols. (1966; reprint of ed. of 1896–1902).

Johann Baptist Villiger

SCHOLASTICISM

I. Nature and Approaches. II. Evolution: A. Pre-Scholasticism. B. Early Scholasticism. C. Classical Scholasticism. D. Later Scholasticism. E. Neo-Scholasticism.

I. Nature and Approaches

Scholasticism is a philosophy, theology and jurisprudence which in the Middle Ages stood for all known science. From the 7th century on, scholasticism developed through the stages of pre-scholasticism and early scholasticism to the classical period of the 12th and 13th centuries, setting up then a tradition lasting for seven hundred years, down to the present day. Post-classical or later scholasticism again reached high-points in Baroque scholasticism and neo-scholasticism. The philosophy and theology of the Catholic Church are no longer dominated exclusively by scholasticism, but it is on the whole basic, though its influence varies from country to country. Scholasticism has therefore known various phases of development and influence, and has been the subject of very different judgments in any given period of ecclesiastical or scientific history. Term and concept, content and method, influence and value have all been variously estimated. Nonetheless, if one considers the method rather than the matter, a consistent structure has persisted which justifies the application of the one word "scholasticism" to these traditions of Western thought which have lasted for so many centuries.

The word "scholastic" comes from the Latin *schola* (Greek σχολή), "school", whence *scholasticus,* meaning first the teacher and then including the students. The word "scholastic" was later applied to the method of teaching used in the schools and to the mentality behind it. In contrast to the spontaneous expositions of liturgical preaching and elementary catechetical instruction, or the spiritual dialogue practised in the monasteries, in contrast indeed to the mystical monastic theology in general, scholasticism organized the "holy Christian doctrine" as a body of knowledge. In the expanding cathedral and municipal schools, teaching became a special profession, demanding expert competence and official qualifications. The schools gradually became bodies which took on the character of autonomous institutes of education, as the new methods of science and teaching developed their own laws. They gave rise then in the 13th century to the great centres of formation which dominated modern Western culture and science, the universities. The organization of traditional learning into a rational body of knowledge is the specific and epoch-making element of scholasticism. This rational procedure in speculation and method and its application in practice and institutions are what have made scholasticism a historic factor in culture and a supremely important phenomenon in medieval thinking, with all its repercussions on the modern era.

1. *The "epochal" situation.* The perfecting of the scholastic method in classical scholasticism came about under the impulse of social and philosophical factors which made it "epochal", that is, it was a change brought about in the historical situation by a general principle. From the end of the patristic era till well into the 11th century, the studies pursued in the monastic schools, for a time the only centres of education, aimed essentially at preserving the traditional heritage, making compilations of new matter where possible and occasionally making excerpts of it for practical purposes. But studies as a whole were strictly orientated to practical and contemplative ends, in the interest of affective piety and the mystical aspiration to God. There was little interest in rational mastery and penetration of the traditional matter, much less in critical, analytical discussion. The recognized authorities were followed, which were primarily the Bible and the official pronouncements of the Church magisterium, and along with these unquestionably infallible sources, the "Fathers", among whom St. Augustine was the most frequently quoted and highly respected. The method taken for granted in theology was the obedient following of authentic or supposedly authentic tradition in general, and the proof from authority in particular, wherever the question of proof was allowed or deemed necessary. The first change was due to outstanding personalities, especially St. Anselm of Canterbury (1033–1109), who put some astonishingly radical questions about the purpose and nature of revelation, renouncing the proof from authority in the matter, and with his principle of *Credo ut*

intelligam, asserted a certain rationality of faith. In this he was not typical of his times, and he stood alone. But he opened up perspectives which were hardly exploited to the full even by classical scholasticism. However, his principle of presupposing a vigorous faith and trying on this basis to grasp it rationally with full assurance of its reasonableness, was a basic interest of scholasticism and entitles him to be called the "Father of Scholasticism". The dialectic of faith and knowledge was to remain the great unsolved problem as between monastic and scholastic theology, and indeed that of medieval theology in general. And under the heading of the distinction and reconciliation of "theoretical" and "practical" reason, Anselm's questioning was to re-echo in the central problems of post-medieval and modern philosophy.

But factors other than influential, learned Churchmen, who were mostly teachers of schools, brought the methodical, rational approach to fruition in classical scholasticism and created a new mentality. There were also social changes. A larger world was opened up by the discovery of new trade routes. The handicrafts expanded their range. The cities flourished. The nobles became a cultured class. Men grew more conscious of their responsible roles in Church and society, if not as individuals. Gothic art and courtly poetry contributed their share, as did the success of the Gregorian reform and the new outlets for religious and Church life offered by the new mendicant orders. The time was ripe for an epochal change in the mentality of the Christian West. A new perspective was opened up which was of fundamental importance for the one Christian Church as it then was in the West — in the same line or in dialectical opposition, as in the Reformation and Counter-Reformation — as it was for the history of man and science in general.

The philosophical framework of the development was first neo-Platonism, in the form transmitted by St. Augustine in particular. Plato was regarded as "the philosopher" but apart from a fragment of the *Timaeus,* little of his actual writings were known. The great change came when further works of Aristotle became accessible. Till the middle of the 12th century, only the *Logic* of Aristotle was known, through the translation of Boethius, and all that was covered was his work on the *Categories* and on *Interpretation.* But now the rest of his *Organum* (treatises on logic) was rediscovered, along with the two *Analytics,* the *Topics* and the *Sophistics,* and this "New Logic" was contrasted with the "Old Logic". At the same time, direct translations of his writings on metaphysics and natural philosophy appeared. Hitherto Aristotle had been known only indirectly on the whole, through the medium of Arab and Jewish philosophers (Averroes, Avicenna, Alfarabi, Moses Maimonides, Avicebron), working mainly in Spain under Arab rule, which meant that Arab translations of Aristotle were translated into Latin. But now Italy and Sicily entered the picture, and direct translations were made from the Greek, chiefly by Bartholomew of Messina and William of Moerbecke, the latter working for St. Thomas Aquinas. It was only this new acquaintance with Aristotle's logic, and above all with his natural history and metaphysics, which created the conditions for the revolutionary adoption of Aristotle by which Christian theology, in spite of the fierce opposition of Church authorities and monastic theologians, was fundamentally stamped, with a swiftness and intensity which in the prevailing conditions was extraordinary. From now on "the philosopher" is Aristotle. The adoption and interpretation of Aristotle as the key to a metaphysical and philosophical understanding of theology was the great achievement of scholasticism. This is what gave it its real significance, and in a certain fashion its full stature. From the point of view of the history of philosophy, this was also the end of scholasticism, though individual thinkers remain important.

2. *Method.* In contrast to the neo-scholastic way of presenting the matter in the form of theses, with its abstract and non-hermeneutical structure, teaching in medieval scholasticism took the form, primarily and on principle, of the reading *(lectio)* of authentic texts, especially from the Bible. The scholastic *lectio* also differed essentially from that of the monasteries. There it was built into the whole structure of the *opus Dei,* and like monastic theology in general, was carried on by monks. Reading and theological exposition were co-ordinated on principle to monastic life and time-tables, and were stamped by the spirit of monastic institutions and their liturgy and spirituality. In the light of this principle, monastic theology stressed the inviolable holiness of the word of God, which no method of logic could attain, much less render perspicuous. It was convinced that the gospel could not be scientifically analysed,

much less construed in terms of rational speculation. Theology was seen as wisdom, not as a science.

Scholasticism, on the contrary, used its logic and its technique of teaching to try to grasp rationally the *lectio*. But Scripture reading was not used merely to furnish theological propositions and theses with biblical citations and arguments. In keeping with the times, it was seen as total attention to the claim of the gospel as the foundation of the life of faith and fellowship. Assent to the word of God was the basic act in the theological effort of the original scholasticism. But here scholasticism found itself faced at once by the problem of the exact meaning of the word of God in the gospel and of how it finds expression in the writings of the OT and NT, as in the rest of authentic tradition. It was precisely on behalf of this necessary assent to the will of God that scholasticism applied the "dialectical method". This at first was merely clearing away linguistic and grammatical difficulties which stood in the way of the understanding of the literary meaning of the text. Harmonizations were attempted by the logic of the *sic et non*. Standing questions and their answers were treated in interpolated comments (taking the literary form of interlinear glosses) or gave rise to longer explanations and lectures (which took the literary form of the *glossa ordinaria marginalia*). In this comment in the form of glosses the dialectical method really came to bear fruit. The scholastics, when interpreting the texts, questioned more and more insistently, and in classical scholasticism with all the energy of their speculative armoury, their basic meaning. They went beyond the concrete difficulties of the texts to reach the basic problems of Christian life and faith, which they finally sought to grasp as a unity in the perspective of a modified Aristotelian metaphysics, by means of the new logical method of argument. A comprehensive system of the *sacra doctrina* was constructed.

The study and interpretation of the text took on a form which was finally stereotyped in a series of steps: question *(utrum)*, provisional answer *(videtur quod)*, objection *(sed contra)* and definitive answer by the professor *(respondeo)*. This technique of teaching and exposition did not simply demand that the student listen in faith. It called for close following and argumentation, though the decision on the question was mostly the function of the teacher. But the method forced the teacher to have reasons for his opinions and to be able to justify them before his colleagues in the *disputatio*. Here professors put forward their *quaestiones* and discussed them in set form, but in a strictly critical way.

This teaching technique gave rise to new literary genres. The glossing of the text gave rise to the *sententiae*, which were combined into collections of "Sentences". These collections of "Sentences" were then generally called *Commentaries*, when the individual thoughts and comments were organized into an ordered whole with each in its logical place. The regular disputations gave rise to the *quaestiones disputatae*, and the extraordinary ones, where anyone could put questions, gave rise to the *quodlibeta*. The *quaestiones*, at first closely connected with the *lectio*, but then becoming independent treatises, were given their major form in the *summa quaestionum*, the *articuli* of which are a series of *quaestiones disputatae* reduced to their essential schemas. Scholasticism was later called the age of the "Summas". The great commentaries and summas with their literary analyses and metaphysical speculation and a structure wholly based on scientific viewpoints were the great medium of self-expression for scholasticism. Its self-understanding was radically determined by faith, manifested in reverence for the infallible authorities, especially the word of God (in the *lectio*) and strict attachment to Christian tradition *(auctoritas)*. Hence came its desire to understand, so vigorously and successfully applied, which released speculative forces *(quaestio)* "moulding to meaning" the truths of faith and establishing theology for the first time as a science, while also gaining basic philosophical insights of permanent validity.

In late scholasticism things began to fall apart. The combination of *lectio, auctoritas* and *quaestio,* which had been worked out with so much genius but had never been deliberately analysed as a hermeneutical principle, was no longer maintained. The potent, genuine and creative self-understanding of scholasticism went into decline. The result was bizarre literary analysis, formalism and nominalism in logic, abstract speculation disjoined from tradition varied by an ill-considered empirical realism, hair-splitting dialectics and forced systematization. This launched the various phases of the anti-scholastic movements, from the *devotio moderna* and the Reformation down to the humanistic, philosophical and theological trends of the modern era.

3. *The self-understanding of scholasticism.* The decline of the authentic scholasticism of the golden age was not due merely to a contingent disavowal of its basic self-understanding. Scholasticism already bore within it, as the development of its methods shows, the makings of the crisis. It was justified no doubt in exposing the misplaced naivety of the monastic Augustinian theology and was therefore able to convince and prevail. But there were many fundamental interests of the older theology which it neglected to its peril. There was a sort of division of allegiance which could not work out well in the long run. Scholasticism agreed with the older theology in presupposing the authentic Christian tradition as the foundation of its self-understanding. But then it applied a rational method of untoward dimensions and, under the impulse of its Greek origins, a non-historical metaphysics. In contrast to their undistinguished successors, this problem had been recognized or sensed by the best thinkers and theologians of classical scholasticism. But even the compromise with the mystical and neo-Platonist Augustinian tradition of monasticism could not really help. The scholastic Enlightenment brought out very strongly the contrast between faith and knowledge, love and learning, tradition and speculation, history and metaphysics, nature and grace. At first, the original scholastic method provided them with a rudimentary set of relationships, but this same method, by virtue of its intrinsic dynamism, was unable really to reconcile them. Indeed, as late scholasticism shows in its nominalist and empiricist trends, it was bound to disrupt the tension. The approach used by scholasticism at an elementary level was not and could not be consciously reflected upon. But as soon as the forces of history had made it the object of conscious attention, the insufficiencies of the hermeneutical and speculative method of scholasticism could not be ignored, precisely because of its lack of understanding as regards its own processes. The balance swung from one extreme to the other in the contrast between faith and knowledge etc.

Even in classical scholasticism, therefore, treatment of such central Christian themes as freedom, the person and history was to a great extent lacking. Not that these realities were not envisaged at all, but they were not included in the system as constitutive elements. As we can see from present-day standpoints, salvation-history did not appear precisely as history, much less as history-qua-revelation in the dialogal process of personal freedom and the dialectic of ecclesial society. These dimensions of the Christian self-understanding could of course only be consciously grasped later. But they were at work as practical problems in the controversies between the various medieval theologies and were latent in the practical self-understanding of scholasticism itself, permitting in the light of modern reflection a balanced judgment on the ancient debates. A simplified historical picture may be given as follows. The Augustinian and monastic theology, which had a far more authentic grasp of revelation as salvation-history, refused to expose itself to the rational questioning of scholasticism, sensing instinctively rather than seeing clearly the consequences of such questioning. And scholastic theology could no longer remain within the framework of the ancient usage, but in breaking away, could not but cloud the Christian self-understanding in favour of formal speculation and institutional rationality — again without seeing clearly what was going on.

These unsolved problems of the reasonableness of revelation and its free historicity, along with the various solutions hitherto proposed, have been the destiny of theology down to the present day. Scholasticism succeeded in laying down for the first time the scientific bases of theology. Its great merit is that it recognized the necessity of this step and set to work on it, which means that it is essentially a theology, not a philosophy. But in doing so it introduced a type of questioning into theology which never found its own true fulfilment and hence could function only as a restorative element. Only by "new blood", this time from modern philosophy, can theology be constituted as a science able to meet contemporary demands. Only the adoption — in the sense of a critical interpretation — of modern transcendental philosophy (Descartes, Kant, Fichte, Hegel), including the existentialist and Marxist reaction to it, can so re-mould the method and content of theology that it need neither set wrong limits to its absolute rationality nor abandon it entirely, nor again gloss over the grace-given historicity of its free thrusts. But this is what will enable it to be a science of faith and the history of faith. Hence it is not a question of simply repudiating scholasticism, but of entering into dialogue with its great representatives, as with modern thinkers. This has already been undertaken within the Church in recent years. But then the question is how such dialogue can be inserted into a teaching philosophy and theology which have hitherto been part of the continuity between scholasticism and the Church, and worked out by scholasticism as such. It is hard to see how the Church can abandon this approach, in favour of which there are so many pedagogical, didactic and historic institutional reasons.

BIBLIOGRAPHY. See bibliographies on *Scholasticism* II A, B, C, D, E, and especially: P. Van Steenberghen, *Le mouvement doctrinal du IXe au XIVe siècle* (1951); id., *Aristotle in the West* (1955); M.-D. Chenu, *La théologie comme science au XIIIe siècle* (3rd ed., 1957); id., *La théologie au XIIe siècle* (1957); A. Grillmeier, "Vom Symbolum zur Summa", *Festschrift J. R. Geiselmann* (1960), pp. 119–69; J. B. Metz, *Christliche Anthropozentrik* (1962).

Eberhard Simons

II. Evolution

A. Pre-Scholasticism

Pre-scholasticism is the term used to describe the theology and philosophy of the 7th to the 11th century, to distinguish it from the preceding patristic theology (see *Patrology* II, III) and the subsequent period of early scholasticism. A number of spiritual trends are combined, of which the common element may be said to be the effort to make use of an imperfectly mastered classical culture in the understanding of faith, while trying to do justice to the special nature of religious knowledge.

1. In most of the countries of Western Europe the 7th and 8th centuries were dark ages for culture. The Roman school system and with it the classical education of the ancient world had almost vanished. The literate were few. The great monasteries alone were centres of learning and its transmission. Here the influence of the Irish and Anglo-Saxon monks was very great. In the cultural centres of their homelands a good Latin was taught, and their devotion to study was characteristic. In the *scriptoria* of their continental foundations they built up huge libraries. The most important scholar of the times was the Venerable Bede, a diligent compiler, who studied the works of numerous Fathers of the Church, putting his own questions and formulating his own answers.

2. The Carolingian Renaissance brought with it a revival of learning (see *Reform* II A).

The goal of this revival was religious. Education was regarded as an integral part of religious culture and religious life (i.e., worship). This was shown above all in the high regard for the study of languages, regarded as the prerequisite of all formation. Along with reading the ancients, students were taught to write once more a correct Latin. The general culture of antiquity, knowledge of natural history and of ancient history penetrated France along with the ancient language. In view of the connection between Hellenism and Christianity, these studies were regarded as a prelude to the science of the faith and urgently recommended to clerics.

The liberal arts played an important part in the school curriculum. They were expected to develop the intellectual powers necessary to the full understanding of the faith. The text-books of Martianus Capella, Donatus and Priscian, as well as the translations, commentaries and theological writings of Boethius were diligently studied. As early as Alcuin, one of the most important organizers of studies in France, there are initial approaches to scholastic exercises, e.g., the learned *disputatio,* which was to play a great part in early and classical scholasticism. Alcuin claimed that even the contents of revelation should be discussed dialectically and tried himself to present the doctrines of the Trinity, incarnation, creation and last things according to a dialectical method, though he did not in fact depart far from the style of St. Augustine and Boethius (*In Topica Ciceronis: PL,* LXIV, cols. 1047 ff.).

Studies were centred on Scripture. The liberal arts were esteemed for the help they gave in understanding Scripture. Most of the writings of the period are commentaries on Scripture. From the British Isles, the most important commentators were Smaragdus, Sedulius Scotus (Scotus = Irish), John Scotus Erigena. There were Agobard and Florus of Lyons; the Germans Rabanus Maurus and Walafrid Strabo; Paschasius Radbertus belonged to the Abbey of Corbei; Dunchadh (Donaghue), Heiricius, Remigius and Haimo worked at St. Germain of Auxerre. The exegesis was strongly traditional. The writers did not presume to offer independent viewpoints. Their main intention was to make the wisdom of the ancient Church available to wider circles. They drew on the Latin Fathers, especially St. Augustine. But some Greek writers were also known, e.g., Dionysius the Pseudo-

Areopagite, through the works of Scotus Eriugena and Hilduin of St. Denis. But independence was shown in the choice of material, the summing up of patristic teaching and its application to new questions, especially those of general theological interest. These included Adoptianism, which was articulated in some Christological formulas of the Mozarabic Church, and Predestination put forward in the form of a conditional positive reprobation by Gottschalk of Orbais, but attributed to the divine *praescientia periturorum* by Rabanus Maurus, Hincmar of Rheims and John Scotus Erigena. In the first of the medieval controversies about the Eucharist, Rabanus Maurus, Paschasius Radbertus and Rathramnus, like Gottschalk, tried to determine the mode of the eucharistic presence. The iconoclast controversy spread to the West as a consequence of the decree of the Second Council of Nicaea (on the reverence of images), which was rejected by the *Libri Carolini* (see *Images*).

3. The political disturbances during the decline of the Carolingian Empire also ended the cultural renaissance. No important works were written in the second half of the 10th and the first part of the 11th century. But a period in which the poems and plays of Hrosvit of Gandersheim had great success and which sympathized with the mathematical and scientific interests of Gerbert of Aurillac (afterwards Pope Silvester II) was not without culture and it would be an exaggeration to call it a Dark Age. The liberal arts were more and more widely learned and esteemed. It was the age of the wandering scholars. Students from all over the West came to Chartres to listen to the master of the liberal arts and biblical and patristic scholar, Fulbert of Chartres.

4. In the second part of the 11th century the teaching of Lanfranc of Pavia and St. Anselm of Canterbury drew students to Bec. Scholarly Churchmen corresponded frequently. Fulbert of Chartres wrote many scholarly epistles and the provocative statements of Berengarius of Tours on the Eucharist raised a storm of epistolary protest, e.g., from Adelmann of Liège, Durandus of Troarn, Guitmund of Aversa, Hugh of Breteuil and Lanfranc of Pavia. The Gregorian Reform with its struggle against simony and lay investiture gave a great impulse to scientific study. The literary controversy meant that the biblical and patristic texts appealed to had to be critically examined, and jurists and theologians were forced by their opponents to try to substantiate their arguments.

5. The main preoccupation of the period was how far the dialectial method of thinking learned from antiquity was applicable to the understanding of the faith. All the important writers used the dialectical method of proof, even the anti-dialecticians, and much more than the writers of the Carolingian Age. St. Anselm of Canterbury wrote a special book *(De Grammatico)* to show how he trained the young monks in dialectical thinking. On the basis of a firm faith, all the tools of human reason were employed to investigate the meaning, coherence and value of the truths of faith. Difficulties began only when conclusions were reached which did not conform to the doctrine of Scripture and the Fathers (Berengarius of Tours, perhaps Roscelin of Compiègne) or when truths of faith were treated with a lack of religious reverence. These abuses brought about an anti-dialectical reaction in the middle of the 11th century, which, while not declaring dialectics illegitimate or worthless, sought to restrict its use (Gerard of Csanád, Othloh of St. Emmeram, Manegold of Lautenbach, St. Peter Damian). The representatives of this trend denied that the laws of thought and nature could provide such absolute certainty that they could be used to reject a truth of faith. Concepts derived from human experience were not to be applied without distinction to God. Intellectual effort was not aimed at mere knowledge, but at a salutary grasp of the faith. In a word, wordly sciences were to be at the service of Christian wisdom.

See also *Dialectics, Hellenism and Christianity, Reform* II C.

BIBLIOGRAPHY. See bibliographies on *Scholasticism* II B, C; also: H. Waddell, *The Wandering Scholars* (1927); id., *Poetry in the Dark Ages* (1948); J. Ryan, *Irish Monasticism* (1931; reprint with new introduction, 1969); A. H. Thompson, ed., *Bede, His Life and Times* (1935; reprint, 1969); C. Burns, *The First Europe: A Study of the Establishment of Medieval Christendom* (1948); F. Ueberweg, *Grundriss der Geschichte der Philosophie*, II (12th ed., 1927), pp. 157–209; P. de Labriolle and others, in A. Fliche and V. Martin, eds., *Histoire de l'Église*, IV (1948); A. Forest, *ibid.*, XIII (1956), pp. 1–73; M. Laistner, *The Intellectual Heritage of the Early Middle Ages* (1950; reprint, 1969); H. Adams, *Mont-Saint-Michel and Chartres* (1959); M.

Deansely, *The Pre-Conquest Church in England* (1961); R. Southern, *Saint Anselm and his Biographer* (1963); L. Bieler, *Ireland, Harbinger of the Middle Ages* (1963); D. T. Rice, *The Dawn of European Civilisation* (1965).

Zoltan Alszeghy

B. EARLY SCHOLASTICISM

1. From the end of the patristic era to the beginning of the 12th century there was, on the whole, little progress on the intellectual plane. Men were content to collect and sift their cultural inheritance, without developing personal initiatives in a critical grasp and estimation of the material. After some abortive efforts in the pre-scholastic period, a change came with Anselm of Canterbury (1033/4–1109), whose methodology of "credo ut intelligam" (*Proslogion,* ch. 1) entitles him to be called the father of scholasticism. But Anselm remains alone in early scholasticism, both in the loftiness of his goal and in its practical implementation. He was concerned with penetrating into the mystery of faith by faith-enlightened reason, without either relying on authorities or rationalizing the mystery. Elsewhere in early scholasticism the proof from authority played a large part, and in the course of the 12th century the *intellectus fidei* became more and more an exercise in deduction, less concerned with the mysteries themselves than with building on the individual truths of faith to make progress in a knowledge extrinsically connected with them.

2. The new departure in theology and philosophy was not due to the discovery of new sources or methods. It was primarily due to the influence of personalities, and was paralleled in all fields of human activity in this epoch. Economic history is characterized by new handicrafts and new commercial routes, the social order by feudalism and the city state; politics by the rise of the national state, the plastic arts by the advent of the Gothic, literature by court poetry and the romance of chivalry; religion, by the success of the Gregorian Reform.

3. The philosophical framework for this new departure was that of neo-Platonism, as represented above all by Augustine, who was the most frequently quoted and most highly revered authority after sacred Scripture. Other sources, though far less important than Augustine, were: Cassiodorus, Isidore of Seville, Martianus Capella, Gregory the Great, Jerome, Denis the Areopagite, John Damascene and Origen. As interest in purely philosophical problems grew, scholars turned also to Plato himself, especially in the school of Chartres (Adelard of Bath, Bernard and Thierry of Chartres, Clarebald of Arras, William of Conches), though only part of the *Timaeus* was available, in the translation of Chalcidius. Against this cultural background it is understandable that Plato was the great philosopher for early scholasticism.

4. Till the beginning of the 12th century, theological formation and study were confined to a great extent to the monastic schools. But then they were joined by the cathedral schools, which rapidly gained great influence on ecclesiastical and cultural life, offering along with theology the liberal arts, law and sometimes medicine. This paved the way for the new departure in theological thought and purpose which has been spoken of above. While the contemplative monastic orders (Benedictines, Cistercians) sought for an affective and mystical union with God — which was also the aim of Anselm, in spite of his apologetical and dialectical method — scholastic theology was primarily concerned with progress in knowledge, also by dialectics. Here the tools of logic were provided by the translations of Aristotle and the commentaries of Boethius *(logica vetus)*. The dialectical method was not pursued for its own sake, as was done to a great extent in the faculties of arts, where it sometimes led to pure formalism in logic and hence evoked the opposition of the anti-dialecticians at the other extreme. The application of dialectics to theology was chiefly effected by Peter Abelard (1079–1142) with his commentaries on logic and his *Sic et non,* where the use of dialectics in theology was explicitly justified and its value demonstrated by the harmonization of conflicting patristic assertions, and by Gilbert of Poitiers (*c.* 1080–1154) with his commentaries on the *Opuscula Sacra* of Boethius. This was against the opposition of monastic theology, headed by the influential Bernard of Clairvaux (*c.* 1090–1153). Abelard was condemned for theological errors at the Council of Soissons (1121) and the Synod of Sens (1141), but Gilbert, who had been delated to the Pope for trinitarian heresy, managed to avoid condemnation both at the consistory of Paris (1147) and at that of Rheims (1148). He emerged the victor from his controversy with Bernard.

Along with such accusations, some of which were justified, while others were based on misunderstandings, there was also a fundamental opposition to dialectics and its use in theology, voiced for instance by Walter of St. Victor. When the rest of the *Organum* of Aristotle was put into circulation about the middle of the 12th century (the *"logica nova": Analytica Priora, Analytica Posteriora, Topica, De Elenchis Sophisticis*), the whole movement received a new impulse and the anti-dialecticians lost ground. However, monastic and scholastic theology cannot always be neatly separated. In Hugh of St. Victor in particular (d. 1141), the most comprehensive theologian of this epoch, and in the school of which he was a representative, both tendencies were happily united.

The specific element in early scholastic theology is the method, which was enshrined in the external form of instruction and in scholarly literature (Commentaries, *Quaestio, Summa*). It was strictly rational in procedure, but gave faith precedence over natural knowledge, on account of the historical situation of fallen man (*homo incurvatus,* as Anselm said). The multiplicity of the themes treated is characteristic. Individual teachers of repute formed schools, as in Laon, where Anselm and Radulf of Laon taught, and William of Champeaux, later founder of the school of St. Victor. At Chartres there were Gilbert of Poitiers (Gilbert de la Porrée), John of Salisbury, Otto of Freising, Alan de l'Isle, Radulfus Ardens and Joachim of Fiore. At Paris there were Abelard, Peter Lombard, Peter of Poitiers, Robert Pourson, Simon of Tournai, Peter of Capua, Praepositinus (Prevostin), Stephen Langton, William of Auxerre; at St. Victor, Hugo and Richard. Each school debated fruitfully with the others. But a consistent view of theology as a whole was impossible for lack of a metaphysics to provide the presuppositions. All that could be done was to collect the theological material in "sentences", harmonize them dialectically and systematize them under various heads. Following Augustine, a general division was made between relative and absolute values *(utenda et fruenda).* Abelard proposed three divisions, under *fides, caritas* and *sacramentum.* In this effort at a systematic division of theology Peter Lombard (*c.* 1095–1160) was important, with his *Libri quattuor Sententiarum.* In keeping with most of the early creeds, he divided this work into four books following the

chronological order of the history of salvation: 1) God, 2) creation, 3) redemption, 4) sacraments and eschatology. The Lombard was not one of the great creative spirits of the 12th century. His work was rather characterized by a balanced and critical selection from the various opinions of the schools and by a perspicuous division of the material. Its purely practical value made it the great manual for theological study and teaching from the end of the 12th century on. Hence the plan he followed became normative, and has remained so in many respects and in various modifications down to the present day.

5. Along with the systematization of the *Sentences,* and the solution of many individual problems the great contribution of the early period for scholasticism as a whole was the development and application of the dialectical method. Special attention was paid to working out a precise philosophical and theological terminology, to which the linguistic logic in this period is an eloquent testimony. Hence ensued also a change of attitude towards Plato—as known in his neo-Platonist and Augustinian guise — which led up to the classical period of scholasticism. The use of Aristotelian logic (Aristotle was known only as a logician to the 12th century, and highly prized as such) and the consequent penetration of some of the metaphysical notions gradually prepared the way for the general reception of his metaphysical writings in the first years of the 13th century. The revelation of the "new Aristotle" was of immense importance for the philosophy and theology of the time, and marks the caesura which must be placed between early scholasticism and the classical period, in spite of a certain continuity. The same period saw the founding of the first universities, at Paris and Bologna, through which a new external framework was also provided for the life of the spirit.

BIBLIOGRAPHY. M. Grabmann, *Mittelalterliches Geistesleben,* 3 vols. (1926–56); C.H. Haskins, *The Renaissance of the Twelfth Century* (1927); A. Macdonald, *Authority and Reason in the Early Middle Ages* (1933); G. Paré, A. Brunet and P. Tremblay, *La renaissance du XIIᵉ siècle* (1933); R. Klibansky, *The Continuity of the Platonic Tradition during the Middle Ages* (1939); F. Copleston, *History of Philosophy,* II: *Medieval Philosophy* (1950); E. Gilson, *History of Christian Philosophy in the Middle Ages* (1955); A. Landgraf, *Einführung in die Geschichte ... der Frühscholastik* (1948); P. Chenu,

Théologie du XII siècle* (1957); J. Leclercq, *Love of Learning and Desire for God. Monastic Culture in the Middle Ages* (1962).

Richard Heinzmann

C. CLASSICAL SCHOLASTICISM

1. *General character.* The difference between classical scholasticism and its earlier form can only be indicated by listing many external and internal elements. External elements: the new stimulus to scientific enquiry resulting from the founding of the first universities; the creation or further development of new literary forms and methods (Commentaries on the *Sentences,* the *Summas,* the *Quaestio* form of argument and counter-argument); the greater importance attached to *ratio* alongside the authorities of Scripture and tradition. Internal characteristics of the new epoch derived from the steadily increasing knowledge of Aristotle, mediated partly by Arabian and Jewish scholasticism then becoming known in the West (Avicenna, Algazel, Averroes, Moses Maimonides) and partly by new 13th century translations from Greek into Latin (William of Moerbecke), whence the Aristotelianism of scholasticism. And the Augustinian-Neoplatonist strand in early scholasticism was further developed. The interweaving and attempted syntheses of these two strands in the 13th century present special problems for research.

Classical scholasticism begins with the question whether theology can be reconciled with the Aristotelian concept of science and with its deductive method. Is an independent philosophy possible alongside theology? What is the highest or most general principle from which all that exists may be deduced (*bonum* or *esse,* various forms of the doctrine of transcendentals)? The various philosophical and theological trends in the Middle Ages are much more distinctive, however, than it was possible to realize even a few decades ago. They can no longer be classified under various simple labels, e.g., the Dominican school as predominantly Aristotelian, or Franciscan theology as predominantly Augustinian-Neoplatonist. One can, however, say with due reserve that the Franciscan Order was more cautious and critical of an Aristotelian view of theology and that Thomas Aquinas and his school maintained a stricter division between theology and philosophy.

New literary forms: the four books of Peter Lombard's *Sentences* became a theological source-book for scholasticism to

such a degree that commentary on them forms a stable element of theological education right down to the period of late scholasticism and even the arrangement of the great *Summas* (and to some extent even of dogmatic text-books down to the present day) was determined by this early scholastic work. This applies, however, only to the formal arrangement and division of the material, not to the philosophical assumptions nor to the main theological emphases in the commentaries on the *Sentences* at any given time. The many extant printed and manuscript commentaries afford eloquent testimony to the variety of theological and philosophical attitudes possible among authors using this literary genre. One of the earliest of such Commentaries to go beyond Peter Lombard was that of Stephen Langton at the turn of the 13th century.

In the *Summas* an attempt was made to attain universality and completeness. Although many *Summae Theologicae* remained unfinished, all of them reveal a tendency to touch in some way on every philosophical and theological problem which could be raised in their day. Individual themes could be dealt with by using a shorter literary form in which questions were collected together (*Quaestiones Disputatae* and *Quodlibetas*). For the question of the essence and methods of scholasticism see I above.

2. *Trends and themes.* An overall picture of the period may be obtained by a brief account of the chief scholastic theologians.

It begins with William of Auvergne (*c.* 1180–1249), Robert Grosseteste (*c.* 1168–1253), William of Auxerre (to 1231 or 1237) and Philip the Chancellor (1160 or 1185–1236).

a) *William of Auvergne,* when Bishop of Paris, founded the first Dominican university chair and so paved the way for the scientific activity of the Dominican school. His main work, *Magisterium Divinale,* provided a general conspectus of Christian doctrine (doctrine of God, Creation, Christology, Sacraments, Ethics) and adopted a polemic style aimed at persuading those who seemed in danger from Arabian-Jewish philosophy. Far from dissolving the faith by rationalizing it, however, William stressed its anthropological significance, since faith provided the individual with contact with human society and the understanding of faith was the common spiritual inheritance of all Christians.

b) *Robert Grosseteste,* first Chancellor of the

University of Oxford and later Bishop of Lincoln, established the first foundation of the Franciscans at Oxford, himself lecturing to the brothers, and may therefore be regarded as the ancestor of the Franciscan school there. Grosseteste wrote commentaries on Aristotle's *Posterior Analytics* and *Physics,* translated the *Nicomachean Ethics* and composed several smaller works, mostly on natural philosophy. His study of the problem of time and eternity had already led him to distinguish non-Christian elements in Aristotle's philosophy from elements useful for Christian thought. His interest in the theory of "illumination", to the new understanding of which he applied scientific thought, linked him with the neo-Platonist tradition. In his cosmogony he tried to reconcile the Christian doctrine of creation with the neo-Platonist idea of emanation, by describing how, once the divinely created light encountered the original matter and began to give it form, one substance must have developed from the other.

c) *William of Auxerre,* Magister in Paris, cautiously introduced Aristotle's metaphysics and ethics into his chief work, his four books *Summa Aurea,* which became an important model for classical scholasticism. He was no less important as a bridge between early scholasticism and classical scholasticism, especially for these theologians who in the period of early scholasticism itself did not so much create "atmosphere" as pioneer intellectual approaches which still awaited development. His *Summa Aurea* had considerable influence on the Dominican and Franciscan schools in Paris. To a rather lesser degree this was also true of *Philip the Chancellor* (of the Bishop of Paris), who treated the whole of theology from the standpoint of the "good", in his *Summa de bono.*

d) The early Franciscan school is represented by the so-called *Summa fratris Alexandri* or *Summa Halensis* which, until the work done by the editors of the critical Quaracchi edition, was regarded as a work of Alexander of Hales (*c.* 1185–1245) but in fact was a composite work by members of his school (Alexander's *Sentences, Glosses* and *Questions,* the *Questions* of John de la Rochelle, those of Odo Rigaldi, anonymous *Questions,* as well as the *Summa Aurea* of William of Auxerre, the most important of the non-Franciscan sources). Alexander, a Franciscan for about 50 years, remained in his post after his admission to the Order and so secured his Order's first chair at the University of Paris.

The most important sections of the *Summa Halensis* were completed in the year of Alexander's death. Slightly revised parts of Bonaventure's *Commentary on the Sentences* were added later, in particular to the doctrine of the state of original justice, in Book III. Book IV, dealing with the sacraments and somewhat poorer in quality than the other sections, was expanded by William of Melitona but never finished. All the fundamental ideas of the Franciscan school, from Bonaventure down to Scotus, are already to be found in this work: the "salvation-history" view that theology has superseded philosophy, because for the Christian thinker with access to revelation, philosophy no longer has any legitimate place in theology except as a method; theology is related to *sapientia* rather than to *scientia,* although an attempt is made to secure for theology the dignity of a science in the Aristotelian sense without identifying it completely with such a science; *pietas* and *affectio* are given priority over the purely speculative intellect and the deductive method; emphasis is on the volitional aspect of theological anthropology. Some of the individual views of this *Summa* incline more to Scotus than to Bonaventure, others were later rejected by Scotus in opposition to both the *Summa Halensis* and Bonaventure. From the very beginnings of the Franciscan school there is not only dynamic development but also discussion and a variety of viewpoints. The importance of this first major Franciscan *Summa* in the scholastic school, even compared with that of Thomas Aquinas, has hitherto not been sufficiently recognized.

So far as its place in the history of thought is concerned, the *Summa Halensis* harmonizes its various sources, with their various attitudes to Aristotelian and Augustinian-Neoplatonist trends, as follows: the conception of being, in the *Summa,* is either neo-Platonist (*diffusio summi boni*) or Aristotelian (knowledge of the particular spheres of being, knowledge of the world, doctrine of abstraction), depending on whether the standpoint adopted moves from uncreated to created being or vice versa. Aristotelian and neo-Platonist modes of thought are used as mutually complementary methods; they do not stand unrelated side by side, as used to be thought. In the *Summa Halensis,* the Franciscan doctrine of matter and form in created things (including the purely spiritual) is interpreted as follows: spiritual and material beings are close together from the standpoint of creatureliness by being metaphysically composite (God alone the *simplex esse*). Even the spiritual is needy, limited, transitory. But since there is no natural immortality of the soul based on the soul's indivisibility and metaphysical simplicity, there is also only, on this view, a mortality of the whole man which is overcome by an *immortalitas ex gratia*. But this immortality by grace depends upon the subjective personal appropriation of the objective salvation-history (Christ's incarnation, death, and glorification) by the individual believer. Such speculative approaches, with their theological reservations about Aristotle, contain *in nuce* a theology of matter, the world and history, which excludes any one-sided intellectualism. Yet it proved impossible for scholasticism to develop such a theology further than the point reached in the *Summa Halensis*.

e) *Albertus Magnus* (*c.* 1200–1280) entered the Dominican Order, taught in Cologne, Hildesheim, Freiburg, Regensburg, Strasbourg, and, during the last years of the life of Alexander of Hales, in Paris. For a short time he was Bishop of Regensburg. He was most at home in the *Studium Generale* of his Order in Cologne, where Thomas Aquinas was his pupil from 1248 to 1252, and where he also died. Albert the Great is known as the "universalist" of the Middle Ages, embodying as he did the knowledge of his age in philosophy, theology, natural science and medicine and producing works in all these fields. But he had no desire to be an encyclopedist; his aim was to penetrate these fields of knowledge spiritually. It is due mainly to him that there is a medieval period in the history of medicine and biology. Although he made a clean sweep of the mythological concepts of nature widespread in his day, it is not surprising that many misconceptions are still found in his works. Albert was concerned especially to distinguish Averroistic Aristotelianism, which regarded itself as the authentic version, from an Aristotelianism based on the re-discovered works of Aristotle himself. But he also turned to the Augustinian-Neoplatonist tradition and gave it an important place in his theology. Because of his personal piety, Albert enjoyed a high reputation as a preacher. Various influential works of late medieval piety were consequently long attributed to his pen, in particular the famous *Mariale*. Albert's interest in neo-Platonism together with his specifically religious writings were the stimulus to Dominican mysticism.

From Albert's first period, his stay in Paris from 1244 to 1248, came in particular his works on systematic theology, the *"Summae" De Sacramentis, De Incarnatione, De Resurrectione, De Bono;* his *Commentary on the Sentences* and the *Summa de Creaturis*. During his Cologne period, from 1248, he was at work on his commentaries on the pseudo-Dionysian writings and on the extant Aristotelian writings and the pseudo-Aristotelian *Liber de Causis*. This work, which lasted until his sixties, took the form of a rendering of Aristotle in paraphrase. Aristotle's ethics, physics, metaphysics, and politics were now accessible to the West in the Christian dress given them by Albert's mind. In his later years, Albert is primarily the theologian once more, writing commentaries on the prophets and the gospels, composing eucharistic works and a *Summa Theologiae,* the authenticity of which has recently been challenged. It would be an error, however, to allow Albert's theological originality to be overshadowed by his philosophical and scientific work. He had a profound understanding of holy Scripture, as his commentary on Luke in particular shows. His exegesis stands out against the background of allegorical interpretation customary in the scholastic period, evincing a marked interest in the literal sense even though tied to medieval conceptions. In respect of this theological work, Albert is in particular a pioneer of an independent Mariology, separate from Christology. He prepared the way for a distinction, though not a separation, between philosophy and theology, yet did not make this a reason for excluding philosophical thought from theology.

f) We turn once more to the Franciscan school in the person of *Bonaventure* (Giovanni di Fidanza, 1217/18–1274). Born at Viterbo, he studied in the Faculty of Arts at Paris, entering the Franciscan Order in 1243. His teachers were Alexander of Hales, John de la Rochelle, Odo Rigaldi, and William of Melitona, so that his intellectual development was entirely within early Franciscan thought. It was probably in 1253 that he became Master of Theology in the University of Paris, but his teaching career was interrupted by the opposition to the Mendicant Orders (William of St. Amour, the great adversary of the Franciscans and Dominicans, becoming Chancellor). When in 1257 he was eventually given a theological chair at the same time as Thomas Aquinas, his call to the generalship of his Order led him to different tasks. In 1272 he became Bishop of Albano. He died in 1274, towards the end of the Council of Lyons.

In independence, comprehensiveness and detail, Bonaventure's *Commentary on the Sentences* ranks as a theological *Summa*. In addition to *Questions* on individual themes and to his *Breviloquium,* an exposition of Christian dogmatics, special mention must be made of his shorter mystical works and his writings on the theology of history, e.g., his *De reductione artium ad theologiam,* the *Itinerarium mentis in Deum* and the *Collationes in Hexaemeron.* In his later period, Bonaventure also concerned himself with questions of Church politics. His countless sermons influenced popular piety, mysticism and religious poetry. He also dealt intensively with the foundation and historical mission of his Order.

In the course of his life, Bonaventure's attitude to philosophy and speculative theology underwent a change. In his *Commentary on the Sentences,* he incorporated Aristotelian thought fully into his theology while maintaining critical reserve and refusing to apply Aristotelian concepts (e.g., hylemorphism) uncritically to theological facts, allowing them a place only where they seemed appropriate and rejecting them where, in his view, they would distort the truth because of the special nature of the theological theme. Scholastic thoroughness, conceptual precision and discrimination were consciously allied in Bonaventure with a theology sought as *sapientia* on the basis of *pietas.* Fundamental to his thought is the concept of *reductio,* i.e., leading back to an ultimate goal. In the origin of all things in God and the return of all things to him, Christ occupies the absolute centre. This explains the Christocentrism found in all Bonaventure's works, sometimes explicitly, whether in his concept of theology or in his primarily mystical *opuscula.* His theology of history, influenced by Joachim of Fiore, provides the background to this Christocentrism. Bonaventure stood apart from the transition in which the older conception of history, which regarded Christ's coming as the eschatological event and the dawning of the last days, was giving way to the newer conception according to which there is a series of six or seven ages before and after Christ, with Christ as the centre of time.

In the course of his career, Bonaventure turned more and more to wisdom as contemplative *sapientia* and made much less

of discursive science. What began as tension-in-unity between *scientia* and *sapientia,* between *meditatio* and *contemplatio,* turns into a mystical ascent. This was the way taken by Bonaventure himself and, on this basis, he adopted in his later writings a more negative position to the Aristotelians of his day, not so much against Thomas Aquinas as against his followers. All his life, Bonaventure was the very opposite of a syncretizer of neo-Platonist Augustinianism and Aristotelianism. In fact his attitude to Aristotle and to philosophical thought was always clear. But his standpoint shifted according to his personal history. This should not mislead us into interpreting the scholastic Bonaventure in terms of the later Bonaventure who prophesied the end of intellectualist theology, for we have to reckon more and more with the originality and independence of the scholastic Bonaventure's clearly defined and firmly grounded attitude to questions of philosophical theology: immortality of the soul based not on the metaphysical indivisibility of the soul but on the dignity of the human person whose true end is the *reductio ad Deum;* graded analogy between created natures and their Creator; co-operation between senses, intellectual activity and illumination; man's self-knowledge as the way to experience of God but not proof of God in the sense of a rational demonstration.

The so-called "middle" Franciscan school, represented by Matthew of Aquasparta, Roger of Marston, John Peckham and Peter of John Olivi, would have been inconceivable without Bonaventure. Unfortunately these theologians are better known for their polemic against Thomas than for the original contributions they undoubtedly made. The difference between the modes of thought in Thomas and Bonaventure was brought into the controversy, despite the fact that both have their validity. This was a historical calamity for which neither of the two great theologians can be held responsible.

g) *Thomas Aquinas (c.* 1225–1274) is seen today without the accretions of various phases of Thomism. He appears less as the "sole arbiter", but for that again, more clearly in the true originality of his genius. He is perhaps the most consistent of all the classical scholastics in constructing a system of his own. He became acquainted with Aristotelian philosophy at the University of Naples and there encountered the Dominican Order into which, contrary to his parents' wishes, he was received in 1243/44. After his studies in Paris and Cologne, he finally received his licence to teach at the University of Paris. During this period he wrote his *Commentary on the Sentences* (differing somewhat from the later *Summa Theologica* in its attitude to many problems), his *Commentaries on Pseudo-Dionysius and Boethius,* his *Quaestiones de veritate,* which for its philosophical clarity is rated among the finest of his works, and the philosophical work *De ente et essentia.* From 1261 to 1265, he taught at the Papal Court at Orvieto and at the Dominican monastery there. The later sixties saw him in Rome, Bologna, and at the Papal Court in Viterbo. During his stay in Italy he completed his *Summa contra Gentiles,* already begun in his Paris days, continued his commentaries on holy Scripture, wrote more *Quaestiones* and the First Part of his *Summa Theologica.* He may also have at this time begun his commentary on Aristotle's *Metaphysics.*

Thomas was once again in Paris from 1269 to 1272, where he was involved in the disturbances about the dangers to the faith from "Latin Averroism" (Siger of Brabant) and became increasingly clear about his own position as an Aristotelian. It was here that he produced his *Quaestiones De anima, De virtute,* and *De malo,* as well as the whole of the Second Part of his *Summa Theologica.* He continued his commentary on Aristotle. In 1272 he organized a *Studium Generale* in Naples for his Order, where he taught for the last time. The two years before his death were taken up with work on the Third Part of his *Summa,* on his commentaries on the Psalms and Pauline Epistles, and once again, on Aristotle. In 1274, Thomas was taken ill on his way to the Council of Lyons and died in the Cistercian Abbey at Fossanova, after having expounded to the monks the Song of Solomon. With his last breath, as it were, Thomas also turned away from speculative theology to mysticism. Reginald of Piperno continued the *Summa Theologica (Supplementum).*

By comparison with the Franciscans, Thomas was much the more "modern", for by distinguishing between philosophy and theology he asserted the independence of philosophy and thus pointed the way to modern philosophy and to the autonomy of the secular spheres. But unlike the Averroists Thomas always sought to harmonize knowledge and faith, philosophy and theology. His primary question was not whether there was any need for an independent philosophy alongside theology, but, on the contrary, whether alongside a — historically prior — philosophy there was any need for an independent theology. His answer to this question was affirmative, in virtue of the salvation of man which the science of faith has to serve. Thus even today it is possible to consider Thomas's philosophy without necessarily having to speak of his theology, whereas in contrast it is hardly possible to discover in his works a theology innocent of philosophy. There are, however, places where he makes less use of Aristotelian philosophical terminology, for example, in the Christology of his *Summa Theologica.*

In his philosophical anthropology, Thomas adhered to the Aristotelian doctrine of the human spirit-soul as the principle of life and, in opposition to the Franciscan doctrine of the *pluralitas formarum,* as the one form of the body. Yet so strongly does Thomas stress the unity of body and soul that he is never in danger of limiting man's personality to the soul. Dependence on sense perception and rejection of innate ideas is basic to his epistemology. According to Thomas, the *intellectus agens,* as a spontaneous activity of thought, draws its intellectual knowledge from sense perception. But sense and intellect are by no means two divided principles, each contributing to knowledge from different sources. On the contrary, the entire individual person, the subject of intellectual and sensible activity, possesses intellectuality in such a way as to posit the necessity of sense perception. There is a unity of the two. Ultimately, human knowledge is, as a reaching out into the world, as openness to being, the guarantee of freedom. Even the famous "five ways" of Thomas, through which he sought to demonstrate God's existence, testify to his idea that there is a connection between all human knowledge and the sensible nature of the world, from the moved to the unmoved Mover, the caused to the uncaused Cause, that which exists contingently to that which exists necessarily, the less perfect to the absolute perfect, the end-directed to the final goal. His argument moves always from finite to infinite being, and is therefore analogical knowledge, since the concept of being in Thomas always has the mode of the finite or the infinite. Since all knowledge of God involves this argument from finite to infinite, the *via negativa* plays an important role in both philosophy and theology.

A crucial point for the relation between theology and philosophy is, for Thomas, the question of the temporal beginning of the world. He regarded it as impossible to demonstrate this temporal beginning philosophically, although he believed he could prove that the world was created; he therefore defended the mode of thought even of philosophers who argued that the world was eternal. Where philosophy was inconclusive, revelation, and therefore faith, must cast the deciding vote. Thomas followed Augustine in defining evil as a lack of a due measure of perfection and therefore as a privation. Modern man finds in this medieval conception a failure to treat the reality of evil seriously.

Central in the contemporary study of Thomas is the problem of the meaning of "salvation-history" and also the question of an anthropological approach in Thomas. It is still agreed, of course, that Thomas is not to be regarded as having an explicitly historical approach, yet it has been shown that by his use of the neo-Platonist scheme of *egressus* and *regressus* he advanced historical thinking far more than had previously been suspected, not only in the Third Part of his *Summa* but throughout his work. Creation, incarnation with grace already at work in history, the bringing home of the world, these are all conceived by Thomas in terms of the economy of salvation and therefore historically, and not merely as necessary modes of being. But he avoids the extremes, on the one hand, of a dogmatic belief in progress based on salvation-history (Joachim of Fiore), and on the other hand, of a theory of an inevitable decline from the source calling perpetually for new reforms. For Thomas, it is the Church which safeguards the connection with the source and at the same time the movement to the goal. He did not deal with the Church in a separate treatise on ecclesiology, but it is constantly present throughout his presentation of theology.

In connection with recent research, we must agree with it in finding the emergence in Thomas of an anthropocentric thought-form in contrast with the cosmocentric Greek, at least inasmuch as Thomas certainly brought out clearly the "presence-to-itself" of the human mind and the self-determination of the human will, thus paving the way for a secular understanding of man. Yet priority may be conceded here to the Franciscans in the attempt to outline a complete theology orientated anthropologically — not a theological anthropology — for the Franciscan school started with man's inner experiences and explained them at the deepest level of sin and grace, so that God is not only its first but, so to speak, its last word.

Apart from Thomas, the main members of the Dominican school of the 13th and 14th centuries were *Ulrich of Strasbourg,* a pupil of Albert, *Hervaeus Natalis* and *Thomas Sutton.* Thomism, however, also spread to the Augustinians (*Aegidius Romanus;* Augustinian school), the Carmelites and the Cistercians.

Opposition to Thomas first appeared within the ranks of his own Order (*Robert Kilwardby, Peter of Tarantaise*) and then chiefly in the ranks of the Franciscans (apart from those already mentioned, *William de la Mare*) and among the secular clergy, in particular, *Henry of Ghent,* the most important theologian of late scholasticism, who taught at the University of Paris and belonged to none of the great Orders.

h) *Henry of Ghent* (1217–1293) spent his whole life debating the theological conclusions derived by Thomas from the study of Aristotle. He derived inspiration for his own thought from the study of neo-Platonism, Augustine, the Victorine school, and even of Arabian Aristotelianism (Averroes, Avicenna, Siger of Brabant). In opposition to Thomas, Henry argued against the unity of form in man. In his view, therefore, the soul could not be the unique informing principle, although he maintained that all other beings possessed only one form. In Henry it becomes especially clear that for him, as for scholasticism as a whole, Christology serves as source for our knowledge of anthropology. According to Henry the numerical identity of Christ's body in life and in death can only be affirmed on the assumption of a *forma corporeitatis,* which must then apply to all men. For the survival of the form of corporeality in Christ's death tells against the unity of form in man. But Henry also proposed another correction. In opposition to the Thomist doctrine of the unity of being in Christ, residing in the *esse suppositi,* i.e., in Christ's being as person, to which the reality of the two natures is subordinated, Henry pioneered a solution for which the way had partly been prepared by Franciscan theology. He distinguished an *esse essentiae,* an *esse existentiae* and an *esse subsistentiae.* When *esse* is attributed to the nature, or to the *suppositum,* it differs in meaning according to whether we are speaking of the creature or of God. In the case of the creature, "being" pertains primarily to the *suppositum,* and to the "nature" only insofar as this partakes of the *suppositum*. In the case of God, however, "being" pertains to the "nature", and to the *suppositum* only insofar as this exists in the divine "nature". For Henry of Ghent, therefore, the *suppositum* is eliminated from the question of the "being" of Christ. According to him, when we refer to the divine and human nature of Christ we have to speak of a twofold being as *esse essentiae*. Only "by (our) reason" can the "being of essence" and the "being of existence" be distinguished in the divine nature of Christ, whereas in Christ's human nature they can also be distinguished "in intention", i.e., with some "objective" reference or "virtually". Consequently, Henry puts the main emphasis upon the human *esse existentiae* in Christ with a view to stressing his true manhood and humanity. The fact that Thomas Aquinas could not bring himself to attribute (its own proper) *esse* or "act" to the human nature of Christ, is probably due to the reaction against Nestorianism. In the case of this particular problem, Henry's position gained increasing support in time. His pupil *Godfrey of Fontaine* shows himself, here as in other respects, partly as Henry's supporter, partly as his opponent. He rejected Henry's position on the unity of form, but accepted that on the question of the unity of being in Christ.

i) *John Duns Scotus* (1265–1308) was the greatest figure of the Franciscan school. He studied in Paris and Oxford, and taught in Cambridge, Oxford, Paris and Cologne. In subtlety of intellect he approaches the other great Oxford Franciscan, *Roger Bacon* (*c.* 1210– *post* 1292), the first empiricist, who therefore also emphasized in the realm of faith the importance of personal experience. Scotus took issue not so much with Thomas as with Henry of Ghent, Godfrey of Fontaine, and Giles (Aegidius) of Rome. His chief work is the *Commentary on the Sentences,* extant in several versions, the most important being the so-called *Opus Oxoniense* or *Ordinatio.* Other important works are the *Quaestiones,* Treatises and Commentaries. As a true Franciscan he regarded philosophy as insufficient in itself. Faith's task is to criticize philosophy and to enrich it in order that it may advance into fields to which it has no access of itself. Among the doctrines of Scotus which have become well known may be mentioned: in philosophy, the univocity of being; in theology, the absolute predestination of Christ, and the freedom of Mary from original sin. In opposition to Thomas, Scotus thought of "being" without any modes, although it is embodied only as finite or infinite being. But the concept of "being" in Scotus is so abstract and without content that it is neutral in relation to finite-infinite characteristics. Scotus therefore did not need to speak of analogy when he simply meant the concept of "being" itself.

Starting as he did from the goodness, love, and will of God, he affirmed that the incarnation would have taken place even apart from the fall of man. It was, so to speak, part of the perfection of creation. As regards the doctrine of the immaculate conception of Mary, it is not clear whether Scotus or William of Ware was first in the field. Mary's freedom from original sin from the time of her conception is explained as a *praeservatio per meritum passionis Christi,* as a *gratia crucis,* which in no way eliminated Mary's need for redemption. Departing from the Aristotelian view, Scotus regarded Mary's motherhood not simply as a passive *materiam praebere* but as an active, causative agent for the incarnation of Christ's human nature. This was the view of previous Franciscan theologians. On this view, therefore, in contrast to that of Thomas, Mary's freedom from original sin is the presupposition of Christ's sinlessness.

3. *Evaluation.* From this survey of the scholastic period, it is clear that starting from more or less the same point (Christian revelation in harmony with human reason), from which there were no deviations, many different interpretations of God, world, and man were developed. The clarity of medieval concepts had a real content and was vigorously applied to reality. This is not to say that we can still manage with only these scholastic concepts and methods today. But it does mean that in its own day scholastic theology was abreast of the times and indeed that its discussion with the intellectual currents of the 13th century gave fruitful impulses to the life of the spirit, despite the Church ban on the adoption of Aristotelian philosophy, at first total but later on increasingly qualified. Theology was the supreme norm, in the light of which philosophy and the profane sciences were allotted their degrees of value. Even if individual theologians were dominated by either the metaphysical standpoint or the "salvation-history" standpoint, the aim was always synthesis, universal intelligibility, and guidance for human life. Classical scholastic theology was never remote from practical pastoral concerns and the direction of each individual

to his salvation, even if it followed the feudal social order of the Middle Ages.

See also *Aristotelianism, Philosophy, Philosophy and Theology.*

BIBLIOGRAPHY. M. de Wulf, *Introduction to Scholastic Philosophy* (1907); id., *History of Scholastic Philosophy* (1952, from 6th French ed.); M. Grabmann, *Geschichte der scholastischen Methode,* 2 vols. (1909–11; reprint, 1956); P. Rousselot, *L'intellectualism de S. Thomas* (1924); É. Gilson, *The Philosophy of St. Thomas Aquinas* (E. T., from 3rd French ed., 1924); P. Glorieux, *La littérature quodlibétique,* I (1925), II (1935); id., *Répertoire des maîtres de théologie de Paris au XIIIᵉ siècle,* I–II (1933); E. Überweg, *Grundriss der Geschichte der Philosophie,* II, ed. by B. Geyer (11th ed.; 1928); M. Grabmann, *Der lateinische Averroismus des 13. Jahrhunderts* (1931); G. K. Chesterton, *St. Thomas Aquinas* (1933); O. Lottin, *Psychologie et morale aux XIIᵉ et XIIIᵉ siècles,* I–IV/3 (1936–44); É. Gilson, *The Spirit of Mediaeval Philosophy* (1936); id., *The Philosophy of St. Bonaventure* (1938; 3rd French ed., 1953); id., *Reason and Revelation in the Middle Ages* (1938); R. Klibansky, *Platonic Tradition in the Middle Ages* (1939); P. Bayerschmidt, *Die Seins- und Formmetaphysik des Heinrich von Gent* (1941); G. Tavard, *Transciency and Permanency. The Nature of Theology according to St. Bonaventure* (1954); É. Gilson, *History of Christian Philosophy in the Middle Ages* (1954); F. Copleston, *Aquinas* (1955); F. van Steenberghen, *The Philosophical Movement in the 13th Century* (1955); id., *Aristotle in the West* (1955); J. Pieper, *The Silence of St. Thomas* (1957); id., *Guide to Thomas Aquinas* (1962); É. Gilson, *The Spirit of Thomism* (1958); M.-D. Chenu, *The Scope of the Summa;* id., *Towards Understanding St. Thomas* (1964); J. Gomez Caffarena, *Ser participado ... en ... Enrique de Gante* (1958); M. de Wulf, *System of Thomas Aquinas* (1959); J. de Finance, *Être et agir dans la philosophie de S. Thomas* (1960); É. Gilson, *The Christian Philosophy of St. Thomas Aquinas* (1961); J. G. Bougerol, *Introduction to the Works of St. Bonaventure* (1964); E. Gössmann, *Metaphysik und Heilsgeschichte: Eine theologische Untersuchung der Summa Halensis* (1964); B. Lonergan, *Verbum. Word and Ideas in Aquinas,* ed. by D. Burrell (1967); K. Rahner, *Spirit in the World* (metaphysics of knowledge in St. Thomas) (1968).

Elisabeth Gössmann

D. LATER SCHOLASTICISM

Late scholasticism was confronted with many different tasks. It grappled with them with varying degrees of skill and offered solutions based on many different principles. It paved the way in many respects for later developments.

1. *The schools.* The great systems of the 13th century were the high-point and the conclusion of a development. But they contained many problems. Their assumptions needed to be critically tested and some parts had to be further pondered and refined. Finally, the huge mass of material had to be cast into typical forms which would be accessible to beginners in their studies. The systems of St. Thomas Aquinas, Duns Scotus and Occam, as well as the theology of St. Augustine, St. Bonaventure, St. Albert the Great and the Pseudo-Dionysius were the main tasks of later scholasticism — tasks which it sought to solve by the team-work of whole "schools".

Like the distinction between classical and late scholasticism, the difference between the various schools of the latter is hard to define. Following B. Geyer (p. 583) one could distinguish in the main three schools — Thomism, Scotism and Occamist Nominalism. Or one could follow M. Grabmann (pp. 95 ff.) and make a longer list, including the Augustinian, Carmelite and Cistercian schools. Some major theologians like Nicholas of Cusa and Dionysius the Carthusian cannot really be assigned to any of these schools (Grabmann, p. 119). The schools were engaged in controversies which were at times passionate. The conflicting fronts finally hardened into the *via antiqua* (which comprised Thomism and Scotism) and the *via moderna* (Occamism). Though Occam's system was initially prohibited, it soon came to take a predominant place, especially in the universities (Geyer, p. 583).

Neo-Platonism had always succeeded in maintaining itself in scholasticism along Aristotelianism. The speculative mysticism of the 14th and 15th centuries was particularly influenced by it, as was Meister Eckhart, who was a major influence in moulding the mysticism of the age (Geyer, p. 531). It should be remembered, however, that in all the schools both Scripture and the *Sentences* of Peter Lombard were zealously expounded.

2. *Basic tendencies.* The tasks which led to the creation of "schools" brought certain basic tendencies into play which affected the various schools in different ways. One impulse to the formation of schools was the strong opposition to a certain "Master" or authority in some quarters, which called forth elsewhere strong support for the authority in question. The various religious orders chose a given master, while Occam had the support of the universities in particular. Hence the schools were marked from

the start by the tendency to polemics and apologetics. Critical tendencies developed along with conservative ones and the two trends stamped the whole period (Geyer, p. 583).

The critical efforts of the age were concerned both with history and speculation. But the fact that since St. Albert the Great and St. Thomas Aquinas medieval thinking was "essentially orientated towards Aristotle" (Geyer, p. 551) told against the development of historical criticism. The Aristotelian definition of science excluded the possibility of history being treated as a science (H. Meyer, p. 189). Historical criticism is represented, characteristically, by the Augustinian theologians, who were less influenced by Aristotle. Nonetheless, the theologians of the time prove again and again to be remarkable masters of patristic and scholastic sources (D. Trapp, p. 185). In the political and ecclesiastical disturbances of the end of the Middle Ages these efforts came to an end (J. Koch in *RGG*, V, col. 1498).

The tendency to speculative analysis predominated so strongly, in contrast to historical criticism, that it may be said to have been characteristic of the end of medieval scholasticism. The system of William of Occam played a large part in this development (Geyer, p. 583).

3. *Occamism*. Occam's attitude was even more critical than that of Scotus. Scotus had restricted the number of truths accepted by St. Thomas as demonstrable by pure reason. Occam recognized no such truths at all. Even the existence, oneness and infinity of God were made pure articles of faith (Geyer, p. 571). The problem of universals may be regarded as the central issue in debate between *antiqui* and *moderni*. The outcome had far-reaching consequences for natural philosophy, metaphysics and theology (Geyer, p. 686). Within Occamism itself, the moderate theologians came to outweigh the extremists.

4. *Ecclesiology*. The theological forces of late scholasticism were considerably hampered by the great conflicts between Church and State and within the Church in the late Middle Ages. Many treatises on ecclesiology were written. The contemporary problems which beset the Church channelled the discussion in certain directions (e.g., the controversies between papalists, episcopalists and conciliarists). But the arguments were based at times on deep dogmatic insights.

Very often it was a matter of defending very practical positions, as in the treatises of Occam on Church and State. But the great ecclesiologists of the time managed to penetrate again and again to the question of the nature of the Church. John of Segovia, Nicholas of Cusa and John de Torquemada ("Turrecremata") displayed a profound understanding of the Church.

5. *The notion of theology*. The refinement of speculative analysis, especially in the logic of Occamism, and its use in theology, called attention in a special way to the scientific character of theology. But the science of formal logic was so predominant that the decisive importance of existentiell questions was lost sight of. The notorious scholastic addiction to debate became widespread. There was a sharp reaction against it even in the late Middle Ages. Many supported Meister Eckhart in his assertion that it was more important to be a master in the school of life *(Lebemeister)* than in the world of books *(Lesemeister)*.

Theology ceased to a great extent to concentrate on its essential themes. In Occamism, the unity of theology and its primary theme were denied on principle. In opposition to these disintegrating tendencies new attention was paid to the question of the central affirmations of revelation and theology. The cross of Christ and the existentiell situation of man became the focus of meditation, especially in the *Devotio Moderna* and mysticism.

6. *Pastoral work*. How strongly the late Middle Ages were interested in pastoral work is clearly attested by the extremely numerous collections of sermons at this period. Very many of these late medieval sermons are constructed along scholastic lines. The didactic element of scholasticism came to the fore with not very happy results. Dry erudition, an artificial division of points, a lack of kerygmatic impulse and of fundamental guiding themes are far too frequently apparent. But it must not be forgotten that along with such inferior productions there were also remarkable examples of learned or simple preaching. A conclusive verdict is impossible because the sermon literature of late scholasticism has not been investigated nearly as much as its theology.

A type of literature which had sprung up in the preceding era now reached its full development. This was the type of book which aimed at preparing simple priests for their pastoral tasks, especially for the administration of the sacrament of penance, by giving them the necessary rudiments of theology and canon law (J. Ziegler). In contrast, for instance, to the "consoling" devotional works of the late Middle Ages and the many books written in the spirit of the *Devotio Moderna,* these writings were very scholastic in type. Some of them were voluminous *Summae,* some were shorter compendiums (P. Michaud-Quantin). The standard work for a long time (1338–1444) was the *Summa de casibus conscientiae* of Bartholomew of Pisa (Ziegler, pp. 14 f.).

Luther's criticism of late scholasticism was not confined to Occamism and Aristotelianism. It was concerned also to a considerable extent with the pastoral writings composed on the scholastic model.

See also *Nominalism, Augustinianism, Middle Ages* II B.

BIBLIOGRAPHY. See bibliographies on *Scholasticism* II C, *Nominalism;* also especially: K. Werner, *Die Scholastik des späteren Mittelalters,* vols. I–IV (1881–87); M. Grabmann, *Die Geschichte der katholischen Theologie seit Ausgang der Väterzeit* (1933; reprint, 1961); H. Meyer, "Die Wissenschaftslehre des Thomas von Aquin", *Philosophisches Jahrbuch der Görres-Gesellschaft* 47 (1934); P. Vignaux, *Nominalisme au XIV*^e *siècle* (1948); J. Ziegler, *Die Ehelehre der Pönitentialsummen von 1200–1350* (1956); F. Ueberweg, *Grundriss der Geschichte der Philosophie,* II, ed. by B. Geyer (13th ed., 1956); M. de Gandillac, "Ockham et la 'Via moderna'", in A. Fliche and V. Martin, eds., *Histoire de l'Église,* XIII (1956), pp. 449–512; D. Trapp, "Augustinian Theology of the 14th Century", *Augustiniana* 6 (1956), pp. 146–274; P. Michaud-Quantin, "Sommes de casuistique et manuels de confession au moyen âge (XII–XVI siècles)", *Analecta Mediaevalia Namurcensia* 13 (1962); H. Obermann, *Spätscholastik und Reformation,* I (1965).

Reinhold Weier

E. Neo-Scholasticism

The revival of scholasticism in the 16th century is sometimes termed "neo-scholasticism" (see *Baroque* II). Its most influential representative was Suarez. But towards the end of the 18th century its force was spent. In the present article, neo-scholasticism means the movement which returned deliberately to Thomas Aquinas, Bonaventure, Scotus or Suarez in order to apply the scholastic method to philosophy and theology. It extended to the middle of the 20th century and is still a decisive force in philosophy and theology in Catholic circles.

1. *Historical presuppositions.* In the 18th century, scholasticism had been almost entirely abandoned in theology and particularly in philosophy, except in some centres of the Suarezian type in Spain and Italy. It had either been replaced by modern rationalism or had lost all connection with the intellectual world by becoming a purely domestic affair inside seminaries and the colleges of religious orders. Efforts were made in France, Italy and Germany from the beginning of the 19th century to stimulate Catholic theology by discussion with Kantianism and German Idealism (Lammenais, Bautain, Gioberti, Rosmini, Hermes, Günther), but failed because of ecclesiastical disapproval. The failure was later explained as due to the fact that the doctrine of the Church and its relevant philosophical structures could not be properly developed, except on the basis of an intensive study of the philosophical and theological tradition of scholasticism. This had been one of the decisive factors in the formulation of Church doctrine and hence was indispensable for a proper understanding of it.

2. *The start of the revival.* The return to tradition, which had been interrupted during the Enlightenment, began in Italy, where some of the older generation had still maintained ties with it. The tradition could thus influence V. Buzzetti (1777–1824), Serafino Sordi, S. J. (1793–1865) and his brother D. Sordi, M. Liberatore (1820–72), C. Sanseverino (1811–65), Cardinal T. Zigliari, O. P. (1833–93) and Don Palmieri (1829–1909). In Spain there were J. Balmes (1810–48) and Cardinal Z. Gonzales y Díaz Tuñón, O. P. (1831–94), in France Domet de Vorges (d. 1910), in Germany J. Kleutgen, S. J. (1811–83) and A. Stöckl (1823–75), in Austria K. Werner (1821–88). By 1860 the revival was so far advanced that scholastic theology was producing works of great value, like the early writings of Franzelin and Scheeben.

3. *Papal commendation.* The movement was given a great impulse by the encyclical *Aeterni Patris* of Leo XIII, 4 August 1879, which dealt with the tasks, sources and methods of philosophy and its relation to revelation. It strongly commended the study of Thomas Aquinas and urged that his doctrine should be the norm of teaching. When the new code of canon law was published in 1917, it prescribed a two-year course of philosophy before the study of theology

(can. 1365, para. 1). Philosophy was to be studied according to the mind of and in keeping with the principles and doctrine of St. Thomas (can. 1366, para. 2). For these reasons, neo-scholasticism is often simply called neo-Thomism. But there was no intention of eliminating the differences between the various Catholic schools. This was made quite clear in the debates of 1914 about the twenty-four theses which had been approved by the Congregation for Studies, and which were supposed to contain the essential theses of Thomism. They were accepted by the Congregation as a "tuta norma directiva", but divergent views in other schools were not excluded, since the truth of the theses was not directly in question but only their compatibility with the faith. The commendation of scholasticism and St. Thomas also runs through the encyclical *Studiorum ducem* of 29 June 1923 and the apostolic constitution *Deus scientiarum Dominus,* 24 May 1931, of Pius XI, and the encyclical *Humani Generis,* 12 August 1950, of Pius XII. It is still heard in the decree of Vatican II, *Optatam Totius* (on priestly formation), though other important aspects are emphasized, especially the biblical foundations.

4. *Institutional expression.* The growth and revival of neo-scholasticism brought with it the development of centres of study which became very influential. There were the Higher Institutes in Rome, the Gregoriana (S.J.), the Angelicum (O.P.), the Antonianum (O.F.M.), the Athenaeum Urbanum (Propaganda Fidei). There were Catholic universities in Milan, Freiburg (Switzerland), Louvain, Nijmegen, Washington, D.C., Ottawa and St. Louis. Other institutes included the Institut Catholique in Paris, the Institut für christliche Philosophie in Innsbruck, the Instituto Luis Vives in Madrid, the Institute for Medieval Studies in Toronto and the various colleges and faculties of the religious orders (e.g., Quaracchi [O.F.M.], Valkenburg, later Berchmanskolleg near Munich [S.J.]). An extensive literary production developed, many of the institutes publishing their own periodicals, text-books and philosophical or theological series.

5. *Historical research.* The revival stimulated research into medieval literature and culture which soon took on wide dimensions. History of philosophy and theology could now include the Middle Ages, hitherto an almost unknown field. This must be con-sidered one of the permanent achievements of the movement. Major editions were undertaken. In historical research into scholasticism the great names are H. Denifle (1844–1905), M. de Wulf, Cardinal F. Ehrle, G. von Hertling, C. Baümker, P. Mandonnet, M. Grabmann, É. Gilson, F. Pelster, M. Landgraf, H. Meyer, F. van Steenbergh. Series of important publications include *Beiträge zur Philosophie des Mittelalters* and *Archives d'histoire doctrinale et littéraire du moyen âge.* Historical investigations showed clearly why Thomas Aquinas should have so central a place. He united the Platonist and Augustinian patristic tradition with the heritage of Aristotle to form a Christian synthesis which was to influence greatly the theology of the Church and the formulation of its doctrine.

6. *Nova et vetera.* Reflection on scholasticism was not meant to be merely the repetition of ancient theses. A closer study of scholasticism was to enable modern science and philosophy to be faced with a proper insight into the development of Church doctrine. From this point of view, the Institut Supérieur de Philosophie, founded in 1882 at Louvain by Cardinal Mercier (1851–1926), paved the way for many developments. Efforts were made to draw on the riches of empirical science for the corresponding philosophical subjects. Mercier worked along this line for psychology, as did also A. Gemelli, J. Geyser, J. Fröbes and J. Lindworsky. Among the students of natural philosophy mention may be made of T. Pesch, E. Wasmann, P. Hoenen, J. Maritain and A. Mitterer. Typical of the discussion of the empirical sciences was the effort to interpret their findings in terms of the ontological categories of scholasticism. This helped finally to bring out the contrast between the world-picture of the scholastics and the moderns. This was a task to which A. Mitterer in particular devoted himself, launching a type of research which showed the relativity of the world-picture behind many of Aquinas's views. These comparative investigations, historical research and divergence among the schools led finally to more nuanced views and critical assessment of scholastic doctrines. The historically conditioned elements could be brought out, and traced into the pronouncements of the magisterium. This work prepared for the forging of links with the modern problems of hermeneutics.

Another approach to the sciences was made along the lines of the French theories of science and the history of science as investigated by P. Duhem. The chief exponent was J. Maritain, distinguishing methodologically philosophy and science and allowing a relative independence to each. This approach claimed support from the theory of relativity, the elementary particles and the scientific views attaching to them. This helped to demarcate the essential contents of scholastic metaphysics and natural philosophy as independent of its world-picture.

7. *Neo-scholasticism and present-day philosophy*. Discussion with modern philosophy began rather as apologetics. A more sympathetic interest began to be shown only in the 20th century. After a phase in which scholastic teaching-matter was extended by taking in later problems — as was done from the start in epistemology, on account of the new setting of the problem — efforts were made to re-state the essential tradition in terms of modern questions and methods. The great pioneer here was the Belgian J. Maréchal, S.J. (1878–1944), who took up Kant and German Idealism and sought to re-interpret scholastic metaphysics in the light of transcendental philosophy. The true content of scholasticism could be presented as an answer to modern questions, an effort which really made possible a fruitful dialogue with other philosophical trends. This line was taken up by A. Grégoire, J. Defever, G. Isaye, A. Marc, etc. It was continued in Germany, with special reference to Heidegger, by J. B. Lotz, W. Brugger, E. Coreth and above all by K. Rahner, who used it to great effect in theology. B. J. F. Lonergan worked along similar lines.

This procedure cannot be regarded merely as the adoption of a particular doctrine into an otherwise predetermined system. It is the project of a new system which is not solely due to the historical and systematic findings of neo-scholasticism. Hence such movements as these are looked upon both as the end and the fulfilment of neo-scholasticism. Fruitful discussion with contemporary thought had been impossible at the beginning of the 19th century, because the discussion had no links with the vital tradition. This defect was now eliminated. The reduced importance of neo-scholasticism in the strict sense may be seen perhaps in how the flow of text-books in scholastic form has

dwindled. They have been replaced by a flood of monographs, independent presentations and essays. But philosophy and theology, as they press forward to confront contemporary problems, ought not to lose touch with tradition. Otherwise they will be exposed to the same weaknesses which handicapped neo-scholasticism in the 19th century.

See also *Rationalism, Kantianism, Idealism, Transcendental Philosophy.*

BIBLIOGRAPHY. F. Ueberweg, *Grundriss der Geschichte der Philosophie,* IV (1924), pp. 623–46, V (1928), pp. 61–66, 176 f., 232–4; J. Zybura, *Present-Day Thinkers and the New Scholasticism* (1926); G. Brunni, *Riflessioni sulla Scolastica* (1927); F. Ehrler and F. Pelster, *Die Scholastik und ihre Aufgabe in unserer Zeit* (2nd ed., 1933); B. Jansen, "Papsttum und neuscholastische Metaphysik", *Aufstieg zur Metaphysik* (1933), pp. 216–40; J. Maritain, *Humanisme intégral* (1936); P. Dezza, *I neotomistici italiani del secolo XIX,* 2 vols. (1942–44); J. Perrier, *Revival of Scholastic Philosophy* (1948); É. Gilson, *The Spirit of Mediaeval Philosophy* (1949); L. de Raeymaeker, *Le Cardinal Mercier et l'Institut Supérieur de Philosophie* (1952); A. Strigl, *Die tragische Schuld der Spät- und Neuscholastik* (1953); G. Söhngen, *Philosophische Einübung in die Theologie* (1955); L. Foucher, *La philosophie catholique en France au XIXe siècle* (1955); G. Rossi, *Le origini del neotomismo* (1957); J.-P. Golinas, *La restoration du Thomisme sous Léon XIII et les philosophies nouvelles* (1959); L. de Raeymaeker, *Introduction à la philosophie* (5th ed., 1964), pp. 177–9, 183–96, 228–304; B. Welte, *Auf der Spur des Ewigen* (1965), pp. 380–409; O. Muck, *The Transcendental Method in Philosophy* (1968).

Otto Muck

SCIENCE

I. General. II. Theory of Science. III. Science and Theology.

I. General

1. *General problems of definition.* There are difficulties about establishing a precise definition of the term "science". The definition itself has to be established scientifically. Moreover, it has to cover not just "science as such", in the singular, but also the various different branches of science. Hence the tendency to try to derive the common features of the various branches of science from one particular science selected as prototype and used as a standard by which to gauge the scientific character of the rest. There is thus a temptation to reduce the original multiplicity of disciplines to the unity of a single

science, or, if this proves impossible, to dispute the claim of some forms of thought to be scientific at all. This tendency affects not only various branches of empirical science which may declare their subject-matter and formal scope to be all-embracing, and claim exclusive validity for their methods. It also affects philosophy which may attempt to regard all branches of science as merely sectional disciplines within philosophy itself, merely a part of its own comprehensive grasp of reality. Moreover, the sciences have only gradually developed in the course of history, and not merely the particular disciplines which exist at present, but "science" as such in the sense of a specific attitude which men may adopt to reality. Each of the new disciplines of course developed its own special character, but, in addition, changes occurred in the general conception of what constitutes a scientific attitude to reality. And it is this general conception which includes the special sciences, forms their basis and finds expression in them. Consequently what "science" has meant throughout the course of its history can only be determined at first by relatively external features.

2. *General characteristics of scientific knowledge.* At the beginning of the history of science in Western Europe, Plato and Aristotle distinguished a hierarchy in human cognition, extending from sense perception of the mutable and individual ($\alpha\ddot{\iota}\sigma\theta\eta\sigma\iota\varsigma$), through experience of habitual regularities ($\dot{\varepsilon}\mu\pi\varepsilon\iota\rho\dot{\iota}\alpha$), to science properly so-called ($\dot{\varepsilon}\pi\iota\sigma\tau\dot{\eta}\mu\eta$), which gives insight into the grounds or principles which universally and necessarily determine a thing (cf., for example, Aristotle, *Metaphysics,* A, 1.).

a) On this basis it may be said that science in the sense of growth in knowledge consists in that mental activity which, by forming judgments (and therefore concepts and inferences), penetrates to the reasons *why* such and such is the case, not just *that* it is so or *how* it is so. These scientific judgments or propositions do not merely claim to be "true" statements, but purport to provide the grounds of their truth (in the traditional sense: agreement of the objective statement with what it refers to). Consequently they provide "certainty" of their truth. This certainty is based on the coherence of one judgment with other judgments and with certain irreducible, basic propositions (axioms). In this way the state of affairs asserted to be the case is regarded as linked with other facts, while the grounds or reasons themselves are regarded as fitting into an explanatory context or pattern (correspondence between propositions and states of affairs, between basic propositions and fundamental laws of reality). Similarly the certainty of the truth of a scientific statement always rests on the state of affairs itself as datum. This, of course, has to be described and stated and fixed in conceptual statements which are then available for repeated reference.

b) Science in the sense of the product of such activity, consists, at any given moment, of the sum-total of well-established true (and probable) statements about an explanatory system of interconnected facts.

This shows, however, that science always involves a domain of objective data, which taken as a whole form the field of scientific inquiry (its material object). Furthermore, science involves a point of view (formal object) from which it envisages the material object under investigation. The material object is of interest in its "significance for", and is grasped "as" so-and-so. Only what is significant from the chosen formal point of view is taken into account, and all other features of the material object which in this respect are unimportant, are passed over. Science is therefore always "abstract"; it never apprehends the full ("concrete") wealth of an individual fact with all it signifies. But that is not a fault on the part of science, which it could or ought to remedy. It is due to the fact that science is concerned with what is more than individual, what is general and fundamental. These two considerations, i.e., the specific character of the material field of investigation and the formal mode of inquiry, determine method, the determinate procedures for forming concepts and propositions and for their combination into a system. Science is never completely without assumptions or presuppositions. It is dependent on objective data, and furthermore its choice of a formal point of view is not made from within an already constituted science. The choice of formal view-point precedes and contributes to constitute a science. To say that science assumes nothing, has no presuppositions, amounts to no more than saying that science admits only those assumptions which can command "general" assent and acceptance, i.e., from "any" thinking person as such. This is taken to be the case because if the general constitution of the human inquirer and the constitution of whatever is under investigation are taken in conjunction, it is considered that all the necessary conditions are present for the acquisition and repeated testing of scientific knowledge. Consequently scientific knowledge is characterized by "universal validity". This means that scientific propositions are intersubjectively valid in principle, i.e., can be communicated to anyone, even if in actual fact they are inaccessible to some because of their intellectual limitations, the direction of their interests, historical conditions, etc. Universal validity also means that as regards content, scientific propositions are "objective", i.e., they contain only what belongs to the reality (the "object") itself, to the exclusion of anything merely subjective, i.e., deriving from the individual inquirer. The intersubjectivity of science means a general intellectual attitude and conduct of thought by which the scientist transcends his individual isolation and identifies himself with every other potential or real inquirer, thus permitting what is under investigation to display itself without falsification just as it is.

3. *Special problems of demarcation of the sciences.* a) These general and relatively external characteristics of science raise a number of problems. It may be asked whether the thing ("in itself") coincides with what it is "for" the knower. In the metaphysical conception of science current in antiquity and the Middle Ages, this was affirmed in principle, even in regard to the natural sciences (which themselves were metaphysical in orientation). According to this view, the being of beings is known immediately to the divine mind, and hence the being of beings includes essentially its knowability to the human mind. The modern philosophical theory of scientific knowledge formulated by Kant, on the other hand, holds that an *a priori* constitutive relation to the human mind (as universal but finite knowing subject) belongs only to beings as phenomena, as objects presented to the mind (as objectivated), not to being as it is essentially in itself (as substance). In fact the empirical science of modern times developed in complete independence of metaphysics, and quite simply and without analysis took "objectivity" to mean the constitution of things "without" reference to a personal subject pursuing science and apprehending them. Objectivity therefore meant precisely the exclusion of the cognitive relation itself in knowledge. In contrast to this, empirical

science at the present time through its own researches is coming to realize that the human knower, both as an intellectual and as a sense-endowed, perceptive subject, is a constitutive and indispensable factor even in the "objective" statements of natural science about nature. This shows that the Cartesian distinction between *res cogitans* and *res extensa,* on which Kant's theory of scientific knowledge was still based, is now inadequate to describe the epistemological position of the natural sciences. The propositions of present-day science in fact do not describe nature envisaged in isolation and abstractly. They are more like "descriptions of our relations with nature", of the "interplay of man and nature", produced in an epistemological situation "in which an objectivation of the course of nature is no longer possible" (W. Heisenberg).

The question therefore arises whether the only presuppositions which science permits, and which are supposed to command "universal" acceptance and assent, can really be assumed in absolutely every thinking person as such, and whether they are valid for all objects whatsoever in every field. This problem is important for the scientific character of theology (both as a science of the "objects" of revealed faith and as a science of the believer in these objects of revelation). But it is even more important in regard to the secular scientific character of historical knowledge, because it means that history can no longer describe its aim in the misleading words of Ranke: "simply to show how things were". There is greater realization that statements made about historical events involve assumptions deriving from tradition and present experience, "pre-judgments" (H.-G. Gadamer). Of course these are not purely arbitrary individual assumptions. But neither are they those of a universal, timeless knowing subject. Consequently the historical event under investigation does not possess the kind of self-contained objectivity and fixity which would mean it could and should be exhausted by progressive additions to knowledge. The epistemological situation here does not seem of course to be characterized by precisely the relation which links nature and the natural scientist, but an analogous relation does appear to link history and the historian (see *Hermeneutics*).

Finally, if science is the methodical, systematic elucidation of the interrelated principles which explain a domain of reality, it must raise the question of what those principles and their interrelations are taken to be, and of how far their domain actually extends. Consequently, not only are the various branches of science distinct, and scientific investigations in the realm of history quite different from scientific investigations in the realm of nature, but a special distinction must be drawn between philosophy, traditionally the universal science *(prima philosophia)* of the interconnection of beings in general in essence and being, and all the "special" sciences of the phenomenal interconnections of beings in nature and history (Kant still speaks of the multiple special forms of "applied philosophy"). Differences in range of subject-matter (material object) and in orientation towards different determining principles (formal object) display differences of method in the various sciences, but these methods are not just various, they are intrinsically diverse just as the sciences are.

b) The "principles" or grounds by which metaphysical philosophy from Plato and Aristotle onwards endeavoured to build up knowledge are the grounds of essence and being in beings in general and in certain realms. Consequently, in this metaphysical tradition the various special sciences were regarded as metaphysical, ontological disciplines (cf. the Aristotelian and Thomistic distinction and co-ordination between πρώτη φιλοσοφία and δευτέρα φιλοσοφία, the later distinction between *metaphysica generalis* and *specialis,* the distinction found as late as Husserl between formal or universal ontology and material or regional ontologies). Whatever the ultimate source ascribed to these principles during the history of metaphysical philosophy (e.g., in the κοινωνία τῶν εἰδῶν under the hierarchical principle of τὸ ἀγαθόν [Plato], in the *divina scientia* of the creator of the world [Aquinas], in the *cogitatio* of the *anima humana* [Descartes], in the absolute subject [Hegel], in the transcendental ego [Husserl]), and whatever the resulting differences in the methods of philosophy as the science of fundamental principles (ἀνάμνησις, *abstractio,* transcendental reflection, immanent dialectic, eidetic and transcendental reduction, etc.), the system of fundamental principles aimed at always formed an "eternal", necessary structure of laws of essence and being. This structure is the basis of all that changes, appears and disappears in space and time under changing conditions, and effectively brings it about that, though changing, the mutable exists at all and is

determinately what it is. It is this regular normative character of the essential ontological foundation of beings (of "things") which is ultimate and primary for metaphysical philosophy. For the various modern empirical sciences, on the other hand, which have detached themselves from any directly metaphysical orientation, the primary and ultimate concern is not why everything in general "is" and is "what" it is, but to discover *why* it happens *as* it does. In other words, the empirical sciences aim at laws which are not eternally necessary laws of being and essence but a factual system of temporal laws of change, laws of motion or phenomenal laws. The latter represent an explanatory system of phenomena. This of course is simply what in fact happens to be the case, but the relation of phenomena to one another is nevertheless "necessarily" determined by it. Consequently, the system of factual relationships (of material phenomena to one another) which the various empirical sciences aim at, under the formal aspect of phenomenal laws, can only be investigated by a process which starts with observation of some phenomenon, then puts forward an explanatory theory which would account for it, and finally tests this hypothetical construction by critical comparison with the observable facts in order to confirm or correct it. In each case, according to the domain of material phenomena that is in question — historical or natural — and according to the corresponding formal orientation of the explanatory system — e.g., according to whether this is assumed to be a mathematical, quantitative system of "natural" phenomena or a qualitative, meaningful pattern of historical phenomena — the result, the range of phenomena included, will inevitably be different for the various empirical sciences and their theoretical constructions, just as the character of the preceding experience of phenomena is not the same for each. There are also necessarily differences in the empirical tests applied to verify the explanatory hypotheses. And the kind of precision of scientific statements which a well-founded theory makes possible, differs from one branch of science to another. Precision in the natural sciences is regarded as demonstrated by what prediction of future events is rendered possible, i.e., what statements can be made about what will be the case, on the basis of general laws, if certain conditions are assumed. The findings of critical history, on the other hand, are intrinsically of such a kind that they take the form of statements about past events, i.e., they aim at giving present knowledge of how it was possible for certain historical phenomena actually to take place. Consequently, the historical disciplines are in principle no less exact than the natural sciences, but they are exact in a sense of their own, which cannot be measured by that of the natural sciences.

c) It is therefore clear that without detriment to the unity of all the sciences (as methodical acquisition of systematically organized knowledge of the determining "grounds" of the factually given), the sciences nevertheless do differ fundamentally, i.e., they differ in what they understand by grounds, fundamental laws and principles. If this fundamental unity and simultaneously fundamental diversity of the sciences is regarded as constituting an "analogy" between them, then the modes in which phenomena are experienced as data and form the starting-point of scientific knowledge must also be analogous, and likewise the various kinds of empirical verification. Consequently, what the various sciences regard as rigour, method and system is analogous in meaning in each case. Even the fundamental and apparently identical terms used in the various sciences are analogous (e.g., "space", "time" and "effect" as used in their physical sense and as used to denote historical dimension, historical time, historical effect). The term "science" itself is analogous. Philosophy in particular, if it regards itself as "scientific", cannot be subsumed under a univocal generic concept of science. And no science is subject to the direct judgment of another and evaluated by it.

This has often been done, of course. To take an example from the natural sciences, biology has been magnified into a comprehensive science comprising not only all the natural sciences but also all the humanistic disciplines (law of the development of life, evolution as the fundamental law both of the whole material and cosmic process and of the history of human cultures — biologism). Psychology too has been proclaimed the standard science among the human sciences and especially the philosophical disciplines (e.g., reduction of the logical normative function of thought to the normality of the process of thought as a psychic act — psychologism). But metaphysical philosophy too calls in question the inalienable independence of the sciences if it attempts to take over already established natural and historical

sciences and their findings into a metaphysical philosophy of nature and of history, in an endeavour to present the laws of nature and history as the evident unfolding of a single intelligible fundamental law, e.g., the single law of the unfolding of absolute Spirit (Panlogicism, with Hegel as its most interesting representative). All such reductions falsify the specific methods of inquiry employed by the branches of science in question. But an equally distorting effect is produced on the science to which they are reduced (e.g., undue historicization of the natural sciences: the concept of what it is scientifically permissible to regard as natural history is itself affected when the concept of humanly purposeful history is equated with the concept of natural history; or, conversely, undue naturalization of the historical disciplines: historical processes admitting of greater or less scope for free decisions are then mistakenly interpreted as necessary processes).

Today the tendency to unitary science and methodological monism comes less from philosophy than from the historical disciplines and natural sciences. The latter are increasingly reduced to physics. The historical disciplines are more and more tempted to identify themselves with social sciences, as branches of sociology, while sociology follows the methodological example of exact natural science because it is dominated by social psychology or social economy or both. We may observe that a reductive relation of this kind to other apparently "more general" branches of science is not necessarily a mistake. The transfer of models from the field of one science to that of another can bring to light entirely new features previously overlooked or insufficiently grasped. It would be mistaken, however, to go on to claim that as a result of such a reduction all the phenomena within the field of the science in question receive a profounder and adequate explanation. It would be wrong to conclude that a single model is obligatory and sufficient for all phenomena in a multiplicity of fields which previously were investigated by a number of independent disciplines. Thus sociology can and will open out very fruitful supplementary aspects for all the historical disciplines (e.g., for history of art, history of religion, political history, etc.). But a total sociologization of these studies (e.g., by explaining all the artistic, religious or political phenomena of human history exclusively by the fundamental laws of social life and by particular social conditions) would leave entirely out of account exactly those features which constitute the precise interest of the subject-matter. The situation is much the same as regards the assimilation of the natural sciences (e.g., chemistry, biology) to physics. This does not simply represent a process of deeper and wider expansion of knowledge of natural phenomena. It points more than anything to a shift in the focus of interest, as a result of which former lines of inquiry or aspects of experience are eliminated as of subordinate or little importance.

4. *Classification of the sciences.* In addition to the division into theoretical, practical and productive sciences, Aristotle speaks of a division into logic (not only formal logic is meant but also what was later called ontology), physics and ethics. All these disciplines, as we noted above, were regarded as philosophical sciences (physics therefore meant philosophy of nature). Kant restored the second of these classifications, but included the empirical sciences which had emerged in the meantime. He lists logic (formal and transcendental), physics (in its "rational part" metaphysics of nature, in its "empirical part" the mathematical science of external nature and of "inner nature" [psychology]) and ethics (in its rational part metaphysics of freedom, of good behaviour or morality, in its empirical part principally practical anthropology). The guiding principle of this division is obviously the fundamentally different yet concordant and analogous regularity of the laws. Thus logic investigates the more universal laws of thought in general, without regard for its material contents; or the general laws of knowledge, i.e., the universal laws of thought in regard to all objects of possible experience. Physics seeks the universal laws which determine natural phenomena in general or in particular domains. Ethics investigates the general moral laws as they ought to apply with absolute obligation purely and simply because they are apprehended as unconditional, but it also studies how they are known under different empirical conditions and what their effective influence actually is.

With the emergence of empirical historical studies under the influence of Romanticism, and the growing interest in individuality in all its forms, the neo-Kantian classifications of the sciences are based on the particular way in which in each case the specific explanatory system stands in relation to the natural or historical phenomena which it determines. Thus H. Rickert distinguishes between the generalizing natural sciences and the individual cultural disciplines. For the former, the individual event is simply an instance of a general causal law which is the principal focus of interest, whereas for the latter, particular events are the unique realizations of a law of value or meaningfulness. (In a similar way W. Windelband had previously distinguished between nomothetic sciences of [natural] law and idiographic sciences of [historical] events.) Other classifications are based solely on difference of method, as for example when the "exact" sciences, i.e., in this context the mathematical sciences (both mathematics as an *a priori* science and the empirical sciences formulated mathematically) are contrasted with the "descriptive" sciences (whether morphological natural sciences or historical or cultural disciplines).

The most influential classification has been that of Wilhelm Dilthey, who drew a methodological distinction between explanation (reduction of natural processes to causal correlations of phenomena) and understanding (investigation of the vital significance expressed in historical phenomena). All these and other classifications of the sciences are quite patently based on an already existent plurality of sciences. Before reflection on the theory of science can begin, each of the various branches of science must already have developed its own particular character. Moreover, this latter does not subsist once and for all unalterably. It changes from time to time in a process which reflection on the theory of science can only follow, not control, still less proclaim to be at an end. On the other hand, these theoretical divisions show that classification cannot be undertaken by one of the disciplines that fall under it. If a theory of science consists merely of reflecting on it from the point of view of one science, there is no possibility of bringing out what distinguishes the scientific character of that discipline from that of others. And if as a result the theory dispenses with the problem of thinking out its own scientific character, it inescapably remains naive and uncritical whatever its subtlety. If, however, reflection on the unity and multiplicity of the sciences is considered properly to belong to a philosophy which recognizes the independence of different ways of gaining knowledge, this testifies in fact to the exceptional position of philosophy in relation to all other disciplines. Even "special" philosophy (philosophy of art, philosophy of science, etc.) occupies this exceptional position, because it is not restricted to a particular field defined and limited by a constitutive "essence", but endeavours to grasp what constitutes this essence itself (e.g., art, religion, politics, history, the inorganic, the organic, nature generally). For the various special sciences, that essence is merely a heuristic means, used without explicit examination to mark a provisional field of inquiry.

But philosophy even in this specialized sense is an *a priori* philosophy of essence, even if it does not, as traditional metaphysics did, regard this *a priori* essence as supra-temporal and eternal, but considers it to be a historical, mutable *a priori* factor, and even if it seeks to grasp it not only by immediate experience but also by having recourse to the analyses of experience carried out by the empirical sciences. Here again a philosophic grasp of essences is only possible because philosophy transcends the limits set to all particular domains by their very nature. Consequently, in comparison with all the special sciences, philosophy is in an exceptional position, chiefly because it is the most universal science of the fundamental and coherent "whole" which comprises all the essential features of all domains of reality whatsoever. This is the case, whatever the ways in which philosophy past and present may have attempted to conceive this "whole" (as universe, soul, God, absolute Spirit, being, etc.). But if philosophy "transcends" all essentially circumscribed domains, this means that instead of being bound by a double limiting and categorized relation to certain material and formal objects, it is directed to what is most formal of all, to this "whole" and its universal and transcendent aspects. This means that for philosophy the concept of method approaches an ultimate limit. So does that of "truth" (as correspondence between state of affairs and cognitive statement, since the totality of all states of affairs is not itself one state of affairs among others), together with the concepts of understanding, scientific knowledge, science itself. Consequently, philosophy sees itself as the ultimate science. It is therefore part of its essential function perpetually to call itself in question, which means to question even the scientific character of its own content. Nevertheless it is the ultimate discipline from which alone both the unity and the independence of the various special sciences can receive just recognition.

5. *Science and its application*. The tradition deriving from Plato and Aristotle stressed that science aims at pure θεωρία, that is, the scientific pursuit of knowledge is guided by truth for its own sake, and aims at the presence of essential reality in the contemplative mind. This service of truth, however, is bound up with the promotion of man's own reality, i.e., education and development of his true humanity. The way of life characterized by ποίησις and the productive knowledge that it involves — τέχνη — fit into the order of social life which is the work of πρᾶξις and moral knowledge, φρόνησις. Action and moral knowledge, however, have their criterion and perfect realization in the intellectual knowledge of philosophical "science", ἐπιστήμη in the strict sense. Human reality is regarded as perfectly achieved when man is in the truth. This inevitably excludes from science in the strict sense any limited practical application, the view that science is a useful means of production, giving power and mastery over reality and potential reality. Even modern "theory" in the empirical natural sciences does not primarily include the application of particular knowledge to the attainment of particular purposes. However, "theory" no longer means intellectual contemplation of essential being as an end in itself. On the contrary, it becomes "a means of construction, by which experiences are brought together into a unity, thus making it possible to control them". And though theory does not concern any specific end pursued by the application of specific knowledge, so that particular practical applications are extrinsic and secondary from that point of view, nevertheless the theoretical knowledge as such is envisaged "from the point of view of deliberate mastery of reality", and taken as a whole is posited as a means, not as an end in itself, as "theory" was in the ancient world (H.-G. Gadamer).

As a result, theory itself has become increasingly "practical". The changed meaning of *praxis* has to be noted, however. The term originally referred to moral action, but now more and more aspects of production (of *poiesis*) enter into it (see *Theory and Practice*). The pragmatical character of modern theory is very strongly reinforced in the empirical natural sciences, because natural science is taken into the service of technology and forms its basis. This is not a one-sided process, but represents a continual advance in science's theoretical understanding of its own nature. Modern technology has its basis in natural science, and the latter accordingly assumes a technological character. Hence theoretical knowledge (science) and its practical application (material production) become two complementary aspects of the same thing, i.e., man's fundamental relation to the world, which he now understands as "work"(control of nature by transforming it).

The process of turning knowledge ("theory") into an instrument is most apparent in the incorporation of the natural sciences into technology, but it affects the historical disciplines as well. This is because the understanding of historical phenomena is increasingly guided by the idea of tracing them to man's "need" to produce such and such phenomena in history in order to preserve his life. Consequently, historical science becomes a partner or even an appendix of natural science. The scientific — and (in Dilthey's sense) explanatory — mind "exploits nature just as the understanding mind (i.e., seeking historical comprehension) exploits history" (A. Gehlen). This becomes even more obvious when historians transfer scientific models to social processes, thus discovering a means of freeing themselves from their primary concern with the past and developing history into futurology and prognostication, and regarding it as a means to construct the future.

In general, however, the determining influence of science on life at the present day is the expression of a conception of reality which, though dominant, is by no means self-evident. In this view, any reality attains its highest presence, manifestation and truth only in man's conceptual knowledge of it. Thus, for example, the understanding of nature achieves its authentic truth in natural science, history is only truly history in the conceptual knowledge of historical science, etc. In contrast to this it might be asked how the various modes of knowledge are mutually irreducible yet fit together into a unity, and furthermore how scientific understanding generally is simply a fundamental (and intrinsically diversified) way in which man and world are true and manifest, an inseparable element in a unity of several equally fundamental human activities. For neither separately nor in conjunction can these fundamental activities be exhaustively theorized, wholly comprised in one concept and one system.

See also *Philosophy, Psychology* I A, *Logic, Metaphysics.*

BIBLIOGRAPHY. B. Bolzano, *Wissenschaftslehre,* 4 vols. (1837; reprint 1929–31); A. N. Whitehead, *Science and the Modern World* (1926); id., *Science and Philosophy* (1947); B. Russell, *An Outline of Philosophy* (1927); *Mysticism and Logic* (2nd ed., 1954); id., *On the Philosophy of Science* (1965); R. Collingwood, *The Idea of Nature* (1945); H.-G. Gadamer, *Über die Ursprünglichkeit der Wissenschaft* (1947); W. Kamlah, *Die Wurzeln der neuzeitlichen Wissenschaft und Profanität* (1948); E. Schrödinger, *Science and Humanism* (1951); id., *Science, Theory and Man* (1957); M. Heidegger, "Wissenschaft und Besinnung", *Vorträge und Aufsätze* (1954), pp. 45–70; W. Dilthey, *Essence of Philosophy* (1954); H. Butterfield and others, *Short History of Science: A Symposium* (1959); S. Toulmin, *Philosophy of Science* (1960); H. Rickert, *Science and History: A Critique of Positivist Epistemology* (1962); A. Gehlen, *Der Mensch* (7th ed., 1962), especially pp. 381–94; K. Popper, *Conjectures and Refutations: The Growth of Scientific Knowledge* (1963); R. Fox and others, *Science of Science* (1963); M. Müller, "Philosophie – Wissenschaft – Technik", *Existenzphilosophie im geistigen Leben der Gegenwart* (3rd ed., 1964); G. McLean, ed., *Philosophy in a Technological Culture* (1965); S. Dockz and P. Bernays, eds., *Information and Prediction in Science* (1965); P. Heelan, *Quantum Mechanics and Objectivity* (1966); H. Nielsen, *Methods of Modern Science* (1967); R. Harré, *The Ideals of Science* (1969); N. Rescher, ed., *Studies in the Philosophy of Science* (1969).

Alois Halder and *Max Müller*

II. Theory of Science

Reflection on science has always formed part of philosophy. It is only in modern times, and especially since Kant, that light on the specific character of human cognition has been looked for from the logical analysis of science. For Kant, this raised the question of the possibility of synthetic *a priori* judgments, which he regarded as an indispensable basis of the universal statements of natural laws made by mathematical natural science; that these are justified is placed beyond all doubt by their success. Later, the following main tendencies emerged in the theory of science.

One line of thought inspired by transcendental philosophy investigates the *a priori* conditions of the sciences. Fichte regarded philosophy as a "theory of science", or "science of science as such". This inquires, "What is the content and form of a science precisely as such, i.e., how is it possible precisely as science?" According to Trendelenburg, all sciences involve "metaphysical presuppositions in their object and logical presuppositions in their method ... The question what justification there is for these presuppositions and how such a conjunction [of object and method] takes place, calls for a theory of science, and this might well be called logic in a wider sense." In this sense, according to K. Rahner, "a question in the theory of science always simultaneously implies the question of the actual nature of science as a human activity". This line of thought is chiefly represented by metaphysical epistemology (see *Knowledge*).

Another tendency is more influenced by the various branches of science themselves and undertakes the logical analysis of these disciplines. Bolzano took what was still a very general view of the theory of science, as "the sum-total of all the rules which we must follow in dividing the whole domain of truth into particular sciences and in their exposition in separate text-books, if we are to proceed correctly". Soon, however, attention was concentrated on questions which emerged in the first place in the course of inquiries into the foundations of mathematics and physics. The primary concern here is not with general philosophical considerations but with detailed investigations of particular concepts and theories. The history of science provides valuable materials for such analyses. Such investigation is now mostly considered part of the theory of science. In what follows an account is given of a few points of view which have been worked out in this field and which can also be regarded as relevant to philosophy and theology.

In contrast to a one-sided domination of theory of science by the natural sciences, the special character of the "human" sciences, e.g., history, was investigated in the Baden neo-Kantian school and by Wilhelm Dilthey. This has assumed great importance for philosophy and theology, chiefly because of the problems connected with hermeneutics.

1. *Axiomatic theory.* Investigations into the foundations of mathematics and science raise the question of the basis on which the meaning and validity of scientific propositions rest. Since the validity of propositions which are derived from other propositions is dealt with in logic, logical analysis is indispensable. Nowadays the techniques of modern logic are used (see *Logic*).

a) *Axioms.* If a body of propositions contains derivative propositions, the propositions can be arranged in inferential order. Underived propositions which serve as basis for further deductions are principles or axioms. Euclid's "Elements of Geometry" are a classical example of a science with an axiomatic structure. Similarly the concepts employed in a science may be examined to determine which can be defined in terms of others, and in this way the basic concepts identified.

b) *Material and formal axioms.* Euclid regarded the axioms as self-evident. This presupposes that the meaning of the basic terms used in the axioms is sufficiently known and that the validity of the axioms understood in that sense is guaranteed by insight. But confidence in an intuitive factor of this kind has been shaken. It has been shown that one of Euclid's axioms, regarding parallel lines, can be replaced by others which are incompatible with it, thus producing non-Euclidian geometries, which can be used in physics. The explanation of this is said to be that scientific theories do not directly mirror the real state of affairs but present a simplified idealization. And so Hilbert inverts the relation between concept and proposition. From the point of view of formal axiomatization the primary question is not that of knowing the meaning of basic concepts which generate axioms. That is a material question of content, not of form. On the contrary, the axioms are primary and the basic concepts are regarded as implicitly defined by them. This means that what is chiefly relevant about the concepts is the relations between them, and these are expressed by the axioms. Consequently, a formal axiomatic system has application wherever an interpretation of the basic concepts transforms the axioms into propositions which hold good of something. If an interpretation of this kind, answering the requirements of the axioms, applies to empirically verifiable facts, we speak of a real model.

c) *Antinomies and freedom from contradiction.* Modes of inference which appear intuitively plausible and which formerly were employed unhesitatingly in mathematics, have been shown to be open to question. It has been proved possible to derive mutually contradictory propositions from them (antinomies). But if a contradiction can be inferred in a system, the system becomes meaningless, for a contradiction entails any propositions whatsoever, and it is no longer possible to distinguish between derivative and non-derivative propositions. It therefore became necessary to formulate modes of inference precisely and to discover whether it is possible to prove that a system which employs them is consistent. Various methods were tried. It has been successfully shown that axiomatic systems of non-Euclidian geometry are consistent. This was done by arithmetization, by reducing them to the non-contradictory character of arithmetic. For this purpose the basic terms of geometry were given an arithmetical interpretation fulfilling the axioms. A logical or mathematical model of this kind is called a formal model. In order to demonstrate the consistency of arithmetic itself, however, a different method had to be employed. Attempts were made (Lorenzen, Hao Wang) to find a constructional solution using only unobjectionable modes of inference and replacing any questionable ones. Objections can be raised in particular to proofs which assume an (infinite) totality of objects (e.g., numbers). Some forms of indirect proof of the existence of something do this, by assuming that a particular attribute belongs to none of the objects or that there is at least one object which possesses it, though which one need not necessarily be known. There are also objections to statements in which a predicate is affirmed or denied of itself, as well as to statements which apply to themselves. The distinction between an object-language and a metalanguage in which we speak about the object-language, eliminates a statement referring to itself, but shows the limits set to any language which has to fulfil strict conditions. Lorenzen endeavours on the basis of his own operationalist standpoint to overcome the difficulty that in order to construct a rigorous language we must already possess a metalanguage, and for the latter to be strictly constructed we must have a meta-metalanguage etc. He argues that learning a language does not always presuppose a language, and that a metalanguage can be introduced by construction.

d) *A priori.* In formalist axiomatic theory, the axioms are conventions; it makes sense to question their utility but not their validity. From the operationalist point of view this has to be qualified to the extent that some linguistic stipulations are required. It is possible to show, however, that other propositions which are usually taken to be mere stipulations necessarily follow from the use of these linguistic conventions. These include, according to Lorenzen, important presuppositions of logic, arithmetic, geometry and even of kinematics and mechanics. They are not empirical propositions, because they are not based on observation; in fact they make it possible to formulate what has been observed. Nor are they merely stipula-

tions and analytic inferences from them. They may be regarded as a reconstruction of what is usually meant by synthetic *a priori* judgments.

2. *Empirical basis.* a) *Empirical verifiability.* The advance of physics to the theory of relativity and quantum mechanics was made possible by submitting certain concepts to critical examination, e.g., simultaneity, correspondence of physical characteristics to sub-atomic particles. The critique consisted in not resting content with the apparently self-evident intuitive meaning but in asking how it is we are able to determine at all whether these terms are applicable or not. This question led to changes of meaning and more precise definition of these terms. Some previously recalcitrant problems were solved as a result. This, and the fact that science is concerned with statements that can be tested, suggest that to determine the meaning of a scientific statement and of the terms employed in it, we have to consider the method by which it can be tested or verified. Analysis of the basis of the scientific validity of scientific statements is therefore of fundamental importance in deciding what they mean.

b) *Theoretical concepts.* Strict application of the principle of verification led to difficulties. General statements of laws are in principle impossible to verify completely. According to Popper, all we require of them by way of test is that they should make possible exact predictions (prognostic relevance) and that it is therefore conceivably possible in principle for them to be proved wrong by the non-occurrence of their prediction (falsifiability). Furthermore, the attempt to define the concepts of natural science in terms of observation encountered difficulties. According to Carnap, disposition concepts ("elastic", "conductor of electricity", "soluble in water") must be introduced by postulates of meaning; the full meaning of such concepts is not completely determined by empirically verifiable statements; instead, some conditions of their correct applicability or inapplicability are stated. This led to the interpretation of empirical scientific theories which is often referred to as the dual schema. According to this, a theory contains both empirical and theoretical concepts, an observation language consisting of empirical terms which can be tested by direct observation, and a theoretical language consisting of theoretical terms, the meaning of which is established axiomatically. Rules of correspondence are also needed to link the two languages and thus permit empirically verifiable statements to be derived from the theory.

c) The logical structure of an explanation in the empirical sciences consists in the logical possibility of deriving the proposition expressing the *explicandum* from theoretical laws, once the particular conditions of the case in question are known. In this respect there is a certain similarity between explanation and prediction.

The following objections have been raised against any over-simplified view of a dual schema of this kind. It is in fact the case that the observation language itself is independent of theoretical elements drawn from rival theories, which observation must confirm or rebut. Feyerabend and Sellars point out, however, that it cannot be concluded from this that the observation language contains no theoretical element whatsoever. It has to be remembered, too, that not everything in the theoretical language established axiomatically is purely arbitrary stipulation. We must distinguish between linguistic conventions, propositions they entail and statements embodying the scientific content of the theory.

d) *Theory and reality*. It is usual to give the expressions of the theoretical language, in addition to the interpretation which answers to the rules of correspondence, another interpretation which satisfies the axioms. This is called a model of the theory. Opinions differ on the epistemological character of such models. A mechanical model used to be considered indispensable, and was regarded as giving a complete grasp of physical reality (interpretation of theory as content). The difficulty of finding mechanical models, and the possibility of presenting different models, have led to the view that models are mere aids to visualization, devoid of any informative value beyond what is expressed in the formalism of the theory (formalist interpretation: a theory is a mere means of representing what can be observed). An intermediate view is that a theory has limited content. Models are thus analogous representations of the reality with which the theory deals. Direct conclusions about reality should therefore not be drawn from the model if they do not follow from the theory itself.

3. *Applications*. Any application of the systems discussed in the theory of science to philosophy and theology, must take into account the different character of these disciplines as compared with the empirical sciences. The difference has usually been over-emphasized, however, with the unfortunate result that little attention has been given to similarities between them. We must therefore confine ourselves to a few indications.

a) *Metaphysical explanation*. While the empirical sciences construct theories from which the *explicandum* can be derived, and thus have prognostic relevance, metaphysics seeks the necessary conditions of the given. Its function is not prognosis but integration. The aim is to express explicitly how a particular conception (philosophical world-picture) provides a unified interpretation of everything which man has to come to terms with in life, and is thus able to offer guidance for the meaningful conduct of life. Philosophical statements are tested (and this is relevant to determining their meaning) by examining whether they do in fact perform this integrative function. Consequently it is not legitimate, for example, to exclude from the start some domain of human experience. Since this verification itself has to be open to the totality of human experience, it is less intersubjective than in the empirical sciences. It is not the business of metaphysics to offer a concrete world-picture, but to bring out what conditions must be fulfilled by conceptions with an integrative function. As regards philosophical views which have emerged at different times in history, we must distinguish between their fundamental meaning which bears the integrative function and the historically conditioned representative models in which this was embodied.

b) *Theology as theory*. If we want to trace a certain similarity between theology and the dual theory-schema, the following approach might be attempted. The observation language is matched by the religious language, in which the fundamental doctrines of faith are expressed. Theology seeks understanding, and for that purpose constructs a system in theoretical language, i.e., the language of theology. The understanding of the faith which this system formulates has to be in harmony with the fundamental statements of the religious language. The distinction between positive and speculative theology would thus correspond to that between experimental and theoretical physics. An attitude of theological positivism towards revelation regards theology as merely a formal systematization of the statements of the sources of revelation. The role of philosophy in theology consists in drawing out what is necessarily implied by particular questions and linguistic conventions. It is chiefly concerned, however, with everything involved in metaphysical explanation. This inevitably demands its integration with the full breadth of human experience and with other philosophical views. This total context must be taken into account in determining the full meaning of theological statements. Furthermore, the theoretical element in the observation language must not be overlooked. This explains the importance of a hermeneutics of the sources of revelation.

See also *Natural Law* II, *Hermeneutics*.

BIBLIOGRAPHY. See bibliography on *Science* I; also: F. Renoirte, *Critique des sciences* (1945); P. Frank, *Modern Science and its Philosophy* (1950); K. R. Popper, *Logic of Scientific Discovery* (1956); O. Muck, "Methodologie und Metaphysik", *Aufgaben der Philosophie*, I (1958), pp. 97–157; id., "Zur Logik der Rede von Gott", *ZKT* 89 (1967), pp. 1–28; id., "Metaphysische Erklärung als ganzheitliches Verfahren", *Akten des XIV. Internationalen Kongresses für Philosophie*, II (1968), pp. 419–25; W. Leinfellner, *Struktur und Aufbau wissenschaftlicher Theorien* (1965); J. M. Bochenski, *Methods of Contemporary Thought* (1965); id., *The Logic of Religion* (1965); R. Klibansky, ed., *Contemporary Philosophy*, II: *The Philosophy of Science* (1968); P. Lorenzen, *Normative Logic and Ethics* (1969); P. Suppes, *Studies in the Methodology and Foundations of Science* (1969).

Otto Muck

III. Science and Theology

The subject-matter of science is virtually unrestricted, in the region of the observable. But it is mainly concerned with systems (the atom, the solar system, the biosphere, etc.) which are more or less isolated from outside interference. The framework of its method is functional causality, that is, the relation of cause and effect is expressed as the regular connection between successive states of an isolated system (see *Matter* II). The features which characterize a system are restricted to measurable quantities (dimensions of space, time, mass, etc.), or reduced to such (force equals mass multiplied by acceleration). The units of measurement (metres, seconds, etc.) are chosen so that they can be reproduced independently of the observer or local and temporal conditions. The laws of nature are the regular connections between the characteristics of a system in its various states. In principle, they can be verified again and again under the same conditions (see *Natural Law* II). They apply to interrelated occurrences in general, but not to unique conjunctures, which are left out of consideration as accidental (marginal or initial circumstances). The laws of nature are general because they hold good in the same way for similar combinations of changeable circumstances. (The law of falling bodies holds for all bodies in a vacuum.) Though general, the laws of nature are not necessarily universal, because they may need to be widened, further generalized or refined to apply to a wider set of variables (transition from the law of falling bodies to the law of gravitation and the general theory of relativity).

Thus scientific concepts and modes of thought are not ontologically grounded. They are based on the fact that they describe correctly phenomena and their regularity and can express the relations between them. The utility, realism and extent of scientific notions and thought-forms are reflected by the totality of the matter which can be adequately grasped by their means. Science undergoes developments. A refinement of concepts and thought-forms can take in a broader field of phenomena and changes in their regular connections. (The revisions of the notions of space and time in the theory of relativity made it possible to combine the mechanics and electrodynamics of systems at rest and in motion. The refinement of the notions of "measurement" and "state" in the quantum theory made it possible to understand the connection between wave and quantum phenomena.) In such developments, the older laws do not become false or useless, since they are still valid in the description of a limited field of phenomena, while they also represent in the main an indispensable approach to the understanding of the wider field.

Natural science is both inductive and deductive. It is inductive inasmuch as the necessity of new thought-forms results from the experimental discovery of new phenomena and laws. It is experience which points to the formation of new or more generalized concepts. But from the formal aspect, natural science is always deductive, because the fundamental understanding of a scientific discipline is only possible when the connection can be seen between the individual statement and the basic principles and laws. The comprehensive registration of facts or a systematic phenomenology is merely a scientific preparation for a working hypothesis or theory. These two aspects then suggest what notion of truth and what criteria of truth hold good for science. (i) The truth of a thought-form is the adequacy with which it can be used to describe and grasp a complex of phenomena or laws and explain their logical structure. The truth of a thought-form is reflected in the extent of the subject-matter which it can explain. (ii) Truth as simplicity (the positivist principle of economy): the number of non-demonstrable principles (axioms) is to be as small as possible, so that the logical connection can be as perspicuous as possible. (iii) Truth as formal correctness: science, insofar as it is deductive, must satisfy the demands of logic. Its axioms should be free from mutual contradiction and independent of each other.

The dogmas of the Church are governed by a mentality which is essentially different from that of science. No doubt the subject-matter of dogma is as unlimited as that of science, since it can comprise the whole order of creation and redemption. Nonetheless, the formal object of a dogma can be characterized in the present context in the following way. (i) Dogma aims primarily at the enunciation of the self-understanding of the Church in its context of salvation. It is the basis by which the faithful identify themselves in each other's eyes (see *Creeds*). (ii) This entails the consequence that dogma is a formula by which membership or otherwise of the ecclesiastical community can be determined, according to the individual's convictions and practices. This aspect of dogma has a strongly juridical character. There is no higher court outside the Church which can be appealed to (see *Infallibility*). (iii) The Church identifies itself with the primitive Christian community and ecclesiastical tradition. Hence dogma is also an essential note of the Church. The comparison of various stages of development must display the unchangeable nature and the laws of growth of the Church. (iv) The Church is in a milieu on which it acts and to which it reacts. This milieu is the living-space of the Church. Hence dogma must also formulate what is beneficial to the life of the community and what is detrimental. It must analyse the structure of the environment and formulate the vital connections between the Church and its surroundings. This aspect of dogma has a historical and sociological character. (v) The spiritual life of the Church is rooted in revelation and tradition. Both roots must be detached from the ancient and mythological world-picture with which they are entwined. Hence dogma has also a philosophical and cultural aspect.

All five aspects show clearly that the formal object of dogma is characterized by concern for the Church and its mediation of salvation, but not by an encyclopedic or profane ideal of truth. In contrast to the natural sciences, the object of dogma is not an isolated system governed by its own laws but above all the historical connection of the individual in the order of salvation with the last end of man and of all creation. In the light of its formal object, the dogmatic formulation is free to make use of either functional or efficient causality as a category. Efficient causality is appropriate to the description of one-directional series of causes, such as the mediation of salvation by the Church to the world about it, from which the "feed-back" is insignificant. Functional causality is appropriate (i) when contrasting dogma and science, since the findings of science are only defined and can only be discussed within the framework of functional causality; (ii) when dogmatic matters are to be formulated in which the Church appears as a functional and vital unity in the history of salvation; (iii) when theology formulates the development of the Church in the direction of the kingdom of God. For in these three instances of causality it would be inappropriate to think of God as (external) efficient cause.

The objects dealt with by dogma are not only matters which can be reproduced and which occur generally (see *Virtue* II, *Sacraments*), but also the unique, non-repeatable salvation-history of Israel and the Christian community, of humanity and of all creation. The concepts and thought-forms used by dogma must meet three requirements. (i) While they need not express fully the content of a given truth or object, they must do so adequately, in terms of the intention behind the formulation. (ii) The formulation must bring out the connection between the matter formulated and the history of salvation and the occasion of the salvific act. (iii) The concepts used must be accessible to contemporary thought and intelligible. They should be represented there by what is "food for thought". The mind of the Church is not just nourished by the past. It must re-formulate its self-understanding again and again in view of the perpetual change in the cultural and sociological structure of mankind. This relation to preaching means that there must be a development of dogma, which is analogous to that which takes place in science. The criteria of truth here are (i) harmony with the sources of revelation and with Church practice throughout history; (ii) unity of purpose with the saving act of God and salvation-history; (iii) the faith professed by the faithful. The question of authority does not arise directly in the contrast between dogma and science.

It appears from the foregoing comparison between dogma and science that they cut across each other in their material object, but differ essentially in their formal objects. Difficulties, especially unreal problems, can arise between dogma and science on the following grounds. (i) In the formulation of a given truth, there may be confusion between functional and efficient causality (creation and beginning of the world; salutary sign and extraordinary natural phenomenon; the soul as the mover and the form of the body; the human will as efficient cause and as a component in a functional unity of the physical and spiritual). (ii) The sources of revelation may be considered under the formal object of natural science (the account of creation, the history of the earth and man, the eschatology of the physical world in the Old and the New Testament). (iii) The findings of science may be considered under the formal object of dogma (mythologization of the evolution of organisms, the expansion of the universe, the second law of thermodynamics). (iv) Dogmatic formulas may use ancient terms which have taken on, under the influence of science, an essentially different meaning in ordinary language or have come to have entirely different connotations.

Some indications may be given of the meaning of these four points.

(i) The notion of creation is meant to express the absoluteness and transcendence of God and the fundamental nature of his relation to the existence and nature of all beings. The biblical formula, "He spoke, and it was made", is not a metaphysical one. The classical formula, "creatio est productio rei ex nihilo sui et subiecti", is taken from efficient causality, but indicates the difference in creation by the addition "ex nihilo". The category of functional causality used in the modern era whittled down the intuitional basis of the formula of efficient causality. Further, it remains an open question whether the chronological beginning is part of the intention of the dogma, or merely a particularity of the thought-forms of efficient causality

which are used in the formulation. Functional causality hardly allows the formulation of a chronological beginning. The relation of God to all beings must be learned by abstraction and analogy from the invariable structures of the dynamics of real and possible systems. The notion of creation points to a relation to the Absolute and hence must be capable of formulation in the widest possible variety of terms. Hence, though different categories of causality may not be confused, they cannot be deduced from one another. So too with the evolution of organisms and of man. It is formulated and defined in terms of functional causality. Its essential notes are found in the special dynamism of the development of certain structures in living things. To mix in notions of efficient causality is not only false methodically, but ignores and distorts the dynamism of life, quite apart from the fact that individual efficient causes within the world throw no light on the all-embracing divine law.

A miracle, as a special event and salutary sign, can only be defined in terms of its purpose and function in salvation-history. Just as the scientific aspect does not fall under the formal object of dogma, so too natural science is as open to a functional connection in salvation-history as the laws of physics to chemical structure and biological information, of which superstructures they in fact are the necessary basis. But if a miracle or the free will is formulated as an instance of efficient causality in a nature which is understood functionally, a confusion of terms and thought ensues, and then an opposition between science and dogma. When the soul is considered as the spiritual and physical form of the human body, this is in harmony with dogma, which defends the unity of soul and body, and also with the functional point of view of natural science. But if the resurrection of man is not considered as God's salvific act, but as the natural right of an immortal effective cause, coming into play to form and stamp the body, there is not only a conflict with science, but the religious assertion of the capacity of the whole man to be saved is obscured.

(ii) The Scriptures of the OT and NT must be considered from the aspect of salvation-history and hence as sources of dogma, not of natural science. Thus the accounts of creation primarily affirm the absoluteness of God against contemporary myths. They do not aim at astronomical data.

(iii) Notions of science as leading to reli-

SCOTISM

gion or of evolution of organisms as salvation-history confuse different complexes of functions and different modes of thought.

(iv) If the primary intention of a dogma has been obscured by the fact that ancient terms (nature, substance, etc.) are now found in new contexts, the modes of thought of science may help to make the original intention accessible to contemporary thought.

See also *Causality, Life* I.

BIBLIOGRAPHY. C. Raven, *Natural Religion and Christian Theology* (1953); id., *Christianity and Science* (1955); E. L. Mascall, *Christian Theology and Natural Science* (1956); C. Coulson, *Science and Christian Belief* (1958); id., *Science, Technology and the Christian* (1961); W. Heisenberg, *Physics and Philosophy* (1958); J. Abelé, *Christianity and Science* (1961); I. T. Ramsey, *Religion and Science* (1964); C. F. von Weizsäcker, *The Relevance of Science* (1964).

Gernot Eder

SCOTISM

Scotism is the term applied either to the doctrine of Duns Scotus or of his school.

1. *Origin.* The controversy among Aristotelians was at its height during the teaching career of Duns Scotus (*c.* 1300), with the ancient Franciscan school (St. Bonaventure etc.) of the Augustinian type opposed to the Thomistic (see *Scholasticism* II C). On 7 March 1277 the Bishop of Paris, Stephen, along with the University, had condemned 219 philosophical theses, including some of St. Thomas's. Archbishop Kilwardby, O. P., declared some theses of St. Thomas to be dangerous. The result of these proscriptions was, as Gilson remarks, that theologians of those days found themselves in the same position as exegetes after the condemnation of modernism (É. Gilson, p. 643; cf. pp. 364, 407–8). Scotus submitted unreservedly to these decrees, as also to the precept of the general chapter of his order, which forbade its members to uphold a doctrine "ab episcopo et magistris Parisiensibus communiter reprobatam" (H. S. Denifle, *Chartularium Univ. Paris.,* II [Paris, 1891], no. 580, p. 58).

The condemnations of 1270, and above all of 1277, reflect the opposition to an independent philosophy, and, as it was thought, to the abandonment of the traditional doctrine. It was a reaction which gave a new orientation to the Augustinian type of Aristotelianism which found its definitive expression in Scotism (cf. J. van Steenberghen, pp. 715, 729).

2. *The essential characteristics of the philosophical and theological system of Duns Scotus.* The penetrating criticism of the *doctor subtilis* was directed against the Franciscan as well as the Thomistic school, and here he was more concerned with contemporary authors than with St. Thomas. Thus he created a system which is neither identical with that of Aquinas nor directly opposed to it; it must be regarded as a parallel to Thomism.

The object of our intellect is *ens inquantum ens;* only the *ens infinitum* is being in the full sense. The first act which is to be predicated of being is that of love, in accordance with the text of Scripture: "Deus caritas est" (1 Jn 4:16). This love indicates the source of action in God, which takes place necessarily *ad intra,* but freely *(contingenter) ad extra.* God sees everything in the *nunc aeternitatis;* he wills everything in one absolutely simple and immutable act, which being entirely rational grasps its objects in an ordered manner. Since God loves himself and likewise wills that there should be *condiligentes,* he wills Christ first of all, the *summum opus Dei,* as the *causa exemplaris* and *finalis.* Mary was foreordained along with Christ and preserved from original sin in view of the merits of her son, the one mediator and redeemer. The love of Christ is revealed especially on the cross and in the Eucharist, *sine qua periret omnis devotio in Ecclesia nec actus latriae exhiberetur Deo (Reportatio Parisiensis,* IV d.8 q.1 n.3; ed. Vivès, 24, 10a).

Just as love is at the beginning of everything, so too our blessedness is in love and not in the vision of the intellect.

Duns Scotus did not demand an independent philosophy. Like the ancient Franciscan school, he upheld a Christian philosophy. The univocity of being, *distinctio formalis, forma corporeitatis,* the freedom of the will were concepts with which he tried to reach a deeper *intellectus fidei* (cf. C. Balić in *DSAM,* cols. 1801–18).

3. *Followers of Duns Scotus.* Scotus's type of teaching attracted the attention of his contemporaries and was not without influence on some of them, as for instance Robert of Cowton, Petrus Aureoli, Alexander Bonini, William of Nottingham (d. 1336), and above all Henry of Harcley (d. 1317) from among the diocesan clergy, though they cannot yet be called Scotists.

52

Some authors enumerate the followers of Scotus according to five periods (cf. A. Bertoni, pp. 433–580). We name only some of them. Among his immediate disciples are: Antonius Andreas (d. about 1320), Alfredus Gonteri (d. after 1325), Francis de Mayronis (d. after 1325), William of Alnwick (d. about 1333), Peter Thomas, Peter of Aquila (d. 1361), John de Bassolis (d. 1333). Others in the 14th century include: Francis de Marchia (d. after 1344), Landolfo Caracciolo (d. 1351), John of Rodington (d. 1348), John of Reading, William of Rubione, Andrew of Novocastro. In the 15th century, the period of the decline of scholasticism, we have the Scotists Peter Tartaretus, Bellatti, Sirect, William of Vaurouillon (d. 1464), Nicolaus d'Orbellis (d. 1471), Maurice de Portu (d. 1513), Trombetta (d. 1518), Paul Scriptor (d. 1505), Gratian of Brescia (d. about 1506), G. Gorris, John of Cologne.

We come finally to the 16th and 17th centuries, the golden age of the school, when there were chairs of Scotism, along with those of Thomism and nominalism, at most universities, especially in Spain.

Hundreds of commentaries on the *Ordinatio (Opus Oxoniense)* were written in this period.

Notable Scotists were: in France, Frassen (d. 1711), Dupasquier (d. 1705), Boyvin (d. 1679), Durand (d. 1710); in Spain, Francis Herrera (d. *c.* 1600), John of Ovando (d. *c.* 1610), Francis del Castillo Velasco, Francis Felix (d. *c.* 1650), Pérez López (d. 1724), Charles Moral (d. 1731); in Italy, Lychetus (d. 1520), Mastrius (d. 1673), Belluti (d. 1676), Faber (d. 1630), Vulpes (d. 1636), Lanterius, Malafossa (d. *c.* 1562), de Pitigianis (d. 1616), Brancatius (d. 1693); in Dalmatia, Benedict Benković (d. after 1520), Matthew Ferkić (d. 1669); in northern Europe, Peter Posnaniensis (d. after 1639), Pontius (d. *c.* 1672), Cavellus (d. 1670), Wadding (d. 1657), Antony Hiquaeus (d. 1641), Hermann (d. 1700), Krisper (d. 1740).

The second half of the 18th and the first half of the 19th centuries show scholasticism in general in decline, and Scotism in particular. It was only in the first decades of the 20th century that Scotism found defenders again in Minges, Garcia, Belmond and Marie de Basly.

4. *Characteristics of Scotism.* Peter Thomas, about 1300, who professed to follow the master *ut plurimum,* blamed the *non scotizantes,* that is, those who wished to interpret Scotus objectively, but ascribed to him doctrines which he did not hold *(vulgus imposuit sibi)* and instead of keeping to the text *(expresse ex textu),* preferred to form their judgments *ex eius intentione* (Vatican Ms. Lat. 2190, f. 51 r–52r). This controversy about the genuine doctrine of Scotus, which ensued from the incomplete nature of his works, was characteristic of Scotism in the 14th century. Single propositions were taken from their context, where for instance Scotus was attacking the determinism of Arab Aristotelianism, stress was laid on freedom, the absolute omnipotence of God and voluntarism, and thus occasion was given to later writers to speak of the influence of Scotism on nominalism and certain theories of modern philosophy. The Christocentric teaching of Scotus, however, and the doctrine of the Immaculate Conception, simply known as *opinio Scoti,* were readily taken over as early as the 14th century. It was on account of these doctrines that the great reformers of Franciscan spirituality (St. John Capistran, St. Bernardine of Siena, James von der Mark) declared Duns Scotus to be the leader of the Franciscan school and the *Doctor Ordinis,* and these doctrines were the chief glory of the Scotist school from the 16th to the 18th century (cf. C. Balić in *Antonianum* 30 [1955], pp. 349–488). Instead of going deeply into the doctrine of Scotus on the Church, the sources of revelation (Scripture-tradition), being as love, Scotists wrote treatises *De formalitatibus;* and because St. Thomas was among the authors with whom Scotus was in conflict on the doctrine of the Immaculate Conception, efforts were made to find points of difference everywhere between Scotism and Thomism. Cajetan was led to affirm that Scotus tried to refute *singula prope verba* of the *Summa of Aquinas* (cf. É. Gilson, "Note sur un texte de Cajetan", *Antonianum* 27 [1952], pp. 377–80).

While some Scotists (De Rada, d. 1608, Macedo, d. 1681, Stella, d. after 1651, Lorte, d. 1724) brought out the contrast between St. Thomas and Scotus, others tried to reconcile the doctrines (Sarnano, d. 1535, Marco da Baudunio), or built up a *summa theologica iuxta ordinem et dispositionem Summae Angelici Doctoris* (De Montefortino, d. 1738) — efforts which in spite of their good intentions must be termed *magni passus sed extra viam.*

Which of the two is the greater theologian? The dilemma *aut Thomas aut Scotus* no longer exists. St. Thomas is the *doctor communis,* but historical research has proved that the *doctor subtilis* was not an adversary of Aquinas. The interlocutors whom he envisaged were contemporary authors (Henry of Ghent, Gottfried of Fontaines, Aegidius of Rome), but not primarily the *doctor communis*. His system is not opposed to that of Aquinas, but is on a parallel plane. As in the past, his system can still perform valuable services for the Church.

See also *Augustinianism, Franciscan Theology.*

BIBLIOGRAPHY. EDITIONS: *Opera omnia,* ed. by L. Wadding and others, 12 vols. (1639), reprint, ed. by L. Vivès, 26 vols. (1891–95); *J. Duns Scoti Opera Omnia,* critical edition ed. by C. Balić (1950 ff.). BIBLIOGRAPHICAL: U. Smeets, *Lineamenta bibliographiae scotisticae* (1942); O. Schäfer, *Bibliographia de vita, operibus et doctrina Joannis Duns Scoti* (1955); V. Heynck, "Zur Scotusbibliographie", *Franziskaner Studien* 27 (1955), pp. 285–91. STUDIES: *Die Kategorien- und Bedeutungslehre des Duns Skotus* (1916); A. Bertoni, *Le bienheureux Jean Duns Scotus* (1919); P. Raymond, "Duns Scot", *DTC,* IV, cols. 1865–947; F. Ueberweg, *Grundriss der Geschichte der Philosophie,* II, ed. by B. Geyer (1927), pp. 504–17; C. Harris, *Duns Scotus,* 2 vols. (1927; reprint 1960); F. van Steenberghen; "Siger dans l'histoire de l'aristotélisme", *Philosophes Belges,* XIII/2 (1942); É. Gilson, *Jean Duns Scotus: Introduction à ses positions fondamentales* (1952); W. Pannenberg, *Die Prädestinationslehre des Duns Skotus* (1954); C. Balić, "Duns Scotus", *DSAM,* III, cols. 1801–18; id., "Joannes Duns Scotus et historia Immaculatae Conceptionis", *Antonianum* 30 (1955), pp. 349–488; J. Bonnefoy, *Le vénérable Jean Duns Scotus: Son milieu, sa doctrine, son influence* (1960); R. Effler, *John Duns Scotus and the Principle Omne quod movetur ab alio movetur* (1962); L. Walter, *Das Glaubensverständnis bei Johannes Duns Scotus* (1968); *Studia Scholastico-Scotistica,* 4 vols. (1968).

Carlo Balić

SCRIPTURE AND TRADITION

A. INTRODUCTION

1. The question of the relationship between Scripture and tradition seemed to have been cleared up for Catholic theology by the declaration of the Council of Trent (*D* 783 f.), which affirmed that the pure gospel was contained and handed on "in libris scriptis et sine scripto traditionibus", and that both modes of the presence of revelation were to be greeted "pari pietatis affectu ac reverentia". (This was repeated by Vatican II, *Dei Verbum,* art. 9, though "Sacra Traditio" was substituted for "traditiones".)

In post-Tridentine times, the declaration of Trent was mostly understood as saying that the content of revelation was divided materially between these two modes of givenness, so that some revelation was contained "only" in "oral tradition". It was assumed that there were therefore "two sources of revelation", differing to some extent in content from one another. This explanation of Trent is not of course to be considered binding. The main justification offered for it was that the extent of the canon, at least, could only be known from oral tradition, and also that many later dogmas of the Church could not be deduced from Scripture alone — not even by a process of explication of what was contained "implicitly" in Scripture, though here it was taken for granted that the process of explication could only be a purely logical operation. This interpretation of Trent's ruling was regarded as one of the most important points of controversial theology with regard to Protestantism and its doctrine of *sola Scriptura.*

2. Within the last twenty years, this position, which had become traditional to a great extent, was sharply called in question by the studies of J. R. Geiselmann and others. They pointed out that the doctrinal tradition, from the Fathers to the time of the Reformation, was by no means unanimous on the relationship of Scripture and tradition. Scripture was in fact allotted a clear priority. In the redaction of the text of Trent, a "partim — partim" had been eliminated, and replaced by a prudent "et". The "traditiones" of *D* 783 f. (always in the plural at Trent) could not be identified with tradition in the present-day sense, and in the sense of the present-day problem. The recognition of the extent of the canon could neither be regarded as an instance of a general relationship between Scripture and tradition nor as a process which had already been explained. In any case, the development of dogma — whether due to Scripture or to an early tradition — was in need of an explanation which was no easier on the grounds of an early explicit tradition (which could be asserted but not proved), than on the ground of Scripture itself. For as regards the dogmas which theologians thought had to be derived from pure "tradition", as not being even implicitly in Scripture, there is in fact no other early attestation, historically verifiable, which could show that they derive from apostolic tradition.

3. The whole question was one of the most keenly debated at Vatican II, especially

during the drafting of the dogmatic constitution *Dei Verbum,* on Revelation and Scripture. There the Council affirms (art. 7) that tradition was at work in the formation of Scripture itself; that a process of tradition continues to go on in the apostolic succession under the assistance of the Spirit (art. 8); that tradition gives testimony as to the canon of Scripture and actualizes Scripture *(ibid.).* The Council goes on to say (arts. 9 and 10) that Scripture and tradition form a unity, because they have one origin — the one divine revelation — and influence one another. Apart from the transmission of Scripture (canon), the actualizing function of tradition is centred entirely on Scripture (insofar as the theme is discussed at all).

It seems clear that the Council deliberately avoids — in contrast to the pre-conciliar draft — any affirmation about the material insufficiency of Scripture. This means in fact, since the opposite had been urged, that the Council had no misgivings about the material sufficiency of Scripture. It may therefore be held that the only task of post-biblical tradition is to transmit the Scriptures as such, to interpret them, to actualize them and to explicate their implications. In other words, to formulate the matter more prudently, tradition functions at all times by listening to Scripture, subject always to Scripture as the critical norm which is universally necessary to distinguish "divine" tradition, the transmission of revelation in Christ, from human traditions. (See further, for the precise nature of tradition, *Tradition.*)

When the Council says that the extent of the canon of Scripture is known from tradition, it must be noted that the formulation of the proposition is positive, not exclusive. The positive affirmation is something which is self-evident, which remains important, however, to exclude a wrong understanding of *sola Scriptura,* according to which the book of Scripture could be "Scripture" in a theological sense outside the Church and its preaching. But it does not decide the question as to whether knowledge of the canon and its extent is based on an individual, propositional truth of faith which as such is neither implicitly nor explicitly in Scripture (which in any case would still not be a matter which could be generalized).

The question might still be raised as to whether the statement of the Council should not in fact be read with an "only", that is, in an exclusive sense. The answer depends on the solution of the difficult problem, which

is still an open one, as to how precisely we are to think of the Church's mode of attaining knowledge of the canon. The knowledge in question cannot be supposed to be due to an explicit statement of the "last Apostle", because there are canonical writings which were produced only after the death of the last Apostle, even though they must still be ascribed to "apostolic times". If we consider that this knowledge came to the Church — not to the individual as such — not just as something "concerned with" or "about" the canon, but as "of the canon", that is, through the canonical Scriptures, this knowledge of the canon need not even be thought of as a special case of the relationship between Scripture and tradition. See K.-H. Ohlig, *Zur theologischen Begründung des neutestamentlichen Kanons* (1969) and B 4 below.

We should proceed along similar lines in considering the statement of the Council (art. 9), to the effect that the Church's certainty about the content of revelation does not merely ("non per solam") derive from Scripture. This again is not an affirmation of the material insufficiency of Scripture, since it speaks of certainty with regard to assent to *all* truths of faith, but not — directly — of the material "source" of given truths of faith. As the statement stands, it speaks of all truths of faith and not just of some, which *ex supposito* are not contained in Scripture. Further, it should be obvious that the whole faith of all individuals in the Church is sustained by the active preaching of the Church, which is tradition, *paradosis.* But this *paradosis* again, precisely as such, has an essential relation to Scripture in post-apostolic times. It is *paradosis* throughout *through* Scripture.

B. Systematic Analysis

1. Though the article *Tradition* must be read in this connection, tradition comes under discussion here, inasmuch as tradition itself is, to start with, as act and as content, constitutive of Scripture. The "oral" preaching of Jesus as the crucified and exalted Lord, a preaching launched by the mission of Jesus Christ, inspired by his Spirit and carried on in faith, is from the start and essentially "paradosis", since it contains the actuality of a unique, historical, all-determining event, and is also addressed to those who did not themselves encounter this event in space and time ("according to the flesh") but could only do so in the word of preaching. Paradosis

is not something added on to the preaching about Jesus the Christ. It is this preaching itself, the attestation of the unique saving deed of God in Christ through the mission, Spirit and faith at work in the preacher, who receives, by hearing, what he says, and says what he thus hears, and who thus stands within a paradosis, a tradition, in both directions.

In the long run, such paradosis cannot exist in the historical situation in which in fact it is always received and handed on, without being committed to writing. And the longer the tradition persists, the less can it do without writing. It becomes Scripture. Scripture is the concrete form taken by the apostolic paradosis, not something else added on to it. As long as this crystallization of the paradosis in Scripture is not necessary, the "apostolic age", the age of the "primitive Church", still runs on. And conversely, this age is ended from the "moment" — which means a certain length of time, between the production of the first and last of the canonical Scriptures — in which the paradosis is only in command of itself by its reference to Scripture.

2. This does not mean that the paradosis is eliminated by a book which then becomes an independent entity and is of itself the herald and norm for the faith of later generations. The authoritative paradosis, the summons to faith, continues. By sustaining itself *through* Scripture, by remaining certain of itself and of its legitimate origin from the apostolic preaching, the paradosis in turn sustains the inspired book in which the paradosis remains concrete.

3. Hence the problem of Scripture and tradition is wrongly put from the outset if it at once takes the form of asking whether the *propositions* of Scripture contain the Christian revelation in full (*sola Scriptura* in a quantitative, propositional sense) or whether in addition some propositions have been handed down "only" through ("oral") tradition — as if there were two materially different "sources" (or "modes of transmission") for Christian revelation. It must be noted that the tradition, which presents *itself* incarnate in Scripture in post-apostolic times, is not originally and essentially a fixed sum-total of propositions, from which further propositions could then be derived through a merely rational process of deduction. Tradition is the persistence of God's revelation, which

both as coming from God and as coming from man (or directed to him) is more than a number of fixed propositions. It is the experience (had) of Jesus Christ, inexhaustible to thought, the ever-incomprehensible mystery of God into which all propositions flow, the real communication of that which is expressed in propositions, through the self-communication of God — in the Spirit, grace and the light of faith (see *Revelation* II).

And this tradition — the transmission of the reality which necessarily of course expounds itself in propositions but is not simply identical with them — continues to be at work inasmuch as tradition, understood in this way, also sustains Scripture. And then again, Scripture, in the proper theological sense, is not a mere book containing many propositional truths (bearing on historical and doctrinal matters), but in fact the event or reality in which the Church gives concrete form to its kerygma, its faith, recognizes it, and submits itself to this objectivation, using it to criticize all other opinions, tendencies, etc., which occur in the course of history. In this way the Church maintains the purity of the true faith which it holds by uttering it in Scripture. It follows that later dogmas — the articulation of the one and abiding faith — need not simply be derived from Scripture in the sense that they are explicitly propounded there "in other words", or that they must be demonstrably and stringently logical deductions in the line of explication of Scripture. It also follows that no later dogmas are independent of Scripture and not subordinated to it. The faith which created Scripture did not eliminate itself by the formation of Scripture (*non sola Scriptura*). Nonetheless, everything in the later utterances of faith must be measured by Scripture, (*sola Scriptura*) since it is in Scripture that the one whole apostolic faith has been objectivated and has given itself, and laid down for all future times, its *norma non normata*.

4. This will appear still more clearly if we turn to the special question as to whether at least the concrete existence of Scripture qua Scripture, the canon, is not a truth which is "only" in tradition and not contained in Scripture. It has already been pointed out above that even if the question were to be answered in the affirmative as in the ordinary theology of the schools (A 1), this thesis could not simply be expanded to a general doctrine of a material insufficiency of Scripture. The thesis thus generalized would

contribute nothing to a real explanation of the development of dogma (see A 2 above). But the generalization itself would not be legitimate, because the theological existence of Scripture (which can naturally not be based on the book itself as such) is of course a different case from other theological assertions (which can very well be all contained in principle in a book). But to give a radical answer to the question and to deal with it correctly, it must be noted that the process of the recognition of the canon by the Church (in contradistinction from that by individuals) is none other than that of the formation of Scripture — and hence of the formation of the canon. In other words, the Church recognizes Scripture as Scripture inasmuch as tradition creates Scripture and recognizes itself as purely and permanently normative in and by the tradition crystallized in Scripture (a recognition ancient, unique and permanently new) — and thus subordinates itself to this tradition. The action of creating Scripture, which is also recognition of the canon, recognizes itself as legitimate, in an indissoluble synthesis of act and object, inasmuch as it sees its work as successful, that is, as producing the purity of faith in Christ.

We are then equally well justified in affirming that tradition recognizes the canon, as in affirming that Scripture attests itself as canonical for the *Church* itself. This is a different matter from saying that the individual could recognize Scripture as canonical on his own — though he for his part had no hand in its formation.

We cannot here reduce the whole relationship between tradition and Scripture to the relationship (an element of which it forms) which obtains between the authority of the Lord and that of the believing Church in general. In this relationship of faith by which the Church believes through the Lord and in the Lord, all that is distinct from Christ (Jesus' words of self-attestation, miracles, the testimony of the original witnesses, etc.) forms an indissoluble unity which comprises both what can have faith-inspiring force only from the authority of Christ in his Spirit, and what mediates this authority to the faithful. If one regards Scripture and tradition as a unity, and as distinct from Christ himself, and if this unity distinct from Christ himself is regarded in the light of this basic axiom of the *analysis fidei*, one has reached the basic standpoint from which the relationship of Scripture and tradition should be envisaged. This unity, with its faith-inspiring

force, is constituted in the final analysis only by the power of the Spirit of Christ, and is itself in fact the mediation of this authority of Christ, in his Spirit, to the Church. Once this is grasped, it remains only to see and accept frankly the simple, straightforward fact that the tradition of the primitive Church (in the actual circumstances) can only abide and hold normative sway through Scripture, of which tradition knows that it has crystallized there, knowing therefore that it is only in Scripture that it is and remains itself. When Vatican II re-affirms that it looks on Scripture and tradition "pari pietatis affectu ac reverentia", it may and must do so, because Scripture and tradition form a unity from the start and are not just brought into relationship with each other subsequently.

BIBLIOGRAPHY. John Cardinal Newman, *An Essay on the Development of Christian Doctrine* (1845); H. J. Holtzmann, *Kanon und Tradition* (1859); M. Winckler, *Der Traditionsbegriff des Urchristentums bis Tertullian* (1897); E. Ortigues, "Écriture et tradition apostolique au Concile de Trente", *RSR* 36 (1949); P. Brunner, *Schrift und Tradition* (1951); G. de Broglie, "Note sur la primauté de l'argument d'Écriture en théologie", in L. Bouyer, ed., *Du Protestantisme à l'Eglise* (1954), pp. 247–50; H. Grass, *Die katholische Lehre von der Heiligen Schrift und von der Tradition* (1954); K. E. Skydsgaard, "Schrift und Tradition", *Kerygma und Dogma* 1 (1955), pp. 161–79; F. Dillistone, *Scripture and Tradition* (1955); J. R. Geiselmann, "Das Missverständnis über das Verhältnis von Schrift und Tradition", *Una Sancta* 11 (1956), pp. 131–50; id., *Die lebendige Überlieferung als Norm des christlichen Glaubens* (1959); id., "Schrift — Tradition — Kirche, ein ökumenisches Problem", in M. Roesle and O. Cullmann, eds., *Begegnung der Christen (Festschrift O. Karrer)* (1959); H. St. John, "Bible and Tradition", *Blackfriars* (1958), pp. 300–9; G. Owens, "Is All Revelation Contained in Sacred Scripture?", *Studia Montis Regii* (1958), pp. 55–65; G. H. Tavard, *Holy Writ or Holy Church* (1959); P. Lengsfeld, *Überlieferung, Tradition und Schrift in der evangelischen und katholischen Theologie der Gegenwart* (1960); K. Rahner, *Inspiration in the Bible* (1961); K. E. Skydsgaard and L. Vischer, ed., *Schrift und Tradition, Untersuchung einer theologischen Kommission* (1963); K. Rahner and J. Ratzinger, *Revelation and Tradition*, Quaestiones Disputatae 17 (1966); G. Moran, *Scripture and Tradition* (1963); Y. Congar, *The Meaning of Tradition* (1964).

Karl Rahner

SECTS, CHRISTIAN

This article simply aims at listing the minor divisions attached in one way or another to the Christian Churches. The word "sect" is not used (as so often) in a disparaging sense, but simply to exemplify groupings which either arrived late on the scene, or are of small numerical size, or are only loosely attached to Christianity in its orthodox forms. For a discussion of the theological interest of the latter, see *Protestantism* I, *ad fin.*

A. CHURCHES AND SECTS IN THE EAST

See *Eastern Churches* D.

B. CHURCHES AND SECTS IN THE WEST

(For the general historical background, see *Reformation*.)

1. *Mennonites; Hutterite Brethren.* These groups developed out of the Anabaptist movement contemporary to the Reformation in Germany. They took their inspiration from the earlier teaching of Zwingli, and made it their aim to restore the perfect apostolic age in a Church consisting only of "saints". They rejected the Church of the masses into which one is born, and hence infant baptism.

a) *The Mennonites* are called after Menno Simons (1496–1561), originally a Dutch priest. Their doctrine is basically Calvinistic. They are now mainly represented in North and South America, their total number being somewhat over half a million. They are generally characterized by their insistence on repentance and conversion, total separation of Church and State, obedience to the State (though rejecting military service and oaths), strict Church discipline and a mainly fundamentalist reading of the Bible.

b) *The Hutterites* (Jacob Hutter, d. 1536) are now found only in the U.S.A. and are distinguished from the Mennonites by their "Adventist" beliefs (see below). Mostly farmers, they still practise community of goods.

2. *The Adventists* are characterized by their expectation of the "Thousand Year Reign" (see *Millenarianism*) and the early return of Christ. They were founded by William Miller (1782–1849) in the State of New York. Basing himself on Dan and Rev, he foretold the Second Coming for 1844. The movement split into groups, of which the main survivor is the Seventh Day Adventists, founded by Ellen White, who interpreted the non-arrival of Christ in 1844 as his entry into the heavenly sanctuary.

The doctrine of the Seventh Day Adventists is not easy to define. They believe in the Trinity, the Virgin Birth, the inspiration and sufficiency of the Bible. Their notion of the sacraments is Calvinistic. The eschatology which characterizes their religion includes the belief that the just will become immortal when Christ comes to inaugurate his Thousand Year Reign, while the godless will be raised up only on the Last Day, to be condemned. Their rule of life follows the Ten Commandments, and includes the observance of the Sabbath (Saturday) and in many groups, abstention from alcohol and tobacco. The General Conference (Washington) represents over a million members throughout the world, who are mostly very active in their propaganda.

3. *Jehovah's Witnesses.* This very vigorous American sect was founded by Charles Russell, a Calvinist who found that his intense study of the Bible did not help him to overcome the scruples engendered by a rigorous doctrine of predestination. In his *Three Worlds or Plan of Redemption* (1877), the first age, under the angels, ran from the Creation to the Flood. The "present monstrous age", under the rule of Satan, was to last till the establishment of the Thousand Year Reign in 1914, to be followed by the eternal kingdom with a new heaven and a new earth.

In 1884, Russell founded the "Zion's Watch Tower Tract Society", Pennsylvania, called since 1896 the "Watch Tower Bible and Tract Society". He founded the "International Bible Students Association" in England in 1914, now operating as the "Watch Tower". The name "Jehovah's Witnesses" came in in 1931. Their aim, according to the statutes, is the spread of "biblical truths" by the distribution of tracts and other means acceptable to the board of directors. They worship Jehovah, the God of the OT, who is regarded as a being of "material spirit". The doctrines of the Trinity and of the immortality of the soul are rejected. The Archangel Michael appeared in the form of Jesus, while Lucifer became Satan, to whose kingdom all secular States belong. Adult baptism and the Lord's Supper are recognized as "sacraments". The organization of the sect, whose propaganda is both highly active and successful, is not very clear. The Watch Tower Society in Brooklyn is at the head, governed by a board of directors with a president. The "Pioneers" are devoted entirely to apostolic activities, while the "Vacation Pioneers" are part-time workers. The "Special Pioneers" or "Missionaries", with more training, are supported by the organization, while the "Pioneers" rely on the sale of Watch Tower publications and gifts from the members. Membership admits to the "Remnant" who will be "co-heirs" with Christ in the Messianic Kingdom.

4. *Revivalist groups.* Since it was always a delicate matter for Protestantism to explain the importance of good works and morality, without which, however, popular piety hardly thrives, revivalist movements gave rise to a large number of Churches and sects.

a) *The Moravian Brethren* (going back in a way to the Bohemian Brethren of 1494, who later had their principal communities in Moravia) took their present form from the movement launched by Philip Jacob Spener (see *Pietism*) *c.* 1670. They are known in Germany as the Herrnhuter Brethren after the *ecclesiola* founded in 1722 by Count Zinzendorf at Herrnhut in Saxony, which considered itself part of the Lutheran Church. Their Pietism exercised a considerable influence on John Wesley (see *Methodist Churches*). They accept the Confession of Augsburg, the doctrine of "Scripture alone" and the Apostles' Creed. Their piety is strongly Christocentric. Their four provinces (Europe, Britain, North and South America) number some 300,000 members, more than half of them in North America.

b) *The Quakers or Society of Friends* (i.e., of the truth) go back to the Anglican George Fox, who felt called to the prophetic office in 1649. The organization dates from 1668, when Fox drew up his *Rule for the Management of Meetings.* True sonship of God is given through a direct interior revelation, the "inner light", held to be superior even to the Scriptures. This entails the rejection of Church, priesthood and sacraments. Worship consists of silent meditation, till the Spirit moves some member of the congregation to speak. Recently, however, religious services can include prayer and preaching by ministers (programmed meetings). Representative "Meetings" are held at various regional levels. Since 1675, the permanent "Meeting for Sufferings" has been the co-ordinating organ for Quaker charitable works, for which they have become internationally famous, e.g., during the Irish Famine of 1845–47 and in various emergencies in the 20th century. This charitable effort is regarded as one of the main fruits of the inner light, and is furthered by such other fruits as personal integrity and strict temperance. Strictly speaking, there

are no creeds or ministry, but Scripture remains basic.

c) *The Salvation Army* was founded in 1875 by the former Methodist preacher William Booth. It is a religious society for the rescue and help of the needy and destitute. The organization, which rapidly became international, is modelled on that of an army, with a "General" at its head. Its faith is Low Church evangelicalism, though without any sacraments, and the major stress is on the moral demands of Christianity and charitable works, for which its organization is both far-reaching and efficient.

5. *The Pentecostal Movement.* The many groups who subscribe to this Adventist and fundamentalist type of religion cannot be said to have any common origin. Many go back to an American movement called the "Latter Rain Movement" (cf. Joel 3:1), i.e., looking for the outpouring of the Holy Spirit (1886). Their type of life is puritanical, and holiness calls for a second perfect conversion after justification. The movement spread rapidly in the 20th century, when the "Divine Healing" publicity roused great interest. The largest group in the U.S.A. is known as the "Assemblies of God, U.S.A.", which is organized on Congregationalist lines. Groups came together to form the "Assemblies of God in Great Britain and Ireland" in 1924. An earlier, more centralized group was the "Elim Foursquare Gospel Alliance" (1915). North America, Scandinavia and Brazil furnish the largest numbers, totalling well over two millions.

6. *The Holy Catholic-Apostolic Church* was organized in the wake of revivalist movements in Scotland and England in 1830–31. It emphasized the charismatic, the restoration of the conditions of the primitive Church and the appointment of "Apostles". The death of six apostles in 1860 led to the splitting-off of the "New Apostolic Church", now chiefly represented in Germany, with some 700,000 members. The apostles are regarded as successors of the primitive apostles, while the chief apostle is the "representative of the Lord on earth". Their sacraments are baptism, confirmation and the Lord's Supper. As the "restored primitive Church of the last days", it awaits the speedy return of the Lord.

7. *The Plymouth Brethren.* This Congregationalist type of fellowship goes back to a

movement in the Anglican Church which rejected the close association of Church and State. Its leader after 1833 was John Nelson Darby, who later formed a stricter branch called the Darbyites. The Plymouth Brethren, so called after their earliest great congregation, are Pietist, fundamentalist and Adventist in outlook, regard the Bible as the sole rule of doctrine and life, and recognize no ordained pastors. Some of the main divisions include the "Open Brethren" and the "Exclusive Brethren", whose hyper-puritanical segregation — going as far as the refusal of dealings with members of the family not belonging to the group — has earned them some notoriety. The exclusivity also extends, even outside this group, to the refusal to practise certain trades.

8. *The Aethiopian Sects* grew up among the Africans as a result of the "Aethiopian" movement towards the end of the 19th century, so called after the biblical account of the conversion of the Aethiopians (cf. Acts 8:26ff.). Many elements of the African religions of nature have penetrated their doctrine, which is adhered to by over 500 sects.

9. *The "Old Catholics"*. Here we understand a number of groups, mostly in America, who depend on *episcopi vagantes,* i.e., on bishops validly consecrated but not members of the episcopalian Churches (see *Old Catholic Church*). The "American Catholic Church" goes back to J. Vilatte, a former Old Catholic who was consecrated by a bishop of the Malabar Church. Some groups in Europe also go back to Vilatte, e.g., the "Église Gallicane" and the "Evangelisch-Katholische Eucharistische Gemeinschaft" associated with Friedrich Heiler. Other *episcopi vagantes* derive their consecration from the Old Catholics, and gave rise to the "Liberal Catholic Church", the "Old Catholic Church in America", the "North American Old Catholic Church" and the "National Mexican Church" (1925). There are about thirty *episcopi vagantes* with more or less stable communities, and many others disengaged.

10. *The Unitarians.* The Unitarians go back to the Socinianism launched by Lelio and Fausto Sozzini at the end of the 16th century (anti-Trinitarian). By the end of the 19th century the Unitarian movement had spread over Rumania, Poland, the Netherlands, England and America. The Bible is not simply the word of God, since revelation is not closed and was never confined to the Jews. Scripture is inspired only insofar as it does not contradict humanitarian reason. The fullest freedom is allowed in its exposition. Unitarians honour in Christ the divinity which dwells within all men. They reject the Trinity, the vicarious expiation of Jesus, original sin, the sacraments — though some are practised as ceremonies — and hell. Heaven is a state of eternal righteousness and love.

11. *The Mormons, or the Church of Jesus Christ of Latter-Day Saints.* This sect was founded in 1830 by Joe Smith in Fayette (N. Y.). Under his successor, Brigham Young, the Mormons migrated to the Great Salt Lake and built up the Mormon State of Utah. The basic principle with regard to revelation is that Mormons believe all that God has revealed and still reveals, while expecting many more important revelations. Many errors have crept into the Bible, and it is supplemented by three other books, including the "Book of Mormon", supposedly revealed directly to Joe Smith. These books confirm the inspiration of the Bible and explain the doctrines which have caused divisions among men for so many centuries. God the Father is the creator of the spiritual substance in man. Jesus Christ is the son of God begotten in the flesh, the saviour of the human race. The Holy Spirit is a purely spiritual being. All three together make up the Godhead. Man is not judged after death, so there is no heaven and hell in the ordinary sense. Faith, repentance and baptism of immersion are necessary to redemption. Baptism for the dead is imparted to a person closely connected with the dead man. Instead of confirmation, the gifts of the Holy Spirit are transmitted by the laying on of hands. The most important of these gifts are speaking in tongues, its interpretation, prophecy and faith healing. Marriage is a contract instituted by God. There is also heavenly marriage for eternity, a marriage with a dead person, which is of great importance because the unmarried cannot be redeemed. In 1895 the earlier practice of polygamy, based on certain notions of the OT, was forbidden by the president of the sect. There are two classes of priests instituted by Christ, the Aaronite priesthood with the degrees of deacon, teacher and priest, which administers secular affairs, and the higher priesthood of Melchizedek, which

concerns itself with spiritual as well as secular affairs. The degrees of the latter are elders, bishops, the seventy, high priests, patriarchs and apostles. The constitution and hierarchical organization are very complicated. The financial administration is very important, since the sect is enormously wealthy, and all members pay tithes. The president is the supreme authority. As the "earthly link with God" he receives the law directly from God. There are nearly two million Mormons at present.

12. *Christian Science or the New Thought Movement.* This is best known by the "First Church of Christ Scientist", founded by Mrs. Mary Baker Eddy (1821–1910), as a "divine metaphysics", "a scientific system of faith healing". Her *Science and Health with Key to the Scriptures* (1875) had a wide success and the mother church was opened in Boston in 1879. The inspired word of the Bible is the "sufficient guide to eternal life", though *Science and Health* is used as a textbook at religious worship. Jesus is the Master and Guide. His great merit is the atonement, the proof of divine love. Belief in the unreality of matter is at the kernel of the system. Sin, illness and death are not real. The reality of sin is simply that men believe it exists. The organization, under a board of directors, is highly centralized, the "Mother Church" in Boston having unrestricted authority. Their newspaper, the *Christian Science Monitor,* is deservedly esteemed for the wideness and balance of its coverage.

13. *Missionary societies.* Outside the framework of the main Christian Churches and communities, there exists an interdenominational type of mission of a peculiar type, which is in some ways the opposite of "sectarian". But the basic and indeed only rule for the admission of members is that they should be "Bible Christians", which is non-ecclesiastical enough to justify their being included here. The main representatives have been the China Inland Mission, founded by Hudson Taylor in 1865, and the Gossner Mission Society (Lutheran). All may be admitted as "brothers" if they take their stand on the Bible. No fund-raising is allowed, and the missions must live by whatever income comes their way otherwise. The missionaries must "let God show them the way". No organization is set up in the homeland to back up the mission. Missionaries are admitted from all Churches and sects, provided they accept the old-time religion of the Bible and are content with what God sends them to live on. There are a large number of such missions today, mostly Protestant fundamentalists, among the 380 missionary societies. They are active and earnest, but cannot be said to further (ecumenical) integration.

BIBLIOGRAPHY. K. Algermissen, *Christian Denominations* (1945); J. Gründler, *Lexikon der christlichen Kirchen und Sekten,* 2 vols. (1961) (bibliography II, pp. 140–6); K. Algermissen, *Christian Sects* (1962); *World Christian Handbook* (London, 1968 ff.).

Johannes Gründler

SECULAR INSTITUTES

The "secular institutes" *(instituta saecularia),* as defined by Pius XII in the Apostolic Constitution *Provida Mater Ecclesia* of 2 February 1947 (*AAS* 39 [1947], pp. 114–24), are the third public state of perfection in the Church, consisting of societies of priests and laity. Their members consecrate themselves to God by binding themselves to perfect charity through the observation of the three evangelical counsels. The object is the exercise of a fruitful apostolate in the world. There are three types of such institutes: clerical, whose members are priests; lay, whose members are men and women; mixed, whose members are priests, lay men and women, in autonomous groups under a priest and general committee.

Since they were first approved, the canonical status of the secular institutes has undergone constant change. From 1949 on, the public character of the institutes and the obligations of their members were recognized. And a clearer grasp of their call in the world showed that "real secularity" was not attained simply by giving up religious dress and common life. In 1962 the workers' mission founded by J. Loew failed to gain approval as a secular institute, because of its common life, public action and group apostolate. This decision brought a profound change with it in the notion of canonical secularity, which was confirmed by Vatican II in the Decree on the Appropriate Renewal of the Religious Life, *Perfectae Caritatis.* It was only on the eve of the solemn session that the secular institutes succeeded in having themselves defined as "non-religious", not merely in the canonical but also the theological sense. They are a secular form of life, not separated from the world.

The Council changed the doctrine of *Provida Mater* on many points. (i) The secular institutes represent a true and perfect consecration of life to God, and not just the life of a third state of perfection, as they had been described in *Provida Mater*. (ii) Their way of life is no longer described as "substantially that of a religious order" — a notion consistent with historical canon law, which regarded the religious life as the genuine state of perfection, which had been given a milder form in the communities of common life and took on a still less exigent form in the secular institutes. These were not obliged by law to have distinctive signs of separation from the world — religious dress, houses, common life. (iii) *Provida Mater* had ordered the secular institutes to co-operate as far as possible with the bishops and to give this co-operation some form of organizational expression. According to Vatican II, the apostolate of the secular institutes is one of "penetration". It is "in the world" that they have to contribute to the growth of the Body of Christ. Their secularity is distinguished from that of the laity. This is the attitude of *Lumen Gentium,* clearly inspired on this point by the doctrine of A. Gemelli, which was also adopted by *Primo Feliciter* (see below).

The essence of this state of life is dedication to God and men "in the world and with the means provided by the world". The dedication and the apostolate are secular. The members of the institutes remain in their ordinary fields of activity and practise a worldly calling, so that they cannot be distinguished sociologically from other citizens. Priests remain secular priests and are incardinated into their own dioceses.

This canonical secularity is the basis of their "apostolic secularity", as described by Pius XII in his motu proprio *Primo Feliciter* of 19 March 1948 (*AAS* 40 [1948], pp. 283–6). It is an apostolate of "presence" in whatever family, social, professional and political milieu the members live. Under certain circumstances, this presence is the only possible form of the apostolate in a given milieu, and is to be understood as an "apostolate of penetration".

Many secular institutes which had had canonical approbation were without this apostolic secularity. To change the constitution *Provida Mater,* which had described the apostolate of the secular institutes as a supplementary one, Pius XII saw that it was necessary to draw on the formula of A. Gemelli to express the fullness of the new secularity. It is based on an apostolate which operates by being present, taking root in and penetrating a given milieu. It seems to be more and more definitely understood as an apostolate of secular institutes who do not rely on co-operation, special houses of their own and works undertaken in common.

This apostolic secularity was clearly confirmed by Vatican II in the decree *Perfectae Caritatis,* which confined the role of the responsible authorities to the general and spiritual formation of the members, but did not assign them a directive and organizational function in the apostolate. It should be noted that neither the pastoral work of priests nor the professional work of layfolk come under the authority of the heads of the institutes. Obviously, the evangelical counsels are put into practice in a very special way by the secular institutes. This has already given rise to a varied field of phenomena, which can be analysed by theological reflection more and more clearly. And such reflection will in turn throw light on the actual experience and practice of the secular institutes.

Discretion, which can at times be observed very strictly, is necessary for any apostolate which aims at really penetrating the world. It can be helpful and even obligatory for an effective and harmonious co-operation in the field of Catholic Action. But this apostolic discretion is never understood as an absolute. The secular institutes put into practice one of the basic aspects of the gospel. They try to be the leaven, the salt, of the earth. Their self-effacement and self-denial recall the grain of wheat which dies in the earth in order to bring forth fruit. They try to re-enact the mysteries of the hidden life of Jesus. They reflect the mystery of the divine, which conceals itself in order to reach more closely into the realm of man's life. The secular institutes represent in a very special way the mystery of the incarnation in the world.

This ideal presupposes a special call. Only a strong character will be able to work on his own in the world and live up to the demands of the evangelical counsels in ordinary life.

The mission of the secular institutes enables the Church to be better informed of the needs of a given milieu and the dangers of various callings. This will help the Church to realize better there the ideal of the evangelical life and to present the message of Christ in a concrete form which is closer to reality.

The organization of the secular institutes presupposes a bond of fellowship which unites the members with one another and with their superiors. These are aided by a board of consultors. They govern the institute in common, according to the laws of the Church and the decision of the governing body which is responsible for the institute.

Superiors are mainly concerned with the formation and the spiritual life of the members. This formation includes, after the first contacts with the institute, lasting from six months to a year, a first period of probation or initiation, mostly a year, then two years' noviceship or possibly three, and finally a third period of probation, involving longer periods of recollection, and maturation through study, which prepares the candidate for his final dedication. These periods of probation normally mean a stay in a house of the institute. Some institutes which are preoccupied with a strict secularity confine the formation of their members to regular meetings in a house of retreats or give courses in their periodicals. These latter types of institute have no common houses, preferring a secretariat or rented headquarters.

Since they belong to a fixed and definite state of life, the members express their obligation to God, the Church and their institute in the form of vow, promise or an oath. This obligation is considered a consecration in the institute. In contrast to religious orders, it is called "secular consecration" or dedication. The vows, like the institute, are public. They are also known as "vows recognized by the Church", and they are received by the superiors of the institute in the name of the Church.

The secular institutes gave rise to a quite normal development. They attracted members who belonged to them in a wider sense, not necessarily practising the three evangelical counsels, but modelling their lives, whether in the married state or not, according to the spirit of the counsels. Some institutes have accepted non-Catholics as like-minded friends and helpers in their human and professional tasks.

Since the secular institutes are a state of life in the Church, they need approbation by the hierarchy. A group which leads a consecrated life can first receive verbal approbation after an experimental period, and then canonical approbation in the form of a decree for the erection of a pious association. If all goes well, a secular institute of diocesan right may be erected, with approval from Rome. If the institute attains a wide degree of influence, it can become a secular institute of papal right by receiving the approbation of the Holy See, first in the form of a "Decree of Praise" and then that of "Definitive Approbation".

In addition, secular institutes which lead a simpler form of consecrated life have been approved on principle by Pius XII. Their form of life is very like that of the secular institutes. But for various reasons they do not desire explicit approbation. Some would regard such approbation as a loosening of their bonds with their milieu. Other groups have not the structure of the secular institutes. They have no superior, strictly speaking, but put themselves at the disposition of the bishop. Others finally form the "secular branch" of religious congregations. Though they live in the world, they are in close spiritual connection with the congregation in question.

Reference may be made in conclusion to the formation of new apostolic groups which live in the closest possible proximity to their milieu, as also to contemplative groups which live a markedly monastic type of life in the world, earning a frugal living during the time not set aside for prayer.

Though only recognized by the Church in 1947, secular institutes first came into existence in the French Revolution. But they were already adumbrated by St. Angela Merici (d. 1540), and several features of the consecrated life in the world are to be found in the Sisters of Charity founded by St. Vincent de Paul. The secular institutes are not just a modern development, though they correspond to the needs and the signs of the times.

See also *Religious Orders, ad fin.*

BIBLIOGRAPHY. DOCUMENTS: *De institutis saecularibus documenta pontificia necnon studia dogmatica, iuridica, historica, practica,* I (1951); J. Beyer, *De saecularium institutis documenta* (1952); id., "De institutis saecularibus bibliographia", *Periodica* 52 (1963), pp. 239–59. STUDIES: A. Gemelli, *Le associazioni dei laici consecrati a Dio nel mondo* (1939); id., *Gli istituti secolari* (1954); *Secular Institutes: A Symposium* (Oxford, 1952); J. Setién, *Institutos seculares para el clero diocesano* (1957); J. Perrin, *Consécration à Dieu et présence au monde* (1958);

L. Alvarez, *El seglarismo y su integridad* (1959); S. Canals, *Secular Institutes and the State of Perfection* (1959); F. Wulf, *Die Spiritualität der Säkularinstitute und die Probleme ihrer Verwirklichung* (1960); H. Urs von Balthasar, "Zur Theologie der Säkularinstitute", *Sponsa Verbi* (1961), pp. 434–69; J. Beyer, "Le rôle du prêtre dans les instituts séculiers", *NRT* 84 (1962), pp. 365–8; G. Reidy, *Secular Institutes* (1962); D. A. Walsh, *The New Law of Secular Institutes* (1963).

Jean Beyer

SECULARIZATION

I. Concept: A. Defining the Notion. B. Secularization as a Historical Process. C. Evaluation. D. The Christian View of Secularization. II. Laicism.

I. Concept

A. DEFINING THE NOTION

"Secularization" comes from the Latin *saecularis,* meaning "worldly", "temporal" or "age-old", and forms a group with "secularity" and "secularism". Since all these words indicate a theory or process whereby things or persons are assigned to the realm of the world, they are often used indifferently. But it is useful and now becoming more common to distinguish them. (i) Secularization has mostly been used for the confiscation of Church property for worldly ends, mostly by the State and against the will of the Church. It has happened again and again in the course of history, for various reasons. In canon law secularization also means granting permission to a professed member of a religious order to live for the rest of his life outside his monastery. (ii) Secularization is now also understood as the process whereby various elements of human life (such as opinions, customs, social forms and even things and persons) or the whole of human life cease to be determined by religion. The result, secularity, then means independence and adulthood with regard to religion. (iii) When secularizing is taken as a programme, when secularity is the mainspring of a world-view, the term "secularism" is used. Secularism would then be a secularizing which did not remain purely secular (as "secularity") but turned into a doctrine of salvation or an ideology. The world-view of a group of English free-thinkers in the 19th century who called themselves "secularists" was propounded under the heading of *Secularism, the Practical Philosophy of the People* (G. J. Holyoake [1854]).

The general history of the terms is as follows. The word "secularization" was first used as a legal term, defining certain political moves, such as had already been the object of negotiations before the Treaty of Westphalia at the end of the Thirty Years War, 1646. It was taken into canon law in the 18th century. When in the 19th century the effort was made to deprive the Church of its influence in cultural matters, especially education, as well as of its material goods, it was only natural that the term "secularization" should be extended to this programme. In France it became usual to speak of the *sécularisation* demanded for philosophy, for instance, while in England the term "secularism" came into use. Secularization and secularism undoubtedly began as slogans of a movement mostly hostile to the Church, and were used in this sense by the Positivism, Materialism and Monism of the times. But they gradually developed a more neutral sense and were then used to describe without value-judgments the historical process of the emancipation of the world from religious tutelage — a process which was increasingly regarded as ambivalent. To avoid ambiguity, or rather to underline the ambivalence of the terms, a distinction was made between secularization and secularism. Secularization is now understood as a more or less neutral term, while secularism is taken to be a false ideology. To mark the difference, however, between process and result, the justifiable, non-ideological result of secularizing is called "secularity", though secularization remains an ambivalent term, meaning in certain modern theological contexts the process or result of a more or less correct emancipation of the world as regards the Church or religion. Since secularization in the English-speaking world is historically relevant only to the suppression and expropriation of the monasteries by Henry VIII in the 16th century, there is no great objection to the new use of the term in the "theology of the world".

B. SECULARIZATION AS A HISTORICAL PROCESS

It is a phenomenon as old and as widespread as religion itself that individuals or groups or even a whole era should at times reject prevailing religious ties and seek to emancipate themselves from them. The phenomenon can take very different forms. One may recall, for instance, how the Egyptian

Pharaoh Akh-en-Aton (Ekhnaton) in the 14th century B.C. set out to abolish the traditional cults and divinities of his kingdom in favour of a more rationalistic system. Or there is the critique to which Greek philosophers, from Xenophanes and Anaxagoras down to Socrates, and then the Epicureans, subjected the mythological notions of the gods in the world around them. The ethnology of religion also shows that there is no religion, even among the primitives, where the doctrines and prescriptions have not been sceptically questioned, at least at times or by individuals, and have only been retained as expedient, but not as unquestionably binding. Nonetheless, like atheism, secularism remained, till the beginning of the modern era, a rare and transient phenomenon. The explanation of the world and the interpretation of human existence was too strongly linked with mythologies. Social life was too firmly based on forms worked out under the influence of religion. Even the manipulation of nature could only be learnt from rules with magical components. It is only in the West in the modern era that secularization became widespread and persistent when as a result of a process which reaches back far into the past and is still not ended, one realm after another of human reality was taken more and more radically out of religion's sphere of influence.

It is understandable that the religious elements tried to stem the process, since not only were worldly realms withdrawn from the religious sphere, but religion seemed threatened with the loss of all links with reality and hence with complete insignificance. The goal of the process seemed to be a secularism which would be the end of all religion. The process of secularization in this conflict may be illustrated from three well-known contrasts which have been used as slogans to sum up and oppose certain worldly and religious spheres. They are faith and knowledge, Church and State, this world and the other world as the end of man (see *Faith, Church and State, Order* IV).

If we follow the developments in these fields since the beginnings of Christianity down to the present day with its trend to secularization, it appears that the process has been more or less the same in all three fields, passing through three stages which may be defined with a fair degree of accuracy.

1. In the message of the NT, the relationship between the worldly and the corresponding Christian realm is such that neither can be said to predominate over the other, to exclude the other or even to be hostile to the other. The doctrine of the NT is simply that the religious sphere is totally different from the worldly, so that neither can substitute for the other since the two are on different planes. Faith has not the function of replacing knowledge. It gives no worldly wisdom, just as it does not suppose it. It merely shows that knowledge, scientific and mundane, has only a relative value. It is not an absolute, on which the salvation or loss of man ultimately depends, though if erected into an absolute and used in order to "boast" against God it becomes foolishness and is opposed to faith (cf. 1 Cor 1:17–2:9; Rom 1:21 f.). And the wise need the gospel as much as the ignorant (Rom 1:14).

The relationship between Church and State or civil authorities is on the same lines. Neither side can displace the other or claim superiority. The State cannot, since "We must obey God rather than men" (Acts 5:29). Neither can the Church, since it is not its task "to judge outsiders" (cf. 1 Cor 5:12). In fact, by accepting the structure of the State without disputing its lawful powers, the Church reduces it to its proper stature (cf. Rom 12:19–13:7 with K. Barth, *Epistle to the Romans* [1933]). And the world is not divided into spheres of influence, allotted to religion and the civil authorities respectively, since we are to "Render to Caesar the things that are Caesar's, and to God the things that are God's" (Mk 12:17). This does not mean that we are to give Caesar one portion and God another, since all that is in the world belongs to God. Two completely different sets of interests are involved which cannot interfere with one another as long as neither of them try to exercise the functions of the other.

It might, however, appear that at least as far as the end of man is concerned, the religious and the secular are opposed to each other on the same plane in the NT, that the tasks of man are distributed between them and that conflict could arise, inasmuch as the State could demand the fullest possible orientation to this world, at the expense of the other world and vice versa. But here too such a conflict appears absurd in the perspective of the NT. Just as faith does not eliminate knowledge or the Church does not make the State superfluous, so too the seeking of the kingdom of God does not absolve man from his earthly tasks. In the NT, the effort to avoid having to fulfil one's everyday and human tasks by appealing to religious obligations is explicitly condemned (e.g., Mk 7:11 f.; 12:40) and the principle is laid down that "if any one will not work, he is not to eat" (cf. 2 Thess 3:10). But again, "the one thing that is needful" shows that to be "troubled and anxious about many things", is a misplaced anxiety (Mt 6:31–34; Lk 10:41 f.), about a relatively minor matter. The striving for worldly ends does not compete with interest in the kingdom of God, as though it could perhaps take its place, but has a different end and object and is in the second place.

In all these instances, the gospel avoids challenging the worldly sphere on its own level and does not seek to exercise sovereignty within that sphere. But the worldly sphere itself is shown to be provisional.

2. The second stage runs from patristic to modern times, and is characterized by the claim of the religious sphere to predominate over the secular, so much so that at times religion seemed to absorb the latter entirely. This approach meant that faith was regarded as containing all that was worth knowing and as a superior type of knowledge (see *Gnosis*), so that philosophy, for instance, could at most be the *ancilla theologiae*. The relationship of Church to State is that the Church, as St. Augustine said, is the pilgrim part of the *civitas Dei,* with an authority surpassing that of the State, which belongs to the *civitas terrena.* The State has merely to serve the Church in the role of the "secular arm". So too the relationship between the earthly and the other-worldly goals of man is described in terms of St. Augustine's image of the two loves: "love of God extending to contempt of self, and love of self extending to contempt of God." It was consequently held that detachment from the world was of itself the direct and unquestionable way of realizing more perfectly the religious end of man (see *World, Church and World*).

3. From the very beginning, this attitude was challenged by objections which grew more and more widespread and finally led to the process of secularization which characterizes the third stage, the modern era. Faith and knowledge, for instance, were already distinguished in classical scholasticism (cf. St. Thomas Aquinas; see *Thomism*) as two modes of knowledge, each with rights of their own, though they were still united in their

ordination to the one truth. But the doctrine of the double truth, upheld by the medieval Averroists and still a force in Nominalism, meant the disruption of this unity. The truth of faith was opposed to that of science, at first as unrelated and then, as contradictory assertions were put forward, as by Galileo, they were regarded as hostile to one another. With the development of science and the proof that it was capable of explaining more and more fields of knowledge, what religion had to say about the world seemed to become more and more superfluous. Faith, regarded in the light of its past as a doctrine dealing also and specifically with the world, was regarded as unnecessary, or at most as competent in the "inward" sphere, though here it was being challenged by depth pyschology. What it had to say appeared as meaningless or at least useless for the world.

There was a similar development in the relationship between Church and State. The unity of the spiritual power and of the civil power which was regarded as dependent on it was initially a reality, and was maintained in Byzantium and the Eastern Church for many centuries. But the claim was challenged by the interpretation given to the "doctrine of the two swords" by the Western Emperors (see *Investiture Controversy*). Here the two powers were said to be derived equally directly from God, a position condemned in the most extreme terms by Boniface VIII in the Bull *Unam Sanctam* (1302). The new theory upheld the "divine right of kings", independent of the Church, and the princes then often subordinated the interests of the Church to those of the State (see *Absolutism*). The Church thus progressively lost political influence over the State, and lost it completely when it was deprived of its last remaining means of imposing strictly political pressure, the Papal States, and when the last links between "Throne" and "Altar" were shattered by the downfall of most of the royal houses. Thus this process also ended in secularity.

There was a corresponding shift in perspective as regards the end of man. Flight from the world, with its neglect of the worldly, bodily and material, and its special connotation of contempt for the sexual, ceased to be regarded as an ideal to be valued for its own sake. Instead, these realms were assigned real values of their own, secondary no doubt at first in comparison to the religious realm contrasted with them, till finally a complete secularization was achieved. It became clear that neither the Church nor the orientation to an other-worldly goal were helping men to master the tasks which were incumbent on them in the worldly realm (see *Social Movements* I, *Rights of Man*). Parallel developments can also be traced in the other realms of human life, mostly in connection with the preceding, as for instance in the realm of art, culture and education, in the understanding of law, authority and history (see articles on these).

C. Evaluation

The historical process of secularization, described above rather summarily as the progressive emancipation of the worldly from a religious sphere which was thus becoming meaningless, contains in fact a number of aspects which must be taken into consideration when a verdict is passed upon it. What secularization means is to be judged chiefly in the light of how religion is understood in the process, especially its relationship to the world (see *Religion* I A).

It might seem that the relationship could only polarize between two extremes, which could be looked upon as representing in their purity the ideals sought after in the second and third stages of the development described above. At one pole the whole world in all its functions is subordinated to religion and governed by its rules (see *Integralism*), at the other religion, insofar as it survives at all, is totally orientated to the other world, with no interest or influence in the worldly realm. In between, there are of course countless other possibilities for the relationship of religion to the world. But this general schema is inappropriate. It is based on a very definite idea of religion and one that is quite inadequate. Here religion is characterized by the fact that it bears on a realm opposed to the profane, the realm of the holy, of which it is the steward. It is a matter of indifference whether this sacral realm regarded as superior to the world has control of the world, or whether it ignores the world in complete detachment from it on the basis of the other-worldly character of the holy. In any case the principle is that man must see in the holy his first and authentic task, to which other duties must always give way. His intramundane tasks are treated as secondary and as liable to come into conflict with his primary task.

This notion of religion, which is poised between Integralism and esotericism, must be contrasted with a view of religion which does not regard the holy as a special realm apart from the profane. As a consequence, the worldly task cannot possibly come into rivalry with the religious one. The holy is realized in the profane, the religious task in the worldly one. But they do not simply coincide, since this would mean the denial of the religious task. And this would lead once more, at least on principle, to the separation of the religious from the worldly realm. The religious task could then only be subsumed under the first type of religion described above. But this remains inadequate, because it does not do justice to the Christian message, just as it has also had a deleterious influence on the history of Christianity, as has been shown.

On the basis of this distinction of two different types of religion two different types of secularization must be envisaged. In the first type, when man finds himself asked to choose between the religious and the worldly task, he is under the impression — justifiable from this notion of religion — that he can only master his worldly task at the expense of the religious one. And his secularization then consists of deciding in favour of the worldly task which he has to recognize as obligatory. But in the second type of secularization, religion sets no new tasks in addition to the worldly one. It merely gives the latter a new meaning and purpose (cf. 1 Jn 2:7f.: "I am writing you no new commandment . . . Yet I am writing you a new commandment"). The rejection of religion, understood in this way, means for the world the denial of the one dimension of this world which can ground this world as a whole. A secularization of this type would not make the intramundane task easier. It would simply make it absurd, since the whole of life would be meaningless. But this is not an outlook which can be endured by many over a long period. If the true religious dimension is persistently excluded, some intramundane substitute will be looked for to give meaning to life. But then, to guarantee an ultimate meaningfulness, some worldly goal will be erected into an absolute. And this will then become a new type of "sacred realm" in contrast to other fields. Another religion is established, in the first, unfavourable sense, and the just interests of secularization are thwarted — unless a new process of secularization is begun, as may be seen to be happening in various atheistic systems.

D. The Christian View of Secularization

The way has now been paved for a verdict on secularization from the Christian standpoint. It will depend on whether Christianity considers itself a religion in the first or the second sense, as proposed above. The history of secularization suggests that Christianity was not always very clear on the point, so that the Christian verdict on secularization will involve a clarification of the self-understanding of Christianity.

1. *The present state of the discussion.* In the years between the two World Wars, when the phenomenon of secularization first became a matter of widespread interest and close investigation on the Christian side, it was mostly rejected out of hand as an anti-Christian movement. This was still the attitude of conservative circles after the Second World War, among circles who were concerned for the preservation of western culture (see *Occident*). Today attitudes are more cautious and nuanced.

On the Protestant side, the influence of dialectical theology has been felt. This was on principle readier to criticize the intramundane claims of religion and the Church than the "secularizing" of the world. Hence even Protestants who tended to emphasize the negative element in secularization (e.g., W. Hartmann, H. Kraemer), acknowledged that it had a positive role to play on behalf of the Church. It was seen as helping the Church to understand itself and its task better, to see itself as homeless in the world and to avoid mistakes when translating the Gospel into the language of the profane world. But there are others, especially F. Gogarten, who regard secularization as "a necessary and legitimate consequence of the Christian faith", though it is to be distinguished from the secularism which adopts in turn religious forms and claims. C. F. von Weizsäcker takes up a similar position, as does J. B. Metz on the Catholic side, the latter pointing out that many modern types of atheism are based on the false assumption that Christianity implies a divinized, not a secular world, and hence that the Christian faith will disappear when its dream-world vanishes. But the true relationship between the Christian notion of God and a divinized world is precisely the opposite: "to Christianize the world means to secularize it".

Another positive attitude to the secularity of the modern era has become well-known under the slogan of "religionless Christianity". This position is based on the severe strictures on religion made by K. Barth, who held that religion was "the concern of the godless". But the real launcher of the notion of a "religionless Christianity" was undoubtedly D. Bonhoeffer who propounded the main lines of thought which have dominated this trend when he was in prison in 1944 under the National Socialists. A list of Bonhoeffer's points enables one to recognize how widely influential they have been: religion as a "historically conditioned and transient form of human self-expression"; intellectual sincerity; the question: "How can we speak about God" — avoiding religion, that is, without the historically-conditioned assumptions of metaphysics, inwardness, etc.? How can we speak of God in "worldly" terms — or is it perhaps no longer possible to speak of him at all as hitherto? (G. Ebeling takes up here the question raised by Bonhoeffer as to the "non-religious interpretation of biblical concepts"; others ask how the word "God" can be introduced in any meaningful way.) God the *deus ex machina,* the stop-gap where human effort fails or at the limits of human knowledge and power; the danger of human existence being reduced to one dimension; the coming of age of the world (which recurs in R. Guardini). One of Bonhoeffer's principles was that we must live in the world *etsi Deus non daretur,* that we must stand before God "like those who deal with life without God". This in fact recalls a saying of St. Ignatius Loyola, that "we must employ all human means with as much prudence and energy as if all our success depended on them". In any case, though perhaps given a one-sided interpretation, it became very popular in the "death-of-God" theology (G. Vahanian, W. Hamilton, T. Altizer and others in America, D. Sölle and others in Germany). Where this meant that God was supposed to be dead and buried in sheer humanism (really, a humanism denying the existence of God — a view not to be attributed without more ado to this trend), Bonhoeffer's point was misunderstood, and was in danger of being made into an ideology, that of a non-secular secularism. J. A. T. Robinson's much-discussed book *Honest to God* is also obviously tributary to Bonhoeffer for its basic ideas as regards a positive evaluation of secularization. In fact most of the important theologians who have discussed the theme at the present day have been influenced by Bonhoeffer in this matter, at least in Protestant circles, where the problem was discussed much earlier and more fully than by Catholic theology.

But among Catholic theologians a positive verdict on secularization is gaining ground and influence, which showed itself at Vatican II, due chiefly to the representatives of this view among the theologians attached to the Council, like Y. Congar and K. Rahner. An example is the Pastoral Constitution on the Church in the Modern World.

2. *Reasons for welcoming a correct secularity.* a) *The true secularity.* One of the reasons why the Christian understanding of the faith now suggests a more positive attitude to secularization may be that it presents itself as the one remaining way of bringing the Christian message to the world of today. According to Bonhoeffer, the "religious" approach will be successful only with a few survivors from the age of chivalry or some intellectuals of doubtful sincerity. But the justifiable effort to be all things to all men is not the only or the decisive motive for the acceptability of secularization. It is welcomed on its own merits, since "it results directly and authentically from the kernel of Christian revelation itself" (H. Zahrnt). This needs to be demonstrated. Here it should be noted that the secularization in question is to be clearly distinguished from a secularism which is an atheistic ideology, offering an answer without recourse to God when asked about the meaning of the whole, the purpose of life, or rejecting the question totally, by declaring it to be absurd or repressing it in silence. What is at stake is the true secularity of the world, which consists of the truth that there is nothing in the world which is too "holy" to be accessible to a worldly approach and must be reserved for religion (religion being then, as we have seen, definitely misunderstood). There is no mystery in the world from which science is barred, on the ground that it can be explained only on "religious" terms (see *Myth, Demythologization*). This does not mean of course that the world and all that is in it is totally comprehensible. The mystery abides universally. But in the realm of action there are no intramundane effects which can be brought about only by "religious" means or practices (see *Magic*). There is nothing in the structure or the order of the world which is taboo, which is to be removed from man's use, as the attitude which could be called "sacralism"

has firmly maintained throughout all the history of religion.

b) *Justification in the light of the Christian message.* The OT already contains, as has often been pointed out (cf. G. von Rad, for instance, or H.-J. Krause, H. Cox) a clear orientation to secularization. It is true that the Israelites lived in a world "which was divided before God into pure and impure, the holy and the profane" (von Rad), where the untouchable ark of the covenant, the inaccessible sanctuary and the chosen people attested the separation of the "religious realm" from the world. But faith in creation, with the claim of God to be Lord of the whole world, the doctrine that the world and all that is in it is created for man, the prohibition of making an image of God to localize his presence in this world, the extension of the promise of salvation to all nations, etc., paved the way for "breaching the pale of the sacral" in secularization (T. Sartory). This tendency came out fully in the NT. In the message of Christ, all the sacral realms within the world, which still seemed inviolable in the OT, were treated as provisional or unimportant, as mere means, or even as impediments to salvation when erected into absolute values. They were thus relativized, often in direct onslaughts: the temple, the "holy place", by the prediction of its destruction (Mt 24:1f.), since the Father was not to be adored there but "in the spirit and the truth" (Jn 4:21–23), and since for Christians God and Christ are the temple (Rev 21:22) as are their own bodies (1 Cor 3:16f.; 6:19; 2 Cor 6:16); so too the "holy times", the Sabbath, since "the Sabbath was made for man" (Mk 2:27), according to Jesus, who pointed to David's having "profaned" the "holy" bread of the Presence to satisfy his hunger. St. Paul says of feast-days and Sabbaths that "These are only a shadow of what is to come" (Col 2:16f., cf. Rom 14:5 and especially Gal 4:10f.). So too the "sacred customs" like fasting (Mk 2:18–20), the rules for pure and impure (Mk 7:1–15), circumcision (Gal 5:2) and so on. Even sacrificial worship and priesthood, in the sense of the OT, are abolished by Christ, as the Letter to the Hebrews shows. In a word, apart from Christ, the NT recognizes nothing sacred about persons, realms, things or structures. The Christian enjoys the freedom of the children of God through Christ and is lord of the world, where everything is holy and unholy at the same time, according to how truly it is in Christ or

69

under the dominion of sin. Hence St. Paul, in his conviction that "nothing is unclean in itself" can formulate the statement which can be regarded as a maxim of Christian secularity: "The world or life or death or the present or the future, all are yours; and you are Christ's; and Christ is God's" (1 Cor 3:22f.).

BIBLIOGRAPHY. See bibliography on *Church and World;* also: D. Bonhoeffer, *Letters and Papers from Prison* (1953); id., *The Worldly Christian* (1967); G. Ebeling, "Die nichtreligiöse Interpretation biblischer Begriffe", *Zeitschrift für Theologie und Kirche* 52 (1955), pp. 296–360; F. Gogarten, *Reality of Faith* (1959); M. Stallmann, *Was ist Säkularisierung?* (1960); G. Vahanian, *The Death of God* (1961); P. M. van Buren, *The Secular Meaning of the Gospel* (1963); H. Cox, *The Secular City* (1965); T. Sartory, *Eine Neuinterpretation des Glaubens* (1966); T. Altizer and W. Hamilton, *Radical Theology and the Death of God* (1966); D. Solle, *Christ the Representative* (1967); id., *Truth within Us* (1968); R. Richards, *Secularization Theology* (1967); K. Rahner, *Schriften zur Theologie,* VIII, pp. 637–66; J. B. Metz, *Theology of the World* (1968).

Albert Keller

II. Laicism

The term "laicism" was coined in France during the struggle for spiritual power under the Third Republic and introduces the problems of the "Church and the World" as they were understood in the 18th and 19th centuries. It is only against this historical background that the attitude of laicism to the relationship of Church and State, for instance, can be properly understood. Laicizing thought was given its classical form in France, though it also played an important role in other countries down to the present century.

The spiritual roots of laicism are to be found in the Renaissance, Humanism and more especially in the Enlightenment. This was the era in which the autonomy and intrinsic value of the world began to be recognized in all spheres — State, society, law, economics, culture and education. The effort was made in consequence to shake off imagined or real ecclesiastical tutelage. Hence laicism has all the characteristics of a movement for emancipation.

The political thought of the era saw the justification of religion and religious societies in the individual's right to freedom of religion and its profession. But since this right obtained only in the private sphere of the person, the freedom of religious groups as such did not follow at once. These were rather assigned the status of an association on the basis of private rights, and hence deprived of public standing in their own right and of their power to influence public life.

One consequence of this process of emancipation and its embodiment in constitutional law was the separation of Church and State, which was completed by the legislation of the Third Republic on 9 September 1905. The concordat of 1801 was abrogated. Diplomatic relations with the Holy See had been broken off in 1904. The Church was deprived of support from public funds, Church buildings became the property of the State, though the local cultic communities, the juridical agents of the cult and its external organization, were allowed to use them free of charge. The financial administration of the cultic communities was supervised by the State. But the dynamism of this emancipation carried it beyond the limits which a neutral State, uninterested in religion, should have prescribed for itself. The educational system of the Third Republic set up a "State religion" of a special type. There had been efforts to provide a substitute religion in the form of an official "Atheism" and a "Theophilanthropism" at the time of the Revolution (1793 and 1795). This issued in 1882 in the abolition of religious instruction in State schools. It was replaced by general ethical instruction on lines laid down by the State. At the beginning, belief in God was still maintained as the necessary presupposition of such ethics, but the "Ligue de l'Enseignement" founded in 1866 demanded that ethics should be purged of all explanations referring to God. Thus laicism became a world-view. The "State Church" celebrated a strange resurrection with a "religion" full of minus signs.

Since the religious orders were the mainstay of the "free schools", the legislation was mainly directed against them. The Jesuit order was banned in 1880. The other orders and congregations were ordered to make application for official recognition on the part of the State. According to the law of 1901, each religious house and all new foundations needed to be licensed by the State. In 1904, all religious communities without exception were forbidden any kind of teaching activity. As in the typical case of France, so too in other countries the question of schools and education was the classical case of conflict between the sovereignty of the laicizing State and the claims of Church life.

The aggressive emancipation on the part of the State provoked a bitter defensive struggle on the part of Catholics. They could not but see the laicizing *Credo* recommended by the State as an unwarranted imposition, and the republican form of the State which upheld this *Credo* as by its very nature a peril. The majority of French Catholics attached their hopes to a restoration of the monarchy, which they soon thought of as the sole guarantee of the external existence of the Church. This political option, meant as a measure of self-defence, inspired the State in turn with misgivings, not always unjustified, that the Church schools were not educating children in loyalty to the new form of the State. State restrictions on freedom of education became harsher and harsher. The aloofness of a great number of French Catholics and their hierarchy was maintained till into the upheavals of World War II. Papal pronouncements were also marked by the character of being on the defensive, though they counselled moderation in the concrete (cf. the warnings of Leo XII; Cardinal Lavigerie). Pius X, in the encyclicals *Vehementer* and *Gravissimo officii munere* (1906), condemned the interference of the State in the proper work of the Church, and hence rejected the law of separation. Pius XI's encyclical *Quas primas* (1925) brought the term "laicism" into the vocabulary of the Church.

On the side of the Church, pastoral prudence prevailed, stimulated by new thinking on the relation of the Church to the world. On the side of the French State, the laws on separation were applied tolerantly, and the tendency to totalitarian claims became distasteful, in view of recent experiences. The way was paved for an agreement. In 1921, diplomatic relations with the Holy See were resumed. The era of controversy within the Church was ended in favour of a line open to dialogue, by the declaration of the French episcopate in 1945.

In the course of this process, the term "laicity" was coined, as a counterpart to "laicism". This "sound, legitimate laicity" of the State (Pius XII, *AAS* 50 [1958]) means the autonomy of the State and public institutions in pursuing the common good, part of which is to guarantee the religious freedom of the citizens and the existence of religious associations under public law. As regards schools and education the Archbishop of Cambrai, E.-M. Guerry, may be quoted: "As regards State schools, laicity means that the school shall not be denominational but neutral and hence shall pronounce neither for nor against religion . . . This is to be distinguished from laicism in the State, which is a philosophical doctrine based on agnosticism, materialism or an ideological atheism by which the State is inspired and with which it seeks to penetrate its public institutions, including the schools" (31 December 1959).

This attitude was ratified by the declarations of Vatican II on the proper autonomy of earthly realities (*Gaudium et Spes*, art. 36), and on the resulting freedom of Christians to choose between political options (*Lumen Gentium*, arts. 25, 36, 37; *Gaudium et Spes*, art. 43). Here the Church is charged to seek a relation of partnership outside the framework of the extremes of the State Church and separation of Church and State. The same principles are the basis of the decree on religious freedom.

See also *Enlightenment, French Revolution, Church and World.*

BIBLIOGRAPHY. G. Weill, *Histoire de l'idée laïque en France au XIXe siècle* (1925); G. de Lagarde, *La naissance de l'esprit laïque au Moyen-Age*, 4 vols. (1934–46); J. Ryan and M. Miller, *Church and State in the United States* (1946); A. Audiert and others, *La laïcité* (1960); L. Capéran, *Histoire contemporaine de la laïcité française*, 2 vols. (1957–59); id., *Histoire de la laïcité républicaine* (1961); id., *La laïcité en marche, 1883–1889* (1961); A. Dansette, *Religious History of Modern France*, 2 vols. (1961); J.-B. Trotabas, *La notion de laïcité dans le droit de l'Église et de l'État républicain* (with full bibliography) (1961); C. Alix, *Le Saint Siège et les nationalismes en Europe, 1870–1960* (1962).

Ernst Niermann

SERMON ON THE MOUNT

1. *St. Matthew.* The Sermon on the Mount, Mt 5–7, is the first and most important of the discourses of Jesus which mark this gospel. It gives a general picture of the "justice" which should characterize the disciples of Jesus and give them access to the Kingdom of God. In the introduction, the beatitudes (5:3–12) constitute a first presentation of the conditions to be fulfilled by the disciples to possess the Kingdom of God. The metaphors of salt and light (vv. 13–16) insist on the good example which the disciples are to give the world by their good works. The first part of the sermon defines evangelical justice as a

justice which surpasses and fulfils the old law. This idea, first enunciated in general terms (v. 17–20), is then developed by six illustrations in the form of antitheses (vv. 21–48). The section concludes with v. 48: "You therefore must be perfect, as your heavenly Father is perfect." The second part exhorts the disciples to practise justice merely to please God (6:1) and applies this exhortation to almsgiving, prayer and fasting (vv. 2–18). A set of diverse recommendations follows: a warning against anxiety about earthly goods (vv. 19–34), against passing judgment on others (7:1–5), against profaning the sacred (v. 6); an invitation to pray to God with confidence (vv. 7–11), to do good to men (v. 12, the "golden rule"), to enter by the narrow gate (vv. 13–14), to beware of false prophets (vv. 15–20). The conclusion is an urgent appeal to put into practice the instructions received (vv. 21–23), an appeal illustrated by the parable of the two houses (vv. 24–27).

2. *St. Luke.* In consequence of a change in the order of the preceding sections, the corresponding discourse in Lk 6:20–49 has been transferred to the plain (v. 17; cf. Mk 3:7, by the sea). The four beatitudes at the beginning (vv. 20–23), which promise the Kingdom to the poor and suffering, are contrasted with four "woes" which exclude the rich and those who are happy in this world from the Kingdom. The first development inculcates the duty of loving one's enemies (vv. 27–36). The recommendations which follow (vv. 37–42) insist above all on fraternal charity. The conclusion (vv. 43–49) stresses the necessity of works, illustrated at the end by the comparison of the two houses.

3. *The literary problem.* The discourse of Lk is much shorter than that of Mt (30 verses instead of 107); all its elements are also found in Mt, except Lk 6:39–40 (= Mt 15:14; 10:24f.), 45 (= Mt 12:34b–35) and vv. 24–26, 38a (proper to Lk). Many items of the discourse as given by Mt are found elsewhere in Lk: Mt 5:13 (Lk 14:34f.), 15 (Lk 11:33), 18 (Lk 16:17), 25–26 (Lk 12:58f.), 32 (Lk 16:18); 6:9–13 (Lk 11:2–4), 19–21 (Lk 12:33f.), 22–23 (Lk 11:34–36), 24 (Lk 16:13), 25–33 (Lk 12:22–31); 7:7–11 (Lk 11:9–13), 13–14 (Lk 13:24), 22–23 (Lk 13:26f.); some appear in other parts of the gospel tradition: Mt 5:29–30 (cf. Mk 9:43–48); 6:14–15 (Mk 11:25); 7:19 (Mt 3:10; Lk 3:9). These observations allow us to conclude that here as in the other discourses of his gospel Mt has made large additions to the basic text by inserting elements taken from other contexts. We cannot, however, identify the traditional form of the discourse with that given in Lk, because his version also contains additional elements, and he may have omitted some things which he did not think would help his Greek readers. The agreements between the two versions attest at least the existence of a more ancient tradition which situated on the mountain a discourse given by Jesus at the beginning of his Galilean ministry, perhaps connected with the institution of the Twelve.

4. *Interpretation.* The two versions of the Sermon on the Mount are composed from different standpoints, which sometimes give very different meanings to the same elements of the gospel tradition. Thus in Lk (6:20) the first beatitude promises the "poor" the consolation which will be refused to the "rich" in the other world (v. 24). In Mt 5:3 it invites Christians to make themselves "poor in spirit" in order to obtain the Kingdom. In Mt 5:25f., the parable of the litigants is an exhortation to concord, while in Lk 12:58f. it is an appeal for conversion. The interpretation of the Sermon on the Mount calls therefore for distinctions. The meaning of the discourse as a whole and of each of its elements must be studied both at the level of each of the redactions as given in the gospels, and at the level of the tradition on which these redactions are based. We must further try to determine the exact import of these teachings in the framework of the preaching of Jesus. A certain displacement of perspectives has taken place: the preoccupations of Christian instruction, which is interested above all in the practical consequences of Jesus' message, do not coincide exactly with those of Jesus as he announces the coming of the Kingdom of God and tries to explain the meaning of his divine mission.

5. *The ethics of the Sermon on the Mount.* The radical and uncompromising character of certain demands of the Sermon on the Mount raises the question as to whether such demands are reconcilable with the concrete conditions of human life on earth. The problem arises only for part of the Sermon on the Mount, especially for the antitheses Mt 5:21–48; but many other declarations of Jesus pose the same problem (cf. for instance Lk 14:12–33). Certain solutions must be

rejected as inadequate: that which holds that these demands are addressed only to certain categories of disciples who are called to a higher perfection or to a particular ministry; that which supposes that they were formulated in view of the imminent end of the world and prescribed an exceptional course of conduct, such as the expectation of imminent judgment would call for; that which maintains that Jesus imposed impossible precepts in order to make man conscious of his impotence and hope for his salvation from God's grace alone; that which sees in these declarations of Jesus the expression of a religious ideal couched in terms of hyperbole, or a way of making man understand the necessity of unconditional obedience to God, without dictating precise lines of conduct. But conduct is clearly the object of these prescriptions, which are presented as an authorized commentary on the Law and as the statement of the conditions required for entry into the Kingdom, in a discourse which insists on the necessity of putting into practice the instructions received. The concrete examples, however, which suppose very well-defined situations, cannot be taken as immediate rules for action. Jesus uses these examples to describe the attitudes which give us to understand what God expects of us and how we are to conform to his intentions in our regard.

See also *New Testament Ethics, Reign of God, Law and Gospel, Works.*

BIBLIOGRAPHY. See the Commentaries on the Gospels of St. Matthew and St. Luke; also: A. Steinmann, *Die Bergpredigt* (1926); M. Dibelius, *The Sermon on the Mount* (1940); C. F. Andrews, *The Sermon on the Mount* (1942); T. Soiron, *Die Bergpredigt Jesu* (2nd ed., 1944); H. Windisch, *The Sermon on the Mount* (1948, from 2nd German ed.); A. N. Wilder, *Eschatology and Ethics in the Teaching of Jesus* (2nd ed., 1950); H. J. Schoeps, "Jesus und das jüdische Gesetz", *Aus frühchristlicher Zeit* (1950), pp. 212–20; R. Bultmann, *Theology of the New Testament*, I (1952), para. 2; P. Bonnard in *Revue de Théologie et de Philosophie* 3 (1953), pp. 233–51; A. M. Hunter, *Design for Life: An Exposition of the Sermon on the Mount* (1953); J. Dupont, *Les Béatitudes*, I: *Le problème littéraire — Les deux versions du Sermon sur la montagne et des Béatitudes* (2nd ed., 1958); II: *La Bonne Nouvelle* (2nd ed., 1969); G. Bornkamm in *RGG* I, cols. 1047–50; J. Jeremias, *The Sermon on the Mount* (1961); W. Lüthi and R. Brunner, *The Sermon on the Mount* (1963); E. Thurneysen, *The Sermon on the Mount* (1965); R. Schnackenburg, *The Moral Teaching of the New Testament* (1965).

Jacques Dupont

SEX

I. Sexuality. II. Sexual Education. III. Sexual Morality.

I. Sexuality

For centuries the prevailing theological teaching attributed no more than a functional character to human sexuality; corresponding to the sexuality of the animal world, it was evaluated chiefly or entirely from the point of view of procreation (see *Birth Control*). On the basis of an anthropology which is concerned with the totality of the person, new points of view for the understanding and evaluation of sexuality present themselves nowadays, leading to changes of emphasis and additional insights and making the current doctrine more complete. Sexuality must be numbered among the essential determining factors in man. It characterizes the entire structure of the human being, whether as man or woman, and affects the behaviour of the individual even in his mental attitudes and processes. As a result of this preliminary enlightenment from the anthropological side, the theologian of today can also find in the witness of revelation an approach to an evaluation of sex in its totality.

1. *Statements in revelation.* a) The statements of the OT have preserved mankind's primal consciousness of his own human nature and his created existence as man and woman. This sexual differentiation has been determined by the Creator and expresses part of what is contained in the assertion that man is made in the image of God (Gen 1:27). In the biblical texts, the problem of body and soul as posed by Greek anthropology is totally absent (see *Body, Soul*). The entire man is created good. Therefore sexuality too as a gift of God is wholly acceptable. Although any projection of a sexual difference on God and the Trinity is inadmissible, the relationship of man and woman united in love reflects something of God's love, in its free giving of itself, and of the unity within the Divine Trinity. In the Yahwist account of creation, the first action of God, in a world seen from a thoroughly anthropocentric viewpoint, is to create man and refer him to an opposite (Gen 2:18–24). Man and woman are to (help) complete each other through communication with the person who is the partner of the opposite sex. Before man comes to the divine "You", he has already met his human partner. The

similarity of sound in the Hebrew terms *ish* (man) and *isha* (woman) could be seen as already pointing to the fact that in this "partnership" there is fundamentally no subordination and superiority. The basis of the poetic, pictorial account of the creation of Eve from the rib of the man is the actual fact of *eros,* the primal experience of the attraction of the sexes to each other. The "two-in-one-flesh" connotes indeed more than a merely passing sexual relationship of man and woman; it expresses the total unity which both form, breaking through even the bonds of blood and family (Gen 2:22–24). Christ was to take up this expression later and base on it his demand for the indissolubility of marriage (Mk 10:6–9). The total surrender in the sexual act is termed in the OT "knowing". In this profound inter-personal meeting both partners reveal themselves in their deepest personal sphere of intimacy; irreversible knowledge and self-revelation come about. But beyond this, man receives from God in principle the responsibility of the transmission of life (Gen 1:28). According to the teaching of the Yahwist, sin not only roused the anger of God, but also caused a disturbance of the order in creation and of the relationship between the sexes. The man, called to account for his insubordinate behaviour, places the blame on his partner (Gen 3:12). The disturbance which sin brought into personal relationships affects the sexual sphere too, within which these relationships come to their most profound realization. Along with this basic teaching, the Yahwist endeavours to give a more exact description of the "wounding" consequent on man's sin, referring among other things to certain aspects of life, conditioned by the cultural environment of the times, which were regarded as an evil and therefore looked on as the consequence of original sin and resulting from human guilt: the desire of the woman for the man, that is, *eros,* as well as the domination of the man over the woman, that is, the patriarchalism obtaining in Israel (Gen 3:6). Also the experience, partly attributable to cultural conditions, of the limits set by modesty in regard to nudity is given a theological significance: the casual naturalness of human relationships is lost (Gen 3:7). Man experiences his nudity as a personal exposure (J. B. Metz).

b) The NT takes up a natural attitude to sexuality and nowhere connects it with the ritual laws of purification of the OT. The ritual laws obtaining in this matter are expressly rejected by Jesus and replaced by a fundamentally new concept of purity (the right intention coming from the heart) (Mk 7:1–23). Through the proclamation of the Kingdom of God now beginning in Jesus, however, the eschatological condition of man is emphasized to such an extent that sexuality and its fulfilment in marriage no longer appear as the only normal or universal way for man in this world; the way of virginity appears beside it as a genuine possibility (Lk 20:27–36). Seen in the religious perspective of salvation-history, sexuality seems somehow left in suspense. In the relationship to Christ, the difference of the sexes becomes a matter of indifference (of like value) (Gal 3:26–28). Following the contemporary evaluation of human sexuality, however, St. Paul was unable to recognize its entire scale of variations and the full richness of marriage; thus in regard to the significance of *eros* he remains more or less insensitive (cf. 1 Cor 7). Yet in general the biblical references to man and his sexuality are very open to the changed understanding of reality in our times; they offer at least in their basic kerygmatic content no encouragement to a dualistic, Manichaistic contempt for sexuality and for a repression of the sexual powers.

2. *Anthropological analysis.* a) A personal anthropology, viewing man in his totality, is nowadays at pains to grasp the meaning of sexuality, not only in the biological sense but in its entirety and to give it its proper place in the total structure of the human person. The sexual difference between man and woman is a constitutive part of human nature; it finds expression in the psychological make-up of the person and may not therefore be regarded in isolation nor in a merely functional way. Everybody lives in the sexual situation, male or female. Sexuality is not something added on to a neutral human nature, but determines the person as man or as woman. Nevertheless one must be cautious in the use of categories such as "the virile" or the "eternal feminine"; for the sociologists (H. Schelsky) point to the extremely varied range of expressions of the female or male role in the different cultural spheres. For the development of human personality, sexuality is of considerable significance. Long before marriage, one comes into the field of force of one's sexuality and is moulded by it. The unmarried person also remains a sexual being. Thus sexuality must be dealt with not only in

relation to marriage; it has a place in all anthropology.

b) The fact that the full man is neither the man nor the woman as such but only man and woman — with due respect for their individual development, but in full equality — points to an essential need for communication with the partner. Only in the differentiation between man and woman can therefore the human potentialities and roles be realized to the full. In sexuality man experiences his insufficiency and his dependence on the "You" of the other — and that, first of all, on the human plane: on the partner of the opposite sex. Inasmuch, however, as sexuality, even when finding its realization and fulfilment in marriage, is still lacking an ultimate fulfilment, it points beyond to something outside the human life-partner. The theologian sees in this a point of contact for the orientation of man to God and his dependence on him. Man achieves the deepest fulfilment only in the meeting with the "You" of God; but this is in final analysis an eschatological fact. This Christian understanding of man as one "called" by God and with a "calling" to fulfilment with God makes possible for the Christian a deeper view and evaluation of human factors and permits him to come to a certain understanding of the transcendental relationship of man through the lack of entire fulfilment in human sexuality.

c) Since sex is grounded in the centre of the human personality, its actuation affects the entire person. Thus the actual primary sex relationships, if they are to correspond to the nature and dignity of man, must always be contained in the framework of eros, in the affection and love which is directed to the entire person of the other, and accepts the other not merely for the sake of one's own need (eros), but also loves them in themselves as persons (philia) and accepts them in their totality. But this acceptance will correspond fully to the dignity of the other person only if it takes place not merely egocentrically in a narcissistic self-love, but is joined to a love (agape) which gives itself, is prepared to make sacrifices and is directed to the "You" of the other, a love which is ultimately a weak reflection of that love of God for man which entirely offers and gives itself. Precisely because human sexuality is not directed by instinct as is animal sexuality, but remains "plastic" (Gehlen, Schelsky), it calls for a formation in philia and agape. Where this is absent, where sex and eros become separated

from the personal, and sexual activity is no longer the means and expression of personal attachment, but sought for its own sake, it loses its natural meaning and legitimacy. Precisely in its indefiniteness as far as natural instinct is concerned and in its openness to formation is expressed the specific nature of human sexuality; its superiority, but also its fragility. To this extent sexuality stands entirely at the service of the personal and must not be separated from it. Sex and eros therefore demand a formation through philia and an integration in agape.

d) The deep personal effect of the sexual act already indicated in the Bible and experienced in life, demands also its acceptance and corresponding integration in the entire human life. The completion of the total sexual self-giving leads to "the giving and receiving of a knowledge and completion which affect the entire person. Where such knowledge and completion take place, those involved cannot part as though nothing had happened. But neither can they enter the total life in common which makes it possible, unless the irrevocable will to share their entire life is present and is expressed in a binding way and accepted by both sides" (Auer). Thus, inasmuch as the sexual act is the expression of the unity of both partners and their total mutual love and acceptance and is capable of bestowing a knowledge which has a most fundamental formative effect, the indispensable prerequisite for its legitimacy is the mutual and publicly proclaimed will to a binding acceptance which is total and permanent. Thus only in validly contracted monogamy is the full meaning of such a self-giving secured.

e) When sex breaks away from the totality of human love, in the attempt to be autonomous and a law unto itself, man experiences "the effects of sin", the dissolution of the inner harmony. Sexuality, valued and activated for its own sake, leads to disrespect for the partner, who is degraded to be the object of one's own satisfaction and therefore deeply wounded in his dignity. Where sex is separated from the personal, it begins a vagabond life; there appears then no reason why the "partner" should not be changed at will. All promiscuity, all sexual chaos, is a sign of a personal crisis on the part of the one concerned.

3. *Formation of sexuality: sublimation.* The enormous excess of energy contained in the sexual drive and the plasticity of human

sexuality indicate that man has the capability of putting these powers at the service of further human purposes, of sublimating them. This redirection does not imply a repression of the sexual impulses but rather a positive re-application of them for other spheres of fulfilment in life. S. Freud describes sublimation as a change in the goal as well as in the object of the drive, so that what "was originally a sexual drive finds a fulfilment that is no longer sexual but has a social or higher ethical value". Freud sees sublimation as the de-sexualization and also the socialization of this drive. Precisely the freely chosen and inwardly accepted sacrifice of the actualization of sexuality, when it represents not a false repression but a genuine acceptance and re-formation of these drives, permits the release of great energies of mind and body which can express themselves in significant achievements of a charitable, religious or cultural nature. "Sublimation is therefore not a mysterious, automatic transformation of sexual impulses into spiritual drives, but the reorganization into a more widely inclusive human attitude" (Auer). It presents itself for everyone as a task and is a prerequisite for the maturing of personality as also for the success of all interpersonal communication. The special nature of human sexuality and the dynamism it contains make it imperative for man that he should not drift in this matter but should provide for a formation and discipline of these powers. A. Thielicke presents it in the following proportions: "The more I am controlled by instinctual drives, the less I seek the unique, unmistakable 'You' of the other and the more I am concerned with the mere unit, the mere numerical 'specimen' of the other sex, to whose individual qualities I am indifferent but whose instrumental significance is thereby all the more important for me." Where no genuine formation of this drive takes place, but only a containment of repression, the road to personal maturity remains blocked, and this can lead ultimately to false attitudes, reactive over-compensations or perversions.

4. *Consequences for moral behaviour.* a) The right evaluation of sexuality demands, first of all, a firm acceptance of one's own sexuality and its development, as well as a knowledge of the power and inner dynamism of sex and *eros,* of the danger of false repressions, and of the place of true sublimation of these powers (see *Sex* II). Hence the encounter with the partner of the opposite sex cannot be treated casually. In correct companionship, which is also incumbent on the unmarried, important forces in both man and woman are released which help towards an integration of the entire sexual faculty and preserve from dangerous repressions. The theological understanding of the two sexes of man explains the importance of *eros* for the maturing of the total personality and for all interpersonal relations. Since all erotic relationships connote a mutual personal self-revelation and a certain surrender, they should take place only in full knowledge of this responsibility, i.e., in remote or proximate preparation for marriage.

b) A right attitude to sexuality forbids all prudery and all exhibitionism; it calls for an acceptance of the sense of modesty. Stress should be laid especially on the total human implication of modesty, namely to protect the intimate personal sphere from unjustified intrusion. While the sense of modesty pertains very essentially to man in his state of threatened dignity, yet the limits of what is included in detail under modesty cannot be determined merely on Christian or religious grounds; it depends very considerably as well on the particular cultural tradition and on what precisely is likely to endanger the intimate sphere of the person. In view of possible developments in the pluralistic society, it will be necessary, without falling victim to nudism, to give careful consideration to the question of training in a casual acceptance of the presence of nudity.

c) Since maturity to full personality and to the necessary integration of the sexual powers takes place only slowly and in separate phases, the question arises whether in this sphere too, that is, in the achievement of personal sexual harmony there may be various stages. May one set limited objectives — or must everything be demanded at once? This implicitly raises the question whether in the sixth commandment there can be *materia levis* in the matter of unchastity. Traditional moral theology has given a negative answer here, without convincing reasons. Unchastity has been reckoned a sin *ex toto genere suo gravis,* which — provided it is committed freely and consciously — never permits of objective levity of matter. In this teaching expression is given to the experience that all freely sought sexual activity develops an inner dynamism which all too easily impels to an egoistic, narcissistic satisfaction of one's sexual impulse. The so-called "*materia gravis* teaching" stems from a time when the sense of true personal love and of *eros* and *philia* had not yet developed, and all erotic encounter was measured in terms of its sexual dynamism. It would be better to re-interpret this teaching that every offence against the sixth commandment is an objectively serious sin, a teaching nowadays rejected by very many theologians, in the sense that sexuality possesses for personal human development and for integration into human society such a decisive significance, that its theoretical or practical rejection in principle entails a serious disorder and thus is to be reckoned as an objectively serious offence against the structure of human existence and action. With regard to the question of guilt, one must also take into consideration, when dealing with offences against the sixth commandment, the modern knowledge coming from depth psychology, and an *imperfectio actus* may frequently be assumed in consequence of disturbance in mind or will. The judgment of individual failures may not therefore be made without taking cognizance of the total basic attitude and intention of the person concerned.

d) Both repression of natural desire for pleasure as well as a hedonistic, auto-erotic acceptance of sex are to be rejected as false forms of behaviour. The same is true of pre-marital sexual intercourse: it could create a disturbance in the psychic balance of the future husband and wife. Pre-marital continence will therefore retain an importance that is not to be underestimated for the maturing of personality and preparation for marriage. A change in the attitude of the Church so as to favour pre-marital inter-course is not to be expected; this would essentially mar the concept of marriage. The step to promiscuity would then be a minor one. Because of the eminently super-individual significance of sex, all cultures, although in different degrees, have been concerned to set up some norms for sexual behaviour. Both a functional devaluation and a magical exaggeration of sex in modern society could be countered on human and Christian lines by a right personal acceptance of sexuality (Weber). But such a considered acceptance of personal sexuality already presupposes a certain view of the world and of man (see also *Sex* II, III).

BIBLIOGRAPHY. sources: Allocutions of Pius XII, especially *AAS* 37 (1945), pp. 284–95; 44 (1952), pp. 779–89; Vatican II, *Gaudium et Spes* (1965), art. 29; Paul VI, *Humanae Vitae* (1968). studies: T. Gilbey, *Morals and Marriage* (2nd ed., 1952); H. Schelsky, *Soziologie der Sexualität* (5th ed., 1956); L. J. Suenens, *Amour et maîtrise de soi* (1959); I. Lepp, *Psychoanalyse de l'amour* (1959); M. J. Buckley, *Morality and the Homosexual* (1959); A. Auer, "Geschlechtlichkeit". *Handbuch theologischer Grundbegriffe*, I (1962), pp. 498–506; S. Freud, *Three Essays on the Theory of Sex,* translated and ed. by J. Strachy (1963); H. Thielicke, *The Ethics of Sex* (1964); F. X. von Hornstein and A. Faller, eds., *Sex, Love and Marriage* (1965); F. von Gagern, *Marriage Partnership* (1966); D. von Hildebrand, *Man and Woman* (1966); L. M. Weber, *On Marriage, Sex and Virginity,* Quaestiones Disputatae 16 (1966); A. Ple, *Chastity and the Affective Life* (1967); J. Guitton, *Human Love* (1967); M. Oraison, *The Human Mystery of Sexuality* (1967); S. Callahan, *Beyond Birth Control: The Christian Experience of Sex* (1968); C. Curran, ed., *Contraception: Authority and Dissent* (1968); P. Harris and others, *On Human Life* (1969).

Johannes Gründel

II. Sexual Education

1. *Its nature and problems.* a) Sexual education can be fruitfully given only in a general framework of moral and personal education. It can neither be value-free nor independent of a determinate view of life, and it presupposes a right attitude to human sexuality. In this there is question, not so much of a moralizing enunciation of the relevant norms, but rather of every form of assistance needed by young people in process of coming to maturity. A form of sexual education which does not concern itself with the question of its own meaning and purpose is a negation of education. Any creation either of taboos or of a false mystique of sexuality should give way to factual communication of the necessary knowledge and an open yet thorough introduction to the important questions of human living, to the significance of sexuality for the development of one's own personality and for personal and social relationships, and in general to the questions of love and marriage. In this there is need for a synthesis of the important questions of living in the light of Christian revelation.

b) Depth psychology forbids us to regard the sexual merely as an autonomous system within the total personality, much as digestion or metabolism; it pertains rather to human nature as such. Therefore the entire human formation and maturity depend to a great extent on the right ordering of the sexual. Any evaluation of the sexual powers which classes them as merely functional, any arbitrary cultivation or isolated enjoyment or use of sexual appetite is therefore to be rejected. Such a cultivation nowadays must be regarded as a one-sided reaction to the negative sexual morality of former times. If sexuality is simply treated from a purely biological, psychological or sociological point of view, little is done for its integration into the person. Any isolated treatment proves disastrous here, because a sexuality that is not properly integrated can through the dynamism of instinct be socially very dangerous.

c) The problem of modern sexual education involves also in every case the confrontation of two different generations.

2. *Starting point and purpose.* a) The starting point and purpose of sexual education is the unity of sexuality and *eros,* of personal love and responsibility of the partners for one another and before society. From *eros,* which is understood as love directed towards the person and encompassing the other person as a totality, arises in the final analysis the preparedness for the permanency of the personal union of love, the effective capacity in fact for marriage. Mere sexuality and the isolated sexual act lack this personal *eros* and involve a degradation of the love between man and woman.

b) For the Christian a true sexual education demands that account be taken of the Christian concept of man and of the Christian ethos of love and marriage. The approach to sexual education will include consideration of salvation-history in its revelations about sin, the need for redemption and the actual redemption and sanctification of man, insofar as they shape the Christian concept of man. Any undue rejection, but also any magical over-emphasis of the sexual is to be avoided. Neither a pessimistic view of man in the sense of a totally corrupted nature, nor a naturalism coupled with a naive belief in progress correspond to the Christian evaluation of man and his sexuality. While upholding a natural, open and healthy attitude to sex, every Christian knows that this sphere too remains endangered by the sinfulness of man.

c) An education directed towards the right ordering of the sexual must be a learning of values. Every increase in surplus sexual energies demands further sublimation, so the adolescent must be provided with increasing help to regulate his drives. Therefore

a deepening of the sense of the dignity of the person is an absolute necessity. In final analysis the aim of a proper sexual education is to make one capable of personal loving contact, with the readiness to assume responsibility for oneself, for the partner and for the new life which may arise.

The young person should also be helped to a critical awareness of the various possible meanings of the word "love", because every meeting of the sexes presupposes a certain degree of maturity.

3. *Methods and "instruction".* a) Sexual maturity depends on the total personal formation and on the life-story of each individual from the pre-genital phase on, on the educative atmosphere of trust within his environment, on the way in which the mother treats the child and on the love existing in the familiy. Sexual education must be given in proper stages. Following the insights of Freud, according to which significance must be attached even to the stirrings of libido in the early years of childhood, the attempt must be made to adapt education to the sexual development in childhood, in youthful years and especially in the years of puberty. And according to each child's capability of assimilating it, care will be taken to give the knowledge suitable to each phase. All untruthfulness in relation to the child's instruction (the story of the stork) as well as all prudishness are contrary to serious sexual education and will take their toll in the course of the child's development. The giving of group instruction on sexual functions creates problems if it is confined to the presentation of purely physical and biological information and does not take account of the formation and training of the entire person. Only knowledge which remains encompassed by the ·total education can help towards the development of the human person taken in his entirety. A competent sexual instruction should have reached a relatively complete stage at the beginning of puberty, that is, before the first pollution or menstruation.

b) Yet mere information is insufficient. The term "sex instruction" often covers a questionable optimism in the matter of giving factual information on the biological and physiological realities. Inasmuch as it concerns the education of the entire human being, sexual education should not be understood merely as "the facts of life". It is precisely the Christian appreciation of man, of his bodily nature and his sexuality, which forbids us to separate the sexual from personal responsibility. The drive of sexual powers, the absence of secure control arising from instinct and the tendency to excess mean that constant effort is needed to integrate these powers in the total personality. If this formation of the sexual powers is not to have a repressive character but is to be an education to love, rightly understood, it will succeed only if it is associated with a certain asceticism in the sense of an integration of the instincts which open the way to true human encounter. The marital relationship of love between man and wife also will be successful only if it has gone through a period of sexual reserve. As long as a sympathetic insight into the meaning and purpose of sexuality is not yet possible for a young person, there is definite need for a corresponding protection and for direction. Along the way towards a proper ordering and formation of the sexual powers there will undoubtedly be stages of development and maturity. A refined form of casuistry will not be capable of determining what in the individual case is right and good or what is contrary to right order, bad and accordingly sinful (see III below). While it is important, in the case of young people, in view of the sudden eruption of the sexual drive, not to over-dramatize and not to speak too quickly of sin in autoerotic behaviour, yet the person in question should be helped to see the "summons" contained in such behaviour. Otherwise a false narcissistic fixation could be carried on even into later years and the young person would find it more difficult to break out of his preoccupation with self and to come to a genuine encounter with the other partner. The release from an infantile egoism demands the rejection of certain projections of unconscious models, especially those of the parent of the opposite sex. If autoerotic behaviour is carried on excessively into the years after puberty, it can be a symptom of a crisis in personality or the expression of an infantile and neurotic character.

4. *Agents*. a) The onus of giving proper sexual education falls in the first instance on the parents. In a healthy atmosphere they must respond again and again to the child's need for information and with constant reference for to knowledge already given, prepare their child for its physical and mental changes. The frequently observed inhibitions and diffi-culties of parents in finding the right words for instructing their children are probably grounded on the fact of experience that the deepest feeling of community between man and wife in the sexual act of marriage remains under the veil of modesty and intimacy, and, as that which is really to be lived and experienced, cannot be articulated. However, too great inhibitions can lead in time to the creation of taboos which have a paralysing effect on the confidence between parents and children.

b) The school too will in the framework of its own work of education be concerned to carry further the knowledge already gained. But the sexual education it provides should be regarded as to a great extent subsidiary. It seems questionable to demand sexual education as a specific school subject, for this is a problem concerning the entire person, which is to be dealt with not only in the sphere of biology but also in other subjects — not least in the framework of religious instruction.

See also *Education* I, II.

BIBLIOGRAPHY. J. King, *Sex Enlightenment and the Catholic* (1944); H. V. Sattler, *Parents, Children and the Facts of Life* (1952); L. Cervantes, *And God Made Man and Woman* (1959); A. Kelly, *Life and Our Children* (1960); id., *Catholic Parent's Guide to Sex Education* (1968); G. Kelly, *The Catholic Youth's Guide to Life and Love* (1962); id., *Your Child and Sex: A Guide for Catholic Parents* (1964); J. Reuss, *Modern Catholic Sex Instruction* (1964); J. Marshall, *Preparing for Marriage* (1966); H. M. Dresen-Coenders, *Psychology of Sex Instruction* (1968); M. and J. Ryan, *Love and Sexuality: A Christian Approach* (1969); F. von Gagern, *New Views on Sex – Marriage – Love* (1969).

Johannes Gründel

III. Sexual Morality

Sexual morality is to be regarded as part of Christian ethics and moral theology; it attempts to explain the purpose and task of human sexuality as well as the moral significance of interpersonal relations, insofar as they affect man in his sexual nature and are of an erotic and sexual character. Human sexuality cannot, however, be rightly explained in terms of finality, but rather from a personal evaluation of man and his relationships. Therefore sexual morality must take its place within Christian moral teaching as a whole and must not be taken in isolation from it as an independent entity.

1. *The traditional sexual morality.* a) The traditional Christian sexual morality was largely based on a narrow view of human sexuality; it was characterized by a predominance of the functional aspect. The significance of sexuality was measured chiefly, and sometimes even exclusively, from the point of view of conception. Thus marriage was seen as the proper place for the actuation of sexuality, since in it the purpose of sexuality, the conception and education of children, is best achieved. For all other spheres of life outside marriage, prohibitions and the injunction to practise continence were the only rules for sexual behaviour.

b) This understanding of human sexuality is based on an approach that is biological in a one-sided way. This approach, under the influence of extra-Christian lines of thought, especially concepts of natural law deriving from Stoicism and from Roman jurisprudence, attempted to derive a norm for human sexuality from the sexual behaviour of animals, bound as they are to definite periods of sexual activity. Besides this, theories deriving from Gnosticism and Manichaeism and the Stoic suspicion of sexual pleasure and desire gained ground, partly unconsciously and partly openly, within the Christian concept of sexual morality. Although Augustine emphasized the natural goodness of marriage and the holiness attached to it by God, yet under his influence the foundation was laid for a sexual pessimism which was to last for centuries. Under the influence of Judaizing Christians, OT ritual purity prescriptions too found entry into sexual morality. At a later period the physiological structure or the "nature of the marriage act" became the normative guide-line for sexual behaviour. Even when an attempt was made to establish further "ends of marriage" and marriage was regarded as a "remedy for sexual desire", yet the biological basis in the conception theory offered no possibility of seeing human sexuality as a value in itself, in its character as a sign and expression of human love and affection and in its foundation in the human person.

c) An over-valuation, lasting into the 19th century, of the male sperm, following the line of Greek biology, knowing nothing of female ovulation and regarding the sperm as already containing the full human life, caused every wilful ejaculation of male seed not leading to conception to be looked on as a moral offence akin to murder. It is significant that, in reliance on Augustine, a "biblical proof" for this was drawn from the account in Gen 38:8–10, according to which Onan neglects his obligation of levirate marriage and is punished by God with death for preventing conception. In this it was overlooked that the intention of the marriage of the brother-in-law was messianic and that the real reason for Onan's punishment was not a sexual offence. Even today the frequently used term "Onanism" for the interruption of the marital act or for masturbation is a relic of this false interpretation.

Inasmuch as extra-Christian influences of these kinds found entry into sexual morality and led to a falsification of Christian ethics, a critical revision of the hitherto accepted tradition seems called for. As well as this, however, the questions of the meaning and purpose of sexual behaviour must be answered anew today and new ideals must be sought for right action in the sexual sphere. These should continue to be determined along the lines of Christian freedom rightly understood, together with the acceptance and formation of one's own sexuality and the responsible entry into interpersonal relations of this kind in the spirit of true Christian love. The Christian will reject in the sexual sphere any trace of contempt for eros and sensual desire, all false asceticism and tactics of mere repression, but also every hedonistic one-sided deification of *eros* and of sexual desire.

2. *The "sexual revolution".* a) The words "sexual revolution" relate to a powerful change that is taking place in our times. Yet it is not merely that, in reaction to a traditional form of Christian morality no longer found convincing, outmoded norms are simply being abandoned and taboos swept aside. Other obligations of more far-reaching significance are becoming the focus of man's attention, as, for example, the rejection of a false repression of sexuality and the demand for a genuine personalization of sexual relations.

b) Sometimes, it is true, the sexual revolution is taken to refer to the theories of those ideologists who, with an optimism that can only be called naive, champion a glorification of sexual desire and expect an uninhibited satisfaction of instincts to result in the disappearance of every form of aggression and in the fulfilment of human living. A. Kinsey — and some biologists and sociologists influenced by him, who in opposition to the compulsion of norms make themselves the champions of sexual realism — strive through lessening the difference between man's scale of norms and his concrete behaviour to achieve sexual relaxation with the hope of lessening thereby social conflict.

c) Wherever "sexual revolution", so understood, disassociates sexuality from the body-spirit unity of the person and submits it to the arbitrary choice and wishes of the individual and to the pleasure of the moment, one has left the realm of sexual morality for that of amorality. An unrestrained sexual promiscuity which rejects all order and all restraints and which leads to a depersonalization, where sexual activity is equated to the needs of eating and drinking, entirely disregarding the facts of personal relationship reduces sexuality to a matter of supply and demand. Sexual intercourse then takes place merely for satisfaction and pleasure "because it is fun". But where sexuality sinks to the level of consumption goods, it causes a destruction of the unity of sex and eros and thus also a loss of meaning in human behaviour which can lead to a disastrous brutalization of sexuality in our society. Every such de-humanization of sexuality renders man incapable of true personal relationships, of a fully human love, incapable of marriage and thus becomes a serious factor in the dehumanization of society (Wendland).

d) The sexual revolution is not to be countered by mere moral prescriptions but through a new understanding of personal love and marriage such as can open for man a way worthy of a human being. Besides this the Christian will allow his concept of man and his understanding of love to be determined by revelation.

3. *Nature and purpose of human sexuality.*
a) There is general agreement on the need for giving form and direction to man's sexual instincts, not, however, on the criteria for providing us with norms of sexual morality. The factors making for morality in sexual activity rest neither on a purely biological foundation nor on any tendency towards development, nor can they be satisfactorily derived from existing behaviour patterns nor from a purely abstract concept of human nature. They must be derived from the personal, social and anthropological aspects of man. Just as in the case of sexual education, so too sexual morality presupposes

a total view of the meaning and purpose of man and his sexuality. With this question of meaning is connected the question as to the nature and dignity of man, the significance of the human person, his social and religious relationships and the sum-total of his obligations. The Christian cannot answer it without the revealed truths of faith.

b) Any explanation of the meaning of human sexuality must also take into account the newly gained insights of the empirical sciences, especially behavioural research and the convergence and divergence of human and animal sexuality. Precisely the specific qualities of human sexuality, its continuous activity outside the mating seasons, the possibility of isolation of sexual desire from conception, the generalized and uncertain nature of human instincts and the consequent possibility of sexual excess, demand for social living, if it is to be human and worthy of human beings, an organic control of the heightened sexual energies. They point to the need for institutionally supported direction and order in sexual relationships. This is but another instance of man's need of education.

c) That nature should be allowed to rule cannot be taken as the norm and purpose of morality, as an outdated sexual morality would have it; nor is the neutralizing but rather the humanization of sexuality the task of man. Therefore sexuality cannot and may not become purely the means to private satisfaction of instinct nor a sort of easily available drug. It gives man a goal beyond himself. In the measure in which sexuality falls into rightly ordered human relationships, and at the same time has regard to its responsibility to one's neighbour, to society and to man's future, it will be successfully "humanized". The liberation of man from his ego in its isolation, the effort towards solidarity, is a necessary step to his becoming himself in a genuine sense.

d) Man in his character as partner in a dialogue, as Christian revelation also sees him, can never meaningfully actuate his sexuality if he sees in it only a purely egocentric value; he must see it in terms of partnership. If he is himself to become a person and rightly develop his own being, the other person is an essential precondition. It is precisely here that man experiences his dependence on the community. Sexuality enables man to put himself and allow himself to be at the disposal of a partner of the opposite sex. "It has the purpose, through this communication, of bringing one's own personality and that of the other partner to their highest perfection. If this dedication is directed at anything less than the total person of the other, there is an incomplete fulfilment of the sexual personality structure" (K. Ruf). Giving and acceptance in an exclusive sense are therefore presupposed if the actuation of sexuality is to experience its full meaning.

4. *The social aspect of sexuality.* a) Although sexuality is to be regarded as a basic structure of the human personality, yet its social aspect ought not to be overlooked. It is the expression of relationship to the other person. Man can fulfil his own existence only in experiencing acceptance by another person. Sex and eros are not merely something individual and personal, they are as well both public and intimate in character. The sexual has accordingly been left in no society to the arbitrary will of the private individual; it has been subjected to social norms. Sexual morality is always social morality, for sexual behaviour has its presuppositions and conditions in the framework of society and its changes. The social aspect of sexuality demands that the needs of the community should also be taken into account.

b) The process of genuine formation and sublimation of the sexual powers leads to a certain de-sexualization and socialization of the instincts. If this is neglected, man's capability for love runs the risk of being subjected to a narcissistic fixation or of being entirely destroyed by uncontrolled instincts. Neither short-sighted repression nor naively accepted satisfaction of these instincts is a help towards human development.

c) If the personal basis and the social aspect of sexuality are not taken seriously, sexual behaviour is directed to the partner in a merely functional way — for the purpose of conception or for the satisfaction of desire. This amounts to a perverting of the sexual powers. This prevents them from attaining to their full meaning because a fleeting encounter is unable to take seriously the other person's true needs.

5. *The establishment of norms of sexual morality.* a) At the present time the question of how to establish norms anthropologically and theologically is the principal focus of interest in sexual morality. Ethnology has shown that the individual normative systems are relative and culturally conditioned in their content. Modern man too no longer accepts unquestioningly the norms presented to him by an authority or community; he wants to know the grounds for their claim to legitimacy. Precisely in the sphere of sexuality he feels himself hedged in by far too many norms, some of them alien to the matter in question. On the other hand sociological and anthropological studies of culture continue to emphasize the basic need for human behavioural norms for guiding the natural instinctual powers and relieving them of burdens, and for ensuring human freedom. This task was and is to a great extent performed by the social order whereby the generally accepted value judgments, the moral and juridical laws, embody an order which is constantly in the process of being re-established. They are the expression of an experience, and a regulative force constructed by the various groups, but are undoubtedly conditioned by the period in which they are established.

b) Neither is Christian sexual morality in a position to derive an absolutely unchangeable system of concrete moral norms from the revelation of the NT preached by the Church, as its most profound source of morality. Rather will it endeavour, by constantly examining present norms in the light of revelation, to bring the manner of life in regard to sexuality into conformity with personal needs. The question of the meaning and purpose of human life and human sexuality must be constantly considered and answered anew from the Christian point of view. This will provide the morally relevant judgments which are derived from the basic structure of man's being and behaviour, or from the nature of man, whereby a system of moral norms is attained which is not rigid but appropriate to the needs of the times, being in keeping with a dynamic and historical understanding of natural law to which a new approach has been made by modern theology.

c) Besides this, the insights of the empirical sciences must be taken into account, insofar as they are morally relevant, as well as the concrete experience of people's moral activity. The norms and guidelines of sexual morality are thus to be arrived at neither entirely deductively nor purely inductively but in a constant dialectic between the two methods.

d) Yet those who content themselves with a morality derived purely from what is done and find their norms in "the normative power of the factual" forego in the last analysis any purpose for sexual morality and any genuine education of man. They overlook the fact that man quite clearly has the capability and the task of actively shaping his development. Both the reality of the factual situation as well as what is possible and necessary are to be taken into account. But the factual behaviour must be questioned as to its normative content; where it is the expression of an inner conviction, the result of an ethos, it cannot be simply disregarded; it is the expression, if often in an oversimplified way, of a justifiable viewpoint. In this context a certain significance in the matter of finding norms must also be attached to statistics.

6. *The Christian command of love.* a) That the command of love is also universally applicable in the domain of sexual morality, and indeed precisely there, is unquestioned. The only problem lies in the content of its fulfilment. In the sacrificial and redemptive love of God for mankind in Jesus Christ the revelation of the NT provides the model and prototype of the *agape* which must be for the Christian the example and standard for all human love. Sex and *eros* find in *agape* their personal and religious integration and meaning. The testimonies of revelation proclaim that human love must be essentially characterized by altruism. Hence an egocentric narcissistic love is radically condemned by Christianity. Every erotic and sexual love which does not have the backing of the total person, which is therefore not prepared to take on responsibility and obligations, cannot be regarded as genuine love. The Christian must constantly measure the relationships to his partner and the claims made on his love against the radicality of the Christian understanding of love. The purification of *eros* through *agape,* that Christian love whose precise nature it is to preserve man from false self-seeking and false surrender to self, and which has as its model and example Christ's self-sacrificing love, remains a life task.

b) For the Christian a still deeper significance of sex, as an element in the history of salvation, is to be found in the fact that man looks to the other person for the formation of his own personality and hence enters into an exclusive and irrevocable union involving the sharing of life's experience and destiny. He thereby creates the precondition for the effectiveness of Christ's salvific action. In marriage one partner becomes the mediator in the salvation of the other. Thus sexuality never possesses a value in itself, but receives it only in becoming the expression of the human will and purpose as a whole.

c) For the Christian, sexuality and marriage acquire a certain relativity seen in the light of eschatology, "for when they arise from the dead men and women do not marry" (Mk 12:25). This is the eschatological attitude of reserve which gives meaning to a decision in favour of abstention from marriage based on freedom and charism, and gives that decision its rightful place; it finds its expression in the particular forms of virginity and celibacy.

d) The radicality of the Christian demand of love appears, however, in the individual case to be an excessive demand if its nature as a gift (as also its character as a "forgiveness" and a grace) is not taken into account. Man has graciously to accept much; in the faith he can be sure of forgiveness for his failings and his tardiness in pursuit of the goal. The thought of forgiveness (cf. Jn 8:1–11) and grace gives balance to the lofty moral demand of Christian love. This demand will then not be felt to be excessive and will not tend to create a neurosis; it will rather have a liberating effect. No matter how much in the course of time sexual morality will again and again adjust to the forms of society, it remains forever confronted with the gospel and is subject to critical judgment in the light of the gospel.

7. *The basic moral attitude.* a) Man's inner readiness to accept his sexuality and assume the role specific to his sex, but also to recognize his own sexual powers in their total personal and social character and to integrate them into the whole of life in all its aspects — this is what is traditionally known as chastity. Nowadays, however, the concept has for the most part lost its positive connotations. These should be restored, since chastity does not just mean "purity" or continence, but the striving after a right ordering and shaping of the sexual powers in the service of the human and social relations of partnership. The aim of chastity is to enable man to love in the personal way that is specific to the sexes and to prepare him to be rightly capable of marriage. Those alone are capable of marriage who are in the true sense capable of love.

b) Inasmuch as sexuality is not an autonomous system within the total personality but a basic human condition, not only is its denial or devaluation fraught with danger, but just as much every exaggeration or isolation, any concept of man, therefore, which so emphasizes the biological and animal sphere at the expense of the development of the personal and spiritual that man is regarded only as a sexual being. Precisely such a basic attitude would be unchaste because a purely functional gradation of values of the sexual powers very soon leads man to claim the right to an isolated enjoyment of sex, to an outlet for the satisfaction of the demands of instinct, to experiments and training in sexual activity, and to indulgence in sex to the extreme of satiety. Such an emancipation of instinct can easily result in a degrading of the partner to a mere object of one's own desires, while merely attempting to avoid serious conflicts by means of purely extrinsic rules of behaviour, e.g.: never hurt the feelings of the other and never conceive an unwanted child (A. Comfort).

c) Unchastity should not be described in a purely functional way, as "misuse" of the sexual powers. It includes every attitude which is not prepared to recognize sexuality in its roots in the total personality and to integrate it in a meaningful way in the entirety of human life, even if this attitude has not yet led to misuse of the sexual powers. Also a one-sidedly biological value-free approach to sexuality must be regarded as unchaste as soon as it lays claim to exclusiveness, that is, as soon as it is seen to be a *pars pro toto* ideology.

d) If, however, the proper basic attitude is present and if it is constantly striven after, even with individual lapses, one can rightly speak of chastity; for the virtue is entirely lost only by an abandonment of the purpose or basic attitude (cf. the Thomist distinction between *incontinentia,* the individual fault or incontinence, and *intemperantia,* intemperance in the sense of unchastity).

8. *Honesty in individual behaviour.* a) For sexual relations honesty is called for above all else. Honesty demands that the individual is sincere with himself and his partner, that he "does not present false hopes, expectations or claims" (Trillhaas). Whoever by appealing to nature seeks an outlet for the unbridled exercise of his passions and instincts, takes neither himself nor his partner seriously as human beings.

b) In this the symbolic nature of the modes of sexual behaviour should be considered individually. Sexual behaviour gets its meaning from the significance which is attached to the individual symbol. It is true that the function of the individual symbols will change according to custom and to the reactions of each person, yet the highest form of bodily union, sexual intercourse, should also be the expression of the highest form of personal union possible to man. This is achieved, however, only if it is also secured and supported by the will of both partners to a mutual bond. To this extent the basic requirement for a full and meaningful exercise of sexual self-giving is the full and irrevocable acceptance of the partner as a person.

c) The experience of bodily pleasure springs from the deeper experience of security in the sharing of life together. It has an ecstatic character. Not the greatest possible sexual pleasure in the orgasm, but the experience of union of two persons is the goal and expression of fulfilment in human sexuality. Inasmuch as the experience of pleasure has only a momentary character and disappears more quickly on the physical level than in mental experience, sexuality urges to repetition. The sign strives for repeated expression, yet it achieves only a premonition of a final and definitive completion which remains as a promise to both partners. If sexuality is regarded as part of the structure of the human person, then its ultimate meaning will not be attained by a merely physical experience of pleasure nor through a temporary personal harmony in the sense of a loving understanding, but only inasmuch as in the mutual acceptance of obligation, it is encompassed in the common responsibility for each other and in the form of a self-giving love shaped by *agape.*

d) Even if the partner declares himself fully in agreement with an uncommitted use of sex in the form of pre-marital or extra-marital intercourse, yet this in fact goes contrary to the meaning expressed in the act. To be sure there are innumerable people who in their use of sex do not come to a knowledge of the uninterchangeable uniqueness of the partner, nor to the experience of a mutual bond and belonging, since they are too selfish to have the openness or attentiveness needed for a genuine love directed to a partner. The wish to belong to the partner "for ever and always" does not even arise in these cases. Yet without a total will to bind oneself no full responsibility for the partner and for the children who may be born of this love can be assumed. Self-giving in this case easily turns to self-surrender. If the sexual act is to be the comprehensive symbol of full mutual love and self-giving, the person too must be fully behind it in knowledge and will. In view of the radical demands of love in the NT all pre-marital and extra-marital sexual intercourse remains therefore wrong and irresponsible (F. Böckle). The significance of sexuality for all mankind and social responsibility give society too a right to a voice in the regulation of the marriage bond. But it will not always be possible to determine juridically the actual beginning of marriage.

e) Since every healthy adolescent and adult comes within the sphere of influence of sexuality, the question arises for sexual morality whether and to what extent there exist certain stages of practical experience of one's own sexuality, different for different individuals, but which could be regarded as stages of development for the maturing person; further, what forms of sexual relationships on the way towards marriage are meaningful and therefore morally permissible. With regard to an evaluation of sexual excitement on a heterosexual basis as in certain kissing games, the question of meaning and moral permissibility cannot be answered by an elaborate casuistry. If fondling and "petting" are understood in the wider sense not as merely deliberately sought sexual satisfaction but as a testing of the erotic response of the partner and as an expression of love, they cannot be globally rejected but could have in certain circumstances a certain justification. However much it is the nature of young people to gather experience, yet the question of meaning and purpose should not be disregarded.

The following should be taken as a principle for pre-marital behaviour: as much physical expression and also erotic and sexually affected expression of love is meaningful and permitted as the individual is in fact inwardly prepared to give. There are very different degrees of extent of the possible bonds between two people, from mere passing or prolonged friendship to the enduring love which is characteristic of marriage. The possibility of self-deception, of the projection of *animus* or *anima* types, demands a corresponding self-criticism and openness for counselling by another. The right ordering and formation of sexuality remains a task of man all his life long; in this, sexual morality can only point to the goal towards which man is directed. Thus there can undoubtedly be certain phases of development and maturity.

9. *Defective forms of behaviour.* a) Insofar as human sexuality is essentially an expression of man's personal other-directedness and union, every sexual activity which is sought for its own sake or which goes beyond the union of mind and heart which is actually there, lacks its full meaning. It becomes a partial or even a false expression. The moral worth of such an activity is measured by the substantial personal value which is present in it. A sexual morality which sees in sexuality only the functions of pleasure and procreation (thus H. Kentler) has abandoned the personal foundation of sexuality and falls victim to an apersonal isolated evaluation of the sexual powers. The egocentricity or narcissism which regards the partner simply as an object of its own self-seeking or which does not see its own sexuality in its social aspect is clearly wrong.

b) A static ideal should not be the foundation for sexual education; one should recognize that there is essentially a development and that man experiences stages in which sexual integration still has the character of the imperfect, not entirely successful or complete. Further cases of defective behaviour should not be judged in an "atomizing" way; the life-story of each individual and his entire basic attitude and approach should be taken into account. For the young person there will be transitional periods of sexual behaviour which must be accepted and worked through. The tendency to repetition and gaining a habit and fixation in defective sexual behaviour should not, however, be overlooked.

c) It is precisely in the years of development that the young person's capability for loving is in danger of being fixed narcissistically or totally destroyed by uncontrolled instincts. Neither a hasty repression of the instincts nor a naively accepted satisfaction of instinctive desire is a help towards human maturity. Masturbation as a form of sexual satisfaction outside marriage, widely practised by young people, should be regarded to a great extent as a transitional phase of sexual development or a reaction to the tension of a strained atmosphere. Insofar as it is not a question of a neurotic fixation, over-dramatization should be avoided. Nevertheless it cannot be regarded as a fully proper form of sexual activity and cannot therefore be simply counselled.

d) The phenomenon of homosexuality can nowadays no longer be approached in a purely negative way. Dealing with homosexuals calls for some form of satisfactory "pastoral" solution. The homosexual is, more than others, indifferent to moral appeals, yet "a great number of them are quite willing and as capable within their limits of entering permanent and 'total' relationships as the 'normal'" (H. Ringeling). In this matter, it seems unimportant whether or to what extent such a trait can be inherited or only acquired. St. Paul condemned homosexuality as a symptom of man's original sin, in keeping with the view obtaining at that time of pederasty as a symptom of corruption and decadence. Where today, however, homosexuality appears more as a disease which cannot be simply "overcome" by moral efforts but seems rather to have an irreversible nature, the attempt will be made to help these people insofar as that is possible. Such a person undoubtedly seeks the totality of the other person, missing, however, the Christian form of encounter with the neighbour (Thielicke). Civil penalties for the practice of homosexuality will therefore be called for only where it is a case of seduction of young people and dependents, of offences against public morality and of the exploitation of homosexuality for profit.

10. *The question of guilt.* a) To answer the question of guilt in individual offences against the right order and use of the sexual powers, one must take into account the insights of depth psychology. Not infrequently they stem from a considerable diminution of knowledge and of free-will. As far as knowledge is concerned, the conditions of sexual tension impair and inhibit the activity of the brain cortex, the seat of mental processes. Reflection is lessened to a greater or lesser extent; the usual caution is forgotten and thought is more and more taken up with the sexual impulse. In such a condition one can no longer speak of clear knowledge. Such a person is also no longer fully clear as to the moral relevance and bearing of his action. The sexual process follows its own proper dynamism. Only after the sexual release from tension and the disappearance of the pressure on the cortex does the "fogging" of thought come to an end (cf. Gagern).

b) Seen from this point of view, it becomes clear that an isolated judgment of individual acts is necessarily insufficient, that instead it is essentially a question of the person's total basic attitude and approach. He who seeks the right order of the sexual and is aware of the dynamism of these powers will not incautiously expose himself to the "proximate occasion". Where, however, in spite of earnest endeavour — in some cases because of previous failure — he is simply once again "overcome", one should also be cautious with the assertion that the individual failure is a grave sin and in case of doubt decide "pro reo".

c) As far as the will is concerned, where there is a right basic attitude, that degree of maturity may often be absent which is necessary for full free consent of the will (a condition for grave fault), especially in the case of young people during puberty. One should not immediately regard every consent as a full consent of the will. It is often a question of an acceptance which indeed is needed in order that an act takes place but which is rather a surrender of a momentarily weaker will in face of the all too powerful sexual impulse. It makes a difference whether a person is seriously striving after the right ordering and integration of his sexual powers or is letting himself be carried along without making any real effort.

d) Decisive for the measure of the wrong attitude and in particular cases also for the gravity of the sin is the measure of the injured or counterfeited love that is involved in the sexual offence. A distinction must also be made in the sexual sphere between real sexual offences and the sexual difficulties which face the young person on the way to a right ordering of the sexual during the process of coming to maturity. The latter may by no means be regarded as insignificant since they can affect considerably the human power of loving and the development of personality, yet one should not see in them the gravest sins. For nowadays the regulation of sexual behaviour is no longer in the forefront of attention in Christian ethics, though this reproach is still sometimes made (as by A. Comfort).

e) The Christian will, however, not be able to deal with the question of guilt without considering also the readiness to forgive demanded by the gospel (cf. Jn 8) and his own experience of forgiveness of sin and guilt, in his faith in the redemptive work of Christ.

See also *Marriage* I, *Natural Law* I.

BIBLIOGRAPHY. T. Gilbey, *Morals and Marriage* (2nd ed., 1952); W. G. Cole, *Sex in Christianity and Psychoanalysis* (1955); D. S. Bailey, *Man and Woman in Christian Thought* (1959); id., *Common Sense about Sexual Ethics* (1962); P. Ricœur, *Sexualité* (1960); H. Thielicke, *Ethics of Sex* (1964); B. Häring, *The Law of Christ,* III (1963) (with bibliography); id., *Marriage in the Modern World* (1965); S. Keil, *Sexualität, Erkenntnisse und Massstäbe* (1966); A. Comfort, *Sex in Society* (1966); W. von Gagern, *Marriage Partnership* (1966); *Sex and Morality. A Report to the British Council of Churches* (1966); R. Atkinson, *Sexual Morality* (1966); R. O'Neill and M. Donovan, *Sexuality and Moral Responsibility* (1967); M. Oraison, *Human Mystery of Sexuality* (1967); H. Ringeling, *Theologie und Sexualität* (2nd ed., 1968); A. Ruf, "Humansexualität und Ehegemeinschaft", *Die neue Ordnung* 22 (1968), pp. 241–52; H. Greeven, J. Ratzinger, R. Schnackenburg and H. D. Wendland, *Theologie der Ehe* (1969); G. Scherer, W. Czapiewski and H. Koester, *Ehe — Empfängnisregelung — Naturrecht* (1969); J. Gründel, *Fragen an die Moraltheologen* (2nd ed., 1969); id., "Das neue Bild der Ehe in der katholischen Theologie", in H. Harsch, ed., *Das neue Bild der Ehe* (1969), pp. 37–73.

Johannes Gründel

SIN

I. Sin and Guilt. II. Punishment of Sins.

I. Sin and Guilt

1. *Introductory.* The gospel proclaims divine salvation in Jesus Christ as redemption and forgiveness of our sins. Jesus calls for conversion as he proclaims and offers the kingdom of God. The Church preached that he died for our sins and as having accomplished purification from sins. We were baptized in his name for the forgiveness of sins. Sin seems therefore to be one of the primary suppositions of the gospel, and in this it is in line with the OT, especially the prophets. But Christian preaching encountered a self-understanding of man in which sin was taken for granted. It has no such place in modern thought. No doubt the optimism of the 19th century, which saw industrial and social progress mainly as an enchanting future, has given way to an experience of the "human condition" and human failure which has become a sort of obsession in philosophy and above all in the novel, the theatre and the cinema. But the word "sin" is not readily used and seems in fact to be avoided. One of the main causes is a reaction against a rationalistic, moralistic and legalistic notion of sin

in a seemingly recent past. But sin also implies a (negative) relationship to God, and hence the notion becomes obscured — or truer — according to the purity of our notion of God. It must be our task to propound in a way relevant today the notion of sin which has and always will have a place in Christian preaching.

2. *The biblical notion of sin.* The most common words for sin in the Bible are the Hebrew חָטָא and the Greek ἁμαρτάνω. The general sense in both cases is to "miss the mark". They are mostly used in ethical contexts in the meaning of "to do evil". In the Bible they very often mean "to do evil against somebody", especially Yahweh. Men do evil against him by transgressing his law, but this law functions in the covenant. Sin is hated by Yahweh as Lord of the covenant, and so its most definite expression is in idolatry, forbidden in the first command of the decalogue and denounced by the prophets. Idolatry sometimes appears as the source of all sins (Exod 20:3; Wis 14:22–31; Rom 1:18–32). Sin is above all revolt (פֶּשַׁע) offence, irritation (כַּעַס) and contempt (נָאַץ) and has the character of a violation of the covenant, and indeed of adultery as regards Yahweh. This OT view was taken over and deepened by the NT, where sin is against the kingdom of God, against Christ (Mt 10:33; 11:20, 24; 12:28–32; Jn 15:18, 23–25), and against the Holy Spirit (Mk 3:28f. par.). But it should be noted that the Decalogue likewise invokes Yahweh when forbidding sins against the neighbour, and that the prophets are not content to denounce idolatry. They are at least as vehement in denouncing injustice against the weak and a worship which is an alibi for social justice. More and more in the OT the command of love of the neighbour came to be placed beside that of love of God, and Jesus ratified the process. Thus Scripture gives us the task of describing sin as directed against God and man. As long as sin is envisaged entirely within the perspective of commands and prohibitions, justice is not done to human freedom. But the prophets display the heart as the seat of man's answer to God. The greatest sin is the uncircumcised or stony heart, or the hard — obdurate — neck. In the NT we find "sin" along with "sins" (in the plural). In Paul it is sometimes a personified might which has entered the world, but it also dwells in men and makes them slaves. In Jn in particular sin appears as the ultimate un-

righteousness, in which individuals but above all "the world" is imprisoned.

3. *What sin is directed against.* Men today react with some justification against the notion of sin in earlier generations, which defined it as "a deliberate transgression of the law of God". This concept can and must be modified from many aspects.

a) First of all, the image must be corrected, if it presents God on the analogy of a civil or ecclesiastical lawgiver and thinks of God's law on the analogy of a positive law (possibly also faultily conceived), as contingent and imposed from outside. God's law is identical with the demands which his creation and salvation make upon us — demands which are identical with creation and salvation themselves. From this we deduce above all that sin is against men. Sinful man offends against what is demanded by his and his neighbour's being.

b) But these demands must not be understood statically, a danger which goes with the concept of "natural law". It is the nature of man to be a person who programmes and constructs himself in history. Hence good and evil cannot be deduced from the tendencies of human nature, where this is contrasted with his personal being. Sin is rather a refusal of the call, of our future, as it is in history, where God's salvation has entered and is realized more and more fully. Rather than define sin as the transgression of a law, we might call it the refusal to commit ourselves in a history of salvation.

c) In the OT and the NT, the "religious" man is told that his sins are not merely setting up strange gods against the true God, but also injustice, harshness, exploitation of his fellows. It is a "blessing" that today we are sensitive to such things. It might be said that sins solely against God are impossible. Every sin is at least against the self (and hence is its own punishment), and God encounters us with his gifts and invitations in our fellow-men, especially in Christ. But it is necessary to stress today that it is God, with his initiative transcending our reality, who meets us in this way. Hence we "offend" and "irritate" God himself in our refusal to commit ourselves to the history of salvation which he wishes to enter on with us. The notion of sin as an offence to God should not be allowed to disappear, unless it seems to imply a strict order of justice between God and man, on the same level — as is apparently the case in most explanations of the redemp-

tion as "satisfaction". But the offence to God must be situated where it really is: God himself is offended in man when we disregard God's summons to love. Just as love of God and man is a unity, so too sin is against both.

4. *The origin of sin in man.* Sin is an ethico-religious act, but a negative one. This implies that what may be said of the moral act may also be said of sin.

a) Sin comes from the free decision taken by man in the kernel of his person, which is called the "heart" in the Bible. But man is always someone who is bodily in the world and he embodies himself more and more, by contact with the world, especially with his fellows. Hence too much attention should not be paid to purely inward sins, as is also the biblical principle. In the strict sense, such sins are never purely interior, any more than other elements. In one way or another, man gives outward expression to the resolves of his heart, and this embodiment deepens his inward attitude. On the other hand, man's body is part of the "non-I", the world, which he makes *his* world, without ever overcoming its resistance. This implies that man's outward behaviour sometimes fails to express his inward resolve, since there remains a foreign element. The difficulty in question gives rise to two limit cases of sin. The first is when only the outward behaviour is in conflict with the demands of morality, while the inward resolution and attitude is not involved. This can be because man acts in ignorance, the significance of his conduct being unknown to him. Or he is not master of his actions.

This limit case is called "material sin", which is therefore not a sin at all but only the appearance — not the manifestation — of it. The second case is the precise opposite. An outward act with a good meaning is deliberately chosen to disguise one's own sinful attitude. This is "hypocrisy", vigorously condemned in the Pharisees in the NT. This surface holiness is a by-product of works-holiness, with which the same group are reproached. The link between the two is not quite accidental, since works-holiness means conduct which follows the norms of morality, but disguises sin by not acknowledging its own need of redemption. In this way, it is also hypocrisy. Material sin and hypocrisy also seem to be limit cases inasmuch as they cannot exist as such for long. Either the bad outward behaviour affects the inward attitude, or the evil attitude will show itself somewhere in outward behaviour.

b) Between material sin and sin from the heart there are many possible degrees. A sinful act can also come about where psychic determinisms regulate the act in part, and our freedom is not fully engaged. To put it metaphorically: the act is on the periphery and not at the centre of our person. Such psychic determinisms may be positive or negative instincts or drives, such as self-assertion, libido, anxiety, which anticipate the free act and obscure one's insight. But ordinary routine can also play a part, if full attention to one's commitment cannot be demanded, because ultimately the decisions required are of little importance.

These considerations have led Catholic theologians to re-think the classical difference between mortal and venial sins. The distinction comes from the practice of the sacrament of penance. It indicates primarily the difference between sins for whose forgiveness the sacrament (in the baptized Christian) is necessary, and sins which can be forgiven without the sacrament (though confession of venial sins is never excluded and has often been recommended by the magisterium). The difference in the gravity of sins, denied by Pelagianism and contested, though with nuances, by the Reformation, is accepted in Catholicism precisely because of the differences it saw in human action with regard to the world (D 106–8, 804, 833, 835). But for centuries scholastic theology could not agree on the standpoint from which the distinction between mortal and venial sin was to be determined. The two types of sin, admittedly only named sin analogously, differ by reason of the freedom of the sinner (full knowledge and free will) and also by reason of the content of the action (grave or light matter). In this view, mortal sin is sin committed with full knowledge and consent in a grave matter, venial sin with less full knowledge and consent or in a slight matter. But in view of what has been said above, it may now be affirmed that there is only one aspect from which the gravity of a sin can be judged: that of full knowledge and freedom or otherwise, or, to use the terms just invoked, whether or not it comes from the centre of our person. Venial sin is then the more or less peripheral sin. The gravity or importance of the act then comes down to its origin — peripheral or central. It is in fact a coefficient of the origin. Infidelity in marriage normally involves a more central resolve than a small theft. This

consideration has already been put forward by K. Rahner, who pointed out that a similar distinction could be noted in morally good acts. Mortal sin, as a decision at the centre of the person, is a break with the vital orientation to salvation, a gambling away of the life of grace. Hence the name of mortal sin. But in the life-history of each man even a central resolve can be revoked, and God continually opens up to us in Christ new chances of conversion. It is only in life as a whole, or in the transition to the next life that sinful decision can be definitive, corresponding to the "sin against the Holy Spirit" (Mk 3:29 parr.), the "sin unto death" (1 Jn 5:16) or the ultimate "lawlessness" (1 Jn 3:4).

c) Every act is revocable, and within each act we may be mistaken about the connection between the inward and the outward element. A wrong outward action need only be material sin, a good action can be hypocrisy, a major offence need not proceed from the centre of our person and it is even possible that a minor offence may embody profound malice. All this suggests that sin is not primarily to be sought in the exceptional act, but in the whole programme of life. This is also true, of course, of virtue and of all categories of virtue and vice. Honesty or falsehood, chastity or unchastity, love or egoism are ultimately realized in a whole life or a period of it, and seldom display themselves clearly in any particular act. Hence the confession of our sins must rather be a life discerned than acts listed, not only in prayer, but also in the sacrament of penance. And the deepest sin is resistance to the summons to rise up from our daily falls humbly and hopefully. It is resistance to the history of salvation which God wishes to verify in each life, even through and out of our sins. Hence in Jn the sin of those who refused to believe in the Son of God was not just that their works were in fact evil, but that they also refused, for this reason, to come to the light (Jn 3:19).

5. *Guilt.* a) What makes sin really sin is guilt. Guilt is the free decision to evil, evil with regard to God and man. We may therefore distinguish in guilt an inward element and a social one, to which *culpa* and *debitum* correspond in Latin. The inward element lends itself to psychological analysis, which can often distinguish between inauthentic feelings of guilt and a real consciousness of guilt. Where the moral norms are more or less imposed by the environment, without

being really assimilated, inauthentic guilt-feelings can multiply (in primitive cultures, but also by reason of a legalistic, puritanical or authoritarian upbringing in our own society). The social element is embodied in juridical guilt, which means being subject to a penalty and (or) being bound to make compensation. This juridical guilt is only ascribed in the administration of justice, in Church and in society, when there are or have been signs of the *mens rea* — or at least, this is the ideal regularly aimed at.

b) This last point indicates that juridical guilt may remain when the *culpa* at the centre of the person has been eliminated by repentance and the bestowal of forgiveness. A repentant murderer still has to pay the penalty. But it is an over-simplification to apply this principle univocally to guilt in the ethical or theological dimension, to guilt with regard to God and man, as when for instance it is maintained that the temporal punishments for sin must still be undergone, though the guilt is already eliminated by forgiveness. It seems truer to say that guilt only remains insofar as repentance does not spring from the centre of the person and take in all levels of one's being insofar as they are accessible to the free act.

c) More difficult to determine than the persistance or disappearance of guilt is, it would appear, its origin. Our consciousness does not precede our will, but is actuated by it, so that we always find ourselves already exercising our freedom in some way. Hence it is impossible to ask where our moral decisions begin in us. Further, in such decisions good and evil are often mixed, so that it is no more feasible to demarcate an age of "original innocence" for the individual than for mankind. If we reflect on the limits inherent to being human, or rather, to the perpetual humanization of man, it becomes clearer and clearer that it is very difficult to draw the line between "finitude" and "culpabilité" (P. Ricœur). Man also feels the perpetual seduction of sin; that he is subjected to "principalities and powers" as well as being a responsible agent; that he is a sort of synthesis of destiny and freedom (P. Tillich). But this need not dim our confession of faith in God and Christ, since the disclosure of a conscience that cannot be fully fathomed (cf. 1 Cor 4:4) is less important than full confidence in him in whom there is superabundant redemption.

6. *"The sin of the world"*. a) We use this Johannine expression (Jn 1:29) to sum up the social nature of sin or solidarity in sin. Even if we prescind from any original sin and its influence on each of us, this solidarity still exists. In Scripture, the whole people of Israel is often considered to have sinned in common, and God was said to have visited the sins of the fathers on the third and fourth generations. Even after Jeremiah and Ezechiel proclaimed the responsibility of each individual before God, a truth underlined by the NT, the link between fathers and children remains. Sin remains a power in the world, and the "world" remains a fellowship of sin. This fits in with our experience of the "contamination" of evil and in general, the "infectiousness" of moral action. One may speak of the sins, or perhaps also the virtues, of a given people or epoch of culture. What does this imply?

b) Guilt, at any rate, because it stems from the personal free act of each individual, cannot pass from one to another. It is not a social characteristic. Hence it is misleading to speak of collective guilt, and to do so is to commit an injustice to individuals. Nonetheless, the influence of one free agent on another is unmistakable. This can be formally described with the help of the term "situation". As a free person, I cannot be deprived of my freedom by the free decisions of others, but they may well place me in a situation which may determine me inwardly even in my freedom. Another can, for instance, disclose a value which makes an appeal to my freedom and he can strengthen its appeal by his example, much more so if he lives out this value. Evil example, on the contrary, deprives me of such an appeal. A value is exposed to doubt and denial. An impulse in the opposite direction is given. This is what the Bible means by temptation or scandal, which is literally the cord or stone placed in someone's path to make him stumble. Such a temptation, when reinforced by social pressure, may be too strong for my moral forces. Still more important is the fact that the persistent absence of positive testimony to a value and the persistent display of evil example can weaken and quench the appeal of the value. The grasp of the value can become so obscure that a real blindness to the value can occur. Such pernicious influences can be seen at work even in adults, who still need the guarantee of others in moral action. They are still more effective on children, inasmuch as they are still dependent on moral education. Children or even a whole generation can even be "born blind" to certain values, when they are born in a milieu where the values in question have been obscured or eliminated. This is how it is possible to speak of the "sins" of a people or a culture, though the sins are to a great extent merely the material sins of individuals born blind to a given value.

c) These affirmations are not confined to the "purely natural" order of things. Grace also comes in question. There are many ways in which man can be of service to the call of grace as it goes out to his fellow. I see in another the concrete reality of what grace asks of me, and the grace given me, the Spirit within me, makes me receptive to the example, the appeal, the message, which come to me from others. This means that sins may work against grace in a given milieu, while grace in turn can inspire a man to break the spell of his milieu, as God has done supremely in Jesus Christ, in a way which is decisive for all milieux. Hence we see sin ruling in many ways in the world, because, according to the vision of Jn, the rejection of Christ consummates and fixes the world in its sinfulness. Such a theology of the sin of the world and of the historical sins of the world might open up a new approach today to the dogma of original sin and possibly determine its interpretation. But apart from this question, it is important as a pendant to the doctrine of redemption, since God in Christ has delivered us from all sins.

7. *Sin, creation, redemption.* a) We have already pointed out that sin casts its shadow before in all man's limitations and finiteness. Nowhere in the world is anything simply a limitation: it is also an evil, the lack of a good which should be there, the missing of a goal. On the analogy of moral evil, but on a lower level, it is customary to speak of physical evil, both in man and under man. But on the infra-human level, it is difficult, if not impossible, to know where one is speaking of *evil,* as may be seen from the Aristotelian principle, "Generatio unius est corruptio alterius". This physical evil is only clearly such insofar as it affects human persons: it might then be termed "cata-strophic" evil. Another form of human evil is tragic evil, which man does to himself or his fellow-man, but not culpably, or at least not directly so. Finally, there is moral evil or sin. These considerations seem to reinforce what was said earlier about the mysterious origin of sin.

b) Analogies can of course be indicated between these different forms of evil, as for instance between physical evil and sin. Teilhard de Chardin pointed to the statistics which suggest that where large numbers are concerned, the good gains on the bad. He thought that this law could apply to good and evil in the human group as well as to biological evolution. And it may in fact be maintained that good — like evil — gains the upper hand insofar as it has become a social necessity. But our whole history shows how much the statistical laws depend on the person for being set in motion, and how the person can again break out of them. Some individuals seem to have had the strange power to launch chain-reactions of evil. But God's redemption works the same way, especially in the liberating life and death of Jesus.

c) If we see evil, and sin in particular, in all creation, the question arises as to how far God is responsible — the question already posed by Job. The answer still seems to be that given in the Book of Job, that it is God's mystery — but that it is not merely a mystery of power but above all of love. The whole of creation must be ascribed to the love of God, and we may affirm with some probability that a created world also involves evil. We must not appeal to God's omnipotence to affirm that he could hinder evil, since the content of God's omnipotence cannot be determined *a priori* by us creatures. But God is not simply the maker of the world, he is also its redeemer who brings it to fulfilment. There he shows that he is on the side of man in the struggle against evil and sin. Jesus, healing and exorcizing by an authoritative word, Jesus dying in weakness, is the deepest revelation of the saving power of God. "Repentance and forgiveness of sins [are to be] preached in his name to all nations" (Lk 24:47).

d) Man always remains exposed to the temptation to sin, even when he has found redemption through faith and repentance (which includes mutual forgiveness). He encounters within himself the concupiscence which is engendered by the inner situation in which he has been placed by original sin — and by the "sin of the world". In its essence, concupiscence is to be distinguished from sin, from which it springs and to which it leads. This distinction is made by the Council of Trent (*D* 792). But in man's actual exist-ence, concupiscence can be recognized in the sinful connivance with it. Hence even a Catholic may say that there is such a thing as *simul justus et peccator.* The magisterium of the Church affirms that the sinner may still have divine faith (*D* 838) and be a member of the Church and of its hierarchy (*D* 646). "The Church, embracing sinners in her bosom, is at the same time holy and always in need of being purified" (Vatican II, *Lumen Gentium,* art. 8).

e) But the priority always rests with redemptive grace. Grace is not merely subsequent to sin, it anticipates it. "We know that any one born of God does not sin" (1 Jn 5:18). The grace bestowed upon Mary, making her a very special case of redemption, was a purely prevenient grace, as the dogma of the Immaculate Conception says (*D* 1641). But the sinlessness of Christ himself is more important (Jn 8:46; Heb 4:15; 7:27). Even this is not to be regarded as a "programmed" incapacity to sin, but as an unfailing constancy in resisting the temptations by which Jesus was assaulted "in every respect . . . as we are" (Heb 4:15). Temptations coming merely "from without" and demanding no inward struggle would be consistent only with a humanity of Christ in which, as the Apollinarists held, the divine Logos replaced the human soul. Such temptation would not have been redemptive, given the nature of our own temptations.

See also *Evil, Theodicy, Original Sin, Metanoia, Concupiscence.*

BIBLIOGRAPHY. TEXTBOOKS AND GENERAL PRESENTATIONS: K. Barth, *Church Dogmatics,* IV/1 (1956); P. Tillich, *Systematic Theology,* II (1957); M. Schmaus, *Katholische Dogmatik,* II/1 (1962), pp. 472–540; J. F. Sagüés, "De Peccatis", *Sacrae Theologiae Summa,* II, ed. by Patres SJ in Hispania professores (4th ed., 1964), pp. 856–1026. EXEGESIS AND HISTORY: J. Guillet, *Thèmes bibliques* (1951), pp. 116–59; A. Landgraf, *Dogmengeschichte der Frühscholastik,* IV/1, 2 (1955–56); I. de la Potterie, "Le péché, c'est l'iniquité", *NRT* 70 (1956), pp. 785–97; L. Ligier, *Péché d'Adam et péché du monde,* 2 vols. (1961–62); G. Quell, G. Bertram, G. Stählin and W. Grundmann, "ἁμαρτάνω", *TWNT,* I, pp. 267–335; A. Gélin and Mgr. A. Descamps, *Sin in the Bible* (1965). STUDIES: M. Waldmann, "Zur inneren Begründung der lässlichen Sünde", *Theologische Quartalschrift* 98 (1916–17); E. Brunner, *Man in Revolt* (1947); H. Rondet, *Notes sur la théologie du péché* (1957); G. Berkouwer, *De Zonde,* 2 vols. (1958–60); K. Rahner, *Theological Investigations,* I (1961), II (1963); P. Schoonenberg, *Man and Sin* (1965); P. Ricœur, *Fallible Man* (1965).

Piet Schoonenberg

II. Punishment of Sins

1. *Preliminary remarks on method and matter.* The theological understanding of what punishment of sin means must not start from a notion based on the penalties imposed by civil law on a criminal for offences against society. The special relationship of God to the world, not that of a particular cause within the world but that of the transcendent origin of the world as a whole, would risk being distorted by this approach. And there are other anthropomorphic notions of God's vindictive justice which make the Christian message of the punishments of sin difficult to accept. The starting-point should rather be from the following considerations.

a) The freedom of man is exercised in the body, in the world. This means that the subjective decision, coming from the free agent as such in its incalculable independence, is necessarily, even in "inward acts", in itself and not just in its consequences, corporeal and mundane, i.e., is exercised "in the other".

b) This "other", being intrinsically constitutive of the free act, has of itself a structure. It is not pure *materia prima.* It forms therefore a prior limiting law for the free act, which submits to it in the very moment in which it alters the matter of freedom.

c) This concrete matter, modified by the free act but still possessing its own laws, is always connected with and united to the world as a whole, with its laws and development. It therefore undergoes the influence of this world as a whole.

d) These objectivations of freedom, which are part of it, which are its embodiment in the body of man, in the world of things and men around him, do not simply cease to be because the free agent rejects his previous decision, "changes his mind". The world, as matter of freedom, does not depend simply on the individual free agent. The new decision, even when the opposite of the first, has to operate in and with the situation which has been to some extent determined by the previous decision (see *Situation Ethics*). The "alienation" which every free decision undergoes through its necessary objectivation in the "other", is an objectivation which on principle could be brought about without a free act, through alien causes. (The same *habitus* of associations, psychic mechanisms, etc., can be set up by free training or by "brain-washing" from outside.) And the inner corporeality of man is always the zone in which the expression from within and the impression from without become one. It belongs to the free subject as an intrinsic component, though it is not simply identical with the free act in its origin. These persistent objectivations of freedom in the corporeal and mundane react upon the free agent, and hence are means whereby the world acts and reacts upon the subject — a mediation which goes to make up the concrete reality of these objectivations. All this is true both of the free act which is morally good and of that which is morally bad.

2. *The concept of punishment of sin.* We may use these considerations to suggest a theological explanation of the punishments of sin. a) The punishments of sin are the persistent objectivations of the bad moral decision, being themselves hurtful because contrary to the true nature of the free subject, and being also the means through which the resistance of the due order of the world (of men and things around the subject) likewise operates as hurtful. From the considerations under 1 above one can see why every sin avenges itself, why punishment (in the sense of penalty, cf. "under pain of") can and must be the connatural, intrinsic consequence of sin. In its necessary objectivations, sin submits — because being finite it can never be autonomous — to the structures of a world made by God. Freedom can never fully eliminate or replace this world and hence undergoes its "punitive" reactions.

Since this avenging setting also includes fellowmen who can themselves act freely, one can see that "punishment" for sin in the sense of civil, penal law can at once be understood as a possible though secondary case of this metaphysical and theological notion of punishment.

b) The punishment of sin, in this sense, appears as the penalty inflicted by God as guardian of the moral order, since the hurtful structures of man and his world which sin inevitably sets in motion are created by God and hence are objectivations and expressions of his holy will. God "punishes" through the good world which he created and whose structures he still upholds when they are abused by finite freedom in an evil act. Since the creature cannot abolish them, they operate to cause pain through the objectivations of sin. It is therefore superfluous and anthropomorphic to imagine that to uphold the moral order by punishing, God would

have to create punitive agents whose sole function would be to bring about the physical evil of punishment. This is true above all of the final situation of man's free history, in which the full and definite reality of man and the world will be directly disclosed, with all "repressions" ended. The radical contradiction between the permanent "supernatural existential" (see *Existence* III B), the permanent offer of God's self-communication in love, and the definitive obdurate refusal opposed to it by the free act will be experienced as the *poena damni*. And this is in fact the only explanation of the pain of loss, since if the punishment is understood as something extrinsically supervening, there would be no desire or need for the vision of God. And the *poena sensus* (which certainly cannot be thought of as merely affecting the senses) in this view of perdition (see *Hell*) consists of the radical contradiction between what the lost obdurately insist on being (and are, "bodily") and the permanent structures of a transfigured world which is their permanent setting. We cannot visualize this permanent, real contradiction which does not affect merely the senses — the "fire of hell". And it is not necessary to do so, either to be objective or to meet the needs of the kerygma today. In putting forward these considerations, we are obviously presupposing the doctrine of St. Thomas, that the punishments of the lost, both "pain of loss" and "pain of sense", are the consequence and not the cause of the definitiveness of the free decision (that of life as a whole) which is of the essence of freedom, since it is a choice of the definitive, not a choice that is to be constantly reconsidered. In the case of the definitive evil decision it is called obduracy.

c) This enables us to understand the difference between "medicinal" and "vindictive" punishment, which again is not to be visualized along the lines of the penal law in force in the State. Every hurtful reaction of reality (in man and his world) to a wrong decision as it affects this reality is of itself a summons to "conversion", to a better decision, more objective and humane, and has therefore a "medicinal" character. Being an expression of the holy will of God, it also has a "vindictive" (retributive) character, which does not of course mean that it must be understood as the angry reaction of a will imposing law merely extrinsically and adding punishments of an extrinsic type. The holy will of God which reacts retributively is the will which creates a good world and sustains it in its objective goodness. Punishment loses its medicinal character (in its effect, not in its essence) insofar as it is confronted with refusal by the free agent, either provisionally or finally through definitive obduracy.

3. *Theological consequences of the notion of punishment of sin.* a) The punishments of eternal loss — a possibility which must be reckoned with for the free agent while still existing in his history, without appeals to a theory of apocatastasis — have been discussed above under 2b.

b) As regards purgatory, the theological notion of concupiscence must also be brought in (see *Purgatory, Concupiscence*). Purgatory then appears as "working out of the system", overcoming, the painful difference between the concupiscent situation of man (not necessarily radically eliminated by death) and the initial good decision for God which has become definitive in death. For the situation of concupiscence which affects man interiorly and exteriorly is partly due to his own free acts. Whether this process of purgation is to be considered a strictly temporal one is a secondary question and ultimately an open one in theology.

c) According to the view of punishment of sin proposed here, the quashing of "temporal" punishment, that is, the punishment co-existing with a good basic decision, actually taken or still possible, cannot be thought of along the lines of a mere "amnesty" — the non-infliction of a punishment additional to the guilt and its natural consequences, to be imposed from without. Hence help in the elimination of the punishments of sin can only consist of a favourable change in the situation within which the sinner has to "work off" the penalties which are the connatural consequences of sin. Or help may be given (through a special grace) to further the total harmonization of the basic decision with the manifold totality of human reality — a harmonization which eliminates the punishment of sin.

d) This principle also enables us to gain a better grasp of the nature of indulgences (see *Indulgence*).

e) The same principle may also be applied to the doctrine of the Council of Trent (*D* 1543, 1580), according to which justification (as the basic decision for God and the existentiell acceptance of the proferred grace of justification) need not always be linked at once with the remission of all ("temporal") punishment due to sin.

BIBLIOGRAPHY. See bibliographies on *Indulgence, Justification, Sin* I, *Penance* II; also: C. Journet, "La peine temporelle du péché", *Revue Thomiste* 10 (1927), pp. 20–39, 89–103; T. Deman, "Péché (Les effets du péché)", *DTC*, XII, cols. 212–25; K. Rahner, "Sünde als Gnadenverlust in der frühchristlichen Literatur", *ZKT* 60 (1936), pp. 471–510; id., *De Poenitentia. Tractatus historico-dogmaticus*, I (4th ed., 1960), pp. 682–729; id., *Theological Investigations*, II (1963); id., *Schriften zur Theologie*, VIII, pp. 447–71; B. Kloppenburg, *De relatione inter peccatum et mortem* (1951); J. Bergmann, *Läuterung hier oder im Jenseits* (1958); E. Quarello, *Peccato e castigo nella teologia cattolica contemporanea* (1958); *Die Sündenvergebung in der Kirche* (An inter-confessional discussion, with contributions from H. Surkau, H. von Campenhausen, K. Rahner, W. Böhme and A. Kirchgässner) (1958); P. Riger, *Sin and Penance* (1962); C. McAuliffe, "Penance and Reconciliation with the Church", *TS* 26 (1965), pp. 1–39.

Karl Rahner

SITUATION ETHICS

1. *History of the problem.* The term "situation" was introduced into the language of moral theology by T. Steinbüchel. It became a sort of technical term when "situation ethics" was condemned by Pius XII (Allocutions of 23 March and 19 April 1952: *AAS* 44 [1952], pp. 270ff., 413ff.; Instructio S. Officii, 2 February 1956: *AAS* 48 [1956], pp. 144f.; *DS* 3918–21).

There is a situation ethics, in the sense of the condemnations here mentioned, when one bases oneself on the concrete circumstances of a moral act to regard as good or justifiable moral decisions which are consciously in opposition to the generally valid norms of the natural law and the revealed will of God, since the link between morals and the order of being is denied. In condemning situation ethics in this sense, Pius XII was dealing with an undoubtedly misguided effort to solve a perpetual problem of moral theology, but one which had only become central with the rise of existence-philosophy.

Morals originally consisted in the main of wisdom sayings and more or less concrete rules of behaviour in typical situations. But with the systematic development of moral theology, the moral act was defined in terms of the end of man. General assertions were made about the nature of man, which were mostly based on experience, and were then used to formulate ethical directives equally valid for all men. The application of these rules to all cases was hardly felt as a problem at first, and where it was explicitly considered, it was not felt to be essential, as when medieval theologians came to speak of the moral difficulties which the OT presented to them. But when the problem of universal applicability came to be felt more keenly in modern times, it was still treated, at least on principle, as a secondary one, though it was in fact in the foreground, especially in the age of casuistry. The controversies about probabilism etc., which preoccupied moralists especially in the 17th and 18th centuries, were undoubtedly a high-point in the earlier efforts of moral philosophy and theology to settle problems arising from the links of morality to its situation. But they did not solve the problems in a decisive way, though one should not underestimate how much the solution of the question of what one is bound to do under pain of sin in doubts of conscience can contribute to the formation of the conscience in a given situation.

When it was difficult to apply general principles to an individual case, medieval theologians usually had recourse to the solution that only the formal moral principles were universally valid *(principia primaria moralitatis)*. The more specific the principles *(principia secundaria moralitatis),* the more limited their field of application. But with the rise of casuistry in moral theology, the concrete case was more and more readily treated as an item to be subsumed under a specifically determined general principle.

When ethical questioning came to be formulated on the basis of the concrete I-World and I-You relationships, that is, when the concrete "intentional" (i.e., object-related) act was taken as the foundation and starting-point, a sort of Cartesian reversal took place in the relation of morality to the situation. The definability and determination of the concrete ethical demand in a unique situation now becomes the central problem of systematic ethics. The interest was now concentrated — to use terms borrowed by Scheler from Bolzano — on "the good in itself" only as mediated by "the good for me". This meant that in theology the question had to be more clearly put as: "How can I know what God wants of me here and now in my unique situation?"

There is undeniable progress here. The moral questioning starts with man in his concrete constitution and his historically changing relationship to his fellow-men and

his environment. Starting therefore with man's situation, it asks how the will of God may be known, that is, it tries to define moral obligations. Scientific study is not confined, as it was to a great extent in the "ethics of essences" of scholasticism, to the general *a posteriori* rules of what is *per se* obligatory. Nor is it just a matter of disclosing the general *a priori* presuppositions of each person, as in the "ethics of disposition" and "value-ethics" of modern times. The new approach also takes in the importance of the subjectivity in its uniqueness and the perpetual historical change of the objective conditions. Thus ethics is completed by an existential ethics, which may also be called a situation ethics and an ethics of responsibility.

The change is due to the individualist and personalist trend in the thought and feeling of our present pluralist age. It is also due to a profounder sense of man's social nature, through which he is so strongly dependent on his social setting and its development. There was also the need to find a valid answer to the historically novel "situation" of modern man, and one which would meet his new understanding of reality. In the ethical situation, what was once a rare marginal case has now become almost the normal one. What most people once thought to be certain, has now become extremely questionable. Other forces making for change in moral theology included transcendental philosophy, phenomenology, existential philosophy, personalism, the theory of science and kerygmatic theology. In all these realms, attention has been more and more concentrated on man as he is in his concrete constitution, his historical conditioning, his facticity and forlornness *(Geworfenheit),* in the freedom of his development and the necessary restraints imposed on him by his dialogue. In Marxist philosophy in particular, and to some extent in existential philosophy, man was considered as completely autonomous and hence as the exclusive norm of moral behaviour.

2. *Systematic analysis.* To understand the just claims of an existential ethics, we must start with a truth which can be verified by reflection. It is that the answer to the question as to the right moral decision in a given moment depends on subjective and objective factors which are by their very nature unique. They may be summed up under the term of "situation".

Each situation is unique because each man, his social setting (human world) and to some extent his environment (biological world), are in the stream of history. For man can only take ethical action inasmuch as he is conscious of himself, his social setting and his environment. But this consciousness is constantly changing. The moral agent is developing subjectively, and his social setting and environment are also developing objectively. He develops in terms of his subjective experiences and decisions, which in turn depend on the constant changes of the environment: he changes, his society changes, his world changes.

Furthermore, the subjective relationship to God is only possible through man's social setting and environment (see *God* II, *Charity* II) and hence is realized in perpetual dependence on the changing situation. This means that a constant change in the concrete ethical claim of God on man must also be taken into account. This claim of God on each man, as manifested by the changing situation, may be called the "hour" (cf. Lk 13:44). It is when a special summons goes out to man in his personal history, e.g., in the situation of choosing a marriage-partner, a walk in life, etc., where he must take a decision which will be essential to his salvation.

What God demands of the individual in a given situation or in such an "hour", is recognized directly in experience, and ultimately in the evident claim of an unconditional concrete obligation. Hence the "hour" only strikes insofar as one clearly recognizes that there is nothing else to be done here and now.

This judgment is infallible insofar as the obligation is evident. It is fallible inasmuch as it is reached through prejudices and pre-assessments, that is, insofar as it is dependent on human contingency and moral maturity. For God necessarily wills that man takes moral decisions, in keeping with his conscience, since personal moral action is only possible on these grounds. And to this extent, the obligation pronounced by conscience is infallible. But then again, the verdict of conscience depends on a limited insight into the claims of a situation, and on the subjective attitude towards fulfilling the obligation. Hence the best that conscience can do is to say what is the optimum of correct moral action for a person in a given situation. It cannot say what is the absolute optimum which might be realized if one could have a clear and full view of the demands of a situation and a disposition to moral action fully in keeping with all demands. To this extent, the verdict of conscience is fallible.

One can be thus orientated in conscience both fallibly and infallibly towards the morally obligatory, because the formal moral good attracts the agent in his virtuous reaction. But then again, this ordination depends on how well, in the concrete, the agent can refer the tangible factors of the situation, the physical, social and mental data, the materially perfect and deficient, to the formal moral good. How well does he know the material good as such? — which is, therefore, the relationship of the physical to the formal moral good, and through this, to the absolute good.

Consequently, man is always infallible in his formal search for virtue, since human action always becomes formally good action though the good intention of the agent, and this, as the subjective intention, is always known, at least indirectly. But since the categories of reality, with all their laws and trends, are only accessible in a limited way to individual and social experience — which may be examined scientifically, however, and formulated in manageable scientific laws — knowledge of the way the categories of reality relate to the material good and hence to the absolute good is always mixed with error or at least limited. This is because our *a posteriori* knowledge is fundamentally limited and dependent on our historical situation, and because our subjective moral disposition is always subject to limits in its perfection. Consequently, the absolute will of God can only be known with a mixture of error or at least only in a limited way.

Hence the reason for the intrinsic limitations of human knowledge of the will of God is to be sought in its experiential nature. Human knowledge moves forward step by step, experience by experience, in historical development. For the concrete ethical decision, this means that it can never be simply deduced from general principles or objectivated findings which would be evident and hence infallibly correct.

Hence it is the task of scientific situation ethics to develop methods which will facilitate an existentiell judgment on a situation, apart from the essential meaning of it. It must work out methods which will assure an optimum of existentiell knowledge of the morally good. This guarantee makes a calculated risk legitimate. And given the elements of uncertainty about the essence and existence of man, due to ignorance or error, in any human situation, such risk is always there.

To determine how man's existence stands to his essence and his existentiell possibilities, the following recommendations are made by scientific theology and the Spiritual Exercises (especially the Rules for the Discernment of Spirits), each in their own way.

a) *The purest possible intention in the moral agent.* This depends on the basic moral intention of the agent, that is, on the faith, hope and love with which he accepts, conditionally and unconditionally and hence religiously, his own self and his neighbour. It also depends on his unconditional affirmation of the absolute truth, goodness and meaning, and hence from the more or less unconditional nature of his theological faith, hope and love. It depends further on the actual degree of perfection in his general moral virtues, which must come into play in every moral act, and finally, on the perfection of the particular virtue which has to be exercised in the actual moral decision (see *Habitus*).

b) If an action is to do justice to a situation, the good intention must be put into effect as objectively as possible. This means that the facts of the matter must be ascertained as correctly as possible, intuitively or by study and reflection, but always drawing on the experience of others, including the authorities, to the fullest extent. But in any case, the knowledge in question has to be attained empirically and must take into account the relative independence of the various categories of reality in the world.

c) A decision as true as possible to the will of God implies that the elements of certainty and uncertainty in the decision have been correlated in the best possible way. This means that one has not tried to substitute virtue for objective knowledge, and, vice versa, that one has not shirked the necessary decisions for want of expert knowledge. For there is morally good action only insofar as it is equally well directed to persons and to things, to this and to the other world. The synthesis of the two realms cannot be merely analytical and deductive, by virtue of the general moral principles which alone make any moral decision possible. The synthesis must also be reached through a structure of imperatives built up directly from experience. Reflection on how rational calculation of risk, e.g., the use of the principle of double

effect, can constantly give a new and optimum balance between inner-directedness and other-directedness, between autonomy and heteronomy, has not yet far advanced. It needs also to be supplemented by the empirical sciences, e.g., the findings of psychology on the motivations proper to persons. And the scholastic teaching on the *virtutes generales* will need to be made accessible again.

As regards ethical pedagogy, it follows that we must go beyond a one-sided Platonizing and rationalizing concept of morality which is based on a religiously and morally unjustifiable desire to base all norms directly on the unconditional and the rationally valid. For man is essentially limited and sinful, and can only act on his limited and one-sided moral insight. The law-making authorities, like the individuals, must be further reinforced in their capacity to make independent decisions and to treat them as obligatory (with due allowance for *epikeia*) — though they are only conditionally and historically valid. Further, by reason of the concrete situation (see *Original Sin, Concupiscence*), there is a predisposition to good or evil, for which allowance must be made in taking decisions. This is a fact which must be brought home more clearly.

See also *Human Act, Existence* I, II.

BIBLIOGRAPHY. See bibliography on *Moral Theology* I; also: E. Grisebach, *Gegenwart, eine kritische Ethik* (1928); E. Brunner, "Grisebachs Angriff auf die Theologie", *Zwischen den Zeiten,* VI (1928); J.-P. Sartre, *Existentialism and Humanism* (1948); id., *Being and Nothingness* (1957); R. Egenter, "Kasuistik als christliche Situationsethik", *Münchener Theologische Zeitschrift* 1 (1950), pp. 54–65; T. Steinbüchel, *Die philosophische Grundlegung der katholischen Sittenlehre* (4th ed., 1951), pp. 226–57, 324–57; id., *Religion und Moral im Licht christlicher personaler Existenz* (1951); E. Brisbois, "Le sartrisme et le problème moral", *NRT* 73 (1952), pp. 30–48, 124–45; F. Hürth, "De Ethica Situationis", *Periodica* 41 (1952), pp. 183–249; *ibid.* 45 (1956), pp. 137–204; G. Klubertanz, "St. Thomas and the Knowledge of the Singular", *New Scholasticism* 26 (1952), pp. 135–66; E. Michel, *Gläubige Existenz* (1952); J. Newman, "The Ethics of Existentialism", *Irish Ecclesiastical Record* 77 (1952), pp. 321–32, 421–31; M. Buber, *Good and Evil* (1953); id., *Between Man and Man* (1965); H.-D. Robert, "Phénoménologie existentielle", *Morale Chrétienne et requêtes contemporaines* (1954); D. von Hildebrand, *True Morality and its Counterfeits* (1955); J. Fuchs, "Éthique objective et éthique de situation. A propos de l'Instruction du Saint Office du 2 Février 1956", *NRT* 77 (1956), pp. 789–818; J. Kraus, *Situationsethik als pastoral- und moraltheologisches Problem* (1956); G. Klubertanz, "The Empiricism of Thomistic Ethics", *Proceedings of the American Catholic Philosophical Association* 31 (1957), pp. 1–24; R. Gleason, "Situational Morality", *Thought* 32 (1958), pp. 533–58; L. Lumbreras, "Ethica situationis et doctrina Aquinatis", *Angelicum* 35 (1958), pp. 139–58; W. Molinski, *Philosophische Grundlagen der Situationsethik* (dissertation, Louvain 1958); W. A. Wallace, *Role of Demonstration in Moral Theology* (1962); id., "Existential Ethics in a Thomistic Appraisal", *The Thomist* 27 (1963), pp. 493–515; K. Rahner, *Theological Investigations,* II (1963); J. Fry, *Immobilized Christian* (1963); J. Bökmann, *Aufgaben und Methoden der Moralpsychologie. Im geschichtlichen Ursprung aus der "Unterscheidung der Geister"* (1964); D. and A. von Hildebrand, *Morality and Situation Ethics* (1966); J. Fletcher, *Situation Ethics: The New Morality* (1966); id., *Moral Responsibility: Situation Ethics at Work* (1967); P. Knauer, "Das rechtverstandene Prinzip von der Doppelwirkung als Grundnorm jeder Gewissensentscheidung", *Theologie und Glaube* 2 (1967), pp. 107–33; R. Gleason, *Situational Morality* (1968).

Waldemar Molinski

SOCIAL MOVEMENTS

I. Social Problems. II. Socialism. III. Christian Social Movement. IV. Christian Social Doctrine: A. General. B. Solidarism. C. Subsidiarity. V. Social Work.

I. Social Problems

While the substance of social doctrine — the doctrine of man as a social being (philosophical [metaphysical] and theological anthropology) — holds good everywhere and in every age, it has constantly to be applied in new and different ways because of constant changes in the milieu, the steady increase of population, the growing interdependence of the members of society, and the transformation of production methods by modern technology. These changes have raised questions which imperiously demand an answer and which are known as "social problems". In the present article we single out certain of these problems that have a particular bearing on the disorders and defects of existing society, and consider what can be done to correct them and establish a more satisfactory order. The social question, then, may be defined as an enquiry into the errors and shortcomings of the present social order, and the remedies for which they seem to call.

The social order has always suffered from some defects and errors. In this sense there has always been a social question. Only in quite recent times, however, did it occur to men to challenge the established order; and it was even later when the social question was really "posed". First men had to realize that much, perhaps most, of the distress prevalent at any given period arises from the faulty organization of society.

A handful of highly cultured men, able to take a wider view of things because of their position as statesmen or ecclesiastics, scholars or directors of major charitable works, were the first to gain this insight; but before very long it had become common knowledge, awakening the public to a passionate concern with the social question. For that very reason, of course, the social question brought conflicts of interest to light, and the proposals put forward for its solution are frequently as much at odds as the special interests — real or supposed — of their sponsors.

It would be most logical to examine the actual or, better still, the potential disorders of society, one by one, indicating the remedy or safeguard in each case. But there are many reasons why such a procedure is not feasible, the chief of them being that we normally become aware of aberrations in social life precisely through the suffering that they cause one section of society or another, just as pain first calls our attention to the fact that we are unwell. In the course of time many different social groups, sometimes those of quite recent origin, have been the victim of the established order, or, more often perhaps, of social change. In each case the sufferings of the unfavoured group, recognized as an injustice inflicted by society, are the focus of the social question at that period — sometimes to the neglect of other ills, less obvious and appalling, which presently fade into oblivion.

Our search has a twofold object: a diagnosis (what exactly has gone wrong and why has this happened?), and therapy — which may either treat the symptoms so as to make the disease more bearable, though without curing it, or stop the pain by getting down to its cause.

When Christianity entered the world, slavery was the running sore in the body politic, and *the* "social question" of ancient times. Yet no one doubted the soundness of the institution; high and low took it for granted; even the philosophers, far from attacking slavery, argued in its defence. The vain attempts which the slaves themselves made to shake off the yoke by violence were simply desperate outbursts of hatred for their masters, in no way inspired by the idea that slavery was immoral and ought to be replaced by a more equitable system of labour. The apostles and the ancient Church did not regard slavery as a social evil, much less make any effort to abolish it. It was enough for them that there was no distinction between bondman and free in the kingdom of God, that the slave had the same right as any other man to freedom in Christ. (The suppression of slavery in the 19th century was unquestionably the achievement of humanitarian ethics, working hand in hand with liberal capitalism.)

As to serfdom — which existed in various forms down to the end of the 18th century in Western and Central Europe and lingered on for another hundred years in parts of Eastern Europe — the medieval theologians not only refrained from condemning it as a social abuse, but on the whole felt it was justified. The Peasants' Revolt in Germany, at the time of the Reformation, was not a protest against their condition but the exact opposite. The revolt (insofar as religious fanaticism was not one of its causes) was a protest against a change in their condition, against the introduction of Roman law which deprived the peasant of the protection he had had under consuetudinary German law. What the peasant demanded was not some ideal social order but his traditional legal status vis-à-vis the landed proprietors, which was now being arbitrarily altered to his disadvantage.

Eventually and by degrees, the labouring masses, the proletariat of free wage-earners that came into being with the rise of industrialism, were recognized as a real social phenomenon, one only to be understood in the context of the whole social framework and the transformations it undergoes. The physical distress, the religious and moral degeneration that prevailed among the proletariat could not fail to attract the notice and arouse the compassion of high-minded men, not least among them zealous priests. For long the problem was thought to be one of unfortunate individuals who had drifted away, or been extruded, from agriculture or a craft and who needed to be restored to their former position in society. But what was involved was the common fate of a whole section of society, not the misfortune of a great number of individuals which could have been eased by the works of mercy or by personal or group education. Industrializa-

tion had set off irreversible changes in the whole social structure and the task was to draw the inevitable consequences from this fact. At first, strangely enough, the rising working classes were not interested in a juster social order that would take account of new circumstances and new needs, but demanded a return to the arrangements for their assistance and protection to which they had had a legal claim in the days of their dependence — just as the German peasants had done before them. Towards the middle of the 19th century it was certain intellectuals, either estranged from Christianity or opposed to it on principle, who first understood the situation, chief among them Karl Marx. But many years passed before this insight gained a foothold in ecclesiastical circles. In fact, despite the social encyclicals of 1891, 1931, and 1961, it has not fully come into its own in the Church even today, when it is beginning to be superseded by events.

For decades the question of the workers seemed to be synonomous with the social question in those countries which led the way in industrialization (England, Western and Central Europe, North America). It was in fact the most insistent of all social problems, and public opinion was so absorbed in it that a number of other social problems of equal importance were almost ignored.

Events took a similar course in countries which were industrialized later or which are only now entering upon that phase of development: an initially unbridled capitalism created (or is creating) intolerable conditions, above all a destitution in a proletariat unwilling to put up with their condition once Marx and Engels have awakened them to class-consciousness. In these countries, then, the social question threatened (or threatens) to bring about the violent overthrow, not only of the social and economic order but of the State itself. Revolutions of this kind have already taken place in a number of countries, other factors, however, playing their part, sometimes a dominant one. The Russian Revolution, for example, owed little to the industrial workers of Russia, who were still very few: it was the work of a band of professional revolutionaries who astutely made use of the discontented peasants for their own ends. Much the same thing happened in China.

There can now be no question of identifying the problem of the (industrial) workers with the social problem. In vast areas of the world, notably in Latin America, the agrarian question gives cause for most concern. But the situation is much altered in the older capitalist countries as well: the once destitute proletariat has disappeared in the "affluent society". It is no longer the working class who are in distress but certain sectors of the middle class, not excluding graduates and professional people.

The position of large families is a very difficult one. Many are in need or live from hand to mouth. Industrial society has increasingly become a "commercialized society", interested only in people who offer some service for which there is a market and which is therefore worth paying for. There is no place in such a society for the family, composed of one person who is commercially active and several people who are commercially passive, being either too young or too old to sell their ability. By definition, in fact, commercialized society is an enemy of the family. It has long been customary in some circles to view the social question as essentially a matter of economics, reducing it in effect to the conflict between rich and poor. But today this interpretation has little to recommend it, and quite misses the mark so far as the position of the family is concerned. The problem of the family — the modern social question *par excellence* — has to do, not with raising the living standard of poor families as compared with that of rich families, but with the arrangements that must in all fairness be made as between large families and small families.

On the other hand the economic factor is the primary one involved in the "international" social question (cf. the encyclical *Mater et Magistra,* nos. 155–77), the gulf between the advanced and the under-developed countries of the world, as it were the two contrasting "classes" of world society. Yet even in this case it is daily becoming more evident that the social question involves more than bread and butter. It is as much an ethical, a cultural, a political problem as an economic one.

There are two ways in which one can try to improve social conditions, just as a physician will treat the symptoms as well as the cause of a disease. One can alleviate the sufferings which the existing order unfairly imposes on certain groups within society (remedial legislation), and one can attack the root of the evil by changing the structure of society itself (social reform). The former approach, though commonly traduced as mere "tinkering with symptoms", effectively stops, or at least restrains, the ravages of social evils in many cases where the cause of the trouble, for some reason, cannot be dealt with (at any rate for the time being). Remedial legislation is indicated, for example, if the root of a social evil has not been ascertained, or if insuperable obstacles prevent its being done away with, or if one is at a loss to replace it with anything better. A social order that is unsuitable or has had its day cannot simply be disposed of like so much rubbish to make room for a nicely planned, prefabricated new society.

In actual practice, the boundaries between remedial legislation and social reform are fluid. Many measures are ambivalent. To make the existing order more bearable, of course, tends to preserve it and to lessen the danger of revolution (the stabilizing effect); but at the same time, imperceptibly at first, the new elements thus engrafted in the existing order by degrees produce such far-reaching changes that the final result is a new society (the reformative effect).

Leo XIII declared the social question a "causa cuius exitus probabilis nullus nisi advocata religione et Ecclesia" (*Rerum Novarum,* no. 13), and his successors have repeatedly insisted that the Church, as well as the State and the parties directly concerned, must contribute to its solution. For the social question is inextricably bound up with problems of the cultural and ethical order. What we are about, after all, is nothing less than forming a society that shall be worthy of man as its "author, representative, and goal" (*Mater et Magistra,* no. 219). In the first place, accordingly, the Church must contribute its sound conception of man as he is actually, ordered to a supernatural end — man in *hoc ordine salutis,* known only through the revelation of which the Church is custodian. Moreover, its doctrine and the religious and moral energies to which it gives rise are best fitted to counteract the selfishness and short-sightedness of individuals or sections of society. This does not mean, as has unfortunately been suggested at times, that the social question is a "religious question". It is neither a religious, nor an ethical, nor an economic question, but simply what its name conveys, "the social question". True though it be that grappling with the social question apart from religion and the Church can only produce fragmentary results, we must not conclude that the problem can therefore be "solved" with the help of religion and the Church. Its solution would mean the establishment of Utopia, the restoration of paradise on earth. Many non-Christian social movements, notably early socialism, have held out that promise, preaching a secularist eschatology. Awareness of original sin and its consequences safeguards Christian social doctrine against such allurements; to this extent, at least, the Church's teaching is thoroughly realistic. But for bringing people down to earth there is nothing like practical work, and therefore it is not only possible but eminently worthwhile for the adherents of Christian social doctrine to join forces over a wide area with those who still dream of an earthly paradise. Very little scope indeed would exist for co-operation with non-Catholic Christians — much less with non-Christians — if the social question were really a "religious question", as integralism would have it, and John XXIII would not in that case have been able to exhort Catholics, as he did with such warmth and magnanimity in *Mater et Magistra* and *Pacem in Terris,* to work together with all men of "good will".

See also *Man, Industrialization, Technology.*

BIBLIOGRAPHY. B. Bosanquet, ed., *Aspects of the Social Problem* (1895); J. Messner, *Die Soziale Frage,* I (1928; 7th ed., 1964); R. H. Tawney, *The Acquisitive Society* (1946); O. von Nell-Breuning and H. Sacher, eds., *Wörterbuch der Politik,* III (1949; 2nd ed., 1958); R. Dynes and others, *Social Problems: Dissensus and Deviation in an Industrial Society* (1964); G. Grundlach, *Die Ordnung der menschlichen Gesellschaft,* 2 vols. (1964); J. Cronin, *The Social Teaching of John XXIII* (1964); id., *Christianity and Social Progress* (1965); J. Höffner, *Gesellschaftspolitik aus christlicher Weltverantwortung* (1964); A. Abell, ed., *American Catholic Thought on Social Questions* (1967).

Oswald von Nell-Breuning

II. Socialism

Socialism is the collective name for a multitude of systems and movements critical of existing society. All of them, it is fair to say, attach as much importance to man's social nature as to his individuality, oppose his self-centredness, emphasize his duties, as a member of the community, towards his fellows and particularly towards the various social bodies to which he belongs. In this general sense, socialism embraces Christian social doctrine and the Christian social movement, which in fact were called "Christian socialism" before there was a Marxist

socialism and are still so called from time to time. Sometimes the term "socialism" is applied pejoratively to doctrines and movements which unduly subordinate man's individuality to his social nature, the private person to society, individual well-being to the common good, whereas Christianity rightly considers man the "author, representative, and goal of all social institutions" (*Mater et Magistra,* no. 219). The most striking example of socialism in this pejorative sense is communism, which so exalts the collectivity over the individual, shows such contempt for human dignity, that the majority of socialists no longer recognize it as the most radical wing of their own movement, repudiating it instead as a betrayal of socialism. On the other hand many who consider themselves socialists attach such crucial importance to the dignity of the human person that it is difficult to decide whether they still lean towards collectivism or simply social reform, the more so as in practice their aims generally coincide with those of the social reformers. Nor is radicalism any criterion in this matter. Thus Catholic social teaching demands that the very structure of society be reformed, whereas many socialist parties, which have long enjoyed governmental power, aim at nothing more than remedial legislation that leaves the social structure unchanged. As often as not, Christian labour unions in underdeveloped countries are far more radical in their aims and measures than socialist unions in advanced countries.

Apart from British socialism, whose roots are Christian, the mainstream of socialism derives from frankly non-Christian sources. Its mightiest current since the mid-19th century, Marxist socialism (communism), has been militantly atheistic from the outset. Socialism was long a religion, or a substitute for religion, for a large section of the working class, who considered the Church the ally of capitalism and therefore the enemy of the working man. It must be confessed that the attitude of a great many Christians, unfortunately including many of the higher clergy (despite the Church's social teaching), was such as to create this impression. Even those socialists not the declared enemies of religion were as a rule steeped in the secular spirit of the age of "free-thinking", which is what Bishop Ketteler meant when he called socialism "the natural child of liberalism". Such is still the outlook of many supporters of socialism today. The present attitude of the intellectual leadership, however, is quite another matter, especially since the socialist parties have largely ceased to speak for the working class alone, becoming truly national parties with broad political aims. Whatever the dominance of opportunists and practical materialists in the actual working of socialist politics, men and women of great integrity, including well-known Protestant theologians, are to be found among the intellectual leaders. The transformation of (non-communist) socialism is also due in some degree to the influence that Catholic theologians have exerted from without.

Before the Church can adopt a definitive attitude towards socialism, some definition must be found that embraces all socialist systems and movements (one author, T. Brauer, identifies twenty kinds of socialism, while another, W. Sombart, holds that there are no less than one hundred) but these only (*definitio conveniens omni et soli definito*). Many such attempts have been made, the most recent and suggestive definition being that of Gustav Gundlach: socialism is "a movement affecting the whole of life, essentially a feature of the capitalist age by reason of its scale of values and its methods, which seeks to secure the freedom and earthly happiness of all on a permanent basis by anchoring these in the institutions of an expertly organized human society from which all trace of heteronomy has been banished" (*Staatslexikon*, IV [5th ed., 1931], col. 1693). Pius XI accepts this definition in his encyclical *Quadragesimo Anno*. He sees the hallmark of socialism in the idea that society was set up merely for human convenience ("solius commodi causa humanam consortionem esse institutam", *ibid.*, no. 118); its whole purpose is to provide men with the advantages to be derived from the division of labour; consequently socialism sacrifices higher human values — notably individual freedom — to the most efficient possible production of material goods, alleging that this loss of freedom in the process of production is more than counterbalanced by the wider freedom men will have to shape their own destiny thanks to the abundance of material goods that will presently be available. The Pope then objects that effect can be given to this purely utilitarian view only by coercion on a grand scale, since no basis for legitimate authority is provided and the authority of God is thus extruded from society (*ibid.*, no. 119). Such a conception is obviously incompatible with the Christian idea of man and the world:

whether in the order of creation or the order of redemption, God is lord of human society no less than he is of the human individual.

There is disagreement as to whether the type of socialism outlined in *Quadragesimo Anno* has ever existed in that form. It is certain that forms of socialism existed in 1931 which did not exhibit the features described in the encyclical and accordingly were not affected by the papal condemnation — the British Labour Party for one (which the Archbishop of Westminster hastened to reassure on this point), and probably Scandinavian socialism as well. Elsewhere, chiefly in the Latin countries, people wondered where this "mitigated socialism" was to be seen which, as the encyclical said, had so far abandoned the class struggle and collectivization as to accord with Christian social doctrine. Evidently what the Pope had in mind was the "revisionist socialism" then widespread in Germany, which was no longer orthodox Marxism but still contained more or less Marxist remnants. Most of its adherents were not religiously inclined and thought that an economy organized on the basis of a good deal of coercion was most likely to ensure the maximum production of goods and their "just" (more equal) distribution. Yet it seems doubtful whether they really believed society was based on nothing more than a convenient division of labour, denied that man is naturally ordered to society and to the values that can neither exist nor be conceived of apart from society, and repudiated any obligation to the common good. However this may be, libertarian, democratic socialism of the present day has been so modified that the purely economic, utilitarian conception of society is odious to it; in the socialism rejected by *Quadragesimo Anno* democratic socialism finds features of capitalism on the one hand and communism on the other, but no resemblance to itself.

The socialist theory outlined in *Quadragesimo Anno* is doubtless what John XXIII calls "formula disciplinae" which "postquam definite descripta est, iam non mutatur" (*Pacem in Terris*, no. 159). But Pius XI had already anticipated the point, and noted that movements arising from such "falsa philosophorum placita" are inevitably subject to change. Hence his verdict that socialism is always incompatible with Catholic doctrine was prudently modified by the proviso, "si vere manet socialismus" (*Quadragesimo Anno*, no. 117). In terms of the "formula . . . definite descripta", the libertarian, democratic socialism of the present day has clearly ceased to be such "socialism". John XXIII bears out this judgment by making only brief and indirect reference to his predecessor's condemnation of "socialism" (*Mater et Magistra*, no. 34) without adopting that position in the doctrinal part of his own encyclical. Of course it does not follow that modern democratic socialism agrees with Catholic doctrine at all points. Much weight must still attach to Pius XI's serious warnings against the "socialism" which he described, tributary to materialism and ending in Bolshevism — that may be a fellow-traveller in many movements today, and affect them in various degrees.

Now that movements have arisen, in the newly independent Afro-Asian countries, which regard themselves as "socialist" but have almost nothing in common with what has been known pejoratively as socialism, even in the broadest sense, it is less possible than ever to pass any global judgment on socialism. What chiefly concerns the new Afro-Asian forms of "socialism" is not criticizing society, much less capitalism, but coming to grips with the multitude of problems that their people inherit. They criticize colonialism rather than the social order. "Socialism" seems to offer them a middle way between the industrialism, imperialism, and colonialism of Western Europe and America, on the one hand, and Russian and Chinese communism, with *its* colonialism, on the other. Were the Church to condemn "socialism" in general, the result in these countries would be the most baneful confusion and dismay.

Nor can it be readily determined whether socialism is a philosophy or has a philosophical basis. Marxism (dialectical and historical materialism) certainly claims the status of a philosophy. For many socialists of the libertarian, democratic school socialism sums up an ethical ideal, which influences their thought and action (though for them socialism is neither a religion nor a substitute for religion). But they do not all derive these principles from the same philosophical source. The Frankfurt Manifesto of the Socialist International, 3 July 1951, and the Godesberg Declaration of the German Social Democratic Party, 1960, state in set terms that one may be led to the socialist position not only by the Marxist social analysis, or some other, but also by humanitarian ideals or belief in Christian revelation; and a leading theorist has said that although there is no socialist philosophy, one cannot be a good socialist without some philosophical foundation. Here is a problem that has still to be resolved: can a large-scale social movement, a political party, prosper if it recognizes or presupposes certain values without seeking any ultimate justification for them — leaving this task to its followers, who may therefore adopt this philosophy or that? Or must the movement, the party, itself take up an explicit philosophical position, thus limiting its support to such of the public as accept that philosophy? The question hardly arises in a society that is philosophically homogeneous, for example a purely Catholic state. But it does where a society is philosophically pluralist, and in this case a socialism which neither is nor aspires to be a philosophy or world-view must frankly face the problem.

Protestant theologians have taken a peculiar attitude towards socialism. Many Protestant ministers support libertarian, democratic socialism, obviously seeing no conflict between its aims and principles and their own faith; numbers of them, in fact, regard this type of socialism as the practical expression of Protestant social ethics. Some well-known Protestant theologians are to be found among the leading theorists of the movement, and certain of them have constructed a "religious socialism". It is more difficult to understand the attitude of many Protestant theologians towards Marxism (atheistic communism). Obviously they do not approve of atheism. But not a few consider that there is much to be said for the communist-socialist critique of our society ("a fact the Popes have never denied": *Quadragesimo Anno*, no. 120), which often rightly condemns conditions that Christians should long ago have set to rights. (Communist) socialism, they say, is a judgment of God upon ourselves. Instead of wishing to take the field against its irreligious elements, we ought to accept the chastisement we deserve, bitter as it is, and remedy our own failings and neglect. The Catholic will answer it in the words of the Lord: "These things you ought to have done without neglecting the others."

See also *Liberalism, Marxism, Totalitarianism, Pluralism.*

BIBLIOGRAPHY. For a detailed bibliography, see *Staatslexikon*, VII (6th ed.), cols. 303–24. — W. Sombart, *Socialism and the Social Movement* (1909); M. Beer, *History of British Socialism*, 2 vols. (1920); C. Joad, *Introduction to Modern Political Theory* (1924); G. D. H. Cole, *Fabian Socialism* (1943);

id., *History of the Labour Party* (1948); K. Renner, *Die neue Welt und der Sozialismus: Einsichten und Ausblicke des lebenden Marxismus* (1946); James Connolly, *Socialism and Nationalism*. Introduction and notes by D. Ryan (1948); id., *The Workers' Republic*. Introduction by W. McMullen (1951); S. Hook, *Political Power and Personal Freedom* (1959); Aneurin Bevan, *In Place of Fear* (1961); R. H. Tawney, *The Radical Tradition* (1964); J. Noyes, *History of American Socialism* (1965); R. Crossman, *The Politics of Socialism* (1965); A. Langner, ed., *Katholizismus und freiheitlicher Sozialismus in Europa* (1965); E. Cheyney, *Modern English Reform: From Individualism to Socialism* (1962); H. Laidlaw, *History of Socialism* (revised ed., reprint 1968).

Oswald von Nell-Breuning

III. Christian Social Movement

The Christian social movement is a recent development, social problems in the modern sense having come to light very late in the course of human history. Aristotle called man a ζῷον πολιτικόν, which is generally translated *ens sociale*. But in fact he and his successors for the next two thousand years recognized only the *societas politica*. For them society and the State were identical. Only in our own day have the two been clearly distinguished, and attention been turned to social problems as contrasted with political ones. There is a growing realization that the sort of life which people will lead in a community depends not merely on the juridical structure of the State but to a great extent on social forces which are non-political (and in this sense "spontaneous"); that together with the State, or even against it, these forces carry tremendous weight either for good or ill. There are many functions which must be left to voluntary associations — formed, it may be, specifically for the purpose — and not to the State, either because the State cannot do these things at all or because it can do them less well. These associations and their activities, the life astir within, we call "movements". Those that spring from the Christian view of the world and from Christian love we call the "Christian social movement". It is to be found at work inside and outside the Catholic Church.

Today the status of the Christian social movement in the Catholic Church is fully acknowledged. Since the time of Leo XIII the Popes themselves have been its leaders. Yet the opposition with which the movement has had to contend from the first still stubbornly persists. First, redemption is commonly interpreted in individualistic terms: the supernatural life of grace which Christ won for the redeemed by dying on the cross is an intensely personal possession of each individual; and since society cannot receive this gift, neither can it have been redeemed by Christ. One can understand the prevalence of this narrow view at a period when the Church was envisaged almost exclusively in juridical terms, as a *societas perfecta* analogous to the State, which was also predominantly regarded as an apparatus of government; so that Church and State confronted each other not as two communities of persons but as two powers, the spiritual and the temporal. But this approach still influences us now that we have learnt once more to see the Church rather as the "people of God" and the *Christus totus*. We are reminded that Christ himself declined the role of a social reformer; that his gospel contains no programme of social reform; that the primitive Church simply accepted the social conditions of that age, obviously unconscious of any mission to improve them. Such principles govern the thinking and even more the practice of many Catholics today, though Pius XI expressly declares that the Church does have a social mission and though Pius XII condemns the opposite opinion as spiritualism and supernaturalism.

Strangely enough, a second grave obstacle in the path of the Christian social movements has been the glorious tradition of Catholic charitable works. From apostolic times the Church felt the spiritual and corporal works of mercy to be its special concern, and they have been carried on in every age under the supervision of the bishops. Thus it was widely supposed, at the beginning, that the Christian social movement wished to extend this charitable aid not merely to needy individuals but also to the poorer classes in general, and ecclesiastical pronouncements were worded in this sense: another new form of the works of mercy seemed to be developing. Indeed the theological virtue of charity may well have inspired these first efforts, and the people concerned may have been chiefly occupied with the works of mercy. But the movement itself was of quite a different nature. By definition the Christian social movement, like any social movement, seeks to establish a just social order and to support the just demands of those individuals and groups whose rights have been infringed. No doubt love must perfect this work (*Quadragesimo Anno,* no. 137), but the work itself is a matter of justice. In fact we may go so far as to say that this work is essentially *profane*, since its object is the creation of a social order for all men without exception and not merely for members of the mystical body — a society which will respect the rights of every man and in which no man shall feel himself an alien. A social movement guided by the Catholic hierarchy might, of course, do much good outside Catholic circles (as a Catholic hospital, for example, will often care for patients who are not Catholics). But if Catholic men and women are to merit the praise which Pius XI has for the pioneers of the Christian social movement (*Quadragesimo Anno*, nos. 19 ff.), then, imbued with the Church's principles and fortified by its sacraments, they must become active and influential in our legislatures and in all other appropriate spheres of public life, recommended by their obvious personal qualifications and not as emissaries of the hierarchy. Recent papal utterances sharply distinguish the Christian social movement from the works of mercy, but in practice the separation is not yet complete. Inertia alone does not account for this fact. Separate as they may be in theory, the borderline between the two domains is blurred in certain areas; a single situation may call for charity to relieve a person in immediate distress and at the same time for social reform so that an injustice may be corrected. This, in fact, was normally the case at the beginning. Leo XIII still regards the workingman as one of the poor, the working class as *miserum vulgus, multitudo egens* (*Rerum Novarum*, no. 29); whereas Pius XI clearly distinguishes between the position of the proletariat — which is not necessarily pauperism — and the destitution widespread in underdeveloped countries (*Quadragesimo Anno*, no. 59).

The social movement is the antithesis of charitable works. It is a movement "from below", a movement of self-help on the part of those who are disadvantaged by the present social order. It does not beg for sympathy. Fully conscious of its own power, the movement is resolved to use this power to secure its just demands and therefore deliberately entrenches itself in strategic positions. By no stretch of the imagination can this militancy, this readiness to seize one's rights if they be not freely given, be considered "social charity". Many, indeed, have thought it anti-Christian, particularly where the workers' movement is concerned. Because Christians failed to read the signs of the times and held

aloof too long, the workers' movement arose in some countries under the auspices of materialist atheism and drew a great part of the working class into its ranks. Here Christian workers founded a rival movement, based on Christian principles, which was recognized as a legitimate part of the movement only after long and bitter conflict. Christian faith, love, and morality do not teach us to acquiesce in social injustice. It is far more Christian to defend one's own rights and those of one's fellows by force when necessary. It is the part of Christian heroism to banish hatred and envy from this struggle, to limit demands to those of justice and the common good, at the same time fighting on a second front against organized atheism which would rob the worker of his faith. Catholics were very slow to realize all this. For decades moral theologians were unable to cope with the problems posed by the existence of the Christian social movement. They could not decide whether it was lawful even to form trade unions or to go on strike, let alone whether particular aims and policies of the unions were legitimate.

Further difficulties arise for a Christian social movement "from below" because Catholics still tend to regard the hierarchy which God has set up in the Church as a model for the structure of civil society. This idea has not only led Catholics astray in political theory but encouraged a mistaken attitude toward social problems. Pius XII (Christmas Message, 1944; Address to the Rota, 1946) dispelled the confusion so far as political theory is concerned; but the mistaken social attitude evidently still persists when, for example, prominent advocates of Catholic social doctrine even today can conceive of co-operation between capital and labour only on the basis that the workers (humanely treated, of course) remain subject to the ultimate authority and direction of those who own the means of production, rejecting out of hand other solutions which take more account of the elementary principle of Catholic social doctrine that labour is not a mere commodity. This state of affairs is aggravated by the fact that the clergy in many countries, especially the higher clergy, are of aristocratic background and have a sense of solidarity with the upper classes, whose feudal mentality they share (often, no doubt, unconsciously).

Thus, despite the unmistakable teaching of the Popes, the Christian social movement still encounters formidable opposition among

105

Catholics. What is perhaps worse, it has to contend with general indifference and with the preconceptions of those who have no quarrel with the established order so long as it appears to serve their own interests. We must therefore prove that a Christian social movement is both legitimate and necessary, showing 1) what relevance the Church and the faith have to human society and its present condition, 2) what there is about the Christian social movement that is specifically "Christian" and enables it to produce different or better results than any other social movement, and 3) what need there is of such a Christian movement.

1. The Church regards itself as "the vital principle of human society" (Pius XII, 20 February 1946). It is not simply one community among the many which together form human society: it is its desire and its mission to be the "soul" of this society, wholly penetrating it with its supernatural life. If society is "that cohesion of men which is prerequisite if they are to achieve anything of objective cultural value", then the Church wishes to orientate this cohesion, from within, towards that ultimate value which is God revealing and communicating himself to redeemed mankind. Social arrangements and conditions, as well as men's conduct in society, fall within the competence of the Church as the custodian and interpreter of the natural moral law, and it must judge of them by this law and *ratione peccati*. And if as Pius XI declares "the whole social and economic organization of present-day society makes it extraordinarily difficult for a vast number of human beings to attain eternal salvation" (*Quadragesimo Anno,* no. 130), then the Church has an urgent pastoral duty to see that these conditions are improved; it will not do simply to preach a change of heart, our institutions themselves must be reformed.

2. Whereas purely philanthropic social movements, for example, seek only to establish a just society — or what they consider such — in the temporal sphere, guided, of course, by purely temporal ideals, the aims of the Christian social movement in this world are always subordinated to the last end of man; its principles are warranted by divine revelation and, in the case of Catholics, by the magisterium of the Church. If the driving force behind other social movements is often the self-interest of a particular section of society, the energies of the Christian social movement ultimately derive from Christian faith and love. Thus the Christian movement generally keeps a sense of proportion and avoids extremism; notably it resists the temptation to identify the interests of one group with the common good. Its attitude is realistic, far removed from the false messianism which expects social reforms to usher in an earthly paradise.

3. Every social movement is based on some kind of world-view or philosophy, conscious or unconscious, sound or unsound, and this world-view directly influences the things men do when their sense of social responsibility leads them to take part in public life; so that any such public activities on the part of a Christian believer are in themselves a part, perhaps anonymous, of the Christian social movement. Certainly, therefore, the sum of the efforts which Christians are making to solve the social problems of our time must be called a Christian social movement. But the co-operation of Christians, if only because of their huge numbers, cannot be dispensed with.

The necessity for an institutionalized Christian social movement, however, is less obvious. Should Christians (Catholics) attempt to discharge their social duties entirely within organizations of their own? Such bodies may have to be created where materialistic humanist socialisms have been first in the field and imbued workers' associations or political parties with a world-view which is not our own or which indeed we find quite unacceptable. When this state of affairs has come about through our neglect, we may be compelled to set up rival organizations which will operate in accordance with our religion or at least will not conflict with it. But even in such cases it will be quite feasible for us to co-operate fraternally with non-Christian bodies so long as their aims and principles are similar to ours, and also with non-Christians in *common* organizations where tolerance is observed by both sides. Such co-operation is not possible with Communists, because their values are totally different from ours, nor with the adherents of any other form of totalitarianism, because all totalitarianism is inherently intolerant. In contrast to the timid reserve of earlier times, John XXIII and Vatican II have urged Catholics to co-operate with others, including non-Christians. In practice special Christian (Catholic) organizations seem to be necessary at the present time in some countries, at least in order to prepare people for their social responsibilities. Whether such organizations are necessary for social action itself will have to be decided in each country according to local circumstances.

What gave rise to the social movements of modern times was the invasion by industrialism of a largely agrarian society steeped in tradition. Conservative and reactionary circles failing to understand what was happening and regarding industrialization simply as a disaster for the peasant and the craftsman, defended the old order as if it were permanently valid, and tried to restore it where it had been destroyed. Hence to this day the Christian social movement is suspected of "social romanticism" — of taking refuge in a world of illusion instead of grappling with hard facts. It was certainly very late in the day when the Christian social movement finally realized that the working class, ever more numerous and more powerful, is destined to become the decisive force in human society. For many years the Christian social movement was — as it still remains in the developing countries — as anti-capitalist as contemporary socialism, though for opposite reasons: whereas the aim of socialism is, as it were, to outstrip capitalism, the Christian social movement was constantly involved in attempts to restore semi-feudal conditions, a patriarchal society. It was often difficult for people imbued with 19th century individualism to perceive that the common good demands the sacrifice not only of customs which are dear to one but also of rights which, though legitimately acquired, have become superannuated.

Pius XI having disposed once for all of individualism *(Quadragesimo Anno)*, the way was open for John XXIII *(Mater et Magistra)* and Vatican II *(Gaudium et Spes)* to focus attention on the common good of mankind as a whole and the world-wide social problems which arise from the co-existence of an "affluent society" in some countries with extreme poverty in others. Today these latter are ravaged by the same unbridled capitalism (not yet tempered by social action) that formerly prevailed in the highly industrialized countries.

Until the 20th century the Christian social movement was mostly confined to the more advanced countries of Europe. In the United States the conditions which would have produced a social movement were altogether lacking until the time of the Depression (1929–33). On the other hand a social movement similar to the European one arose in a number of developing countries where the colonial powers had set up industries, and a Christian social movement began to stir among the native élite who had been educated in mission schools. In all the Latin countries, and throughout the developing world, the Christian social movement directly faces the Communist threat and has thus to fight on two fronts at once. In order to compete at all with Communism it must take on a revolutionary, anti-capitalist guise, which makes it the more difficult to work out a sound, positive programme with goals that can actually be achieved.

The Christian social movement also exists outside the Catholic Church. Among the Eastern Orthodox there is scarcely a trace of it. The mystical and contemplative mentality of these Churches tends to discourage social action. There has been no scope for it anyway either in Tsarist Russia or in the present Soviet bloc. The movement for social reform initiated in the mid-19th century by some prominent Anglicans (F. D. Maurice, C. Kingsley) met with little success at the time but exercised considerable indirect influence in the development of trade unions and working-class education, whereas the social conscience of the Non-Conformists played an important part in the formation of the British Labour Party.

Today (with the exception of those under Communist rule, as observed above) a powerful and resolute social movement flourishes in all the Churches which have joined the ecumenical movement. The way was paved for it by the Stockholm conference on Life and Work, 1924, and its theological bases were worked out at the conference on Faith and Order held at Lausanne in 1927. The conferences at Amsterdam (1948), Evanston (1954), and New Delhi (1961) each made important contributions to the movement. The Churches of the World Council of Churches, unlike the Catholic Church (*Mater et Magistra,* nos. 186–99), are frankly prepared to sanction and encourage the official steps which are being taken to limit the number of births in countries already suffering from over-population. In other respects, however, there is a remarkable unanimity, so far as practical aims and policies are concerned, among the members of the World Council and between them and ourselves; the "responsible society" which they seek to establish is in effect what we mean by solidarity.

See also *Spiritualism, Supernaturalism, Justice, Industrialization, Romanticism.*

BIBLIOGRAPHY. A. V. Woodworth, *Christian Socialism in England* (1903); G. E. Raven, *Christian Socialism, 1848–1854* (1920); G. Goyau, *Autour du catholicisme social,* 4 vols. (1924); G. C. Binyon, *The Christian Socialist Movement in England* (1931); A. M. Knoll, *Der soziale Gedanke im modernen Katholizismus* (1932); M. B. Reckitt, *Faith and Society: A Study of the Structure, Outlook and Opportunity of the Christian Social Movement in Great Britain and the U.S.A.* (1932); A. M. Crofts, *Catholic Social Action: Principles, Purpose and Action* (1948); H. Rollet, *L'action sociale des catholiques en France 1871–1901* (1948); J. B. Duroselle, *Les débuts du catholicisme social en France* (1951); J. N. Moody, ed., *Church and Society: Catholic Social and Political Thoughts and Movements 1789–1950* (1953); K. von Schuschnigg, "Origins of Christian Social Reform in Central Europe", *Social Order* 4 (1954), pp. 409ff.; 5 (1955), pp. 29ff.; M. P. Fogarty, *Christian Democracy in Western Europe 1820–1953* (1957); K. Brüls, *Geschichte der katholisch-sozialen Bewegung in Deutschland* (1958); G. Beuret, *Die katholisch-soziale Bewegung in der Schweiz* (1959); World Council of Churches, *The Official Report of the World Conference on Church and Society, Geneva, 1966* (1967).

Oswald von Nell-Breuning

IV. Christian Social Doctrine

A. GENERAL

Christian social doctrine is usually taken simply as the equivalent of the social doctrine of the Catholic Church. Whether there exists as well a Protestant social doctrine comparable in extent and importance or only a Protestant teaching on social ethics, is disputed even among Protestants themselves. Scarcely even the rudiments of a social doctrine can be found in the Eastern Churches. In this article we deal chiefly with Catholic social doctrine. At the end we give a brief sketch of its Protestant counterpart.

1. *Concept.* Catholic social doctrine, as it is taught in papal and other Church documents, as well as in the popular and scientific writings of Catholic scholars and exponents, can be defined as "that unified body of teaching, in the Christian dispensation, on the organization of terrestrial human society as a whole and in its individual parts, which sets a standard for the progressive ordering of society by man through the exercise of his natural social powers" (G. Gundlach in *Staatslexikon,* IV [6th ed.], col. 914).

"In the Christian dispensation" both philosophical and theological knowledge is possible. In Catholic social doctrine, as it is at present, knowledge by use of reason clearly predominates. Thus it is — at least in the present stage of development — almost entirely social philosophy and only in a very limited way social theology. It needs further development on the theological side — if for no other reason than to keep abreast of Protestant social ethics whose line of argument is basically theological, proceeding as it does from sacred Scripture. Statements taken directly from the *depositum fidei* will be only very rarely applicable to concrete situations; in general a social theology will present conclusions *ex ratione theologica.*

The human society with which Catholic social doctrine is concerned is that of this world.

Insofar as it is social philosophy, Catholic social doctrine must build on the basis of experience supplied for the most part by the empirical sciences, especially biology, physiology and psychology. There is a particularly close relationship with the empirical social sciences ever in process of expansion. Of these, the science known as sociology has always been liable to the temptation to regard itself as a philosophical science or as a substitute or heir to philosophy. This calls for an attitude of critical reserve or even opposition, yet it does not entail rejecting the fruits of sociological investigations, provided they have been reliably conducted and critically examined.

In contrast to the empirical social sciences, the Catholic social doctrine deals with the "ordered structure" of society. This means that it is a social metaphysics or ontology and therefore also a *normative* science or *deontology* of society. This gives it also its position in the disputed question of value judgments. As a theoretical science it rests on the basis of the *philosophia perennis* and thus accepts "essentialism", in contrast to positivism and neo-positivism which wholly reject it. Its metaphysics is based on the axiom: "ens est unum, verum, bonum". There is knowledge not only of *being* in general, but of *essences (quod quid est),* and from these flows essential knowledge about what are values and what are not, especially about ethical values and their opposite, about what ought to be and what ought not to be. Not everything that has been regarded as knowledge of the essential has proved to be so; therefore Catholic social doctrine always examines expository statements very carefully before it draws normative conclusions from them. It is also very conscious of the need to guard against wishful thinking, since it distorts the vision of the facts and even much more insidiously insinuates itself into normative judgments. But it will never allow the spheres of being and duty, or the knowledge of being and knowledge of duty, to be isolated from one another. Nor is it content to systematize in a scientific way ethical norms — in this case social ethics — and test them for logical coherence: in contrast to all types of positivism, as well as to the prevailing Protestant opinion, it holds essentially to this: the principle of social order, or, what amounts to the same thing, the norms of social ethics are capable of being known by our *intellect,* although experience shows they are generally known clearly only in the light of revelation *(necessitas relativa revelationis).*

Although man is, and will remain, in many ways a riddle for us, yet Catholic social doctrine has a convincing answer to the question: "What is man?" From what man *is* (not this or that man, but man as such), it deduces what befits or behoves man *(honestum)* and what is unworthy of him *(turpe),* what is his relationship to his fellow-man and to God, namely that God's will binds him, that he *must* do what is *honestum* and *may* not do what is *turpe.* We express this briefly as follows: we have a *concept of man* and from this concept follows logically our *concept of the order of society.*

Revelation teaches us that man is not only a natural image of God, but is called as well to a supernatural likeness to God and to his sonship in grace, to be brother and co-heir to the incarnate Son of God, member of his mystical body, the Church, of which he is the head; also that his Church is not only *Christus totus,* but also a society, taking its place among other societies. All this is a very substantial enrichment by revelation of our knowledge of man. What follows for social doctrine in general and especially for the understanding of the *socia(bi)litas* of man is a matter on which opinions vary.

The Church itself, as a social structure, has been hitherto almost exclusively studied from the specifically juridical point of view *(societas perfecta);* there is as yet scarcely any social doctrine *about* the Church. From its object this would be social theology. The address of Pius XII of 2 February 1946 to the College of Cardinals made a beginning, but this has not been followed up.

The relations of Church and society, Church and State, which are so frequently discussed, also presume that God has revealed himself in Jesus Christ and has founded this one Church. This section of the doctrine is left for the most part to the teaching of fundamental theology or dogmatic theology on the Church. As for marriage, the usual practice is to deal only with natural marriage in social doctrine, and in doing this the supposition is made that the unity and indissolubility of marriage can be proved from reason; sacramental marriage of baptized persons, including its demands on State and society, is then left to other disciplines, especially canon law.

The notion of "person" is basic to the entire social doctrine. Yet on this there is a fundamental dispute as to whether the *mysterium SS. Trinitatis* enables us to go beyond what is ascertainable by philosophical analysis and to deepen the concept of the person in the sense of being open to others, in contrast to the enclosed nature of the individual; also whether it is permissible to draw analogical conclusions from the intratrinitarian relationships to the social relationships between human beings. *If so,* we would arrive at a radically theological social doctrine; *if not,* social doctrine would remain as a whole a philosophic science with certain "additions" of a theological nature.

Whatever may be said about this, the method used by the Popes, and especially by Pius XII, of developing the doctrine philosophically and of taking the motives for action from the world of faith, has great practical advantages. In this way the Popes could address themselves not only to believing Catholics but to all — apart indeed from that relatively small group who adhere to a philosophy which sets an unbridgeable chasm between the world of being and the world of values and in whose judgment to conclude from being to duty would be a flagrant offence against logic. In fact the papal pronouncements reach the ears of a very wide circle of unbelievers and are received with great interest. There is this also to be said: a theologically derived social doctrine would convey the image of a society all of whose members have the Catholic faith and live according to its teachings, whereas we live in an ideologically pluralistic society, and it is in the shaping of this society we must co-operate. We may not impose on this society an order, corresponding indeed to our convictions, but which would do violence to those who think differently and would prevent them from living according to their conscience. We must build with others a society we can feel at home in, because it will give us a fair deal, above all in allowing us to live according to our conscience, but also one that can be accepted by others as well, because it is fair to them too and does not expect from them anything they would have to reject as being against their conscience. A social doctrine that is built on sound human reasoning and addresses itself to all men of good will, has the chance of giving a lead and indicating goals which for the widest circles are not only acceptable but will actually be accepted. If in recent decades so many of the social teachings of the Church, with which it once stood in direct opposition to the spirit of the times and consequently almost alone, have come to be universally accepted, if neo-liberalism and neo-socialism converge ever more closely on Catholic social teaching, it seems even providential that the Popes have chosen this road (which remained that of Vatican II in spite of its theological effort).

2. *Content.* Catholic social doctrine sees in man the personal dignity proper to his nature but just as essentially it views him as directed to society ("naturally social", see above). Society does not exist outside or even above men who are bound by the social bond, but entirely *in* them and *for* them.

This results in that peculiar mutual relationship of individual to society which is formulated in the principle of solidarity: the individual is by his nature ordered to society and this, in turn, to him. Briefly, this means "mutual involvement". Every single individual is as a member — at least as long as he is a member — inextricably involved in its destiny; and the society can in turn not loose itself from its involvement with its members; the normative aspect follows: every individual shares in the responsibility for the success or failure of the community; this in turn bears responsibility for all its members ("each for all, all for each"). Thus the principle is fundamentally a principle of being and derivatively an ethical principle (see B below).

The relationship of individual and society is more exactly determined by the principle of subsidiarity: society should be helpful to its members, especially its ultimate members, the individuals, that is, it should promote their own activity, not suppress or absorb their individual life. This *gravissimum principium* (*Quadragesimo Anno,* no. 79) works in two ways: on the one hand it opposes collectivist, especially totalitarian, tendencies and on this side it must continue to be applied in present-day society; on the other hand — whence its name: *subsidium afferre* — it demands from social groups that they give their members generous help, especially help to self-help. Insofar as Catholic authors expound this principle in different ways, there is question less of different views than that some stress one side and others the other. The strange attacks of Protestant authors rest on obvious misunderstandings. The principle has been given surprisingly sympathetic attention by democratic socialists (see C below).

The central idea of Catholic social doctrine is the *bonum commune.* Unfortunately this term is used in two different senses by the scholastic followers of St. Thomas and those of Suarez. There are two words in English for this concept: common good and common welfare. The common good is that value or sum of values which forms the goal of all the activity of a particular society; this can be a very limited utility value, or it can be the sum total of all the cultural values attainable by man. It is in this elevated sense that Thomistic authors used the term "common good" which then consists in the *perfectio naturae specificae humanae.* The "common welfare" in contrast to the common good is "an organizational and organizing value". It consists in this, that a society is rightly organized, i.e., in such a way that it can fulfil its functions, and is thus enabled to co-ordinate and activate the powers of its members too with a view to securing the common good. In this sense the Suarezians speak of the *bonum commune;* usually the papal documents too use this terminology, indeed *Mater et Magistra,* no. 65, defines *bonum commune* in this way. Thus understood, the common welfare is a most important value in the service of the good, whereas the common good is a value in itself.

These differences which have their following in the two schools of thought we have mentioned, make themselves apparent only when the social principles and especially the notion of the *bonum commune* are subjected to a deeper and more speculative analysis and evaluation; otherwise they appear only occasionally, e.g., in the teaching on the right of ownership, which the Thomists see as justified by the *bonum commune,* whereas spokesmen of the other school derive it from the personal nature of man and *end up* with the consideration due to the *bonum commune.* Perhaps it can be said with all due reserve that in general the one school sees the problem more from the objective point of view and the other more from the subjective, just as ethical principles (principles of moral theology) can be thought of either from the point of view of the law as a pre-existing, objective norm, or from conscience as the subjective appropriation and realization of morality.

In its details, Catholic social doctrine deals with the different societies, especially the family and the State as *societates naturales.* The former is nowadays clearly taken to mean only the *societas coniugalis et parentalis.* It is more difficult to determine what is intended in speaking of the *res publica* ("State") and especially when it is called a *societas perfecta.* Nowadays, especially since *Pacem in Terris,* one must include the complex of international and supranational institutions; many statements about the "State" include also member groups, especially those "political" communities with more or less administrative autonomy. With regard to the so-called *corps intermédiaires* or *puissances intermédiaires,* especially in the question of whether they belong in the sphere of the State or of private associations or in a third group, there is a division of views: in *Quadragesimo Anno,* following in this German legal thinking, the latter opinion is held, for *Mater et Magistra* whose thought is more in accord with Roman law, "public" and "private" are sufficient without a third principle of distinction.

Popes and bishops have *on particular occasions* made statements on social matters. Thus all official Church documents are written for an occasion and, as such, are not complete or systematic textbook expositions. It is clear from them how the circumstances of time and current interest determine the matters dealt with. Leo XIII directs his attention to the question of the workers in the capitalist industry of Central and Western Europe and to a limited extent of North America. Pius XI takes up the question of the entire social order, but still chiefly from the point of view of industrial capitalism.

John XXIII includes and emphasizes agriculture and also the service industries and, since the Church had even under his immediate predecessors become more and more world-wide, addresses himself to world problems, especially those of the developing countries. This illustrates clearly how Catholic social doctrine, in keeping with the definition given at the beginning, is concerned with the structures of society as a whole and in its various parts and with the task of promoting social order in an ever-changing world.

3. *Binding force.* The views of Catholic experts are not sufficient to constitute Catholic social doctrine; binding force pertains only to the official doctrinal and disciplinary pronouncements of the Popes and the bishops. The teaching authority of the Church can propose doctrine for acceptance, the disciplinary authority can impose binding decrees. The Church claims teaching authority, as Pius XI expressly states, "in omnibus, quae ad regulam morum referuntur", but rejects it just as certainly "in iis quae artis sunt" (*Quadragesimo Anno,* no. 41). In the social, economic and political spheres too the Church has to proclaim and authentically interpret the natural and revealed moral law; this also necessarily includes the assertion of those essential truths from which moral and juridical norms flow. It can also proclaim all other truths which are necessarily (not only logically) connected with the truths of faith. On purely factual matters, however, e.g., on the situation of social groups, conditions of production, distribution of income and wealth, etc., it has only purely human knowledge such as every research worker can acquire for himself; its statements on these matters and the claims it deduces from them will therefore have only that degree of certainty that pertains to the available information, the experts consulted, etc. The result is: the Church enunciates basic principles and norms in virtue of its own God-given teaching authority; in exercise of its pastoral office it applies these norms to those concrete situations and cases demanding a solution; the validity of these applications depends in each case on a judgment which has no more than human certainty. Often this judgment is dependent in turn on preliminary questions of a clearly specialized, technical nature (*quae artis sunt),* for which the Church in default of supernatural illumination is dependent on the competence of the experts. A particular

case of this which regularly occurs is when it is a question of judging whether a certain course of action is permissible or not in view of its probable good or evil consequences. In *Mater et Magistra,* no. 239, and again in *Pacem in Terris,* no. 160, the Church expressly requires the obedience of the faithful when the hierarchy apply the principles of Catholic social doctrine to concrete cases; in the last mentioned passage the part and task of the expert *(prudentia)* is admirably enunciated, after which the Church if necessary *(cum opus est)* gives judgment on the question which falls within *its* competence, namely that of morality. Vatican II emphasizes even more decisively the independent responsibility of the experts and urges the pastors of the Church to respect their due freedom ("observanter agnoscant", *Lumen Gentium,* art. 37).

To determine correctly the degree of binding force, consideration must be given to the measure of authority claimed by the statement itself; further, its purpose and the circumstances in which it is given, what are the tacit assumptions and therefore limitations it includes, and much besides. In order to be able to appeal to it in controversial issues without running the risk of interpreting it in an arbitrary way, it is always necessary to make a study of the problem itself.

With its social doctrine the Church throws light on social life with its needs, its confusions and its injustices in order to stimulate our thought and still more our consciences; the Church cannot and will not give patent remedies nor a panacea to solve the "social question".

4. *Excursus: Protestant social doctrine or social ethics?* However much the Protestant Churches may differ in their definitions of the Church, they are united in holding they have no ecclesiastical teaching authority. A social doctrine which would be the binding official teaching of the Church is therefore excluded. If there is such a thing as Protestant social doctrine at all, it could only be a set of propositions accepted more or less unanimously by Protestant Christians. The content and object of study of this would be the same or similar to that of Catholic social doctrine. Whether the Protestant view of the faith permits such a set of teachings is disputed among Protestants themselves. Some Protestant authors, especially in the U.S.A., hold fast as Luther did to the natural law and so to

the conviction that even in the state of fallen nature human understanding is capable of assimilating the pertinent factual and theoretical knowledge and to recognize the idea of God it expresses. The corpus of knowledge built up by these authors is thus, as far as the matter is concerned, social doctrine in the same sense as ours and shows a wide measure of agreement in content with ours. The position is widely different in Continental Europe where the vast majority of Protestant theologians understand original sin and the *sola scriptura* principle in such a way that the very notion of a social order is inadmissible, much less an intellectual knowledge of that order. Thus fallen man must rely on the directions found in sacred Scripture. This entails a great effort to search the Scriptures for relevant social statements. In fact Protestant theologians have got a great deal out of it. Sacred Scripture proved to be a much more fruitful source than at first appeared; nevertheless a complete systematic social doctrine can by no means be derived from it. To give answers to urgent practical questions, therefore, Protestant theologians are forced, starting from the insights gained from sacred Scripture, to go on to make use of other premises taken from experience or from the relevant sciences. Often in these cases the text of the sacred Scripture is little more than a connecting link for a series of ideas and chains of conclusions which, when viewed closely, are seen to rest on intellectual knowledge. In such cases, there is little or no difference between this and our natural law mode of argument. In particular the documents of the Conferences of the World Council of Churches of Amsterdam (1948), Evanston (1954) and New Delhi (1961) appear to the Catholic reader to be genuine natural law conclusions, but this is disputed by the majority of Protestants.

Divergence of opinion between Catholic and Protestant social doctrine or social ethics stemming from these differences essentially concerns marriage. Also in connection with the State, especially civil authority ("rulers"), many Protestant groups hold, in deference to biblico-theological considerations, views contrary to Catholic teaching. In general one can say that in questions which are still controversial, the division of views does not fully coincide with differences of belief but runs counter to them. In comparison with the great dogmatic differences, which exist not only between different Protestant Churches but also between more orthodox and more liberal theologians in the same Church, there prevails in general on the Protestant side in attitudes and demands of social ethics a surprising measure of agreement. In most of the practical questions Catholic social doctrine and Protestant social ethics are very close together and fight shoulder to shoulder.

BIBLIOGRAPHY. M. Weber, *The Protestant Ethic and the Spirit of Capitalism* (1930); F. Cavallera, *Précis de la doctrine sociale catholique* (1931); O. von Nell-Breuning, *Die soziale Enzyklika* (1932); T. S. Eliot, *The Idea of a Christian Society* (1939); A. C. F. Beales, *The Catholic Church and International Order* (1941); T. O'Kane, *A Catholic Catechism of Social Questions* (1946); G. Toniolo, *L'odierno problema sociologico* (1947); O. von Nell-Breuning and H. Sacher, *Wörterbuch der Politik*, I–V (1947ff.); V. A. Demant, *Theology of Society* (1947); R. Kothen, *L'enseignement social de l'Église* (1949); J. Azpiazu, *Fundamentos de sociología económico-cristiana* (1949); R. Grob, *Grundzüge einer reformierten Sozialethik* (1950); M. Rader, *Ethics and Society: An Appraisal of Social Ideas* (1950); J. F. Cronin, *Catholic Social Principles* (1950); J. M. William, *Catholic Social Thought* (1950); M. Clement, *Introduction à la doctrine sociale catholique* (1951); E. Troeltsch, *Social Teaching of the Christian Churches*, 2 vols. (1951); E. Barker, *Principles of Social and Political Theory* (1952); R. Niebuhr, *Moral Man and Immoral Society: A Study in Ethics and Politics* (1952); J. Hutchinson, *Christian Faith and Social Action* (1953); A. Fagothey, *Right and Reason: Ethics in Theory and Practice* (1953); W. Shanahan, *German Protestants Face the Social Question* (1954); H. D. Wendland, *Die Kirche in der modernen Gesellschaft* (1956); O. von Nell-Breuning, *Wirtschaft und Gesellschaft heute*, 3 vols. (1956–60); J. Schasching, *Katholische Soziallehre und modernes Apostolat* (1956); A. Utz, *Sozialethik* (1958); R. Miller, *American Protestantism and Social Issues (1909–1939)* (1958); J.-Y. Calvez and J. Perrin, *Église et société économique. L'enseignement social des papes de Léon XIII à Pie XII* (1959); J. F. Cronin, *Social Principles and Economic Life* (1959); W. Stark, *Social Theory and Christian Thought* (1959); E. Welty, *Handbook of Christian Social Ethics*, I: *Man in Society* (1960), II: *Structure of the Social Order* (1963); F. Karrenberg and W. Schweitzer, *Spannungsfelder evangelischer Soziallehre* (1960); H. D. Wendland, *Der Begriff Christlich-sozial: Seine geschichtliche und theologische Problematik* (1962); G. Gundlach, *Die Ordnung der menschlichen Gesellschaft*, 2 vols. (1964); J. Newman, *The Christian in Society* (1964); J. Messner, *Die soziale Frage* (7th ed., 1964); J. F. Cronin, *The Social Teaching of Pope John XXIII* (1964); P. Riga, *Peace on Earth: A Commentary on Pope John's Encyclica* (1964); E. Morgan, *The Social Conscience of a Catholic* (1965); id., *Social Commitment* (1967); J.-Y. Calvez, *The Social Thought of John XXIII* (1965); J. Bishop, *Latin America and Revolution* (1965); P. Bigo, *La doctrine sociale de l'Église: recherche et dialogue* (1965); N. Monzel, *Katholische Soziallehre*, I: *Grundlegung* (1965); G. Irvine, ed., *Christianity in its Social Context* (1967); H. Cox, *The Church amid Revolution* (1967); J. Maritain, *Integral Humanism* (1968); W. Gibson, ed., *Social Ethics* (1968); *La Lettre* (Paris), *Christianisme et révolution* (1968).

Oswald von Nell-Breuning

B. SOLIDARISM

Solidarism is that system of securing social order which is equally opposed to individualism and collectivism and which takes its name from the socio-philosophical principle of solidarity. Individualism puts the entire stress on the individual, so that the community appears to be nothing more than the sum of the individuals. Collectivism, on the other hand, puts all the stress on society so that the individual is recognized as significant only as a member of the totality. Solidarism makes it its aim to secure a balance between individuals on the one hand, who retain even as members of society their personal value and autonomy, and the total social entity on the other hand which is a unit of social order, not indeed with a unity of substance, but a real unity nonetheless, and, as such, is much more than a mere logical, numerical unity. To our abstract way of thinking the one-sided nature of either individualism or collectivism is much easier to grasp than solidarism with its balanced emphasis on both sides. Yet the reality of the latter is a matter of universal experience. Even the vocabulary we use has difficulty in expressing this double reality without over-emphasizing the one side or the other.

Since it is a question of a real content, the principle of solidarity must first be formulated as an ontological principle. In this sense we speak of community involvement: all individuals are involved as members of the social totality in the common social destiny of this totality; similarly the totality (society or community) is inextricably involved in the destiny of the members. This real involvement exists quite independently of our awareness and acceptance of it; even if the individual or the totality deny it or act against it, it continues to exist unaltered, indeed it is in these circumstances that experience confirms its existence.

This unalterable real content must obviously have consequences for practical life and attitudes; from the ontological principle of common involvement there follows the *deontological* principle of common responsibility: every individual as

113

member of the community must "respond", i.e., stand responsible for the welfare of each and every member. The name "principle of solidarity" (solidarity = *obligatio in solidum*) expresses, not the ontological content of mutual or common involvement but directly the juridical, ethical content of common responsibility which is in fact an *obligatio in solidum*. Each must also be prepared when needed to make up for the defective or absent performance of others. This not too happy choice of name should not cause us to overlook the fact that the principle is primarily socio-metaphysical (theoretical) and only secondarily juridical and ethical (normative).

According to the teaching of solidarity, man is not accidentally but essentially an *ens sociale*. This holds not only for the *ordo naturalis* ("man as he comes from the hand of the Creator"), but also for the *ordo supernaturalis;* the mystical body of Christ is, as a consequence of the real participation of the members in the divine life of the head, not indeed a substantial unity but yet much more than a mere unity of order (here language touches the limits of its capacity for expression).

The *solidarisme* of the 19th century in France had laid chief emphasis on the ethical content. What was known in Germany as "Christian" solidarism was developed as a strictly socio-philosophical system by H. Pesch, S. J. (1854–1926) and further expanded by Gustave Gundlach, S. J.

Sometimes solidarism and Catholic social doctrine are used simply as equivalent terms, but this usage has also been strenuously opposed. The concept of man is unquestionably the same in solidarism as it is in Catholic social doctrine and all essential conclusions agree as well. The leading ideas of the encyclical *Quadragesimo Anno* and especially the account it gives of society are based on the principle of solidarity. But *Quadragesimo Anno* and the pronouncements of Pius XII do not exhaust the contents of Catholic social doctrine. The encyclical *Mater et Magistra* throws a new light on many things. All those parts of solidarism which go to build up a distinct system are Catholic social doctrine; nevertheless solidarism is not *the* Catholic social doctrine.

See also *Society* I, II.

BIBLIOGRAPHY. H. Pesch, *Lehrbuch der Nationalökonomie,* 5 vols. (1905–23); F. H. Mueller, *Heinrich Pesch and his Theory of Solidarism* (1941); A. L. Harris, "The Scholastic Revival: The Economics of Heinrich Pesch", *Journal of Political Economy* 54 (1946), pp. 38ff.; G. Gundlach, "Solidarist Economics", *Social Order* 1 (1951); R. E. Mulcahy, *The Economics of Heinrich Pesch* (1952); O. von Nell-Breuning, *Verantwortliche Gesellschaft (Festschrift Karrenberg)* (1964).

Oswald von Nell-Breuning

C. SUBSIDIARITY

1. If the principle of solidarity ("solidarism") is the structural principle of every conceivable society, the principle of subsidiarity is the appropriate, equally universally valid, principle of competence (i.e., being qualified to act in a given sphere). Because structure and competence are bound together of necessity in the closest possible manner, and because both are ultimately determined by the *bonum commune* of the current social pattern, both principles are deducible from the concept of the common good as the supreme guiding star of all social philosophy; but at the same time each is deducible from the other.

2. *Subsidium afferre* means to give help. Everything that a community does for one of its members should be of genuine assistance. The acts of assistance that are truly helpful will be those that the recipient really needs, because he is incapable of fully supplying his own needs. Such assistance is all the more helpful when it puts the individual in a position to help himself, thus making itself superfluous. Assistance on the road to self-help is also given when a person is relieved of burdens or tasks of a lower order so that he may be free to perform a higher service. This is true of individuals as of the relationship between the larger (comprehensive) to the smaller (circumscribed) social group. In periods of spreading totalitarianism and megalomania the principle of subsidiarity defends the rights of the small social group. This defensive function of the principle may be specially relevant today, but it is only the converse of its positive substance: a society that is orientated, in the spirit of the principle of subsidiarity, to the good of its members, should always act as the true servant of its members. Negatively, this implies that society should limit individual initiative only to an extent that is absolutely unavoidable; positively, that society should take in hand everything

that can be done only, or can be done better, by society than by the individual or group. Long before the encyclical *Quadragesimo Anno* (1931) proclaimed the principle of subsidiarity as "in philosophia sociali gravissimum illud principium", Abraham Lincoln had formulated it thus for practical use: "The legitimate object of government is to do for a community of people whatever they need to have done but cannot do at all, or cannot so well do for themselves in their separate and individual capacities. In all that people can individually do as well for themselves, government ought not to interfere." Wherever sound reason rules there is not the slightest danger of the principle of subsidiarity being contradicted, for fundamentally it is nothing else than the application of the classic axiom: "Omne agens agendo perficitur."

Nonetheless objections are raised against the principle of subsidiarity from the most diverse quarters. Some Protestant authors maintain that it is a "Catholic" principle and hence unacceptable to them; and even among Protestant theologians who have thoroughly examined the principle we find the most astonishing misunderstandings. What they read into the principle of subsidiarity or presume to see lurking behind it is certainly not propounded by any of its advocates and least of all by Christian social teaching. That serious and well-intentioned authors can arrive at quite ridiculous expositions of the principle of subsidiarity can only be explained by the fact that politicians appeal to this principle when alleging that their solutions of practical political problems are demanded by Catholic social teaching. This is a violation of logic. Principles as such are abstract: practical political measures must be concrete. These can indeed be measured against principles, but can never be deduced from a principle. Concrete solutions must always be worked out in terms of the concrete problem. An apportioning of competence that is not in harmony with the facts annuls the effect of help offered, thus offending against the principle of subsidiarity: an apportioning that agrees with the fact facilitates and enhances the help offered, thus agreeing with the principle of subsidiarity. It is completely erroneous to try to delimit the spheres of operation of diverse social groupings, that are not related as member to whole, with the aid of the principle of subsidiarity. The sphere of operation of each social grouping is determined by its specific *bonum commune;* and insofar as spheres overlap (e.g., functions that fall to the competence of both Church and State), the delimitation is made not with the aid of the principle of subsidiarity, but has to be referred back to the comprehensive *bonum commune* that embraces both. Being a formal and not a material principle, the principle of subsidiarity has nothing to say about the spheres of function of social groupings, but does make affirmations about the (vertical) apportioning of competence within one and the same social entity or complex of social entities (e.g., federation and member States, union and affiliated unions, State and voluntary social groups). The word "subsidiary" can perhaps give rise to misunderstanding: used as a rule in the sense of "subordinate" or "substitute", it suggests the restrictive idea that the assistance of the community is intrinsically undesirable and ought to be offered only in the most extreme cases, when all else has failed. The French, however, with their distinction between *subsidiarité* and *suppléance* are not liable to make this mistake.

3. A quite fundamental problem is that of the so-called competence over competence: whose business is it to regulate competences by positive legislation? If this authority is vested in the supreme legislature, then — although it is a question not of free discretion but of discretion governed by the principle of subsidiarity itself — there arises unavoidably the danger of the abuse of power attendant upon centralization. Nonetheless this may be the only proper solution. Those who hold ultimate responsibility for the well-being of the whole community must be in a position to regulate competence and to vest in themselves those competences that they require in order to be able to offer to the members who make up the whole community the assistance due to them. When John XXIII in *Mater et Magistra* and Paul VI in *Populorum Progressio* call for a supreme world authority they are speaking completely in harmony with the principle of subsidiarity. In view of the pressing and burning problems and tasks of today, humanity as a whole, still insufficiently organized and hence incapable of action, is justified in taking over from States and international and supranational institutions the competences which it needs in order to possess the power of action that will enable it to fulfil the tasks which have accrued to it.

4. As a social-metaphysical principle the principle of subsidiarity applies without exception to all social groupings — not merely to those possessing a democratic structure (in the philosophical sense), but also to the two hierarchical social groups: the Church of Christ (considered as a *societas*) and the family, i.e., the community of parents and children. Parents, educators and teachers will be true to their function, will provide genuine help to children, only if they aim at producing in them independence and autonomous responsibility. This is also true of the Church in respect of the relation between those in ecclesiastical office and the laity (Vatican II: Decree on the Apostolate of the Laity).

See also *Social Movements* III, IV B, *Society* I–III, *Social Philosophy, Totalitarianism, Marriage, Church* III, *Laity* II.

BIBLIOGRAPHY. J. Maritain, *Man and the State* (1951); *Aufgaben und Grenzen der Staatsgewalt. Stellungnahme der . . . deutschen Bischöfe* (1953); A. F. Utz, *Formen und Grenzen des Subsidiaritätsprinzips* (1956); O. von Nell-Breuning, *Wirtschaft und Gesellschaft heute*, I (1956); H. Weber, "Subsidiaritätsprinzip", *RGG*, VI, cols. 455 f.; A. Freemantle, ed., *Social Teachings of the Catholic Church* (1963); J. F. Cronin, *The Social Teaching of John XXIII* (1964); A. Aaron, ed., *American Catholic Thought on Social Questions* (1967).

Oswald von Nell-Breuning

V. Social Work

1. *Notion.* Social work originally meant all work for the relief of distress and the betterment of certain underprivileged classes. Reflection and experience logically led people to consider the causes of distress, the "social question". Answering it is the business of the social sciences, which provide the principles underlying social policy and social reform. The highly developed modern industrial States have worked out three main systems of assistance, adapted to the social principles and economic circumstances of each State: social work (formerly "poor relief"), on individual cases, social insurance, and pension schemes, the latter two giving a claim to an income on the basis of one's former earnings. There is a clear trend towards establishing an income which guarantees "social security". But a due proportion must be preserved between the gross national product and spending on social security.

Christian social doctrine with its principles of solidarity and subsidiarity, its "predilection for little things" (Theodor Becker), and its "opposition to all gigantism and coercion" (Ludwig Heyde), is of great importance in the struggle between individual initiative and Statism. Its sobriety and moderation keep it on a middle course. The question of how to distinguish between a just social order ("welfare State") and the paternalistic State must be seen against this background. The answer is essential to a sound notion of social work. By "social work" we mean the "case work" that is undertaken by the national administration, local authorities and voluntary organizations.

2. The aim of social work is to help human beings. "The ultimate source, representative, and goal of all social structures is and must be the human person, which by nature has an imperative need of social life" (Vatican II, *Gaudium et Spes,* art. 25). We have the following definition from the Social Committee of the Council of Europe: "Social work is an activity that seeks to bring about better mutual adjustment among individuals, families, and groups, and between them and the society in which they live. It works towards this goal by making systematic use of individual ability, the relations among individual people, and the various forms of assistance which society offers."

The abilities of the individual derive from his mental and physical dispositions. This, whenever help is given, must be borne in mind as well as the interaction between soul and body. Whereas human relations in the age of farming and handicrafts were uncomplicated and comprehensible, in the conditions of industrial society (with work at a distance from the home, paid according to the worker's efficiency, and demanding the utmost concentration; division of labour obscuring the contribution of the part to the whole, etc.) men become anonymous, alienated, and isolated. The family is the society which can offer most help; its cohesion is proved time and again in the moment of need. Groups in the parish, neighbourhood, or factory, among those of the same occupation, among young people, among wives and mothers, among the elderly, do not form spontaneously; they must be set afoot and stimulated. It is the business of social work to support and encourage these groups everywhere.

3. *Functions.* First a social worker must understand why people fall upon evil days.

The reasons in our time are usually complex. Among certain groups of people several causes interact. Thus mothers break down through overwork. Helplessly and at haphazard, outside assistance is called in, which does not correspond to their means. Extra work outside the home seems the sole recourse, but it only speeds up the fatal cycle. Or young people have outwardly or inwardly outgrown the family circle. Tired of a parental control that does not always treat the individual suitably, they leave the confining safety of the nest. Not winning recognition, experiencing failure, they take up with untried companions, sometimes with delinquents or at worst with criminals. We watch in sorrow and alarm as the burden weighing down these groups of people, who are supposed to ensure the continued existence of our society, grows heavier and heavier. Again, children have to be fostered out because their parents, grown solitary in a "faceless" society, have neglected them, often inculpably. Only with an exact case-history, a careful diagnosis, and individual counselling and care can one gradually solve such tangles. Data on the past are often unavailable or hazily remembered.

The growing number of old people adds new problems. Life-expectancy lengthens, but for all their accumulated experience of life old people feel more helpless than ever in this changing world. There is a growing number of the footloose and homeless, "vagrant and elusive" (Frank). They fit only momentarily, or not at all, into the social or natural order, which they find meaningless. Workers from other countries and cultures are allowed in, uprooted from their native soil, but not integrated into their new surroundings. Advances in hygiene and medicine raise other questions. Do we succeed, for instance, in making life "worth living" for the physically or mentally handicapped through their own work, their own earnings, and a certain independence? Social work tries to "foster a better adjustment" in and with these individuals and groups, which we have mentioned as examples. That must be done within the framework of the pluralism, as to principles and outlook, which governs all who are involved in the business of assistance ("adjustment"), whether actively or passively. Ideals diverge widely. Consciences have been formed to differing degrees. Personal responsibility always remains, although many wrong decisions and attitudes also result from outward circumstances and the social environment. People who often have a retarded sense of values must be brought to recognize values. New troubles may ensue from social work. People waver between conflicting emotions: wanting to share in the general prosperity, they hand their children over to strangers; wanting to be healthy and re-integrated into the labour-process, they also want to keep drawing accident benefit as if it were an annuity; they want to stay in the country, in the old family home, and they become commuters to a town job that pays a steady cash wage.

"Concern for" others, however noble the motives behind it, cannot cope finally with these problems. "What a person can do for himself is of more use to him than anything others do for him" (Krause).

4. *Methods*. Over the past few decades new methods of personal assistance have been worked out.

a) *Individual assistance*. "This is the art of applying scientific data on human relations and experience in handling the latter so as to marshal the individual's abilities and also tap sources of help in the community apt to effect a better adjustment of the client to his whole environment or part of it" (Swithun Bowers).

b) *Group work*. "It is based on knowledge of the behaviour of individuals and groups, of the terms of corporate life and social relations" (Lattke). Anyone may take up personal relations with anyone else in the group. This gives people an opportunity for personal development and new social responsibility.

c) *Community work* is the endeavour "to co-ordinate public agencies for social work and adult education in the broadest sense, so as to foster personal relations among individuals and groups" (Peter Kuenstler). The last of the three methods to evolve, community work has already given a good account of itself in satellite towns and newly-settled areas, as well as in new parishes. Neighbourhood activities are always encouraged, so that as far as possible no one shall be alone and friendless. These methods, being based on the nature of man as a person, are also limited thereby. If one lifts them out of their original social and philosophic context they are likely to become "mere rules of casuistry; for in all work with other people the essential thing is the proper balance between considered and spontaneous behaviour" (Krämer).

117

For these methods to be effective there must be a team, a group of collaborators with differing insights and experience but united in tolerance and perfect discretion. It is hardly possible any longer for the individual as such to help his fellows in any real and lasting way.

5. *Kinds of assistance.* Obviously social workers have always tried to adjust their help to the needs of the person seeking it. The discoveries of science, especially of the sciences dealing with man, changes in human thought and human structures, have "awakened a deeper, more ambitious desire: the person and the social group want a life that is really free and worthy of man, drawing on all that the modern world can offer in such abundance" (*Gaudium et Spes,* art. 9). Accordingly, a variety of "individualized forms of assistance" have been developed, like "care, training, and counselling; efforts addressed to the person himself, his will to help himself, his better judgment" (*Sozialenquête der Bundesrepublik Deutschland* [1966]).

The stress is now on prevention. In Germany, for instance, help for convalescent mothers has become a whole movement; every year 180 special nursing homes restore some 2 million mothers to health with a few weeks' treatment and spiritually reorientate their lives (the 63 Catholic nursing homes for mothers have joined to form the Catholic Workers' Association for Convalescent Mothers, Freiburg im Breisgau). Case workers may take over the whole burden of house-keeping in certain situations of intense strain. A young person must be increasingly free to fend for himself, not simply be protected by isolation; "orphanages" have turned into "children's villages". Counselling services for families and parents (marriage-guidance councils), for students and apprentices (advice on the most suitable school and type of secondary education), for employers on social relations in their factories, and other advisory councils are more and more numerous. Most widespread of all are advisory councils on the training of children; with good reason, as the figures show that 80% of the children and young people with whom social workers have to do are the victims of the social conditions they must live in (Loofs).

6. *Legislation.* For the conditions in various countries, see the bibliography, below. — Most modern States are fully aware of the necessity of "counselling", to educate and help independence, as well as of immediate material help. Legislation can make certain provisions for such counselling, but clearly, counsel will be of little help where the recipient refuses to welcome it. Hence one of the main tasks of social work is to convince people of their need of expert advice. Nowhere, it may be said, is the network of advisory panels spread wide and tight enough. And where such guidance is available, very often the existence of it is unknown to those who most need it. Social workers must therefore also seek out those who need the help of counselling. It has been suggested that legislation should include the duty of notifying the authorities of certain definite types of needy cases which can have irreparable consequences if neglected. But such compulsion is not the correct way. More will be achieved by a policy of "active tolerance". The payment of supplementary benefits of various kinds may be an occasion of giving guidance, diplomatically offered. The general principle of reducing compulsion to the minimum is most relevant here.

7. *Personal problems.* How effective social work will be largely depends on the people who undertake it. Whether they are professional social workers or voluntary helpers, they are the kind of people who wish to serve others. But the service we are discussing can beget a feeling of superiority, which again may insensibly turn into an appetite for power, that special temptation of people whose work is looking after others. Those whose formation has been such that they recognize and accept their own limitations, can resist the temptation. Mere training is not enough. Alice Salomon, founder of the profession in Germany, called social work a charismatic profession demanding "a universal education". Since the professional social worker must not only cope with individual cases but often give general answers to the social problems of our time as well, his training must be broad and thorough. In Germany it covers three years at a technical college *(Höhere Fachschule);* in other countries of Western Europe and in the U.S.A., 6 to 8 terms with university connections. "The question arises whether we should go on regarding the profession of the social worker as one ancillary to medicine, pedagogy and psychology, or accept it as an independent profession with a field of its own, like those others" (Isbary). There is a clear trend,

probably inevitable, towards giving social workers university training.

Most of the training centres that were founded by private initiative in Western Europe, the U.S.A. and Latin America in the early 1900's are run by religious or philanthropic bodies. Social work is one of the ways in which the Church, the people of God, can work "from outside" on the world of today.

8. *Problems of organization.* Organization can be a great help or a dangerous distortion in social work. Among the organizational problems are: the co-ordination of internal services with the field service; dependence on a superior in Church, State, or voluntary organization whose training and experience usually differ from the field-worker's; co-operation in mutual respect between officials and voluntary workers; above all harmony between State social workers and those of the religious bodies. Imaginative social work can be stifled by the tangled growth of competing organizations.

9. *International co-operation.* In 1927 the International Conference for Social Work (ICSW) was founded to pool the experience of social workers and foster the movement in each country. The Catholics had led the way with their International Union in 1925 (UCISS = Union Catholique Internationale de Service Social). Every two years since 1928, except during the Second World War, international conferences have been held on themes broad enough to stimulate the delegates and provoke an exchange of views. Each country has a national committee, apart from the Communist countries, which are not officially represented. This committee draws up a preliminary report on the chosen theme of the international conference. Very valuable and illuminating material can be had from each national committee. A general report on each world congress is provided in English, French, and the language of the country where the congress has been held.

Investigations by UNESCO have shown that illiteracy, the economic structure, and national income are closely connected, and that urbanization and industrialization automatically reduce illiteracy. This correlation bears directly on the state and intensity of social work in industrialized countries, in largely agrarian ones, and in those with a mixed economy (*Illiteracy in Mid-Century,* UNESCO publication [1957]).

Vatican II sums up the meaning of social work as follows: "All must regard their neighbour as an 'alter ego', be concerned above all things for his life and the means necessary for him to live as befits a human being ... Today in particular we must be a neighbour to every man, ready to serve him in practical ways" (*Gaudium et Spes,* art. 27).

BIBLIOGRAPHY. M. Richmond, *Social Diagnosis* (1917); id., *What is Social Case Work?* (1922); A. Salomon, *Soziale Diagnose* (1927); P. Jostock, *Grundzüge der Soziallehre und der Sozialreform* (1946); S. Bowers, *Nature and Definition of Social Case Work* (1949); G. Hamilton, *Theory and Practice of Social Case Work* (1954); H. Lattke, *Sozialarbeit und Erziehung* (1955); A. Young and E. Ashton, *British Social Work in the Nineteenth Century* (1957); F. J. Bruno, *Trends in Social Work, 1874–1956* (2nd ed., 1957); National Conference of Social Welfare, *Community Organization* (1958); W. Friedlander and others, *Concepts and Methods of Social Work* (1958); W. Friedlander, *Individualism and Social Welfare* (1961) (France); F. Klein, *Das Bundessozialhilfegesetz* (1961) (German Law); *Social Work Practice,* 6 vols. (1962 ff.) (U.S.A.); L. Woodroofe, *From Charity to Social Work* (1962); E. Ferguson, *Social Work: An Introduction* (1963); National Association of Social Workers (U.S.A.), *Building Social Work Knowledge* (1964); L. Lurie, ed., *Encyclopedia of Social Work* (1965); K. K. Jacob, *Methods and Fields of Social Work in India* (2nd ed., 1965); M. Kamphuis, *Die persönliche Hilfe in der Sozialarbeit unserer Zeit* (1965); D. Donnison and V. Chapman, *Social Policy and Administration* (1965) (Great Britain); S. Dasgupta, *Social Work and Social Change* (1967); American Public Welfare Association, *Public Welfare Directory* (revised annually); P. Kaim-Caudle, *Social Policy in the Irish Republic* (1967); *A Guide to Voluntary Service* (Great Britain), H. M. Stationery Office (1969).

Marianne Pünder

SOCIAL PHILOSOPHY

1. What is social philosophy? Having experienced social life, man can ask what is the nature and essence of it (or of society, as the quintessence of social intercourse). To go "behind" and "beyond" experience in this way will also evoke the question as to the meaning of social life for the person. If there is such a meaning, the question also arises as to the values embodied in social life and in its aptness to promote values.

The philosophical systems soon took in the social element. The thought of antiquity was taken up by scholasticism and handed on to the present day in social ontology. Philosophy of law and of the State have always been included in social philosophy, to which Hegel and Marx made large contributions. The 19th century expression "social philosophy" designates primarily "systems, theories and trains of thought which envisaged social reforms of a utopian nature" (von Kempski). Movements such as liberalism and socialism reflect the social philosophy which upholds both the freedom of the individual and his essential links with society, as do social thinking, values and action. The persistent notion of the organism finds its ultimate expression in "universalism". Phenomenology and value-ethics, like existence-philosophy, offer new insights into social reality. The various approaches show that the registration of social facts is not enough. Their interpretation in the light of social reality as such appears essential for the due fulfilment of human existence and demands its own special scientific treatment.

Christian thinking, posing the question of the origin and nature of created being, developed a social philosophy on the basis of Aristotelian and scholastic doctrine. It rejected individualism and collectivism, and carried over the notion of natural law into neo-scholasticism. The general result is designated "solidarism". Existence-philosophy and value-philosophy were used to deepen and extend the ontological orientations of Christian social philosophy. Light was thus thrown on the richness of values in personal fellowship, as also on the social character of personal existence. Evolutionist or dialectical principles have left little mark hitherto on Christian social philosophy. *Quadragesimo Anno* (nos. 14, 110) speaks of a "new", "Christian" social philosophy. The natural knowledge of man and society, including social institutions like the State, law, property, etc., is understood to have revelation as its background. Thus Christian, and indeed all social philosophy is closely related to social ethics, since social reality always imposes tasks to be realized. By virtue of its origin, Christian social philosophy is closely linked with studies of natural law, the effort to formulate rights and duties based on the social nature of man. Social philosophy tries to throw light on the nature of man insofar as it is social and finds fulfilment in fellowship.

2. Certain principles follow, which show that the philosophical questions are multiple.

In terms of the Aristotelian categories, social being appears as a relation (accidental or transcendental) and as a state of being-

together *(esse unum in pluribus)*. The relation is seen as orientated to human values in general ("intentional" relationship). Others attach it to social ethics, seeing all members of a community as orientated to the common good, where they find their fulfilment. The phenomenological and personalist view of society defines social reality by the term of "togetherness" *(Mitmenschlichkeit)*.

The social orientation of man means more than that he is ready for the perpetual exchanges with others which are necessary for life. It means that giving and accepting enrich human nature. Existential phenomenology defines human existence as "being there through others and for others" (Kwant). Man's social dimension is not just one among others, but a primordial determination without which man cannot be. "The whole person is social and the whole social reality is personal" (Plattel).

Society, the concrete realization of the social factor, is seen in social philosophy as a unity of order and relationships (among persons who by nature can and must combine). Values are not excluded by this notion, since the attainment of values is as it were the goal of social union: social welfare is the common *good*. In the value-ethics of phenomenology society or fellowship itself appears as a value, the basic value of human existence, since values exist only in fellowship. Fellowship attaches man to the realm of values. The basic social attitude is love, and it takes the form of personal fellowship: existence and intercommunication in love. Utilitarian teamwork is necessary, but will be all the more perfect, the more it is a personal fellowship.

Social philosophy also deals with social structures or laws, universally valid social principles. There is disagreement as to their number or how they can be organized into a system, but there is wide agreement on the following. The principle of solidarity affirms the due and necessary social links. The principle of subsidiarity tries to determine the various fields of competence of social activity and is declared in *Quadragesimo Anno* (no. 79) to be "a most important principle in social philosophy". The principles of unity and totality try to demarcate the body social, and to allot persons their place in the order of the whole. The principle of the common good gives the purpose of an activity which is in keeping with the social reality. The principle of the dignity of the person is at once the basis and goal of the social reality.

Social philosophy also deals with the

development of society, which must be considered as a historical entity. Thus progress, freedom and obligation must be constantly re-considered. The notion of order must be applied to the facts of social evolution.

3. *The importance of social philosophy.* The interpretation of social existence is now the task of sociology rather than of social philosophy. But social philosophy is a help to sociological interpretation, which has recourse to it "when the analysis of the social system presents insuperable difficulties" (R. König). But sociology does not attribute scientific value to social philosophy as such. Nonetheless, this has a scientific value, beyond the role allotted to it by sociology, when it investigates the social nature of man in all its dimensions and does not confine itself to the social structures which are historically or immediately apparent. It has a critical function when it is based on an understanding of man which takes in his total relationship to the world, society and God. It can then transcend the tensions of individualism and collectivism, egoism and altruism, person and community, freedom and obligation, which dominate so many social systems and attitudes. It can point beyond the accidental or contemporary, beyond the historically-conditioned, to what is permanent in man as such — of which the social quality is unconditional.

Certain forms of social thinking, in terms of organism, mechanism, processes, etc., have been borrowed from science and technology. These can be criticized by social philosophy, which can bring out the truly personal and social nature of man. It will also retain, and even augment its importance, against behavioural sciences based on mathematical and technological views of a "planned society", if it succeeds in grasping and propounding the full riches of personal and hence social being.

See also *Social Movements* IV.

BIBLIOGRAPHY. R. F. Ervin, ed., *Science and Society* (1952); G. Simpson, *Man in Society* (1954); D. Riesman, *Individualism Reconsidered* (1954); R. König, *Soziologie* (1958); J. von Kempski in E. von Beckerath and others, eds., *Handwörterbuch der Sozialwissenschaften* (1956–65), IX, cols. 527–32; K. Kapp, *Towards a Science of Man in Society* (1961); T. Parsons, ed., *Theories of Society* (1961); P. Winch, *Idea of a Social Science and its Relation to Philosophy;* W. Stark, *Fundamental Forms of Social Thought* (1963); J. Giers, "Die Sozialprinzipien als Problem der Christlichen Soziallehre", *Münchener Theologische Zeitschrift* 15 (1964), pp. 278–94; M. Ginsberg, *Essays in Sociology and Social Philosophy,* 3 vols. (1956–66); F. Eggleston, *The Search for a Social Philosophy* (1966); M. G. Plattel, *Social Philosophy* (1966); T. Segerstedt, *The Nature of Social Reality* (1966); R. C. Kwant, *The Phenomenology of Social Existence* (1967).

Joachim Giers

SOCIAL SCIENCES

1. *The term and scope.* The "social sciences", a term in use in England and France from the early 19th century, obviously embrace a number of sciences which deal with social matters. The difficulty in defining the concept and scope of the social sciences is in the word "social".

Man with each of his fellows, man with society, man with his material background (of economics) and the being of man himself is something to be conceived "socially". Hence if "social" and the relevant sciences are applied to the life of men in common, the scope is immense, since such life is made up of language, history, culture and so on, which would all then need to be treated under the social sciences. Hence it is better to restrict the object of the social sciences to "social life as such" (Geck). It is the knowledge of what makes up human life together, the laws it follows, the goals it pursues.

The notion and scope of the social sciences will depend on the tasks which fall to common life. This means that the sciences must be to some extent open to variation, which will be displayed in the different relationships of other sciences to the social ones. In the present state of the subject, the social sciences have in common the scientific approach to social questions, but differ in methods and goals. Sociology is generally regarded as a basic science here. The question of the unity of the social sciences remains open, while the question of a basic normative social science is debated. But even if no such norms are arrived at, the social sciences help to form the social consciousness in general and hence are important for social life.

2. *The subjects.* However the various fields covered are ranged together, they will at least supplement each other. From the fundamental aspect of society as a whole, the problem of social life in general, the sciences are social philosophy, sociology, social biology or human and cultural ecology, and

social pedagogy. Most of these fields are so complex that further sub-divisions are necessary. Social history treats of the growth and relationships of social groups, social research studies behavioural factors at the present day, with the help of social statistics and sociography. Since the methods of social research follow those of the natural sciences, mathematical and technical apparatus and thought-forms are becoming of greater importance.

The realms in which social life are crystallized are studied in theories of the State and political economy, while the theory of law and political science are also of importance for social life. Philosophical principles (philosophy of the State, philosophy of law) and ethics (economic and political) enter in when the material is distributed between these fields, but the scientific presentation of such principles is not generally a matter for the social sciences, being dealt with rather in social philosophy and social ethics. Social ethics has to treat of the fundamental values in social life and must again be divided into various disciplines.

Efforts to systematize the social sciences are based in Christian thinking on philosophical and theological principles. The scientific and normative approach to social life are combined. The effort is "both to explain and present systematically social reality, and to work out social norms" (J. Höffner). So too, on the principle of the link between "being" and "ought", basic social sciences (on the nature of society and behavioural sciences) are distinguished from subsidiary ones, such as study of law, economics and cultures (G. Ermecke). And the various levels of social reality demand individual research, which means that the social sciences have a certain order, in keeping with the Christian understanding of them. If social ethics is decisive, with its interest in the common good, the social sciences are linked with each other insofar as they contribute to this common good. Christian social doctrine is not social science but part of theology. It deals with the same matter, social life, but now in the light of revealed truths and the salvation bestowed in Christ. The social life is seen within the total order of Christian existence.

3. *Development and methods.* There are many social sciences because social life is complicated and all processes must be considered and explained. Earlier thought linked social life to philosophical or ethical systems, and even economics and public offices were essentially considered as parts of ethics and natural law. In the 19th century, the strictly social element was singled out for scientific investigation, especially the processes which were relatively independent of civic or political life.

Concern with society in the early socialists meant also proposals for the reconstruction of society. Social science reached a provisional climax in A. Comte, leaving behind it, in its quality of sociology, the theological and metaphysical stages of knowledge and making the scientific or "positive" study of men, humanity and their future its object. But before the social sciences could develop independently, the encyclopaedic view of the theory of the State had to differentiate the sciences of law, economics and society, though this could not be done without some overlapping. The philosophy of law stimulated social thinking on an organic basis (G. W. F. Hegel, C. Krause and H. Ahrens). R. von Mohl directed attention to "middle-class" society, while K. Marx noted the class-war. Systematic attention was paid to the organic foundations of social doctrine, and political economy influenced the tasks and and methods of the social sciences, through the efforts of the recent historical school (G. Schmoller and others).

Important discussions arose between the social scientists who considered that their task was also political and hence one of value-analysis (G. Schmoller) and those who denied that the social sciences had to make value-judgments or set goals (e.g., M. Weber). Social economy, according to the former, had practical goals corresponding to value-judgments, since objective as well as subjective values could be determined, with binding force for scientific investigation as well as for the moulding of society. Without denying subjective value-judgments, the others demanded on methodological grounds a strict distinction between knowledge and value-judgments, between research and the setting up of goals. The debate continues, and is taken up by sociology in its own way: "How can freedom from value-judgments be achieved in sociology?" Here the scientific history and the social presuppositions are elaborated: "What social conditions give rise to the postulate of a value-free science?" The knowledge that in the quarrel about values the whole integrating function of the social sciences was at stake, hence their meaning for social life, led eventually to a shift of perspective. The unjustifiable confusion of social data and value-judgments is still rejected, but views on the application of the social sciences and also on their acquisition diverge widely. The neo-positivism of the Vienna Circle, of R. K. Popper and others distinguishes between facts and decisions or norms which cannot be reduced to facts — a "critical dualism". Social science can use its analyses to offer practical alternatives for limited, predetermined purposes, which are technically feasible. Hence it has no little value for social practice as a source of information. But others assign social science a wider task of counselling, based on the fundamental goals of social life. In a strictly normative social science, corresponding presuppositions must be established.

4. *Prospects*. The discussion about the evaluation and application of the findings of the social sciences is hardly yet closed. Some decisions go beyond the categories of the practical or impracticable, the expedient, the foreseeable and realizable, to indicate what is morally possible or permissible. A normative social science claims to proceed from "basic judgments of value". A sense of responsibility demands the profession of "basic interests" and "basic decisions" which are in keeping with the meaning of human life.

Such meta-sociological premises cannot be easily determined. But they cannot be rejected as unscientific, if the correct methods are used to apply basic insights to experience. They will derive from the interpretation of human and social life in general, so that an ontologically and metaphysically orientated social doctrine cannot be disregarded. Social life will become further differentiated. The findings of the individual sciences will multiply. Planning for the possible and necessary in human social life will become more comprehensive. Under these circumstances, one cannot do without the unifying function of the basic positions which are socially mandatory.

BIBLIOGRAPHY. E. Seligman, ed., *Encyclopaedia of the Social Sciences,* 8 vols. (1938); K. R. Popper, *The Open Society and its Enemies,* 2 vols. (1945; 4th ed., 1962); M. Weber, *The Methodology of the Social Sciences* (1949); Q. Gibson, *The Logic of Social Enquiry* (1950); G. Weisser, "Normative Sozialwissenschaft . . .", *Soziale Welt* 7 (1956), pp. 2–26; K. R. Popper, *The Poverty of Historicism* (1957); L. Ward, *Ethics of the Social Sciences* (1959); J. Höffer, "Versuch einer Ortsbestimmung der christlichen Gesellschaftslehre", *Jahrbuch des Instituts für christliche Sozialwissenschaft* 1 (1960), pp. 8–18; D. McEwen, *The Problem of Social-Scientific Knowledge* (1963); J. Gould and W. Kolb, ed., UNESCO *Dictionary of the Social Sciences* (1964); UNESCO, *World List of Social Science Periodicals* (3rd revised ed., 1966); D. Braybrooke, ed., *Philosophical problems of the Social Sciences* (1965); J. Gould, ed., *Penguin Survey of the Social Sciences* (1965); R. Rudner, *Philosophy of Social Sciences* (1967).

Joachim Giers

SOCIETY

I. The Social Group. II. Fellowship. III. Common Good. IV. Public Opinion.

I. The Social Group

1. *The problem of definition.* Society — to give a preliminary verbal definition — is the totality of interactions between individuals, no matter how combined, insofar as this totality constitutes a system with its own internal processes, the development therefore (whether naturally or artificially) of a unified relationship between a number of people. As such a unified relationship between human beings, between beings, that is, who have the free disposal of themselves, and over whom no one has disposal except to the extent that they themselves in free responsibility put themselves in the hands of others, the functional structure of society is not to be thought of as the mechanical or organic integration of many into a functional relationship. The factual relationship is rather to be considered, in principle, as a conscious one, to which the individuals consciously relate. Thus the members of society always interact in such a way that they relate primarily to their own interaction and then by means of it to one another. This means that society, being human, is the basic development of a unified relationship between the individual and his quasi-natural interaction with others, both elements being equally basic to it.

This essentially double nature of the relationship implies the impossibility of a real definition of society which would be valid for all times. Inasmuch as such a definition is an attempt to determine the relation of the individual to his relationship with other persons, a theoretical correlation between the related person and his relationship, and thereby the consciousness of the social process itself, it is always an element of that which it attempts to define. The definition then modifies what has been defined (and that by necessity, insofar as the latter, the fact of relationship, is present in personal society merely as a consciously perceived element of the total process). The definition becomes part of the objective substratum of the social process, and calls for a constantly renewed assimilation if it is not to contradict, even in its very form, the "essence" of society as the expression of relationship. This formal definition sees society as so essentially a historical reality that all attempts to objectivate it in a definition must be taken as a historical and momentary element of society. This means that any definition must be regarded as an element of a definite social process and the latter as essentially constituted through its own historical self-explanation.

2. *Historical development as the content of modern dynamic society.* In antiquity and in the Middle Ages man was more or less taken for granted as the ζῷον πολιτικόν *(ens sociale, animale politicum)* and socio-philosophical reflection concerned itself essentially with the problem of the *best* society: the optimal organization of the *polis* as the environment of the citizen who exercised his freedom in this public sphere; the most successful order of law as guarantee of the world-wide *Pax Romana;* right order in the hierarchical gradations of Christendom. Society could therefore be taken simply as the correlative to the "individual" considered in his immediate and thus independent self-consciousness. This concept became problematic only at the time of the Renaissance with the rise of civil society in the sense of a functionally constituted community of autonomous individuals. Such a society finding itself "homeless" in the framework of the quasi-natural law prevailing in the ordered society of the Middle Ages, found an adequate understanding of itself in the claim of modern philosophy, after Descartes, to deduce the entire world structure from the ideas of an *ego cogitans* formed prior to any world reality and providing a basis for all thought, and accepted this as its only explanation. A result of this conceptual development was that for the first time the need, theoretical as well as practical, arose of abandoning the notion of society as a given self-evident reality and of finding an explanation by reconstructing it in its original meaning starting from the thinking subject. This called for a fundamental self-analysis on the part of society. In professional philosophy (as for example in

Leibniz) this novel problem was reflected in the attempt to relate the universality of self-consciousness, now for the first time apparent, which could accept nothing "outside" its own self-determination and the world it opens up to the plurality of such "windowless" egos. This found direct expression in the theories of early liberalism on the "social contract" (in Hobbes and Rousseau, though in very different forms) which explained society by means of personal interactions after the model of a contractual agreement, and accordingly demanded from social institutions, especially the State, merely that they should regulate (thus Montesquieu in explicit detail) as a functional association based on freedom, the relationships between the individuals and their induction into a social totality by way of a contract.

With this basically new beginning, traditional society was superseded not only theoretically but also in practice, inasmuch as society is not just neutral material, but a correlative expression of its theory, the latter being an element of the former. The revolution in the understanding of social relationship led naturally in the liberal movement in England and America as well as in the French Revolution to an upheaval in those social institutions in which civic society consciously created its own social order. This implied not merely a change in power relationships but an epoch-making change in the meaning of society and thus, insofar as society is essentially a conscious relationship, in the nature of society itself. Since that time society refers itself in its development no longer to some predetermined order imposed on it without its own free disposition but *exists* now only to the extent that it systematically reflects its own meaning, comes to a rational understanding of its own functioning and expresses institutionally what it has thus understood. What exists from now on is a purely self-reflective society, autonomously determining its own nature as society. This also implies inversely that basic reflections on the meaning of society enter *ipso facto* into the development of society.

Such a development on the part of society implies first of all on the practical level a fundamental change in the functioning of all institutions of authority. Where it came to an understanding of itself civic society no longer acknowledged, and modern society in general since then does not acknowledge in principle, any authority which it has not itself legitimized, but subordinates all power to its own functioning. In this way it reduces the power of the State especially to a pragmatic reality. This it does in two ways: firstly, the power of the State can no longer have any meaning but that of functional administration, and secondly, the use of power by this administration must justify itself before the dynamic process of modern society (by whatever means of democratic formation of opinion this comes about). The juridical public system retains this function of service in all those areas of social life it wishes to take over, indeed precisely there inasmuch as all institutions, now no more than the externalization (and thereby the assurance), of the balance between the individual and the social element immanent in him, exist and function only to serve a total social expression. Thus society in turn makes these institutions its own and thus can reach even the intimate non-social areas only insofar as they are institutionally secured and expressed. While in the course of time the meaning of practically all public spheres — the judicial system including legal sanctions, social welfare, education and even science, etc. — has undergone this change (or is undergoing it), in the bourgeois society of the West only the capitalist principle of private profit as the motive power of economic life still resists assimilation into a modern fully-institutionalized social process. Consequent on a tradition inherited from the deism of early political economy, which assumed a pre-established harmony between individual interests, a directly personal factor, private ownership of what are means of relationship in society is not seen in the context of its social function and as a result has not come to an integration into a total social process which would be not just arbitrary but expressed in legitimate institutions. This is a "bourgeois" inconsequence which results in fatal irrationalities similar to those arising from the naiveté of the Communist reliance on a State system without true relationship to the individual. Besides the immanent development of its functions through institutions on a democratic basis, modern society also implies in principle systematic self-analysis through scientific reflection. It was no accident that sociology came into existence along with civic society, and is an integral factor in modern society in general. Sociology is seen, as empirical research, and also (inasmuch as all empiricism tacitly or expressly presupposes a formal object) as an *a priori* systematic science. As such, sociology defines society, in the most general and preliminary way, as a self-sustaining system of interactions, and accordingly indicates, as the basic constitutive processes of every empirical society, firstly the biological preservation of the species based on a division of functions, and secondly the "culture", the personal dimension of interaction, which, if it is to be possible, calls for a consciousness of values held, at least formally, in common, as a meeting place of rational ideas. It inquires into these basic forms of social activity, these being the chief formal ways in which society expresses itself, as to the nature and degree of variation they exhibit, the interdependence of these varying individual processes and their expression in institutions, as well as the "cultural" integration of society in an accepted understanding of itself. Society is thus seen as a role-play in which social needs and expectations reveal a comprehensive system of functions, and it is only in the execution of these that the individual becomes socially expressive and intelligible.

Social science, however, reflects a certain naiveté as long as it is regarded as being merely theoretical (with occasional subsequent possibilities of application), and does not from the beginning claim to be illuminating, both historically and factually, as an intrinsic factor in the modern social process. Understood in this way (as in the Marxist tradition of social criticism), theoretical social science has the decisive function of critical investigation of all those hindrances to social relationship, whether they are subjective or collective, which resist the total self-realization of society, by blocking the social process in its function of creating relationship, and thus introducing alienation into the dynamics of society. It is especially necessary, where appeal is made from such hindrances to relationship to extra-social authorities, to unmask such appeals as ideological determination foreign to its nature and so to pave the way for assimilation into a true relationship. In this sense society may and can nowadays be personal, thereby entering into the historically irreversible phase of absolute self-reflection, only if it scrutinizes itself constantly for ideological trends (see *Ideology*). A society of this kind demands, in the interest of its absolute self-expression, besides the practical removal of all resistance to social interaction and to its scientific investigation, that it should be based on an enlightened understanding of the fundamental conditions of interaction between individuals and so of the nature of society in general; an understanding which monadology has merely shown to be a philosophical desideratum. Such absolute reflection of society began in the inter-personality theory of German Idealism, especially that of Fichte and Hegel, with the insight into the inter-personal relatedness of one's own personal immediacy itself. It saw that self-consciousness is constituted essentially by freedom, that is, by the responsible query as to the meaning and justification of one's own reality, and thus in the context of an absolute criterion for legitimacy in general and subject to its claims. It also saw that the absolute criterion of meaning and purpose can be apprehended only through a concrete historical claim by another person on one's own freedom, whereby the ego in principle both materially and formally becomes part of a concretely historical and contingent process. In factual interpersonal contact, the dialectical tension between the absolute nature of the formal claim to meaning here disclosed and the material contingency and defectiveness of meaning (with its view of self and the world) as actually experienced — this being the true significance of that dialectic between the individual and his capacity for relationship that constitutes society — shows both to be factors equally basic to the fundamental process of relationship itself. Thus society, as the essence and perfection of the fundamentally primary relationship, transcends itself essentially (and here is probably the place for the problem of Church and State) to seek fellowship. The latter is that outgoing in interpersonal relationship in which the assertion of purpose and meaning takes material form in a unity in which all free men, relating to and through each other, correspond and contrast (see *Charity, Virtue* II), and in which nothing is held back in the process of mutuality. Such a *societas perfecta* as a total communication is the goal aimed at in principle by modern society with its basically critical attitude to ideology.

See also *Society* II.

BIBLIOGRAPHY. See bibliographies on *Social Movements* IV A, *Church and State, Social Philosophy, Sociology*; also: T. Hobbes, *Leviathan; or the Matter, Forme and Power of a Commonwealth Ecclesiastical and Civil* (1651), ed. with introduction by M. Oakeshott (1946); C. de Montesquieu, *De l'esprit des lois* (1748), E. T. by T. Negent (1949); J.-J. Rousseau, *Du contrat social* (1762); id., *Political Writings*, ed., with introduction and notes by C. E. Vaughan, 2 vols. (1915); G. W. F. Hegel, *Grundlinien der Philosophie des Rechts* (1821), E. T.: *The Philosophy of Right*, by T. Knox (1942); A. Comte, *Cours de la philosophie positive*, 6 vols. (1830–42); id., *System of Positive Polity* (E.T., 1875–77; reissued 1966), 4 vols. (1822); K. Marx, *Das Kapital*, 3 vols. (1867 ff.), E.T. from 3rd German ed. by S. Moore and E. Aveling, ed. by F. Engels (1886); F. Tönnies, *Gemeinschaft und Gesellschaft* (1867; reprint, 1963); E. Durkheim, *Les règles de la méthode sociologique* (1894), E.T.: *Rules of Sociological Method* (8th ed., 1950); T. Litt, *Individuum und Gemeinschaft* (2nd ed., 1924); M. Weber, *Wirtschaft und Gesellschaft*, 2 vols. (1925), E.T.: *The Theory of Social and Economic Organization*, by A. Henderson and T. Parsons (1947); M. Scheler, *Die Wissensformen und die Gesellschaft* (1926); T. Parsons, *The Structure of Social Action* (1949); id., *The Social System* (1951); O. von Nell-Breuning, *Einzelmensch und Gesellschaft* (1950); W. Ziegenfuss, *Gesellschaftsphilosophie* (1954); J.-P. Sartre, *Critique de la raison dialectique* (1960); J. Höffner, *Christliche Gesellschaftslehre* (1962); M. Horkeimer and T. Adorno, *Sociologica*, II (1962); M. Theunissen, *Der Andere* (1965); N. Monzel, *Katholische Sozial-lehre*, I, II (1965–67); E. Topitsch, *Sozialphilosophie zwischen Ideologie und Wissenschaft* (2nd ed., 1966).

Konrad Hecker

II. Fellowship

1. *Notion.* It is part of the primary experience of man to know himself comprised within a fellowship, by virtue of which and in view of which he exists (even if only by denying it). The essence of his finite "nature" is not only to be with and for himself (at least in self-consciousness) but also to be with others. Since therefore he is not capable of self-realization except in fellowship, fellowship is a basic concept in theological and philosophical anthropology. As a basic determination of human existence fellowship is qualitatively different from all sociological headings such as group, community and society, which can only be regarded as derivative forms of fellowship or as means to that end. Man is never just himself. The "I" can only exist and be defined in terms of the "You" and "We" (and vice versa): communication is an intrinsic constituent of personal self-realization. Hence freedom as self-determination is always circumscribed by fellowship, and fellowship is a condition of the freedom of the individual (on the polarity of person and fellowship, see *Person*). Thus fellowship cannot be understood as a mere aggregate of individuals, nor as the self-realization of a comprehensive principle of

unity which extrapolates individuals as multiple moments of itself. Fellowship is a proper, primordial type of existence in the unity of the individual with the whole and the whole with the individual. And this mode determines and permeates all elements of human existence. Fellowship does not come about primarily in view of an end extrinsic to itself (a common purpose, utility, etc.), nor is it essentially subsidiary. Throughout the relativity of constantly changing modes of existence and the play of varying ends and ideas, the primary ground of fellowship can be seen as personal life itself, in its ever greater fulfilment (see *Order* IV).

2. *Characteristic proprieties.* Since fellowship is an essential of human existence, it is never an artificial product, but like life itself, the result of an irresistible force which is law even throughout the various forms given it by free decision and is ultimately not dependent on arbitrary choice. Every fellowship has some sort of constitution which allots the individual his determinate place therein (see *Authority, Unity*). All human fellowship, in the concrete, is no doubt subject to the limitations of the finite: it can be genuinely realized only with a few, and all the forms it takes are necessarily restricted. But as a trancendental determination of human existence it is in principle not subject to any bounds. There is a dynamism in all true fellowship which of itself strives to integrate all communities, all men and all history, without prejudice to the particular forms which its finite nature requires. The tendency to depth and concentration does in fact always conflict with the principle of comprehensiveness. But as a transcendental note of being, fellowship in itself and in its affirmation (love, loyalty, etc.) participates in the absolute character of the personal (see *Personalism*).

3. Fellowship take various concrete forms in keeping with the dimensions of the being of man (finitely infinite, spirit-soul) in its historical plurality, which thereby consciously finds itself fulfilled in various ways. On the level of the sexually structured personality there is marriage and the family; on that of historical origin and orientation in spiritual, cultural and political unity there is the nation and state; on that of interpersonal relationship, friendship and brotherhood; on that of man's radical and all-embracing dependence on God, there is

religious fellowship (community of faith and worship, see *Church* II, *Religion* IA). The interpenetration and mutual relationships of all these traits in man himself are reflected in the resulting forms of society. Then there are also derivative forms, emotionally or rationally motivated, which can be termed fellowship only in an analogous sense: scientific associations, work-teams, companies formed for profit, self-defence and so on.

4. Since all human society must take on finite, concrete form, though essentially and in all its notes based on a transcendental relationship to the infinite and incalculable being of God, all society is essentially conditioned by a fellowship in and with God which man is impotent to set up and which remains historically unattainable in this world. This is reflected negatively in the imperfectibility of all society in the world and positively in the inner dynamism and the extrapolation which are orientated to the "kingdom of God". Society's immanent tendency to the infinite throughout all its forms and characteristics is the reason both for the utopian nature of all societies and for their possible mutual rivalries. If a society as a whole or in one of its essential characteristics claims to be an absolute, and refuses to allow for the difference between essential claim and external particular realization, the ideological perversions of society result, such as collectivism, totalitarianism, mass society, individualism.

5. *Theological aspects.* Since man is essentially social, the history of his salvation, though personally unique and immediately related to God, is just as primordially a community history of salvation, which is the foundation of individual salvation.

The history of salvation did in fact take the form of God's absolute, personal self-disclosure, in a grace which set up immediate fellowship with man. Hence this personal fellowship with God always signifies the individual in the community and in view of the community, while the community is likewise there only for the individual.

The basic theological and existential (ontological) aspects of the community of salvation will then throw light on its concrete forms (covenant, synagogue, community, Church), its concrete notes (especially those of the Church; see *Communion of Saints*) and on the constituent salvific events which form and affect this community of salvation both as to its individual members and as a whole (see *Revelation, Sacraments*).

See also *Man, Individualism, Collectivism.*

BIBLIOGRAPHY. E. Stein, "Individuum und Gesellschaft", *Jahrbuch für Philosophie und phäno-menologische Forschung* 5 (1922), pp. 116–283; G. Walther, "Zur Ontologie der sozialen Gesell-schaft", *ibid.* 6 (1923), pp. 1–158; H. Plessner, *Grenzen der Gesellschaft* (1924); H. Seesemann, *Der Begriff der* κοινωνία *im Neuen Testament* (1933); E. Brunner, *God and Man: Four Essays on the Nature of Personality* (1936); id., *The Divine Imperative* (1937); F. Hauck, "κοινός", *TWNT,* III, pp. 789–809; J. Wach, *The Sociology of Religion* (1944); M. Buber, *Between Man and Man* (1947); F. Ebner, *Das Wort und die geistigen Realitäten* (2nd ed., 1952); V. Bellezza, "Il singolo e la communità nel pensiero de Kierkegaard", *Nietzsche e Kierke-gaard* (1953), pp. 133–89; F. Tönnies, *Community and Society* (1957); M. Scheler, *On the Eternal in Man* (1960); R. Guardini, *The World and the Person* (1965); M. Theunissen, *Der Andere* (1965); A. Darlap, "Fundamentale Theologie der Heils-geschichte", *Mysterium Salutis,* I (1965); J. O'Mal-ley, *The Fellowship of Being: An Essay on the Philosophy of Gabriel Marcel* (1966).

Adolf Darlap

III. Common Good

1. *The problem today.* The problem of the common good has been the subject of lively debate in recent years among students of Christian social doctrine. The debate bore on the relations between person and society (or more generally, between the individual and the fellowship of which he is a member), and on the relation between the good of the individual and the general good. One group defended on principle the priority of the common good *(communitarians),* while others *(personalists)* maintained equally forcibly the priority of the good of the individual. Communitarianism bases itself on an organic notion of order upheld in the Middle Ages, under the influence of Greek philosophy. Personalism is more akin to the modern notion of the value and dignity of the human person, and of the inviolability of human rights as against society and above all as against the State. But it integrates this view in a conception of solidarity which assigns priority to the full realization of the personality with all its rights and dignity. Both trends are fundamentally in agreement, being sharply opposed to a liberalist individ-ualism, from which Christian personalism

must be distinguished by reason of its "solidarism", and also opposed to totali-tarianism, from which Christian communi-tarianism must be distinguished basically, since it includes the notion of the inviolable dignity of the human person. The com-munitarian view is associated with E. Welty, C. de Koninck and A. Utz, the personalist with G. Gundlach (who stressed its specifical-ly solidarist element), J. Maritain, I. Esch-mann and G. Wildmann. The problem of the common good was then dealt with in Pius XII's allocutions on human rights, in John XXIII's encyclicals *Mater et Magistra* (1961) and *Pacem in Terris* (1963), in Vatican II's discussions of the limits to the rights of person and society in the matter of civil and religious freedom.

2. *The notion of the common good.* To under-stand the problem and to try to solve it, the concept of the common good must be analysed and the various meanings discerned which may underlie the concept. It may first be understood transcendentally. God himself, as the first cause and last end of creation, is the *bonum commune* of the universe. The primacy of this common good of the order of creation is not open to discussion. But it does not affect our question, which aims at comparing the common good with the good of the individual within the various orders of society.

The common good of a fellowship or society is the apt inner structure which enables it to harmonize the different interests of all its members, and to preserve the rights of each person for the common good of all. Considerations as to how the common good and the good of the individual are to be defined and contrasted have led to the following descriptions of the common good.

a) The common good, as an objective institution, comprises the objective well-being of an organized fellowship. This common good, when truly and correctly understood, is essentially ordained to the good of the individual, but is not identical with it. The objective well-being is the condition of society which enables the individual to develop himself properly in order to attain his personal well-being. The notion is defined as follows by John XXIII in *Mater et Magistra,* no. 417: "The common good comprises all the conditions of social life through which men may better and more easily attain their own personal fulfilment." See also Vatican II,

Dignitatis Humanae, art. 6. It is therefore essentially ordained to the good of the person, but not identified with it.

b) A second opinion takes the common good to be the common benefit enjoyed in common by all the members of a community, the commonwealth or common weal. The common good is then the essence of its well-being, which is more than the sum of the benefits enjoyed by each individual. This common weal is ensured by all on behalf of each, and by each on behalf of all, in general and mutual solidarity. It is possessed by each individual in his degree, insofar as he is a part of the whole.

This position has been developed chiefly by A. Utz, in order to be able to maintain the absolute primacy of the common good without falling into totalitarianism. The common good immanent to a society would then be the prosperity, the sufficiency of goods of all types, available to all the members of the community. It is therefore the combination of the personal well-being of all and of each individual, insofar as this well-being is a unity and not just an agglomeration, provided in common (by all for each and by each for all) and enjoyed in fitting proportion (by participation) by each individual, as part of a whole.

c) A third opinion, that of personalist solidarism, describes the common good as the good of all in common solidarity. It is common, insofar as it has been achieved in solidarity and each individual possesses it in a fellowship of love with the others. But it is not common in the sense that the personal achievement of the individual has to be ultimately considered as part of a whole, this whole being qualitatively different, belonging to a higher order. The person must be seen as a totality who is adapted and ready for the fellowship of love in human solidarity. And the fellowship which embraces the individuals is not a whole composed of parts. It is personal communication, openness for others in love.

All these definitions, however, share to a certain extent the same theory, and hence meet the same problems when it comes to determining the practical application of the notion of the common good. The common good changes materially in the course of history and so gives rise to various conflicting programmes for its embodiment. But these concrete programmes react in turn on the formal definition, so that the definitions given above may well reflect concrete decisions previously taken.

3. *Common good and personal good.* When one compares the objective, institutional good of the organized society with the personal good of the members of the society, the persons who constitute it, there can be no doubt — in the light of the rights of the person — that the common good is ordained to the personal good and is subordinate to it. Even when personal well-being has to be subordinated partially to a common good rightly understood, the common good in question has its ultimate ontological basis in the personal good of the individuals as members of the society. "The State is for man, not man for the State" (Pius XII, encyclical *Divini Redemptoris: AAS* 25 [1937], p. 79; cf. *Mystici Corporis: AAS* 35 [1943], p. 221; Vatican II, *Gaudium et Spes,* art. 26).

But if the common good is really to serve the individual and his immediate well-being, how is it to be procured? What should be the relation of the individual to the common good? And consequently, what should be the relation of public institutions to the common good? A certain part is played here by historical conditions — the stages of cultural, moral and spiritual development of the human person at different epochs. Hence, for instance, in the notion of the common good as understood in the Middle Ages, with its stress on the idea of the organism, certain human rights were not given adequate consideration, though this does not mean that the notion in question should be treated as totalitarian. But it is impossible to overlook the deficiencies of social structures and ethical standards, which were partly a matter of historical conditioning, and hence are not wholly a matter for blame. The conviction that human rights are inviolable, and that even — and particularly — the State cannot justly proceed against them, is one of the basic principles of modern thought, but it is a conviction which was achieved only through a long historical process. And it is an essential and invaluable element of the common good when rightly understood. This fundamental truth has been re-iterated by the magisterium of the Church in recent times (e.g., Pius XII, *AAS* 41 [1949], p. 556; John XXIII, *Pacem in Terris: AAS* 55 [1963], pp. 273f.). It presupposes a changed attitude towards the State as guardian or depositary of the common good. St. Thomas Aquinas, who in this matter remained tributary to Greek thought, ascribed to the State an educational function which was to colour the whole ethical life of the citizens (*De Regimine Principum,* 1, 1, c. 14 and 1, 2, c. 4).

Vatican II distinguishes between "common good" ("welfare") and "public order", the latter being only a part of the former, and being ·itself composed of three elements, protection of the rights of all, peaceful fellowship in true justice, the due maintenance of public morality (*Dignitatis Humanae,* arts. 6, 7). The State has the positive duty of furthering the common good with all the means compatible with freedom — a duty which extends to the area of international relations, as is stressed in *Gaudium et Spes,* arts. 83–90 and in the encyclical of Paul VI, *Populorum Progressio,* 20 March 1967. The State has powers to compel and prescribe, but these are limited by the demands of "public order".

See also *Rights of Man, Totalitarianism, Personalism.*

BIBLIOGRAPHY. F. Suarez, *Disputationes Metaphysicae* (1597), disp. VI, E. T.: *Disputation VI, on Formal and Universal Unity,* by J. Ross (1965); E. Welty, *Gemeinschaft und Einzelmensch* (2nd ed., 1935); C. de Koninck, *De la primauté du bien commun contre les Personalistes* (1943); I. Eschmann, "Bonum commune melius est quam bonum unius", *Medieval Studies* 6 (1944), pp. 62–120 (On the value of the person in Aquinas); C. de Koninck, "In Defense of Saint Thomas", *Laval théologique et philosophique* (1945) (reply to Eschmann); O. von Nell-Breuning, *Wörterbuch der Politik,* I (2nd ed., 1954), pp. 51 ff.; A. Utz, *Sozialethik* (1958); G. Gundlach, *Staatslexikon,* III (6th ed.), pp. 737–40; G. Wildmann, *Personalismus, Solidarismus und Gesellschaft* (1961); J. Messner, *Das Gemeinwohl* (1962); J. Maritain, *The Person and the Common Good* (1966).

José María Diez-Alegría

IV. Public Opinion

1. *The concept.* a) The concept of public opinion derives from the socio-political sphere and denotes the process as well as the result of the formation of opinions and attitudes on the part of the general public. It is expressed formally in certain constitutive acts (e.g., by means of elections), informally in special groupings (e.g., pressure groups) and, in the mass media, partly formally and partly informally. The objective character of public opinion depends on the type of the political society. Totalitarian forms, by means of restrictions on freedom of speech and by

sanctions, enforce a uniformity of public opinion. And how democratic a society is. basically depends on the freedom to express and form opinion there. Accordingly, for the existence of a genuine public opinion it is essential that, besides a certain plurality of opinions, the process of formation of public opinion should have free scope.

b) By analogy with this socio-political concept, that of public opinion in the Church must also be considered, although it must be borne in mind that in comparison with the State and society, the Church is a more homogeneous and unified group which has special doctrinal and disciplinary characteristics. This difference arises from the different nature and purpose of the Church. Nevertheless there is no doubt that not all ecclesiastical structures can be *a priori* regarded as of divine right. They arise in many cases in connection with what were primarily feudalistic-monarchical structures, and the conclusions to be drawn from these historico-political implications on the need for adaptation to more modern constitutional forms have not yet been carried to completion. In order not to mix theological argument with the ideological justification inevitable in such a period of reflection, we find it more appropriate to adopt a primarily sociological approach.

2. *History and state of the problem.* a) The categories of *private* and *public* derive from Greek and Roman antiquity. The city (πόλις) and public affairs (κοινά) are strictly separated from the home (οἶκος) and private life (ἴδια). The public sphere obtains in the market place (ἀγορά, *forum*) both in speech and in action. Birth, death, the work of slaves and the life of the woman constitute the private sphere under the rule of the master of the house. (οἰκοδεσπότης). Freedom, virtue, emulation, fame and truth are to be found only in the light of the public sphere and public opinion is the articulate expression of public life. Especially in the notion of the State as *res publica* and in the definitions of Roman law, the structural distinction between public and private was preserved right down to our modern civil society. Kant, with the formulation of the principle of publicity as the mediation of politics and morality, sought to harmonize the antitheses. Hegel and Marx posed the problems of this theory by pointing out the lack of orderly relationship between society and State, inasmuch as the State and the public sphere can no longer

be identified. In 19th-century liberalism serious doubts were raised as to whether it was possible to have an objectively guaranteed concordance of the contradictory opinions in public life and whether public opinion did not take the form of coercion to conform rather than a critical check on the use of power (J. S. Mill, A. de Tocqueville). Public opinion increases in quantity to an enormous extent but declines in its effectiveness as a corrective. Idea and ideology can no longer be precisely distinguished. The intellectual élite and the upholders of representative democracy strike out in all directions to counteract the disintegration of public life.

This is still relevant to the modern problems of public opinion, since its critical reaction is more necessary than ever, while its objectivity is increasingly in danger, through manipulation, through a bewildering plethora of information, through the commercialization of news in the late-capitalistic society. The public sphere has changed from being a forum of opinion to a market for the culture and entertainment industry, in which news becomes a commodity to be bought and sold. The special dialectic of public opinion now consists in the creation of the need for information and the satisfaction of that need by way of supply and demand, deeply penetrating and exposing the most intimate sphere of private life. The supposed congruence of public opinion and reason as formulated in the thesis *vox populi vox Dei* has lapsed, if indeed it ever existed; yet it needs to be preserved as a controlling factor if there is to be any check on power and authority. A unified theory to reconcile these contradictions does not exist. Many programmes must be ruled out because of the uncritical use of historically obsolete categories.

b) Modern life can be divided generally into two areas of communication, two forms of public opinion: the area of *informal,* sociopolitically unofficial, personal opinions, and that of the *formal,* institutionally authorized, official opinions. Both areas of opinion have a varied scale of internal reliability: the informal ranges from mere prejudice to the automatically accepted opinion of the groups manipulated by the techniques of the entertainment industry; the formal include declarations, statements, decrees, etc. There is little life in public opinion in either realm, in the former because it has little weight, in the latter because it is the privilege of the authorities. Contact between the two realms

is through the mass media or through individuals, without of itself establishing communication. Instead of communication, there is the spread of collectivized views; instead of public opinion, there is the presentation of manipulated information. An effective public opinion today can take only the form of critical publicity; in this the areas of formal and informal communication must be brought into contact with each other so that the internal flow of opinion in one complex is channelled into the other and transformed by it, i.e., internal and external public opinion must be brought into communication with each other and social consensus and conflict become the object of public controversy. Such a public opinion could be an effective check on the use of power and provide a maximum of rationality.

3. *Public opinion in the Church.* This sociopolitical control of public opinion cannot fail to affect the role of public opinion in the Church, insofar as it is a question, not of particular tendencies, but of efforts to mediate the antitheses of freedom and necessity, subject and object, individual and institution. The argument which is often adduced to defend the non-democratic, hierarchically authoritative condition of the Church (namely, that the revelation of God in Jesus Christ, the normative aspect of sacred Scripture, and the implications arising from the apostolic succession for the offices of teaching, sanctifying and giving pastoral care, are *a priori* incommensurable with a quasi-parliamentary or plebiscitary model of public opinion), has the character of an ideology, for, in the first place, it is a historical fact that public opinion had weight even when the Church was a Church of the masses, and, secondly, political systems have entered into the constitution of the Church. Most essentially, however, this concept rests on the premise of the unhistorical character of the truth, on a misunderstanding of the hermeneutical realities, and the disregard for the tension between general norms and a concrete imperative.

Since in the modern situation of public opinion the interaction of those in authority and those under authority demands a continuing reflection on this relationship and a critical adjustment of it, there is lacking in the Church to a very great extent an effective public opinion. To effect a liaison between authority and obedience should be the task especially of theology and preaching. Yet it

131

frequently does not go beyond a verbalization of this problem, because it is itself functionally related to the official Church. In spite of the many post-conciliar attempts to re-structure public life in the Church and in spite of a theology committed to the freedom of the individual, the sociological view presents the unyielding picture of an authoritarian popular Church as it developed (apart from many quantitative modifications) in the early Middle Ages: strict centralization, close correlation of *lex divina* with Church discipline, preaching in the form of declaration as an authoritative process of proclamation, and finally the formation of conscience as an instrument of behaviour control. In addition there exists a peculiar dialectic of free critical speech in the public life of the Church: it serves in fact rather to consolidate the existing situation than to change it effectively, inasmuch as the presence of verbal criticism is taken as establishing free public opinion, and also as an alibi for the lack of effective change in what has been criticized. Finally, it may be remarked that the absence of a widespread, effective public opinion has been often reflected under the surface in the unduly private and inward-looking tendency of theology (see *Political Theology*).

4. *Possibilities of establishing a public opinion in the Church.* The attempts hitherto to direct the change in the structure through increased representation (mass media, especially television), through advertisement by means of professional public relations, through symbolic demonstrations (Pope's journeys, conventions, Catholic congresses, etc.), or through increased collaboration of the laity in parish councils, are entirely insufficient and are often seen to be in themselves questionable, especially if only "the representatives themselves are represented" (C. Schmitt). Vatican II emphasized, in very general terms it is true, the right to free expression of opinion and to information in State and society (*Inter Mirifica*, ch. I), yet did not mention the right to information within the Church, and the traditional form of Catholic publications and publicity within the Church is criticized only slightly and in a passing way. More significantly, the expressions in *Lumen Gentium* of the tendencies to decentralization (arts. 23–27), to equality and the brotherhood of all the faithful precede the hierarchical differentiation (art. 32). Notable too is the desire to give ex-

pression to the dignity of the laity. The distinctions of hierarchy and status are, however, strongly expressed right at the beginning (art. 18) without being followed by a theologically adequate justification for the distinctions of order based on sacred law. Yet in general, a new tendency predominates, that of emphasizing collegiality in completion of the statements of Vatican I. To provide a fruitful public opinion in ecclesiastical life will call for an increasing desacralization of authority within the Church, the transformation of proclamation by monologue into dialogue, the change of passive pious exercises into informative Church services, as well as exegetically critical exposition of the Scriptures. Within the change from the traditional Church of the masses to a Church of convinced Christians, the need for disciplinary measures of control will disappear; the abolition of the Index may be regarded as the first step in this direction. Further, those who hold authority in the Church will be drawn into the increasing crisis of authority and will see themselves forced even to the revision of certain statements in face of the requirements of specialist scientific evidence, whereby the extremely broad spread of expert knowledge will give public opinion a new efficacy. The differences between the various cultural areas in the one Church make a greater pluralism necessary. The one-sided emphasis on the private sphere in Christian practice of the faith and Christian ethics cannot be reconciled with the trend to "one world": public life in future will need global structures. Finally, this universal communication in the Church, in public opinion, is a realization of the relationship of dialogue between Church and world which was adumbrated by Vatican II.

See also *Authority, Communications Media, Idea, Ideology, Laity* I.

BIBLIOGRAPHY. Lord Acton, *The History of Freedom* (1907); W. Bauer, *Die öffentliche Meinung und ihre geschichtliche Grundlage* (1914); C. Schmitt, *Römischer Katholizismus und politische Form* (1923); J. Huizinga, *The Waning of the Middle Ages* (1924); W. Albig, *Public Opinion* (1938); P. Lazarsfeld, B. Berelson and N. Goudet, *The People's Choice* (1944); B. Berelson and M. Janowitz, eds., *Public Opinion and Communication* (1950); C. W. Mills, *Power Élite* (1956); K. Rahner, *Free Speech in the Church* (1959); id., *Theological Investigations,* II (1963); id., "Demokratie in der Kirche?", *Stimmen der Zeit* 182 (1968), pp. 1–15; V. Key, *Public Opinion and American Democracy* (1961); F. Wilson, *Theory of Public Opinion* (1962); A. Montaldi, *Le rôle de l'opinion publique dans la communauté Atlan-*

tique (1963); R. Lane and D. Sears, *Public Opinion* (1964); J. B. Metz, *Theology of the World* (1968); H. Bahr, *Verkündigung als Information* (1968).

Werner Post

SOCIOLOGY

1. *Historical review.* Social phenomena have been the object of thought in all social systems. The writings on social philosophy are an outstanding example of this. With the rise of industrialism and secularization and the loosening of previously accepted social ties, the social foundations themselves came to be questioned. This, as well as the constantly increasing complexity of social structures, demanded an independent science with its own methods, not the least of whose functions would be to help in the solution of the "social questions" that had arisen. Sociology is thus strongly orientated to the investigation of modern society, without at the same time neglecting the historical and theoretical aspects.

The name "sociology" was introduced by Comte who believed he had discovered in the three-stage-law (theology, philosophy, positivism: in the third stage are found the sociologists) the principle of evolution underlying history. Spencer, relying on anthropological research, attempted to found a sociology parallel to physiology and biology (Darwinism). An organic and biological approach, together with some romantic notions, are found also in Lilienfeld, Schäffle and Worms. Parallel with these are impulses in the direction of reform which also led to the first great empirical investigations (L. von Stein, Le Play, Booth, etc.).

Two important influences came to bear on sociology: one from Hegel who in his philosophy of law called bourgeois society a "system of needs" and analysed the chief relevant factors in its method of work and production; the other influence was that of Marx who understood the industrial system as a capitalist society which must yield to the classless society. Although his prognoses of pauperization, the increasing proletariat of workers and the disappearance of the middle class were not fulfilled, yet he was correct in his recognition and exact analysis of a number of important phenomena of industrial society (see *Marxism*). Among the critics of the belief in progress and the political theories of the universalist, speculative sys-

tems of Saint-Simon, Comte, Marx, Spencer, etc., were Durkheim, Pareto and Max Weber, who are nowadays reckoned among the classical writers on sociology. They asked that the science should be more modest in its claims and have a more exact empirical base. An example was given by Durkheim in his *Suicide* (an investigation of the correlation between suicide and adherence to a group, especially a denominational one) in which he described the condition of "anomy" as the collapse of the normative structure. The charge of sociologism has been made against his *Rules of Sociological Method,* in which he explains all categories of thought including religious concepts as products of the particular social environment. For him the comparative method ("the indirect experiment") seemed to be the only method of investigation worthy of sociology.

Pareto put the emphasis in his theory of social action on the analysis of non-logical activities. In these there is present a constant factor, the irrational impulses ("residues"). The variable factor consists in the apparent explanations which serve as ideologies ("derivations"). According to Pareto the ruling élites are superseded by the social groups striving for power, in a competitive struggle in which the ideologies play an important part ("circulation of élites"). Max Weber achieved in a universal survey a synthesis of systematic and historical sociology, the influence of which is powerfully felt even today. He rejected the Marxist thesis that the economic conditions of production are the primary determinant of human thought and sought to establish that the spirit of capitalism arose from the Protestant ethic and therefore from ideas originally inspired by religion. Besides the sociology of power (charismatic, traditional, rationally legitimized authority), he dealt with such problems as economic sociology and the sociology of religion (embracing all the great religions). His chief attention was given to the increasing rationality of modern society and the "desacralization" of the world (see *Secularization*). Following Dilthey, Weber saw the task of sociology as the provision of insight into rationally orientated activities. The natural sciences, which set up rules of causality for events that "explained" individual happenings, were unable to understand the attitude of the individual. Critical objections can, however, be also made to Weber, as for example against his partly contradictory theory of knowledge constructed under the influence of neo-Kantianism, as well as his demand for freedom from value-judgments in science. The concept of sociology as a cultural science proceeding by way of understanding and insight found favour in Germany, among others with Sombart, Freyer, Alfred Weber, and in the United States with Sorokin and Znaniecki. They hold that sociology has to do with immaterial objects (symbols) which must be defined as cultural values. In sociology a social reality recognizes itself. A causal explanation cannot throw light on a social object, or is at best merely complementary. On the other hand a large number of sociologists, especially in the U.S.A., because of their general empirical approach, tended towards neo-positivism and behaviourism. The most important representatives are Lundberg and Chapin. They asserted that there is no scientifically relevant difference between natural science and sociology. They devoted their attention especially to the construction of social "laws". Chapin developed, for example, a gravitational model thought to apply both to physical objects and social groups. This approach resulted in a considerable extension and refinement of techniques, but led at times to a neglect of sociological theory.

The present position of sociology is determined by an increasing institutionalization of sociology (multiplication of chairs of sociology, expansion of institutes, specialized courses) since 1945. Sociological publications in every field have grown enormously and are scarcely any longer capable of being dealt with even in an international survey. A phase of frequently exaggerated expectations from sociology on the part of other sciences including politics, seems to be succeeded by a critical phase. Sociology itself too has voiced criticisms of an excessive institutionalization. In most Western countries (France being a relative exception) the American influence is outstanding although it is now slowly diminishing. Empirical research finds ready acceptance, as do new techniques, some of which are mathematical (Lazarsfeld, Guttman). The increasing influence of the great European representatives of sociology such as Weber, Durkheim, Pareto and Simmel, as well as that of Freud, has led to a higher value being set on sociological theory in the U.S.A. This development is linked especially with the name of Parsons. Influenced by the functional school of ethnology (Malinowski, Radcliffe-Brown and Linton), he gave new life to the old thinking in terms

of organism under the name of structural-functional theory and developed a large conceptual complex reminiscent of the formal sociology of von Wiese. Merton was among those who later rejected this theory as being unable to bridge convincingly the gap between the basic empirical concept and the developed schemata of classification. Instead, the development of theories of the "middle range" was sought, leaving the question open, however, as to the criterion for the determination of the "middle". Inquiries into structure were also pursued by a French school chiefly under the influence of Lévy-Strauss (see *Structuralism*). This is directed towards the linguistic sciences and engages principally in analyses of systems of meaning, but neglects the question as to how far these coincide with the social phenomena to which they refer. While the line of development aiming at insight has now scarcely any followers, dialectical sociology stemming from the Hegelian left (Adorno, Habermas, Marcuse, Lefebre, Mills, etc.), and in the Eastern bloc (Markievicz, Szczepanski, Hahn, etc.), has developed in opposition to the empirical approach. Invoking the support of Marx, the significance of social philosophy is stressed (Horkheimer, Lukacz, Schaff, Garaudy). Hermeneutics too can now be inserted into the chain of explanations (Habermas, appealing to Gadamer). Politico-revolutionary analysis has taken on a new lease of life, whereas the non-Marxist sociologists sometimes merely appear as upholders of the status quo.

2. *The nature of sociology*. Sociology is the science of "social activity". Since this social activity is always directed towards social systems, sociology can also be called the science of social systems (groups, institutions, society). Through its orientation to social systems, social activity attains a relative constancy and becomes a sort of repeated experiment. It can therefore be assessed by other active participants and becomes capable of scientific analysis. Since the social process is relatively independent of the individual, the object of attention in sociology is not man as an individual but man as fulfilling a certain social function (role, office) and thus as representative of a social reality. Representation also entails the realization and living portrayal of group norms (aims and obligations). These arise from group consensus based on tradition, as well as from individual insight into the social system,

insofar as its existence is recognized as meaningful. Sociology thus attempts to arrive at an understanding of the norms and normative models which are independent of the individual and are transmitted to him in the socializing process (see *Education*), and which determine human activity and mould man as a member of a group. Consequently, the object of sociology does not consist in the "interpersonal", in mutual relationships and social processes, but primarily in the study of the complex of norms which is relevant to human activity. The extent or duration of a social system cannot be precisely laid down. It reveals itself in every case only through its functions, in the last analysis through the individual activities directed to a particular objective. These in turn are to be grasped only against the background of the total system and its central norms, i.e., its structure.

The social functions can be described in terms of the individual, e.g., calling or profession, and then subdivided in terms of the various qualifications and functions within a given calling. They can also be grouped in major units, such as the workshop, department, firm, industry and society in industrial sociology. These functions always include, besides the individual functions (roles), empirical objects of the most varied kind (e.g., implements, machines), which in turn influence the norm structure. The more general functions too can be represented by individual persons in such a way that the entire complex of objects and means is combined with the people who are active in them. Thus leadership, authority, power and status emerge, in any particular instance, primarily as a participation in the effective presence of the social group, and secondarily as the power to give orders and impose sanctions. Only after the norms of a social system and its functional differences have been analysed is it possible to understand social change, conflicts, deviate behaviour, integration and disintegration, social classes, mobility, manipulation, repression, etc.

From this it is clear that the structural significance of individual problems cannot be grasped and the thread of understanding is lost in a welter of empirical data, if a strict separation is made between social philosophy and sociology, since every social system can be grasped only in a wider structural context. Seen ideologically, sociology exists only when partial aspects are explained in terms of the "whole". Besides philosophy, closely allied to sociology are social psychology, pedagogy, history, economics, jurisprudence, demography and social anthropology (ethnology). The two last-mentioned sciences can also be reckoned as subdivisions of sociology.

The areas of research of sociology are "general sociology", the basic problems such as norm, role, group, power, social change, etc., and "special" (or hyphenated) sociologies. The areas of research have developed in connection with urgent social problems in dependence on the interests of the researchers. There are no sharp lines of division between general and special sociology. Thus the conditions of industrial workers in the 19th century aroused attention. Among the most important branches of research are industrial sociology, urban and rural sociology, family sociology, political sociology and the sociology of religion. Nowadays the chief topics of research, apart from general theory, are youth and education, leisure and work, the developing countries, population and town planning, the media of communication, and, a recent arrival, revolution. Further areas of research are the sociology of law, of knowledge, of organization, of minorities, and of deviation. Every social sphere can in principle be made the object of a special sociology (e.g., art, the military forces, old age, sport, medicine, etc.). A special place is taken by research into ideologies which investigate all expression of mental activity in terms of the social background and seeks to expose ideologies as an instrument of social struggle. It has led at times to a general suspicion of ideology which renders an objective scientific discussion and the attainment of an attitude of proper self-criticism difficult or impossible. If all that is achieved is a "ritual of criticism" (Dahrendorf), sociology can easily become uncritical if it does not reveal its standards of criticism and the system corresponding to them. If every universal view of things, every form of group consciousness is termed an ideology, this lends itself to a relativism for which the distinction between ideology and truth is a matter of indifference.

3. *Method.* The discussion of method has always figured extensively, especially in Europe (Germany, France) and the U.S.A. The chief themes are: a) the nature of the object of sociology; b) the nature of the empirical bases of sociological theories and c) the so-called "value-free" judgments.

135

The present position is that there is a dispute over method between the representatives of an empirical approach under the influence of neo-positivism or "logical positivism", and the upholders of dialectical sociology. The former accused dialectical sociology of arbitrariness, since it did not, they said, subject its assertions to the test of direct personal observation, while dialectical sociology in turn accused its opponents of the uncritical use of empirical techniques, without attending to the relevant problems, attaining neither to historical depth nor to a critical perspective. Each side also suspects the other of ideology.

A further objection to the empirical approach is that the claim to the discovery of what are held to be purely scientific "laws" is a false interpretation. Here too in fact it is always a question of investigation of structure, not the revelation of isolated "universally valid" causal laws of the "if, then" type, since the factors affecting the result can never be fully isolated. An isolation of the sociological factors is all the less possible as knowledge is historically structured and on principle all-embracing and is therefore open to influence from all sides. Against dialectical sociology it can be objected that in many cases it opposes a system developed from the matter itself (this is less true of the realistic research sometimes found in Communist countries) and seeks to belittle it as "ontology". The attempt to come to grips with its tenets often remains fruitless because these are then dialectically cancelled and the utopia of the classless and stateless society is taken as a historical and philosophical guideline.

Sociology is not individual analysis. It gains its understanding by observing the behaviour of individuals and groups, taking account of symbolic meanings, and arguing to underlying normative patterns which reveal the structure of a given system. This is the basic method by which "typical", "ideal" concepts are arrived at — "the crowd" as such, the "shop floor" as such, etc. What counts in each case is the total social phenomenon, which gives the elements of the structure their significance and rank. In order to arrive at a suitable evaluation, all known relevant factors must be taken into account. By means of such criteria sociological analysis is enabled to illuminate in a critical way the individual social phenomena. In the theory arising out of the formation of empirical typifying concepts it is not possible always to escape subjectivism. Never-

theless it can meet the demand for interpersonal verification. Sociological theory may be said to be justified by experience when arguments based on all available information converge on the object of research. Thus the criterion of sociological theory lies in the effective grasp of the social phenomenon by means of the conceptual framework inherent in the theory. Under these circumstances the consistent demand since Max Weber (especially in post-World-War-II Germany, less among American sociologists) for the omission of value-judgments in science is difficult to uphold, if it is to mean anything more than the abstention from unfounded subjective opinions, because scientific theory is essentially to be understood as a measurement which attributes to the parts of the structure their position, their value, or their significance. The abstention from evaluation would be equivalent to an (impracticable) abstention from the understanding of the relationships within the structure. But if the structure in its theoretical analysis essentially contains evaluations, then there no longer exists an unbridgeable gap between sociology on the one hand and ethics and politics on the other.

Among the empiricist schools of sociology there is a lack of agreement as to whether the immediate testing of hypotheses in experience should be undertaken as a verification (thus under the influence of Carnap, for example) or as a "falsification" (following Popper). The demand for verification of hypotheses is problematical because social phenomena do not repeat themselves. Besides, even a multiplicity of factual judgments gives no ground for a generalized statement. The demand for falsification of hypotheses through observation has little point for the reason that in principle everything is capable of falsification, that is, there are always (unforeseen) conditions in which the expected does not happen. Both empirical lines of approach also make the systematic construction of a theory seem open to question, since they undervalue the conceptual aspect which cannot be subjected to an empirical test. Concepts must be determined before an hypothesis can be formulated. Therefore hypotheses can never be a substitute for a structured conceptual framework. Neither can "laws" of universal validity be derived from a multiplicity of statistical correlations, for these are an indication of relations between the various elements of a structure the significance of which can be discovered only by an analysis of the total structure. The relations which are given the name of "laws" are usually no more than trivialities which are never valid for all circumstances and sometimes not even for the majority of cases, e.g., "the more contact, the better understanding between people" (Homans). Yet for a particular situation they can have a prognostic value. The mathematical model constructed so as to include a number of dependent factors always falls far short of the reality and neglects of necessity the historical and symbolic components in social activity. Yet these considerations do not imply a rejection of refined techniques. They are rather merely a reminder that their justification and use must be undertaken in full realization of the total structure to be investigated and the total knowledge available.

Among the many empirical techniques and methods of approach special mention must be made of observation, questioning, experiment and scale measurement. In observation we distinguish according to the relation of the observer to the object (mostly a group), between participant and non-participant; according to the method of recording, between checked and unchecked; and according to the knowledge of the group members into concealed and open observation. This technique has been frequently used in ethnology and in the sociology of youth. Questioning is done either in writing, (and this has many disadvantages) or orally through an interview. Various forms of interview are used in the various stages of the investigation: the interview in depth to reveal all the important problems involved, the pre-test to evaluate and check on a questionnaire and finally the interviewer's summing-up in the actual result. According to the degree in which the order of questions is laid down in advance we can distinguish standardized and non-standardized interviews; according to the degree in which categories of possible answers are set out or not we can distinguish "closed" and "open" questions. The experiment is less used in research but it is of great importance for questions of scientific theory. We distinguish projective (planned in advance) and *ex-post-facto* experiments (available statistical material is evaluated). The problem is always how to come by the relevant factors and to isolate the situation. Scale measurement involves the setting up of criteria and standards for measuring value-differences (e.g., opinions). One essential is that the measure-ment of intensity cannot be derived from a counting of heads. The theory of scale measurement cannot be isolated from the discussion in scientific theory of the formation of concepts, nor does the questioning of experts provide a solution. Important types of scale measurement are comparison of pairs, the polarity profile, Thurstone's method of simultaneous intervals; important scales are the Likert and Guttman scales.

Decisive for all techniques is the indication of validity (correspondence of research intention and research result) and reliability (formal accuracy of measurement, agreement of results of constant observations in constant conditions).

Among the lines of approach (with typical aims and research procedures) are opinion research, content analysis (of newspapers, radio programmes, etc.), individual case studies (investigation of an object with the help of all available techniques) and sociometry (measurement of popularity and unpopularity in small groups).

See also *Science* I, *Social Philosophy, Positivism*.

BIBLIOGRAPHY. GENERAL AND HISTORICAL: V. Pareto, *Trattato di sociologia generale* (1916); id., *Sociological Writings*, ed. by S. Finer (1966); M. Weber, *Wirtschaft und Gesellschaft* (1922), E.T.: *Economy and Society*, ed. by G. Roth and C. Wittich (1968); T. Parsons, *The Structure of Social Action* (1937); id., *The Social System* (1951); L. and J. Bernard, *Origins of American Sociology* (1943); R. Linton, *The Cultural Background of Personality* (1945); J. Leclercq, *Introduction à la sociologie* (1948); R. K. Merton, *Social Theory and Social Structure* (1949); H. Schoeck, *Soziologie, Geschichte ihrer Probleme* (1952); H. Becker and A. Boskoff, eds., *Modern Sociological Theory in Continuity and Change* (1957); J. H. Fichter, *Sociology* (1957); G. Gurvitch, ed., *Traité de sociologie*, 2 vols. (1958); C. Lévy-Strauss, *Anthropologie structurale* (1958; revised ed., 1968), E. T.: *Structural Anthropology* (1963); P. Winch, *The Idea of a Social Science and its Relation to Philosophy* (1958); H. Johnson, *Sociology: A Systematic Introduction* (1963); W. Sumner, *Social Darwinism*, ed. by S. Persons (1963); P. Berger, *Invitation to Sociology* (1963); A. Inkeles, *What is Sociology?* (1964); G. Lundberg, *Foundations of Sociology* (1964); T. Abel, *Systematic Sociology in Germany* (1965); F. Jonas, *Geschichte der Soziologie*, 4 vols. (1968–69); J. Monnerot, *Sociologie de la révolution* (1969); P. Abrahams, *Origins of British Sociology* (in preparation). METHODOLOGY: E. Durkheim, *Les règles de la méthode sociologique* (1885), E.T.: *The Rules of Sociological Method* (8th ed., 1950); M. Weber, *Gesammelte Aufsätze zur Wissenschaftslehre* (1922); id., *Methodology of the Social Sciences* (1949); S. Stouffer and others, *The*

American Soldier, 2 vols. (1949); W. Goode and P. Hatt, *Methods in Social Research* (1952); P. Lazarsfeld and M. Rosenberg, *The Language of Social Research* (1957); M. Duverger, *Méthodes des sciences sociales* (1961); W. Siebel, *Die Logik des Experiments in den Sozialwissenschaften* (1965); id., "Werturteil und Messung", *Jahrbuch für Sozialwissenschaft,* 17 (1966), pp. 1–15; D. Willer, *Scientific Sociology: Theory Method* (1967); F. Znaniecki, *Method of Sociology* (1967); H. and A. Blalock, eds., *Methodology in Social Research* (1968); R. Mayntz, K. Holm and P. Hübner, *Einführung in die Methoden der empirischen Soziologie* (1969). REFERENCE BOOKS: A. Cuvillier, *Manuel de Sociologie* (1950); E. Willems, *Dictionario de Sociología* (1950); G. Gurvitch, *La sociologie au XXe siècle* (1957); W. Bernsdorf, ed., *Internationales Soziologenlexikon* (1959); F. Fairchild, *Dictionary of Sociology* (1962); R. K. Merton, L. Broom and L. Cottrell, eds., *Sociology Today,* 2 vols. (1962); J. Gould and W. Kolb, *A Dictionary of the Social Sciences* (1964); M. Duncan, ed., *Dictionary of Sociology* (1967); D. Sills, ed., *International Encyclopaedia of the Social Sciences,* 17 vols. (1968); W. Bernsdorf, ed., *Wörterbuch der Soziologie* (2nd ed., 1969). PERIODICALS: *American Journal of Sociology* (1895 ff.); *Année sociologique* (1896 ff.); *American Sociological Review* (1936 ff.); *Cahiers internationaux de sociologie* (1946 ff.); *Kölner Zeitschrift für Soziologie und Sozialpsychologie* (1948 ff.); *Soziale Welt* (1949 ff.); *The British Journal of Sociology* (1950 ff.); *European Archives of Sociology* (in English, French and German) (1960 ff.).

Wigand Siebel and *Norbert Martin*

SOUL

1. *Concept.* The doctrine of the soul, as an expression of man's self-understanding in general, is part of the subject-matter of general anthropology. Here it means, within the framework of a comprehensive notion of man (though one that is always coloured by its times), the constitutive element by which human existence is capable, by nature, of attaining selfhood. If freedom, decision, responsibility and knowledge are essential determinations of man, so that he not merely has his freedom and consciousness but actually is these acts as he exercises them, then his nature, the principle of his acts, which goes beyond any actual exercise of them, must in itself make his basic activity possible. The soul is human nature in its self-awareness and hence the primary force of the subjectivity.

It is of the substance of man. Its primordial act likewise has substantial significance (see *Person* I). This act, with its history, is embedded in the fundamental context of existence. Man *is* what he makes of himself,

and his being is what he could really become. Personal development, the "history of the soul", is itself a fundamental process.

From this, the following general determinations may be deduced. The soul itself is not man (see *Platonism, Origenism, Augustinianism*). It is one of his principles of being (see *Aristotelianism* I, *Thomism*). It is substantial in character, contrary to the assertions of psychological actualism. As partial cause (formal, because a principle) of (the whole of) human nature, it stands in a primordial relationship to its material, corporeal constitution. The material principle, to which the soul essentially belongs, as its form, can be designated as the "prime substance" of the soul, on account of its priority to it, even genetically (see *Evolution* II B). When it reflects materiality itself (and not just some material object), it gains distance, as in the animal soul, and then when the specific difference intervenes, when the reflection is substantial, it is called spirit. It is independent in character, though its essence is always intrinsically determined by its origin, which is also the reason of its individuality. (Hence St. Thomas treats *materia prima* as the principle of individuation.) As spirit, it is the intrinsic form of the body and so possesses a so-called natural immortality.

The coming-to-be of the soul gives a view of the primal ground. For the soul's "material" origin brings with it its perpetual [dependence] relatedness. Since then matter appears in the soul as a relation, the substantial nature of the soul's transcendence reveals the equally substantial transcendence of all reality — as a natural process (see *Creation*). The coming-to-be of the soul is the substantial mirror of the coming-to-be of the finite world. The (natural) function of the soul shows why its concept was so important, from the Christological controversies of early times to the "psychological" doctrine of the Trinity in St. Augustine and in the mysticism of the Middle Ages.

2. *The concept of soul in biblical and Western thought.* Strictly speaking, the problem of anthropology was not posed by biblical thought. Thus the soul (נֶפֶשׁ, ψυχή) does not appear as a metaphysical principle, but means simply "the vitality of the flesh". Man himself becomes a soul (Gen 2:7) and when he dies he is a "dead" soul (Num 23:10), the soul of a dead man (Num 6:6). The soul comes directly from God (Gen 24:14).

The anthropology of the NT is on the same lines. In St. Paul, flesh (σάρξ) and spirit (πνεῦμα) do not simply indicate the opposition between body and soul, but contrast man (cf. 2 Cor 7:5) in his frailty and sinfulness with the divine might (Rom 8:1ff.; 1 Cor 1:26) which redeems him. (Each of these parts, flesh and spirit, like "body" [σῶμα] and soul [ψυχή], always stands for the whole man.)

Ancient Greek philosophy thought differently. Matter was understood to be eternal (Plato, *Timaeus;* cf. *Platonism*) and God was regarded, from the point of view of his activity, as demiurge. Hence everything which proceeds from him (the forms which determine the constitution of things in the world) are themselves supposed to be twofold. The soul is a "mixture" of the changeable and the unchangeable (*Timaeus,* 41) and is composed of a trichotomy of reason (λογιστικόν), heart (θυμοειδές) and worldly desire (ἐπιθυμητικόν). This gives rise to the (moral) problem of rising above matter. The body was the prison of the soul, and later matter was understood as evil itself (see *Gnosticism, Manichaeism*). Man's soul was to be guided by the eternal truth of the spirit, by means of an unworldly existence, to the pure contemplation of the forms, to find its true self (see *Transmigration of Souls*). But for Plato man is then one with God (from eternity?) and hence immortal, pre-existing, separated in his "essence" from the world. This then gives rise in Aristotle (see *Aristotelianism* I, *Hylemorphism*) to the problem of how the "active intellect" (νοῦς ποιητικός, *intellectus agens*) is united with the "receptive" intellect (νοῦς παθητικός, *intellectus passibilis*) and of whether there can be an "individual" immortality (see *De anima* and its Averroistic commentators), since the lower and truly human(?) part of the soul dies. Against this background, the Stoics thought of the soul as refined matter, within the framework of the great world-reason, and Plotinus thought of it, in its various phases, as an emanation of the divine.

Ancient Christian thinkers took up this anthropology. They put forward the thesis (due to Hebraic thought?) that the soul was mortal, since otherwise it could not be a created thing (so Justinus, Tatian and Irenaeus). Tertullian, to bring out its connection with the whole world, called it a *corpus sui generis,* thinking of the body as an intersocial reality.

But this relationship can be fitted into Greek thought. No doubt the spirit (νοῦς) is the decisive element. But as Origen says (*De Principiis*), the pure spirit (pre-existing) falls into sin with the first movement of its will and must then lead a miserable existence, corresponding to the gravity of its sin, in the world, as a soul (ψυχή). Man is therefore doomed by nature to live by going out of himself — an "ek-static" existence. Poised between heaven and earth, he is ordained to be a superman, in order finally to transfigure the flesh by means of his soul, which by virtue of the redemption and with the help of asceticism is transformed into *pneuma.*

This Greek notion prevailed in the following period. It was given its most forcible expression in St. Gregory of Nyssa and above all in St. Augustine. The soul, in its spirit (*mens*), participates in divine wisdom, which it exercises in contemplation.

Nonetheless, the controversy with Platonism continued, even in the early Middle Ages (cf. Gilbert of Poitiers, Hugh of St. Victor). In the doctrine of St. Bonaventure a distinction was introduced into Augustinianism, with the doctrine of *materia spiritualis.* The definitive turning-point, now conceived of in Aristotelian terms, came with St. Thomas Aquinas. For when Aquinas went beyond the old distinction between matter and form to distinguish between being and essence (the "real distinction" between essence and act), he saw in the very actualization of matter by spirit a resultant reality distinct from both, the human person. Here the *anima,* as the *forma unica corporis,* is given its proper metaphysical place. This explains how the *conversio ad phantasma* is necessary for the human spirit, and conversely, how it is possible to re-live the immanent divine life in the actuality of the true self (the *scintilla animae;* cf. Eckhardt).

Further developments did not maintain this position, but still confirmed it in some ways. Insofar as the "ontological difference" (see *Being* I, para. 1) was lost sight of, Western thought fell victim to a dualism of body and soul hitherto unknown and now applied on the anthropological level. The soul was *res cogitans,* in contrast to a *res extensa* (Descartes). The soul became an attribute and mode of the divine substance (see *Spinozism*), a self-contained monad (Leibniz), an infinite striving (Lessing), the incomprehensibility of the absolute (see *Kantianism*), knowledge and deed (Fichte), the self-explication of the Idea (Hegel), a mystical potency (Schelling), the will to power (Nietzsche), the difference between the ego and the superego (Freud), existentiality (Jaspers), thereness ("being there") (Heidegger), the primordial realization of the future (Bloch). These are all various types of the effort to use what was no longer called soul to grasp the basic law of reality — in the subject (cf. H. Urs von Balthasar). Christian theology was drawn into this process (see *Tübingen School, Personalism, Dialectical Theology, Transcendental Theology*). The soul, now considered as subjectivity — which is why its immortality is denied on the Protestant side — remained the human potency for the absolute.

3. *The magisterium.* The dogmatic definitions are concerned almost entirely with the relation between soul and spirit.

The first point made is that man has only one soul (ψυχή), which is rational (λογική) and hence that one cannot speak of two souls (Constantinople IV, *DS* 657). This, the *anima intellectiva,* exists as a different individual soul in each man ("non est anima unica in cunctis hominibus") and it is immortal precisely as an individual (Lateran V, *DS* 1440). In reply to the question (of the Greeks) as to how spirit and body are united, it is affirmed that the *anima intellectiva* is of itself (and not through the *anima sensitiva:* P. Olivi) the *forma corporis* (Vienne, *DS* 902). This does not affect the Franciscan doctrine of the *pluralitas formarum corporis,* which rather makes its presence felt when the dogma goes on to affirm that after death and before the resurrection (compare the doctrine of John XXII, *DS* 990–1, which at first sight seems different) the soul can see the essence of God *nulla mediante creatura,* by a *visione intuitiva,* and possesses (individual) bliss *usque ad finale iudicium et ex tunc usque in sempiternum* (Benedict XII, *DS* 1000–1; see *Beatific Vision*).

The fundamental principle is strongly emphasized that the soul is created directly (*DS* 3896) by God, from nothing (*DS* 685). Hence it is not part of the divine substance (*DS* 201, 285, 455), and never leads a precorporeal existence (*DS* 403, 456), though conversely, *as such,* it has not a material origin (*DS* 360, 1007, 3220). It is the vital principle in man (*DS* 2833) and is higher than the body (*DS* 815). The spirituality of the soul can be proved (*DS* 2766, 2812).

Man as a whole is said to be (primarily in connection with Christology) soul, body and spirit (νοῦς) (*DS* 44, 46, 48). He consists of spirit and body (*DS* 800, 3002), or of soul and body (*DS* 250, 272, 900).

The basic affirmation is that the spirit of man is created by God and forms the soul of his body, in an essential relation to it, whether this relation is understood in an Augustinian or a Thomistic way. It was not till Vatican II that the magisterium broke out of the body-soul schema and came into line with the approach of the modern era. The key-word is now person and not soul. Man is "one" in body and soul. In his "interiority" he transcends the totality of things. "Thus, when he recognizes in himself a spiritual and immortal soul, he is not being mocked by a deceptive fantasy . . . he is getting to the depths of the very truth of the matter" (cf. *Gaudium et Spes,* art. 14).

4. *Present-day problems.* a) The "Greek" tradition argues from the nature to the subject, while today one goes from the subject to the nature. Nonetheless, even here the question of the essence cannot be evaded, since it is the means of revealing the absolute priority of the person. This priority can be grasped if the activity of the person determines once more the character of the nature. By means of the soul, the morality of the basic act becomes an essential element of the nature thus "characterized" (see *Original Sin*).

b) The "soul", understood as standing for man, is a fundamental theme of theology in the context of sin and redemption. But since theology considers the person in its basic constituents and sees there the factors which give rise to the moral decision, the real sphere of theology only begins where man exercises his basic faculties and transcends himself in his orientation to the absolute. Theology has the task of explicating this transcendental capacity of man. It includes psychology insofar as it must set in motion fundamental complexes within this realm, but it is essentially different from it inasmuch as it does not make these complexes function in relation to others but transcends them by taking them into the order of conscience.

c) The origin of the soul supposes physical causes. But if in general the divine activity and the development of the world are intrinsically connected, transcendent and immanent causalities must merge where the world in itself transcends itself absolutely. This self-transcendence can be described as the creation of the soul, and here phylogenesis and ontogenesis are intrinsically connected.

See also *Evolution, Body, Spirit.*

BIBLIOGRAPHY. See bibliographies on *Evolution* IV, *Person* II; also: F. Diekamp, *Die origenistischen Streitigkeiten im 6. Jahrhundert* (1899); B. Jansen, "Die Definition des Konzils von Vienne", *ZKT* 33 (1908), pp. 421–87; A. E. Taylor, *A Commentary on Plato's Timaeus* (1928); E. Dinkler, *Die Anthropologie Augustins* (1934); W. Gutbrod, *Zur paulinischen Anthropologie* (1934); J. Hempel, *Gott und Mensch im Alten Testament* (2nd ed., 1936); É. Gilson, *The Spirit of Medieval Philosophy* (1936); H. Urs von Balthasar, *Apokalypse der deutschen Seele*, I–III (1937–39); R. Schaerer, *Dieu, l'homme et la vie d'après Platon* (1944); J. Pedersen, *Israel, its Life and Culture*, I (1946); S. Petrément, *Le dualisme chez Platon, les Gnostiques et les Manichéens* (1947); W. Jaeger, *The Theology of the Early Greek Philosophers* (1947); W. Davies, *Paul and Rabbinic Judaism* (1948); H. Karpp, *Probleme altchristlicher Anthropologie* (1950); W. Eichrodt, *Man in the Old Testament* (1951); J. A. T. Robinson, *The Body* (1952); R. Onians, *The Origins of European Thought about the Body, the Mind, the Soul, the World, Time and Fate* (2nd ed., 1954); A. Pegis, "St. Thomas and the Unity of Man", in J. McWilliams, ed., *Progress in Philosophy* (1955), pp. 153–73; id., *At the Origins of the Thomistic Notions of Man* (1963); P. Teilhard de Chardin, *The Phenomenon of Man* (1959); id., *Man's Place in Nature* (1966); D. Lys, *Nèphèsh: Histoire de l'âme dans la révélation d'Israël* (1959); M. Bailey, "Biblical Man and some Formulae of Christian Teaching", *Irish Theological Quarterly* 27 (1960), pp. 173–200; T. Boman, *Hebrew Thought compared with Greek* (1960); *L'âme et le corps*, ed. by Centre catholique des intellectuels français (1961); *La nature humaine. Actes du XIe congrès des sociétés de philosophie de langue française* (1961); C. Tresmontant, *La métaphysique du Christianisme* (1961); G. von Rad, *Old Testament Theology*, I (1962); T. Zaner, *The Problem of Embodiment* (= Phaenomenologica 17) (1964); A. Ahlbrecht, *Tod und Unsterblichkeit in der evangelischen Theologie der Gegenwart* (1965); K. Rahner, *Theological Investigations*, IV (1966), pp. 221–52; id., *Spirit in the World* (1968); E. Coreth, *Metaphysics* (1967); C. Moeller's commentary on the Pastoral Constitution on the Church in the Modern World in H. Vorgrimler, ed., *Commentary on the Documents of Vatican II*, vol. V (1969), pp. 1–114.

Elmar Klinger

SPINOZISM

Spinozism is the name given to a line of thought which goes back to Benedict (Baruch) de Spinoza (1632–77), combining elements of Jewish and neo-Platonic philosophy with Cartesian principles to form a rationalistic and monistic doctrine of salvation. Its central theme is based on the conviction of the essential unity of reality, which Spinoza reduces to a single substance, called *Deus sive natura*, God or nature. Thought and extension are not independent substances but "attributes" or aspects of substance; they embody two wholly parallel orders of the same reality. For the same reason there can be no causal connection between the "modes" of thought and the "modes" of extension, between ideas and things, soul and body. Both are devoid of any real existence outside the one substance of which they are determinations distinguished in purely negative ways. So all reality has to be studied by a geometric method that is likewise strictly inherent in and dependent on substance, and it is from this monistic vision that we derive our idea of the tasks that are set human thought and human activity. Man's senses and imagination first lead him to regard things as substances, though they cannot in fact exist in themselves and can have reality only in the one substance. Hence man must rise above discursive to intuitive knowledge. In the latter, the highest form of knowledge, it is given to man to grasp the true, which is the *index sui et falsi* and from which all true ideas necessarily proceed. In the ethical realm, man must free himself from the chains of sensuality and passion and gain strict mastery of his emotions through reason. In this way he comes finally to the *amor Dei intellectualis,* in which he attains his true good and his happiness. Such convictions led Spinoza to interpret revelation largely in terms of rational ethics. In the Bible he distinguished between a core of truth connatural to the heart and mind of man, and beliefs which seem valid only to men who are still unable to rise to life on a purer and higher plane. This attitude, combined with his assertion of the radical unity of substance, his polemics against any kind of teleology in God or nature, and his absolute denial of human freedom, explain why Spinozism was considered from the outset to be atheism, on the one hand becoming the subject of violent theological controversy and on the other encouraging naturalist and rationalist trends in religion.

Thus there was lively discussion of Spinozism in Holland (Kuyper, Bredenburg, etc.), France (Lamy, Jacquelot, Boulainvillier, etc.), and England (Cudworth, Henry More, Toland, Clarke, etc.). Finally, thanks above all to Bayle's enormously successful article (1697), the idea spread through all Europe that Spinoza was a "thoroughgoing atheist", with the paradoxical result that his system was even more carefully explored. All this culminated in the "Spinozist renaissance" in Germany during the last decades of the 18th century. Leibniz had given his full attention to Spinoza's thought, Wolff had devoted a study to him which in many respects is still fundamental today. And Lessing professed himself a Spinozist — mainly for theological reasons — at the end of his life. But it was above all in the atmosphere of the *Sturm und Drang* period and early Romanticism that the naturalist themes of Spinozism were enthusiastically taken up. What attracts men like Herder and Goethe is not so much Spinoza's actual system — which they tend to mix with Leibnizism and neo-Platonic elements — as his sense of the profound oneness of reality, in which they find an invitation to regard all the forms of nature and of history (taken in a positive sense, not as mere *modi*) as so many manifestations of a primordial force ever driving on towards higher forms of life. And the charge of atheism laid against Spinoza because of his critique of theism actually inspired later theologians to look for a non-anthropomorphic conception of God more in keeping with the naturalism and idealism that were daily gaining ground. (Among the more important of these thinkers were Hölderlin, Schelling, and Schleiermacher.)

Even thinkers who would by no means call themselves disciples of Spinoza, and who, like Jacobi, rejected his strictly determinist and mechanist monism held that he gave the clearest and fullest formulation of a philosophical idea with which all philosophy is forced to reckon (Jacobi himself, Fichte, Hegel, and others). Spinozism makes an important claim on modern philosophical and theological thinking. It has not the importance which it had a hundred and fifty years ago, in the age of Goethe, especially in the religious field. There are few points of contact with the dialectical, existential or explicitly theistic forms of modern thought. But in contrast precisely to this predominantly "subjective" trend, Spinozism gives a sense of objectivity, which a fundamentally "anthropocentric" thought is in need of, if it is to be fully legitimated.

See also *Jewish Philosophy, Neo-Platonism, Cartesianism, Rationalism, Monism.*

BIBLIOGRAPHY. B. Spinoza, *Opera,* editio critica by C. Gebhardt, 4 vols. (1925); G. Bohrmann, *Spinozas Stellung zur Religion* (1914), pp. 59–81 (Spinoza in England); H. Wolfson, *The Philosophy of Spinoza,* 2 vols. (1934); A. Shanks, *Introduction to Spinoza's Ethics* (1938); L. Roth, *Spinoza* (2nd ed., 1954); S. Hampshire, *Spinoza* (1956); A. Oko, *Spinoza Bibliography* (1964).

Valerio Verra

SPIRIT

1. *Preliminary note.* Spirit is one of the fundamental concepts in the history of philosophy, which might indeed be called, as in German, the "history of the spirit". If the full extension and depth of the concept is to be grasped, it should not be constricted within the limits of a definition. The "historicity" which is an essential property of the spirit and the "history" which is its essential actuation must both be considered if we are to understand the concept in terms of the problems it sets to modern thought (see *History* I). This will bring to light the hermeneutic circle involved in the process — the interrelationship between the spirit's understanding and its being understood. For this reason we shall begin by tracing the main changes which the concept has undergone in the history of philosophy, understood as the self-understanding of the spirit.

2. *On the history of the concept.* The philosophical concept of spirit was first worked out in Greek thought, though there is no one Greek word which has all the connotations of our "spirit". The word πνεῦμα "wind, breath" came to be used for the "breath of life" but except in religious and poetical use never quite lost its etymological meaning. It was the word νοῦς which underwent the changes of meaning in which the specifically Greek understanding of spirit was arrived at, which was to have such influence on Western thought. For Anaxagoras, νοῦς was the active principle of order in all things, but he had been preceded by Parmenides, who enunciated the principle of the correspondence of being and spirit which was to dominate all subsequent philosophy: νοεῖν was understood as "to perceive" and "to comprehend". In the development of Plato's thought, the spirit is both the faculty which enables man to contemplate the changeless eternal world of forms and — in the later Plato — a cosmic potency, the world-soul, the rational order of being. Aristotle takes νοῦς as the activity (ἐνέργεια) which is characteristic of man: as the specific mode of human self-realization, it already foreshadows to some extent the later *ratio* — the independent human "determination" of all reality. In his famous view of the origin of the spirit as "from without" (θύραθεν) Aristotle presents the spirit, in its relationship to being and God, as purely external and in the nature of an object. Western metaphysics is henceforth dominated

by the notion of spirit's being "in" and "above" man. Spirit is experienced and expounded as something detached from the "world" (space, time, movement) and ordained only to "being", which is considered as a perpetual presence, independent of space, time and movement.

For later developments, it is important to observe that the notion of spirit underwent a decisive change in Christianity, though the notion was always determined by its Greek origin. The richness of meaning which the notion of spirit offers us today is undoubtedly due to the confrontation of the Greek experience of existence with that of the Bible and Christianity — the "destiny of the West", as M. Müller called it — a confrontation which did not result in a total synthesis. For St. Augustine, the spirit (mens, animus) is not simply the Greek νοῦς: it is the acies mentis, the apex of the mind, the personal, dynamic point of contact and encounter between man and God. But Platonism is still a mighty force, and he allows the Christian experience of existence to be coloured by the metaphysics of the ideae aeternae immutabiles. In St. Thomas Aquinas, the spirit (mens, spiritus) is understood, anthropologically, as the individual substance: spirit is spirit-soul, that is, the form of the body, in terms of an Aristotelian hylemorphism re-interpreted scholastically. But this anthropological aspect is not the only one in St. Thomas. He also assigns the spirit its place in the larger whole of a hierarchical metaphysics of being and the Christian doctrine of creation. Being and spirit tend to coincide, and actually do so, in complete identity, in God, whereas the human spirit is "all things, but only in a certain fashion" (quodammodo omnia). Beings can be understood only in the spirit, since it is the "light" (lumen) in which the excellence of man's essence is founded. This "light" refers man to the "uncreated light", of which it is the imprint (impressio), revelation (manifestatio) and likeness (similitudo) "in" man. Corresponding to the natural and supernatural order, this light is either natural or supernatural.

Modern developments of the notion of spirit are characterized by the tendency to treat it as one with the subject. The profusion of meanings with which the spirit had been enriched in the course of its history gave rise to a varied vocabulary. Thus Descartes speaks of res cogitans, Leibniz of the "monad", Kant of the "transcendental consciousness", Fichte of the "ego" — and so on. The climax of this development was reached in German Idealism, which claimed to merge the whole history of the spirit into the absolute dialectic of being and spirit. Hence for Hegel, spirit is the "loftiest concept", the "supreme definition of the absolute". The spirit alone is the true and the real, it sets antithesis and synthesis in motion, it is the unity of all oppositions. Hence, as the self-determination of the spirit proceeds, all determinations are, as Hegel says, "spiritualized", "made fluid": they are absorbed into the growing self-awareness of the spirit, which attains its perfection in the concept of absolute knowledge, which is the self-awareness of absolute freedom.

Dissatisfaction with the Hegelian system of the absolute spirit was voiced from three stand-points, which gave rise to a correspondingly threefold development in the understanding of spirit. With Kierkegaard the biblical and Christian background makes itself felt once more (see below). Marx and dialectical materialism regard the spirit as the reflection of material nature. Dilthey tries to define the life of the spirit according to its concrete forms and contrast their special nature and methods with all natural processes ("the sciences of the spirit"). At present the concept of spirit is used in many senses according to the schools or traditions followed. Two questions arouse particular attention. The first arises from the "historical consciousness" of the 19th century and is the fundamental one about the "historicity" of human existence, which poses indirectly the question as to the "historicity" of thought (see below). The second is posed by the "evolutionary" view of the world taken by modern science and asks about the place of man and hence that of the spirit in the cosmos (cf. P. Teilhard de Chardin).

3. *Suggested solution.* a) When we try to explain the notion of spirit in terms of today's thinking of the problem, we encounter a remarkable difficulty. The very school of thought, which, following Heidegger, now poses the question of being and of the historicity of thought most radically, avoids using the notion of spirit at all, or to any significant extent. The reason for its exclusion is its origin in the Greek metaphysics of the West. However, a justifiable criticism of Graeco-Occidental metaphysics with its disregard of time and history, should not make us lose sight of the decisive change brought about in the Greek concept of spirit by the biblical and Christian experience.

Apart for instance from St. Augustine (see above), Kierkegaard must be mentioned as one of the most important witnesses to a concept of spirit which is not simply Greek, but biblical and Christian in its essential relationship to time and freedom. His remark "that the Greeks did not grasp the notion of the spirit in its deepest sense" suggests that our task should be to understand the conjunction of spirit and history from the standpoint of the Christian experience of time.

b) The notion of spirit derives from a primordial human experience of which it is the interpretation. Spirit is what distinguishes man from all other beings. It is "presence", growing historically more intense. Man is not just one being among others: he is the being in whom the meaning of being is disclosed as he makes his concrete and manifold affirmation of being. As he says "is", he expresses his transcendence with regard to all beings, a transcendence which is orientated to being. In his openness to being, which is experienced *a priori* but always mediated historically and which constitutes the basis of all transcendence, man arrives at that primordial selfhood in which he distinguishes himself in knowledge and will from all beings and finds his essential freedom.

This experience of "historicity", today being expressly formulated for the first time, forbids us to base the notion of spirit on that of some changeless and eternal being. Being is no longer experienced merely as a timeless entity, to be grasped and represented in objectivating concepts, but as the genesis of history and meaning. It is a self-disclosing "event" — which should not, however, be taken as implying any ontological "actualism". Thus the spirit is openness to being, or rather, it is the "medium" or "place" where the self-communication of being — experienced as an event — makes its meaning known and its absolute claim felt. Spirit is therefore the presence of being to itself, a presence primarily historical in the sense that it releases history. This presence must be simply interpreted as the fathomlessness of being, which alone makes room for truth and freedom: the mystery which is at the disposal of none. Thus being discloses itself historically in the sense that it creates history. In doing so, it remains the mystery which is not at the disposal of man. And this alone is how the personal self-disclosure of God can be (see *Potentia Obedientialis*) and is

in fact always experienced in his salvific action in history (see *Salvation* III, *Grace, Nature and Grace*). He is "absolute spirit": not in the sense of an objectified changeless "self-possession" remote from the world and history, but as the incalculable personal "origin", to which the finite human spirit always feels itself referred, and to whose rule and claim it knows itself to be subject in its experience of thought and freedom (see *Participation*).

Excluding therefore all ideas of an immediate knowledge of God as object (see *Ontologism*), we may further understand the human spirit as the immediacy of the finite to the infinite, of the conditioned to the absolute, of the temporal to the eternal: which means in the concrete that the spirit must be understood as an immediate relationship to God. This does not imply a sealed-off "inwardness". The immediacy or immediate relationship to God is and always remains a fresh self-realization *as history* (M. Müller). In its character of immediacy (immediate relationship to God), the spirit is the ultimate historicity itself, from which all history originates: history being understood as the dialectical development in time of man's relationship to himself and to things. This peculiar relationship between the spirit (as such immediacy) and its self-realization (in its history) must be borne in mind, because it marks the radical difference between the view here put forward and Hegel's dialectic of the absolute spirit. The spirit being immediate relationship to God realizes itself in its history not by an Hegelian process of "self-elimination by transformation" but by maintaining this inviolable relationship with God in which it fulfils itself. Thus in contrast to Hegel we understand the spirit essentially as *personal spirit:* which gives rise to the problem of the relationship between persons or subjects.

c) The view of the spirit here put forward makes the spirit "greater" than man: as Pascal says, "l'homme passe infiniment l'homme", not in the sense that it is alien or extrinsic to man, but in the sense that man is only what he is by being thus "greater" than himself. The most essential thing in man is not a self-sufficient subjectivity, but a constant opening out beyond himself, which we may call his being "there", the presence of being disclosing itself historically as mystery. Thus the various historical interpretations of spirit (see section 2) are subsumed and transformed in this understanding of spirit, which has been gained from the experience of historicity.

We see therefore the spirit both as that which immeasurably surpasses man and as that which remains his most essential element. And the question now is how we are to understand his concrete structure as it is manifested in the multiplicity of its components. The various acts in which man fulfils himself point to *two basic spiritual faculties:* rational intellect and will. The source from which they originate is the spirit — St. Thomas had already called this process *resultatio, emanatio.* Since the spirit must fulfil itself through these two faculties, it includes a sort of unity in duality, a double intention or direction swinging between two poles, in which it "must throb as though in two pulses" (W. Kern). *Knowledge* represents the element of perceptive appropriation, but the outgoing urge of *love* is the element in which the spirit obtains its most characteristic determination. The two functions may be distinguished by reflective reasoning. But the more concrete the exercise of their essential activities, the more fully are they integrated with one another, as interpenetrating modes of the one total tendency of the spirit.

d) The human spirit reaches its complete concrete reality only in its "attachment" to the body, which is not, however, to be regarded merely as an extrinsic medium or instrument, but as its "expression", its way of being "there". The specifically human finiteness of the spirit is manifested in this concrete act of being "there". In this connection we may mention briefly that our starting-point, the historicity of the spirit — by which history is first set afoot — allows us to take in and go beyond the Greek way of understanding the Christian doctrine of *angels,* the so-called "pure spirits". We are now enabled to think out the nature of the angels more thoroughly — and more biblically. This is true above all of their "relationship to the world and history" (K. Rahner), which remains essential, though other than that of the human spirit.

e) Spirit as the self-realization of the immediacy of the presence of being also implies an essential relationship to the *material cosmos.* The spirit is the self-presentation of being as the unlimited whole. There can be therefore and there is nothing "outside" the spirit. And since it can only realize itself by means of material things, the cosmos is at once absorbed into the dialectic of the spirit, of which it is the "extended embodiment".

It follows that the history of the spirit and the evolution of the cosmos do not draw further and further apart but come constantly closer together. The human spirit first appears "inside" the cosmos and its evolution, whose history therefore precedes the spirit and (in a certain way) outruns it. But this does not mean either that the human spirit is an immanent product of evolution, derived from a purely material process, nor that it is an alien element in the cosmos. The human spirit is not to be thought of as an object within the world, just as one "thing" among others. By its very nature it is the presence of being, that which first gives rise to history and meaning. Hence it is clear that the human spirit always spans the history of the cosmos, inasmuch as it can give meaning to the whole history of the cosmos — even retrospectively. And this is not a process extrinsic or indifferent to the cosmos, since the cosmos is only addressed as cosmos by the interpretation of the spirit: that is, the cosmos only "comes to itself" "in" the spirit. Hence the history of the cosmos is always opened out to the spirit: indeed, it culminates in the spirit and is "fundamentally always a history of the spirit" (K. Rahner). Thus we may not think of the spirit as merely the product of a material process, as dialectic materialism maintains, misapprehending completely the nature of the spirit. Yet the peculiar history of the blending of spirit and cosmos in unity only becomes comprehensible in the light of an act which spans both: the creative act of God (see *Creation*).

See also *Pre-Socratics, Platonism, Aristotelianism, Thomism, Metaphysics, Hylemorphism, Idealism, Marxism, Existence* II, *Body, Soul.*

BIBLIOGRAPHY. M. Müller, *Sein und Geist* (1940); id., "Ende der Metaphysik?", *Philosophisches Jahrbuch der Görres-Gesellschaft* 72 (1964), pp. 1–48; W. Cramer, *Grundlegung einer Theorie des Geistes* (1957); A. Marc, *L'être et l'esprit* (1958); W. Kern, "Einheit-in-Mannigfaltigkeit: Fragmentarische Überlegungen zur Metaphysik des Geistes", *Gott in Welt. Festgabe für K. Rahner,* I (1964), pp. 207–39; P. Teilhard de Chardin, *Man's Place in Nature* (1966); K. Rahner, *Spirit in the World* (1968).   *Lourencino B. Puntel*

SPIRITUALISM

Spiritualism is a general term covering both certain philosophical statements of the reality and power of the spirit and of its relation to the material and corporeal world (1); and also certain tendencies and attitudes in the social and individual life of men in religious matters (2). The more common meaning in English (= "spiritism"), interest in certain abnormal phenomena attached to mediums etc., is not dealt with here; but see *Psychology* IV.

1. *Spiritualistic tendencies in philosophy*. In the history of philosophy, spiritualism is used to characterize opinions opposed to materialism. It is the position which maintains that the spirit is an independent, non-derivative reality and not subject to causal determinism. Some extreme positions regard the spirit monistically as the sole reality and discount the material and corporeal as mere manifestations of the spirit (see *Monism*). Various opinions may be adduced under this heading. Platonism maintained a dualism as between the world of forms and of the senses. Neo-Platonism developed this further, with its notion of the ascent of the soul to the spiritual and the primordial One. Psychological spiritualism maintains a fundamental opposition between soul and body, based on a radical separation of spirit and matter. The soul is purely spiritual, without any other activities apart from the spiritual ones (R. Descartes, F. P. Maine de Biran, N. de Malebranche). The various philosophies which strive to understand matter as the self-explication, product or epiphenomenon of the spirit (G. Berkeley, G. W. von Leibniz, German Idealism) are efforts to go beyond this dualism.

The positivistic tendencies of the 19th century (see *Positivism*), which rejected all metaphysics and all knowledge outside the bounds of experience, was opposed by a philosophy which investigated the ground of the possibility of the experience of the positive "datum" and proposed to see there a fundamental spiritual principle. So for instance R. H. Lotze, M. Wundt, F. Paulsen in Germany; in France, as the precursors of the later existence-philosophy, F. P. Maine de Biran, F. Ravaisson, J. Lachelier, and then H. Bergson and M. Blondel and the *philosophie de l'esprit* of L. Lavelle and R. Le Senne.

These philosophies are at one in refusing to accept, in view of the multiplicity of the manifestations of reality, a metaphysical dualism. They search for a unifying basic principle behind the contrasts. They find this basis, underlying all reality in all its forms, in a spiritual principle, in contrast to the materialism which maintains that all reality can be reduced to and derived from matter and material forces.

The explanation of this principle, which is the one unifying ground of all reality, takes different forms. The unity is explained as a unity of origin. The origin is distinct from the being of things, but the unity does not eliminate differences and contrasts within the various realms of being. An openness for the spirit is assumed, as the intrinsic relation to this origin. On the other hand, the unity is also explained as a unity of substance and essence, which then, consistently, eliminates the distinctions between the various realms — between absolute and contingent being, in the God-world relationship (see this article, and *Pantheism*). And in the realm of the contingent the difference between knowledge and being, matter and spirit, being and action, individual and community is also eliminated. This has important consequences for the self-understanding of man, for his notion of freedom, society and the world.

2. *Spiritualism and religious life*. Spiritualism and spiritualistic tendencies in the self-understanding of man have less marked effects, in the religious and especially the Christian realm, with regard to doctrine, as for instance in the development of a definitely spiritualistic theology. They are mostly at work in the realm of actual religious life, where they bring about certain emphases and shifts of accent in preaching, piety and the forms of religious fellowship. What is at stake here is in general the meaning of redemption for the material creation, and in particular the significance of signs, rites, symbols and social structures, both for the mediation of salvation and for the religious act. Here we can only indicate briefly the way such accents are displaced, without addressing ourselves fully to their many historical manifestations and justifications.

a) While it is true that the oneness and totality of the redemption, taking in the whole of creation in its salutary effects, was never explicitly contested within the Church, the history of Christianity shows certain trends in the opposite sense. The work of salvation may be restricted or reduced to the "soul" of man, the consequence being that the truth of the resurrection of the flesh, with its bearings on the significance of earthly realities and the worldly activity of Christians, is left in the background. Such restriction is evident in the description of the mission of the Church as the "cure of souls", in the role accorded to the laity and their worldly activity within the Church, in the fashion in which the Church lives in and presents itself to the world. To ward off such false spiritualization, Vatican II recalls the cosmic and historical dimension of the redemption (*Gaudium et Spes,* art. 45, citing Eph 1:10) and takes this theological principle as its basis when speaking of the Church in the world, of the proper share which the laity have in the mission of the Church, of the significance of history, culture, etc., in the order of salvation.

b) The "spiritualizing" view distorts the intrinsic relationship between the order of creation and the order of redemption. And the religious act ceases to be understood as a total activity of the whole man in all his dimensions, including therefore body, world, history and society. Instead, the spirit, understood in a mystical or a rationalistic sense, becomes the sole or at least the primary element in the constitution of the religious act and the formation of religious fellowship. And then the demand is made that the relationship to God should be direct and pure. Mediation through the word and the sacraments becomes questionable or indeed repugnant. The historical, social presence and tangibility of the work of salvation is lost sight of. Body and soul remain opposed to each other without intrinsic relationship. So too there is a split between man's fragility (see *Original Sin*) and his justification by faith, between the gospel and the order of the world and morality, between faith and works. Religious life is restricted to the sphere of private inwardness.

c) Such spiritualization makes itself manifest above all in the understanding of the hierarchical office in the Church, of worship and of the sacraments. A supposedly direct relationship to God reduces the ministry to no more than a function ensuring good order. Anything beyond this is suspect, as an undue interference in the relation of man to God. The saying of our Lord that the Father is to be adored "in the spirit and the truth" (Jn 4:23) is not merely understood, in line with the prophetic tradition of this saying (cf. for instance Hos 6:6; Jer 7:21; Is 1:11; 58:6), as a demand for the purification of worship, eliminating a merely external performance or superstitious and magic approaches. The purity and authenticity of adoration, in the spiritualistic view, consists in the rejection of all cultic forms. The

necessity and efficacity of the sacraments are also lost sight of. They are reduced to mere symbols and reminders, which bring home imaginatively to the faithful the inner process of salvation.

d) In the realm of ethics, spiritualistic tendencies show themselves in the radical elimination of an "ethics of law" in favour of an ethics of the disposition. The "figure of this world" is rather endured patiently than moulded actively. The attitude towards decisive realms of human existence, such as power, marriage and property, is rather one of anxiety and withdrawal than of active and critical responsibility.

Spiritualism remains a constant danger to Christianity, and is not due merely to external influences. The task of grasping intellectually and translating into practice the whole range of the mystery of the incarnation is constantly threatened by a spiritualizing theory and practice. Such tendencies are clearest in times marked by a rigidity of attitude and a stress on externals which call for reform and enlivenment. But then they can prove to be positive contributions to the complex historical process which allows itself to be moulded by faith. The necessity of not just dismissing such trends but of welcoming them seriously and using them as critical correctives in the constant reform of the Church also holds good — in an analogous way — of the relationship to the communities outside the Church which claim to uphold a pure spiritual religion and a direct relationship to God.

See also *Religious Act.*

BIBLIOGRAPHY. See bibliographies on *Religious Act, Body, World;* also: H. Heimsoeth, *Die sechs grossen Themen der abendländischen Metaphysik* (1922); G. Thils, *La théologie des réalités terrestres* (1952); P. Tillich, *The Theology of Culture* (1959); A. Auer, *Weltoffener Christ* (1960); M. Merleau-Ponty, *The Phenomenology of Perception* (1962); H. Urs von Balthasar, *Who is a Christian?* (1967); J. Splett, *Der Mensch in seiner Freiheit* (1967); K. Rahner, *Spirit in the World* (1968); J. B. Metz, *Theology of the World* (1968).

Ernst Niermann

SPIRITUALITY

I. Concept: A. Biblical Foundations and Historical Developments. B. The True Notion of Spirituality and Some Illuminating Contrasts. C. Spirituality: the Objective Redemption as Mystery. D. Consequences. II. History of Christian Spirituality:

A. From Jesus Christ to the Development of the Kerygma. B. Development and Consolidation. C. The Intermediate Period. D. A Unified Society and Culture. E. The Struggle for the Individual. F. Inward-Directed Development. G. Concluding Remarks. III. Special Features: A. Meditation. B. Examination of Conscience. C. Spiritual Reading. D. Spiritual Exercises. E. Spiritual Direction.

I. Concept

A. BIBLICAL FOUNDATIONS AND HISTORICAL DEVELOPMENTS

1. *"Spirit" in Scripture.* Both the term and the content of what is generally referred to as Christian spirituality have their origin in the NT. Judaism had already combined in רוּחַ *(pneuma, spiritus, spirit)* a number of associated meanings which are important for us. Spirit was the life-force stemming from God with its psychological and dogmatic intelligibility — with an ever clearer accent on "the religious individuality". And spirit was the power of Yahweh in its significance for the people of God — either as a prophetical and eschatological gift (1 Sam 10:6; Is 11:2; Joel 3:1f.), or hypostatized as the Wisdom of God (Wis 1:6; 7:22). In the NT there grew out of the Christ-event an understanding of the "Spirit" that was both new and of a piece with what went before. It appears timidly at first in Mk and Mt where there is evident a hesitancy to connect the uniqueness of Jesus, "the fact that God himself is really present in him as nowhere else" (E. Schweizer), with the extensive experience of the Spirit within the community after Easter. A new theology of the Spirit developed, as Lk then shows, after the supremacy of the Lord as bestower of the Spirit (4:14ff.; 24, 49; Acts 2:33) was seen more clearly and as he was recognized as Lord of the Spirit-filled community. The relation of the Spirit of the Church to the eschatological reality of the Lord was seen to be one of identity. When Lk depicts the Spirit as the presence of Christ establishing his Church, the accent is still on the extraordinary. The Spirit is "the special gift" which brings about in the faithful, individually and collectively, the manifestations "which are essential to a missionary activity which is still going on and growing, and indeed, which make this activity possible" (E. Schweizer). Paul definitively completes this identification of the exalted Lord with the *Pneuma* (2 Cor 3:17). To be united to Christ is to enter into the sphere of the Spirit (1 Cor 6:17); faith in the Lord is from and in the Spirit (1 Cor 2:10ff.); the renunciation of circumcision, the "flesh", the self-righteous observance of the law, is service of the Spirit of God and glorying in Jesus Christ (Phil 3:3–6). In concrete terms it is called: praying in the Spirit (Rom 8:15ff.; Gal 4:6); the fulfilment of the whole law through the Spirit (Rom 8:4; in Gal 5:19–23 the *works* of the flesh are contrasted with the *fruit* of the Spirit); the building-up of the Church through the gifts of the Spirit (1 Cor 12–14) and through love of the neighbour (Gal 5:13–15; 1 Cor 13). While St. Paul focuses his gaze more intently upon the consummation which is yet to come (Rom 8:11; 1 Cor 15:35ff.), and upon the pledge of what is yet to be given (Rom 8:23; 1 Cor 15:35ff.), St. John stresses the present salvation in the Spirit which means judgment for "the world", but rebirth in the Spirit of truth and love for the faithful (3:3–5; 4:23f.; 6:63; 14–16; 20:19ff.). This experience of the Spirit, as Christians drew new inspiration from the incomparable figure of their Lord, gave rise, especially in the late Pauline and the Johannine writings, to a deeper insight into the divine and personal individuality of the Spirit. And the "spirituality" of Christian existence, in the individual, the community, and the Church as a whole was more clearly recognized.

2. *Pneumatikos,* spiritual, became thereby — with a basis supplied already by St. Paul (1 Cor 2:13–15; 9:11; 14:1) — a technical term for Christian existence. The neologism *spirit(u)alis* appeared early in Christianity. In spite of shifts of meaning, restrictions and extensions, the adjective has retained down to our own time the sense of "at the core of Christian existence". Throughout the Middle Ages and far into modern times, one might consider it *the* distinctive description of the typically Christian. This was also true of the corresponding words in the Romance and Germanic languages.

3. The corresponding noun, *spiritualitas,* the formal and creative element of the core of Christian existence, is found as early as the 5th and 6th centuries, appears in the 12th and 13th centuries in the great poets, and by the middle of the 13th century gave rise to the corresponding French *espiritualité* and the like. But it was only in the 17th century that the French *spiritualité* was established in its technical sense to indicate the personal

relation of man to God. Here the subjective side of this relation was more and more stressed. The banality, however, of the word when one speaks of Christian spirituality and Christian spiritualities, is only the product of our own time, as also is, unfortunately, the anaemic unreality which is almost always connected with the word "spirituality".

B. The True Notion of Spirituality and Some Illuminating Contrasts

This short survey of the biblical basis and the historical development of the word shows sufficiently the dialectical tension of what "spirituality" should mean, and which is only inadequately expressed in static concepts. It is rooted in the coming of divine revelation, in the historical concreteness of revelation in Jesus Christ, and in the ecclesiastical tradition through word and sacrament. It means the personal assimilation of the salvific mission of Christ by each Christian which is always in the framework of new forms of Christian conduct and is comprised within the fundamental answer of the Church to the word of salvation. The inner fullness of Christian spirituality, as demanded by the biblical "Spirit", and the deformations which need to be corrected, can be best discussed in the light of concrete historical problems. This will also help to bring out key-points which will give content to a concept only formally outlined so far.

1. *Enthusiasm and institutions.* St. Paul had to censure the Christians of Corinth for the "enthusiasm" (in the sense of Knox's book) in misinterpreting the gifts of the Spirit. Ecstatic spontaneity, raptures, and abnormal reactions seemed to be the supreme experience of the Spirit. This heady misconception never became again a real danger for the Church as a whole, after the Montanist difficulties of the 2nd and 3rd centuries, although the mania for the extraordinary and miraculous remained a temptation, one that our Lord himself had had to warn against (e.g., Mt 16:1–4). Behind all this there is a supernaturalism which wants to see as well as believe in the promise given in Jesus Christ. The opposite danger, however — often proceeding from the same root — of turning every expression of "Spirit" into an official institution or even of equating the official institution with charism, and laws and institutions with spirituality, is

much more real in actual Catholicism. The great examples in the history of piety shows us that genuine spirituality can only develop in the tension between office and charism. The movement of St. Francis of Assisi centring on the ideal of poverty allowed its enthusiasm to be guided along an orderly course by ecclesiastical restrictions; St. Ignatius of Loyola, who formulated the rules of *sentire cum ecclesia* was long under suspicion of being an *Alumbrado*. Too much juridical regulation of spirituality and the absorption of all initiative or spontaneity by officially established traditions undoubtedly meant that many initiatives could find no place in the Church and that their spirituality, in part genuinely Christian, found homes outside it.

2. *Spiritualization and rationalization.* Another danger had its source in the attempted philosophical penetration of the spiritual life (cf. Evagrius Ponticus, Meister Eckhart). The emphasis easily came to be placed on the rational element — as can be seen from the very terminology: spiritual-mental-intellectual. Christianity, instead of being seen as integrating man, was made an intellectual and theoretical process, an approach that is quite compatible with a "mysticism of the obscure". This danger, which appears so clearly in history, ran parallel over long stretches to the institutionalizing tendency already indicated. It did not, however, result so much in a juridical regulation of the spiritual life, as in a frequently esoteric "watering-down" of the spiritual. As a result, the word "spirituality" still carries with it today the flavour of the enfeebled, the ascetically de-materialized, and the aesthetically esoteric. The opposing danger of turning spirituality into an unspiritual life-force is so foreign to Christianity that it need not be seriously considered (cf., however, isolated racial deformations of the Christian message). Yet related phenomena such as the stressing of the irrational or exaggerations of an emotional or pietistic nature are clearly perceptible in the history of Christianity. Along this same line one could also mention the modern attempts — especially outside of the Catholic Church — to free Christian spirituality from the objective, articulate and historically tangible, and to base it rather on the subject and his decisions, commitment, or free and unanalysable acts. What is of permanent value in all these attempts is the stress on the incalculable role which the individual person and his commit-

ment play in spirituality. The danger here is the resolving of the tension between the original, objective saving acts and the subjective appropriation of them, in favour of the latter.

3. *Dualism*. For the sake of completeness we must mention a third source of danger inseparably connected with those already mentioned. Very early, Christian spirituality took a perilous course through a dualistic conception of man as body and soul. Up to the present day a great part of spiritual literature had been unconsciously dominated by the ideal of the "spiritual" man who, purified of all material concerns, strives to attain to the pure realm of the soul and the spirit. Behind this lurks an ontological misinterpretation of the Pauline tension between spirit and flesh. Certainly the Gnostic-Manichaean disqualification of the body is today shunned in Catholicism. Some indeed are apprehensive, not without justification, of the backlash of an imprudent glorification of the body. But one could scarcely maintain that theology has completely overcome the Greek conception of the two-layer man. The image is suggested by language, and sustained by the indispensable kernel of truth within it. To an even greater extent this accusation is true of spiritual theology and still more so as regards ordinary "edifying" books. A re-thinking cannot be achieved merely by the superficial adoption of more modern terminology. It demands of spiritual theology that same intellectual effort which has produced such obvious fruits in the many new approaches to dogmatics. It cannot be done without the critical dissection of forms of thought which have been valid for centuries. See *New Testament Theology, Old Testament Theology, Existence* II, *Language, Sociology, Psychology.* It is at the same time, however, important to be warned against any reduction of spirituality to the psychological or the sociological.

C. Spirituality: the Objective Redemption as Mystery

1. *Preaching and the sacraments as the origin.* Christian spirituality — that one can today also speak of a spirituality of a Thomas Mann or of Marxism cannot be dealt with here — draws its vitality from the salvific deed of God in Jesus Christ present in the Church and transmitted through its preaching and sacraments. Some of the elementary considerations, then, can be better elaborated in terms of this other pole of the dialectical unity of Christian spirituality, the objective salvific deeds which are alive in the faith of the Church, rather than through reflection upon the believing man. A glance at the historical development will justify this orientation of spirituality to the content of faith and the object of worship. The Christianity of the 1st century was, for instance, so closely bound up with Scripture and the "objective" sacramental events that what was understood as "sacrament" was the whole fullness of the mystery, the mystery of the liturgy as well as the mystery of life inspired by worship. It meant, therefore, the mystery of Christian existence as well as that of the salvific events; behind the datable historical event, it meant the divinely willed personal confrontation of the individual Christian with Christ through the mediatory activity of the Church.

In the modern *theologoumenon* of the *res sacramenti* a meagre though central kernel of the ancient sacramental theology of the Christian life, actual "spirituality", is still alive. The words of Scripture were likewise the support of the Christian faith. The doctrine of the three or four senses of Scripture brought it into lively contact with the faith of the individual. It is true that the NT antithesis between Spirit and letter (2 Cor 3:6; Rom 2:19; 8:7) was interpreted in a one-sided way with reference to the problem of understanding Scripture (Origen). (Primarily this was meant to contrast the impotency of the law with the life-giving Spirit of Jesus Christ.) But the concrete way of thinking inspired by the four senses shows that the notion of the economy of salvation was still basic. In modern terms, the letter meant the superficial sense which was still existentielly unassimilated and hence also accessible to those without faith; allegory was the dogmatic reality of salvation-history intended by the letter; the moral sense was the existentiell assimilation of this in Church and private life; typology was directed towards the eschatological salvation in Jesus Christ, which is at the same time present and still to be hoped for. In the 12th and 13th centuries this unity was split up into what we would today call dogmatics and spirituality. At the same time the theology of the Scriptures also became an independent science with the result that in the late Middle

Ages spirituality was continuing ever more noticeably along a track that was far from both Scripture and dogma. From the four-fold fullness of meaning there remained finally only empty moralizing or free speculation using verses of Scripture as points of departure. The way lay open for a psychologizing spirituality. Even this could not preserve the unity of integral existence and broke up, especially since the 17th century, into the partial disciplines of ascetical and mystical theology.

It was only in our time that attempts were again made to re-establish the former unity. In the task which still remains to be done, one cannot skip this historical development and the individual disciplines. Nevertheless, it remains essential to restore the unified form which alone gives each of these disciplines their meaning.

2. *Preaching and sacraments as source of life*. What we have briefly described as the development of reflection upon "spirituality" also had its clear counterpart in spirituality as it was actually lived out. This could be spelled out in a history of meditation (from attentive reading of Scripture to abstract pondering on philosophical truths), a history of eucharistic piety (from the common liturgy with its repercussions to devotion to the "prisoner of the tabernacle"), a history of mysticism (from the reading and active response to Scripture and the *rara hora, parva mora* of St. Bernard to *contemplatio infusa*). A result of this would be even clearer evidence that spirituality is "the dimension of mystery within the objective dogmatics of the Church" (Balthasar). The two poles, then, seen in their original unity are: the fullness of revelation which unfolds in the Church, and man in his personal existence. It would also be clear that the spiritual life is not a simple concept but one that springs from and derives its sense of direction from the saving events, from Christ who is present in the word and the sacrament. Scientific and theoretical reflection on spirituality consequently cannot be content to be one discipline alongside of or subordinate to other theological disciplines. Spirituality is a general science that cuts across all the rest and bridges all subjects relevant to theology. Always directly flowing from the font of revelation in Christ, it brings all such subjects into the life of the individual. Therefore it naturally arranges the other disciplines according to their bearing on actual Christian existence.

D. CONSEQUENCES

1. *Unity and plurality of Christian spirituality*. From such a description of spirituality which merely tries to echo the biblical message of life in the Spirit, there are several important conclusions. The question of there being one or many spiritualities (Bouyer, Daniélou) is merely a matter of the point of view. There is obviously only one Christian spirituality if I begin my consideration of this "cross-sectional" science on the level where the Christian message is first addressed to men. However, were one to consider the lowest level of its actual realization, to use the image of the pyramid, there would be as many spiritualities as there are alert Christians. Between these two levels lie those great patterns of religious conduct which have exercised formative influence in the course of Church history (and already in the biblical writings) and which have often been charismatic and exemplary realizations of Christian spirituality for a given time or for a given task.

2. *Spirituality and personal life*. On the basis of this truth and of the general conception of spirituality which was sketched above, it will also be clear that concrete spiritualities can be grasped less as doctrine than as personal existence. Just as the one Christian spirituality can be defined most clearly in terms of the person of Jesus Christ, so too these great group-forming spiritualities within Church history are all charisms of God which are embodied in a man or a group rather than in a doctrine — an incarnation that is irreducible to conceptual analysis. That these "divine imperatives" also took on didactic form and were written down is self-explanatory, since the whole man, individually as well as socially, is addressed by the "divine imperative". Yet even today the most fruitful spiritualities seem to grow rather out of actual Christian existence than out of ideas.

3. *Trinitarian circumincession of spiritualities*. This personal crystallization and the interplay of spiritualities gives rise to a unity and diversity of Christian attitudes which, as Balthasar has shown, are ultimately based on the trinitarian unity of God. Though the fullness of Christian spirituality is experienced in each case, in the individual or in a group, there are within this very fullness real differences as between persons and between

groups — differences around which communities build up. This unity-and-diversity which eludes logical categories must be allowed for in the present-day discussion of lay and religious spirituality. An absorption of the one into the other would contradict the trinitarian basis of its diversity in the same way as a reduction to categories or a chaotic dissociation. Historically, the position of the spirituality of the religious life or the counsels has been clearly that of the symbol and exemplar which leads to true Christianity (K. Rahner). Whether this contrast with lay spirituality is still valid depends in the last analysis upon the Christian existence itself which is charismatically bestowed by God, and not upon theological reflection upon it. It should, however, be clearly indicated that though theological reflection must rethink many of the attitudes of the past in this context, it cannot find there any discrediting of the layman in the relation between the lay, priestly and religious states as it was properly understood, for example, by the great religious teachers of the past (in terms of that necessary relation between unity and diversity which we have indicated).

4. *Service in the Church as the common element of spirituality.* This necessary relation between unity and diversity within Christian spirituality has a deeper parallel in the one life of the individual Christian. The word of God — if we may include within this biblical expression the whole event of revelation and its transmission in history — is only fully the word of God if it finds its realization in the obedience and action of the Christian (cf. *res sacramenti*). Likewise, the Christian is only fully a Christian when he looks away from his own existence to lose himself, listening to God's word, in prayerful and active service of the Kingdom of God, each according to his own call. This unity prior to and present within all diversity is Christian spirituality. It is that spiritual reality which is already transmitted through the Church and as the Church, in which each Christian is inserted. It is precisely in the case of the great, independent personalities of Christianity that it can be demonstrated that the distinctiveness of the figure, unmistakable though it is, arises out of a deeper-seated unity. It is from this unity also that the epochal changes in spirituality must derive their justification, and the same unity contributes to the radical changes that seem to be the stigmata of our times. It is the unity of the Spirit of Christ who "breathes where he wills" and in the way he wills and who always, nevertheless, gives himself in entirety. This intertwining of the many individual strands in the one pattern of the spirituality which is already given and ever to be renewed reveals the essentially ecclesial form of all Christian spirituality. It shows how it is grounded in the social as well as in the personal being of man and how it is built up in actual fulfilment in the grace of that Spirit who is both given to each and who remains ever the same. As the Spirit is the Spirit of Christ, there is also an equally essential eschatological dimension to spirituality. For in it the Christian directs his gaze towards the Lord who is both present and yet to come.

5. *Unity of activity and passivity.* Having recognized the Spirit as the determinant we can now approach the concepts, often presented as opposites, which have played such a great role in spirituality: asceticism (from that of ordinary life to preparation for the mystical union) and mysticism; action and contemplation, doing and suffering, achievement and gift, possession and striving for, etc. These opposites retain their importance and had, indeed, to be newly considered in modern anthropology and theologically deepened. However, we are today more aware than ever of their provisional nature with regard to the one thing which is at the heart of Christian spirituality. In the Scriptures many texts (cf. Gen 2:7; 1 Cor 2:10ff.) hint at the mystery of the Spirit, who is both God and of God and who is nevertheless bestowed upon man as his truest self. Theological reflection has fixed this truth in what can only be a dialectical formulation, namely that a man is wholly himself, his own to possess — and therefore action, deed, achievement; and also that he is just as much a gift of God — and therefore contemplation, passivity, and searching. In the actual spiritual life, however, this contrast, which in the last analysis is also at the basis of "asceticism and mysticism", is eliminated in the personal encounter with God. The analogous encounter between man and man already suggests the original identity of activity and passivity.

Since the spiritual life, in spite of all human achievement, is always first a divine imperative, any prediction of the course of modern spirituality could only tentatively be deduced from the signs of the times and without speculative finality. Perhaps one could offer, however, the following formulations as typical of the direction of spirituality in our time: a more intensive commitment within the world, especially in the area of its social need; diametrical to that, a more intensive conscious-personal responsibility; stressing of the dialogal; and all of this in an open-mindedness that is today allowing Christianity to look more and more to other religions and even to atheism. But perhaps all this is but an expression of the one fact that today God reveals himself as perhaps never before as the hidden God. To live this with complete openness for the incalculable imperative of God is Christian spirituality.

See also *Asceticism, Mysticism I, Holy Spirit, Enthusiasm.*

BIBLIOGRAPHY. On the historical part, see *DSAM;* L. Tinsley, *The French Expressions for Spirituality and Devotion: A Semantic Study* (1953); E. Schweizer "πνεῦμα", *TWNT,* VI, pp. 387–560, with bibliography; H. de Lubac, *Exégèse médiévale,* 4 vols. (1959–64); C. Mohrmann, *Études sur le latin des chrétiens,* 2 vols. (1961); J. Leclercq, "Spiritualitas", *Studia Medievalia,* III/1 (1962), pp. 279–96; M. de Certeau, "'Mystique' au XVIIᵉ siècle: Le problème du language 'mystique'", *L'homme devant Dieu,* II (1964), pp. 267–91; L. Bouyer, F. Vanderbroucke and J. Leclercq, *History of Christian Spirituality,* 3 vols. (1964–69). On the systematic developments, everything should be included which contains new approaches to spirituality, though most of this literature, characteristically, does not stem from the strict field of spirituality. Here we note only: H. Urs von Balthasar, "Spiritualität", *Verbum Caro* (1960), pp. 226–44; K. Rahner, "Über die evangelischen Räte", *Glauben und Leben* 37 (1964), pp. 17–37; L. Bouyer, *Introduction to Spirituality* (1964), with the discussion between J. Daniélou and L. Bouyer in *Études* (1961), pp. 270–4, 411–15; *Rivista di ascetica et mistica* 10 (1965), pp. 309–532 (special nos. 4–5, introductory essays on spiritual theology).

Josef Sudbrack

II. History of Christian Spirituality

Any thumb-nail sketch of the history of Christian spirituality bristles with difficulties. There are so many facets to depict: theology (where, for instance, some authors have neglected St. Irenaeus), liturgy, religious custom, asceticism and mysticism in the strict sense, psychology, sociology, ethnology and other supplementary disciplines; the endless variety of spirituality in individuals, groups, trends, periods, etc.

In spirituality, the subjective act, the *individuum ineffabile,* corresponds to the articulated propositions of dogmatics and the detailed customs of the liturgy. Hence any "historical synthesis" which is not to be a banal generalization must be somewhat personal and selective. Its value will be not in its completeness but in its usefulness as a basis for dialogue in interpreting the facts.

We concentrate in the following on Western Catholic Christianity.

A. FROM JESUS CHRIST TO THE DEVELOPMENT OF THE KERYGMA

Though it is difficult to depict the life of Jesus in terms of concrete situations and definite propositions, it is absolutely certain that his disciples knew him and his message as the presence of the Kingdom of God. There was a unity of the aloofness of God and the immediacy of God; of the *tremendum* of cross, judgment and *eschata,* and of the *fascinosum* of miracles, doctrine and person. All this is stamped with the seal of the definitive in the resurrection, through which the Lord goes and the Spirit comes. The history of spirituality is the development of this *individuum ineffabile.*

a) The first key is provided by the expectation of the imminent end. The one experience of the "Not Yet" and the "Now Already" is explained more and more definitely in terms of dates and numbers. The millenarianism of patristic times, the threats of judgment from visionaries and penitents, the "Kingdom of the Spirit" announced by Joachim of Fiore and the modern "Adventist" type of movement are further echoes of this explanation.

b) The "eschatological presence" proclaimed in the Johannine writings forms the counterpart to this expectancy. It has dangers of its own, which flared up in the "enthusiasm" of certain Corinthians, in Montanism, and in certain modern movements.

c) The presence of Christ in the Spirit, at once far and near, is the synthesis provided by St. Luke. This leaves the Church open to undue institutionalization of its eschatological dynamism and of its "enthusiasm" in the possession of the Spirit. But the doctrine of the sacraments, as in St. Ignatius of Antioch, which has often been impugned, is its legitimate embodiment.

d) In Scripture itself, the Spirit already begins to take on concrete form in the hierarchy (ministry) and dogma. The constant temptation of spirituality is to under-estimate them, while they themselves are tempted to forget that their function is merely ministerial.

e) The crystallization in terms of moral precepts (see *Sermon on the Mount*) stems from the Wisdom tradition. The dangers involved are reflected in the Letter of St. Clement, e.g., in the watering down of imperatives to an ethic of two degrees of perfection.

f) The theology of martyrdom has two main points. Death is testimony, asceticism is kerygma. But even this can produce short-sighted views, in the line of individualism and loss of eschatological perspective. Cf., for instance, Acts 7:56, "*I* see — [*now*] — the heavens open"; Phil 3; St. Ignatius of Antioch.

g) Scripture, the backward look to the Lord, and the Eucharist, his presence in the Spirit, unite the two tendencies and obviate their dangers.

B. DEVELOPMENT AND CONSOLIDATION

a) The theory of the coming Christian life remains unimpaired in the salvation-history of St. Irenaeus, as in the Syrian and Antiochene school (St. Ephraem, St. John Chrysostom) with its interest in positive scholarship. But it was otherwise in the Alexandrian school (Origen, St. Athanasius, St. Cyril, the Cappadocians). The "pious" theology of Monophysitism was inspired by this neo-Platonist approach. The word of Scripture reveals a "spiritual" sense, and the world becomes a cosmos spiritualizing itself towards the first principle (the ἕν of Plotinus). Spirituality describes and experiences this way of spiritualization.

b) This is clearly embodied in monasticism in all its forms — the anchorites (St. Anthony), the coenobites (Pachomius, St. Basil) and the type of monastic life generally adopted (Evagrius, Cassian). The Syro-Palestinian style of the wandering preacher (Mt 10) quickly developed into asceticism. Under the influence of the theology of martyrdom, it took the form of flight from the world into the desert. Its theoretical justification was worked out by the Alexandrian School. The crude concepts of spiritual realities in the Messalian school left scarcely a trace. The opposing trend from neo-Platonism became the basic principle for the Christian effort. The task to be mastered was the total renunciation of all that was earthly,

to make ready for the "spiritual" encounter with God.

c) After the turning-point under Constantine, there was a sense of public responsibility, which should not be regarded as a falling off from a higher state. It was rather the effort to master the world, as inspired by the Bible, in place of a spirituality which was inclined to flight from the world.

d) St. Augustine set in motion the great occidental, anthropological reversal, which was to remain more or less static in theory till Luther and indeed until existential theology.

C. THE INTERMEDIATE PERIOD

a) The chaos of the Barbarian Invasions and the triumphant progress of Islam revealed the superficiality of Christianization.

b) The mainstay of religion and civilization was monasticism (Lerins, St. Martin of Tours, St. Columbanus). The future lay with the synthesis of humanity, discipline and religion achieved in the Rule of St. Benedict. St. Gregory the Great was inspired by its spirit when he wrote his allegorical interpretation of Job, whose prudent asceticism was to make it the handbook of the Middle Ages.

D. A UNIFIED SOCIETY AND CULTURE

a) The Carolingian reform and renaissance saw much compilation and cataloguing of past records. "Germanic" traits became visible: love of the tangible (Eucharistic controversies), juridical interests (development of the Curia), dedicated following (veneration of the saints, effort to excel), emotional freedom (devotions), individualism (penitential theology).

b) Monasticism stamped the next centuries. Beside the intellectual approach of St. Anselm of Canterbury, there were the eremitical movements represented by St. Peter Damian and the Carthusians, and the disciplined organization of Cluny.

c) The interpretation of Scripture as applying to individual mysticism came to a peak in St. Bernard and the Cistercian theology (William of St. Thierry). Other components were enthusiasm for the Crusades and the poetry of love (Minnesingers).

d) Among the communities of clerics, the Premonstratensians and the Victorines Hugo and Richard tended to form systems and stressed the organic nature of salvation-history.

e) The piety of the mendicant orders was of a more active type. Under St. Francis of Assisi, the poverty of the wandering preachers was diverted from heresy to become a prop of the Church. The intellectual and practical efforts of St. Dominic to combat the heretical trend led to a great thrust forward in theology.

f) The high-point here was reached with St. Thomas Aquinas, O.P., St. Bonaventure, O.F.M., and then Scotus, O.F.M. It was prepared for by the *Sic-et-Non* dialectic of Abelard. But this "rationalization" forced spirituality to seek "non-theological" forms.

g) Great women like Hildegard and Hedwig had already striven for interiorization. The trend is clear in German mysticism (Eckhart, Suso, Tauler), in Ruysbroeck, and in English and Italian circles ("The Cloud of Unknowing", St. Angela de Foligno). Other trends were the ecstatic mysticism of certain nuns and the "dark night" mysticism, stemming from the Pseudo-Dionysius, among the Carthusians.

h) Nominalism (William of Occam) sought to break with neo-Platonism, through attention to the individual, linguistic logic, natural science (at Oxford), democracy. It gave rise to the *devotio moderna* and its methods of prayer (G. Groote, *The Imitation of Christ*), which began as a lay movement.

i) Other positive contributions came from reform movements in the religious orders. Nicholas of Cusa sought for a new spiritual unity, which was also the aim of the best forces in Humanism and the Renaissance.

j) Lack of intellectual insight in popular piety brought with it many dangers: superstition (in adoration of the sacred host), witch-hunting (the Inquisition), superficiality (copious accounts of visions, ignorance of the Bible), materialism (see *Relics*), subjectivism (devotion to the Sacred Heart), moralizing (in preaching), emotionalism and eschatological fears.

E. The Struggle for the Individual

a) The spirituality of the movement for reform (see *Reformation*) should not be thought of in terms of pietistic withdrawal or more world-directed revivalism, still less in terms of Gnostic or fanatical developments. Luther sought to underline the irreplaceable individuality of the believer. Nominalist in philosophy, he stressed the personal conscience, with the watch-word; *ego eram ecclesia*. The recourse to Scripture

signified the direct approach to Jesus. Even his theology of sin and grace stemmed from an unflinching confrontation with the infinite power and mercy of God. Calvin was clear but cold, disciplined but harsh, while Zwingli displayed humanistic traits (see *Calvinism*).

b) The Society of Jesus, founded by St. Ignatius Loyola, became the direct opposite, though the original intention was otherwise. Even here there are superficial distortions, but the encounter with God can be clearly seen as a unity in tension: strong individuality (illuminative way [cf. the Alumbrados], discernment of spirits), and determined objectivity (methods, obedience, service). The initial impulse did not come fully into its own in the theory of spirituality, but it may still be seen at work in Probabilism, with its stress on the individual conscience, Molinism (with its stress on freedom) and missionary adaptation (cultural emancipation).

c) Spanish mysticism at its peak provided a description of the encounter between God and man which was psychologically accurate and religiously transcendent, in the notion of grasping and being grasped. The spontaneous freshness and prudence of St. Theresa of Avila found objective expression in the work of founding monasteries and letter-writing, as also in devotion to the humanity of Jesus. The poetic and speculative tendency of St. John of the Cross shows its churchmanship in his recourse to Scripture and the classical authors.

F. Inward-Directed Development

Till the time of the Reformation, spirituality was combined with the outward and the interior life of the Church. As the Church sealed itself off — even the Baroque was inspired by a defensive reaction — men looked inwards. There is no need to describe individual figures (mostly French; see *Mysticism* II D) and schools (independent movements were lacking). Controversies hardened into official condemnations, but kept to the old lines. They were mostly differences of emphasis within the same basic principle.

a) *Survival of the past.* Even in scholarship the influence of German and Flemish mysticism persisted, in spite of writings being put on the Index, and gave rise to tensions within religious orders (S.J., O.F.M.Cap.). The use of the patristic armoury was often masterly (Arnauld, Bossuet and Fénelon). More than ever, the classical author was the

Pseudo-Dionysius (especially among the Carmelites).

b) In the controversy *De auxiliis* which opposed Dominicans and Jesuits, Jansenism and Quietism, the debate concerned the corruption of man, the irresistible nature of grace or the over-estimation of man (P. Charron). The roots of "abandonment", resignation even to hell (Molinos, Mme Guyon) and of the courtly spirituality (the king's confessors, Père Joseph) are to be found here. In moral theology, the controversy between Rigorism and Laxism was concerned with the claims of law or personal responsibility (see *Moral Theology* III). Controversies about the frequency of Holy Communion and the definitiveness of confession *(renouvellement)* were consequences of the actual practice. The differences are not fully explained by men's different pictures of God. Kindness was the key-note of St. Francis de Sales, strictness that of Saint-Cyran. The stress on the humanity of Christ and the *états* of Bérulle contrast with the destruction-theory of his disciple Condren. The Jansenists overstressed the Lordship of Christ in contrast to Pascal's love of Jesus. Much partisanship was due to political intrigues.

c) Religious communities remained the mainstay of spirituality. In the 16th, 17th and again in the 19th century they were increased by an astonishing number of charitable and educational foundations (St. Vincent de Paul, St. John of God; Maria Ward, St. Angela Merici, St. John Baptist de la Salle, Ignatius Rice, St. John Bosco). New apostolic congregations, such as the Redemptorists, flourished alongside the old. Missionary works stirred the enthusiasm of large masses of the people.

d) The theory of spirituality was directed towards the inward life. It has been preoccupied down to the present day (cf. *DSAM*) with such questions as infused and acquired contemplation, the difference between asceticism and mysticism, the priority of will or intellect, direct vision, paramysticism, etc.

e) Spiritual direction (Lallemant) and spiritual friendship (St. Jeanne de Chantal) rose to new heights — though there were some morbid exaggerations (the nuns of Loudun).

f) There were many other notable figures: missionaries at home and abroad, popular preachers, penitents (St. Paul of the Cross, de Rancé), martyrs (England, America), pastors (the Curé of Ars), visionaries (from St. Margaret Mary Alacoque to the children at La Salette, Lourdes, Fatima, etc.). The interior life remained predominant.

g) The people were taught a large number of institutionalized devotions: the Sacred Heart, Mary, the Sacred Wounds, the Eucharist, the Apostleship of Prayer, etc. The weakness was not so much exteriorization as juridicalism and regimentation.

G. Concluding Remarks

The new and promising approaches of recent times stem from a return to the sources or from openness to the world.

a) The trail was already blazed in the 19th century. The organic notion of theology (see *Tübingen School*), Traditionalism, the theological principles of German Idealism, Americanism (I. T. Hecker) and various pastoral efforts (Sailer; and see also *Josephinism*) were at one in trying to bridge the gap between theory and practice, in other words, to further spirituality. The Syllabus and the Modernist controversy proved that the time was not yet ripe. The "real assent" of Newman pointed onwards, as did the "little way" of St. Theresa of Lisieux.

b) New forces came into play in the 20th century with the liturgical movement (which remained for a long time over-preoccupied with the past) and the new interest in Scripture, which had been preceded by flourishing patristic studies. The youth movements remained inward-directed in their common life. Fruitful discussion with natural science ensued (R. Guardini, E. Przywara). Catholic Action flourished in the Latin countries. In matters of spirituality, Vatican II merely worked over old questions such as the "state of perfection".

c) The tasks of today can be described in terms of four principles developed outside the Church.

(i) *The new hermeneutics.* In many respects the "Death-of-God" theology must be dismissed as a mere fashion, but it is a reminder that it is not only the encounter with Scripture but the encounter with God as well which demands as a prelude some hermeneutical consideration. This is even truer of spirituality (see *Prayer, Sacrifice*), though the task has hardly been even perceived as yet.

(ii) *The new picture of man.* Psychology and anthropology make it impossible to confine spirituality to the "interior life" as its main interest. The indissoluble bonds which link human willing and knowing to pre-personal and social facts make all purely interior data suspect. The modern interest in the objective, in hard facts, must point the way to the reality of revelation and to concrete tasks.

(iii) *The new world-picture.* The shaping of the world is displacing more and more the acquisition of knowledge as the human task. Following Blondel and others, Teilhard de Chardin surmised that the encounter with God would take place in action, rather than in preliminary knowledge. This has little if anything to do with the ancient distinction between action and contemplation.

(iv) *The new picture of society.* The religious conscience of the individual is linked to society and its shaping of the future. This has been brought clearly to the fore in the debate with Marxism. The biblical truth of the social nature and social effectiveness of Christian faith (i.e., of the Church) has thereby been rediscovered (see also *Political Theology*). It is to be hoped that this controversy will bring theology as a whole nearer to the exercise of faith, i.e., to spirituality.

See also *Asceticism, Mysticism, Hermeneutics.*

BIBLIOGRAPHY. See bibliography on *Spirituality* I, and especially L. Bouyer, F. Vandenbroucke and J. Leclercq, eds., *History of Christian Spirituality,* I (1964), II, III (1969).

Josef Sudbrack

III. Special Features

A. MEDITATION

1. As opposed to the terms "mental prayer" and "contemplation", the traditional term "meditation" is increasingly employed nowadays, even outside the domain of Christian life and spirituality. Its meaning ranges from a psychosomatic technique and therapy acquired by yoga exercises and the practice of auto-suggestion, to ordinary intellectual and personal reflection, or even to advanced forms of religious and comprehensive awareness which ultimately go beyond prayer in the narrower sense and disclose transcendence. The increasingly clear demonstration of the markedly meditative attitude of the higher religions of the East and the interpretation of the findings of depth psychology and the experiences of psychotherapy may serve critically to test the great traditional experiences of meditation in the store of the Church's wisdom, to free them from partial oblivion and awaken them to new efficacy in contrast to certain mistaken developments of Christian spirituality. Critical and discerning discussion by the Church of psychotherapeutic experiences of meditation was made difficult by the (non-scientific) pansexual basis given to psychoanalysis, while dialogue with the higher religions of the East, especially with the various forms of Buddhism, was long hindered by one-sided, narrow dogmatic perspectives. The time should now be ripe, for it has been prepared by detailed studies, for a critical and discerning discussion, especially as increasing stress in every domain calls for a comprehensively meditative mode of life. This would not, however, mean aiming only at the highest forms of meditation. It would have to open up practicable paths which, for example, would take account of somatic and psychological factors and, generally speaking, of what is provisional in human existence, giving it its legitimate importance as an inevitable intermediary stage. The time has come to develop in theory and in practice new and comprehensive ways of meditation, and to give them organized structures in the Church.

2. Christianity was rooted in the salvation-history of the people of Israel, with its meditative liturgical spirituality. The early Church was marked by its experiences of the Pneuma. The mysteries of salvation were re-enacted in the celebration of the liturgy. From the beginning, therefore, it had a decided feeling for meditation (*anamnesis* and eschatological expectation). Parallel to the intellectual and historical development of Christianity, this dimension took shape in accordance with the new situations as they appeared. The process was promoted by the Fathers, and after the Constantinian turning-point, received public and legally constituted form, particularly in the liturgy and in the rules of Western monasticism. The cloistered life, understood as the *Opus Dei,* became in East and West the decisive basis and transmitter of meditation in the wide sense. The different views on the conduct of Christian life in the great contemplative orders, the varying influence of Christian ideals, the appearance in the Middle Ages of the "evangelical" mendicant orders with

a new spirituality of their own, and the increasingly numerous foundations of monasteries and schools, diversified the practice of meditative life. The resulting multiplicity of ascetical techniques and methods of meditative prayer was at the same time a response to the actual demands which arose through the Christianization of the Latin and Germanic peoples. As examples of historically important meditative movements, we mention German mysticism, the *Devotio moderna,* Spanish mysticism, the Ignatian Exercises, Pietism, the French School and, in our days, the "little way" of St. Theresa of Lisieux.

Astonishing similarity to the statements of Christian mysticism is found particularly in Buddhist texts. Buddhism is less a religious society with a consistent theoretical and institutional structure than various ways of deliverance through meditation. Theravada Buddhism seeks *Nirvana* as goal of deliverance, by rigorous, methodically practised techniques, aiming at the destruction of the notion of the "I", as the real source of suffering. This is done by a very subtle watchfulness with regard to the body, to all feelings and states of consciousness including their objects, with the determination, persevered in even into death, to achieve absolute abstraction. And this resolve ultimately seeks to abstract even from its own determination, in order to merge absolutely in "nothingness". Zen Buddhism, on the other hand, also seeking the deliverance of blissful enlightenment, only uses absolute abstraction as an element in panspiritualization which makes possible universal communication. The way leads through moral purification and perfection, and through alert and profound emotional tranquillity to comprehensive concentration which, mediated by the celebrated *zazen* (correct sitting-posture meditation) and *kōan* (a special exercise in concentration), opens out a life of stillness and silence and is completed in loving detachment and generous selflessness, an ascent of the mind to the universal unity and universal communication of blissful enlightenment. Amida-Buddhism practises trustful invocation of the merciful saviour whom the self longs for with ardent devotion and to whom it gives and unites itself in order to enter into the total light and life of the Buddha-nature—a term which, as in Mahayana Buddhism generally, means the fathomless ground of all reality.

Buddhism as a mode of life and a vital wisdom is permeated by the conviction that no strict statement is possible about the ground of all precisely because it is the ground of all and itself without ground. For this reason Buddhism was for long dismissed in too sweeping a way as a monism or cosmic pantheism by Christianity, which attributes decisive value to personal and historical mediation of the divine life. The light thrown by scholarship on the higher religions of the East, as well as radical reflection by Christian theology on its own understanding of revelation (which alone makes possible an interpretation of the testimony of Christian mysticism), shows how difficult are the problems of the mediation of salvation, deliverance, and of that mysterious reality present but at the same time hidden in all, which in Buddhist terms is the Buddha-nature, in Christian terms, God-Christ. For Christianity, of course, it is decisive that the mediation of salvation is historical and personal, incarnational. Nevertheless, even here God must be seriously seen as that total reality which precisely in itself as total reality cannot be further mediated and communicated, which breaks through all representations and formulas and which is perhaps what the Buddhist himself means when in dialectically hyperbolic statements he emphasizes the absolute impossibility of mediating the absolute, which as a consequence has rather to be interpreted pantheistically. Conversely, Buddhism is also quite aware of the problem of historical and personal mediation. Whatever may be the outcome of theoretical and critical discussion between the two higher religions, only a mediation of salvation by love, which also knows absolute detachment in death yet accepts even this, not for its own sake but for the sake of the life manifest in it, reveals that blissful "nothingness" which is not absolutely death but all-embracing, creative life.

3. Although the Christian conception of revelation regards as decisive its historical, personal mediation in Jesus of Nazareth as the Kyrios of history and cosmos, it is a paradoxical fact that the theory of meditation current in the Church does not give much prominence to this historical and personal mediation. On an Aristotelian and scholastic basis, it regards man as a being of a special kind who as such is rooted in being as true and as good. As opposed to a "philosophy of being" aiming at a false immediate contact with God, an adequate Christian theory

of meditation must bring the absolute spirit-source of human existence into harmony with its concrete temporal and historical character, and then show systematically and hermeneutically that man lives essentially (not merely theoretically, in a secondary way) as a radical question, but one which as such is mediated by personal and social dialogue. And this question is dependent for its explication on meditative awareness. This concentration of human awareness and freedom, in which the radical question emerges as the guiding-line, means that the past, the unconscious, and the temporality of human existence as a system of dialogal, historical, personal relationships, are simultaneously rendered present and perhaps transformed. Only in such a present, rich in manifold relationships, is the relation to God actually realized. This is the medium of all historical, personal contact, the *logos* of all dialogue. Such an actual intermediary person exemplifies the specific character of the self as such, namely, consciousness and freedom. The intermediary person as *dia-logos* is not merely an abstract universal but, rather, the concrete truth of every person realized personally in each instance. Consequently this is the medium and the root of all reality, and therefore the centre of integral meditation.

Theologically, the *dialogos* can be understood as the cosmic Christ who, mediated by his historical bodily incarnation in Jesus of Nazareth, is the pneumatic glorified Kyrios of eschatological history. Only the personal mediator understood as Christ makes God himself visible as his ground, God who, because he is beyond all relationships and therefore all intermediate reality, is "nothing and all" (Eckhart). An awareness of this kind, which does not overhastily claim to be grounded in the light of being, but must first recognize its indispensable multiplicity of relationships if it is to attain its own identity and thereby find the presence of God, comes in various modes of meditation on the religious interests of the moment. And in this respect a fundamental distinction can be drawn between natural and religious (Christian) meditation (P. Dessauer). Natural meditation is again determined in various ways according to the reality which it seeks to mould and heal. Yoga meditation, for example, is the awareness of one's own body and its functions; meditation may evoke past consciousness or the unconscious. It is scientifically elaborated in psychotherapeu-

tic meditation. Philosophical meditation opens the mind to philosophical evidence. The various kinds of natural meditation develop their own particular conceptions of their purpose and methods. In principle they are possible to everyone. Everyone can represent to himself and concentrate on the realities which confront him in his interior history (cf. P. Dessauer). Religious and Christian meditation, incorporating on occasion natural modes of meditation, in a special and explicit way renders the act of realization itself present, through the means offered by redemptive history and by the Church's liturgy generally. Such meditation has to develop its own special practical and theoretical self-awareness. Its inner dynamism gives rise to the special problems which are dealt with in detail in the classical tradition of Christian spirituality and mysticism.

4. The practice of meditation by its very nature is concerned with awareness, not, as in one alienating form of meditation, with being directly absorbed in something else as such. It does not mean absolute indifference, as a not uncommon nihilist misconception of Ignatian detachment would suggest. Nor does it mean extinction of personal life, as in a false, largely unconscious view of the *theologia crucis*. Meditative awareness is different from an empty, distracted or preoccupied consciousness, as well as from rigorous concentration (where it is not a question of self-awareness) and can be described as a concentrated, recollected state of mind in and through which alone other contents are communicated. This recollected and mediating consciousness is inherently directed by the radical question which each human being is and lives; disclosure of this is itself eminently a task for meditation. The urgency of this question, which addresses its summons from the vital centre itself, is dulled if particular interests smother the connections which it has with all the dimensions of reality that concern the self. Courage for personal conversion and sensitivity to truth are a presupposition as well as a result of a meditative attitude to life (see *Metanoia, Conversion*). Without historical, concrete, dialogal openness to truth (and not merely of the theoretical and detached kind), and without the awareness of transcendence which it implies, the dynamism of meditation ceases and the ensuing sterility means that the depth of human reality is lost sight of.

Consequently, what is needed is a heuristic, vigilant alternation between concrete, practical moral commitment and retirement with recollection. In this way existentially critical awareness repeatedly renews its strength. The primordial consciousness of truth manifest in the radical question, and the irreplaceable guiding principle which it implies, will not normally be discovered and confidently followed without concrete external human guidance. Otherwise the exercitant, on an apparently but not really Christian impulse, may overhastily push forward to the final goal of meditation, recklessly and dangerously committing himself, or else be held up in some cramped domain. The condition of society produces many unconscious deformations, conflicts and complexes which narrow men's minds and restrict their freedom and make it difficult for them to achieve meditative concentration, even if they deliberately do everything they can to attain it. Consequently, a special hermeneutics of human reality should be developed for this purpose. This would not leave the various special sciences to deal with the concrete characteristic features of human reality (e.g., dreams) which are the most direct expression of the primordial question, but would bring out their regulative and constitutive significance for man. This might prepare the way for a more individual kind of pastoral care, providing initiation and guidance in the meditative life. It would also call for the courage to unmask taboos falsely imposed on the forces liberated by meditation; it would require trust in the spontaneity which meditation promotes, even though this cannot be regimented. An integral practice of meditation, incorporating all the available technical methods, is still a desideratum for the Church and for theology, despite what is already available. That is in fact a symptom of the present crisis in the meditative life of the Church.

See also *Mysticism, Prayer, Spirituality* III D.

BIBLIOGRAPHY. J. Maréchal, *Études sur la psychologie des mystiques,* 2 vols. (1924–37), E. T. of vol. I (1926); F. Heiler, *Prayer* (1932); R. Garrigou-Lagrange, *Christian Perfection and Contemplation* (1937); T. Merton, *Seeds of Contemplation* (1945); *New Seeds of Contemplation* (revised ed., 1949); id., *Mystics and Zen Masters* (1967); C. Happich, *Anleitung zur Meditation* (3rd ed., 1948); E. Herrigel, *Zen and the Art of Archery* (1953); id., *Zen and the Art of Archery* with *The Method of Zen* (1960); F. Melzer, *Meditation in Ost und West* (1957); M. Eliade, *Yoga* (1958); J. B. Lotz, *Meditation im Alltag* (1959); J. Dechanet, *Christian Yoga* (1960); H. Urs von Balthasar, *Prayer* (1961); H. Dumoulin, *History of Zen Buddhism* (1963); A. Graham, *Christian Zen* (1963); P. Dessauer, *Natural Meditation* (1965).

Eberhard Simons

B. EXAMINATION OF CONSCIENCE

The notion of examination of conscience starts with recognition of the fact that man is a moral being, responsible for his actions. Examination of conscience corresponds to a natural structure in man, for it is the way to self-knowledge with a view to personal perfection. Hence we find forms of examination of conscience at every higher stage of human development and in all higher non-Christian religions, even in some philosophical systems which regard it as a means of self-education or psychotherapy.

In harmony with the ethical teaching of the NT, examination of conscience finds its most perfect expression and highest ideal in the spiritual practice of Christianity. Christian spirituality has developed a method which allows examination of conscience to mature in an atmosphere of recollection, of the presence of God, and of prayer. The best known and most widely used is that provided by the *Spiritual Exercises* of St. Ignatius (nos. 24–43). Following ancient Christian tradition he recommends a general and a particular examination of conscience, the latter in respect of specific points that are of importance to the life of the person in question. According to some theologians, the chief result of this schematization has been the rejection of, or at least a resistance to, the practice of examination of conscience.

The end of examination of conscience is not self-knowledge for its own sake. Examining his conscience in the light of grace, a man places himself with his sin and guilt in the presence of God, in order to know himself and accept himself humbly and realistically, and then to plead in contrition for the forgiveness of his sins from the mercy of God. Examination of conscience is a precondition of the confession of sins in the sacrament of penance and is recommended as a daily practice by the tradition of the Church and by spiritual writers. It is commended to everyone, but specially to those who are appointed to bear witness through their special vocation as ministers of the Church (cf. *CIC,* can. 125, n. 2, and the motu proprio *Rubricarum instructum* of John XXIII; cf. also D 92, 543, 547, 606, 618, 638). By examination of conscience we are held to an ideal of a life that is worthy of the gracious act of redemption in Christ. Because all sanctification is a work of grace, by examination of conscience a man strives to uncover the obstacles that stand in the way of grace, and to make the resolutions that will dispose of these obstacles. Thus, examination of conscience is a ceaseless striving for the spirit of *metanoia* and conversion. The Christian who practises this discipline frequently achieves an interiorization of his spiritual life, an awareness of his spiritual condition and, through the alertness of his heart, a greater openness to, and readiness for, grace. With anxious and scrupulous people examination of conscience can precipitate deeper disturbance and the aggravation of their pathological mental condition.

See also *Education* V, *Psychotherapy, Contrition, Conversion, Metanoia, Spirituality* III D, E.

BIBLIOGRAPHY. See bibliography on *Spirituality* III D; also: G. Sepiéter, *L'examen de conscience* (2nd ed., 1932); A. Delchard, "Examen de conscience", *DSAM*, IV, cols. 1789–1838; T. Müncker, *Die psychologischen Grundlagen der katholischen Sittenlehre* (4th ed., 1953); B. Häring, *The Law of Christ*, 3 vols. (1961–66); G. Siewerth, *Wagnis und Bewahrung* (1964), pp. 201–46 (on the formation of conscience).

Jesús María Granero

C. Spiritual Reading

1. *Concept.* a) Biblical faith is very closely connected with the written word. The experiences of God of the "first" generation, the patriarchs and prophets, etc., find expression in writing, are meditatively developed in constant contact with the written word, and form the nucleus round which all subsequent piety crystallizes. The NT (and the OT transmitted by it) plays a similar part for the second and third generations of Christians. The Lord is announced to those who know him through earthly intermediaries (though directly and immediately in the spiritual and personal order of grace), in kerygmatic, liturgical and dogmatic formulations, and this happens most closely and with normative force in Scripture. Consequently the reading and hearing of the authentic, inspired word is one of the fundamental activities of Christianity.

b) The further we go back in history, the more clearly we can see the identity of scriptural reading with theological reflection and the actual exercise of faith in life (see *Spirituality* I–III, *Liturgy*). Because, however, the testimony of the words of Scripture is only a medium for the greater, incarnate Word, contact with Scripture develops a rich variety of forms: liturgical listening — meditative reading; concrete personal search for the summons contained in the word of God — authoritative exposition; preacher's paraphrase — effort to establish the authentic text; meditative consideration of the character of Christ — apologetics in defence of his reality. Genuine "spiritual reading" belongs to this context.

c) The break that was made in this unity can be precisely traced in history; it consisted in isolating spirituality from its connection with Scripture — though of course the separation was never absolute. The growth of a literature of works of piety (in the East in the 5th and 6th centuries, in the West in the 12th and 13th centuries), and the division of *lectio* into *lectio divina* and *lectio scholastica*, stand at the beginning of the dissociation (see *Biblical Exegesis* III). It ends with practices and theories (cf., for example, O. Zimmermann, *Lehrbuch der Aszetik*), in which Scripture no longer forms the matter of spiritual reading.

2. *Theological reflection.* a) There is no doubt that scriptural reading is the prototype which provides the norm and orientation for all spiritual reading. Consequently all genuine spiritual reading may be regarded as in effect "anonymous" scriptural reading.

b) The centre of the spiritual reading of Scripture is Christ. The words of Scripture find their meaning when the letter of Scripture (including the theology of Paul, of the Synoptics, etc.) opens out upon the Word made man. One reason for the spiritual sterility of some exegetical works is that this "bearing witness to the Lord" (cf. Mk 1:1) is not taken seriously.

c) The abundance of additional spiritual books has its root in the Christocentricity of Scripture. Fuller knowledge of the Lord can only be attained in the testimony of Scripture, and prompts the production of further writings which take their standard from Scripture but are wider in scope. These may be variously characterized. Central among them are testimonies to the actual experience of Christian life (see *Saints* II, IV). A division in tabular form, suggested by I. Behn, would be: mysticism: the articulate expression of the act; mystagogy: guidance to the act;

mystology: reflection on the act. This must take its bearings throughout from Scripture.

d) The manifold character of spiritual literature should lead to elucidation of the role of tradition, society, etc. No more than passing reference can be made to liturgical reading (hearing). Ideally, it would be a combination of communal action and private meditation, kerygma and prayer, praise of God and penance, hearing and reading.

e) Hearing and reading are fundamentally identical ways of encounter; phenomenological comparison between them can make clear their basic unity. Hearing (see *Obedience*) faces God's summons; reading (see *Spirituality* III A) opens out one's own world to give precedence to the Christian message.

3. *Practical aspects.* The practice of spiritual reading must be judged in relation to the "sacramentality" of the words of Scripture which in an analogical way extends to subsequent spiritual writings.

a) Spiritual reading stands between mental cultivation and prayer. Only its dynamic impulsion towards prayer makes it spiritual reading. Spiritual reading is only achieved by those whose level of spiritual culture is not lower than their general human and intellectual culture.

b) This makes clear our duty as well as our freedom in regard to spiritual reading. On broad theological grounds, but only in this very wide sense, it is scarcely possible to dispute the duty of spiritual reading. But it is important to note that this obligation can only be met if interior freedom is preserved in view of the mass supply of spiritual reading on the market. The criterion of choice should be spiritual joy or inner attraction.

c) Difficulties mostly have their origin in the spiritual sterility of many works on the Bible or in the reader's inadequate mental attainments. Yet such difficulties may also be one of the crosses which characterize Christian life.

In good spiritual literature the process of actualization of the gospel has to take place. Consequently, the wide range of available spiritual literature must not be sacrificed to one-sided biblicism; the fruitfulness of the words of Scripture, resulting from inspiration, has to be operative precisely in spiritual literature; that is where it achieves its actual efficacy.

BIBLIOGRAPHY. For a historical orientation see B. Crouzel, *Origène et la connaissance mystique* (1960); for studies of liturgical themes see *La Maison Dieu* (1945 ff.); for studies of developments in spirituality see L. Bouyer, *La spiritualité au moyen âge* (1961). SPECIAL STUDIES: D. Gorce, *La Lectio Divina*, I: *Jérôme et la lecture sacrée dans le milieu ascétique romain* (1925); M. van Assche, "Divinae vacare lectioni", *Sacris Erudiri* 1 (1948), pp. 13–34; B. Smalley, *The Study of the Bible in the Middle Ages* (2nd ed., 1952); id., *English Friars and Antiquity in the Early Fourteenth Century* (1960); P. Vandenbroucke, "Sur la lecture chrétienne du psautier au Ve siècle", *ibid.* 5 (1953), pp. 5–26; P. de Leturia, *Lecturas ascéticas y lecturas místicas entre los Jesuítas del siglo XVI* (Archivio italiano per la storia della pietà II) (1953); J. Leclercq, *L'amour des lettres et le désir de Dieu: Initiation aux auteurs monastiques du moyen âge* (1957); M.-D. Chenu, "Lecture de la bible et philosophie", *Mélanges Gilson* (1959), pp. 161–71; H. de Lubac, *Exégèse médiévale*, 4 vols. (1959–64); *Los monjes y los estudios* (1963), by various authors; J. Leclercq, "Lecture priante", *La liturgie et les paradoxes chrétiens* (1963), pp. 243–69; F. Vandenbroucke, "La Lectio Divina du XIe au XIVe siècle", *Studia Montis Regii* 8 (1966), pp. 267 ff. For later developments see the handbooks, e.g., A. Tanqueray, *The Spiritual Life* (1951). THEOLOGY AND PRACTICE: H. Urs von Balthasar, "Wort, Schrift und Tradition", *Verbum Caro: Skizzen zur Theologie,* I (1960), pp. 11–27; id., *Herrlichkeit: Eine theologische Ästhetik,* I (1961), especially pp. 511–35; K. Rahner, *Theological Investigations,* IV (1966), pp. 357–67; III (1967); id., *Schriften zur Theologie,* VI (1965), pp. 111–38; VII (1966), pp. 511–15; P. Emery, "L'Écriture méditée: Quatre degrés: lecture, méditation, prière, contemplation", *Lumen Vitae* 20 (1965), pp. 619–31.

Josef Sudbrack

D. SPIRITUAL EXERCISES

1. *Origin, nature, and method.* Spiritual exercises have developed in the course of the centuries in accordance with the spirituality of each era. Thus the essential elements we shall discuss here took shape gradually: retreat for a precisely fixed period, methodical procedure in the light of certain themes under the direction of a retreat-master, and the working out of a definite resolution about how to follow Christ.

Very early the example of Jesus in the wilderness and the apostles awaiting the Holy Spirit (Acts 1:13) moved many bishops and devout souls to withdraw into solitude for a considerable time. Euthymius (d. 473) was one of the most zealous promoters of this movement, which had become widespread by the 6th and 7th centuries. During the Middle Ages many religious houses had special cells or even "hermitages" for guests who wished to undertake spiritual exercises. It was the desert Fathers who first gave these exercises set forms — meditation, examination of conscience, and ascetical practices — which were more deeply studied and precisely regulated in the 13th century. But it was only the *devotio moderna,* especially under Mombaer and Cisneros, which laid down in detail the ways and degrees of contemplation (usually taken as seven), without, however, establishing a single, invariable method applicable in other spiritual spheres.

As Pius XI points out in the encyclical *Mens Nostra,* St. Ignatius Loyola took over unchanged the heritage of patristic and monastic tradition. He singled out the most important elements for a method of contemplation and produced *Spiritual Exercises* remarkable for their balance and harmonious unity, which serve the one purpose of "finding in peace God our Lord". He based himself on Scripture and the experiences of the spiritual life, as Paul III says in the bull of approbation. Ignatius is not guided by theory but by the facts of redemptive history. He does not begin by defining creation, sin, and vocation but sets forth the facts of creation, sin, and our divine vocation as found in Scripture and dogma. Thence he proceeds to theological conclusions and the personal problems of the retreatant. He aims at presenting the basic Christian doctrines — Trinity, creation, redemption, grace, original sin, the reality of the Church — as vital truths. The retreatant is to understand that he is subject to God's continuous influence from the outset. Under the light given him by God, the retreatant recognizes the meaning of creation, of history and of his own life. He learns how profoundly he is committed to sin, but also encounters most vividly the offer of redemption through Jesus Christ. The two components of this deeply moving experience bring him to a "change of heart" (see *Metanoia*). In bestowing deliverance, Jesus draws the redeemed into his mission. In the further course of the *Exercises,* the retreatant participates, in meditation, in the life, death and resurrection of Jesus and is to allow himself to be penetrated more and more profoundly by the "spirit" of Jesus, his mind, feeling and will. In the measure in which he becomes inwardly open to "having the same mind which was in Christ" (cf. Phil 2:5), which also means attaining critical awareness through the "discernment of spirits", the retreatant can hear the call which assigns him his particular task in the Church. Thus the *Exercises* serve the growth of love, which finds God in all things and recognizes what must be its own special way of serving God in all things throughout a whole life.

This effort is made in direct union with the Lord, under the guidance of the retreatmaster, according to rules that Ignatius lays down in his book, which is meant to be neither a book of piety nor the theoretical exposition of a system, but a spiritual guidebook, the fruit of the "glorious enlightenment" which Ignatius experienced in 1522 at Manresa, in whose light "all things seemed new to him . . ., as if he were a different person with a new mind" (*Autobiography,* no. 30). In the years that followed he several times revised the Manresa outline (until its approval by Paul III in 1548), making it into a handbook for retreat-masters. He was influenced in the course of the revision by other books (especially the *Imitation of Christ*).

The *Exercises* aim at a complete renewal of the individual, and through him of society. So although they were originally given not to groups but only to individuals, they not only wrought a profound change in the outlook of these few people but also led to reforms in many dioceses, religious houses and other ecclesiastical institutions, especially as community exercises were very soon being given on an Ignatian basis. Every retreat-house (the earliest founded was that at Alcalá in 1561) became a spiritual centre with an extensive influence. St. Charles Borromeo based the reform of his clergy on the Ignatian *Exercises.* The Asceterium set up at Milan in 1569 started a powerful movement which affected all sorts of people in practically every Catholic country through the labours of the great 17th-century missioners. New and larger houses (the first of which was opened at Vannes in 1659) made it possible to give regular courses of exercises, so that more and more of the faithful took part. The spread and effectiveness of the *Exercises* were due in no small measure to their constant recommendation by thirty-six Popes in more than 600 pronouncements of various kinds. Pius XI named St. Ignatius the patron of retreats (25 July 1922) and in the encyclical *Mens Nostra* (20 December 1929) called the Ignatian *Exercises* "the wisest and most comprehensive handbook of spiritual direction, . . . the soundest guide to inner conversion and deep piety".

Ignacio Iparraguirre

2. *Spirituality*. We shall discover the spirituality and teaching-method of the *Exercises* by studying the text and the part they played in the author's spiritual life (cf. the *Autobiography* in particular). The main divisions of the first manuscript (autumn, 1522) are: the "Kingdom of Christ", the "Two Standards", the history of sin, the examination of conscience, the substance of the rules for the discernment of spirits. Peter Faber gives us the first written statement of their aim: "modus ascendendi in cognitionem divinae voluntatis". Recognition of the particular claim of God on the individual concerned and "the election" of a life more and more responsive to that claim are at the centre of the *Spiritual Exercises* of St. Ignatius.

The pedagogy designed to lead to that end begins with the sinful frailty of man and his situation between the claim of God's will and the counter-claim of the world. The discernment of spirits is meant to shed light on the situation, raise one above specious ideals and motives, and free one to gaze on the will of God in the shape of his incarnate Son. This enlightenment and penetration is a process of interiorization, which leads to "sentire", a knowledge of the heart which transcends both rational knowledge of the truths of faith and an affective grasp of them. The hearing of the call of God takes place at the core of the personality. Along the way of human guidance (retreat-master) the goal to be attained is that "he himself, the Creator and Lord, shall communicate himself to the soul devoted to him . . . and dispose it for the way in which it can serve him better in the future".

From this knowledge of the heart issues the "election", which is more than an application of general rules to the particular case by means of discursive reason. It is the interior harmony between man's pure openness to God and a concrete object of choice. Constant exercise of such "election" then produces that "ordering of life for the salvation of the soul" which the grace of God assigns the individual in question.

The clarity of the call heard within becomes still more compelling through "contemplation of Christ our Lord" (second to fourth week). The image of Christ in the *Exercises* originated in the *eximia ilustración* by the river Cardoner (Manresa, 1522). Its content comprises the dynamism of the divine persons in the Trinity and their traces in creation; the incarnate Son of God, archetype and end of all created things, founder of the order of redemption and abiding presence in man and the world; and the mediating role which the Lord's glorified humanity has to play in the work of redemption. It follows from this Christological view of things that both the world and the Church are the scene of experience of God, each in its own way; that God's will must be sought in both domains and that God can be sought and found "in all things". Accordingly "sentire", that key Ignatian word for spiritual knowledge, has as it were a "hypostatic structure" (Hugo Rahner) which rules out all infatuation. So the full, undiminished visibility of the work of redemption in Christ and his Church is the measure of the motion of the Spirit which the individual experiences and sets the scope within which we make our election in following Christ. (The main function of the retreat-master should be to determine the field which the Church assigns to the individual.) We find this basic principle of the Ignatian election in the *Rules for Thinking with the Church,* of which numbers 1 and 13 still hold good, though the others are less relevant now. "Ordering one's life unto the soul's salvation" is in the nature of service ("*mystique de service",* de Guibert). But the service of God is that of the creator and Lord, and hence the *Exercises* say that the world is the place where this service is to be performed. Thus every project for life ("fruit of the *Exercises*") which we envisage and decide on by our "election" must include a spiritual solicitude for our fellow-man, in keeping with God's turning to man to redeem him in Christ. This turning "outward" of the person concerned to save his own soul is what particularly characterizes the spirituality of the *Exercises*.

See also *Discernment of Spirits.*

BIBLIOGRAPHY. TEXT: Critical ed. in *Monumenta Historica Societatis Jesu,* III/1 (1919), E. T. by W. Longridge (1950), J. Corbishley (1963), L. Puhl (1968). COMMENTARIES: L. de la Palma, *Camino espiritual,* 2 vols. (1628); F. Suarez, *De Spiritualibus Exercitiis* (1592, 1910); I. Diertins (1687); A. Denis, 4 vols. (1891–93); H. V. Gill (1935); W. Longridge (1919), E. Przywara, *Deus Semper Major,* 3 vols. (1938–40) (in German); H. Pinard de la Boullaye, 4 vols. (1950–54); K. Rahner (1965). BIBLIOGRAPHIES: I. Iparraguirre, *Orientaciones bibliográficas sobre S. Ignacio de Loyola* (1957), pp. 75–101; J.-F. Gilmont and P. Daman, *Bibliographie Ignatienne (1894–1957)* (1958). STUDIES: H. Bernard, *Essai historique sur les Exercices spirituels de S. Ignace* (1926); I. Iparraguirre, *Historia de los Ejercicios de S. Ignacio,* 2 vols. (1946–55); H. Pinard de la Boullaye, *Les étapes de la rédaction des exercices* (7th ed., 1950); F. Wulf, ed., *Ignatius von Loyola: Seine geistliche Gestalt und sein Vermächtnis* (1956); G. Fessard, *La dialectique des exercices spirituels de Saint Ignace de Loyola* (1956); P. de Leturía, *Estudios Ignacianos,* II (1957), pp. 3–186; J. Lewis, *Le gouvernement spirituel selon S. Ignace de Loyola* (1961); E. Hertsch, "Exercitia spiritualia in der evangelischen Kirche", *Theologische Literaturzeitung* 86 (1961), cols. 81–94; L. Verny, *Spiritualité et engagement: Une retraite de trente jours* (1962); J. de Guibert, *Jesuits: Their Spiritual Doctrine and Practice* (1964); J. Simons, *Retreat Dynamics* (1967); D. Stanley, *Modern Scriptural Approach to the Spiritual Exercises* (1967); H. Rahner, *Ignatius the Theologian* (1968); id., *Spirituality of St. Ignatius Loyola: An account of its Historical Development* (1968).

Ernst Niermann

E. Spiritual Direction

Spiritual direction began in the monasticism of the early Church, first among the hermits who needed counsel in their isolation and then in the monasteries, where charismatically gifted elders devoted themselves to spiritual direction — as did also superiors, which could give rise to conflicts. The notion of the superior as the "spiritual father" seems to have developed more strongly in Western than Eastern monasticism. In the Society of Jesus the superior was spiritual father by virtue of his office. Other orders followed this practice. A number of abuses arose, especially where spiritual direction and sacramental confession were combined. Another trend then set in, and finally spiritual direction and the office of superior were made distinct.

Even in the ancient Church, layfolk also entrusted the direction of their souls to monks. But spiritual direction outside the monasteries only became important in the spiritual movements among the laity which characterized to some extent the period from the 12th to the 15th century. Layfolk could also assume the task of spiritual direction, as did for instance St. Catharine of Siena and Nicholas of Flüe. The great age of spiritual direction was the 17th century, especially in France, with such figures as St. Francis de Sales, St. Vincent de Paul, Père de Bérulle.

One hears of a "crisis" of spiritual direction today. And there is an undoubted need to seek for new ways. One form is discussion in small groups: discussion of meditation during spiritual exercises in common, *la revision de vie,* "sensitivity training". Such discussion is possible only in homogeneous groups. It does not replace the spiritual direction sought by the individual from a counsellor in private, but makes it more adequate, especially by the possibilities it holds out of better social adjustment. Given the present-day distaste for the institutionalizing of direction by assigning it to a special official, real progress is possible through this new departure.

There is need above all for a reappraisal of the nature and tasks of spiritual direction. It is both a "humanist" and a "spiritual" process. "No man is an island": man is only himself in contact with his fellow-man. This is the anthropological ground for spiritual direction. As is well known, the mere verbalization of a problem can already "cut it down to size". In the Church, the body of Christ, men are even more intimately related to one another. This is the theological ground for spiritual direction. Hitherto, as a rule, the theological and "spiritual" element was perhaps unduly stressed. Very often, too little attention was paid to the fact that spiritual growth is only possible, as a deliberate personal commitment, within a framework laid down by nature and personal history. It is true that spiritual direction must be concerned with spiritual initiatives, with disposing for the incalculable encounter with the mystery of God and his word, whose impact is never quite the same in any two cases. It is essentially concerned with the discernment of spirits and the finding of the will of God in a concrete situation. Nonetheless, all these things must be integrated into a man's life as a whole, and the spiritual cannot be treated as a sort of superstructure on top of the human element. Spiritual direction cannot be confined to the religious realm, as though this existed in isolation, but must deal with the whole man and his actual problems. The main tasks of spiritual direction may therefore be outlined as follows: a) to help the individual to self-knowledge; b) to help him to self-acceptance; c) to help him to detachment from his own ego; d) to help him to find the actual will of God.

a) The spiritual director cannot be asked merely to ratify the subject's opinion of himself. The subject must be ready to accept without resentment or defence mechanisms aspects of his character which he himself does not recognize, at least under their true names, and is not perhaps anxious to admit. He must be convinced that the value of spiritual direction depends essentially on his own readiness to be humbly frank. This is mainly what the spiritual director has to go on, which means that he must first be ready to listen attentively. This is the only way in which real dialogue is possible. The director tries to place what he hears in an objective perspective, analysing it and throwing light on it, so that the enquirer can feel that he is understood. The answer to the question, "Who am I really, and where do I stand?", is best based on a straightforward account of the life-story of the enquirer, not centred, as in confession, on the question of guilt, faults and sins, but comprising the whole evolution of a life. This should be able to throw light on the deeper structures of a man's nature and character, as well as on the aspects which at once meet the eye. In the course of the discussions, it will probably be necessary to take up past history again and again. At the first meeting, the director, usually, though not necessarily a priest, will probably mainly try to listen receptively to what he is told.

b) All self-knowledge, and especially when it is sought for religious motives, implies immediately an ethical demand. The enquirer must be ready to accept himself as he has seen himself to be, to face what he is, to bear the burden of his real self. Human beings tend almost inevitably to create an image of themselves in accordance with their wishful thinking, to play a "role" of their own choosing and then go sour when facts are stubbornly resistant. Nothing less than a real conversion is needed if the searcher is to accept the profounder self-knowledge which he gains with the help of another. Here too the director must give guidance and encouragement. This invitation to conversion should not be primarily a call for ascetical effort. The director tries to show how pre-existing dispositions interact on each other, and what elements of imbalance are present. He has to distinguish structures of mind and character which are religiously neutral from the moral and religious attitudes by which alone a man's value is determined. There is then still much to do in the line of furnishing religious motives to help the subject to accept the inadequacies and disequilibrium of his nature, to bear his own burden — in a word, to carry his cross after Christ.

c) Once the process of self-acceptance has begun, it releases the forces which help a man to stand back as it were from himself and exercise a healthy self-detachment. The spiritual director then has a new task. He must help the enquirer to recognize the projections of the self-seeking ego for what they are, to rid himself of fictive life-styles and take up the programme indicated by his real qualities as revealed by his actual life-story, the way of life ordained for him by God. This means striving for the inner attitude which the tradition of spirituality has described as abandonment, resignation or indifference (St. Ignatius Loyola) — terms which could be misleading. Here the discernment of spirits plays an important part, to which the spiritual director should be equal.

d) This brings us to the real aim of spiritual direction, the finding of the will of God "for me", in the whole programme of life and in the new situations to which it constantly gives rise. This is the interest to which the Spiritual Exercises of St. Ignatius are devoted. The will of God, the will of his grace, follows the lines of each man's nature, even where, and indeed above all where, the self must be crucified for the sake of its ultimate fulfilment. When a man is in harmony with himself, he is profoundly in harmony with God, though it always remains true that reason and grace cannot totally coincide in this spiritual process. Self-fulfilment passes through the incalculable and hence impenetrable "mystery of the cross". "He that would find his life must lose it." The life of the individual, like the history of the race, contains so many obscure challenges and barely decipherable potentialities that it is the main task of the spiritual director to try to help the enquirer to find the will of God in the actual circumstances of his life.

Spiritual direction and psychotherapy are essentially different, since the former is concerned with eternal salvation and the latter with the healing of illness. Nonetheless, in practice the boundaries are fluid, since the spiritual director cannot exclude the element of healing, and the therapist should not prescind entirely from man's religious salvation, above all when he is dealing with someone whose fundamental attitude is that of a believer.

See also *Spirituality* III D, *Discernment of Spirits, Psychotherapy*.

BIBLIOGRAPHY. H. Bacht, "Seelenführung in der Krise", *Glauben und Leben* 26 (1953), pp.

422–36; A. Plé, "La relation (de la psychothérapie) dans la direction spirituelle", *La vie spirituelle,* supplément 68 (1964); A. Godin, *Pastor as Counselor* (1965); id., *Priest as Counselor* (1968); R. Hostie, *Pastoral Counselling* (1966); J. Laplace, *Direction of Conscience* (1966).

Friedrich Wulf

STATE

1. *Concept and elements.* This term, which nowadays is commonly, though not exclusively, used for the political community, came into general currency from the 16th century onwards. Previous to this, terms such as πόλις, *civitas, regnum, regimen* prevailed (the "government" is still the more usual term in the English-speaking world). It signifies the permanent supra-familial way of life of a human grouping which is historically individualized through a variety of factors, cultural, geographic and biological, and in which the positive legal order, the regular adaptation to constantly changing conditions of life and the care of these conditions assume a predominant significance. This makes it easy for us to arrive at the four essential elements of the social structure "State". The concept of the State demands: a) an indefinite number of people in and with their families (and extended families), and with their property, who have the enduring will to live together for the sake of their well-being, i.e., a people; b) a territory permanently settled by this people; c) a public authority with power of ultimate decision which exacts obedience and is capable of enforcing its legislative and executive measures for the protection of each and all and of warding off dangers from without; d) permanence, i.e., the general will to live together remains the same through the succession of generations and is not affected by "constitutional changes". Naturally a people retains the right to join with other people in a federation, thus abdicating its full sovereignty, even to the extent of entering a world federation — this can even become an inescapable duty. Under this general concept of State can be subsumed the rudimentary forms of political life among primitive, pre-historic peoples as well as all others, including the powerful modern States and even a world State.

2. *Justification for the State.* The experience of history as well as philosophical considerations show that the "State" is a necessary social structure, demanded by man as a body-soul unity with dominion over the earth. It is just as necessary as the permanent fellowships of marriage and the family are to bisexually reproductive mankind. Nevertheless the State and family are two essentially different social structures, in the nature and purpose, in the authority and power that they possess, and in their duration. Both are natural and necessary, yet the traditional teaching on the State (based on a particular concept of man and the consequent views of the social and political nature of man) has defined the State as a perfect society *(societas perfecta)* and the family as an imperfect society. Perfect society means, firstly, that the State has its own proper end (purpose), the common good, and, secondly, that it has all the means needed for attaining its end. A State is juridically independent of other States, although juridically subject to international law (that the people, the State and any confederation of States are subject to the universal natural law is self-evident). This is the so-called "sovereignty", i.e., the power of decision about the independence and security of civic life, about the protection and enforcement of the positive, i.e., the historical, order of law, about the constant reform of law and of the social order according to the principles of social justice (since positive law is always in danger of becoming "injustice": *summum ius, summa iniuria*). In taking cognizance of its legislative, juridical and executive functions, the civic power must constantly decide how to secure the right order in human relations, what is right and not right between individuals, families and groups, when an ethical duty should be made into a legally enforceable obligation. With regard to the concept of sovereignty a distinction must be made between a formal and material element. The individual State can transfer to an international organization decisions in the social sphere, e.g., the *ius belli,* or it can remain neutral about religion, i.e., in the sense of religious freedom and separation of Church and State, and can abstain from all interference in the religious life of its citizens; it can join with neighbouring States in alliances, international treaties, even to the extent of a federation of States, all of which implies renunciation of certain sovereign acts. Since the notion of "sovereignty" is historically an emotive word, we use instead the notion of independence; little is changed in the reality.

3. *Origin of the State.* The origin of the State is rooted in human nature. The saying of Aristotle that one who does not live in the *Polis* is either a god or a beast, is still true. Man is a corporeal person, therefore bound by the need to provide for himself, for the security of life, freedom and property. He who is responsible for someone's bodily sustenance can all too easily rule over him, and he who has no property, all too easily *becomes* property. Taking a general view of the notions of life, freedom, i.e., self-initiative, mode of living, free choice of profession, of partner in marriage, of dwelling-place, of a voice in public affairs and the right of acquiring property, one must conclude to the necessity of a State which is governed according to the rule of law. We transfer to an elected or otherwise selected group the "monopoly" of making, reforming and implementing law, making it powerful enough to resist every private "power" that would attempt to make a private right absolute, guaranteeing for its part a public, secure, speedy and equitable legal process, and thus protecting the public peace and the security of private rights. This raises, however, the constant dilemma of the problem of power. Public power, i.e., civic power, must be strong enough to render superfluous all use of force in the private defence of rights and interests (with the exception of self-defence), yet not so powerful that instead of being the servant of human rights it becomes arbitrarily destructive of them. This is the special task of constitutional law which determines the more detailed practical regulations for the legislature, executive and judiciary, settles their sphere of competency, and safeguards in the list of basic rights the essential personal rights and guarantees due legal process as well as the jurisdiction and limits of the organs of State. In spite of a constant tendency in this direction, power is not and cannot be the aim and purpose of the State; this is, above all, justice. Men have time and again dreamed of an anarchical community, without power and without domination. Such communities were always short-lived and not infrequently turned, under a "charismatic" leader, into dictatorships or totalitarian States.

4. *Historical origin of the State.* We must distinguish between the natural origin of the State and its historical beginnings. In the last half-century we have seen the rise of dozens of States, through the dissolution of previous States according to the principle of "national self-determination"; through the federation of smaller States; through successful revolt and international recognition; or through the more or less voluntary relinquishing of colonial power. This is not what is meant in the question of the historical origin of the State, for these "new" States suppose previous States or colonies dependent on States. The question of the historical origin of "the State" is not a question of the historically documented act of origin of a concrete State but rather how we may conceive the origin of "the State" in general. The phenomenon of the State exists either because of a biologically necessary development according to the law of nature, without the co-operation of free human acts, or it has been the result of free human action (if we exclude the myths of the divine foundation of the State). In the first case there is no problem for political philosophy, but only one for natural philosophy. In the second case the free acts can be regarded either a) as stemming from human nature, so that the act is free, yet the intentional content of the act appears objectively demanded for the perfection of the idea of man, or b) as a fully free act of people coming together, an act neither objectively called for nor ethically demanded, but at most the consequence of functional objectives.

The social or political contract provided for political philosophy a suitable juridical form for such acts: the State arose through a contract, e.g., through general acceptance of the decisions and, in cases of arbitration, recommendations of the revered head of an extended family. This always implies a status contract, i.e., a new (i.e., independent of the will of individuals) form of community living, objective in its moral content, which is more perfect in view of the nature of man. Thus this status contract cannot be dissolved nor be bound by conditions which contradict the status. The mutual duties and rights of the State and its citizens have thereby an objective existence and present no problem of acceptance for the succeeding generations. Neither is it necessary to imagine a *status naturalis* in which all too frequently typical civil institutions, such as private ownership, money, etc., are more or less developed (John Locke).

The social contract may also imply acceptance of a particular form of government, of positive law or constitution, as several medieval philosophers have taught — otherwise a second contract of subjection must be presumed. What is essential is that those who are uniting to form a State become one "people" and that the power to form a constitution rests with them, i.e., that the people united in this way are the holders of political power from the point of view of natural law; that consequently the forms of government and the constitutional law insofar as it is not just declaratory of the natural law, is positive mutable law, and therefore there is no such thing as a monarchy of divine right or a formal republic, or a direct democracy which is the only legitimate form of government. That at least was the meaning of the scholastic doctrine of transference of political power. The social contract of Hobbes sought only to create the *deus mortalis,* the entirely absolute sovereign who would guarantee unconditional order, civic peace and security, based on absolute obedience or, rather, absolute external conformity. Locke's social contract supposed that the natural rights (to life, freedom and property) were already recognized in the state of nature, but would be better secured in the *status civilis.* Civic power was to be restricted to this function. Rousseau's intention was to use the theory of the social contract to reform the corrupt, inequitable society and to make natural rights and "civic" rights effective for direct democracy, to circumvent the problem of authority and obedience through the identification of subject and citizen, over whom the *volonté générale* with its totalitarian tendencies held control. Its powers were unlimited, except perhaps by accidental circumstances.

The important and essential differences between the old teaching on the contract and the theories of Locke, Hobbes and Rousseau, as well as the differences between these theories themselves, arose from an understandable fear of "revolution". The dominance of monarchic-conservative and legitimist tendencies (e.g., the problem of the Papal States) meant that they were not sufficiently appreciated in the 19th century. The transference theory held by most of the Fathers and the medieval and modern scholastics fell into disfavour. Its place was taken by the "designation" theory. It has become once again in the 20th century for the most part the *opinio communis.*

5. *The purpose of the State.* That the common good is the goal of the State or the organic unity of the various goals pursued by the State has been generally recognized since the time of Plato and Aristotle, both of whom declare the realization of justice to be the first and most important task of the State. The preambles of modern constitutions often define very well the common good. Thus, for example, the U.S. constitution of 1789 says: "We the people of the U.S.A., in order . . . to establish justice, ensure domestic tranquillity, provide for the common defense, promote the general welfare and secure the blessings of liberty to ourselves and our posterity, do ordain and establish this constitution for the United States of America." To establish the justice of internal social order, founded as a secure order of freedom and law, nourished and motivated by the moral order, without, however, being identical with the order of law, is the first task of the State, with corresponding rights and duties on the part of the public power and of the citizens. The objective positive law and the subjective positive rights, having their justification and legitimacy in the objective natural law and the natural rights of the person, are both essential constituents of the common good. To this extent every State embodies the rule of law, independently of the historical form of the State or government. Right is not identified with or at the mercy of the State, which lives within lawful right. Its power is the "servant" and protector of right.

The common good is at the same time more than merely a positive order of law; the latter is itself upheld by the specific political and social virtues: by the free moral obedience of free citizens, by their loyalty, i.e., by the social justice displayed in mutual assistance freely given which counterbalances the divisive influences of positive law and the hardness of its "mine" and "thine", by the professional ethic in independent lesser societies in social and economic life, by all the virtues whose seed-bed is the family. In the (social) market economy State with its technologically conditioned and far-reaching division of labour and specialization, the common good cannot be realized through civil law alone, i.e., through freedom of contract and property, since this freedom can be preserved only under the supposition of equality of bargaining power. Under the iron law of wages of classical national economics the money wage bore no relation to the work done and so arose the problem of the workers and the social question in a society centred on the market. To arrive at an equitable sharing in common welfare in these circumstances, social reformers have created modern social legislation on the basis of distributive justice, founded and protected workers' organizations, furthered the "redemption from the proletarian existence" by means of positive policy on ownership and more just distribution of the national income. To meet the demands of the concrete common good, the State subsidizes public and private schools at all levels, promotes equality of opportunity for the gifted, supports the arts and social recreation; for the sake of the common good, i.e., for the sake of general moral standards, it must regulate the dangers brought about by unlimited freedom of the mass media of social communication; for there is no public freedom without personal responsibility. Also in regard to more material things such as public buildings and amenities of all kinds, streets and parks, squares, playing fields and nature reserves, the State must act for the common good.

The two forms of justice affecting the common good are legal justice, which defines the duties of the citizen in regard to the general welfare, and distributive justice, which requires from the public authorities an equitable attention to the welfare of all citizens; they are the classic virtues to which nowadays social justice is added. They find their function *mutatis mutandis* also in the community of nations.

The central value of the common good helps also to meet the problem of the legitimacy of public power and of the right of active resistance to tyranny; also the question of the primary legitimate holder of public power. A tyrant is a ruler who habitually offends gravely against the common good by eliminating the rule of law, by arbitrarily depriving whole classes of citizens of their natural rights, or by misusing his power for adventures abroad. In such cases the people, whose common good is so grievously injured, have the right to active resistance, which naturally, since a people is always an organized and not an anonymous mass, is activated by groups specially capable of this and objectively called to it. Whether each individual act of resistance is legitimate depends on the concrete emergency in each case. Unfortunately, since the period of absolutism, the classical doctrine of the right to resist has been neglected in political theory and in moral theology; and with it the

related teaching on the historical origin of the State, the holder of public power and the doctrine of transference.

A realistic attitude will never accept the over-simplified antithesis of individual and State, for the individuals are necessarily, by their very nature, not only members of the family community, but also of many other communities freely created in proportion to the general cultural development. In the exercise of their rights of self-determination and self-government these communities serve economic, professional, cultural, pedagogical, religious, and even recreational purposes. Each community has, for its part, its own partial common good which is under the protection of the general political common good and is to be furthered by it. The relationship of these two areas of common welfare to each other is determined by the principle of subsidiarity. The means and form of practical application of this principle are dependent on the stage of cultural development. Nevertheless the danger of the "universal provider" State in which all social services and tasks are performed by the State bureaucracy must be avoided, just as since the creation of a social, economic and cultural policy, the "night-watchman" State of economic liberalism, confining itself to the protection of the right of property and freedom of contract, has been abandoned.

6. *State and society*. From this vantage point a basis can be found for the solution of the problems of State and society, State and nation, State and Church. In the modern State the basic rights encompass more or less exactly a sphere of general social life, the free determination of which is in principle guaranteed through the initiative of the individuals and of groups through voluntary organization. The State as an order of law provides the individuals with certain legal institutions, e.g., private and common ownership, the contractual and corporative nature of associations, and guarantees them the protection of the general laws, always of course subject to the preservation of public order. These innumerable organizations of freely associating citizens go to make up the freely organized private society, to be distinguished from the State as governmental organization. The distinction implies therefore directly a system of government devoted to freedom, in contrast to the totalitarian State which necessarily rejects these differences.

7. *State and nation.* The democratic and egalitarian tendencies of the French Revolution gave rise to the principle of national self-determination. The national State was the ideal. In fact there existed and still exist, especially in the new States that arose from the previous colonies, both the multinational State and the a-national State, e.g., the U.S.A., Canada, etc. The nation forms no more than an especially powerful factor for integration, which can easily degenerate into a virulent nationalism with universal claims, with all the dangers which the era of nationalism has conjured up.

8. *State and religion.* In contrast to the State of antiquity and to the Roman Empire in which the State included the religious sphere and became the means of salvation, the entry of Christianity into history meant that the State and the Empire were de-sacralized; the State or its ruler was no longer the guarantor of salvation. The State should apply itself to the temporal, the *felicitas terrena,* the organization of this world. This explains the fierce reaction of the Roman Empire and its rulers against the little *secta Christianorum,* but also the wish of Constantine to make the Church, now grown great, to be a guarantor of the Empire. But Christian teaching refused to base the State on anything but natural law. In the sphere of revealed religion and the divinely founded Church the State has no jurisdiction. "Non eripit mortalia qui regna dat coelestia": the natural rights and duties of the citizens are not changed by the *status gratiae.* But the Church must stand firm, in all historical forms of the relationship between Church and State, for freedom to teach, to provide pastoral care, to exercise its mission and administer the sacraments, for itself and its members, in the pluralist society and its political form, the religiously "neutral" State, that is, in the "lay" State.

9. *Public power.* The State as the universal, permanent *unitas ordinis,* bringing together individuals, families, and communities, is unthinkable without the public power, protecting effectively the common good in time of conflict and enforcing law. Love and the spirit of friendship can and should infuse social life and keep it active. Yet even those who love, and even saints, will always have opposing opinions, honestly arrived at, about what is concretely to be done; law and authority, and power of execution based on them are essential among men. *Ubi societas ibi ius; ubi ius ibi auctoritas et potestas.* The incarnated person, man, lives necessarily in perpetual danger of body and soul from nature and from his fellow human beings; he yearns for *secura libertas.* But if law becomes ineffective, there is the threat of a *bellum omnium contra omnes,* which can only be overcome by the effective *power* of law. The public power comes into being with the social contract and in natural law its wielder is the people who have come together in unity. It is they who, in the interest of the better realization of the common good, can transfer or delegate the public power to one person (monarch) or to a group, as happens, e.g., in the *Lex Regia* of Roman law. By this teaching, the various forms of State or government are historically conditioned and derive from positive law. No form, not even the democratic, is of natural or divine law.

10. *Forms of State.* There is no one single legitimate *form* of State. The only exclusive principle of legitimacy, and therefore of legitimate change of form of the State through revolution, is and remains that which best realizes the common good according to the circumstances. This may also legitimize an originally unlawful revolution, if the form of State thus established does in fact achieve the common good in a permanent manner. The doctrine of designation was popular in the 19th century. (Political power is not transferred from the public, but the holder is "designated". This view became anchored in Church law after the defeat of Conciliarism, which was rooted in the idea of the Church as a corporation.) But the notion is not fruitful, and is too historically conditioned — by anti-revolutionary ideas, fear of Rousseau's false doctrine of the sovereignty of the people with its infallible common will, etc. Few would support it today.

As a result of the foregoing, the "indifference" of the Catholic Church to the historical forms of the State is understandable. These are based on human law, their ultimate legitimation is the concrete realization of the common good to which the people, in the form of State historically developed, have an unconditioned right. The *Ecclesia Universalis,* called to teach all nations, can adapt to all human cultures and civilizations. It recognizes the State as supreme in its sphere; it knows that in the changing forms of State, the people, the members of which it is its divinely appointed task to lead to salvation, live on, characterized by many non-political factors. The social, constitutional State, legitimated by the democratic principle of the consent of the citizens, with the institutions of human and civic rights, division of powers, and accountability of government to the people or to its elected parliament, i.e., the dependence on law ("the rule of law"), appears to have thus solved the problem which Abraham Lincoln formulated as follows: The government must be strong enough to protect us, but not so strong that it could oppress us.

11. *State and community of nations.* The State as it historically exists is the way of life of a group of people who are characterized by many non-political factors, cultural, linguistic and mental, as well as material (e.g., geographical, economico-technical). Therefore there will always be a multiplicity of States, which will possibly in the future form federations in increasing numbers. States are therefore on principle members of the highest and true community, the community of mankind. The character of the State as "perfect society" by no means excludes this trend. Vitoria and Suarez, who rejected a world dominion of Emperor or Pope, saw true States even in the "uncivilized" (as they were called later) tribes of Indians. Although they seem to do so, States do not live in a state of nature (in the sense of Hobbes), exclusively controlled by power factors, but in a community with a specific common good (cf. *Pacem in Terris*) and a positive law based on the natural law, the *ius inter gentes,* as Suarez called it, which, by virtue of the comity of nations and international treaties, positively regulates the relations of States. One may call the law of nations imperfect since its implementation in cases of conflict depends on the injured member and his right to go to war. Therefore it was necessary to formulate strict conditions for the just war, which, however, are insufficient today in view of the means of mass destruction. Total war is not intelligible, even as an a-moral, purely utilitarian use of force, since in the end no one survives to enjoy the conquest. Neither should it be forgotten that the greater part of the law of nations is a law of peace, regulating the peaceful communication between the nations and their citizens, finding common standards in communications, in health regulations, in traffic, in commercial law, in cultural co-operation for the protection of human rights, etc., the smooth functioning of which is taken for granted (in times of peace).

International law, as we have said, is imperfect to the extent that it lacks security and the capability of progressive adaptation through a legislature to an international life developing largely independently of it. And it cannot be effectively implemented through courts of final appeal backed up by coercive power. It is (still) a law of co-ordination, not of subordination, i.e., the putting into effect of the law is still too dependent on the goodwill of the States. That is the reason why prohibitions of war (e.g., Kellogg Pact) are ineffective. Rather must means be provided, partly through diplomacy and much more through the development of legal institutions, to make war progressively superfluous as the *ultima ratio.* There will always be "conflicts"; the problem is to settle them justly and equitably by peaceful means. Historically no war has been in itself inevitable, but it became this at a particular moment and conjuncture in history.

The Christian will therefore welcome all attempts to solve conflicts peacefully, and all efforts of mind to arrive at timely knowledge of possible conflict. Just as in the inner life of the State there is need of a policy, i.e., the constant reform of the concrete order in mental and cultural, in legal and moral, in social and economic affairs, based on the virtues of justice and charity, so too in the world community there is need of this constant reform of order, especially as it is endangered here by national egoism and pride of intellect and will. The *ordo juris positivi,* anchored in treaties and protected by power, must, if civil strife within the State and wars between nations are to be avoided, be capable of change or reform in the light of the *ordo iustitiae,* by peaceful means. This may be humanly difficult, but it is not impossible; for the general development has already created conditions which make possible a political action which seemed impossible before World War II and the threat of a third World War. Why should charity and humble justice not be able to achieve in the direction of the good what hatred and diabolical hybris have been able to do for evil?

See also *Person* II, *Society, International Law, Natural Law* I, *Rights of Man, Church and State, Absolutism, Power, Law* III, IV, *Resistance, Revolution, War.*

BIBLIOGRAPHY. F. Suarez, *De Legibus* (1612); cf. *Francis Suarez: Selections from Three Works: A Treatise on Laws and God the Law-Giver; A Defence of the Catholic and Apostolic Faith ... Work on the Three Theological Virtues* (1944); T. Hobbes, *Leviathan* (1651); J. Locke, *Two Treatises on Government and Law* (1690); J. J. Rousseau, *Contrat Social* (1761); O. Gierke, *Political Theories of the Middle Ages* (1900); id., *Natural Law and the Theory of Society, 1500–1800*, E.T. with introduction by E. Barker, 2 vols. (1935); id., *The Development of Political Theory* (1939); L. Hobhouse, *The Metaphysical Theory of the State* (1918); L. Duguit, *Law in the Modern State* (1919); H. Laski, *Authority in the Modern State* (1919); id., *The Foundations of Sovereignty and Other Essays* (1921); id., *The State in Theory and Practice* (1935); R. McIver, *The Modern State* (1926); R. Lowie, *The Origin of the State* (1927); V. Lenin, *The State and Revolution* (1932); H. Magid, *English Political Pluralism* (1941); R. G. Collingwood, *The New Leviathan* (1942); H. Kelsen, *General Theory of Law and State* (1945); H. Rommen, *The State in Catholic Thought* (1945); M. Weber, *Civitas Gentium* (1947); id., *Economy and Society* (1968); J. Maritain, *Man and the State* (1951); R. Gettell, *History of Political Thought,* revised by L. Waniless (2nd ed., 1953); E. Voegelin, *Order and History,* 3 vols. (1956 ff.); H. Finer, *The Theory and Practice of Modern Government* (1954); H. Blackham, *Political Discipline in a Free Society* (1961); O. von Nell-Breuning and H. Sacher, eds., *Wörterbuch der Politik,* I (2nd ed., 1962), II (2nd ed., 1957); A. Cobban, *Rousseau and the Modern State* (2nd ed., 1964); G. Gundlach, *Die Ordnung der menschlichen Gesellschaft,* I (1964), ch. 5.

Heinrich A. Rommen

STATES OF MAN, THEOLOGICAL

1. *General concept.* "State of man" is here understood in the theological sense – not in the biological sense of "natural state" or the like, nor in the ecclesiological sense of the lay, clerical or religious state, nor again in the social sense of class or calling. We are dealing with the fundamental inward and outward situations of man in the history of salvation which determine his relation to salvation and are constituted either by the free action of God or of man or of both.

2. The realities comprised under the term "states of man" — the state of man before the Fall; the state of original sin; the state of redemption and so on — were always before the minds of the faithful. Hence there was always a doctrine of the states of man, though not in these terms and not a system of its own, simply because the Christian faith, both individual and collective, always thinks in terms of the history of salvation. Hence it

always had to dinstinguish phases in the relationship of man to his final salvation.

From the Middle Ages on, this doctrine was systematically developed, but it has not even yet been worked out as a generally accepted "system" dealing with these states of life, where they all would have their definite place and where all the distinguishing marks would be clearly distributed. (On the history of the question, see *LTK,* IX, cols. 1013–16; the word "status" in the sense of a phase of the history of salvation, as used here, does not occur in the documents of Vatican II.)

3. In the ordinary terminology, these states sometimes mean a temporal succession of phases in the history of man's salvation, such as the *status viatoris* and the *status comprehensoris.* They sometimes bring out various aspects of the same phase and situation, as for instance when the *status naturae lapsae et reparatae* is spoken of, to indicate that the present order of salvation has as its determinants both original sin and the redemption. They sometimes designate situations which precede the free decision of the individual, and sometimes situations which can only be brought about *by* such a decision. Thus we have the *status peccati* and the *status justificationis* — situations brought about by the decision of man with regard to the absence of sanctifying grace or justification in the sinner or with regard to grace freely accepted. Sometimes real and concrete states are meant, but again, sometimes a merely abstract situation which can be defined only negatively, as in the *status naturae purae.* All these disparate aspects and principles of distinction make it almost impossible to combine the states of man into a single system which would be clear and logical.

4. But the fundamental distinctions with regard to the states of man can no doubt be arrived at on the following principles. A distinction must be made between situations which exist prior to the individual free decision, and those which are due in some way to human freedom. And then again the difference between the various historical phases (not aspects) of the history of salvation, individual and collective, must be borne in mind. We can thus make the following distinctions, which correspond to a division found in St. Thomas, *Summa Theologica,* III, q. 13, a. 1 ad 2, between the *status innocentiae, culpae, gloriae.*

a) *The original state (status iustitiae originalis).* This is the situation which was originally prior to the whole history of human freedom, being the possibility of freedom as created by God. It was the nature of man elevated by the grace of the self-communication of God, in which man was ordained to the vision of God as his goal. It was the situation of the "beginning" as such (see *Creation* IV).

To bring out clearly the supernatural character of this situation, produced as it was by the self-communication of God (see *Nature and Grace*), we say that God could have created man even without this grace (*D* 2318). This allows us to conceive of the abstract possibility of a pure state of nature *(status naturae purae),* with which, however, the state of the sinner may not be even materially identified in the real order of things.

The grace which constituted this primordial situation of salvation may be considered the grace of Christ. This means that this grace, decreed by God in his will to self-communication, attains by its own nature its historical climax and eschatological manifestation in the incarnation of the Logos. Thus the beginning, the initial state, has essentially a Christological character. The question as to whether and how this "paradisiac" state was "chronologically" prior to the state of salvation-history cannot be discussed here. But in any case prudence is called for with regard to any notions of the primitive state (the "history of origins") which would simply make it a stretch of time homogeneous with the time of salvation-history, which would bring up difficulties from modern palaeontology. We can form an idea of the original state only by an aetiological deduction which works back from our own situation in the order of salvation, and only insofar as our conclusions are valid.

b) The state of fallen and restored nature *(status naturae lapsae et reparatae)* is the state of salvation-history as it still runs its course, identical in fact with the *status viatoris.* This is the situation of the history of salvation, as brought about by original sin and the redemption of man. It should be an elementary principle that the situation of original sin and that of redemption should not be conceived of as successive phases of the history of salvation. They are two aspects of one and the same situation, that of the actual history of salvation. The divine salvific will which brought about the original state

with its ordination to Christ continues in force (see *Existence* III B, *Grace*). There never was a time in which man was not "objectively redeemed" *(intuitu meritorum Christi).* And there was no period or situation in this history which was not also affected by the "sin of the world" (see *Original Sin, Sin* I, *Concupiscence*). This state can exist in three ways, with regard to human freedom.

i) It can exist simply in the form of a prior datum, that is, prior to any free decision in its regard. This is how at any rate we should think of the situation of the child before coming to the full use of reason. We need not now ask whether and how there is a difference in this situation of salvation-history according to whether the child is baptized or not. At any rate, the situation of the unbaptized child is not solely determined by original sin. It is also affected by his "objective" redemption. He is to be baptized, not merely because he is in a situation affected by original sin, but also because he is redeemed — not just in order that he may be redeemed. It is this state of redemption which is to be made manifest in an ecclesial and sacramental way (see also *Limbo*).

ii) This state may exist in the form of a sinful refusal of the salvific will of God. It may be the ratification of the element of original sin which affects the situation of the history of salvation. This is the *status peccatoris (status peccati).*

iii) The state may exist in the form of the acceptance of the existing grace (through faith, hope and love) and a rejection of the element of original sin in the situation of the history of salvation. This is the *status iustificati (status iustificationis),* which comes about in and through the personal decision. This may be without the baptism of water, but it achieves its full historical and social manifestation in baptism and full membership of the Church (see *Eucharist* I).

c) The state of fulfilment, in the vision of God, is called the *status comprehensoris,* the *status patriae.*

5. The one state of the history of salvation as it runs its course may be divided, from the point of view of collective history, into the phases before and after the historical manifestation of Christ. (It may also be divided in the same way from the point of view of individual history, though the phases in individual history need not coincide chronologically with those of collective history.) These phases may be described in Pauline

terminology as the time of the law and the time of the gospel *(status legis — status evangelii [gratiae]),* though it should be noted that this subdivision does not ultimately range the fundamental components of the one salvation-history in chronological sequence (nature, grace, sinfulness, origin from Christ, origin from "Adam"). The temporal sequence is in the explicit awareness of these components in the history of revelation, and hence the distinction deals with how this awareness was possible before or after the historical Christ-event (this awareness itself being also, however, an element of salvation-history and hence of the situation itself with regard to salvation). It is indeed possible to subdivide the *status legis* again into a *status legis naturae* and a *status veteris legis,* with St. Thomas, *Summa Theologica,* III, q. 60, a. 5 ad 3; q. 61, a. 4 ad 1. But this terminology could easily give rise to misunderstandings, since the *natura* in question is not *natura pura.* It was a situation in which all the basic components of the situation created by salvation-history were present (in a pre-Christian way). And again, the Old Law, being the law of the OT, did not affect the general situation of all men with regard to salvation. Hence this last subdivision is valid only for the special history of salvation and revelation in Israel before and after Moses, i.e., the history of the patriarchs and the history of the covenant of Sinai.

See also *Salvation* III B, C.

BIBLIOGRAPHY. See bibliographies on *Grace, Nature and Grace, Order* IV, especially: H. Renckens, *Israel's Concept of the Beginning* (1964); I. Willig, *Geschaffene und ungeschaffene Gnade* (1964); M. Schmaus, *Das Paradies* (1965); K. Rahner, *Theological Investigations,* IV (1966); M. Seibel, "Der Mensch als Gottes übernatürliches Ebenbild...", *Mysterium Salutis,* II (1967), pp. 805–40, with bibliography; H. de Lubac, *The Mystery of the Supernatural* (1967); H. Waldenfels, *Offenbarung* (1969).

Karl Rahner

STATES OF THE CHURCH (PAPAL STATES)

1. *The rise and development of the Papal States* to some extent runs parallel to that of the idea of the primacy. Although the papal possessions became a State strictly speaking only in the 8th century, its roots reach back into earlier centuries, if not actually to the time of Constantine. The intensification of the cult of Peter from the 5th century onwards, both in Rome and beyond, resulted in lavish gifts on the part of the Emperor and nobility. Known from the 6th century as the *patrimonium Petri,* this large area of land in the possession of the Roman Church was mainly concentrated in Lower Italy and Sicily but extended far beyond Italy. By his centralizing policy, Gregory the Great succeeded in greatly increasing the yield of this property and, during the troubles attendant on the Barbarian Invasions, made it the basis of an extensive social welfare activity. By the disappearance of the Byzantine authority, the military defencelessness of Italy, and the deepening spiritual estrangement caused by the Eastern Empire's hostility to images, a political vacuum was created in Central Italy and administrative and governmental functions gradually devolved upon the spiritual authority. In the first instance the Pope made himself responsible for maintaining food supplies and internal order in Rome and its neighbouring territories. During the persistent Lombard attacks even the defence of Rome, militarily and diplomatically, passed to the Pope. Respect for the prince of the apostles afforded more effective security than such measures as the rebuilding of the city walls (completed under Gregory III) and the coalition with the equally isolated Ravenna, Spoleto and Benevento. The Pope carried on peace negotiations with the Lombards as the real ruler of the Duchy of Rome.

Political separation from Byzantium took place under Stephen II. When in face of a Lombard ultimatum the Pope was sent no aid from the Emperor, he first followed the Emperor's ambassadors to negotiations at Pavia in 753 and then, when the negotiations broke down, continued his journey alone into France to see King Pepin. At Ponthion, in response to his plea for protection, the Pope was given a sworn promise of aid and, by the undoubtedly genuine Treaty of Quercy (754), was guaranteed possession of Rome and Ravenna with Venetia and Istria, as well as of Spoleto and Benevento, once the Lombard kingdom was destroyed. In return, Pepin was given the title of *patricius* (which he did not make use of), denoting his protective sovereignty over Rome. After Pepin's victory in 756, Ravenna and the Pentapolis (on the Adriatic from Rimini to beyond Ancona) were "restored" to St. Peter. Together with the Duchy of

Rome, these territories henceforth constituted the Papal States, in which a papal administration was set up and officials and people owed allegiance to the Pope. However, the extent of the claims made by the papacy on the basis of the "Donation of Constantine" (produced at this time) and on the basis of the promises made by Pepin and later by Charlemagne, was never matched by the restitutions made by secular rulers, not even when Charlemagne renewed the promise of Quercy in 774 and expanded the Papal States in 781 and 786 by adding Southern Tuscany, the Campagna and the city of Capua. Further south only the patrimonies were restored. The Papal States, henceforth separated from the Empire, thus acquired their definitive form under the sovereignty of the Pope. The Eastern Roman Emperor answered this "apostasy" by the complete exclusion of the Pope from the Byzantine sphere of jurisdiction, in particular by subordinating Lower Italy, Sicily and the vicariate of Thessalonika to Byzantium ecclesiastically.

The character of the new State, which was more the visible embodiment of an idea than a real power, was revealed in its chequered relationship with the Western Emperors. To protect the papal sovereignty, the *patricius* Charlemagne had come to Rome in 800; by his coronation he became overlord in Rome and in the Papal States, intervening in administrative and legal matters. Although autonomy was guaranteed by the pact of Louis the Pious (817), the *Constitutio Romana* of 824 set up a joint commission, responsible to the Emperor, to control the administration. It required a newly elected Pope's sworn allegiance to this constitution, thereby making the Papal States part of the Carolingian Empire. The fall of the Empire revealed the fundamental defects of an elective State, the tension between the Roman nobles and the *familia S. Petri*, the danger of rivalries between Rome and Ravenna, and the vulnerability of the Papal States in face of the Saracen invasions.

John VIII was driven to build a small papal fleet. The additions to the Papal States and the considerable measure of autonomy which Charles the Bald secured for it remained, however, practically meaningless. The inroads of feudalism resulted in the almost complete independence of large parts of the Papal States under the sovereignty of their previous lords. In an upsurge of Roman civic pride in freedom, usurpers arrogated to themselves the title of *patricius*. From the 10th century onwards, the Papal States, dominated by the "patrician" families, barely included more than Rome, the Campagna and Southern Tuscany.

John XII appealed to Otto the Great for help against Berengarius I, who occupied the Exarchate and the Pentapolis. Otto restored papal sovereignty to its former extent by a treaty in 962, but in actual fact only Ravenna in the Exarchate was restored. Clearly the Roman Church lacked the necessary means to administer a large territory unaided, and only repeated intervention by German rulers from Otto I down to Henry III prevented the Papal States from becoming a hereditary princedom of noble Roman families; even so, during the Roman rebellions in the time of Otto III, the Pope was unable to remain in Rome.

Only the nomination of Popes by Henry III created the conditions which enabled the Reform Popes from Leo IX onwards to regain real sovereignty over the Papal States. Now real expansion took place. Benevento submitted to papal authority; Spoleto and Fermo were added under Victor II. The basis for the Gregorian Reform was of course broader than the Papal States. There existed a number of vassal states owing allegiance to the Pope near or beyond the borders of the Empire, and having diminished sovereign rights, beginning with the Norman kingdom under Leo IX and Nicholas II. Under Gregory VII feudal links were established with Dalmatia, Russia and Aragon; England, Poland, Denmark and Spanish counts paid Peter's Pence.

The Pope, who established an army of his own, the *militia S. Petri,* sought by these feudal rights to increase the number of vassals available for advancing his religious and ecclesiastical plans. These *fideles S. Petri,* gained partly by an appeal to the Donation of Constantine, and the bequest of Mathilda of Tuscany, made sometime after 1076, alone enabled the Pope to struggle against Henry IV and provided the necessary shield for implementing the Gregorian Reform.

Later Papal policy was aimed more at purely territorial matters in Italy and inevitably became involved in difficulties and conflicts not only with the Normans but also in the North. The bulk of Mathilda's *allodia* (freehold estates) lay in the region from Siena to Mantua. They were first occupied on the Emperor's behalf, until Lothar III in 1136 had himself invested with them by the Pope, while Mathilda's feudal estates, Ferrara in particular, passed to the Papal States immediately following the Countess's death (1115).

The Concordat of Worms (1122) not only secured the return of all the property and *regalia* of St. Peter, it also meant the recognition of the political independence of the Roman Church. This independence was expressed in the imperial dignities already accorded to the Pope in the *Constitutum Constantini,* the purple robe worn by a newly elected Pope at his investiture and the tiara with the gold circlet which he wore in certain processions. But there was some opposition to complete State sovereignty on the part of the democratic movement of the Roman community and in the efforts of the Hohenstaufen Emperor to restore the *honor imperii.* Whereas to counter the former the Emperor's help was essential, the 12th-century Popes were able to block the Emperor's political designs and to maintain their sovereignty in the Papal States by means of alliances with the Lombard cities. Favourable circumstances (the struggle for the German throne) and Innocent III's dominant personality produced a radical change, even if only for several decades. Appealing to ancient grants recorded in the property archives of the Roman Church, the Pope sought for the "recovery" of the lost territories. He managed to secure for the Papal States Spoleto, the March of Ancona and a strip of land in Southern Tuscany. More ambitious plans seemed legally secured and near to realization by reason of the promises of Otto IV (1201) and the Golden Bull of Eger (1213). Yet with the attachment of Sicily to the Empire the danger at once became apparent that the Papal States might be caught in a vice and succumb to the far-reaching plans of the later Hohenstaufens. When the papacy's own troops ("Soldiers of the Keys") failed to prevent the occupation of the Papal States by Frederick II, the Pope appealed finally to Charles of Anjou. A swift succession of pontificates and the ambition of the new vassal-ruler of Sicily, chosen as Senator of Rome and nominated Papal Vicar for Tuscany, greatly increased the difficulty of restoring papal authority in the Papal States, even when Rudolf of Habsburg's concession made possible the extension of the Papal State around the Romagna (the former Exarchate).

If the 13th-century Popes found it impossible to consolidate their control in the Papal States, it is hardly surprising that in the following century, and especially during the Avignon Exile, anarchy and disorganization should have become widespread, with the Ghibellines and Guelphs striving with each other for power. In Rome itself Cola di Rienzi proclaimed a republic. It was only with difficulty that the Popes were able to control their State through legates. The establishment of another State of the Church on the Rhone seemed more important to them. Here, the county of Venaissin had been in the possession of the Holy See since 1274. In 1348 Clement VI purchased the city of Avignon which was within the county. Avignon and Venaissin remained in the Church's possession until the French Revolution. From 1309, when the papacy settled in Avignon, the Popes scarcely entertained any notion of a return to Rome, yet they sought to restore their sovereignty in the Papal States. Cardinal Aegidius Albornoz took charge of these efforts in two legations (1355–1367). The Aegidian Constitutions, the fruit of the Cardinal's labours, assured a certain civic autonomy and remained the civil code of law for the Papal States down to 1816. But fresh rebellions broke out after the Cardinal's death and not even the return of the Pope to Rome was able to quell them. Papal rule was only restored with Martin V. He accomplished this with great skill and in 1429 he forced the ever unruly Bologna to recognize papal sovereignty. He believed that a reorganization of administration was essential for the reform of the Church and with this in view he sought trustworthy assistants. He thought he could find such helpers in his own family and therefore furnished these with innumerable tenures. His policy was continued by Nicholas V.

Under the Renaissance Popes the Papal States reached their maximum secularization. As a secular power they were involved in the affairs of the petty Italian States. All efforts to preserve their neutrality in the squabbles between these States and amid their constantly changing alliances were frustrated by the intrigues and conspiracies of the *nepotes* by which the Pope was drawn into military conflicts with France and Venice. The unrestrained nepotism of Alexander VI did eventually result in the overthrow of the *de facto* rulers in the Romagna, the Marches and the Campagna. These rulers were replaced by the single rule of Cesare Borgia.

177

STATES OF THE CHURCH

After the Pope's sudden death, however, his conquests reverted once more to the Church. Julius II completed the overthrow of the local overlords, recaptured in the war against Venice and France the territories which had been lost, enlarged the Papal States with Modena, Parma and Piacenza, and tried to weld this hitherto amorphous mass of kingdoms, vassal States and autonomous States into a unified structure under a single authority. Although Paul III once more made the Farnese a family power by the conferment of Parma and Piacenza, once the last of the princely vassals died no more great feudalities were conferred in the Papal States in the 16th and 17th centuries (Ferrara 1588, Urbino 1630) following Pius V's prohibition of such donations.

The Papal States of the next centuries acquired their distinctive character from the Catholic Reform and Counter-Reformation and from absolutism. They were now administered without apparent difficulty by a Secretary of State and a *camerlengo* (chamberlain), supported by a special congregation. The administration, completely in clerical hands, revealed many defects; in particular, almost the whole of the financial resources were used for the city of Rome alone, for the work of the Curia, and for occasional nepotism (Urban VIII), to the detriment of the provinces, governed by legates and lacking both a uniform administration and uniform legal practice. The income of the Papal States (from duties, indirect taxation, and, since Clement VII, also from pawnbroking) decreased appreciably in the 17th century. In the 18th century the Papal States were anachronistic in structure and administration, despite all efforts at reform; its citizens lacked any "national consciousness" and there existed no supporting stratum of middle class citizens.

The French Revolution was the beginning of the end for the Papal States. They had long since lost their religious character in the eyes of the world. But the Revolution refused in principle to accord them any spiritual authority whatever, regarding them simply as the largest State of Italy, with which the French Republic soon found itself at war. After the Peace of Tolentino (1797) the legations of Bologna, Ferrara, and the Romagna were lost to papal rule. In 1798 what was left of the Papal States was occupied, the Roman Republic proclaimed, and the Pope taken prisoner. Napoleon declared Rome a free, i.e., imperial city,

and annexed the Papal States to the Kingdom of Italy. An indirect renunciation of the Papal States in the Concordat of Fontainebleau was explicitly withdrawn by Pius VII a few weeks later. After the overthrow of Napoleon, Consalvi succeeded in completely restoring the Papal States (1815). Limited administrative reforms were followed by a period of reaction even in the economic and technical fields. Excluded from real responsibility, the laity either formed secret societies or else gave their support to the national efforts of the Italian Romantic movement. The Popes failed to recognize the spontaneous vigour of the Risorgimento and, after the unhappy gesture of Pius IX, were unwilling to abandon any part of their sovereignty or to place themselves at the head of a war against Austria. The presence of foreign troops in Rome, therefore, while it could delay the revolutionary movement in the Papal States, could no longer master it. An internal democratization was equally impossible. A democratic constitution in a State under a Pope endowed with universal jurisdiction seemed contradictory. In 1860 the Marches and Umbria were annexed to the Kingdom of Sardinia. On the outbreak of the Franco-Prussian war, the French troops left Rome. Following merely token resistance, the armies of the Kingdom of Italy occupied the Eternal City on 20 September 1870. Papal sovereignty was abolished by popular vote; the Papal States were incorporated into the Kingdom of Italy. Since the papacy refused to recognize this act and rejected the legal guarantees, the "Roman question" remained a major political issue for the Italian State, an unredeemed legal right for the papacy, and a divisive ferment between liberal and conservative Catholicism. No satisfactory solution was found until the Lateran Treaty of 1929, which resulted in the creation of a symbolic Papal State, the *Città del Vaticano*.

2. *Significance and problematic aspects.* Seldom has the merely relative value of historical forms been so clearly demonstrated as in the case of the Papal States. In its first centuries, the then unarmed Papal States seemed a quite essential embodiment of the spiritual authority of the Petrine office. As a base for the spread of the Church in the West they were the cause of a further deepening of the gulf between Rome and Byzantium. In the Middle Ages they afforded some guarantee, often insufficient, of the autonomy of papal

power, but at the same time forced its rulers to follow a selfish policy to maintain their territorial integrity. The ensuing struggles intensified, while the Church's religious influence lessened, until the fall of the Hohenstaufens. When during the confusion of the 14th century the Papal States ceased to be the base of the papal finances, the Avignon papacy was driven to establish a complex tax system. The recovery of the Papal States once again required the expenditure of nearly 40% of the papal income. Only when two-thirds of the Curia's income once again came from the Papal States was it possible to renounce part of the *annates* and other levies. In the 15th and 16th centuries the existence of the Papal States made possible an independent religious policy (transfer of Councils to Ferrara and Bologna), whereas the territorial and financial base was too small to permit large scale activities against the Turks or in the Thirty Years War. Even the leadership of Italy in its struggle for unity slipped from the hands of the successors of Julius II.

On the other hand, the Papal States were a factor hindering the spread of the Reformation in the greater part of Italy. In other respects, in the Post-Tridentine period the Papal States rather posed problems than shaped policy in international politics. After the French Revolution, they seemed to the Enlightenment an outmoded anachronism, while believers saw them as an indispensable guarantee of the Pope's spiritual authority in face of the irreligious and even antireligious modern State then emerging. They seemed not just an instrument but an ultimate safeguard for the effective exercise of the Church's teaching office (a different view was taken by Döllinger, etc.). In the concern to maintain the Papal States, which involved Italian Catholics in a painful matter of conscience, increasingly urgent social issues were for long ignored, of course. The loss of the Papal States, while intensifying the respect and support of the Catholic world for the Pope, tempted politicians to try to turn it to their own advantage. All such efforts were brought to naught by Pius XI's generous solution of the problem. A Papal State in the medieval sense would have been intolerably alien to the Second Vatican Council's understanding of the Church.

See also *Absolutism, Reform* II C, D, *Avignon Exile.*

BIBLIOGRAPHY. SOURCES: A. Theiner, *Codex diplomaticus dominii temporalis S. Sedis,* 3 vols. (1861–62; reprint, 1963); P. Fabre and L. Duchesne, *Liber censuum,* 3 vols. (1889–1952); N. Miko, *Das Ende des Kirchenstaates,* II (1962). LITERATURE: In addition to the Histories of the Popes by Pastor, P. G. Schmidlin, Caspar, Haller, Seppelt and the articles in *Enciclopedia Cattolica,* XI, *Catholicisme,* IV, *LTK,* VI, see especially M. Brosch, *Geschichte des Kirchenstaats seit dem 16. Jahrhundert,* 2 vols. (1880–82); G. Schnürer, *Die Entstehung des Kirchenstaats* (1894); L. Duchesne, *Les premiers temps de l'État Pontifical* (4th ed., 1912); E. Dupré-Theseider, *L'idea imperiale di Roma nella tradizione del medioevo* (1942); A. Ventrone, *L'amministrazione dello Stato Pontificio 1814–1870* (1942); O. Bertolini, "Restitutio 756–57", *Miscellanea P. Paschini,* I (1948), pp. 103–71; E. Griffé, "Aux origines de l'État Pontifical", *Bulletin de littérature ecclésiastique* 53 and 59 (1952 and 1958); W. Ullmann, *The Growth of Papal Government in the Middle Ages* (1955); P. Partner, *The Papal State under Martin V* (1958); L. Dal Pane, *Lo Stato Pontificio e il movimento reformatore de settecento* (1959); G. Filippone, *Le relazione tra lo Stato Pontificio e la Francia rivoluzionaria,* I (1959); E. E. Stengel, "Die Entwicklung des Kaiserprivilegs für die römische Kirche 817–962", *Abhandlungen und Untersuchungen zur mittelalterlichen Geschichte* (1960), pp. 218–48; D. P. Waley, *The Papal State in the 13th Century* (1961); L. P. Raybaud, *Papauté et pouvoir temporel, 1730–58* (1963); R. Mori, *La Questione Romana 1861–65* (1963); N. Miko, *Das Ende des Kirchenstaates,* I (1964).

Hermann Tüchle

STOICISM

1. *General description.* a) The political and social changes in the time of Alexander the Great and the diadochi, at the end of the 3rd century B.C., brought about the disintegration of the Greek city-state and thus the loss of the inner force which the Greeks of classical times had found in their bond with their *polis* and its religion. All possibilities of the intellectual life seemed to have been exhausted by the speculative work of Plato and Aristotle, and by the empirical research of the latter and his school. It was therefore practical questions of the conduct of life which occupied the attention of the two schools of philosophy which were taking form in Hellenism, the Stoics and the Epicureans, the "Stoa" being more important and extensive than the "Garden". The intellectual disciplines were mainly studied for the sake of ethics. For the educated, philosophy took the place of religion. It looked for a new way of providing man with

security. The question of the purpose and end (τέλος) of man became predominant. Man was no longer considered in the light of the city-state, as when Aristotle had defined him as an *ens sociale* (ζῷον πολιτικόν), and ethics ceased to be regarded as part of political life. Man took refuge in the inner life, to avoid dependence on outward conditions. Epicurus was content with an individualistic attitude which made "pleasure" (ἡδονή — the totality of sense perception) the term of reference of all action. But the Stoa regarded the individual as a member of the one human race (*animale communale*, ζῷον κοινωνικόν) where there was no distinction of nation or class. The unity of man with himself, in which he finds his happiness (εὐδαιμονία) and goal (τέλος), necessarily presupposes a general consent to the one law which binds all men equally. This law (νόμος) is identical with the divine reason (λόγος) which guides the universe.

b) Though some of the leading Stoics like Zeno and Chrysippus were of Oriental origin, the thesis of Pohlenz, that Semitic elements were at work along with Greek thought in Stoic doctrine, has not met with much acceptance. The influence of the Socratic schools, especially the Cynics, was important. In natural science and theology, the Stoa took over important traits from Heraclitus.

2. *Doctrine.* Wisdom (σοφία) is defined as the "knowledge of things divine and human", philosophy (love of wisdom; see *Philosophy*) as "training in the art necessary to life". It is divided into logic, physics (natural science) and ethics. The relationship of the parts is illustrated by the metaphor of an orchard. Physics, of which theology forms part, is like the trees growing up towards heaven, ethics like the nourishing fruit and logic like the protective walls.

a) *Logic.* Logic comprises dialectic and rhetoric. Dialectic creates the basis for correct action, since it enables man to know what is formally and materially true. Since both language and thought are manifestations of the authoritative Logos (the later Stoics distinguishing the Logos formed within [ἐνδιάθετος] from the Logos thrusting outwards in speech [προφορικός]), dialectic comprises linguistics and grammar as well as formal logic and epistemology. The corporeal sounds (σημαίνοντα) are to be distinguished from the incorporeal concepts or thoughts (σημαινόμενα, λεκτά), which in turn are different from real things. Names were deliberately given to things by the first men, according to the norm of nature (φύσις).

The names of the five cases in grammar go back to the Stoics. Their theory of the tenses was not based like that of Aristotle on the succession of time (past, present, future) but on the types of action, according to which the Stoics distinguished repetition and continuance (χρόνοι ὡρισμένοι) from the simple act (ἀόριστοι). Propositions were divided into simple and compound (copulative, disjunctive, hypothetical), the proposition (ἀξίωμα) being defined as "a complete sentence which is either true or false". Their doctrine of hypothetical and disjunctive conclusions, based on that of the Megarians, is the foundation of modern propositional logic.

There can be no knowledge independent of sensible perception. The effect made upon the organ of sense by the material object becomes a representation (φαντασία) when reason (τὸ ἡγεμονικόν) takes it into consciousness. The representation only becomes significant for knowledge and action when the Logos, after preliminary examination, acknowledges it in willing consent or composition (συγκατάθεσις). The consent is only justified when the representation reflects the object in a way which would be impossible without the real existence of the object. This "cataleptic notion", which according to Zeno enables an object to be "grasped", which necessarily "comprises" our assent according to Chrysippus, is the criterion of truth (Chrysippus).

The soul at birth is like a *tabula rasa,* and receives its contents through perceptions. The multiplicity of similar representations stored up in the memory gives rise to the empirical general notion. With the help of analogy, composition and negation, non-empirical concepts can be formed from the empirical ones. The formation of concepts proceeds either by methodical reflection or spontaneously. The natural impulse gives rise to the "innate ideas" (προλήψεις or κοιναὶ ἔννοιαι) which are found in all men (imperfectly, even before the full development of reason) and which are the presupposition of all other knowledge.

b) *Physics.* Strictly speaking, only the corporeal can be said to exist. It is divided into the passive (πάσχον) or matter (ὕλη) and the active (ποιοῦν), the latter being thought of as artistically plastic fire (πῦρ τεχνικόν), as penetrating breath (πνεῦμα) or as tension (τόνος). Like the microcosm of man, the macrocosm, represented as a finite sphere, is a living being endowed with reason. Its substance is eternal. Its present order will be maintained only till the return to the primordial state of fire in the conflagration (ἐκπύρωσις), after which the same cosmic process begins again. Since the pneuma pervades the whole world in various states of purity and force, there are degrees in the structure of being. The formation and development of particular things are caused by the *rationes seminales* (λόγοι σπερματικοί) which come from the cosmic mind. Lower beings exist for the sake of the higher, which need the lower to exist. The human soul, which according to many Stoics is perishable, comes into being by generation. It is divided into the dominant reason (τὸ ἡγεμονικόν), the five senses, the faculty of speech and procreative ability.

Terror and admiration at natural phenomena and the order of nature bring about in men the spontaneous, innate pre-notion of the divinity (πρόληψις). The philosophical proofs of the existence of God (from the structured degrees and the finality of all beings) are merely to show that the notion is justified. The reconciliation of the philosophical notion of God as the Logos, Fire, Spirit, which permeates the world, with that of popular religion is performed by the allegorical interpretation of the myths. Later a distinction was made between the theology of the poets, the philosophers and the State. The providence of God, which is deduced from the purposefulness of the world, guides all things to what is best for man. All events, including the mental life of man, are determined by the chain of causality (εἱμαρμένη, destiny). This makes scientific divination possible. The problem of how this determinism can be reconciled with the self-determination of man, which was taught very emphatically in Stoicism, was grappled with, though not satisfactorily answered.

c) *Ethics.* Every living being has a perception of itself along with its external perceptions. This means that it finds itself appropriate to itself (οἰκείωσις) and strives to develop its own proper being. For man, this is the Logos. The development of the Logos is man's true advantage (ἀγαθόν), which is identical with the morally good (καλόν) and happiness (εὐδαιμονία). Happiness is independent of all that is morally indifferent (ἀδιάφορον). But within the range of the indifferent there is a difference between what is fitting for our nature (προηγμένα) and

what is contrary to it (ἀποπροηγμένα). The goal of human life is harmony with the Logos which is man's characteristic faculty and the universal law of nature from which all positive laws derive. (Zeno's formula, "to live harmoniously", ὁμολογουμένως ζῆν, was given an explanatory addition by Cleanthes, "to live in harmony with nature", and by Chrysippus, "to live following nature".) The natural affinity (οἰκείωσις) goes beyond the individual ego to take in all men because they are akin to one another through their rational nature. The Stoic is a cosmopolitan, a citizen of the whole world to whom none is a stranger. All men have the same rights by virtue of the Logos which is their nature.

Knowledge of good and evil, φρόνησις, is an essential element of all virtues. The virtues are indissolubly connected with one another, and like all faults, of equal importance. Each of them is indivisible. It is either possessed in its entirety or not at all. Between the morally perfect acts which are done for the sake of the moral good (κατορθώματα) and wrong actions (ἁμαρτήματα) come the mediocre actions (καθήκοντα) which are in keeping with man's nature but are not performed for the sake of the moral goal.

Passion (πάθος) is a faulty judgment (Chrysippus) or an urge going beyond due measure by reason of a faulty judgment (Zeno). Since it is an illness of the Logos, it must be entirely quenched (in impassibility, ἀπάθεια). (The Middle Stoa went back to the Aristotelian doctrine of the right mean in the passions.) The best defence against passion is to recognize that there is nothing good or bad apart from the moral order, and to be prepared for anything that may happen. Men are divided into three classes, the sages, the fools or the worthless and the advancing (προσκοποῦντες). While the fool is torn apart inwardly, the wise man is in harmony with himself and the cosmic law. If he can no longer bear his external life or can fulfil his moral task only by surrender of his life, he will depart this life voluntarily after having weighed all the factors.

3. *History.* a) *The Early Stoa.* Zeno of Citium (*c.* 334–263 B.C.), a pupil of Crates the Cynic, began his teaching about 300 B.C. at Athens, in the "many-coloured hall" (στοὰ ποικίλη) decorated with the paintings of Polygnotus. He was followed as head of the school by Cleanthes of Assos (*c.* 331–232), whose Hymn to Zeus is the loveliest testimony to the "cosmic" piety of the early

181

Stoa. The system of the older Stoa was completed by Chrysippus from Soli in Cilicia (*c*. 281–208), who was famous for his skill at dialectics and his literary productivity.

b) *The Middle Stoa*. The founder was Panaetius of Rhodes (*c*. 180–110 B.C.), who went back to Plato and Aristotle and thus modified the ethical rigorism of the Stoa. Panaetius was the inspiration of the philosophical circle around Scipio Aemilianus which was so important for the intellectual development of Rome. His work *On Correct Behaviour* (Περὶ τοῦ καθήκοντος) was used by Cicero in his *De Officiis* and was thus an essential element in the development of Roman ethics and the ideal of humaneness. His pupil Posidonius of Apamea (*c*. 135–51) was a philosopher, a student of nature, a geographer and a historian. He saw the cosmos as an organism held together by "sympathy", in which all things react on each other in a vital relationship.

c) *The Later Stoa*. L. Annaeus Cornutus (1st century A.D.) has left us a *Compendium of Greek Theology* which employs the allegorical method of the ancient Stoa in interpreting the myths. In Musonius Rufus (*c*. A.D. 30–108) and his pupil Epictetus (*c*. 50–120), interest in systematic speculation gives way to ethical directives. L. Annaeus Seneca (4 B.C. – A.D. 65) was also preoccupied with rules for good living, but took an interest in natural philosophy. The *Meditations* of the Emperor Marcus Aurelius (121–180) were the high-point and the end-product of the later Stoa. Stoicism ceased to exist as a system soon afterwards. Some of its thought was taken over by middle Platonism and neo-Platonism.

See also *Wisdom, Logic, Dialectics, Providence, Indifference, Neo-Platonism*.

BIBLIOGRAPHY. EDITIONS: H. von Arnim, *Stoicorum Veterum Fragmenta*, 4 vols. (1905–24; reprint, 1964); M. van Straaten, *Panaitii Rhodii Fragmenta* (1952; 3rd ed., 1962). GENERAL WORKS: R. D. Hicks, *Stoic and Epicurean* (1910); E. Bréhier, *Chrysippe et l'ancien Stoa* (1910, 1951); id., *The History of Philosophy*, II: *The Hellenistic and Roman Age* (1965); E. Bevan, *Stoics and Sceptics* (1913); K. Reinhardt, *Poseidonius* (1921); id., *Kosmos und Sympathie* (1926); id., "Poseidonius", in Pauly-Wissowa, *Realenzyklopaedie*, XXII/1 (1953), cols. 558–826; E. Zeller, *Die Philosophie der Griechen*, ed. by F. Lortzing and others (1920–23), III/1; J. Moreau, *L'âme du monde de Platon aux Stoiciens* (1936; reprint, 1965); M. Pohlenz, *Die Stoa*, 2 vols. (1948–49); B. Mates, *Stoic Logic* (1953, 1961); K. Barwick, *Probleme der stoischen Sprachlehre und Rhetorik* (1957); S. Sambursky, *Physics of the Stoics* (1959); M. Laffranque, *Poseidonios d'Apamée* (1964); L. Edelstein, *The Meaning of Stoicism* (1967).

Friedo Ricken

STRUCTURALISM

Structuralism, both as a method of analysis and as an ideology into which the method constantly degenerates, has spread from France to become a typical phenomenon of our times, and as such is of interest to the Christian preacher.

1. *History of the method*. The history of European thought may be said to have gone from substance to structure, from a notion of being characterized by intrinsic determination and independent existence to another perspective which can be defined only with difficulty. Possibly its first expression was given it in the "structural psychology" of W. Dilthey. As formulated by his disciple E. Spranger it ran: "A reality has a structure or systematic build, when it is a whole in which each part and the function of each part contributes significantly to the whole, in such a way that the build and function of each part is determined in turn by the whole and hence is only intelligible in the light of the whole" (E. Spranger, *Psychologie des Jugendalters* [19th ed., 1949]).

This rather philosophical analysis of psychological structure, studied in the works of the Swiss psychologist Jean Piaget and his disciple Lucien Goldmann, gave French structuralism the categories of totality and function. Still more influential were the Marxist categories of the all-important infrastructure with its dependent suprastructure, and the Freudian subconscious which secretly determines all our actions. But of decisive importance for C. Lévi-Strauss, the father of French structuralism and for his followers, whom alone we consider here, was structural linguistics as founded by the Swiss scholar, F. de Saussure and developed by linguistic circles at Prague (N. S. Troubetzkoy, R. Jakobson) and Copenhagen. Earlier linguistics had been mainly concerned with the genetic approach, tracing the origins of the various languages and the changes of their elements in successive stages. The new approach inclined to take a "synchronistic" view, describing a linguistic system and investigating its determinant structure while prescinding from historical change. Marxist and Freudian categories could be verified in structural linguistics, inasmuch as language was regarded as the great social phenomenon. And the meaning attributed to it on the conscious level of vocabulary, grammar and proposition could be ultimately traced to an unconscious process of composition. This process was supposed to follow certain rules, which could be investigated by modern linguistics and reduced to a few basic rules of universal validity.

2. *Structural analysis.* Hence this structural analysis derived from linguistics is primarily concerned only with the systems of signification which man has created. Unlike psychology and the natural sciences, it does not ask how far a given system of signs corresponds to the "objective reality" which it indicates *(le structurel).* The aim of structural analysis is to discover within any given closed system of signification the rules according to which it is composed and functions. This "structuralist process" can be described with some degree of simplification in two stages. The first stage, that of dismemberment or *découpage,* discloses the "elementary structures", the smallest units, from which a given system is built up. Following a basic presupposition taken over from linguistics, these units are not to be defined by their "substance" but by distinction and limit, their manifold relationship to the other units. Even the elementary particle of a system must be regarded as a "structure", in which the smallest change modifies the whole. The second stage, that of *agencement,* arrangement, is concerned with finding in these elementary structures the rules of association and composition by which the units become a system. More precisely, it seeks the typical *form* of a given system.

3. *Applications.* De Saussure himself indicated some fields other than language to which structural analysis could be applied. "Language is a system of signs which express ideas. Hence it is like writing, the deaf and dumb alphabet, symbolic rites, etiquette, military signals and so on, except that it is the most important of such systems. One may therefore envisage a science which studies the life of signs in the framework of social life . . . We shall call it semiology (from the Greek *sēmeîon,* 'sign'). It will teach us what signs consist of, the laws by which they are governed" (*Cours de linguistique générale,* In-

troduction, ch. III, para. 3 [3rd ed., 1968], p. 33). Structural analysis can in fact be applied to any system of signs. The stroke of genius which made Lévi-Strauss famous was that he applied the principles of structural linguistics to the seeming confusion of the various systems of marriage laws among certain primitives and reduced them to the principle of the swap. But literary systems of signification were more manageable, and Lévi-Strauss then took up the myths, while students of literature applied structural analysis to poetry. Art, fashion, the cinema, advertizing and the press can also be analysed in this way, and also philosophical and theological systems, the Bible presenting itself as especially suitable.

4. *Ideology.* Structuralism becomes an ideology when the methodical principles are made universal and absolute, and when methodical abstractions become negations on an ontological level. The discovery of the role of the unconscious in the composition of systems of signs leads to the massive negation of all deliberate activity on the part of the human subject and the affirmation that freedom and responsibility are an illusion. To this Sartre replies: "The initial disintegration, which makes man disappear behind the structures, evokes itself a negation: man appears behind the denial. A subject or subjectivity exists, at the very moment when the effort is made to go beyond the given situation, by preserving it. This transition is the real problem. One must try to understand how the subject or subjectivity, on a transient basis, constitutes itself by a continual process of interiorization and renewed exteriorization."

Prior to all attributions of meaning, and outside the scope of man's disposing, there is a universal code which underlies all systems of signs. Hence the question of the special meaning of an arrangement appears as secondary or even insignificant, as a sort of jig-saw puzzle within the framework of an unchangeable universality of meaningfulness or futility. As Paul Ricœur said to Lévi-Strauss: "You deny that there is any 'message', not in the sense of cybernetics, but in the sense of kerygma. You despair of meaning, but you save yourself by affirming that even if people have nothing to say, they at least say it so well that their language can be subjected to structural analysis. You save meaning, but it is the meaning of the non-sense, the admirable syntactical arrangement of a discourse which says nothing. You combine agnosticism with a hyper-intelligent view of syntax. This makes you fascinating and disturbing at the same time" (*Esprit*, November 1963, p. 652). The constancy of structures, which change merely in externals, and their one-dimensional character which means that there are no differences of level, leads to the emptying of the categories of "history", "development", "progress", "revolution", "infra-human", "human" and so on. Man himself appears finally as merely a "machine, more perfect perhaps than others, which is working at the dissolution of an original order and hence reducing organized matter to a state of inertia which will one day be final" (Lévi-Strauss).

We may conclude with another remark of Sartre, who finds that "man is perpetually 'beyond' the structures by which he is determined, because what makes him what he is, is something else again. So I fail to understand how one can stop at structures. To me, this is a logical scandal."

See also *Language, Meaning, Order* I.

BIBLIOGRAPHY. C. Lévi-Strauss, *Structural Anthropology* (1963); id., *Totemism* (1963); id., *Tristes Topiques* (1964), E. T.: *World on the Wane;* id., *The Savage Mind* (1966); id., *The Elementary Structures of Kinship* (1967); id., *The Scope of Anthropology* (1967); N. Chomsky, *Current Issues in Linguistic Theory* (1964); R. Barthes, *Système de la Mode* (1967); "La pensée sauvage et le structuralisme", essays by J. Cuisenier, N. Ruwet, M. Gaboriau and P. Ricœur, and discussion with C. Lévi-Strauss, *Esprit* (November 1963), pp. 545–652; L. Althusser, *Lire le Capital* (1966); M. Foucault, *Les mots et les choses* (1966); J. Lacan, *Écrits* (1966); A. Greimas, *Sémantique structurale* (1966); E. Leach ed., *The Structural Study of Myth and Totemism* (1966); J. Piaget, *Le Structuralisme* (1968); G. Schiwy, *Der französische Strukturalismus* (1969); id., *Strukturalismus und Christentum* (1969).

Günther Schiwy

SUAREZIANISM

By Suarezianism is meant the trend of thought in Catholic Scholasticism which derives from the Spanish Jesuit Francisco Suarez (1548–1617). Suarez taught philosophy (1571–74) and theology (till his death in 1617) in Segovia, Valladolid, Rome, Alcalá, Salamanca, and Coimbra (from 1597). His works (26 volumes in the Vivès edition) had a considerable influence even on his con-

temporaries. Jesuit professors were quick to adopt him as their master, though he was never officially appointed or recommended as such. His philosophical writing (*Disputationes Metaphysicae* [1597]) became a classical text in European universities in the 17th and 18th centuries, to some extent even in Protestant faculties.

The Suarezian school (insofar as one may speak of a school) tried to take a middle of the road position among the Thomist, Scotist and Nominalist schools then flourishing. Their efforts were furthered by Suarez's strongly analytical mind and by the historical situation. Suarez had tried to give dispassionate consideration to every opinion, even the most extravagant, on every point. This earned him the reproach of eclecticism, but there can be no doubt of the independence of his judgment. Certainly he is less systematic than the other great scholastics; what mainly holds his work together is his intellectual honesty and the sharp precision of his distinctions. On the whole, he is nearest to St. Thomas, in the catholicity of his outlook and in his basic doctrines, where, however, he allows himself a wide range of freedom. He is also notably influenced by Scotism and Nominalism. He was therefore the object of fierce polemics during the neo-Thomist revival. He did not lack defenders, but the controversy did not shed much real light on the positions. Today a calmer estimate of him is beginning to emerge, but much basic research is still wanting.

1. *Metaphysics.* Suarezian philosophy is still far from the radicalism of Descartes. It is still the philosophy of a theologian who calmly presupposes the theist and spiritualist medieval view of the universe and seeks to convey it by a rational and orderly method which will also help to explain Christian dogma. It was a considerable advance for Suarez to have set forth his material as a treatise on ontology (though he did not use that term, and included what must be called natural theology), independent alike of the theological tractates and the commentaries on Aristotle.

One of his traits is certainly realism; but not in the sense that he ascribes to the structures of thought, formally as such, an importance of their own, but rather in his consistent conviction of the absolute primacy of the particular. Hence his characteristic concreteness, and his acceptance of "the intellectual intuition of individual sensible things" as the primal knowledge (presupposing the traditional, i.e., realistic value of sense perception). Suarezians see in this a rightful liberation from the excessive "Platonism" still at work in the great medieval syntheses. Their adversaries regard it as the typical impact of Nominalism, undermining the validity of abstract knowledge. It is only fair to admit that Suarez speaks of conceptual knowledge in a more balanced way than Occam. But subsequent history has shown that the more critical spirit in which they approach the earlier systems represents a valuable gain. At the same time one must agree that some perceptions of great value in the Platonic inheritance are lost in Suarez: for example, the "fullness" (illimitation) of the notion of being. This makes access to the problems of infinity more difficult. Today we realize that the cause was probably a narrowing of logic, which (as in Scotus) gave the concept priority over the judgment. Generally speaking, the concreteness of Suarez failed to exploit the metaphysical values inherent in the structures of human knowledge (and their dynamism). So in face of the radical critique at the base of modern philosophy, Suarezianism is in a favourable position, on account of its critical solutions (such as *distinctio rationis cum fundamento in re*). But it lends itself less readily than Thomism to the application of the transcendental method, and hence to a new basis for metaphysics.

The systematic development of Suarezian metaphysics is guided by the postulate of the conceptual unity of all in the supreme concept of being. But Suarez preserves an essential descending order in his ultimate divisions (God — creature; substance — accident): an order realized in the creature's dependence on God and the accident's inherence in substance. In these divisions, therefore, there is an "analogy of intrinsic attribution", defined precisely by the existence of this descending order. If the emphasis on unity evokes Scotus, the "intrinsic attribution" must now be recognized as an essential element in St. Thomas's "analogy of being". Suarez understood it better than Cajetan. In the problem of substance and accident, Suarez's solution follows St. Thomas's. In the question of man's conceptual knowledge of God, Suarez, in contrast to St. Thomas, adheres to the order of reality *in itself* (first God, then creatures) rather than to the order in which we *predicate* (for by nature,

according to St. Thomas, our concept corresponds to created reality, and must be purified before it can be applied to God). So Suarez rejects the analogy of proportionality. The great merit of Suarez is his insistence on the metaphysical importance of the dependence of everything on God as its cause. Thus his "intrinsic attribution" answers to a total, systematic view of reality in which "radical dependence" occupies the place usually taken by the "real composition of being and essence" in the Thomistic system. Without entering into the problem of this distinction (which Suarez, on the grounds aforesaid, thinks is not a "real" distinction), we may say that it seems preferable to regard "utter dependence" as the ultimate metaphysical characteristic of creatures. One might even show that it comes closer to the essence of St. Thomas's complex notion of "participation", as now understood in historical research.

Rather than as the Infinite, the Suarezian system envisages God as *ens per se necessarium*, which corresponds to St. Thomas's *ipsum esse subsistens (esse est actualitas . . . et propter hoc perfectio)*, though not so profoundly analysed. The *ens necessarium*, the existence of which, Suarez holds, must be accepted once we accept the existence of anything (whether or not there be an infinite series of contingent causes), is unique (one by virtue of its essence because existing by virtue of its essence). It is therefore the "supremely perfect" and "infinite", since it is or is the source of every perfection.

Suarez can be considered the metaphysician of Molinism, because of his theory of "concausation" without any intrinsic union of the causes, and his explanation of the principle *agens qua tale non mutatur* which cuts the ground from underneath the postulate of a *praemotio* (see *Grace and Freedom*).

2. *Dogmatic theology.* Here Suarez's most remarkable contribution is to methodology. He helped to develop the positive method and to work out the "theological notes" attached to propositions. But apart from these elements, which had a historic impact and of which all schools of theology made use, the following traits, which can hardly be formed into a system, are the most characteristic elements in his theology.

a) The supernatural character of the acts of the theological virtues affects their formal object, and is therefore psychologically relevant — a position of St. Thomas which is held very widely today and which Suarez upheld when it was generally opposed. In this context Suarez's *analysis fidei* is subtle and profound; if its logical formulation leaves something to be desired, it demonstrates penetratingly that the *primum creditum* is always God as he reveals himself.

b) Like all Molinists, Suarez stresses the active part played by a created person's human powers in the acts of supernatural life; thus he holds that the *potentia obedientalis* is also something active, though without prejudice to our complete dependence on God's initiative and on the operation of his grace.

c) When discussing the dogma of the Trinity, Suarez does not hesitate to speak of an absolute subsistence and of the being and real perfection of the relative subsistences — once more his concrete realism. Suarez does not see any incompatibility here with the oneness of God or the infinitude of each divine person, because in his own special perfection each person equivalently possesses that of the others.

d) On the incarnation, he thinks that the humanity of Christ lacks the "mode" of subsistence which (as *realiter* distinct from the nature) would have made him a person in his humanity as such. As to the classic question about the purpose of the incarnation, he takes a position midway between St. Thomas and Scotus.

e) Modern historians, including those who have no great affection for Suarez, all agree that he made an essential contribution to the theory of rights and law (especially in his *De Legibus*). His two main principles, which were undoubtedly highly original and had a very great influence, were (i) that the community is the primary repository of authority in the genesis of all society, and (ii) that the *ius gentium* or "natural (international) law" is prior to all positive political measures. Here he followed some hints of Vitoria. Suarez provides some principles in these matters which could be highly instructive in the present effort to construct a supranational society.

See also *Thomism, Scotism, Nominalism.*

BIBLIOGRAPHY. K. Werner, *Franz Suarez und die Scholastik des letzten Jahrhunderts,* 2 vols. (1861; reprint 1962); R. de Scoraille, 2 vols. (1912–13) (biography); E.-M. Rivière, *La bibliographie des ouvrages imprimés et inédits de F. Suárez* (1918); L. Mahieu, *Suárez, sa philosophie et les rapports qu'elle a avec sa théologie* (1921); H. Rommen, *Die Staatslehre des F. Suárez* (1927); G. Smyth, *Jesuit Thinkers of the Renaissance* (1939); J. Fichter, *Men of Spain: Francis Suarez* (1940); F. Suarez, *A Selection from Three Works* (1944) (*Laws, Apologia for the Catholic Faith, Theological Virtues*); J. Hellin, *La analogía del ser y el conocimiento de Dios en Suárez* (1947); id., "Lineas fundamentales del sistema de Suárez", *Pensiamento* 4 (1948), pp. 123–67; P. Múgica, *Bibliografía Suareciana* (1948); J. de Vries, "Die Erkenntnislehre des F. Suárez und des Nominalismus", *Scholastik* 24 (1949), pp. 321–44; J. Iturrioz, *Estudios sobre la metafísica de F. Suárez* (1949); L. Pereña Vicente, *Teoría de la guerra en F. Suárez,* 2 vols. (1954); N. Öry, "Suárez in Rom", *ZKT* 81 (1959), pp. 133–62; J. Gómez Caffarena, "Sentido de la composición del ser y essencia en Suárez", *Pensiamento* 15 (1959), pp. 135–54; P. Monnot and others in *DTC,* XIV/2, cols. 2638–728 (with bibliography); S. Castellote Cubells, *Die Anthropologie des Suárez* (1962); B. Hamilton, *Political Thought in Sixteenth Century Spain* (1963) (Vitoria, de Soto, Suarez, Molina); E. Gemmeke, *Die Metaphysik des sittlichen Guten bei F. Suárez* (1965).

José Gómez Caffarena

SUBJECTIVISM

Subjectivism is the tendency in philosophy not to attribute the validity of the judgment to how things display themselves as they are, but to certain conditions in the subject who judges, though these conditions do not serve to exhibit the thing. Subjectivism can be at work in various realms: epistemology, ethics, aesthetics and religion. Formally speaking, the subjective conditions affecting the judgment may be such that they are accessible to empirical research. Or again, they may be open only to transcendental reflection. Thus one may distinguish between an empirical and a transcendental subjectivism.

1. Empirical subjectivism is based on the fact that thinking and judgment are often dependent on one's personal qualities — a certain psychosomatic constitution, which has been further stamped by education and a series of free decisions — and by one's membership of a given race and civilization. This is an observation which as it stands is neutral and justified. It becomes subjectivism only when it goes on to affirm that these subjective influences cannot on principle be overcome, or at least that we can never be certain of overcoming them. This gives rise to the two basic forms of empirical subjectivism, relativism and scepticism. Relativism is content with the mere sub-

jectiveness of the judgment: "It is so for me." Scepticism is always doubtful of its own objectiveness: "But is it really so in itself?"

The two attitudes can only be stated insofar as their proponents envisage the real truth — either to reject or doubt it. Hence the affirmation presupposes its contrary and hence is self-stultifying. But this consideration of principles is not enough to guarantee the objectiveness of any given judgment in particular. Nonetheless, it gives a reasonable hope that truth may be attained by vigorous investigation. And it also teaches us to be reserved about our own judgments, especially when there are positive reasons for suspicion. These two truths should make us ready for dialogue. But the purpose of the dialogue must always be to have sight in common of the thing itself, though perhaps in an irreducible plurality of perspectives.

The basic principle is that the validity of the judgment can only be based on the relation to the reality in question, and that this relation remains ultimately intact, in spite of being conditioned in so many ways, since man, as along as he is a man, abides in the truth. And this principle is the norm to be applied to all types of subjectivism. The truth of a reality, the value of an action, the beauty of a work of art, the holiness of a religious "object" are determinations which are within the objects in question and not merely projected upon them because of one's tastes or the like. Hence such determinations are also "intersubjective". They must be acknowledged by all the persons involved and unlike the pure interiority of the indefinable free act or the passing feeling, must be capable of enunciation to some extent in objective propositions (scientific theory, ethics, aesthetic canon, religious dogma).

2. The conditions on which the validity of knowledge is dependent, according to transcendental subjectivism, cannot be demonstrated in empirical research. They represent the possible answers to what Kant called the "transcendental" question (*Critique of Pure Reason,* B, 25): what is it in the subject which makes the objectiveness of the object possible? Thus, while in empirical subjectivism the subject was envisaged as the source of the lack of objectivity, in transcendental subjectivism the subject appears as the source of all objectivity and hence truth.

It is in fact true that every object, as such, is the result of an objectivation. It is only through the models and considerations sketched by the interested subject that the object of a given science can take shape. But this objectivation must be subordinated to the claims of the matter to be presented, which is in fact possible — as already appears implicitly in the considerations upon empirical subjectivism. Knowledge is true, not insofar as the object is constituted by the subject, but insofar as in the object the reality itself becomes apparent. A subjectivity not fully at the disposal of objectivity, i.e., of the manifestation of the thing itself, would be subjectivist in the wrong sense.

3. It is at once the strength and limitation of our subjectivity that we can create a free space for things where they can be themselves and show themselves. But the supreme achievement of this liberating activity of the subject is not the objectivation of beings, but the love which actively brings the other to be within the space of one's own life. It is here in fact that the subject learns that his subjectivity is not pure mastery of self but has to be liberated for such self-determination in each case. For it is only through the experience of being itself accepted that it becomes capable of accepting the other in its otherness. But since such recognition is a reciprocal matter and hence cannot produce itself, the power of subjectivity as such is seen to be a gift. Human thinking which refused to recognize its character of gift would be subjectivist in a third, metaphysical sense.

See also *Kantianism, Transcendental Philosophy, Relativism, Scepticism.*

BIBLIOGRAPHY. G. Hegel, "Glauben und Wissen, oder die Reflexionsphilosophie der Subjektivität", *Works,* Jubilee ed., ed. by H. Glockner, I (1951), pp. 277–433; K. Jaspers, *Von der Wahrheit* (1947); id., *Perennial Scope of Philosophy* (1949); id., *Truth and Symbol* (part of *Von der Wahrheit*) (1959); F. Battaglia, *Il problema morale nell'esistentialismo* (2nd ed., 1949); M. Heidegger, *Holzwege* (1950); id., *Nietzsche,* 2 vols. (4th ed., 1961); E. Cassirer, *Problem of Knowledge: Philosophy, Science and History since Hegel* (1950); F. Gogarten, *The Reality of Faith* (1959).

Gerd Haeffner

SUBSTANCE

1. *Historical survey.* According to Aristotle, substance (οὐσία, ὑποκείμενον) is the chief object of metaphysics (*Metaphysics,* VII, 1;

1028b, 2ff. and 6f.), because it is what primarily exists and is the first of the categories, to which all the others are intrinsically related. More precisely it signifies that which stands by itself, the ultimate bearer of all that belongs to a being (cf. *Categories*, I, 5; 2a, 11f.; 2b, 15ff.). This conception was further developed by the scholastics. It was opposed by the empiricism which was foreshadowed by Nicholas of Autrecourt and fully elaborated by David Hume. According to Hume, the idea of substance arises solely because constantly associated phenomena are designated by a common name. Positivism and neo-positivism represent a similar view. Encouraged by the ambiguous definition given by Descartes, extreme rationalism in Spinoza arrived at a monism of substance; there can only be the one, uncreated, infinite or divine substance, and creatures are merely its modes. Spinoza was outdone by G. Leibniz, who reduced everything to the monad as the simple subsistent; the one infinite monad renders possible many finite monads each of which mirrors the whole universe, but only from its own angle. Kant endeavoured to arrive at a synthesis of his predecessors, counting substance among the *a priori* categories of the understanding; these are valid only of the phenomenal object; what defines substance is subsistence; its sensible schema, however, is real duration in time. This is over-emphasized: "In fact the proposition that substance persists is tautological" (*Critique of Pure Reason,* A 184). N. Hartmann accordingly takes substance to be the persistent substratum which he considers is only to be found in the inorganic realm. It is known *a posteriori*. It applies to the thing-in-itself. Living beings, on the other hand, are not substances, for they neither endure nor are they a substratum, but are based on the inorganic. H. Bergson viewed everything in terms of *élan vital* and *durée;* instead of persisting solidly, things occur in perpetual flow; rational thought divides this into particular states which, it is true, must be unified by a persistent substratum. With M. Scheler, who restricts substance to the realm of things and excludes it from persons, the philosophers of existence and the existentialists raise man as personal existence or activity above persistent substance. According to Heidegger's fundamental ontology, "ex-sistence" is the substance of man (cf. *Sein und Zeit,* p. 212), i.e., his οὐσία is the destined communication of being, thanks to which he "stands out" or is "present there".

As atomic physics shows, particles and waves, mass and energy merge into one another; corporeal substance appears to evaporate more and more into processes, becomes rather than is.

2. *Doctrinal discussion.* Etymologically, substance is what stands beneath, that is, what forms the basis of appearances, unfolds itself in them, discloses and simultaneously conceals itself. Substance means in fact "that which stands of itself", the independent subject, the real being or *that which* is. It is contrasted with accident or appearance, which essentially inheres in substance as its support and only occurs as a further attribute of the real being or as the channel through which something is or appears. The distinction between substance and phenomenon derives from the fact that the same being explicates itself in many and ever-changing appearances. Here substance is a finite category, which stands in need of completion by the accidents; it is contrasted with the infinite substance beyond the categories, which alone is the whole. According to Aristotle, the "first substance", the particular (τόδε τι: *Metaphysics* V, 8; 1017 b, 25), is substance in the full sense; derived from this is "second substance", or substance as a universal. Platonism, on the other hand, regards the particular as second, and the universal as first substance; the latter, however, is not a concept formed from the particular, but the form or exemplar antecedent to it. By its very notion, substance only excludes dependence on a substratum, not dependence on a cause; there can therefore be substances which are caused, i.e., created substances. Strictly speaking, substance denotes only the substantial whole; yet essential parts which go to constitute this whole (e.g., body and soul) are also spoken of as substantial. Although substance usually stands out as what is relatively persistent in contradistinction to its changing appearances, anything that exists in itself, even if it only lasts for an instant, is truly a substance.

The principle of substance states that if anything whatsoever exists, there is substance; for the inherent presupposes that which exists in itself, and appearance that which appears. Finite substance is evidenced in human responsibility; if a man were merely an attribute of something else, the latter would be acting through him; it would bear the responsibility, not the man himself. Man's substance does not exclude the process of historical change, but is actually its ground; this comprises the claim of being which endows substance with its specifically human character. Since this claim is absent from the infra-human, substantial independence diminishes stage by stage and the individual is more immersed in nature as a whole. Consequently substance is least clearly marked in the inorganic realm; it can appear as mass or energy, and can be thought of as particle or wave. It is scarcely to be distinguished from events or processes, and it is also difficult to determine whether one or more substances are involved. Nevertheless the existence of inorganic substance is not to be gainsaid. On the notion of substance in the doctrine of the Eucharist, see *Transubstantiation*.

See also *Empiricism, Positivism, Existence* II, *Being* I, *Body, Soul*.

BIBLIOGRAPHY. Aristotle, *Metaphysics,* 2 vols., ed. by W. Ross (2nd ed., 1924); B. Bauch, *Das Substanzproblem in der griechischen Philosophie* (1910); R. Jolivet, *La notion de substance* (1929); J. Hessen, *Das Substanzproblem in der Philosophie der Neuzeit* (1932); D. Parker, *Experience and Substance* (1941); A. Marc, *Dialectique de l'affirmation* (1952), pp. 541–53; N. Hartmann, *New Ways in Ontology* (1953); R. McCall, *The Reality of Substance* (1956); W. Büchel, "Quantenphysik und naturphilosophischer Substanzbegriff", *Scholastik* 33 (1958), pp. 161–85; J. B. Lotz, *Ontologia* (1963), nos. 536–97; P. Heelan, *Quantum Mechanics and Objectivity* (1966).

Johannes Baptist Lotz

SUNDAY

1. *Theological significance.* Sunday is a gift of God's grace. Even the natural elements contained in Sunday were planted in man's nature by the Creator. The seven-day rhythm emerged through the combination of man's spiritual urge towards order and his biological and psychological needs. Similarly, the duty to worship God is part of being a creature. According to Jewish belief, the holiness of the Sabbath stemmed from the Sabbath in Paradise, when man could renew his strength and lay before God in adoration and jubilation the crown of his dominion over all creation which was his because he had been created in the image and likeness of God (Gen 1:26, 28) (Guardini).

Sunday already appears as a gift of God in its prefiguration in salvation-history, the *Jewish Sabbath* (Col 2:16; Heb 8:5). The Sabbath was entirely due to the initiative of Yahweh (cf. Exod 16:4–5). By his command to cease activity (the original meaning of the word) God releases man from the yoke which work has become as a result of original sin (Gen 3:19) and undertakes himself to provide for man (Exod 20:8–11). The Sabbath is a commemoration of the deliverance out of Egypt (Deut 5:15) and is thus also a sign of Passover and covenant (Exod 31:12–17; Is 56:1–6; Ezek 20:12). It is therefore a sacred reality, "sanctified" by God himself (Gen 2:2–3), modelled on the creator's own rest and a sign that the Lord sanctifies his people (Exod 20:12). In its eschatological aspect which is particularly clear in the writings of the prophets (Is 66:22–23; Ezek 43–45) the Sabbath foreshadows its ultimate fulfilment in Sunday. During the exile Israel used the Sabbath (and circumcision) to mark itself off from its pagan surroundings.

The origin of *Sunday* has practically nothing to do with the spread of the planetary week in the West at the beginning of the 2nd century. Sunday also began independently of the Sabbath: in the beginning it existed side by side with the Sabbath (Acts 2:42–47 etc.) which continued to be observed by the early Church in Jerusalem (Acts 2:46 etc.) and by Judaizing Christians (Gal 4); for a long time there was no rest from work on Sunday. The old Sabbath ended with the Passover of the Lord, but as a type (like the temple etc.) it had its fulfilment in Christ (2 Cor 1:20). Thus Sunday really is an "original creation", as Congar calls it, a gift of God's grace through his Christ who rose "on the day after the Sabbath, the first day of the week" (Mk 16:2), who always appeared to his disciples on a Sunday (Jn 20:11–18; Lk 24:15, 34; Jn 20:26; 21:3–17; Acts 1:10) and sent them the Spirit on a Sunday (Acts 2:1 ff.). These accounts have important theological and pastoral aspects: the Lord always appears on a Sunday and always when the disciples are assembled (Lk 24:33; Jn 20:19, 26; Acts 2:1); he eats the messianic meal with them (Mk 16:14; Lk 24:30, 41–43; Jn 21:9–13) and gives them his messianic authority (Mt 28:18–21; Jn 20:21, 22–23).

Sunday is thus the weekly Easter, the "celebration of the paschal mystery on the eighth day which is therefore rightly called the day of the Lord or the Lord's Day" (Vatican II, Constitution on the Sacred Liturgy, art. 106). The new people of God participate in the victory of Easter. They experience a true liberation from sin, death, and the devil. They are led towards the glorious freedom of the children of God (Rom 8:21) and so incorporated into the new covenant. Hence the close connection between Sunday and baptism and the even closer one between Sunday and the Eucharist. St. Augustine uses the word *sacramentum* for Sunday (*In Joannis Evangelium*, XX, 2; *PL*, XXXV, col. 1556). Sunday is a commemoration and, at the same time, "presence": the faithful come into contact with the works and the merits of the Lord and are filled with the grace of salvation (cf. Constitution on the Sacred Liturgy, art. 102, para. 2). "Thus the Lord's day is the original feast day" (*ibid.*, art. 106), in fact the only feast the early Church celebrated before one of these Sundays was especially chosen for the celebration of Easter, while other feasts were introduced later.

Sunday, like all sacred signs, is not merely a commemoration but a promise: it is the "eighth day" (cf. Jn 20:26; 1 Pet 3:20, 21), our introduction to the new order which began with the resurrection (cf. 2 Cor 5:17; Gal 6:15; 2 Pet 3:13; Acts 21:1, 5); it is the beginning of the cosmic fulfilment and eternal life. This eschatological aspect gives Sunday an air of waiting for the final fulfilment. At the same time it is also an "advance participation" (cf. Constitution on the Sacred Liturgy, art. 8) in eternal life, casting its light into our own time.

2. *Sunday observance*. The present threat to the sanctification of Sunday (see *Secularization, Industrialism, Leisure* I, II) poses the pastoral problem of how to reshape Sunday creatively, holding fast to tradition as properly understood, without clinging to outdated, changeable elements, but bringing out the essentials as clearly as possible. For this we must first of all abandon some false pastoral attitudes which are more harmful than the threats from without. The sanctification of Sunday has been presented far too one-sidedly as a duty, while it would be far more convincing to base it on the values discussed above. God first "sanctifies" Sunday (in the sense of Jn 17:19) and man's task is the corollary of this gift. Thus Sunday, once it is recognized as a help and as the basic feast-day, becomes a source of joy and real leisure (Constitution on the Sacred Liturgy, art. 106). Some fundamental changes of attitude will be necessary for this: "Other feasts should not

be given preference ... for the Lord's day is the basis and essence of the whole liturgical year" (*ibid.*).

Religious worship and rest from work which are of very different origin and value must not be presented as of equal importance. For a long time Sunday existed without rest from work. As Congar points out, if the dramatic times of the martyrs were to return, it would still be possible to continue the weekly celebration of the resurrection; it might be more difficult, but the real essence of Sunday would stand out far more clearly. It is of course desirable that worship and rest should continue together; we must respect the fact that man needs rest by nature and it is only logical that on the day of the risen Lord creatures and earthly activity should give way to God by a cessation of work. Freedom from work in this sense means freedom from sin (Jn 8:31). Material rest is prefiguration and presupposition for rest in God. However, God's rest is not inactivity, but a fullness of life and bliss and a highly active joy in his works. The ultimate reason for rest is the eschatological dimension of Sunday (cf. Jn 13:1). The sense of eternal fellowship in love experienced on Sunday promotes the works of mercy and the apostolate.

The paschal mystery must cease to be a peripheral matter and must once more be seen to be the living centre of all pastoral work and the very essence of Christianity (cf. Constitution on the Sacred Liturgy, arts. 5, 6, 102, 104, 106, 107). Any sanctification of Sunday which is too one-sidedly individualistic must be corrected by a healthy ecclesiology (Vatican II, Dogmatic Constitution on the Church). Sunday is not a matter for the individual, but for the community. On Sunday "the Christian faithful must meet together" (Constitution on the Sacred Liturgy, art. 106; cf. art. 10) because it is the day of God's people when the Church is there through word and Eucharist, in the assembly which is to be proclaimed as the epiphany of the Church. It is essential that Christians should assemble (Mt 18:19-20; Jn 11:52; Eph 1:9ff.) and the early Christians were noted for this (Pliny the Younger, *Letter to Trajan,* 10, 96); missing the assembly (cf. Heb 10:25) means reducing the Church (*Didascalia Apostolorum,* 13). From the methodological point of view it is not only useful but necessary to consider the Sabbath as a prefiguration of Sunday in the history of salvation.

BIBLIOGRAPHY. J. Hessey, *Sunday: Its Origin, History and Present Obligation* (1860); H. Dumaine, in F. Cabrol and H. Leclercq, eds., *Dictionnaire d'archéologie chrétienne et de liturgie*, IV, cols. 858–994; S. McCasland, "The Origin of the Lord's Day", *JBL* 49 (1930), pp. 65–82; C. Callewaert, *Sacris Erudiri* (1940); J. Nielen, *Das Zeichen des Herrn: Sabbat und Sonntag in biblischer und urchristlicher Bezeugung* (1940); "Dimanche et célébration chrétienne", *La Maison Dieu* 9; P. Duployé, M. Chevrot, H. Féret, J. Daniélou, Y. Congar, R. Guardini, M. Michaud, A.-G. Martimort, G. Boulard, G. Michonneau, A. Robeyns, and P. Parsch, *Le Jour du Seigneur* (1948); J. Hild, *Dimanche et vie pascale* (1949); A.-G. Martimort, "Structure de l'assemblée chrétienne", *La Maison Dieu* 20, pp. 153–75; J. Wagner and D. Zähringer, *Eucharistiefeier am Sonntag* (1951); J. Jungmann, *The Mass of the Roman Rite*, 2 vols. (1951) (see Index); O. Procksch "ἁγιάζω", *TWNT*, I, pp. 112–16; K. L. Schmidt, "ἐκκλησία", *ibid.*, III, pp. 501–36; E. Lohse "σάββατον", *ibid.*, VII, pp. 1–35; K. Rahner, "Der Tag des Herrn", *Statio Orbis* 2 (1961), pp. 195–7; T. Maertens, *C'est fête en l'honneur de Jahvé* (1961); H. Oster, *Le mystère pascal dans la pastorale* (1964); B. Botte and others, *Le Dimanche* (1965); O. Rousseau, "La revalorisation du dimanche dans l'Église catholique depuis cinquante ans", *Miscellanea liturgica in onore di S. E. G. Lercaro* (1966); W. Rordorf, *Sunday: The History of the Day of Rest and Worship in the Earliest Centuries of the Christian Church* (1968).

Henri Oster

SUPERNATURALISM

The collective term, supernaturalism, designates a number of theological trends of the late 18th and the first half of the 19th century, which strove to defend against Naturalism and Rationalism the supernatural character of revelation and its special importance as a source of knowledge which was not to be reduced to natural reason.

1. *Historical background.* Supernaturalism was part of the Church's reaction to the emancipation of the world (see *Secularization*), or rather, to the intellectual abandonment of the unity of the medieval order. It was one of the efforts to re-think and re-formulate, in the upheavals of the modern era, the position and justification of revelation and Church. The movement for emancipation had given rise to a Naturalism which in the explanation of the world, of man and his history, culture, knowledge and morality only saw as legitimate the categories which had been worked out for the understanding of nature. Nature thus became a closed system, whose origin and development could be variously explained, but which was fully accessible to one and to one only principle of knowledge, human reason, which could grasp its meaning and purpose. "Supernatural" interventions of God, as for instance in the form of historical revelation, were either excluded on principle or the possibility of recognizing them as such was denied. (It may be noted that this attitude reflects to some extent, negatively, the relationship between nature and the order of supernatural revelation as described by the theology of the time, which was at least basically "extrinsecist" in its approach.)

The necessity of revelation for man's salvation was denied, since nature itself contained all that man needed and made it accessible to his reason. Nature thus became unlimited, infinite and non-historical. It was seen as fulfilling all the metaphysical needs of man. There was no place for the supernatural in the understanding of Christian revelation. Faith became a sort of irrational underworld, imposing taboos, alienating man and hindering progress. Religion became an element in the immanence of nature. It was one of the main tasks of Naturalism to explain the genesis of religion within the framework of the development of nature (cf., for example, D. Hume, *Natural History of Religion* [1757]). An enlightened social order assigned religion and religious associations a precise place, subordinated to the system, in the education and perfectioning of man. The Deism which originated in England in the 16th century and then spread to the Continent was also part of this naturalistic world-view. Though it recognized the existence of a personal Creator, the denial of any further influence of God on the world was a further confirmation of the self-contained character of nature and of the possibility of explaining it by reason alone. Rationalism may not have denied the simple possibility of supernatural revelation. But as regards the content, it made the critical reserve that nothing could be admitted which did not prove capable of being grasped by the categories of reason. Hence it led at least in practice to the reduction of revelation to reason and nature. Theology became philosophy and Christianity was no more than natural religion (see *Deism, Rationalism*).

The supernaturalistic approach in theology, which brought with it a hardening of conservative and integralist attitudes, was a reaction to this Naturalism and Rationalism.

It was engendered in a climate of scepticism which put forward radical doubts about the power of reason and the optimism of the Enlightenment. A further factor was the shock caused by the total political upheaval of the French Revolution. The resulting vacuum was filled by views of God and the world which were tinged with Romanticism and Idealism and turned the pages of history backwards in a search for a sound and happy world. This was very attractive for conservative circles in the Church and politics (see *Romanticism, Revolution and Restoration*). The opinion took form that humanity or the Church could only maintain and defend itself if the natural powers of reason were down-graded, and the existing plurality of systems and sources of knowledge were reduced to some postulated unity.

2. *Supernaturalism in theology.* Supernaturalistic traits were manifested in the Protestant Churches chiefly in Pietism and its attitude towards ecclesiastical orthodoxy. Theologians went back to a biblicist Lutheranism in order to preserve the supernatural character of biblical revelation and to uphold the doctrine of justification against rationalistic efforts to whittle it away (see *RGG,* II, cols. 623f.; V, cols. 791–9; VI, cols. 589f., 813). Within Catholic theology, supernaturalistic trends showed themselves especially in Traditionalism and Fideism. Traditionalism held that the certainty of human knowledge could be guaranteed only by the authority of a divine revelation which had been given to the first men and which had to be handed on to all generations in an uninterrupted tradition, the channels being language, folklore, society and the Church. Such tradition was absolutely necessary for man, since his individual reason was physically incapable of attaining the only truths which could give meaning to his existence. Metaphysical and religious and moral truth could only reach man through a tradition coming "from outside", to be accepted by him in faith and confidence, based either on the divine authority or on the universal testimony of the human race. Fideism had its own special position with regard to the relation between reason and the act of faith. Its low opinion of reason led it to deny any co-operation of reason in the genesis of the act of faith. It distrusted all efforts to penetrate rationally the truths of faith and rejected the traditional apologetics with its logical argumentation. The only element relevant to salvation was the dedication of the heart in faith (see *Fideism, Traditionalism*).

3. *Supernaturalism in Church life in the 19th century.* Though supernaturalism contributed little to theological reflection, it had important consequences for the self-understanding of the Church and the moulding of its relationship to the world, as for the attitude of individual Christians. The "necessity" of revelation on the grounds of the feebleness of reason, its role as tutor and practically as guardian of the underdeveloped, the inability to distinguish and allow their proper independence to the various realms of reality led to the attitude known as Integralism which stamped the Church in the 19th and at the beginning of the twentieth century, and which is still a force to be reckoned with. The effort was made to answer the many different questions which the age put to the Church by a simple appeal to the faith. The magisterium of the Church was thus assigned importance even in fields in which it had no competence, and the Church became involved in futile and indeed harmful disputes (see *Church and World, Church and State*). The consequences of an attitude which put too much stress on revelation in seeking norms for Christian behaviour in fields which had even a remote connection with faith and morals are well known: the effort to mark off ghetto-like special Christian realms in the midst of the world, resistance to external influences, conservatism within, clericalism and restorative tendencies in political matters, a growing alienation and inward dissociation of the very levels of the population which gave the century its special stamp. The Church had to undergo the reproach, not always unjust, that it had perverted the faith into a totalitarian ideology.

4. *Critique of supernaturalism.* As an answer to the questions posed by Naturalism and Rationalism, and as a contribution to a new orientation of the Church's life of faith, supernaturalism was inappropriate. It opposed to the overestimation of reason an overestimation of revelation as a source of knowledge. A closed system was opposed by another, equally closed, equally incapable of seeing and explicating in their mutual contrast the necessary distinctions between the order of creation and redemption, between revelation and its historical forms, between faith and knowledge, Church and world and so on. The dialogue demanded so

urgently by the times between theology and the profane sciences could not be launched on such premisses. Blindness to the plurality of systems and orders of knowledge and to the relative independence of the partner in the dialogue could only make the latter feel that he was under a modern type of tutelage. Misgivings must also have been aroused by the would-be pious description of man as the receiver of revelation. The belittling of his reason — in which Kant's critique of reason was so readily used as a proof — and the purely passive role attributed to his receptivity made faith appear as a blind assent, obscuring the responsible decision of the hearer of the word. This approach made revelation so "necessary" that the very core of its supernatural character, the free, gratuitous, historical intervention of God was lost sight of, and revelation again appeared as "natural", in the sense of being immanent to the world. (This of course betrayed the formal identity of the basic approach both of naturalism and supernaturalism, the denial of a plurality.) Further, the well-intentioned but misleading formula, "the moulding of life by faith", was incapable of stemming the quick spread of a "schizophrenia" in the individual Christian, who was torn between his ecclesiastical and his worldly attitudes, on the basis of constantly conflicting claims on the part of the Church and of the world.

It was undoubtedly no easy matter for the magisterium of the Church to bring itself to condemn supernaturalistic tendencies and to plead the cause of reason, since the upholders of supernaturalism thought that they were loyally dedicated to the cause of the faith. The Fideism of Bautain was condemned in 1840 (*D* 1622–7) and the condemnation of the Traditionalism followed in 1855 (*D* 1649–52, against Bonetty). The First Vatican Council formulated a comprehensive pronouncement against Rationalism and supernaturalism (*D* 1781–1820). It insisted on a twofold order of knowledge ("It has always been and still is the unanimous conviction of the Catholic Church that there is a twofold order of knowledge, differing not only in the principle of knowledge but also in its object" [*D* 1795]), and described the role of reason in the genesis of the act of faith. In view of the persistence of integralist attitudes and practices, great importance must be attached to the development of this pluralist principle and of its dialogal structure in the Pastoral Constitution of the Second Vatican Council on the Church in the Modern World (*Gaudium et Spes,* especially arts. 14–17; 33–39; 40–45).

See also *Spiritualism, Pietism.*

BIBLIOGRAPHY. See bibliographies on *Enlightenment, Fideism, Naturalism, Rationalism, Traditionalism;* also: E. Troeltsch, *Christian Thought: Its History and Application* (1923); E. Hocedez, *Histoire de la théologie au XIXe siècle,* 3 vols. (1947–52); E. Hirsch, *Geschichte der neueren evangelischen Theologie,* V (1954) (chs. 47 and 48); K. Barth, *From Rousseau to Ritschl* (1959) (E.T. of 11 chs. of *Die protestantische Theologie im 19. Jahrhundert* [2nd ed., 1952]); M. Grabmann, *Geschichte der katholischen Theologie seit dem Ausgang der Väterzeit* (2nd ed., 1961), section III; L. Scheffczyk, *Theologie im Aufbruch und Widerstreit* (1965); E. Husserl, "Phenomenology and the Crisis of Philosophy", *Proceedings of the Aristotelian Society, London* (1965); B. Welte, *Auf der Spur des Ewigen* (1965), pp. 380–409 (on Catholic theology in the 19th century); P. Hünermann, *Der Durchbruch geschichtlichen Denkens im 19. Jahrhundert* (1967).

Ernst Niermann

SUPERSTITION

I. The Problem. II. Magic. III. Astrology.

I. The Problem

1. *Notion.* The word "superstition" primarily means an inverted, a "wrong" faith, but also a "sham" or deficient faith. What will be called superstition in any particular case depends on the outlook of the observer. Generally speaking, any religion or worldview is tempted to dismiss as superstition manifestations of a belief that conflict with its own norms or notions of belief. A "scientific" world-view which is thought absolute will look on all religions as superstitions. Apart from the fact, however, that assuming the world to be wholly explicable through reason must itself be acknowledged a superstition, because it is beyond the powers of natural science to tell us what life means, this assumption continually spawns superstitious counterfeits of religion. Within Christianity superstition means either misinterpreting important parts of the gospel in a magical sense or obscurely clinging to elements of paganism (natural religion) in Christian practice, or else abusing the forms of Christian faith in a flight from the insecurity of life and from the decisions it demands of us.

No doubt "superstitious" elements are inevitable in any religion, since transcendental religion (and therefore Christian faith as well) has to objectify itself in categories which are essentially inappropriate to it and which it must always outstrip, though it cannot leave them behind altogether (see *Analogy of Being, Mystery*). But superstition only enters the picture when men cease trying to rise above the categories of religion, as they must constantly do, and (consciously or not) cling to them for "safety" as to something no longer "transparent" (that no longer points beyond itself).

2. *Superstition in the history of religions.* Superstition presupposes a magical world-picture, or the remnants of one. It assumes the existence of forces inexplicable in terms of the laws of nature (however those forces be conceived of in particular). Man feels subject to such forces and tries to manipulate them by magic. Studies in the history of religions have solidly established the timelessness of superstition and its various forms — soothsaying, oracles, the popular interpretation of dreams, significance of certain dates or days, and so on. The recognition of magic and superstition demands a clear rejection of the magical interpretation of the world, the result either of a higher, more cultivated stage of religion or a more scientific outlook. This can be verified by the classical Greek and Latin texts on superstition (δεισιδαιμονία – servile fear of the gods instead of rational worship): Hippocrates, *De Morbo Sacro,* I; Plato, *Republic,* 364 b–365 a; Theophrastus, *Characteres,* 16; Plutarch, *De Superstitione;* Cicero, *De Divinatione,* II, 148; Pliny the Elder, *Naturalis Historia.*

The OT condemns every kind of superstition (cf. Exod 22:18; Lev 19:26, 31; 1 Sam 28; Is 8:20; Jer 27:9; Dan 2:27f.), as a sign of lack of trust in the only God, Yahweh, and an affront to him. But it recognized that the revealed faith was constantly jeopardized by superstition, mainly through Jewish contact with Canaanite nature-worship.

The gospel pronounces judgment on all superstition, all devils and demons (Mk 1:25–27 par.; 3:15; 5:13; 6:7 par.; Mt 12:28 par.; Lk 8:29; cf. Acts 13:10ff.; 19:13–19). St. Paul ranks idolatry among the works of the flesh (Gal 5:20; cf. 1 Cor 10:14 and Col 3:5).

3. *The phenomenon.* Superstition is especially prominent in the limit situations of life — birth, love, sickness, death —, in situations of heightened anxiety or fateful decision (magic relating to fertility, love, or healing; necromancy, etc.). It is one of man's despairing attempts to explain his baffling existence and escape its insecurity and anxiety. It can reveal an obscure knowledge of the numinous depths of existence and his ordination to transcendence. But primarily superstition distorts man's view of the absolute sovereignty of God, since it is inspired by the idea that by his own expert ritual words and acts he can propitiate the gods or forces on which he feels his enigmatic existence to depend. This egocentrism precludes the religious confidence which looks for everything from God's absolutely free power and goodness. Superstition and magic and the like may also offer an apparent security, which silences the real questions of life before they are articulated at all. This also explains why many people today are drawn to superstition (horoscopes, for example). The economic, social, and scientific complexity of the world now overwhelms the individual. He feels helpless, an insignificant, expendable factor in social processes which seem to be inescapable. This induces a passivity which gratefully clutches at the superstitious explanation that everything depends on an enigmatic but sovereign fate which gives meaning even to the absurd. This view spares men both intellectual effort and commitment. So superstition is one of the factors that make it difficult or impossible for a man to develop his religious, moral, and social personality. It is always a symptom of personal crisis. The resignation and complacency produced by modern commercialized superstition (plus other factors we cannot discuss here, such as general scepticism and economic affluence) mean that it cannot be an introduction to the true faith, although theoretically it might be. The poverty and shallowness of what superstition has to say about the background of human existence prevent men summoning up the courage of the real faith which would overcome fear, doubt and despair.

4. *Superstition and Christian faith.* Christian faith is constantly obliged to redefine itself vis-à-vis superstition. Custom and belief in the Churches are always in danger of degenerating into magic and superstition, for various reasons. Either a) custom and the belief underlying it may be relics of paganism which Christianity has not really been able to legitimize; or b) they may be relics of earlier phases of belief and science which

have now been left behind (see *Inquisition* II, *Superstition* III); or c) legitimate custom may become superstition because faith is misinterpreted (e.g., using the sign of the cross as a charm, mechanically reciting series of prayers, certain ideas about Mass and Communion). Being at once bodily and spiritual, man seeks to express and explain himself not only in words but also in sign, symbol, and image, and therefore many customs that Christianity has assimilated can be justified so long as their meaning and practice do not contradict the spirit of the faith — that salvation is found only in Jesus Christ, through the decision which must be fully personal in the believer. This truth can be obscured where Christianity mainly consists in the habit of observing a weight of accumulated traditions. Such habits offer apparent security but it collapses under any serious strain — not always yielding to a sounder grasp of the faith and a realization of one's personal freedom and responsibility. It is therefore the task of the Church to watch itself constantly and to educate the faithful to a faith fully conscious of the nature of Christian life and strong enough to endure fear and doubt and to transform them. In certain cases pastors of souls will only overcome superstition if they do not merely unmask and condemn it but recognize it as a symptom of deeper human distress which must be taken seriously and understood in order to be cured.

See also *Missions* II, *Religious Customs*.

BIBLIOGRAPHY. J. H. Newman, *An Essay in Aid of a Grammar of Assent* (1870), pp. 389–408; S. Baring-Gould, *Strange Survivals* (1905; reprint, 1968); E. W. Budget, *Amulets and Superstitions* (1930); B. Bonnerjea, *Dictionary of Superstitions and Mythology* (1927); J. von Negelein, *Weltgeschichte des Aberglaubens*, 2 vols. (1931–35); K. Zucker, *Psychologie des Aberglaubens* (1948); E. and M. Radford, *Encyclopaedia of Superstitions* (1948; 2nd ed., 1961); C. Ratschow, *Magie und Religion* (1955); F. Buri, "Glaube und Aberglaube", *Theologische Zeitschrift* 12 (1956), pp. 206–36; P. Bauer, *Horoskop und Talisman: Die Mächte des heutigen Aberglaubens und die Macht des Glaubens* (1963); A. Lang, "Religionsersatz", *LTK*, VIII, cols. 1173ff.; C. Brunner, *Science, Spirit and Superstition,* revised ed., by W. Bernard (1968).

Bonaventura Kloppenburg

II. Magic

The word "magician" comes from the Persian Magus, of unknown meaning, which was first applied to a caste or tribe of priests among the Medes (cf. the Levites) (Herodotus, *History,* I, 101). From his associations with the Babylonian priesthood, the Magus was then understood as an astrologer, an interpreter of dreams and a wizard. Magic then came to mean the art of enchantment, sorcery, the mysterious power of producing marvellous effects by compelling the aid of preternatural forces.

1. *History of religion.* The exact definition of magic, its distinction from religion or its place within religion, has been and still is debated. Certain actions are supposed to bring about directly, by compulsion, certain (preternatural) results. More precisely, according to A. Bertholet, they are the direct means of hastening, or bringing to a head, such results. The actions in question are simply the putting in practice of a dynamistic view of the world, and this is probably the kernel of the definition of magic (cf. *RGG,* IV, col. 596).

Magic is therefore concerned with the gaining, imparting or warding off of power. The experience of power in general and in certain distinguished beings or phenomena in particular forms the background and origin of the theory and practice of magic, though the actual historical origin of magic cannot be explained, and no chronological schema can be drawn up to show the transition "from magic to religion" (see 3 below).

Defensive (apotropaic) magic, like more positive forms, can use the method of transferring power by touching or by mimicry, as in sympathetic magic. Stones, plants, animals and above all men, especially distinguished men, are bearers of the power in question, which can be attached to parts as well as to the whole. The power may lie, for instance, in the shell of the tortoise, the tooth of the lion, in the blood, hair or spittle of the man. The power contained in the breath of life is most conspicuous in the magic word, which effects directly what it says, especially in blessings and curses. The name plays a special role here, and in the higher cultures also the written word, letters, formulas committed to writing, numbers and combinations of numbers, geometrical forms like the square and the five-pointed star.

Since the limits of the person are so vague here, the boundary between contact magic and sympathetic magic is fluid, as when, for instance, damage done to the footprint of

195

an enemy is supposed to harm the enemy himself. In sympathetic or homeopathic magic, like produces like. This includes the painting or dancing of hunting scenes, which are to ensure the success of the hunt, the wood or clay figures placed in Egyptian tombs to do the work demanded of the dead, and above all, the wax or other models which are to be stabbed to bring about the death of the person depicted.

Both methods are used in "white" and "black" magic, white magic being those practices which are considered (in a certain society) as helpful and permissible, black being understood as aiming at harmful and criminal ends. In both forms the aim is to gain or to control or pass on certain powers, for example by "drawing off" an evil and dangerous force which has caused illness or sin. The wider the fields of force are supposed to be, and the more the analogies taken in, the more comprehensively and systematically, and with increasing refinements, the theory and practice of magic appear. They range from the smoking of tobacco by the Indians to bring about the formation of rain-clouds, to the complicated "sciences" of astrology and sooth-saying.

2. *The Bible*. As in all religions, including Christianity (see below), magical practices occurred in Israel (cf. 1 Sam 28:3–25, where Saul assists at the conjuring up of the dead; 2 Kg 21:6 etc.). But they were explicitly forbidden and combatted by "the law and the prophets", which practically identified them with idolatry. For the law, see for instance Exod 22:17; Lev 20:27, where the death penalty is mandatory; Deut 18:9–12; for the prophets, see Is 44:25; Jer 27:9; Ezek 13:18–23, etc. Neither miracles nor prophecies are magic (Exod 8:12–15; Num 23:23; Deut 13:2–6). The word of God is mightier than all magic (Wis 16:5–14; 17:7 ff.). But reforms are always needed to eliminate magical abuses (cf. 2 Kg 18:4, where King Hezekiah destroyed the "pillars and the Asherah", and even "the bronze serpent that Moses had made").

The NT with its summons to repentance and message of liberty (freedom from the "principalities and powers") is sharply opposed to all magic. For particular concrete instances, see Acts 8:9 ff. (Simon Magus), 13:6–11 (Bar-Jesus), 19:19 (book-burning at Ephesus). The miracles of Jesus and the apostles, as the duel with Bar-Jesus shows in particular, are not stronger types of magic but mighty deeds of God ("the finger of God", Lk 11:20). That the actions are placed entirely in the service of God and are inspired by prayer — their "dialogue" structure — forms the decisive difference with regard to magical practices.

3. *Philosophy and theology*. The automatic working of forces on the one side, the sense of personal relationships and the reality of freedom on the other — these are the distinctive and permanent criteria as between magic and religion. It is to be noted that the personal relationship with its respect for freedom comes to the fore, and indeed in a special way, in the desire to influence the "Other", the powerful vis-à-vis, by urgent prayer, sacrifice and so on. But it need hardly be emphasized that it is very difficult to draw the line between them in practice.

At any rate, no attempt will be made here to distinguish between a "magical" and "rational" outlook on the world. For one thing, the conventional distinction between magical and rational by no means coincides with the distinction between magic and religion. Magic when contrasted with rationality is understood as a certain cloudiness in the picture of the world, where people do not succeed in distinguishing clearly enough between subject and object, the animate and the inanimate, individual and universal, etc. But considered reflection on the permanent "body-spirit" nature of man and especially on its historicity shows how limited and questionable is the distinction when made in these terms, which have to a great extent ceased to be taken for granted in the scientific world. Instead of speaking of the "magic" world of the primitives, the various cultures are to be investigated in detail, and we had not to wait for Structuralism to see the analogies with magical world-pictures in our own civilization (see *Structuralism*). (Structuralism started in fact from the acknowledged existence of such parallels.) And here we do not just mean the horoscopes without which no popular newspaper can compete, but also organizational structures and notions of society, representations and symbols which have a thoroughly "rational" and well thought out character.

If the distinction between "magical" and "rational" is questionable — and indeed certain forms of rationalism can be diagnosed, on planes extending beyond those of individual psychoanalysis, as magic using other methods — it will be difficult to disqualify certain practices as magical in contrast to the truly religious. How much of what is stigmatized as magic is really "science" (medicine etc.), mistaken no doubt, but still a legitimate non-religious effort to use means to an end? And conversely, an apt and successful use of means to an end, in spite of all its rationality, can really be magical, if it represents and takes the place of the specifically religious goal, as for instance when it offers full "salvation" to men. A non-rational, magical objectivation can safeguard the experience of the mystery behind the world and man, in spite of all its inadequacies, while certain rational views fail to grasp this experience properly and merely explain it away, so that it is buried from sight in a positivist world-view. Nonetheless, the irrational is not of itself religious, just as the irreligious is not necessarily rational — one need only think of the many forms of "profane" magic in use today, from charms, mascots and horoscopes to the technology and sociology which present themselves as doctrines of salvation.

Hence to say that someone dabbles in magic, it is not enough to note that, rightly or wrongly, he recognizes the presence of (strange) forces acting upon the existence of man and that he tries to master them. He must in practice or theory try to separate these forces from their ultimate relationship to the one free and sovereign God. He must try to make their manipulation entirely independent of his personal adoration and inconditional obedience to the one personal God (cf. A. Darlap in *LTK,* VI, col. 1275). But since the world and man and hence religious reality exist on many planes and in many dimensions, and since it would only be a higher type of magic to try to reduce them to a homogeneous unity, even "for the glory of God", to make our tasks easier, the danger of magic is a permanent threat to man in his situation of freedom. The danger affects man in his situation of body-spirit and his inter-personal situation in general, where person is embedded and bound up with nature (see *Concupiscence*). One thinks of such phenomena as compulsive washing or other repetitive tics in individuals, or of the role of advertisement, propaganda and mass suggestion in society.

Basing ourselves on the considerations put forward above, we may now define magic comprehensively as the theory and practice of a direct natural determination of freedom. It is the effort to determine the *free* agent, in contrast to the scientific effort, however "science" may be understood. It is *direct,* in contrast to the normally mediated, "bodily" relation to freedom. It may be hard to distinguish in fact between the free play of freedoms and the effort to use *nature* to influence freedom. And again, the "natural", being a dimension of reality and a realization of freedom, cannot be simply dismissed as magical in contrast to "pure" freedom.

This truth also applies in the religious realm. In keeping with the "incarnational structure of grace" (K. Rahner), signs, institutions and tangibility (see *Sacraments* I, *Sacramentals, Religious Custom*) are essential elements of religion. The free religious act takes place essentially in symbolic form (see *Symbol*). The effect of the sacraments, *ex opere operato,* does not mean any magic automatism, but comes from the free, historical and faithful promise of Christ. (Their "validity" is guaranteed, but this opens up a free interpersonal exchange without simply guaranteeing its "fruitfulness".) Nonetheless, there is a constant tendency or temptation to "be of little faith" and so try to reduce everything, from concepts to worship, to the level of things that can be manipulated as though by magic — rationalistically and irrationally. Faith and religion is therefore constantly set the task anew of "discerning the spirits", of self-criticism which will be as inexorable as it is prudent and tolerant in ridding itself of magic.

BIBLIOGRAPHY. *HERE,* VIII, cols. 245–321; *DBS,* V, cols. 732–9; *Billerbeck,* IV, pp. 529–53; see the bibliography to *Structuralism;* also: J. G. Frazer, *The Golden Bough: A Study in Magic and Religion,* 13 vols. (3rd ed., 1911–36; abridged ed., 1922 ff.); L. Lévy-Bruhl, *Primitive Mentality* (1923); W. J. Perry, *The Origin of Magic and Religion* (1923); F. Graebner, *Das Weltbild der Primitiven* (1924); K. Preuss, *Der magische Mensch (Homo divinans)* (1928); R. Allier, *Magie et religion* (1935); H. and H. A. Frankfort, J. A. Wilson and T. Jacobsen, *The Intellectual Adventures of Ancient Man* (1946); E. de Martino, *Il mondo magico* (1948); H. Webster, *Magic* (1948); L. Chochod, *Histoire critique de la magie et de ses dogmes* (1949); H.-J. Schoeps, *Aus frühchristlicher Zeit* (1950), pp. 239–54; M. Bouisson, *La magie* (1958); F. Arnau, *Macht und Geheimnis der Magie* (1965); J. Splett, "Symbole et liberté", in E. Castelli, ed., *L'herméneutique de la liberté religieuse* (1968), pp. 103–23.

Jörg Splett

III. Astrology

Astrology ("reading of the stars") assumes that there is a regular connection between the position of the stars at the moment of a person's birth and that person's character and destiny. Astronomy investigates the natural laws governing heavenly bodies.

1. The following are some of the objections to astrology raised by various specialized sciences:

a) Over a period of more than two millennia, not one of the several thousand most reliable horoscopes known has ever been proved to be accurate.

b) Astrology connects a person's destiny with the stars partly on the basis of astrophysical ideas that are demonstrably false, and partly by reading a fateful significance into mere names (Mars = war or death; Venus = love, etc.).

c) It is arbitrary to assume that the stars affect a person only at the moment when the umbilicus is severed.

d) There is no reason why the celestial sphere should be divided into "houses", particular areas that are supposed to govern the main concerns of human life (such as marriage, friendship, profession, and so forth).

e) Cases where a horoscope appears to have been accurate are readily explained by the laws of chance.

f) The methods of individual astrologers vary so widely that a number of practitioners have been known to interpret a single horoscope in as many different ways.

Newspaper horoscopes, in particular, bristle with contradictions. Most professional astrologers dismiss them as worthless.

In France, Belgium, Denmark, Sweden, the U.S.S.R., Italy and Switzerland it is an offence to practise astrology as a profession.

Whereas the rules of astrology are quite arbitrary, it is a demonstrable fact that heavenly bodies, above all the sun and the moon, do affect the earth and thus indirectly influence human life.

The researches of M. Gauquelin (in 1955) have proved the claims of astrology to be baseless. On the other hand, scrutiny of the dates of birth of some 24,000 prominent people in various walks of life seems to suggest that Mars, Jupiter and Saturn may have influenced their entry into the world. The laws of probability fail to account for these statistics. As yet, however, no evidence for a causal connection has been forthcoming.

2. The psychological aspect of astrology tells us nothing about the stars but something about human nature. "Astrology", says T. W. Adorno, "faithfully reflects the mysterious world of our experience." Practically all the serious threats to our life, all the personal qualities that shape our fate, reappear in the heavens — the twelve "houses"; the planets, named after the gods of antiquity who were the religious projection of human necessities (Mercury for money and one's profession; Jupiter for power and influence, etc.); the signs of the zodiac, whose names are considered symbols of human characteristics.

The irrational nature of astrology gives it a considerable appeal. Instructions and advice that seem to come from the depths of the universe, guidance from this mysterious "other world" to help one through life, inspire a fear which apes the reverential. The opinion of C. G. Jung on this matter deserves more notice than it has received: "Results apparently due to more than chance are interpreted as a synchronistic phenomenon, that is, as a meaningful coincidence which derives from archetypally founded expectations on the part of the experimentor . . . In situations that bring an archetype to life — and astrology is one such situation — the figures are brought into line with emotional expectation under the influence of some accommodating factor. Such synchronizations, such 'significant accidents', have a background of a causality, freedom and meaningfulness in nature which is correlated with necessity, automatism and meaninglessness" (*Zeitschrift für Parapsychologie* 1 [1957], pp. 91–92). Jung also says that the attributes of the signs of the zodiac are myths, psychological images projected into the sky, where they seemed to be "discovered" (as is the way with projections). He regards astrology as a largely parapsychological phenomenon.

3. The opinion of some astrologers that the stars do not control a person but simply give him certain inclinations, is not without interest from the philosophical point of view. Supposing that the stars did affect people, their influence on human behaviour would simply be comparable with that of other factors in the environment (such as the weather) and would not destroy the freedom of the will.

4. From the theological point of view, astrology is a serious matter because it is practised as a "substitute religion". Thus it is

a superstition that blocks a person's way to confident faith in God. Instead of constantly shaping his own destiny by personal decisions as God wishes him to do, man takes refuge in servility to an anonymous master. Priests who have the care of souls should not underestimate the influence exercised by the "clergy" of this substitute religion. Prophecies of misfortune to come are particularly dangerous because they may give rise to a compulsion to see them fulfilled.

See also *Psychology* IV.

BIBLIOGRAPHY. P. Saintyves (= E. Nourry), *L'astrologie populaire* (1937); K. Prümm, *Religionsgeschichtliches Handbuch* (2nd ed., 1954); M. Gauquelin, *Cosmic Clocks: The Scientific Implications of Astrology* (1967); id., *The Scientific Basis of Astrology* (1968).

Johannes Fasbender

SYMBOL

1. *Term and concept.* Etymologically, the word "symbol" comes from certain usages in ancient law. Two parts of a ring, staff or tablet served, when they were brought together συμ-βάλλειν, to identify legitimate guests *(tessera hospitalitatis),* messengers and partners. Thus the word came to have the meaning of "treaty", and in ecclesiastical language could designate the common profession of faith, the fixed and obligatory formulas or creeds (the "symbols") and then the instruments, images and acts in which the faith was expressed. Through the study of religion, psychology, art, literature, the theory of science and logic, the concept has been extended and varied so considerably that it can take in the operative signs of logical calculations (as in "symbolic" logic). Leaving aside the terminology of formal logic, it may be said that a symbol is distinguished from a sign, which is the broader, more formal concept, by being more "adequate", either in the nature of things, or because chosen "by convention" for its aptness. The symbol is closer to the thing signified, and is less arbitrary than the sign. This distinction between sign and symbol will not always be clear in practice. But it serves to indicate the special quality, the meaningfulness of the symbol, in contrast to the sign which merely points to something else. But the distinction also serves to indicate the limitation and ambiguity inherent in the symbol.

2. *Philosophy.* a) *The anthropological approach.* The symbol in the sense so defined stems from man's essential constitution as spirit-body — and hence at once, and indeed by the very nature of the body — a social being. Hence the innumerable symbols adopted must be investigated for the symbolization which posited them, just as the spoken word is referred to language, speech — the "speaking word", λόγος, by virtue of which man is man. The symbol in this original sense of symbolization, i.e., as is still to be shown, the simultaneous positing of and experience of symbols, would then appear as the (self-)realization of freedom. Hence the symbol does not refer to something else. A reality appears in it — in "the other of itself" — which is there and present but not fully exhausted by this appearance. In such an anthropology Hegel's notion of exteriorization (of the concept, which by nature tries to "manifest itself") becomes the "real symbol" of K. Rahner. Its primary case is the human body and the bodily acts which go with personal attitudes such as love, faith or hatred.

But the element of interpersonality in the positing of the symbol must be stressed just as definitely. As freedom acts, it necessarily addresses itself with its "word" to another. But even prior to this, freedom is never solely activated by itself. Hegel has also shown that form implies limitation, that limit can never belong to one alone but means two at least, and hence that the I only comes to itself (self-awareness) in its encounter with another I. Against German Idealism, however, we must note, with the later Fichte and the dialogal philosophy of the 20th century, that the "self-discovery" in the encounter with the other is not "one-way" but essentially "two-way" traffic. Just as the I finds itself in the You, so too the You in the I, in the common symbol; and the two not only find themselves and each other, but also their mutual reference, their being-in-common. And this common being is realized in a common act. For each, the positing of the symbol is simultaneously experience of the symbol and vice versa.

In the symbol, freedom is realized (in the "medial" sense of activity and receptivity) as a "two-in-one" (or "many-in-one") reality. In this duality or multiplicity in unity its further determinations take root: its riches, its limitations, its historicity. The limitation of the symbol is that it differs in a way from what is symbolized (or better: from what gives itself symbolic form in it). Tillich, for

199

instance, rightly rejects the expression, "merely a symbol", since the symbol is "more" than it tangibly is and says, being appearance, presence, self-positing of ... Nonetheless, it is not simply that which is positing itself in it there. If the symbol is confused with what it symbolizes, the deformations of fetishism and image-worship appear: the symbol becomes an idol. But if the real presence of the reality symbolized in the symbol is not recognized, the deformations of "pure interiority" follow, iconoclasm in the widest sense: the symbol is reduced to a mere signal, sign-post or "code-number". But even qua symbols, no symbols may be erected into absolutes as though given in the nature of things. Since they are expressions of freedom, they are historical, which means that they can become out of date and empty as soon as freedom — individually or epochally — take a different shape. Hence no system of symbolism, except the most purely formal, is possible. Anything can become a means of self-expression, not arbitrarily but in the framework of historical existence, oblivion of which reduces symbol to allegory. This is the field for empirico-historical research into symbolism in religion, art, literature, law, politics, folklore and science, in the individual and the supra-individual mind.

b) *The world as symbol.* This anthropological approach brings us to the gradation of symbols, from the body to the freely-chosen word or expressive gesture. (It also allows for the distinction between the symbol in the strict sense and the concept, as well as for the question of technics and symbol, which likewise goes beyond mere opposition.) In this way, the symbol, like every other basic concept, shows itself to be analogous and comprehensive. The symbol thus appears in the dimension of the world, as is already suggested by the question of the demarcation of the body from the world. It has an integrating function in the structure of the symbolic form which it anticipates (see *Play*). Further, the anthropological approach enables us to have some understanding of nature and the world in general as symbol. This is not to be dismissed as naive anthropomorphism. Biology investigates symbols in animal behaviour, in animal forms (Portmann) and in the structure of plants (e.g., the insectivorous orders). Apart from such intrinsic traits here and there, man has always regarded the flow and fabric of the world as also symbolic of himself and of the Wholly Other, the holy. Art in particular gives expression to the former attitude, where the results of comparative folklore and depth psychology are also relevant. The second point of view is given expression in the cults and myths of religion. But in fact, art always helped to interpret the latter feeling, and religion the former, e.g., in the myths of the creation of the world from the body of a primeval giant or man. And in a similar way, thought inspired by the Christian tradition can take in expressly the unity of the two moments. Since according to Scripture (Gen 2:19f.) Adam gave the beasts their names, i.e., their nature, it need not be subjectivist Idealism to affirm that the world, including man, being the "word" of the creator, is only this word when it is perceived by man. This means that it is a word which from the start is uttered by both. The world is therefore a symbol of the interpenetration of finite, created freedom and infinite creative freedom. They are not partners on an equal footing, but it remains true that the creative freedom does create freedom and hence gives itself a "partner", so that the world is really the history of "the two". But such lines of thought can only be adequately established by theology.

3. *Theology.* The creatureliness of things — created for the glory of God, which becomes articulate in man — is the basis of their kinship, their "similarity" (in the analogy of being), which enables one to be represented or depicted by another. And as creatures, they are all in their own way *vestigia Dei,* the visible manifestation of his invisible nature (Rom 1:20). But the great original symbol of Christian theology, the fulfilment in a superabundant way of the *imago Dei* in man, is the incarnate Logos, to see whom is to see the Father (Jn 14:6–10). Hence Christ did not proclaim liberation from symbols but the redemption of the symbol. Here the symbol displays, at its most intense, its historicity, its interpersonal nature and its difference in an identity which is dialogal, personal and "pneumatic". Its richness and fullness is such that of itself it resists the temptation of idolatry, though this may not be fully verified in its assimilation, and it cannot be emptied out to be left as a mere code-number. Above all, here symbolic form and symbolic reality are identified. At least in Christ the symbol effects what it signifies. It is not merely validly posited and received, but also fruitfully — to use, not inappropri-

ately, the terminology of the sacraments. In the incarnation the symbol has lost the ambiguity which was its deepest limitation and which it could never have transcended by itself.

Possessing such fullness, this symbol likewise has "universal validity". It has the power proper to the symbol, unlike the concept, to evoke, to summon and claim, to give meaning, in a way which knows no epochal, cultural or any other limits. It remains the "middle" of history, not because it is the most universal concept, but because it is the "name" for all things (Phil 2:9–11 — the *universale concretum*). The incarnationally symbolic character of this middle is then the law of its historical development in the visible Church, creed, sacraments, sacramentals and so on. As has already been indicated, this history also presents the temptations to which the symbol exposes men. But in principle they have already been surmounted (Mt 16:18; 28:20), though only "in hope" (Rom 8:24). The "new earth" without a temple (Rev 21:22) is not yet an unveiled reality and hence the division between sacred and profane continues. But the new earth will not mean the end of the symbol but its fulfilment: the pure "coincidence" of the kingdom of man and the kingdom of God, the kingdom of the Son and the kingdom of the Father (1 Cor 15:18), an immediacy given by the fact that the Son made man "remains".

Finally, this ending of the symbol is fulfilment in the sense that it does not lead to the perspicuousness of having "seen through" everything, to a finally successful grasp in knowledge, but to the rapt recognition of a freedom which bestows itself. The gap of seen and unseen which characterizes the symbol is here finally disclosed, not as a dichotomy between two "worlds", which still has to be bridged, but as primordial freedom in the act of giving itself without abandoning itself. For it is only in this way — where it does truly give *itself* — that it is revealed as the holy mystery.

See also *Holy, Analogy of Being, Identity-Philosophy, Images, Myth, Incarnation, Sacraments.*

BIBLIOGRAPHY. E. Cassirer, *Philosophy of Symbolic Forms,* 3 vols. (1953, 1955, 1957); H. Looff, *Der Symbolbegriff in der neuern Religionsphilosophie und Theologie* (1955); F. Hermann, ed., *Symbolik der Religionen,* 12 vols. (1958–62); P. Tillich, *Theology of Culture* (1959), ch. v; id., with others, *Symbolism in Religion and Literature* (1966); *Symbolon: Jahrbuch für Symbolforschung* (1960ff.); M. Eliade, *Images and Symbols* (1961); G. Vann, *Myth, Symbol and Revelation* (1962); H. Urs von Balthasar, *Herrlichkeit* (1962ff,) (4 vols. so far); B. Welte, *Auf der Spur des Ewigen* (1965); K. Rahner, "Theology of the Symbol", *Theological Investigations,* IV (1966), pp. 221–52; C. Jung, *Man and his Symbols* (1967); J. Splett, *Sakrament der Wirklichkeit* (1968).

Jörg Splett

SYNCRETISM

1. *The term.* The word "syncretism" was first used by Plutarch (*De Fraterno Amore,* 19) to describe a combination of Cretan communities against a common enemy, a rare and in fact historically uncertain event, as the Cretans were usually fighting among themselves. The term began therefore by signifying a political alliance in which mutual differences were overlooked in the face of a threat to all. The term then occurs again in the 16th century in Erasmus (*Opus Epistolarum),* who derived it from a verb συν-κεράννυμι (which does not occur in classical Greek) and transposed it into Latin. Subsequently, it was generally applied to an eclectic mixture in philosophical and theological doctrines. The humanist Cardinal Bessarion was described as a syncretist for his efforts to reconcile Plato and Aristotle in the 15th century; the theologians who tried in the 16th century to harmonize Thomism and Molinism were "syncretists", and the term was applied to G. Calixtus and others in the controversy between Lutherans and Presbyterians in the 17th century.

From the 19th century on, the term has chiefly been used in comparative religion, meaning a fusion of different godheads, cults or religions. Used in its strict sense, it points to the fusion of Oriental mystery religions with the religions of Greece and Rome in Hellenism.

2. *Forms and motives.* a) The forms and motives of syncretism are closely connected.

(i) Within a given religion, syncretism appears first of all as the fusion of godheads (theocrasy). Traits belonging to different gods are transferred to a certain god who is then revered as the supreme god, such as the Babylonian Marduk, the Egyptian Isis or the Persian Mithra in pre-Christian times. Egypt was the main scene of such fusions, the priests deliberately promoting amalgama-

201

tions of gods and cults to bring together the various local religious heritages. All gods came to be viewed as manifestations of one divine unity, of which Ammon, for instance, was the name, Re the visage and Ptah the body. The notion here is that one invisible divine force dwells in a number of personal, anthropomorphic forms. The phenomenon of one god being personally present in various forms also occurs very early in India. In the *Atharvaveda* (14, 4, 1 ff.), the following description is given of one godhead: "He mounts to heaven as Savitâr, he ascends to the clouds in the guise of the great Indra . . . He is Vâyu with the towering clouds. He is Aryaman, he is Rudra, he is Mahâdeva, he is Agni, he is Sûrya, he is also Yâma, the great (god of death)." Such syncretism goes beyond the identification of one god with another in polytheism, and paves the way for revealed monotheism, inasmuch as it takes account of the mysterious character of the holy.

When contact comes about between cultures through migration, trade, common settlements, colonization, etc., the possibilities and forms of syncretism multiply. Along with the fusion of godheads, religious forms and interpretations are borrowed, gods and cults are identified, exchanges ensue which end in the synthesis of different religions.

(ii) In nearly all civilizations, and particularly in those resulting from acculturation, there are syntheses in the religious realm composed of native and foreign elements. Rites are taken over from one culture to another, as in Israel during the reign of Manasseh (*c.* 693–639 B.C.).

(iii) Going beyond this stage of partially unconscious borrowing, sometimes whole groups of gods are made interchangeable or identified with each other. Antiochus IV of Commagene (1st century A.D.), whose ancestry was both Persian and Macedonian, had the gods of both peoples sculptured on the Nemrud-Dagh, where they appeared as equivalents. He identified, for instance, Mithra and Apollo.

(iv) Hellenism was the great age of syncretism. The attempt was soon made to compare the gods of the Egyptians, the Phoenicians and the "barbarians" with those of the Greeks, and later with those of the Romans. In Alexandria, under the Ptolemies, the Egyptian god Usar-Api (Osiris-Apis, already a syncretistic figure) was linked with legends from various cults, and identified with Asclepius, Zeus and Pluto (cf. Tacitus,

Historiae, 4, 83 f.). Under the name of Sarapis he became a god for Greeks and Egyptians alike. This type of phenomenon became characteristic of the influence of the Oriental mystery religions on the West in imperial times. The worship of Isis attained great importance. She was goddess of the world, and was revered as Cypris (the Greek Aphrodite) in Cyprus, as Diana (the Greek Artemis) in Crete, as Proserpine (the Greek Persephone) in Sicily and as Ceres (the Greek Demeter) at Eleusis (cf. the litanies addressed to Isis in Apuleius, *Metamorphoses,* 11, 5, and the hymns of Mesomedes). The Persian cult of Mithra became one of the most important religions of the pagan world. It was a blend of Oriental, Roman and later even of Christian elements (cf. the identifications of the Heracleia of Tyre in Nonnus, *Dionysiaca,* 40, 369 ff.). The Magna Mater, Attis, Cybele and other gods worshipped in Asia Minor were naturalized in the Empire, disseminating mystery-cults which have often been interpreted as cultic processes of death and resurrection, rebirth and divine sonship, illumination and redemption, divinization and immortality. In the 3rd century A.D. the many Syrian, Hellenistic and Western cults were amalgamated into a pantheistic solar religion (cf. Macrobius, *Saturnalia,* I, 17, 2).

Special doctrines of this period may be seen in the Hermetic writings and Gnosis, which were syncretist in origin and nature. In the Hermetic myth, Hermes Trismegistos (the Greek version of the Egyptian god Thoth) was regarded as the mediator between the transcendent sphere and the material world, and as the author of religious revelations. The revelation-discourses of the *Corpus Hermeticum* combine Egyptian, Platonic, neo-Pythagorean, Orphic and Jewish notions into a peculiar cosmogony, anthropogony and soteriology. The origin of Gnosis (in the strict sense; see *Gnosis*) is more problematical. But this religious movement of late antiquity presents a picture of man and the world which clearly betrays at least Iranian, Jewish, Stoic and Christian influences. Efforts were made in Stoicism and neo-Platonism to justify syncretism. The thesis was put forward that all gods were of equal value, being different abstractions of the essentially one God, and that all religions were the same, being concrete representations of eternal ideas. Nonetheless, the religious forms of late Hellenism were perversions, tending to become essentially private cults or astrological pantheisms.

(v) A certain syncretism may also be noted in the religions of the Far East and of early America, for which a few indications must suffice. In India, there was at least a partial mixture of Islam and Hinduism. In China, Confucianism and Taoism drew gradually together, combining also with Buddhism from the 5th century A.D. In Japan, since the time of Kôbô, A.D. 774, Shintoism and Buddhism combined to be the mainstays of the ancient national religion.

b) The motives of syncretism are as various as its stages.

(i) Certain geographical, economic and linguistic factors promote the process of religious amalgamation, especially where a cosmopolitan outlook, as in the empire of Alexander, favours cultural contacts, dissemination of a language (the Greek *koine*) and the interchange of gods. But one of the basic causes is also a policy of religious tolerance, an instance of which is the rock inscription of Behistun, engraved by order of the Achaemenid King Darius of Persia, in Old Persian, Elamite and Babylonian. This may be contrasted with the exclusive monotheism of Judaism.

(ii) On the plane of religious piety, syncretism appears as an effort to fill in gaps in a given religion.

(iii) Syncretism also plays a role, in the form of adaptation, in the general process of the explanation of religion and in the missionary work of the Church. One may recall, for instance, the accommodation to the formulas and notions of Persian religion in the designation of God as the "God of heaven" in Ezra 6:10, which was intended to win the toleration of the Persians for the Jewish notion of God. Another instance would be the methods of adaptation used for the famous "Chinese rites". Christianity has no doubt since St. Paul's speech on the Areopagus and down to the missionary theories of modern times, during its controversies with the various philosophies (Platonism, Epicureanism, Stoicism, neo-Platonism), as with Gnosticism and the doctrine of the Logos, as also in its efforts at adaptation in non-Western lands, frequently assimilated heterogeneous elements. But this process cannot be seen as syncretism (see *Hellenism and Christianity, Missions* II).

3. *Theological interpretation.* Syncretism has been interpreted as an epiphenomenon linked with the cultural development of man, in line with the Stoic, neo-Platonist and humanist view of the equality of all religions; or as a deliberate fusion of godheads, due to a profound change in religious ideas (K. Prümm); or as a result of the general dynamism of religion (G. van der Leeuw). But this is to leave it on the plane of the phenomenology of religions. An approach to a strictly theological explanation is only possible where it is no longer seen as an aberration due to superstition and unbelief, but as a positive moment in the objectivation of man's transcendental experience of grace and salvation (see *Salvation* III).

BIBLIOGRAPHY. J. Réville, *La religion à Rome sous les Sévères* (1886); F. Cumont, *The Oriental Religions in Roman Paganism* (1911); J. Geffcken, *Religiöse Strömungen im 1. Jahrhundert n. Chr.* (1922); H. Schaeder, *Studien zum antiken Synkretismus aus Iran und Griechenland* (1926); K. Latte, *Die Religion der Römer und der Synkretismus der Kaiserzeit* (1927); J. Geffcken, *Der Ausgang des griechischen-römischen Heidentums* (2nd ed., 1929); R. Pettazoni, "Sincretismo e conversione nella storia della religione", *Bulletin du comité international des sciences historiques* (1933); G. van der Leeuw, *Religion in Essence and Manifestation* (1938); H. Bonnet, "Zum Verständnis des Synkretismus", *Zeitschrift für ägyptische Sprache und Altertumskunde* 75 (1939), pp. 40ff.; J. Moffatt, *HERE*, XII, cols. 155–7; F. C. Grant, *Hellenistic Religions: The Age of Syncretism* (1953); K. Prümm, *Religionsgeschichtliches Handbuch für den Raum der altchristlichen Umwelt* (2nd ed., 1954); H. Bell, *Cults and Creeds in Egypt* (1954); G. Lanczkowski, "Zur Entstehung des antiken Synkretismus", *Saeculum* 6 (1955), pp. 227–43; R. Bultmann, *Primitive Christianity in its Contemporary Setting* (1956); P. Hacker, "Religiöse Toleranz und Intoleranz im Hinduismus", *Saeculum* 8 (1957), pp. 167–79; K. Latte, *Römische Religionsgeschichte* (1960); M. Nilsson, *Geschichte der griechischen Religion*, II (2nd ed., 1961); D. S. Houécard, "The Wider Ecumenism", *Aylesford Review*, VII (1965).

John Charles Maraldo

T

TAXATION, MORALITY OF

Taxation means the paying of money according to law for the support of government, or the levying of such payments. Tax laws range from municipal ordinances to the decrees of the supreme authority.

1. *Authentic and false response.* Response to taxation is commonly minimal compliance, if not outright refusal. Such a response is value-blind, understandable though not excusable. Tax structures are so complex that paying taxes has become totally impersonal, e.g., the routine filling of an income tax report. The citizen sees tax law as a despoliation, a restriction of freedom to use what is his. The tax system may be value-blind as well, i.e., organized to maximize revenues independently of the capacity of the taxpayer to pay. From such regressive taxation results an unjust burden on, say, the lower income group. The tax system is blind to the value of distributive justice.

The antidote to such insensitivity to value by government and taxpayer is twofold. First, public servants must reawaken to the principle: the society exists for the person. A regressive tax system imposing a disproportionate burden on one group in society makes these persons mere means to an end, the public good. Second, taxpayers must achieve a heightened sense of community. Tax law, as all law, helps to erect the external structure necessary for human existence. This external community makes possible the realization of man's ultimate value as a person within the union of love with God and men. Without taxes no community, for community requires peace and order in society, education

and food for all. Taxes make these values a reality.

Beyond these social values there are the moral values of justice, obedience and love. Justice assures to the person an integral human existence. This means that human needs are fulfilled. Today man's material and spiritual exigencies are greater than in earlier times. Government services become progressively more necessary to supply these increased needs, a theme ably developed in the encyclical *Mater et Magistra* of John XXIII. Government must collect adequate revenues to finance these public services.

The material goods of the universe have a common destination, the whole human community. Justice requires that this destination be more equitably achieved, that economic imbalances be redressed. Thus a prosperous sector of an economy, e.g., industry, must assist a depressed sector, e.g., agriculture; a developed economy ought to provide capital for an underdeveloped nation.

Next there is the value of obedience. Obeying the law is not merely bending one's will to an impersonal edict. It is a response to a person, the public official, whose function is community service. Ultimately it is a response to the Father in heaven incarnated in the legislator, who mediates to man the Father's command. "For he (the authority) is God's servant for your good . . . Therefore one must be subject" (Rom 13:4–5).

Finally taxation is an expression of the biblical teaching, "Love your neighbour as yourself". In today's complex and over-populated world private works of charity do not exhaust the demands of love. Without public provision for health, employment and housing, the neighbour cannot adequately be fed, clothed and sheltered. Tax systems are necessary for such public institutions to function.

2. *Scriptural teaching.* "Let every person be subject to the governing authorities . . . Pay all of them their dues, taxes to whom taxes are due" (Rom 13:1, 7). Note that the rulers to be obeyed are pagan, for Paul is writing to the Christians of Rome. Exegetes, both Catholic and Protestant, interpret this duty as owed to the Emperor, to provincial governors and local magistrates as well. The teaching of Paul expresses a moral imperative, not a counsel.

Taken in isolation the text envisages rulers in lawful possession of power and exercising it for the good of their subjects. But after Rome turns against the Church Paul reiterates the same duty: Tit 3:1; 1 Tim 2:1–2. He echoes faithfully the teaching of Jesus: "Render to Caesar the things that are Caesar's" (Mt 22:21). The Church has interpreted the Pauline injunction as a perennial principle, not as a mere temporary directive.

3. *Moral immunity from tax obligation.* Do all tax laws impose a moral imperative, and in the full amount required by law? Rom 13 does not so state. Paul speaks of paying taxes in general. Positive law is of its nature generic. As such it cannot reflect the unique ability to pay of each subject. Moreover, not all tax laws are just. Governments do not always readjust tax burdens to changing economic conditions. Also there is widespread tax delinquency in some countries, resulting in conscientious taxpayers rendering more than their just share. There is room, then, for interpretation of one's duty and for responsible decision as to the paying of taxes.

One may not, however, apply the judgment of moralists of one country or time to another. A classic example is the moral opinion: purely positive laws do not bind in conscience. Moralists do not apply this view to tax law today. In developed economies it is inapplicable to income taxation, which provides such a large portion of public welfare funds. Nevertheless moralists still accept, as excusing from tax obligation, inability to pay and proportionate hardship. For these confer the standard authors. With the wide variation in tax structures from nation to nation, more specific guidance must be sought in the moral studies of each economy.

BIBLIOGRAPHY. S. Weston, *Principles of Justice in Taxation* (1903); F. Hamm, *Zur Grundlegung und Geschichte der Steuermoral* (1908); O. von Nell-Breuning in *Staatslexikon,* V (5th ed., 1932), cols. 123ff.; VII (6th ed., 1968), cols. 698ff. (with bibliography); id., *Sittliche Grundsätze zu Steuerrecht und Steuermoral* (Akademie der Diözese Rottenburg) (1954); S. Scailteur, *Le devoir fiscal* (1950); G. Gilleman, *The Primacy of Charity in Moral Theology* (1959), pp. 253–79; B. Häring, *The Law of Christ,* I (1964), pp. 252–85.

Robert H. Springer

TECHNOLOGY

1. *General concept.* The Greek word τέχνη embraces all "artificial" production of things by man, as opposed to their spontaneous, "natural" growth and development. Starting from this, technology can be taken as synonymous with "art" in the widest sense, in contradistinction to "nature". It is one of the basic ways in which the world of nature is freely and consciously transformed into the world of man, a cultural process, therefore, which consists essentially in material production. Within this category of "artificial" activity, especially in view of the progressive differentiation of culture in relatively autonomous "areas", technical production in the narrower sense is to be found: technology and its products, called "instruments" because they have a functional, instrumental purpose (in contrast with art and its products whose nature is symbolic and representative). The more specialized uses of the term technology in the 19th and early 20th centuries derive more or less from this original meaning: technology considered as an extension of the "instrumental" power of the human limbs; technology as the use of raw materials and the forces of nature in the satisfaction of material needs according to certain rules discovered through experience (traditional technology) or through scientific experiment (modern technology); modern technology, therefore, is "applied science", as a system of means to economic or other human purposes.

2. *Modern technology.* The increasing prominence given to technology as an object of philosophical analysis (of history and of anthropology) is the result chiefly of the experience in so many forms of the famous "crisis", the decisive factor in which was seen to be the influence of technico-scientific thinking and technico-economic activity on

social living, on the relations between the peoples of various countries, as well as on their attitudes to their own traditions and to those they hold in common with others. A revolution was seen to be in progress, the result of which seemed to be the disappearance of the very foundations of the ordered way of life stemming from the traditions of Western Europe. Though the forces of dissolution and of reconstruction were seen in retrospect to have been operative over a long period, it was not possible to have a conceptually clear picture of them. By relating the problem of technology to the problem of Western European history and to that of world history, which is only now emerging and becoming possible as a unified entity, it became apparent that the earlier approach — that which regarded modern technology merely as a direct continuation, an intensification and expansion of the craft production which is common to all regions and to every stage of civilization — had been entirely inadequate.

Technology has indeed always existed. Technology in that very general and not very enlightening sense (which regards historical differences merely as "stages of development" of a single process) has indeed existed from the dawn of human history. If we think of it purely in terms of the development of technical procedures, whether taken one by one or all at once, we overlook the epoch-making difference that marks the precise nature of technology at any particular period of history and especially in modern times. For these methods of procedure with their appropriate instruments and knowledge of the natural world have not just a certain coefficient in an abstract line of development. In fact, the reality and significance of nature and the knowledge of nature, of an instrument and the production of objects, of work in general in its concrete existence (and not only in its most formal definition) are determined by how and as what man at any period understands himself and understands the actual world which he desires to shape. For this reason modern technology, in an age of automation and atomic reactors, an age bringing the machine era to its perfection, cannot be adequately explained in terms of a process of the accumulation of discoveries of means and of methods. This colossal quantitative accumulation and expansion — which is the external reality of modern technology — is rather, precisely as an external perceptible reality,

to be itself interpreted in the light of the actual origin, and therefore the specific "qualitative" difference, of the understanding which our culture has of itself and the world in modern times.

This means, however, that modern technology is not something that is found in the world as an important phenomenon, or even as a most important cluster of phenomena: the position is rather that the modern world is itself basically a technical world, "modern" culture is itself technical culture, and only insofar as this technical change of the world has extended (even geographically), does the "modern", the "today", the present exist. If culture is man's communication of his own essential reality to the world, this means that now technology is the basic form and expression of this self-communication. Technically moulded attitudes and ways of imagining and producing things are to be found not only within the narrow radius of technical plants, research laboratories, and production centres; their power is now greater, now scarcely hidden any longer, and they show it by the fact that they have begun to penetrate all dimensions of human society right down to the intimacy of private and family life. As a result of this penetration, a change is brought about in the entire order and significance of the world itself in which this process of thought and action goes on. Thus the "end of modern times" (R. Guardini) connotes also a new, perhaps lengthy period of man's fundamental relationship to the world, marked by positive knowledge and power, the epoch of the complete disclosure of the world to absolute technical reality (A. Weber) in a process from which "no sector of culture and no nerve in the human organism will remain immune" (A. Gehlen). Technical reality, the methods of production as well as its product in the various stages of a system where everything is regulated almost "soullessly" and ultimately by the system itself, makes itself the model to explain everything that exists and that happens, whether non-human or human. It makes itself the norm for what is to be regarded as true and as real. Even living human reality itself is subjected to this norm, and the expressions of human reality, knowledge and science, work and profession, leisure and recreation, etc., are drawn within the ambit of its insatiable drive towards achievement and are regarded as justifiable insofar as they serve the purposes of this appetite for power.

Nature (as source of raw materials and of energy), work (as the directed co-operation of all, and also as the form of behaviour which characterizes and sets a standard for life in general), and man (as a member of this modern society with its division of labour and other typical phenomena) unite in the one closed efficiency-system of the technical world (Max Müller).

Thus technology, going beyond its own sphere, comes to be the goal of that basic activity and the determinant of that basic attitude of man to the world which is winning increasing acceptance and already to a large extent characterizes our time. In the pattern of knowledge that is typical of this attitude, the "know-how" is no longer a complementary element, side by side with and indeed subordinate to personal "culture" and religious truth. Rather, this knowledge, this science of power, efficiency and work (uniquely and rightly confident of its success), now claims exclusive validity and consequently seeks to invade all areas of human life. Not from a neutral, formal definition of "technical", artisan production or methods, but only from the actual nature of modern technology as it penetrates man's life and world, and seeks to encompass it totally, can the astounding technical achievements and their overwhelming significance for the general mentality be grasped. These so frequently analysed phenomena can be understood only if they are seen as being themselves technically determined in reference to one another. They have been, to be sure, most clearly perceptible up to the present where they have arrived at their logical term in the entire social organization; nevertheless, insofar as they are already operative tendencies, they transcend the opposition between the political systems of East and West, for example in the drive for ever more perfect specialization and simultaneous centralization of automated production; in the growing bureaucratization, rationalization and standardization of the processes of living and of social relations; in the functionalization of these processes and relations and their corresponding loss of significance in themselves and their reduction to being merely the reward and goal of collective planning; in the axiomatic assumption that anything and everything is capable of manipulation and control; in the desire (although mostly unconscious) for the finalization of history, which is understood as the successful overcoming of all material obstacles and the dissolution of all social differentiation etc. These are all elements in the build-up of an understanding of the world such as H. Freyer among others has analysed. The uniformity of these and other phenomena that follow in the wake of a technology that claims exclusive validity as the basic form of truth and reality for man and the world, is well known. Divergent explanations, however, are given of the source of this process. Is it to be taken theologically as man's task in creation (F. Dessauer), or anthropologically as grounded solely in that human will to dominate and control which excludes everything accidental and intractable (M. Scheler)? Or is it to be seen as a matter of the "history of being", the "destiny" which alone makes possible and activates the unlimited will to bring everything under control and which comes to man out of the traditions of the West (M. Heidegger)?

A philosophical analysis that sees the essence of technology in the modern development we have outlined does not necessarily lead to the conclusion that this development has already penetrated fully and established itself in our present-day reality; nor does it follow that modern man's technical outlook on himself and the world has made permanently secure its inherent claim to exclusivity (nor even that this is possible). We do, however, assert that this process of the substantial modification of life through technology and the importance attaching to it is what in fact characterizes our present world. We hold too that all non-technical thought and action, insofar as they retain contemporary significance, do so only in confrontation with the general technical attitude which is shaping the world. They make use of its potentialities, thus falling to that extent at least under its influence, or they forego them deliberately in individual cases. Further, a society which, in keeping with its general traditional aims, tries to resist the total organization of its powers, gets the impression that today a society is possible and even already exists, which is prepared to go to the ultimate in the technical modification of all life, one which appears, even in principle, of superior efficiency; for the technical approach to the world creates this impression and shares it itself. This is quite independent of how far the technical development has actually gone or whether it has reached or can reach this position of superiority.

3. *Modern technology as a problem*. Through the conquest of nature man has in fact won a hitherto unknown freedom from the pressure of natural forces, even those within himself. Increased production of goods, shortening of working hours, progress in all aspects of medical science, means of communication spanning space and time, etc., make his life easier and make it possible to live more intensely. Granted this much, the critical question then arises as to what is understood by living intensely or completely, or by the full reality of human life. In the light of a particular, non-technical concept of man, modern technology can be a danger to human existence, and this can happen in spite of the increased security it gives, which it is neither possible nor desirable to eliminate. This danger does not consist in technical culture preventing "nature" (human and non-human) from being nature any longer. Wherever man lives, even in the most "primitive" cultures, nature is drawn into the sphere of human thought, desire and action and is changed, or else it remains an entirely alien element, threatening and hostile to man. Neither is the danger to be found in the "revolt" of the modern technical means against their inventors. Such a danger, arising as it does from the instrumental nature of these means, even though it is admittedly increased with their complexity and the great quantity of energy they bring into play, is to be dealt with, at least in principle, on the technical level. Neither a culturally weary romanticism asserting the unquestionable "unnaturalness" of technology, nor the demand for an "exorcism" of technology, which itself implies the acceptance of the personification of the technical means, meet the case. The real danger is rather that modern technology, while it opens the way to a higher level of human existence by surmounting the obstacles of natural forces, itself prevents the attainment of this higher level.

The curtailing of working hours brings increased leisure. But the technical environment remains a world of work and extends its influence to this leisure as time for a "break", for respite from and for work, as planned and organized entertainment (as opposed to recreation). The modern techniques of news-reporting, transport and co-operation extend the reach of communications so as to make ever more perfect communication possible. But communication itself falls under the influence of a theory and practice of merely transmitting information, standardizing opinions and manipulating consciousness. Technical means of research can serve as ways of making discoveries in the sense of the highest knowledge for truth's sake; in fact, this purpose is diluted or pushed aside by the actual method of research used in society and by the tendency to view knowledge and science first and foremost as a form of positive knowledge capable of being used as a path to power and of providing a suitable basis for such an approach. Philosophy is to reduce itself to a scientific justification and explanation for the positive technical world and society. Education loses its place of prominence in favour of technical training which seems more necessary and more deserving of promotion. Art becomes a marginal phenomenon or is reduced to the level of an ideological instrument in the scheme of technical purposes. Religion is regarded as a waste of effort, except insofar as it seems capable of being used provisionally as a means of securing order, providing leadership and preserving peace and tranquillity. Thus the real danger of technology and of the world which it regards as the only valid one and the only one worthy of extension is that, in the planning and realization of this world, he who plans and realizes is himself drawn into his own plan and process. This happens in such a way that man gains mightily in real power and freedom of action through the reduction of nature, of man himself and his social relations to factual and objective terms, but this he does no longer in his own person but merely as a member of the social efficiency-system. The danger is that only this purely socially functional reality will be recognized as of decisive importance, whereas that which cannot be reduced to a function or to a mere object, such as the individual in himself and in his relations to others and as a person in the community will find little or no place.

The multiplication of tasks of this conditional, functional nature distorts man's vision of the sole unconditional task of his freedom imposed on him personally (nor can he be relieved of it by anybody) with his life and with his death, that death which is the term for him of every such disposition in his regard and the final closure on all intervention on his behalf. The danger is, therefore, that the perfecting of technology in the world with the fascination of its undoubtedly great achievements would entail the dehumanization of man, not leading him to acceptance of himself in reconciliation, but rather to a permanent alienation in the world of nature and in the process of its conquest. The technico-scientific capacity of all things for being objectivated and manipulated, once actually experienced and established, inhibits the admission of recurring or even new basic experiences. Now insofar as it is precisely these basic experiences which are concerned with the acceptance of tradition or of new historical events, the fully technical world involves the assertion of a present without tradition and indeed without future, together with the subjection and in principle the termination of history. In place of a readiness for new historical development not calculable in advance, there is only the justifiable expectation of progressive evolution of what has already been implicitly and in principle secured. Realization is only a question of measurable time, not of immeasurable history. The ineradicable search after an immediate personal meaning for suffering and happiness, life, love and death, etc., meets a vacuum. The technological mutation of the world, which takes the substance from this immediate personal search and discovery of meaning in life, produces then the phenomenon of loneliness.

In considering the frequently posed question of what is "to be done" in this situation, it must be clearly recognized that the technical world is an actual human progressing development, which cannot be simply skipped over, whether "backwards" or "forwards". Therefore all attempts to shield man from the "dangers" of technology find themselves in an ambiguous position inasmuch as they can themselves appear to be technico-organizational activities, and indeed become such activities whenever, even in a spontaneous, well-intentioned way, they are inspired by the view that technology itself as a whole can be brought under "control", that is, that it can be regulated in technical fashion. Admittedly there are vitally important problems within our technical world, e.g., that of "control of production" (above all in the sphere of atomic armaments). But it is just as necessary to ask ourselves whether the importance of things is to be judged solely from the point of view of man's desire to establish his technical domain, with its smoothly efficient functional system of production and con-

sumption, or if it may not still be possible for man to have experience of a privation in his life which cannot be "removed" by any system of universal security, or to long for some essential, giving meaning to life, which it is beyond the capability of technical excellence to bestow. Only from this entirely different basic experience and search for meaning can the essential postulate and promise of technology be countered. Only here too can it be seen how it comes about that in a fully technical world which denies its own historical roots and so makes itself absolute, on the one hand, for example, all suffering which lies deeper than bodily need is overlooked or made little of, or at most can appear as a troublesome but manageable "disturbance". We see too how it is, on the other hand, that in such a world all thought, action or construction not serving to increase power or not having some measurable utility value, is played down as "unproductive" and relegated to a fringe area where its social effectiveness is marginal. Alternatively, it is, as far as possible, directed back into the technical system and harnessed to its purposes. It is the task of philosophy and theology, of medical science, education and pastoral care, to address themselves to this modern historical process in its many forms. If in this connection there is question of "adjustment", it must be understood in the sense that what is already actual (work and life, man and society, the traditional and the future) should be taken seriously, but taken seriously precisely in that enlightening, helpful contradiction, which not merely confirms the existence of this reality but also provides that which this reality tries to exclude from itself and yet truly needs.

See also *Culture, Tradition, Leisure* I, *Time* B, *Meaning*.

BIBLIOGRAPHY. J. Bernhart, *Der technische Mensch* (1946); A. Weber, *Farewell to European History: Or the Conquest of Nihilism* (1947); S. Giedion, *Mechanization Takes Command: A Contribution to Anonymous History* (1948); J. Ortega y Gasset, *Dehumanization of Art* (1948); id., *Man and Crisis* (1958); N. Berdyaev, *Towards a New Epoch* (1949); id., *Fate of Man in the Modern World* (1959); G. Marcel, *Le déclin de la sagesse* (1954); M. Heidegger, "Die Frage nach der Technik", "Wissenschaft und Besinnung", *Vorträge und Aufsätze* (1954); F. Jünger, *The Failure of Technology* (1956); F. Dessauer, *Streit um die Technik* (1956) (with bibliography); A. Gehlen, *Die Seele im technischen Zeitalter* (1957); H. Arendt, *The Human Condition*

TEMPTATION

(1958); M. Müller, "Philosophie – Wissenschaft – Technik", *Philosophisches Jahrbuch der Görres-Gesellschaft* 68 (1960), pp. 309-29; id., "Person und Funktion", *ibid.* 69 (1961), pp. 371–404; H. Freyer, *Theorie des gegenwärtigen Zeitalters* (1961); id., *Schwelle der Zeiten* (1965); O. Spengler, *Man and Technics* (1963); *Tecnica e casistica* (Atti del Convegno indetto del Centro internazionale di Studi Umanistici . . . a cura di E. Castelli) (1964); W. Armytage, *The Rise of the Technocrats* (1965); M. Brown, *On the Theory and Measurement of Technological Change* (1966); R. Guardini, *The End of the Modern World* (1968, translated from the 7th German ed., 1959).

Alois Halder

TEMPTATION

1. The nature of temptation is to be understood from the fact that man as a defective being is ordained to a perfection which transcends him. The impelling tendency to personal and therefore moral perfection is his mental orientation under the impulse of grace towards his fellow men and towards God. It comes to realization in the ordination of all human acts to the end of man, in proportion to his openness to the transcendent, that is, to the mystery of God, experienced though not capable of being comprehended. This ordination of man to perfection is exposed to many dangers, since man includes in his make-up a whole complex of tendencies which, by reason of the inner affectivity specific to each of them, have an impulse towards immanent fulfilment in relative autonomy unless they are directed by free, intelligent human acts to the demands of the person in his self-transcending development. The need for a conscious integration of the various particular tendencies arises from the fact that, in consequence of the unsureness of our human instincts and our state of concupiscence the tendency to realization of particular urges can come into prominence consciously and emotionally in a one-sided way. It is here that the possibility of temptation arises. Thus temptation always consists, in the last analysis, in the danger of jeopardizing the optimal dynamic orientation to a persistent growth in perfection by acts which would adversely affect this growth. The reason for such temptations can be extrinsic, e.g., endocrine changes, unexpected fantasies of imagination or of memory, conditions of emotional excitement resulting from repressions, etc.; but they can also result from human disappointment through others, the experience of one's own limitations, false

ideas of the will of God, and other factors of the superego and of the environment, none of which are directly subject to control.

Man is not directly responsible for the occurrence of such temptations. Temptations in this sense are rather an inevitable fact, the result of our dependence on pre-existent structures and external realities. Their occurrence is neither morally good nor bad. They are to be distinguished in principle from a conflict in conscience where a divergence occurs between several objective duties for which one has assumed moral responsibility. In a temptation, on the other hand, a value comes to the fore which is not related to the person as a whole but to a particular tendency, a merely conditionally moral value therefore, whose realization (at least in the form it takes at the time of temptation) is seen as running counter to the wellbeing of the person.

Thus if there is to be question of temptation, the particular value must not enter into the foreground of consciousness to such an extent that a choice between it and the personal value is no longer possible. That would be the case, if, as a result of ignorance or error, reflection on the significance of the particular value is not possible, or if a compulsive fixation arises of a neurotic or psychotic kind and so the freedom of choice is removed (see *Illness* II). It follows that there is no question of sin in yielding to such tendencies (which are contrary to the wellbeing of the person). Correspondingly, a limited direct responsibility exists where the instinctive desire which causes the temptation is so strong — no matter for what reason this may be — that the insight into the importance of the temptation is lessened and the power of the will to overcome it is hampered. When people yield to such temptations, we speak of sins of weakness.

These temptations arising from extrinsic reasons can on their part induce internal urges which are injurious to the optimum personal development and which can induce repressions which thwart the desire to know. This is the case when a person freely gives into temptations or instinctively yields to them (e.g., to bad influences in upbringing). Insofar as these urges are instinctive, one is not responsible for the resulting temptations. But if they are caused by freely yielding to extrinsic temptations, one is responsible for them, since the cause of them is freely accepted (e.g., cases of addiction, morbidly fostered hate complexes, etc.). Thus the

210

possibility of intrinsic temptations arises finally from man's pre-existing structures, both transcendental and empirical, as well as from the personal development of each individual.

Furthermore, with his limited intellect man cannot have an over-all picture of his potentialities. His decision to pursue a particular course of self-realization, therefore, is always affected by risk, inasmuch as he can only have a limited view of the effects of his decision and can therefore fail in it. The best possible moral decision is when the risk is so calculated that the factors of security and insecurity in action are held in balance. From the point of view of depth psychology, temptation always occurs when instincts have not been integrated and the tendency arises to attempt this integration in too anxious or too light-hearted a way. In the first case, trying to be too sure, a man will fail through not making full use of his capabilities; in the second he fails through overconfidence by going inconsiderately a-gainst existing structures and so negativing his capabilities. Temptation therefore always imperils the transcendental dynamism of human action. When temptation is overcome, this dynamism is free to operate again, and on a deeper level. According to whether the temptation affects man in the kernel of his existence, or only peripherally or as regards his fuller perfection, the act involved is morally grave or of less importance. It makes no difference whether the different degree of danger is due to the importance of the object to the person tempted, or to his degree of freedom with regard to the action.

2. Temptation is explained in the Bible a) as a *testing by God*. Especially according to early statements of the OT, God makes trial of the fidelity of his chosen people (Exod 15:25; 16:4; 20:20; Jg 2:22; 3:1–4) and of individuals, e.g., Abraham, whose temptation is constantly held up as an example (Gen 22:1; Ecclus 44:20; 1 Macc 2:52; Heb 11:17), or Job, whose fear of God Satan is allowed to test through sufferings (Job 1:11ff.; 2:5f.; see also the resultant temptations, Job 7:1; 10:17; 16:10; 19:12). In the later Wisdom literature there is more emphasis, under Hellenistic influence, on the notion of tempta-tion as a means of purification and education (Wis 3:5; 11:9; see Ecclus 2:1–6; 4:17; 33:1; cf. Jas 1:2, 12; Heb 11:17, 37).

b) *As seduction by the powers of evil.* Thus the diabolical temptation of our first parents (Gen 3:1–7). The Jewish thought is clearly that behind the evil tendencies of man there lurk the temptations of the devil and his evil spirits, which can be overcome only by the help of God.

This idea of the devil as the great tempter gains ground in the NT. It underlies the petition in the Our Father (Mt 6:13 = Lk 11:4) and the command of Jesus to his disciples in Gethsemane (Mk 14:38). St. Paul too sees underlying temptations the action of Satan (1 Thess 3:5; 1 Cor 7:5), but testifies at the same time that God gives the power to overcome temptation (1 Cor 10:13). Similarly the Apocalypse ascribes temptation to Satan (Rev 12:9; 13:14; 19:20; 20:3, 8, 10), while Jas 1:13f. affirms expressly that temptation does not come from God. In the Apocalyptic literature temptation is regarded as a characteristic of the eschatological tribulations (Dan 12:10; 1 Pet 1:6; 4:12; 2 Pet 2:9; Rev 2:10) and, especially in He-brews, as to be overcome in Christ (cf. 4:15; 2:18; see also Rev 3:10), since in Christ and in the reign of God which he has brought, Satan's rule over this aeon is ended.

3. Since temptations always consist in the danger of diverting man from the course he should pursue towards perfection, for the *moral victory* over temptation what is most needed is the will to perfection and therefore the openness to grace, which expresses itself in a love for virtue in general and for particular virtues. For in this way the integration of individual drives into the service of man's perfection is accomplished.

Since the immediate cause of temptations is, first and foremost, from extrinsic factors, the moral effort must concentrate on directing these factors. Yet it should be clear from the start that subjection to temptation is given with our nature as creatures, and is not removed by grace. But grace permits us to be calm in the face of temptations in reliance on God's help, so that our being tempted must, in the final analysis, be borne with humble resignation. Yet there are many means of overcoming temptations corresponding to their multiple causes. In extreme cases, resort should be had, for example, to medical treatment and psychotherapy. But there will always be need of avoiding unnecessary occasions of sin (Eph 5:15) in prudent consideration of one's own weakness and in responsibility for the tasks incumbent on each. Often the best way to deal with tempta-tions is through suitable distraction. Above all else there is need of the constant correction of the unrealistic prejudices and bias which settle in the superego. Besides, there is need of as unconditional a love of truth as possible and of the good in general, as well as patient and open-minded confrontation with the empirical realities (see *Health* II).

To overcome temptations caused by extrinsic factors there is need of constant formation of conscience. This must, in order to reduce or eliminate temptations, aim at the most reasonable balance possible between satisfaction of instincts and their sublimation, since only in this way will the necessary balance between openness to the transcendent and dependence on the immanent be maintained and proper account taken of the dynamic and historical character of the moral imperative of the unique occasion. For only thus will overestimation or underestimation of our own capabilities be avoided and our attachment to existing structures put at the service of personal perfection in the best possible way.

This means, further, that the temptations arising from intrinsic factors can be neutralized only to the extent to which voluntary false attitudes are corrected as far as may be through an approach to their causes that is both prudent and resolute.

4. A balanced pastoral training must avoid a biased simplification in its view of talents and tasks regarded as a source of temptation, since such a simplification always carries with it a projective interpretation of reality, repressing one or more of its aspects and thus in effect misinterpreting it. Prayer, as recommended by Scripture (Mk 14:38), constant watchfulness (Lk 8:13; 21:36) and above all firmness in virtue (Lk 22:28; cf. Mk 13:13; Rev 2:10), which is a means to steadfastness (Jas 1:2f.), will be the best help towards this balance. This presupposes that one seeks in directness and simplicity what is good and true insofar as it is capable of being known and put into effect in a concrete way and thus endeavours to master life in reliance on God's help who does not wish our failure in temptation but our success (Rev 3:5).

5. *Temptation of God* consists, a) from the biblical point of view, in wantonly provoking God's anger through lack of trust in divine providence. Thus when the chosen people murmured in the desert and doubted God's willingness to save them (Exod 17:2, 7; Deut 6:16; 9:22; Ps 95:8–11; Heb 3:8f.). In the NT Jesus rejects as a tempting of God the demand that he should understand his messianic mission in a worldly manner (Mt 4:7). 1 Cor 10:9 and Heb 3 warn the faithful not to tempt God as the Israelites did of old. In Acts 5:9 the attempt to deceive the Christian community is seen as a temptation of the Spirit of the Lord and in 15:10 St. Peter says that it is tempting God to try to burden pagan converts with the yoke of the law.

b) From the point of view of moral theology, tempting God is to be regarded as a provocation of God which is a betrayal of hope, inasmuch as it does not wait for salvation from God but tries to master human destiny by its own power and volition. It can express itself in many forms, ranging from the presumptuous reliance on the constant readiness of God to forgive, so that salvation is no longer hoped for in "fear and trembling" (Phil 2:12), to superstitious judgments about God. It is based ultimately on a false image of God which negatives and makes an idol of the sovereign mystery of God's love for us in freedom.

6. *The temptations of Jesus* related in Mk 1:12f.; Mt 4:1–11; Lk 4:1–13, need to be analysed with the help of form-criticism, to bring out the underlying messianic understanding of Christ. They imply that Jesus would betray his messianic mission if he succumbed to the temptation of not appearing, in spite of his messianic dignity, as the obedient servant of God and the second Moses withstanding the rebellious Israelites. The temptations of Jesus by the Pharisees (Mk 8:11; 10:2; 12:15; Lk 10:25) also have the purpose of putting the messianic mission of the Lord to the test. In contrast, the temptations of Jesus in Gethsemane (Mk 14:32–42 parr.) explicitly deal with Jesus' capability of being tempted, which in Heb 2:18; 4:15 is explained as a sign of his becoming like to us in all things, sin alone excepted. Jesus withstands the temptation through the acceptance of the suffering (cf. Heb 5:7–9) — the possibility of his succumbing is clearly excluded — and becomes in this way a model which makes it possible for us to follow him.

See also *Human Act, Devil, Concupiscence, Moral Theology* III.

BIBLIOGRAPHY. H. Seesemann in *TWNT*, VI, pp. 22–33; P. Valloton, *Essai d'une doctrine* de *la tentation* (1954); I. Owen, *Temptation and Sin* (1958); "La tentation", *Lumière et vie* 10, no. 53

(1961); B. Häring, *The Law of Christ*, I (1961); E. Grünewald, "Tiefenpsychologische Aspekte zur Situation der Versuchung", *Gott in Welt*, II (*Festschrift K. Rahner*) (1964), pp. 568–78; J. Dupont, *Les tentations de Jésu au désert* (1967) (with bibliography).

Waldemar Molinski

THEODICY

1. *The problem of theodicy*. It is not necessary to recall, much less demonstrate, that the world is stamped by misery and suffering, by evil in all its forms. There is no need therefore to "show the interest" of the question. It is an importunate one, today as ever at its most tormenting in the suffering of the innocent, especially what has been called the "absolute evil" of the suffering of children who are exposed to it not only inculpably but without even the possible defence of fleeing it. And today as always the existence of evil is regarded as the decisive proof against the existence of God. An age which has made empirical verification the ideal of knowledge must find this experience incontrovertible. The hypothesis of theology is falsified by the experimental facts of history. The result of the experiment seems obvious. Nonetheless, before entering into any details, the question arises as to whether there is in fact such a result — as to whether one has really come to a "result" at all. The experiment is carried out on man. And therefore it is still on principle "open", not because it is still going on, but because it is happening to him, in his freedom. He *and* his answer (his answers) are an intrinsic part of the result in this question.

2. *The various answers*. a) Dualism, one of the fundamental answers, was formulated in its most extreme form by Eastern religion. In the Parseeism of Zarathustra, good and evil are divine powers locked in conflict. But this notion had a constant influence on Western thought, from antiquity, Gnosticism and Manichaeism down to the later Schelling. Plato was the first to give a survey of the various earlier attempts to explain evil: the ἄπειρον (non-limited or neutral, indeterminate) of the Pythagoreans, the universal tension of opposites in all reality (Heraclitus), man in the sins of his pre-existence (Orphism, Empedocles) or the ignorance due to man's bodily state (Democritus, Socrates). For Plato, as for the Stoa, God is in no way the cause of evil (θεὸς ἀναίτιος), which is due to the human will (αἰτία ἑλομένου); cf. *Republic*, X, 617 e. But since he has to make evil (cosmic evil due to matter or anthropological due to the passions) unreal, merely apparent, in order to force it into his monism, even Plato's thought is coloured by a latent dualism. This dualism stands out clearly in the theory of emanations in neo-Platonism, which sees evil as the growing distance between things or degrees of being from their origin. This is to identify evil with the very existence of beings, in contrast to the (transcendent) One, from whom nonetheless beings emanate, or strictly speaking, which flows out into beings.

b) Insofar as neo-Platonism is the final and possibly supreme effort of Greek thought, the Greek answer to the problem of evil may be contrasted with the Jewish-Christian as being "cosmological", while the latter is "historical". It is apostasy from the almighty and good God. And the moral explanation of evil given by the Stoa is also bettered, since the incidence of freedom is not reduced — by an illogicality — to a monistic rationalism, but seen as a "dialogal" historical freedom (see *Freedom* II). Evil now appears as a punishment, though also as a testing-ground. But the limits of this explanation are clearly seen. It must fall silent before the incomprehensibility of God (as in the Book of Job), whose "works", whose "power" is made perfect therein (cf. Jn 9:3; 2 Cor 12:9).

c) This message of an almighty, good God who still permits evil is given by the early Christian thinkers as a real answer to the questions of the more or less dualistic religions which it encounters. Lactantius (*De Ira Dei*, 13) defines the problem by affirming (i) that God either wills to prevent evil but cannot (which would be to deny his omnipotence) or (ii) that he can, but does not will to (which seems to deny his goodness) or (iii) neither wills to nor can prevent it, or (iv) can and wills to prevent it (which is belied by the reality of evil). The attempted answers to (ii) resort to elements of Greek philosophy sometimes only imperfectly detached from their dualistic context — above all the interpretation of evil as a privation. New efforts are made to underline freedom and the resulting possibility of sin, into which God has to set men as he creates them (cf., for example, St. Irenaeus, *Adversus Haereses*, IV, 37, 1: βία θεῷ οὐ πρόσεστιν, "It is not in the nature of God to coerce"; Tertullian, *Adversus Marcionem*, II, 6f.). God's permission of the *real* misuse of freedom does not seem to be fully explained in this way. Early patristic efforts to formulate an answer within the framework of Jewish-Christian revelation with the help of Greek philosophy crystallized in a form which has remained authoritative to a great extent down to the present day in St. Augustine.

d) St. Augustine was preoccupied from his youth by the question of how there should be such perversity in human life in spite of God's sovereign power (*De Libero Arbitrio*, I, 4; *Epistola* 215; *De Ordine*, I, 1). His efforts were permanently coloured by the debate with Manichaeism, to which he had adhered for nine years (*Confessiones*, IV f.). Against a background of a highly acute sense of evil (cf. *Confessiones;* and e.g., *De Civitate Dei*, XX, 2), he denies all proper being to evil: "All that is is good. Hence evil, which I am trying to define, is not a substance" (*Confessiones*, VII, 18). His recognition of the goodness of all things may have been due to neo-Platonist writings. But his uncompromising certainty, which included matter (*De Natura Boni*, 18) was due to the Christian metaphysics of creation (see *Creation* I). Hence though he tries to forestall the Manichaean question as to the origin of evil by discussing its nature (*De Natura Boni*, 4), the divine origin of things is the basis of his interpretation. It follows that evil is *contra naturam*, since all nature as such is good (*De Civitate Dei*, XI, 17; *De Libero Arbitrio*, III, 36). It is a falling away from essence and nature, from its norm, order or character. It is a tendency to non-being; corruption, lack, "privation" (*De [Moribus Ecclesiae Catholicae et de] Moribus Manichaeorum*, II, 12; *Contra Epistolam Fundamenti*, 39; *De Natura Boni*, 4). This was the "positive" statement of St. Augustine's fundamental position: "Non est ergo malum nisi privatio boni" (*Contra Adversarium Legis et Prophetarum*, I, 5). The nature of evil is that it has no nature. It can only be real in the good. It is a dialectical testimony to the goodness of its underlying nature. If evil destroyed its good sub-stratum (sub-stance), it would eliminate itself into nothingness (*De Civitate Dei*, XI, 9, 22; XIII, 3: XIX, 12 f.; "Etiam voluntas mala grande testimonium est naturae bonae", XI, 17).

No less important in itself and in its consequences was the definite view of the types of evil taken by St. Augustine. "The word 'evil' is used in two senses: for what man does and for what man suffers. In the former case it means sin, in the latter punishment of sin" (*Contra Adamantum*, 26). Moral evil, wickedness, is evil without qualification, and indeed ultimately the only evil (*Contra Fortunatum*, 15). Physical evil, being the punishment of sin, is just and good (*De Civitate Dei*, XII, 3), a gift of God's goodness, a merciful warning (*ibid.*, IV, 1). St. Augustine did not close his mind to the suffering of the innocent. It was to purify and test them (*ibid.*, I, 8) and a proof of the solidarity of man in original sin (*ibid.*, XXII, 22) (see *Original Sin*). He also essayed a natural explanation of physical evil, especially in the non-spiritual realm, in the "finitude of the lower creation" (*Contra Secundinum Manichaeum*, 15). There is a necessary order of degree in which the particular serves the perfection of the organized whole, whose beauty is brought about by contrasts etc. (*Confessions*, VII, 19 — still in *De Civitate Dei*, XVI, 8).

God has nothing to do with (moral) evil. Its cause is simply "the will of the angels and then of men as they turned from the unchangeable to the changeable good" (*Enchiridion*, 23). The possibility of this evil is contained in the finite spirit's freedom which is nonetheless the great privilege of its nature: "He who is good by the free decision of his will is better than he who is good by necessity" (*De Diversis Quaestionibus*, 83, 2). The question remains as to why in fact sin is permitted. The solution, that even the sinful spirit still has a greater value than all non-spiritual beings (*De Libero Arbitrio*, III, 12, 16, etc.) does not carry conviction. The question is only underlined by the categorical "It is good that there should not be only good, but also evil" (*Enchiridion*, 96). However, *after* the permission of evil, it may be postulated, to some extent *a priori*, that God can and must will to bring good out of evil: "Bene utens et malis de malis bene facere", "Making good use even of evils to bring good out of evils" (*Enchiridion*, 27; 100; cf. *De Civitate Dei*, XXII, 1; *Epistola* 166, 15; "Even in our evil works the works of God are good": *De Musica*, VI, 30). Though evil — in the form of sin above all— is against the will of God, it is not absolutely outside his will. It is included in the indirect will which permits it (*Enchiridion*, 95 f.; *De Civitate Dei*, XI, 17; XVIII, 51; XXII, 2; *De Correptione et Gratia*, 43; *Sermo* 301, 5, etc.). St. Augustine merely suggests how God transforms evil into a greater good. Peter's denial, for instance, leads to progress in knowledge and humility (*De Correptione et Gratia*, 25; *Sermo*, 285, 3).

e) St. Augustine's view, with its neo-

Platonist components reinforced by the Pseudo-Dionysius (*De Divinis Nominibus,* IV, 18–35), remained unchallenged. Exceptions such as the optimistic emanationist system of Erigena (*De Divisione Naturae,* III, 6) or the views of Abelard (*Theologia Christiana,* V, 1321) and of Nicholas of Cusa (*De Ludo Globi* [edition of 1514], I, p. 154) on the best possible world, did not change the picture. St. Thomas Aquinas (*Summa Theologica,* I, q. 48f.; *Contra Gentiles,* III, 4–15; *De Malo*) developed St. Augustine's notion of evil with a consistency, logical and ontological, steeled by Aristotle (*Metaphysics,* IX, 9f.). He clarified the key-notion of permission (*Summa Theologica,* I, q. 19, a. 9; for its basis, cf. *ibid.,* q. 48, a. 2 ad 3; but contrast *I Sententiarum,* 46, 1, 3 ad 6), and also the indirectness of the origin of good "from" evil (*ibid.,* with a slight correction of St. Augustine), and stressed the essential deficiency of second causes, as "discharging" Providence of liability (*Contra Gentiles,* III, 71, 77). In essentials, Duns Scotus (*II Sententiarum,* 26–31) and Suarez (*Disputationes Metaphysicae,* IX, 9f.) agree with St. Thomas.

f) In 1710 appeared the *Essais de théodicée sur la bonté de Dieu, la liberté de l'homme et l'origine du mal* of G. W. von Leibniz. The term (first mentioned in a letter of 1697) thus came into philosophical and theological usage (cf. Rom 3:4f.; Ps 51:6; Milton, *Paradise Lost, ad init.,* "To justify the ways of God to man" [1667]). It became the usual term for all efforts to solve the problem of evil. The title indicates the whole problem and the questionability (also in the sense of whether it is worthwhile) of undertaking to "justify God" at the bar of human reason — though Leibniz, like Kant after him, did not exclude considerations derived from the theology of revelation. (Kant defined theodicy as "the defence of the supreme wisdom of the author of the world against the accusations brought against it by reason on the ground of the repugnant in the world" [*Schriften,* VIII, p. 255].) After Leibniz, theodicy in the strict sense became generally an explicit treatise, mostly part of the philosophical doctrine of God. (The historical circumstance, that "theodicy" flourished in Germany, especially in the 18th century, before Kant, and for a long time afterwards in England, and the way it concentrated the questions of God, man and the world, may have contributed to the use of "theodicy" to designate the whole treatise on the philosophical knowledge of God. It

displaced for a time the title "Natural Theology", which has now come back into use, though this too is not a very happy expression [see *Natural Theology*].)

But Voltaire's criticism of Leibniz's optimism in *Candide* is really more than a counter-position: it rather shows its real meaning, i.e., its fatality. The divine necessity by which this world — one might almost say, *faute de mieux* — is to be accepted as the best of all possible worlds, corresponds to the theory of the *malum metaphysicum* — a dispassionately objective and abstract thesis which ultimately is the same, at least in a certain respect, as the pessimism of Schopenhauer, the theory of the impotence of the spirit in the later Scheler or the present-day talk of the "absurd". It all comes down to what T. Haecker has called the specifically Western hindrance to a genuine theodicy: the tragic world-view (*Schöpfer und Schöpfung* [2nd ed., 1949]) — making the finite as such tragic.

g) Protestant theology emphasizes that it is not God who has to be justified to man, but man to God, which means *by* God. But traditional lines of thought from Christian theodicy are not excluded. Luther says that God produces good through evil (*WA,* LVI, p. 331). But from Zwingli down to Barth there is an undue tendency to identify real causality and mere permission of evil in God; so too in Baianism and Jansenism. For M. Flacius evil was the true reality of fallen man.

Some rare voices were raised among Catholics against the supposed vaporizing of evil by treating it as a privation; see Cajetan (*Commentarium in Summam Theologiae,* I/II, q. 71, a. 6; q. 72, a. 7); so too in the 19th century J. Kuhn and H. Klee. Lamennais (*Esquisse d'une philosophie,* II, 1, 4) took up again Leibniz's notion of *malum metaphysicum.* The "solution" of the problem of theodicy given by the redemption through Christ (W. Trillhaas in *RGG,* VI, col. 746) is discussed in scholastic theology on the occasion of the motive of the incarnation (e.g., de Lugo, *De Incarnatione,* 7, 2, 13). In more recent times it was discussed chiefly by Barth (*Church Dogmatics,* III/1 [1958]).

3. *The permanent question.* The answers, it was noted, are here part of the data. What is the result?

a) Modern theodicies may be described as pessimistic or optimistic. Both approaches assume that evil cannot be hindered. A different reason is given in each case. The

215

optimists hold that evil is intrinsic to the structure of the world, being the necessary pre-condition of a totality of a higher value. This is to relativize evil and to make it a means to an end. It takes the sting out of theodicy and makes it a justification of the cosmos — a "cosmodicy". It is no doubt a valid point, and one which was copiously considered by tradition, that much physical evil has an intrinsic usefulness and purpose in the existing world. (Pain, for instance, functions as an alarm. But even here it has been asked, why does it hurt so much? — to say nothing of useless pain.) But what is one to think of such a world order? The attempt to upgrade this world to the best of all possible worlds fails on philosophical and theological grounds. The perfection of the material world always admits of a higher perfection. The exclusion of the infralapsarian character of the world, manifested to some extent in its constitutional deficiency, means in any case that the additional (physical) evil, insofar as it is the consequence of sin, and above all sin, evil itself, is emasculated and reduced to the ontological level.

In contrast to this effort to minimize evil, pessimism exaggerates it and erects it into an absolute. But this distortion or evacuation of the theistic notion of God makes all theodicy pointless. Every effort to hypostatize evil is belied by the priority of the true, good and beautiful essentially intrinsic to all human speech, thought and values, and attested even in the fundamental notion of evil and pessimism, all contrary data notwithstanding. Pessimism in particular, which in its most definite forms elevates evil to the rank of an evil primordial will, shows that the central problem of theodicy is the problem of moral evil, or, in theistic terms, the permission of sin. However, the pessimistic notion of evil as the inescapable destiny of man in the world, the view of the world as a tragedy, has some merit. It can help one to gain a deeper understanding of the Christian theodicy inspired by salvation-history and Christology, and hence of the "sin of the world" which modern individualism, even on the moral plane, tends to be unaware of.

b) Each human being comes into the sphere of influence of sin, a "hamartiological" determination of this world, which Pauline theology affirms to be the world-wide effect of the first sin of man. If it may be assumed that in the original state of man his nature, pure, sound and true, was to have been directly the (quasi-) sacrament of his holiness-in-grace, then after sin, which destroyed both his sanctity and his soundness, the convulsions of nature had to be the effect and sign of the status of the world, now without grace and wholeness, not being in Christ. Thus the world, insofar as it is affected by the Fall, is also a *sacramentum diaboli*. Since the soundness of peace and joy ceased to be directly the sacrament of salvation through its sinful misuse, redemption from sin could only be and be expressed in the opposite, in disaster, suffering and death. The mystery of the cross was necessary and its meaning begins to dawn here. The ambiguity of physical evil in the light of original sin — it is both the product of finite material nature and the destiny brought about by sin — is left behind by the free historic act of redemption. It is given the clear sacramental character of mediating the new salvation (cf. W. Kern, *Geist und Leben* 32 [1959], pp. 58f.).

c) This seems to pose the problem of evil and theodicy in its most extreme imaginable (or unimaginable) form. The cross of Christ as the consequence of sin makes all metaphysical tragedy-writing anaemic. But it is precisely the statement of the problem in this infinitely acute form which is the "solution". The problem of the sin of man becomes the mystery — or scandal — of the love of God. Just as sin was the occasion of the cross *(in ordine executionis)*, so too the cross is the inner ground *(in ordine intentionis)* of the permission of sin. Even between human beings, when one fails in love and the other overcomes the disaster by forgiveness, love takes on a new and finer depth and inwardness, the unique morning freshness of love redeeming and redeemed. And this can only be through the free will to love of the one who has not failed. But it could not have been at all without the failure. If this is so, then it was "necessary" (cf. Lk 24:26) that Christ should have been the incarnate revelation of the love of God in some similar way. By becoming sin and curse for men (cf. 2 Cor 5:21; Gal 3:13) he was to create them anew, raising them up out of sin, conquering evil by patiently redemptive, crucified love, which thus radiated and was revealed as infinite power.

The harmartiological dimension of evil is transformed into the staurological reality of Christ (on the cross), like the death of man carried over into the death of God. See St. Augustine, *In Joannis Evangelium*, 12, 10, and *Sermo* 350, 1: "Being killed (as man) by death he (God, in his humanity) killed death." The paschal confession of the *felix culpa* has its biblical foundation in St. Paul's proud affirmation that the greater the power of sin, the greater is the power of grace (Rom 5:20f., with the rejection of all the fallacies of a mystique of sin, Rom 3:8; 6:1). The decisive text of the gospels with regard to the key-notion of the permission of sin is the parable of the prodigal son (Lk 15:11–32; cf. for instance Lk 7:36–50; Jn 12:24f.; 2 Cor 12:9). The achievement of Christ has basically replaced the disruption of sin and its consequences, by recapitulating the disruption, that is, by re-living and repairing it. The Christian optimism which believes in the power of God's love will be one with Christ in suffering — not brushing aside — all sense of pessimism — and in breaking through it to transform it into the resurrection. The problem of evil coincides with that of the motive of the redemptive incarnation of God in Christ. This is what gives it its rank and scope, which goes far beyond the acquisition of this or that virtue, like patience "out of" persecution or contrition "out of" sin.

d) When dealing with the problem of evil, it is not enough to make the formal *a priori* statement of philosophy that evil *must* be reconcilable with the infinite power, wisdom and goodness of God. An effort must be made to give also a concrete and hence historically verifiable answer. And this must ultimately be a theological answer, one given by God himself. But the nature of the proposed "solution" must be kept in mind. It is never merely intellectual and speculative.

To speak of the cross in such terms as were used above must not be allowed to cloak the fact that sin is revealed — including forgiven sin and indeed in the light of this forgiveness — as what ought never to have been or be. Love does not need sin. What sort of love would that be! But the triumph of love is the disclosure of sin as sin, that is, as utter worthlessness: worthless as repugnant and absurd, as ineffective and hence in every sense of the word meaningless. This is the only approach in which sin remains sin without being made to mean something else. Wickedness and evil are taken for what they are.

But in this same approach love takes on a new dimension with regard to evil. The meaningless, while given no chance to justify itself, is taken into the service of meaning. Here too, therefore, it must be firmly maintained that seemingly conflicting data are reconciled, though how it is so cannot be satisfactorily explained to the full. That it is so and how it is so are not equally clear, as in so many cases. But this should not lead theodicy to fall into the vicious circle which is one of today's greatest dangers: that the insistent experience of evil should cloud the clear conviction of the existence of God which is to overcome its darkness. In any case — in response to the experimental disproof of God mentioned above (1, *ad init.*), the equally unquestionable instances of meaningful purpose must be insisted on. This is not a matter of choosing between optimism and pessimism according to which of them offers the best figures, as may be seen from the true nature of such experience (see *Meaning*). But the character of suspense and "hope" in this experience needs to be brought out better than was mostly done hitherto. (The attempts of the Augustinian medieval tradition etc. to integrate somehow the actual damnation of angels and men, e.g., to the glory of God's vindictive justice, may be taken as read, not superciliously, but without any further speculative interest.) The complete intellectual clarification of evil would actually bar the way to the explanation of it which can be sensed. To grasp it fully intellectually would be to cease to grasp it as it ought to be grasped, as an abiding question (see *Hope*).

For if here the answer is part of the result of the experiment, so too is the answer which each one makes to the previous answers. And the answer is not only the commitment which obtains in all knowledge and experience (as the actuation of the *cognoscens* as well as the *cognitum in actu*). It is a fully practical and active hope. Evil is a summons to action. This does not solve the question. The question remains. But just as such action can take place only in hope, and not in despair, true hope exists in the face of evil only as the fighting hope which is struck as it strikes. If there are questions which are not to be "answered" but lived (R. Guardini), evil is one of them. Hence the train of thought leads back to the "staurological" consideration (3c), not in the sense of an answer but in the sense of a listening to the abiding question. Thus the question remains a summons. Love is that by which evil is made good.

BIBLIOGRAPHY. See bibliographies on *Evil, Meaning, Providence, Sin* I; also: G. W. Leibniz, *Essais de Théodicée* . . . (1710; E. T. ed by D. Allen, 1966); G. Philips, *La raison d'être du mal d'après St. Augustin* (1927); M. C. D'Arcy, *The Pain of this World and the Providence of God* (1935); J. Jolivet, *Le problème du mal d'après St. Augustin* (1936); W. Grundmann, "χαχός", *TWNT*, III, pp.

469–87; L. Lavelle, *Evil and Suffering* (1940); J. Maritain, *St. Thomas and the Permission of Evil* (1942); T. Deman, *Le mal et Dieu* (1943); C. S. Lewis, *The Problem of Pain* (1944); W. Greene, *Moira: Fate, Good and Evil in Greek Thought* (1944); S. Petrément, *Le dualisme chez Platon, les Gnostiques et les Manichéens* (1947); A.-D. Sertillanges, *Le problème du mal*, 2 vols. (1948–51); M. de Coursey, *The Theory of Evil in Saint Thomas* (1948); C. Joad, *God and Evil* (1952); M. Buber, *Good and Evil* (1953); J. A. Sanders, *Suffering as Divine Discipline in the Old Testament and Post-Biblical Judaism* (1955); M. Scheler, *Liebe und Erkenntnis* (1955); G. Harder, "πονηρός", *TWNT*, VI, pp. 546–66; B. Lonergan, *Insight* (2nd ed., 1958), pp. 657–703; K. Barth, *Church Dogmatics*, III/1 (1958) (creation as justification); B. Welte, *Über das Böse* (1959); C. Journet, *The Meaning of Evil* (1963); W. Brugger, *Theologia Naturalis* (1964), pp. 369–90 (with bibliography); J. Maritain, *God and the Permission of Evil* (1966); E. Lohmeyer, *The Our Father* (1966); J. Ricœur, *The Symbolism of Evil* (1967); W. Eichrodt, *Theology of the Old Testament*, II (1967) (see index under "Sin", "Evil"); W. Kern, "Theodizee: Kosmodizee durch Christus", *Mysterium Salutis*, III/2 (1969).

Walter Kern and *Jörg Splett*

THEOLOGICAL METHODOLOGY

I. Principles: A. Preliminaries. B. The Internal Dimension of Theological Epistemology. C. The External Dimension of Theological Epistemology. D. Concluding Remarks and Prospects. II. Loci Theologici.

I. Principles

A. Preliminaries

Various expectations are likely to be aroused by this title. In English it may suggest that general questions are to be discussed concerning the status of religious propositions from a viewpoint which need not be that of Christian faith, or even where it is, would not be chosen with traditional Catholic distinctions, say, of natural and revealed theology in view, but rather discussions concerning the validity of religious statements considered as forming a class alongside the classes of empirical and poetic statements. For discussions of this kind see *Religion* I C, *Faith* I, *Religious Experience*, *Apologetics* I, *Fundamental Theology*. This article is concerned with the epistemological structure of ecclesial theology, and takes for granted at least the existence of a continuing tradition of systematic theological articulation of the gospel in the Catholic Church. However, it would be unsatisfactory simply to refer to other articles without some brief discussion of the

system of categories which supports this distribution of topics, since a theological epistemology should at least be concerned to examine its own epistemological status as well as that of theology itself (see *Theology* I).

Clearly theological epistemology consists in a reflection upon theology considered as an autonomous intellectual discipline or "science". So long as the scientific character of theology in general, or indeed the specific scientific procedures familiarized by tradition or custom, were not in question, it was possible for a treatise of theological epistemology to take shape and lead an independent existence, even generate its own conventional disputes, without reference to questions of general epistemology, or even to theology itself. It is commonly the case that treatises on methodology at best rationalize inventive intellectual procedures already being practised, or more often simply ossify these procedures in a theoretical structure long after they have ceased to be practised or even relevant. Treatises of this irrelevant kind are still being written in our day by Catholic theologians (which is the only reason for mentioning them), after the closed world of Catholic theology has been notably breached by new creative theological thinking, by intensive investigation of some areas of the history of theology and the pressures of secularization. These latter pressures are intensifying, and should be welcomed insofar as they force Catholic theologians to reconsider the nature of their task of communication with the world, and in particular the structure of theological meaning.

The acceptance of a necessary division of labour, then, must not be taken to prejudge the question as to whether a different approach to theological epistemology may not be more in accordance with a world in which traditional categories are increasingly being revised. Such an approach would not be able to assume in advance the theological distinctions delivered to it by tradition, but would have to adopt a critical role in regard to them. For in the most general terms, the task of theological epistemology, like that of theology itself, is to establish communication between Church and world, in such a way that the internal ecclesial perspectives open out upon and are open to perspectives which emerge immanently in the course of a secular history to which the Church's theology, and revelation itself, provide no immediate key. Theology is an encounter of Church and world in which the meaning of the gospel becomes articulate as an illumination of the world; and the exploration of the structure of this meaning in theological epistemology must itself be the continuing actualization of such an encounter (see *Church and World*).

No such ambitious claim is made for this article, above all because the new movements in theology make it too difficult to practise that reflexive role of a methodology which consists in making and correlating maps of territories already explored by others. This metaphor is already a simplification, for it transposes into the spatial order a problematic which is temporal and historic; now it is in this latter order, as we shall see, that the theological problem itself today becomes increasingly explicit and that the solutions begin to take shape.

We shall assume, then, in what follows, that there is a "special" theological epistemology and methodology concerned with the reflexive analysis of theological structures of meaning delivered to us by a continuing tradition of theology practised in the Church, and it is only by implication and on particular topics that we shall take into account problems of meaning and knowledge in general. This special theological epistemology, then, will share with all theology the double *a priori* of ecclesial faith, which will serve as its internal dimension; and in the external dimension proper to all theology it will be concerned to authenticate the claim of theology to intellectual autonomy while assuming without detailed discussion its claim to be "intellectual" at all, i.e., to propose meaning and truth. That is to say, the basic question as to whether theological statements mean anything *at all* will not be discussed here.

B. The Internal Dimension of Theological Epistemology

Reception of the Church's continuing tradition of theology is a matter of faith. This is not of course to say that every proposition in every theological system is an object of faith; but faith is a presupposition of insight into the meaning of these diverse theologies, of understanding that they are unified in the object or the realm of their concern — very simply, are trying to talk about the same things. This is a point of some importance now that we are more ready to admit the existence of plurality and even profound

discontinuities within the single continuing tradition. It is no longer seriously possible to offer an anonymous handbook, however large, and call it simply "Catholic Theology"; it was not long ago that even Karl Barth, with some justification, seemed to suppose that this was so. Communion, ordinary or extraordinary, in the Church in faith, offers access to a universe of meaning, not open to those who reject this communion. So the Church as a continuing historical institution, and active spiritual communion of faith in the Church, together form the double *a priori* of theological meaning. This ecclesiality of faith is of course realized in different degrees, while in all degrees tending by an inner impulse to the union of communion; and the continuing validity of the expression "Catholic theology" is due to the self-defining activity of the Church from time to time in excluding theological articulations of faith declared not to be Catholic: the *positive* unity of Catholic theology is not itself capable of exhaustive theological articulation but is the one *reality* of God, Christ, the Church. The Catholic theologian accepts this power of the (hierarchically structured) Church community to define itself and its authentic witness with respect to what it is not in such a way that the *a priori* of ecclesial faith for a Catholic theologian can be partially exhibited in a series of historical monuments which are moments of the Church's explicit self-definition. The Catholic theologian's world of meaning has fixed points which are themselves meaningful and not just ineffable (see *Magisterium, Council, Pope*), though these points do not fall into a systematic order among themselves, do not exhaustively display the *a priori* of ecclesial faith, and are ultimate only in the simultaneous alternatives they exclude (i.e., they are open to interpretation within perspectives which are not their own).

Now this faith is not merely the immanent life, in part explicit and in part implicit, of a historic community and a culture in which men creatively bring their own meaning to light; the unifying sense of the whole world of meaning accessible in faith is transcendental disclosure of this meaning to and for men, intrinsically communication to men of meaning as gift. In the traditional theological terminology, this is the dimension of the theological world of meaning which is called revelation or gospel. The meanings entertained and exchanged in this community inform the community — not only in its language but also in its conduct, its institutions, its rites, its art and music — in such a way that while remaining human meanings (this will be examined when we look at the external dimension of theology) they are in principle capable of unification in no human meaning but only in an ultimate meaning, the Meaning of meaning, God. Further, this ultimate Meaning has declared itself historically as Word made man, Logos and First of many brethren, Son of God and Son of man; and in doing so has associated with this figure in human history other men who would scripturally embody in their witness to him the eschatologically ultimate character of this self-declaration of Meaning. This self-declaration is an ἀρχή, an absolute beginning: it is the beginning of the gospel (cf. Mk 1:1; Lk 1:2; Jn 1:1), which is permanently present in the communion of faith, permanently recoverable as spring and source in the meanings entertained and exchanged in the community. The scriptural deposit of the primitive multiplicity of meanings of the one ἀρχή is continually made present by informing new complexes of human meaning; in its own unity in multiplicity — the "theologies" of the NT (and OT) writings — it offers a pregnant instance of the nuclear character of the complexes of ecclesial meaning. For every explicit Catholic life is a "theology", a project and a declaration of the Meaning of Catholic meanings; and theology as "science" and autonomous discipline can only reflect upon this lived meaning by being itself an instance of lived meaning.

C. THE EXTERNAL DIMENSION OF THEOLOGICAL EPISTEMOLOGY

The Word which unifies the multiplicity of Christian meanings is offered to us through those meanings not only for our consent (or refusal) but also for our assent (or denial). At one and the same time it invites us, by our consent and assent, to depart from where we are (cf. Gen 12:1) to find ourselves in some "higher" or "deeper" truth, to ascend the degrees of the "ontological comparative" (Fink) to find ourselves "in the Truth", "in Christ". Perhaps it is only in the formal system of modern mathematics and logic that truth is reduced to the display of the internal consistency of axioms and postulates; but even here there is the possibility of "applications", as in the part played in information theory by the "truth-table"

systematization of the naive Yes-No, assent-dissent, character of human statements. At any rate, both the Yes-No character of statements and their claim to "significance", to depth of truth, are prominently and actively present in theological statements (see *Logic*).

In this section we shall be concerned with the human dimension of theological meaning and its twofold truth, especially insofar as this meaning has been deliberately given structure by the reflexive activity of a theologian's mind. Just because the primitive NT witness to the ἀρχή, itself assumed into the ἀρχή, is language and articulate at all, it is not only "revelation" but also "theology", since the gospel, no matter how communicated, is proposed to us as human communication, ordered and unified by a human mind. Even the synoptic gospels, as has been clearly shown in recent years, are not just collections of narratives and *logia,* but each exhibit a unifying constructive intention proper to the evangelist. But even if we had nothing but random collections of sayings and narratives of isolated incidents, there would still be implicit in them a comprehension of the world. In the Pauline texts in particular, it is possible to analyse the constructive and supporting function of concepts available in Hellenistic civilization; and in the Johannine writings one can learn to overhear the resonances of a variety of pursuits of the divine at the end of the 1st century integrated by John into a concentration of meaning in the Word made flesh. But John is not only a poet of Jesus; as theologian *par excellence* he is at least as insistent as any NT writer on the exclusive and decisive character of his witness in the rejection of false teaching.

The Pauline and Johannine testimonies provide us with two very different styles of theological "construction", both deriving from and referring to the same ἀρχή (compare Jn 1:1–18 with Col 1:15–20, and again Heb 1:1–4). We may study even in that human meaning which is revelation a human evolution and amplification which continues to be revelation. The rediscovery and appropriation of the *literary* complexity of the NT writings is the absolutely primary prerequisite of any theologizing today if we are to overcome the split between "exegesis" and "theology" and avoid certain misguided forms of "biblical theology" (neither biblical nor responsibly theological) due to the uneven growth of the Catholic mind for many centuries. For the diversification of meaning in creative literature and its inner integration there into a complex unity of insight and comprehension helps us to understand diverse possibilities of organization in the biblical literature. To recognize that saga, gospel and novel are different literary genres should not mean that we must forget the novel when we study saga or gospel. It is also through a sense of the insights afforded by creative literature that we can best appreciate the historicity of the NT witness, its character as *Ereignis,* illuminating event. The special significance of literature here is that unlike plastic art und music, it retains not only the invitatory aspect of truth, the appeal to traverse the degrees of the depths of being, but also a continuity with those pragmatic or empirical uses of language which emphasize or isolate its Yes-No aspect. It is this Yes-No or propositional-logical use of language which has dominated Catholic theology for centuries until our own day. Both the dialectic and logical grammar of early scholasticism and the newer "scientific" logic of Aristotle's *Posterior Analytics* in classical scholasticism helped to construct a theological world in which meaning was articulated as argument and not as insight. The effect of this one-sidedness may still be seen today in textbooks for theological students, ordered in the form of theses to be proved or defended (so a modern French series still in course of publication). Even if syllogistic demonstration is no longer thought to be the normal or the ideal mode in which to manipulate all meaning or manifest all truth, there still seems to be some uneasiness about wholly abandoning a theological style which prized clarity and decisiveness above exploration in depth.

This uneasiness has its real justification. As we have seen, the Church community has repeatedly had to establish its own identity by a process of self-definition involving exclusion. The revealed truth of God has an identity *in* the world. The offer of truth to the Church and by the Church is not only an invitation to ecstatic vision but it also defines the way to that vision. The truth of the Church's witness is still human truth and as such finite; what it excludes is not nothing, for only all-inclusive, infinite Truth could have only nothing to reject. But in this "ecumenical" age of the Church we have learned to exclude from within, as it were, by taking up into Catholic truth whatever has its rightful place there, by fulfilment rather than anathema. No Catholic theology then can afford to abandon argumentation and the precision which it demands; yet exclusive emphasis on this Yes-No character of truth, and still more, its syllogistic style, would impoverish theology unduly. After all, there seems to be no lack of dispute and controversy in other disciplines, such as history and letters, which do not lay down such artificial standards of rigour; and such disputes are not always about nothing. As has been seen in the theology of the development of dogma, a theory of the amplification of meaning by syllogism alone has the most pernicious effects. In our own times the problems of missionary adaptation and more generally of the communication of the gospel to a new and changing world have made it necessary to take more seriously the complexities involved in the exchange, amplification, translation and reintegration of meaning.

It has appeared in what has been said that the construction of a theological structure of meaning is bound to employ methods which are at least similar to those employed in other disciplines. In the investigation of the Scripture, for instance, it must practise the ordinary techniques of historical and literary criticism; explicit logical theory can at least serve as a negative check and an instrument of analysis; the justification of particular propositions may remind us of the procedures by which decisions are arrived at in law, thereby bridging the gap between procedures of verification in theology and in the natural sciences. The question arises whether there is anything uniquely characteristic of theological method in the construction of theology. We may take as our point of departure Collingwood's useful distinction between a proposition as a mere statement and that same proposition as an answer to a question. Certainly this distinction serves to show the interest of the commonest of the scholastic procedures: the use of the *quaestio* as a technique of exploration by interrogation first of conflicting authorities and later of conflicting chains of argument as well. Every theological statement can be put to the question simply by putting it in interrogative form: *utrum* . . . As an answer to a question the proposition has a new epistemological status as part of a *structure* of meaning. The questions now arise as to the proper sources of the meaning which is so structured, the nature of the structure, and the perspectives which sustain the structure.

The question of the proper sources of

221

theology as an autonomous discipline has already been touched on under B. Here it is only necessary to inquire into those complexes of meaning through which revelation is communicated, in regard to the possibility of ranking them according to some principle. Where theological structure is held to be strictly demonstrative, the complexes are ranked according to their probative force as *loci theologici*. Thus a sort of general theological criteriology can be set up, sometimes pretending to a high degree of refinement, as in the elaboration of theological qualifications. The manifest artificiality of an excessive refinement sought after more for its own sake rather than for the benefit of theology itself should not blind one to the general importance of this discussion (e.g., what exactly is the status of various papal pronouncements on contraception? What difference is made to Mariology as a whole by the definition of the Assumption as a dogma?). Yet as soon as we remember that the original complexes of meaning are not merely isolated items waiting to play their part as arguments in the structure of a demonstrative theology but have their primary value in diversely mediating revelation in a historic process of communication, then we must critically examine the idea of a theological structure of meaning which could tend to distort revelation in this way. In the classical moment of Latin theology it was possible for St. Thomas Aquinas, more decisively than any of his contemporaries, to determine the structure of theology as an Aristotelian science, in which the articles of faith, dependent upon the divine vision itself, served as principles for the body of actual or potential theological conclusions which could be drawn from them. It may be observed that St. Thomas's actual practice, like Aristotle's own, was fortunately a good deal less rigid than his epistemological theory. The science of theology was seen as another form of the single *sacra doctrina* delivered to us by the (glossed) Scriptures; but this mediation was conceived of as taking place through the summary of the Scriptures in the Creed, such that wherever Scripture dealt with historical particulars not enunciated in the Creed, it had merely illustrative or supplementary value. Once again, fortunately, St. Thomas's practice was much more generous and genuinely historical than this theory. But in the last resort it is an archaic theory of meaning and of language which supports both the theory of probative arguments and the theory of theological structure as an Aristotelian science: the theory that meaning is accessible and manipulable only in the form of essentialist concepts. In spite of the considerable sophistication of medieval logical grammar, in spite of St. Thomas's own developments of this grammar in an ontological sense in his theory of analogy, the theory of meaning implicit in all scholastic theology is dominantly "ontic", tied to the specific natures of the cosmic world. Concepts, in St. Thomas's epistemological theory, are still "similitudes" of natures; historical meaning is not genuinely meaning at all, for it is only in the generality of the concept and of "science" that meaning can be authentically realized.

Thus a critical examination of the presuppositions of the epistemology of scholastic theology leads us to reconsider both its theory of the original complexes of meaning and its theory of the adequate and appropriate structure for that meaning. But before making some suggestions of our own, we must further consider the perspectives which sustain the structure of meaning in a more than logical sense. This is the question of the "hermeneutic locus" of a theology discussed by Protestant theologians like Fuchs and Ebeling. In simple terms, any theology which is to be more than biblicist, a mere rearrangement of biblical themes, must adopt general perspectives within the horizon of which complexes of meaning acquire mutual significance. In St. Thomas's theology, for instance, such a perspective is supplied by the order of creatures to the Creator as *principium et finis,* Origin and End. St. Thomas himself mentions another perspective, the whole Christ, which has been taken up in our own day, as seeming to offer a more biblical schema, and there have been many rather naive attempts since the first shock of Darwinism died away, to adopt the schema of generalized evolution, as by Teilhard de Chardin. It would be a mistake to regard the adoption of a generalized theological perspective as a matter of detached and deliberate choice. The perspective must present itself with the ultimate obviousness which only the sense of an epoch can supply. Certainly this must be so if the theology is to speak to men of its time and to provide a context for continued theological debate; but the fundamental ground for the articulation of the perspective must lie deeper than the individual theologian's own conscious and reflexive mind; he must be guided by a kind of prophetic insight into that order of relevance which is taking shape in history under the sway of Providence. Such a perspective, appropriate to the epoch into which we are moving today, might be provided, we suggest here, by the schema of God as the Meaning of meaning. This is in fact the perspective within which this article has been written.

D. CONCLUDING REMARKS AND PROSPECTS

The notion of a theological epistemology, as we have seen, is itself historically conditioned, as indeed is the notion of a general philosophical epistemology. There is a "family-line" of investigations to which the (primarily 19th-century) notion of epistemology belongs, and whose lineal descendants today form the family of investigations into meaning: Heidegger, Wittgenstein, Merleau-Ponty, Gadamer. This work of philosophical reflection was preceded and is today accompanied by an "ontic" preoccupation with meaning in such diverse fields as linguistics, existential analysis, behaviour studies, social anthropology or ethnology, literary criticism, to name only a few. The search for identity in the new nations of the post-colonial era, in a tension between traditional religions and new technology, is a preoccupation with the redefinition of meanings. The personal search for the "meaning of life" has to be conducted within the transcendental horizon of the question of the meaning or truth of Being and its historicity. If we reject the God "out there", we must equally reject the God "in here", and learn to put the God-question as a search for ontological meaning (see *God-World Relationship*).

These general reflections are intended to support the suggestion that the reformulation of theology taking place in our time demands a corresponding reformulation of theological epistemology. If the schema of God as Meaning of meaning is accepted as a possible perspective for theology, and thus as a possible formula for "natural" theology, our view of the complexes of theological meaning and their structural reintegration in an autonomous theological "science" can no longer be governed by an archaic theory of meaning. Theology, while continuing necessarily to practise the onto-theo-logical mode in which its formulations have been uttered historically, must become explicitly aware of its own existence as a kind of meta-theology; the theological epistemology corresponding to this meta-theology would be an explication of the "meta", the dimension of this meta-theology in the historical process of ontological meaning. We may ask, but only from our "epistemological" viewpoint, what such a meta-theology would look like, since it seems that there are only anticipations of it today.

It would certainly involve the "destruction" of all previous theologies and their "recapitulation" in a history of meaning which is also a history of being. This would even include the revealed biblical "theologies", although these would continue to retain their privileged place in the history of theological meaning. The considerable body of work which has been done in recent years on the history of theology is an important first step towards this "destruction", but too little of it has faced up to the real ontological problems involved in this apparently historicist relativization. We have to ask what is the *meaning* of this historic succession of theologies (and of the sterile repetition of unimportant variants), and we have to ask this question not within a presupposed perspective of any one of them but ask it radically as part of *the* theological problem of the meaning of God and man for one another. The substantive ("ontic") answer to this question we already have in Jesus Christ, and can have no other. It is the ("ontological") meaning of this substantive meaning we must continually search for without expecting any final answer. Thus the ἀρχή of this meta-theology would be the λόγος – εἰκών – μυστήριον τοῦ θεοῦ, the Word-Image-Mystery of God, the divine Wisdom, ἀγία σοφία. How could this ontological meaning become articulate? What "structure" could it have in a single mind? In fact it could only exist as a total human culture, the progressive discovery of a single human identity in Christ as the historic process of the diverse but related processes of self-discovery going on in distinct cultures all over the globe in response to the challenge and threat of a uniform technological mass-culture. There is at least a single discernible adversary, not to be subdued by the mere repetition of traditional truths, Christian or other. The individual theologian could only make contributions to such a theology-as-culture, and only possess it as his own "culture" according to his own capacity, and not as a *Summa*.

The cultural "structure" of such a meta-theology is as much or as little a *logical* unity as a song or a smile. It is a comprehension of the depth of meaning or truth in the affirmation of particular truths; it is a standing fast in holiness, a "Thy will be done". It passes into music, the inarticulate, into silence. At the same time, precisely because this theology is concerned with the ontological dimension of truth in its cultural structure or organization, it will need to proceed dialectically, by exclusion as well as affirmation, to the inclusive truth of humanity in God. Thus its historic destiny is to "make known through the Church the manifest wisdom of God" (Eph 3:10) in that process by which God "recapitulates all things" (1:10) in Jesus Christ, the ontological meaning and identity of the multiple history of man.

BIBLIOGRAPHY. M. Grabmann, *Die theologische Erkenntnis- und Einleitungslehre des heiligen Thomas von Aquin auf Grund seiner Schrift "In Boethium de Trinitate"* (1948); J. Beumer, *Theologie als Glaubensverständnis* (1953); M. D. Chenu, *La Théologie comme science au XIIIème siècle* (3rd ed., 1957); M. Polanyi, *Personal Knowledge* (1958); H. U. von Balthasar, *Skizzen zur Theologie,* I: *Verbum Caro* (1960); Y. Congar, *La Foi et la Théologie* (1962); R. Roques, *Structures théologiques de la Gnose à Richard de Saint-Victor* (1962); J. Ratzinger and H. Fries, *Einsicht und Glaube* (1962); E. Fuchs, *Hermeneutik* (3rd ed., 1963); M. D. Chenu, *La Parole de Dieu,* I: *La Foi dans l'intelligence* (1964); G. Ebeling, "Der hermeneutische Ort der Gotteslehre bei Petrus Lombardus und Thomas von Aquin", *Zeitschrift für Theologie und Kirche* 61 (1964), pp. 283–327; F. Mayr, "Prolegomena zur Philosophie und Theologie der Sprache", *Gott in Welt (Festgabe für Karl Rahner),* I (1964); J. M. Robinson and J. B. Cobb, *The New Hermeneutic* (1964); H. G. Gadamer, *Wahrheit und Methode* (2nd ed., 1965); B. Welte, *Auf der Spur des Ewigen* (1965); G. Ebeling, "Hermeneutik", *RGG,* III, cols. 242–62; id., "Theologie und Philosophie", *RGG,* VI, cols. 782–830; E. Schillebeeckx, *Revelation and Theology,* I (1967), II (1968); H. Schlier, *The Relevance of the New Testament* (1968).

Cornelius Ernst

II. Loci Theologici

1. The name *loci theologici* is given, on the analogy of Aristotle's *Topics,* to the most general headings or viewpoints in theological epistemology and methodology. Aristotle's *Topics* are concerned with the basis of dialectical as opposed to scientific proof; this basis is found in generally recognized maxims which later were called *loci communes*. According to A. Gardeil, these

τόποι re-appear in the Spaniard Melchior Cano O.P. (1509–1560), the classic author on theological proof, as *loci* based not on objective insight but on authority. As a matter of historical fact, in A. Lang's opinion, Cano drew rather on Cicero, whose *Topica* are aids for the orator to gather materials in support of his case. The influential work of Rudolf Agricola (d. 1485), *De dialectica inventione,* drew largely on Cicero, and was used both in the *Loci Communes* of Philipp Melanchthon (concerned more with content) and the formal *De Locis Theologicis* of M. Cano. Basing himself on the traditional divisions of theology, Melanchthon was concerned with headings under which the doctrines found in Scripture can be subsumed. *Loci* of this kind were composed on the Catholic side by John Eck and others. Cano, on the other hand, starts from authority and reason as the fundamental sources of theology and seeks the places where theological truth is to be found.

2. The *loci* according to M. Cano: a) *Sacred Scripture*. Cano follows the Council of Trent as regards the proof from Scripture. His text is the Vulgate, his Canon that of the Council, his interpretation is determined by the common consent of the Fathers. Inspiration is a sure guarantee of the inerrancy of Scripture in all its parts and doctrines.

b) *Tradition* is justified by Cano on the ground that some truths are only obscurely contained in Scripture or not at all. Moreover, he holds that the living word is superior to its fixation in writing. He regards as sacred tradition what can be traced back to apostolic times — that which does not owe its origin to a Council or Pope. An uninterrupted chain of witnesses since the earliest times is an equivalent proof. What the Church today universally teaches or what is believed everywhere in the Church, can only derive from apostolic tradition.

c) The authority of the Catholic Church rests on its infallibility in questions of faith. This is manifested by the universality of a *dogma*.

d) The authority of *councils* depends on papal confirmation. Only general councils with such confirmation teach infallibly.

e) The authority of the Roman *Church*. Cano expounds the proof for the primacy of Peter, his infallibility and that of his successors, that is, as he demonstrates, the Bishop of Rome. As a private person the Pope is capable of error. In virtue of divine assistance his definitive decisions in questions of faith and morals are held to be infallible if he imposes them on the whole Church. Here the subsequent definition of Vatican I is clearly anticipated.

f) Individual *Fathers* can indicate a probability in questions of faith. A majority among the Fathers does not count against the objection of others. But unanimity in the interpretation of Scripture and teaching on matters of faith constitutes a conclusive patristic proof.

g) *Theologians.* Cano finds himself obliged to defend scholastic theology against the attacks of classical scholars and Protestants. The agreement of many scholastics in favour of a thesis has no authority as against the objections of others. Universal agreement on their part in a matter of importance would make the contrary opinion open to serious doubt. Unanimity of view about matters of faith and morals has some claim to validity.

h) As well as these *loci* properly so called *(proprii),* there are extrinsic ones *(alieni),* which correspond to reason. The first of these is natural insight or evidence. By this Cano simply means indubitable, generally recognized truths.

i) The unanimous opinion of all *philosophers* as such is valid. The question whether preference is to be given with Augustine to Plato or with Thomas to Aristotle, is decided by the Dominican Cano in favour of the latter.

j) A new element with Cano is the explicit attention given to *historical proof.* He accepts as valid what is confirmed by credible witnesses and what by prudent standards can be taken to be true, particularly if the witnesses agree and are acknowledged by the Church.

Cano's *loci* encouraged a trend towards positive theology. Their drawback was their merely extrinsic juxtaposition, but Cano overcomes this by numerous intermediate links. However, he tends to make the various elements of a theological proof too independent.

As well as dealing with *inventio,* the discovery of theological truth, Cano also discusses *judicium,* judgment, in connection with the various theological notes and censures which he attempts to assign to the different truths of faith in accordance with their origin. He follows an accepted custom by concentrating above all on characterizing the doctrines opposed to them and rejected by the Church. His idea of heresy must be considered too wide. He includes in it not only what contradicts the Church's teaching, but also any rejection of the consequences that follow from it. He regards as heresy the rejection of Christian truths which are not of faith, whose *de fide* character is maintained by only a few theologians; he sees heresy even if opposition to the doctrine of faith is not clear and manifest. Every proposition which in any way favours such opposition is suspect of heresy. He regards as evil-sounding or offensive to pious ears any doctrine which is insufficiently grounded, and as scandalous, any which is contrary to good morals. With these censures Cano provided a pattern for theology down to the present time, though his classification has not been followed in every detail.

3. *The loci at the present day.* Contemporary theology usually classifies theological proofs under four heads: proof from Scripture, from tradition, from the teaching of the Church and from theological reasons. The pronouncements of the Church's magisterium above all serve as the basis for the doctrine itself. Theology is a part of the Church, a part of its mission of teaching, and can therefore only expound the Church's teaching. This teaching has of course not merely to be proved from Scripture and tradition but also to be understood in depth, and adapted to contemporary thought.

The first and proper place to seek for theological proof is sacred Scripture. The text of the OT is frequently uncertain even today. Nevertheless it is superior to any translation even for the purpose of theological proof. The text of the NT has now been established with such certainty that the Church can have recourse to it in the same way as formerly it used to appeal to the Vulgate.

The question of the canon is just as controverted as ever. For the Catholic Church it was determined by the Council of Trent. In the interpretation of the process of fixing the canon, the norm that has to be used from the ecumenical point of view is the Christian character of its content. Those who do not refuse to regard Catholics as Christians will also count works of early Catholicism such as the Letter of James, the Pastoral Letters or Acts as genuinely Christian books.

The question of inspiration has to be thought out afresh today. A. Bea and others explain it as God's making use of the human author, God being the authentic author of

Scripture. K. Rahner thinks in more general terms of the primitive Church, which enjoyed God's special assistance at its foundation, of which the NT is an element. As regards the OT, N. Lohfink holds a view which locates all inspiration in the foreshadowing of Christ. For the NT also an interpretation of inspiration needs to be worked out which would make every word of Scripture audible as the Word of God. In this way the understanding of inspiration refers us to correct exegesis. In the Lutheran view the necessary hermeneutics primarily concerns the doctrine of salvation; in the Orthodox view it concerns the traditional understanding of Scripture, and in the Catholic view it centres on its official interpretation. These three points of view need not be mutually exclusive, for the Church, and within it the Fathers, always present and interpret the words of Scripture as the word of salvation.

The dogmatic scriptural proof cannot, like exegetical exposition, be content to establish the sense of the particular passage as far as this can be derived, with due regard for the literary genre, from its context in the whole work, from its period and from the whole of Scripture. Dogma is only fully stated in its historical form if its scriptural justification proceeds from the basis of the two Testaments, grounds the OT on the NT and makes clear the historical line followed by the preaching of saving doctrine. Consequently the teaching of the various individual writings and groups of writings is to be expounded separately. In the OT the starting-point should be the saving proclamation to Israel, the exodus from Egypt, the Sinai covenant and the manifold witnesses of God's deeds and words. These have to be expounded in the light of their NT fulfilment by means of the links manifested in the NT. The starting-point for the interpretation of the NT is the saving event concerning Jesus Christ, primarily his death and resurrection but also the incarnation of the Son of God, his holy life and his words.

Tradition is understood nowadays, by J. R. Geiselmann and others, no longer simply as the preservation of a possession entrusted for keeping, but rather as its living development in history. Even where genuine tradition grew alongside Scripture, it has long since become one with the doctrine of Scripture in a living process of faith and teaching. Vatican II left undecided the question as to whether tradition completes Scripture or merely interprets it. In theological argument, tradition should be presented as the development of the doctrine contained in Scripture. The process of tradition occurs by way of spirituality and teaching, and above all through discussion with other views. The authentic function of living tradition and the proof from tradition is to make the truth of salvation stand out dialectically in contrast to differing views.

Theological reasoning in the narrower sense *(ratio theologica)* has the task of assigning individual doctrines their place in the doctrinal structure of Christian dogma. It has to take its criteria from the great themes of the Christian proclamation of salvation. Consequently saving doctrine becomes the centre of all theology. And thus it also incorporates the *loci communes* in Melanchthon's sense; for he always understood by them the most important doctrines of theology.

See also *Spirituality* I, *Theological Notes, Theology* I, *Tradition.*

BIBLIOGRAPHY. P. Melanchthon, *Loci communes rerum theologicarum seu hypotyposes theologicae* (1521; ed. R. Stupperich, 1952); M. Cano, *De Locis Theologicis* (posthumous, 1563; ed. M. Cucchi, 1890); A. Gardeil, "La notion du lieu théologique", *Revue des sciences philosophiques et théologiques* 2 (1908), pp. 51–73, 245–76, 484–505; id. in *DTC,* IX, cols. 712–47; A. Lang, *Die Loci Theologici des M. Cano und die Methode des dogmatischen Beweises* (1925) (with bibliography); id. in *LTK,* VI, cols. 1110ff.; H. Fries and J. Ratzinger, eds., *Einsicht und Glaube (Festschrift G. Söhngen)* (2nd ed., 1963); M.-D. Chenu, *La foi dans l'intelligence* (1964); J. Feiner and M. Löhrer, eds., *Mysterium Salutis,* I (1965) (especially ch. 3, on the permanent presence of revelation in Scripture and tradition, and ch. 4, on the presence of revelation through the Church); H.-G. Gadamer, *Wahrheit und Methode* (2nd ed., 1965); W. Kasper, *Die Methoden der Dogmatik* (1967).

Eberhard Haible

THEOLOGICAL NOTES

A. The Notion and its Importance

It is part of theology and its methodology to discuss the rank, and degree of certainty, of a theological proposition and to describe its situation in terms of its relation to revelation. A proposition is qualified positively by certain "notes" and negatively by certain censures. On the assumption that theological notes are not merely to be registered historically, their meaning and purpose can be indicated only within an ecclesiastical hermeneutics which both points to the understanding of Church documents and theological texts, and brings to light the process of understanding, exposition and application which is carried on in and by the Church.

This is at once enough to explain why the notes are called "theological". The method pursued is not or should not be the qualification of theology by non-theological factors (e.g., influenced by Church politics). And one should not be misled by a wrongly understood claim to universality to apply too hastily theological labels to non-theological propositions.

But theology must here be understood not in the narrow sense of a theology of the schools, but as the process of self-understanding in the whole Church and the concomitant reflection. In this sense the theological notes provide an indispensable guide in dialogue within the Church and in the dialogue of the Catholic Church with the Christian Churches in general, as also in the dialogue of the Christian Churches with the non-Christian world. The theological notes serve to explain the importance which attaches to the declarations of the Church, of its magisterium and of theology. In the orientation of dialogue, the various grades of notes and censures are particularly helpful. It may seem indeed that when the authority of the magisterium covers the designations *de fide divina (et catholica)* or *haeresis,* all dialogue is at an end. For here the uncompromising challenge of kerygma and dogma is met with, and dialogue within the Church is left behind by the incomparable dialogue between the self-revelation of God and man. But one must also consider that the encounter of God with man in human terms implies the accessibility of the word of God in the word of man — more precisely, in the human theological dialogue which is inspired by the faith and understanding of the Church.

Accordingly, even after the solemn proclamation of a dogma the process of understanding and expounding it continues in the Church. And after the exclusion of a false doctrine and the imposition of anathema and excommunication, the truth hidden in or summoned forth by the error continues to act and to influence the dogmatic development of the Church (cf. the exegesis of 1 Cor 11:19; see *Schism* I). One must therefore consider the value of theological notes from

the point of view of the *propter nos homines* which attaches to the word of God; from the point of view of the essentially social nature of man and of the socially constituted Church, where there is need throughout of mutual understanding and regulated speech; and from the point of view of historicity, which points to the need for a "note" to meet a given situation aright and also to the limits of such a note.

B. The Traditional Notes and Censures

1. *The historical conditioning.* The individual notes and censures are as clearly stamped by their historical origins as is the whole process of qualification. It is clear in particular from the highest possible qualifications, the article of defined faith or the rejection of a heresy, that the Church was meeting a challenge in history, either from doctrinal falsity or from intense controversy among theologians. The time of origin gives its historical form to the note and its particular conditioning, which impose on later times the burden of distinguishing and understanding. But the lower notes, e.g., *haeresim sapiens,* are still more clearly marked by theological schools and by particular fears and troubles of a given time. Then the possible political implications of a theological note should be considered. Sometimes the note was meant to serve the unity of faith in the wider sense of Church discipline or even the political unity of a kingdom. Hence even dogmatic assertions are combined with "rules for speaking in the Church". And in the formulations of the Middle Ages in particular, a broader sense of *fides* and *haeresis* must be presupposed (A. Lang), which was used to serve the concrete unity of the discipline of the Church. This perspective may also be noted in the confessions of the Reformers *(Formula Concordiae).* On the other hand, when political interests and Christian confession are strangers to one another, as in the primitive Church and perhaps in the secularization of the present day, there is a concentration on the expression of faith as such: negatively, on the rejection of heresy and positively, on the possibility of a preaching in accord with the times.

2. *Historical phases.* The beginnings of Christianity, and its first thousand years to a great extent, are marked not by degrees of notes and censures but by the discussion of

the true faith and the orthodox doctrine, and hence by the condemnation of a heretical position by an "anathema", mostly pronounced by the Church when assembled in synods. St. Paul already utters an "anathema" against the preaching of "another gospel" (Gal 1:8). Mt 18:27, however, does not speak specifically of a doctrinal censure. More significant in Scripture is the indirect rejection of heresy by the choice and form of the *logia* transmitted, reflecting a given *Sitz im Leben,* and the denunciation of sectarian groups (in the Epistles, e.g., 1 Jn 2:22; 4:2f.). The Pastoral Epistles strive explicitly to uphold the apostolic heritage (1 Tim 6:20; 2 Tim 1:14) and reverence for "sound doctrine" (1 Tim 1:10; 2 Tim 4:3; Tit 1:9; 2:1; cf. 1 Tim 4:6, 13, 16; 6:1, 3; Tit 2:7). Accordingly, in the first centuries, condemnations were directed against heresies and total apostasy from the faith. The great Councils led to a nuanced description of Catholic orthodoxy in the Christological and Trinitarian controversies and thus gave rise to a specialized — though frequently misunderstood — set of concepts for the demarcation of a heretical position. Nonetheless a wider sense for such notes and censures cannot be excluded, even well into the Middle Ages, though there were at times the first steps to listing "lower" notes (e.g., in St. Thomas Aquinas, *Contra Errores Graecorum, Prooemium* [*Opuscula Theologica*, I, no. 1029]: "non recte sonat"). This technique of distinguishing the various notes was prepared for by scholastic philosophy, and was worked out systematically from 1270 on. The oldest known list of censures is from 1314, and the oldest known commentary on theological notes is from William of Occam. In the 14th and 15th centuries the University of Paris (like Louvain and Cologne later) exercised an acknowledged right of censure, which was of great influence in episcopal, papal and conciliar measures (as at Constance). One can see how an institutionalized and respected theology can stamp the teaching of the Church. The break-up of the scholastic tradition in the late Middle Ages and the coming of new heresies often occasioned a multiplication of censures, as by the Council of Constance against Wycliffe and Huss (*DS* 1151–95; 1201–30); Martin V, in the Bull *Inter Cunctas* (*DS* 1247–79, especially 1251).

Special importance attached to the Bull *Exsurge Domine* (*DS* 1451–92, especially 1492) directed against Luther (which according to recent research did not always meet his points). The Council of Trent aimed at bringing out the *fides catholica* but not theological opinions. Subsequently the magisterium levelled various censures against Jansenism and Quietism (cf. *DS* 2269; 2332; 2390). The censures used in the Bull *Unigenitus* against P. Quesnel were comprehensive, while the Bull *Auctorem Fidei* applied various censures in detail to different points (*DS* 2600–2700). In the interest of "peace and charity", and ultimately of freedom, the Popes sometimes forbade theological schools to apply censures to each other (cf. *DS* 2167; 2510).

In the 18th and 19th centuries the magisterium made increasing use of the encyclical (the first of the modern encyclicals dating from 1740), of censorship of books (the Index) or of declarations *(responsa)* of the Holy Office. To sum up, it may be said that "the magisterium never had an official list of censures or theological notes but rather followed, though with reservations, theological custom" (cf. A. Kolping in *LTK,* VIII, col. 916).

But post-Tridentine theologians showed a tendency to elaborate and define precisely the various notes and censures. Here the great names are M. Cano, F. Suarez, O. de Castro, J. de Lugo and the Salmaticenses (cf. J. Cahill). Catholics engaged in controversial theology (Veronius, Holden, etc.) tried to bring out as clearly as possible the essential truths of faith in contrast to theological opinions (missing at times the essential historicity of dogmatic concepts), in order to confine the debate with Protestants to certain formulas, and ultimately to serve the purpose of reunion. Systematic presentations of theological notes and censures began to appear at the beginning of the 17th century. In 1709 Antonius Sessa (Panormitanus) listed a total of sixty-nine theological notes. C. L. Montaigne, C. du Plessis d'Argentré, D. Viva, J. Gautier and M. Tournely worked on the same systematic lines. Efforts were made in the time of the Enlightenment to separate essential dogma from "incidentals", especially scholastic conclusions. The Tübingen School in the first half of the 19th century took little interest in the minor theological notes, but concentrated instead on dogma and its development, and on the "symbolic" (credal) doctrine of the Church, in dialogue with Protestantism. But the rise of neo-scholasticism brought with it a meticulous distinction between the various notes and censures; so J. Kleutgen, C. Schrader, J. B. Heinrich, J. B. Franzelin, H. Hurter and J. Perrone. The systematic elaboration reached a peak with M. J. Scheeben. Along with the directives of canon law (canons 247; 1395–1405), the manuals of dogmatic and fundamental theology (apologetics) were of importance in the 20th century, up to the Second Vatican Council.

3. *A survey of the most frequently-used notes.* The enumeration, division and evaluation of the various notes and censures vary from author to author. The following may be taken as typical.

a) H. Quilliet *(DTC)* and G. Marsot *(Catholicisme)* distinguish censures (and the corresponding positive notes) i) with regard to the truth of revelation: *haeresis, haeresi proxima, error, propositio temeraria;* ii) with regard to the form, e.g., *piis auribus offensiva;* iii) with regard to the effect, e.g., *scandalosa, blasphemica.* Censures of the first type are understood to be perfectly applicable if the form (second type) demands it.

b) The division given by A. Lang seems more comprehensive. According to the quality of certainty, he distinguishes (i) formally revealed truths, (ii) virtually revealed truths and (iii) the "indirect doctrinal account" of the Church. There are corresponding degrees of certainty: doctrines solemnly defined by the Church; doctrines guaranteed by the ordinary magisterium or the instinct of faith in the Church; doctrines professed in theology; doctrines not yet fully stated or guaranteed. With regard to quality (i) of certainty, this leads to the following notes (or degrees of censure): "veritas de fide definita (haeresis manifesta); veritas de fide (haeresis); veritas fidei proxima (haeresi proxima); secundum sententiam probabilissimam, probabiliorem, probabilem, secundum opinionem communem, verissimiliorem, verissimilem: de fide." With regard to quality (ii) we have: "veritas catholica definita (error circa fidem); veritas catholica (error); sententia theologica certa (theologice erronea); secundum sententiam probabilissimam etc.: veritas catholica." With regard to quality (iii) we have: "veritas de fide ecclesiastica (propositio reprobata); veritas de fide ecclesiastica (propositio falsa); sententia certa (falsa); secundum sententiam probabilissimam etc.: de fide ecclesiastica.

c) A distinction was always made between infallible and non-infallible, though mostly accompanied by efforts either to maximize or minimize the bearing of the note. This has been brought out more and more clearly in recent theology, the censure of heresy being kept distinct from all other censures. All other notes are shown clearly according to their various grades on a lower level than that of the infallible doctrine of the faith (and of heresy). Within the non-infallible notes, the authentic declarations of the organs of the magisterium are distinguished from the notes applying to theological assertions. As well as these distinctions, the various designations of the traditional notes follow the official declarations of the Church (cf. *DS, Index systematicus,* H 1 d) or the classics of post-Tridentine and neo-scholastic theology.

4. *Authors, form and binding force.* a) Authoritative notes and censures are given by those who have jurisdiction in the external forum. Hence the supreme organs for notes and censures (and exclusively so for infallible matters) are the Pope and the Ecumenical Councils. Limited competence attaches to the Roman Congregations, Provincial Synods (episcopal conferences) and the individual bishops and major superiors of religious orders. The whole people of God is charged with the safeguarding of the true faith. Theologians have a special responsibility and thus are especially qualified to give theological notes — as the University of Paris did in the Middle Ages — though their authority is not one of jurisdiction. Their notes have the weight of "professional" opinions and have often influenced the magisterium.

b) Notes and censures can be given in detail (one note attached to one proposition) or in combination (several censures attached to one proposition) or comprehensively (one or more censures coming at the end of several propositions). They can be aimed at the actual words of a proposition *(sicut jacent)* or at the intention of the author *(in sensu ab auctoribus [assertoribus] intento).* Then, a given work could be condemned (by being placed on the Index of Forbidden Books) or the *opera omnia* of an author, which was a condemnation of his whole theological conception.

c) Infallible propositions have binding force when defined by a Council with the Pope, or by the Pope when speaking *ex cathedra* in the faith *(ex sese;* see *Infallibility).* Authentic (non-infallible) notes demand "the religious obedience of the will and intellect" (Vatican II, *Lumen Gentium,* art. 25).

Other theological notes, being given by theologians, have the authority of their professional expertise and of the "common doctrine".

C. New Questions — New Notes

This survey of the traditional notes has also served to show their limitations, which are especially clear when one tries to classify the complex ecclesiastical and theological reality of the present day. Vatican II not only brought up new questions which are not dealt with in earlier documents of the magisterium, but also produced texts which present a problem in the matter of their binding force and theological notes. In deference to the wishes of John XXIII, the Council made no solemn definitions. It was finally content to recall the normal rules of interpretation, and noted that at the Council in question, the only binding definition would be such as was clearly affirmed as such (cf. *Lumen Gentium, Notificationes;* also art. 25). In general, the various assertions, even in the two dogmatic constitutions (on the Church and on Revelation), must be recognized as authoritative doctrine, which bind in conscience but are only *de fide divina* where they repeat earlier definitions, or truths of faith directly recognizable as such from Scripture. The titles *(constitutio, decretum, declaratio)* also give pointers to the status and authority of the Council's teaching. The title and scope of a "pastoral constitution" have a special meaning, since its point is not (derivative) doctrine, but concrete, charismatic directives for the Church (K. Rahner).

Some encyclicals which have appeared since Vatican II *(Mysterium Fidei, Populorum Progressio, Humanae Vitae)* have given rise to renewed reflection on the theological note to be attached to encyclicals. No one denies that it is possible in principle to have an infallible *ex cathedra* decision in the form of an encyclical, under the usual conditions acknowledged by the magisterium and theologians and with the appropriate formulation. But in the cases in question there is unanimity in affirming that that which is not infallible can be fallible and is reformable. This means that the encyclicals are recognized as official, authentic utterances which must be taken seriously by all Catholics and accepted with respect — though perhaps by means of an equally serious fundamental discussion. A letter of the German bishops in 1967 "to all who are charged by the Church with the preaching of the faith" considers the possibility of error "in non-defined utterances of the Church, which can themselves vary widely in the degree in which they bind". It goes on to say: "In order to safeguard the true and ultimate substance of the faith, (the Church) must give doctrinal directives, even at the risk of error in detail, which are binding to a certain degree but which are not of defined faith and are therefore to some extent provisional, even to the point of possible error" (no. 18). It may therefore be supposed that in many pronouncements of the ecclesiastical magisterium on practical moral attitudes the notion of "magisterium" is to be taken in a wider, non-specific sense. It is not doctrine "in a matter of morals" but exhortation in which Pope and bishops exercise their pastoral responsibility (cf. J. David). In concrete matters of social ethics in particular, the Church will register and pillory the yawning gap between existing social conditions and an ideal determined from the gospel (E. Schillebeeckx). It will strive to pin-point the negative, what ought not to be, but in details it will only be able to give highly contingent directives, inspired by dialogue with the profane sciences. It will thus show itself primarily as an "institution of social criticism" (J. B. Metz; see *Political Theology*).

A further question discussed today is that of the note to be attached to authentic doctrinal documents (such as catechisms) which are published by the authority of a local Church. It is the question of their authority within the region in question (diocese, province, etc.), outside it and in the whole Church.

D. Problems of Systematic Theology

1. *The faith of the whole Church.* Theological notes must be considered today more than ever in the perspective of the whole Church and its faith — primarily therefore with an eye to the whole Catholic Church, but also in view of the separated Churches. The theological basis for this approach is the notion of the people of God, whose totality constitutes the Church and whose "instinct of faith" is itself a decisive factor in the grasp of dogma. "Through the instinct of faith inspired and nourished by the Spirit of truth, the people of God, under the guidance of the magisterium and following it loyally, receiving thus truly the word of God and not of men (cf. 1 Thess 2:13), holds fast unfailingly

to the faith once handed on to the saints (cf. Jud 3). Through this instinct it penetrates more and more deeply and correctly into the faith and applies it more fully in life" (*Lumen Gentium,* art. 12). If this instinct of faith, with which the laity is also equipped (cf. *ibid.,* art. 35), has a great part to play in determining the supreme note, *de fide,* it is all the more active in the acquisition of non-infallible theological knowledge. Hence the whole people of God contributes (or should be invited to contribute) to the reaching of correct theological notes. This partnership is today possible on account of the modern means of communication and the resulting dissemination of theological culture. The notes will therefore serve all the better to demonstrate the identity of the faith throughout the changes of its formulation. It is therefore the task of the theological notes, on their highest dogmatic level, to bring about and assure the *consensus fidelium,* which can only be attained through freedom of conscience and today less than ever can consist merely of formulas imposed only from without. Hence the theological background against which the identity of the faith is articulated can and must be very broad and diversified.

2. *Pluralism in theology.* If the preaching of the faith is to have contemporary relevance, that is, if revelation is to be intelligible to the very different types of culture in which men and nations live today, theology cannot shirk the effort to master the many types of speech and thought-form in use today. Otherwise it will fall victim to a dogmatic positivism or an equally positivistic biblicism. It is necessary "to do philosophy in theology" (K. Rahner); see *Philosophy and Theology.* This is a help to the understanding of the faith within a given cultural framework (philosophy, individual sciences, pre-scientific thought-forms). But it cannot but hinder the understanding of the plurality of theologies in question. The charge of communicating revelation makes it more difficult today to communicate the understanding of revelation. So too there is proportionately less chance of testing adequately the orthodoxy of the assertions of another school, i.e., of giving them a theological note. It is therefore necessary that if a theological note is pronounced, it should only be the fruit of dialogue between schools and trends, inspired by love of the one faith and by a corresponding desire to reach mutual understanding. In this matter, an apt

use of the principle of subsidiarity in the Church can be of service. This would mean that the bishops, and the regional authorities such as episcopal conferences, would have more say in a further realm, that of the theological notes and censures. But these would have to call in as advisers theologians of all shades of opinion, insofar as they were representative in the region in question. The papal magisterium (and its organs) would have the special task of dealing with strict questions of faith, which as such affect the whole Church, and would intervene within the framework of the principle of subsidiarity or act as the highest court of appeal. For this the supreme magisterium would need the services of a world-wide theology, and the preliminary studies of regional authorities and of theologians established and emancipated in their ecclesiastical function. Here too it should be clear that the pronouncements of the holder of primatial authority which affect the whole Church are to be distinguished from those which he makes as Patriarch of the West, as metropolitan of the Roman province of the Church or as diocesan Bishop of Rome.

What has been said above is particularly true of the necessary censures — even when uttered after profuse and expert discussion, which must of course always come first. It must be confidently recognized that through the assistance of the Spirit, the true faith is upheld in this way by the ecclesiastical authority — especially in its supreme doctrinal pronouncements, which are infallible. But at the same time, the possible good faith of those censured must be allowed for, as also for the historically-conditioned element in the understanding of an actual expression of the faith — a historicity which is not done away with by ecclesiastical authority. The formula might perhaps say that after careful examination it is not possible at present to see that a given thesis corresponds to the understanding of faith in the Catholic Church. In this way a censure would be pronounced with the whole authority of the existing Church — which obliges precisely in the present — while at the same time the way would be left open for future progress in the understanding of the faith. This could mean a better explanation of the censured thesis and hence a consensus not previously reached.

3. *The horizon of law and gospel.* It is not merely because of ecumenical interests that

theologians should consider the matter of theological notes in the Pauline framework of "Law and Gospel". The *analogia legis* must be noted in all discussion of the "law of believing", and all unnecessary notes should be avoided. When Vatican II gave no dogmatic definitions, it was conforming on principle to this demand. In loyalty to the gospel, which believers should experience as a liberation, the effort today should rather be to restore the many truths of faith to the unity of the word of God, that is, to search for a "short formula" as the circumstances demand, "a brief summary of the Christian faith" (K. Rahner). This is better than branching out into a growing number of definitions, and would obviate the need of picking one's way through a maze of notes and censures. This would lead to greater respect for the ordinary magisterium in which no formal pronouncements are made, and it would also accord free theological opinions their due right. Thus a certain reserve in allotting theological notes will be a testimony to the gospel, to the many-sided working of the Spirit in the doctrine, faith and life of the Church, and ultimately to the *Deus semper maior,* who cannot be comprehended by any human formulas.

See also: *Hermeneutics, Magisterium, Dogma* I, *History* I, *Tübingen School, Neo-Scholasticism.*

BIBLIOGRAPHY. H. Quilliet, "Censures doctrinales", *DTC,* II, cols. 2101–113; G. Marsot, "Censure doctrinale ou théologique", *Catholicisme,* II, pp. 800 f.; S. Cartechini, *De valore notarum theologicarum et de criteriis ad eas dignoscendas* (1951); A. Lang, "Der Bedeutungswandel der Begriffe 'fides' und 'haeresis'" (Councils of Vienne and Trent), *Münchener Theologische Zeitschrift* 4 (1953), pp. 133–46; id., *Fundamentaltheologie,* II (4th ed., 1968), pp. 251–64; H. E. W. Turner, *The Pattern of Christian Truth: A Study on the Relation between Orthodoxy and Heresy in the Early Church* (1954); J. Cahill, *The Development of the Theological Censures after the Council of Trent, 1563–1709* (1955); J. Salaverri, "La potesdad de magisterio ecclesiastico...", *Estudios Ecclesiásticos* 29 (1955), pp. 155–95; K. Koser, *Franziskanische Studien* 38 (1956), pp. 66–77 (on Occam); K. Rahner, "What is Heresy?", *Theological Investigations,* V (1966), pp. 468–513; id., *Schriften zur Theologie,* VI, pp. 104–10 (on the collective discovery of truth); id., in H. Vorgrimler, ed., *Commentary on the Documents of Vatican II,* vol. I (1967), pp. 186–217; id., *Schriften zur Theologie,* VIII (1968), *passim* (Vatican II as challenge to theology; philosophy in theology; historicity of theology; magisterium and theology after the Council; the short formula of the faith; dialogue in the Church); J. McKenzie, *Authority in the Church* (1968); J. David, *Neue Aspekte der kirchlichen Ehelehre* (1968), pp. 71–93.

Johann Finsterhölzl

THEOLOGUMENON

1. A theologumenon is a proposition expressing a theological statement which cannot be directly regarded as official teaching of the Church, as dogma binding in faith, but which is the outcome and expression of an endeavour to understand the faith by establishing connections between binding doctrines of faith (see *Analogy of Faith*) and by confronting dogmatic teachings with the whole of secular experience and all a man — or an age — knows. Such a proposition need not necessarily materially differ from one which is actually of faith. It can be implicitly contained in a truth of faith, in the intelligible perspective involved in the latter, in the historical origin of the conceptual apparatus it employs, etc. (see *History* I; *Dogma* II; *Hermeneutics*).

2. Such theologumena are absolutely necessary for theology and the formulation of the faith. That can be seen from the mere fact that even the official teaching of the Church does not and cannot consist only of dogmas in the strict sense, but enunciates theological statements without (yet) absolutely committing the faith to them. These are theologumena which have become generally accepted, sociologically speaking, in the Church. Such theologumena must be made because otherwise actual understanding and really practical efficacy of the articles of faith in the proper sense would not be possible at all. Theologumena are necessary because revelation does not comprise all knowledge of reality in its origin and degrees, and because the one human being in the unity of his consciousness and active self-awareness cannot really understand and personally assimilate something that bears no relation to the unified world of his own knowledge. What is revealed can, therefore, only really be known and personally assimilated in function of a man's secular knowledge (see *Faith, Faith and History*).

3. From this it is clear that revelation when received by man (since it does not absolutely alter his situation) is itself always conveyed partly by theologumena. Revelation speaks in confrontation with the present state of

valid knowledge, with the experience and the world-view of the actual hearer. It makes use of the systems of concepts available, the materials of representation, the helps to understanding, the perspectives and the ways of approach to comprehension easily accessible at a given time. In short, revelation, occurring in human cognition, necessarily uses theologumena (at least as glosses). They are not the element of binding dogma contained in the meaning of a statement, but the intellectual frame of reference inevitably expressed simultaneously with it, and by means of which what is dogmatically meant is understood, correctly but in a certain perspective.

4. Anyone who makes statements involving faith does not need to, and in fact cannot, adequately distinguish by reflection in them the dogmatic proposition from the theologumenon. Otherwise he could completely eliminate the theologumenon; and similarly he would have to be able adequately to become aware by reflection of the historical presuppositions of his own thought; whereas neither of these is possible. Nevertheless we are always implicitly aware of the distinction: for example, by knowing the identity of what is meant in a plurality of types of representation which themselves cannot be reduced to unity; or by concomitant awareness of the secular origin of the assumptions involved in the theologumena or of the unimportance of these for the central affirmations of the faith etc. The history of reflection on this distinction is the history of theology itself. Not that the latter is a history of the elimination of theologumena in favour of a "pure" theology of "merely" dogmatic statements. But it is a history of perpetual changes in theologumena, faster or slower, of greater or less fundamental a kind as the case may be. Ultimately that history is identical with that of men's historical growth in the knowledge of truth. This does not mean that in regard to dogma something is eventually recognized as erroneous which previously was believed to be absolutely true, but that the *conversio ad phantasma* which makes possible and supports all cognition, is a turning to the totality of historical experience, which itself changes. The enduring identity of the knowledge of the truths of faith ultimately rests on the fact that what throughout this history seeks, finds and fulfils itself is the one nature of man given in transcendental experience. This nature, supernaturally elevated from its origin, is always oriented towards God as absolute, and thereby possesses the abiding element of the eternal truth which itself assumes ever clearer historical form in the history of this supernaturally transcendental human nature, until the historical appearance of absolute truth in Jesus Christ.

See also *Theology* I, *Theological Methodology* I.

BIBLIOGRAPHY. See bibliographies on *Dogma* I, II, *Hermeneutics, Theological Notes, Theology* I; also: B. Welte, "Homoousios Hemin: Gedanken zum Verständnis und zur theologischen Problematik der Kategorien von Chalkedon", *Chalkedon,* III, pp. 51–80; Y. Congar, *La foi et la théologie* (1962); E. L. Mascall, *Theology and Images* (1963); H. Urs von Balthasar, *Karl Barth* (2nd ed., 1962), especially part III; H. R. Schlette, "Dogmengeschichte und Geschichtlichkeit der Dogmen", *Geschichtlichkeit und Offenbarungswahrheit* (1964), pp. 67–90; H.-G. Gadamer, *Wahrheit und Methode* (2nd ed., 1965); B. Welte, *Auf der Spur des Ewigen* (1965), part III; K. Rahner, "What is a Dogmatic Statement?", *Theological Investigations,* V (1966), pp. 42–66.

Karl Rahner

THEOLOGY

I. Nature: A. Introductory Remarks. B. The Nature of Theology. C. Theology and the Other "Sciences". D. Special Questions of Modern Theology. II. History: A. The Theology of the Beginning. B. Theology within a Definite and Homogeneous Culture. C. The Theology of the Future.

I. Nature

A. INTRODUCTORY REMARKS

1. On the history of theology see *Theology* II.

2. The general principles of the theory of knowledge which are important for the understanding of theology can only be given in outline here.

a) Man's conscious and articulate knowledge of himself (scientific and pre-scientific) is not the whole of his self-understanding, but the interpretation of a self-understanding grasped directly and historically in the act of existence. (One may compare logic or ethics. Man does not act logically or responsibly for the first time when he studies logic or ethics, scientifically or pre-scientifically.) Such reflective knowledge is not just a leisurely afterthought, but an element of existence itself and of its history. Man as he speaks and lives with other human beings necessarily reflects on himself, though in historically different ways. And this conscious knowledge reacts on his original self-understanding and helps to change it. The original self-understanding itself has again a number of constitutive elements of a transcendental and historical character, which need not be gone into here.

b) Truth can exist only in intersubjectivity. To see what is meant here by truth, one must not just think of isolated propositions which are considered correct because objective. The understanding of such propositions is possible only within a non-thematic but real horizon which is represented by speech or language and all that this implies. But this speech is essentially the work of intersubjectivity. Hence the question of truth is always posed within the framework of intersubjectivity and is indeed the question of this intersubjectivity itself. But it is always inspired by the latter and its components and presuppositions, which can never be exhaustively grasped by reflection.

c) Theoretical and practical reason form a unity in difference which again has a history which can never be totally perspicuous and amenable to the theoretical reason. In this unity in difference, theoretical and practical reason form together man's single faculty of knowledge. By "theoretical reason" we understand primarily the reason which grasps "metaphysically" the transcendental necessities and tries "scientifically" to systematize empirical experiences and bring them into definable functional combinations (though such reason, when compared to the technique of present-day science, may well be still at a pre-scientific stage). By practical reason we mean the knowledge which is ultimately immanent to the free — and hence not arbitrary — decision by which man always lives, one way or the other, and which can be gained only in such decision. The probing mind must never forget that it reflects this totality of practical and theoretical reason and can never grasp it exhaustively, if for no other reason than that the act of reflection itself cannot be again the object of reflection.

d) The notion of science — in the widest sense, including philosophy and theology — has itself a history. And the historically conditioned and changing notion of what a science is and what it can and ought accomplish helps to determine the actual pursuit of these sciences. Because of the unity of human consciousness all sciences depend on one another, whether consciously or not. Theology, for instance, is to some extent determined by the history of all the sciences and their historical self-understanding.

B. The Nature of Theology

1. a) *A definition.* Theology is the *science* of faith. It is the conscious and methodical explanation and explication of the divine revelation received and grasped in faith. This methodical reflection is possible and necessary because the "official" revealed word of God already contains a conceptual and propositional element which as an element of faith and its responsible communication to others demands further explanation, reflection and confrontation with other truths. Hence revelation is intrinsically amenable to reflection. If "science" is understood to be methodical reflection (along lines appropriate to the subject-matter in each case), it is absurd to deny theology the character of a science.

Three reasons may be noted in particular.

(i) Beyond what has been said above, there is no mandatory and permanent notion of science known to history. The limitation to experimentally verifiable facts — of the natural sciences, mathematics, quantities, fields outside value-judgments — is arbitrary, a mere matter of terminology, and would deprive theology only of a claim to be scientific in a way foreign to it.

(ii) Theology has a special subject-matter which can be distinguished from all others: the act and "content" of Christian (and ecclesiastical) faith. This subject-matter is at least a psychological and historical fact which may be methodically investigated, even if it is rejected as an ideology and an error, even if then reduced to a part of the science of religion. It would be methodical reflection on the phenomenon of culture known as religion.

(iii) The fact that Christian theology reflects on the act and content of faith in the light of faith does not deprive it of its scientific character. For total commitment is compatible with critical reflection which excludes nothing *a priori* from its critical questioning. The critical reason has the intrinsic ability to recognize that while it investigates the pre-critical presuppositions of existence, it can never grasp them exhaustively. It can recognize that no theoretical reason can exist outside the sphere of a decision of the practical reason which can never be exhaustively grasped.

b) Theology is the science of the *faith,* or rather, the science of the Christian faith.

(i) There are various interpretations of the Christian faith, not merely in theology as such but even within the propositional element which is part of the faith as such. There are various "confessional" theologies. Since in spite of these differences there is *one* Christian faith which is really one and the same behind the various propositions in which it is objectivated in the confessions and which is also sufficiently objectivated conceptually in the confessions (in the confession of Jesus as Lord), there is a Christian theology which, as the science of the faith, is really one.

(ii) Theology is the science of faith inasmuch as the Christian faith is the basis, norm and goal of this science. It is concerned with the faith as act and content *(fides qua* and *quae)* and presupposes it in the Church and in the student of theology. Faith is the goal, because the methodical reflection is not an epilogue indulging speculative curiosity but leaving the object, faith, itself untouched. The Christian must be able to answer for his faith to himself and his fellows, and methodical reflection is the form which this responsibility takes in the individual and collective situation. It is the actual account which we must give ourselves and others of the truth of our hope (cf. 1 Pet 3:15). Thus the science of faith actually becomes part of the faith (of which critical responsibility is a moment). Otherwise it would be reduced to a mere science of religion. This does not mean that faith and theology cease to be independent. For theology as such does not produce faith and it does not transform it into a higher, perspicuous system of a Gnostic or rationalistic type. And while faith is the *auditus* and the *intellectus fidei,* which involves a critical reflective element, especially faith as preaching, this is not at once a systematic and methodical reflection, like a strict science. Since theology is in this sense the science of faith, it has a sense of its own inadequacy which it works out and must keep on working out conceptually. It has a sense of the infinite transcendence of the word of God in faith with regard to all theological propositions. And this sense is part of the radical self-understanding of theology. Since theology reflects and serves the giving of a critical answer for the faith, it is essentially orientated to testimony and preaching. Hence all theology is "kerygmatic". Otherwise it is merely speculative philosophy of religion. In spite of its essentially kerygmatic character, its relation to preaching, it is a science of critical reflection, not directly meditation (as prayer) or exhortation. It is precisely as critical reflection that it serves preaching.

Its relation to faith, the full act of human existence in freedom, makes the science of faith a "practical" science, not in the sense of being a second-class science accompanying a higher intellectual science of the "theoretical reason", but in the sense that "practical" describes better the one totality of its knowledge. Theology is practical above all because it is orientated to the acts of hope and of love, which contain an element of knowledge which is unattainable outside them. It is true, no doubt, that the practical end of theology is also the desire of selfless knowledge which aims at a *sapere res prout sunt.* But this knowledge is ultimately attainable only in the act of hope and of love. Orthodoxy and orthopraxis combine to influence one another in a basic inexpressible unity which can only come to light in practice, because knowledge is only sound when it has surpassed itself and become love — which is its way of surviving as contemplation.

(iii) Since theology is the critical and methodical reflection on faith, the immediate "subject" (agent) of theology is not simply man endowed with the supernatural *habitus* of faith, but man as rational, in keeping with the distinction between faith and theology. But since theology is to remain the science of faith, faith must be the subjective inspiration — and not merely the object — of this operation of human reason. Thus the "subject" of theology may be described as the *ratio fide illustrata (D* 1799), though here *ratio* is not to be taken in a rationalistic sense.

c) Theology is an ecclesiastical science of faith. Since human intersubjectivity is at its peak in faith (A, 2, b), while faith, the hearing of the revelation directed to the people of God, is the faith of the Church and faith within the Church, theology is necessarily ecclesiastical. Otherwise it ceases to be itself and becomes the prey of the wayward subjective spirituality of the individual, which is today less fitted than ever to be the cohesive force of a community. Since the faith of the Church is necessarily linked to the historical word of divine revelation, Church theology is necessarily dependent on Scripture and tradition. Since the Church, *as* the community of faith, is an institutional society, Church theology is essentially related to the magisterium in the Church. Theology does not thereby lose its critical function with regard to the Church and its life of faith. Indeed, it is only because it is an ecclesiastical science, and hence an element of the Church itself, that theology can and must exercise its function as the Church's self-criticism, the constantly renewed effort to purge the faith from all that is merely human and questionable or historically transient.

d) As an ecclesiastical science, the whole of theology may well have a "political" aspect and be in this sense "political theology". This does not mean (or does not only mean) that the Church has a critical task in face of society, presupposing a corresponding reflection. Still less is political theology the preparation for "political action", an unjustifiable interference in the relative autonomy of worldly society and its politics. But if man's existence is equally individual and social in its essence, and if all theology is related to man (being reflection on the faith in which anthropocentrism and theocentrism combine, by virtue of the self-communication of God to man), theology cannot be restricted to the private salvation and the interiority of the individual. In all its concrete realms, it must consider the social relevance of its utterances. Social does not here refer only to the profane background within which and for which the Christian lives his Christian existence (see *Political Theology*).

e) Theology is a historical science. This does not merely mean that it has to do with "historical matter". And it does not exclude the transcendental element in theology. It means primarily that theology is and remains perpetually linked to the historical event of salvation which took place once and for all. Man's salutary relation to this event — his "contemporaneity" with it — is not brought about by theology. This is the work of the kerygma and of faith. But since faith as such already contains an element of reflection which becomes articulate in theology, and since theology is always orientated to this element as to its starting-point and goal, theology itself has the character of a historical science in the highest sense. The historical is not just the starting-point of a deductive theology, as was assumed in the Middle Ages, but the very object of theology (see *Salvation* III). This also means that theology has an essential relation to the future. For the historical here has the character of promise and cannot really be understood apart from this character. Since therefore all salvific events are hope-inspiring promises, eschatology is a structural principle of theology as such. It is not merely a treatise at the end of dogmatics

— though this does not mean that dogmatics and eschatology could be simply identified.

2. *The "formal object" of theology.* In earlier times, the "formal object" of theology was much debated. It was assumed that theology was so unified a science that it had one single formal object from which it drew its unity. For this reason, and also to justify theology as a deductive science, medieval theology gave as the formal object "God in his Godhead" (cf. St. Thomas Aquinas, *Summa Theologica,* I, q. 1, a. 7). This view is acceptable if God is understood here in his self-communication. If this is correctly understood as at once the central saving event and word of revelation, and as the inner principle of the faith which inspires theology, the mysteries of the Trinity and incarnation and of justifying, divinizing grace are already comprised in it and hence the fundamental mysteries of salvation are considered together. And since salvation and revelation are the history of this divine self-communication — creation being merely the constitution of its recipients — theology as critical reflection on salvation can also be comprised within this formal object. There is then no reason to reject "God as God" as formal object, on the ground that it would eliminate theology as a historical science (as reflection on the anamnesis of the history of salvation). If God communicating himself is taken as the formal object of theology, there are advantages for a transcendental understanding of theology, since the formal object and the subjective principle of theology (God as the uncreated grace of faith) would clearly be the same. In any case, *Deus sub ratione deitatis* is not the basis of a merely deductive theology, since the divine self-communication is only accessible to our conscious reflection in the history of salvation and the *word* of revelation. Hence this classical definition of the formal object of theology is not very helpful when one tries to grasp the nature and methods of theology.

3. *Divisions of theology.* The division of theology is not merely a matter of listing systematically the ordinary disciplines studied in theology. A division along the lines of a genuinely theological theory would raise the question of a basic reform of theological studies and lead perhaps to the discovery of tasks which are in fact overlooked by theology. The ancient division into *theologia*

(the doctrine of God in the strict sense) and *economia* (the doctrine of creation and salvation) is no longer in use. It overlooked in any case the simple fact that we only know "God in himself" through what he does for us in the history of salvation, and that the *economia* is really the *theologia,* because it is the history of the self-communication of God. The usual division is into historical, dogmatic and practical theology. The first would be closest to the *auditus fidei,* the second would be the *intellectus fidei,* and the third would deal with the *praxis fidei* in the life of the Church (see *Pastoral Theology*). But this division causes difficulties. That the three elements overlap is a difficulty inherent in the matter itself and merely testifies to the unity of theology. But it is difficult to fit the history of the Church, for instance, into this schema. It is, of course, a historical science, but it does not seem really to belong to the one "historical" theology (see *Bible* I A, B, *Dogma* III, *Theology* II) which is directly connected with the *auditus fidei.* Church history might be considered history of dogma insofar as the Church preserves and attests revelation in all that it is and experiences (cf. Vatican II, *Verbum Dei,* art. 8). Or it could be considered as the presupposition and hence a subsidiary discipline for practical theology, since the past must be known if norms are to be drawn up for the immediate tasks of the Church. But is this what is really understood by Church history? Or is it only a theological science in a broad sense, so that the problem really does not arise?

Moral theology, as usually understood, should no doubt be considered a part of systematic (or dogmatic) theology, i.e., under the heading of theological anthropology. Or it could stress how historically conditioned are its concrete affirmations and demands and be understood as the ethical actualization of the basic Christian attitude in each changing situation. It could then be considered in its entirety as part of practical theology, while systematic theology would continue to perform its ordinary dogmatic task of reflecting on the ultimate religious attitude (see *Virtue*), out of which moral theology grows as part of practical theology, in keeping with the needs of the situation. The study of canon law is to be regarded as part of practical theology, concerned with the human law of the Church, as *ius conditum* and *condendum,* which is part of its vital structure. The true place of the *ius divinum* would rather be within dogmatic ecclesiology. (On the nature of fundamental theology as a discipline of systematic theology and on its place within theology as a whole see *Fundamental Theology.*) There is no need to consider here the precise place of other usual disciplines within theology as a whole. Subjects like liturgy, ecumenical theology, Christian social doctrine, Christian archaeology, the science of religion, etc., are either parts of a more comprehensive theological discipline or of subsidiary disciplines or combine the tasks of several disciplines for practical, technical reasons.

All this should not give the impression that a scientific theory of theological study has been catered for by the division outlined above. For one reason, the actual divisions of theology as now usually accepted have generally arisen without much considered reflection, in the wake of similar profane sciences and hence not from a genuine theological impulse.

C. THEOLOGY AND THE OTHER "SCIENCES"

1. The relation of theology to the *science of religion* in all its forms has already in fact been touched upon, to some extent; and it is the same in many respects as the relation of theology to philosophy and the modern anthropological sciences. The science of religion is as independent of theology as is philosophy, and represents an important subsidiary science for theology.

2. *Theology and philosophy.* As the history of theology shows, the intellectual self-understanding of man (see *Philosophy*) which precedes the *auditus fidei,* accompanies it and derives from it (going beyond the interpretation of a purely revealed anthropology), has had a very great influence on theology. And conversely, the philosophy of the Occident at least (which is a force everywhere in the modern world-culture) is historically unthinkable without the history of revelation and Christianity. Theology was not the intrinsic norm of philosophy, but in the actual course of history, it was theology which to a great extent opened up to philosophy its own possibilities. It is not easy to determine the basic relationship between the two. Insofar as there is a valid distinction between nature and grace, philosophy exists in its own right, though this means that the study of philosophy must go on within theology itself and that theology cannot simply assume the existence of a

ready-made tool in the shape of a rounded-off philosophy with which to work. Theology and philosophy differ, as Vatican I said (*D* 1795), in their *principium* and their *objectum*. Theology is based on the grace of revealed faith and regards the revealed mysteries of God, while philosophy proceeds from natural reason and is concerned with the objects accessible to this. Since philosophy cannot consider Scripture, tradition and magisterium as sources and norms of knowledge, this distinction of the *duplex ordo cognitionis* is easily understood.

It must be remembered, however, that philosophy, on principle, can exclude nothing from its critical questioning. It cannot omit the phenomenon of the Christian faith without giving up its claim to be universal and hence ceasing to be itself. Then, it is true that the object of Christian theology can only become a conscious certainty through the word of revelation (of a conceptually explicit kind). But it is there in the universal self-communication of God (see *Existence* III B, *Grace, Revelation*), implicitly, in the experience of grace. Hence natural reason is always subject to the finality of grace, whether accepting or rejecting it. It follows that natural reason is not so untheological in its principle and object as may be suggested by the fact that in its philosophical reflection it has no explicit norm in revelation and dogma. All philosophy is in fact carried on unconsciously either in faith or unbelief — at least when one considers not this or that proposition of philosophy, but the ultimate mental horizons within which any proposition is situated and is given meaning. For there is in fact no one who is neutral with regard to grace. And there is philosophy in all theology because grace can be real only in nature and each hearing of revelation contains at once an element of interpretation which is to some extent determined by the self-understanding with which the hearer comes to revelation — by his "philosophy". Hence philosophy, which contains a secret element of theology undecipherable by philosophy itself, can have a very positive relation to theology. Transcendental philosophy in particular easily passes over in the concrete to transcendental theology. It has a maieutic function with regard to theology. "Philosophy is an inexorable but by no means arbitrary questioning of the unquestioned. It is a fruitful negation which criticizes and cross-questions the conventional canons of the 'evident truths' of each age. It fights against the

creeping absolutism of the individual sciences as they trespass beyond their categories. It is a protest against the anonymous dictatorship of the factual, a summons to break again and again with the seemingly obvious. To adapt a saying of Hegel, it can look on itself as 'its own age summed up in a question'. Philosophy therefore may be said to take the side of the ever greater possibilities of human existence, which can never be reduced to the merely factual. It thus discloses, even if only in a negative way, the concrete, historically changing 'openness' of the human mind (see *Potentia Oboedientialis*), on which faith itself must always base itself in its responsible proclamation of its hope" (J. B. Metz in *LTK,* X, cols. 69 f.; see also *Philosophy and Theology*).

3. *Theology and the modern sciences.* In earlier times philosophy had a monopoly in mediating man's self-understanding to theology. Things are now different. There is a large number of anthropologically important sciences outside philosophy, important for human self-understanding and hence for theology, and regarding themselves (at least *de facto*) as autonomous and not as branches or subordinate parts of philosophy. This uncompromising and to some extent irreducible pluralism of anthropological sciences, which may be interpreted theologically as a "situation of gnoseological concupiscence", is of great importance for theology. These sciences, today at any rate, are partners in dialogue with theology and must be accepted as such by it. The dialogue is not just concerned with reconciling the findings of modern science with theological assertions. It is above all the confrontation of theology with the mentality of the modern sciences, above all the exact natural sciences, a task which theology has far from mastered.

D. Special Questions of Modern Theology

1. *Theology and ideology.* Like all study of the "metaphysical" and "transcendent", which cannot be verified by the methods of the exact sciences, theology is suspect to many scientists, sociologists in particular (from Feuerbach and Marx on) as being an ideology in the modern sense of the term. This suspicion cannot be dismissed off-handedly. Theology is the human *intellectus fidei*, historically conditioned and hence infinitely different from God and his word. And it is in

the concrete always a theology carried on by sinners. It can be culpably suspect of ideology insofar as it is tributary to the ideologies of each age and society. Recognition of this possibility and indeed of this partial truth is part of theological knowledge itself. But the word of God which is voiced in theology and the preaching of the Church is not an ideology but the most radical critique of ideology. Christian theology is concerned with the *Deus semper maior,* the one absolute future (see *Hope*) who surpasses infinitely all this world's thrusts and systems but is really there as such for us in grace and hope. It is a theology of willingly accepted death as the dawn of the absolute future. As such it contradicts all ideologies which refuse to recognize their limitations and only maintain themselves against the greater reality which embraces them by arbitrary obduracy, purely speculative evasiveness and intolerance. Such a theology "when it finds or finds itself opposed by other universal interpretations of the world and of existence, cannot simply reject them pugnaciously and intolerantly. It must try to discover in them, and benefit by, something of the ever greater possibilities of the faith which can never be exhausted purely speculatively. These are to be searched for less in the content than in certain patterns of thought and consciousness which have been historically voiced in such philosophies and world-views. In such ideals theology, with its shortcomings due to sin, and with its own principle of looking for the Spirit to breathe where it wills, may find one of its own potentialities which it has forgotten or missed or failed to discover" (J. B. Metz in *LTK,* X, col. 71).

2. *The role of theology in the Church of today.* Theology is for the preaching of the Church. All preaching today presupposes some methodical reflection and hence theology. Hence all priests and above all the bishops must be theologians. This does not mean that there must always be a group of professional theologians at the top by divine right. But once this is admitted, there are two points to be noted. Theology and skill in theology are not the preserves of the priestly or episcopal office-holders because they have their own specific task of preaching in the Church. A broad and deep knowledge of theology (such as is needed in the Church as a whole at least today, and always, on principle) presupposes gifts of nature and grace which are not found everywhere and are not necessarily found in all office-holders. Hence there can be important "charisms" of theology even outside the hierarchy. The "charism" of teaching is not linked with the office of superior in the NT (Rom 12:6–8; 1 Cor 12:28f.). Then, at the present time, the preaching of the Church as a whole presupposes a theology with so much scientific and technical preparation that it must be carried on by professors of theology — or whatever one likes to call them. Whether they are priests or layfolk is a secondary question. They must have had a specialist formation and have a certain special professional ethic. The Catholic Church cannot and ought not be a "Church of professors", but it cannot be today a Church without professors. Whether such an ecclesiastical professorial body can or should be given concrete form as an institution, e.g., as consultors to synods, as groups attached to the Roman Congregation for the Doctrine of the Faith, so that they can speak clearly in the Church, is another matter. There is no need to discuss further here the legitimate freedom which must be accorded to the theologians in their work.

3. *The pluralism of theology today.* There have always been "schools" of theology upholding contradictory opinions, starting from different assumptions and developing different patterns of thought. A pluralism of this type in theology is not new and it has always been a principle in the Church that it should be either tolerated or expressly approved of. But theologies today are displaying a pluralism of a different type, one that cannot be now reduced to unity. Formerly there were controversies between the schools and to some extent different patterns of thought, not recognized as such, however. But fundamentally they knew each other, spoke more or less the same language, and could try to clarify their differences and eliminate them in a higher synthesis. The materials and methods of theology — linguistic, historical and speculative — were accessible to all — or completely outside their range of interests. But today the intellectual and social environment of theology is different. Methods are different. There are so many different starting-points and languages in philosophy that no single individual can master them adequately. The mass of material in exegesis and history of dogma is such that no single individual can take in and master "theology", even as it is at present.

Theology has become many theologies. They need not be contradictory. If they are to be Christian and Catholic, they must abide by the one perpetual confession of faith of the Church, in the obedience of faith. The ancient creeds (which were also in part the result of "theology") are in fact more important than ever, since they can hardly be replaced by new formulas which would be "existentielly" understandable by all at once. But the theologies remain multiple, because the whole of present-day theology, with its various disciplines, terminologies, approaches, problems and audiences, cannot be even approximately grasped by the individual. Team-work can help, but in the intellectual sciences, where the procedures and the findings cannot be separated, it cannot fully overcome this pluralism. It has come to stay. There will be more and more theologies, which will not be able to follow each other adequately, though this of course does not mean that they will be simply juxtaposed without influencing each other. On the contrary, a new type of effort at mutual tolerance, mutual influence and mutual criticism will be necessary, much more than hitherto. The magisterium, hitherto nourished too exclusively by a certain type of Roman theology, will have to find new ways of controlling and fostering this pluralism.

4. *Theology and modern "irrationalism"*. Much more than in former times, theology must now envisage readers and hearers whose whole culture inclines them to "relativism", scepticism and positivism. Where religion is accepted, it is relegated to the realm of the irrational where it is no longer exposed to rational questioning and objections. Such attitudes and the corresponding interpretations of religion and its theology existed earlier (see *Modernism*), but they did not as today stamp the whole mentality of an era. If theology is really to give an account of the faith to a given age, it must see this situation clearly and take it into account. Fundamental theology and dogmatic theology must be much more of a unity than formerly, because the credibility (and existentiell assimilability) of the individual truths of faith means at least as much for the credibility of the fact of revelation as this does for the former. Theological statements must be modest and prudent and when treating the individual themes of theology must not forget its general principle of mystery and the merely analogous nature of its concepts with regard

to its object. Theology must take care to see that its individual propositions are related to the real kernel of faith and revelation, in terms of the hierarchy of truths. It must make this kernel intellectually and existentielly assimilable and on this basis articulate the various individual dogmas, without making its task too easy by simple recourse to the formal authority of the magisterium. For the magisterium itself is only credible by virtue of the manifest credibility of the whole of revelation.

BIBLIOGRAPHY. See bibliographies on the articles referred to above; also: the introductions to the textbooks, especially K. Barth, *Church Dogmatics,* I (1949); E. Brunner, *Dogmatics,* I (1949); M. Schmaus, *Katholische Dogmatik,* I (1960); Patres SJ in Hispania, *Sacrae Theologiae Summa,* I (5th ed., 1962); H. Thielicke, *Der Evangelische Glaube,* I (1968). — E. Petersen, "Was ist Theologie?", *Theologische Traktate* (1951); G. Söhngen, *Die Einheit in der Theologie* (1952); id., *Der Weg der abendländischen Theologie* (1959); J. Beumer, *Theologie als Glaubensverständnis* (1953); E. Fuchs, *Was ist Theologie?* (1953); H. Köster, *Vom Wesen und Aufbau katholischer Theologie* (1954); G. Wingren, *Die Methodenfrage der Theologie* (1957); G. Woods, *Theological Explanations* (1958); Y. Congar in *DTC,* XV, cols. 341–502; id., *La foi et la théologie* (1960); A. Kolping, *Einführung in die katholische Theologie* (1960); G. Ebeling, *Word and Faith* (1963); id., *Theology and Proclamation* (1966); id., *God and Word* (1967); J. M. Robinson and J. B. Cobb, *New Frontiers in Theology,* I–III (1963–67); H. Thielicke, *Between Heaven and Earth* (1965); M. Nédoncelle, *Is Theology a Science?* (1965); T. P. Burke, ed., *Word in History* (1966); W. Pannenberg, *Grundfragen systematischer Theologie* (1967); E. Schillebeeckx, *Revelation and Theology,* I (1967), II (1968); R. Latourelle, *Théologie, science du salut* (1968); J. Moltmann, *Perspektiven der Theologie* (1968); M.-D. Chenu, *Faith and Theology* (1968); Y. Congar, *History of Theology* (1968); H. Fries, *Bultmann-Barth and Catholic Theology* (1968); P. Neuenzeit, ed., *Die Funktion der Theologie in Kirche und Gesellschaft* (1969); H. Grass, *Theologie und Kritik* (1969).

Karl Rahner

II. History

The history of theology can be regarded as forming with the history of dogma a part of Church history. Or it can be regarded as forming with exegesis a presupposition and element of historical and systematic theology. But as a branch of Church history, the history of theology would have to contain many elements which would not be directly of use to systematic theology. Patrology, if not treated merely as the history of literature in patristic times, may be regarded as the first section of the history of theology, that is, as history of theology in the patristic age. Or the history of theology may be begun at the point when the "Fathers" end and the theologians begin, that is, with early scholasticism. Just as patrology could be treated as a history of patristic literature, a similar procedure could be followed in the history of theology. But then it would be merely a history of theologians and of theological literature as such, which would be a useful undertaking, and one that is too little attended to. Nonetheless, the history of theology should be a theological undertaking. As such, it is obviously akin to the history of dogmas (and of the Councils), and this is its usual framework. But there is a radical difference between the two, corresponding to the difference between dogma and theological proposition. The history of dogma cannot of course be described without recourse to the development of theology. But the history of theology remains separate, being in fact the history of theologians, theological literature, theological propositions, schools and institutions, various theological concepts, thought-forms, methods, motives, etc., in spite of the fact that history of dogma and history of theology are usually in fact treated together. History of theology in this sense can then be divided into the history of the various disciplines, history of exegesis and so on. And since the history of theology has a history of its own, it can be part of its own subject-matter.

The division of the history of theology into periods to bring out the characteristics of each age encounters the same difficulties as the division of Church history. Since the history of theology is an essential part of Church history and reflects it because dependent on it, it seems obvious to consider that the divisions should be the same in each case. But the periods of Church history as such provide only very extrinsic divisions for the history of theology. And the problem is only displaced a little, since the objective divisions of Church history are still a debated problem. It must further be noted that it would be a false approach to assume beforehand that the periods in question should be more or less of equal length. Under these circumstances, the division to be outlined below may be considered. It is primarily concerned with systematic theology, since this is the clearest reflection of the spirit of a given age, insofar as it is influential in theology.

A. THE THEOLOGY OF THE BEGINNING

The word "beginning" is here used not just in the sense of the initial stage of a period of time, but in the sense of *principium,* the "whole in a kernel", if for no other reason than that this was the period of the unique historical event of Jesus the crucified and risen Lord, the permanently valid centre to which all theology is referred. It is difficult to divide this period from the following one, but the theology of the beginning could be seen as coinciding with the time of the primitive community, the time of the apostles, the origin of the NT. But this period could perhaps be extended to the moment when theology crystallized in a particular culture as the self-understanding of a Church which may be regarded as in some way national or established. In this first period theology is still ambivalent, still stamped by the OT and the environment of Jesus, but also thinking in terms of the civilization and religion of Hellenism. Two subdivisions may be made in this period.

1. *The history of the theology of the New Testament* (see *Bible* I A, 2; *New Testament Theology*). This is usually given in introductions to the NT, exegesis and biblical theology. But it is really part of the history of theology, since even within the NT we find theology and development, whose normative function is, however, guaranteed (K. Rahner, *Theological Investigations,* V [1966], pp. 33–41). It is the time of the first and permanently normative reflection on the original experience with Jesus of Nazareth. The OT was still a vital starting-point for theological argument, the experience with Jesus was being transposed into the first type of Christology, the "Christology of descent", the notion of salvation through grace alone was being worked out, it was becoming clear that between Easter and the return of Jesus there was the Church, and the Church was becoming conscious of itself as an institution *iuris divini* (*ibid.,* pp. 219–43).

2. *The history of theology between the NT and the theology of the imperial Church,* i.e., *c.* 100–300. The Church has left the ambit of the OT. Practically its only partners in dialogue are Hellenism and the Roman Empire. The Apologists tried to speak to the cultured in their own language. The first attempts were made to draw up theological systems — some major ones, like

241

that of Origen. Technical theological terms came into use. In the struggle against Marcion and the Gnostics, further thought was given to the continuity and discontinuity of Christianity with its OT origins. A defensive front was formed against the religious philosophy of the times (see *Gnosticism, Docetism*). In the struggle against Montanism and Novatianism and the controversy on the re-baptism of heretics an ecclesiology began to take shape which would do justice to the juridical development now clearly established. The demarcation of the canon of Scripture was begun and became the subject of theological reflection.

B. THEOLOGY WITHIN A DEFINITE AND HOMOGENEOUS CULTURE

The conversion of the Roman Empire introduced a very important period of Christian theology which reflected the cultural unity and character of the society in which it flourished. This unity did not of course mean that theology had not to deal with schools, controversies, schisms, heresies and contradictions. But all had the same geographical and cultural background and the same mental horizon, mostly accepted unreflectingly. It was a mentality of very complex components, being the heritage of the ancient Hellenistic and Roman culture, while also marked by the Christian message and — later — by the characteristic new approaches of the Germanic peoples. This whole age, the end of which one may put at the Enlightenment or the French Revolution, or perhaps in our own times, forms a definite unity, in spite of all its differences, when compared to the theology of the beginning and to the theology which is now slowly taking shape. The whole period may be subdivided into three phases: a) the dialogue of Christian faith with a well-defined culture, historical and regional; b) the objectivation and systematic articulation of the objective truth of faith (the Middle Ages); c) the subjective (transcendental) and historically-minded reflection on faith and the truths of faith (modern era).

But first we must consider the unity of this period which lasted for more than fifteen hundred years. The basically common character, in spite of differences which went as far as bitter struggles between orthodoxy and heresy, is only now beginning to stand out clearly as we pass out of this period and the new age is ushered in only reluctantly

by the mind of the Church. It is not obvious, for instance, that the theology in the future — like that of the past and for the same reasons — will be accompanied by a history of dogma which leads to new dogmas. It is not obvious that it will be almost indissolubly linked to a special period of cultural history and derive from the unity of this cultural horizon a unity (latent for the most part) which overrides all "cleavages". It is not obvious that this culture, being itself tributary to Christianity, will be a protection to faith and theology. But in any case the past age and its theology had a unity which marks it off clearly from the era upon which we are now entering. It should also be borne in mind that the late Middle Ages, the theology of the Reformation and the Counter-Reformation, the theology of the Baroque period and of the Enlightenment are the consequences of earlier, epoch-making decisions taken in the seminal years of the Middle Ages (B. Welte, p. 418) and were only gradually replaced after the Copernican revolution in thought brought about by Kant.

1. *The theology of the Roman Empire, East and West.* This theology bore the marks of its times: neo-Platonism and Roman imperial and juridical thinking (see *Alexandrian School, Patrology* II, *Cappadocian Fathers, Patrology* III). But there was no betrayal of the original Christian truth, because this great Christian fact, the presence of God himself in the world, kept on breaking through the mental horizons of the time, the notion of the degrees of being where God was the "supreme" and hence the most remote and "other-worldly" reality. The inherited mental horizons are there, but constantly called in question, however unconsciously. Since it was a theology of degrees of being, of order and of the "Empire", it was less concerned with history and hope, less a theology open to an unknown future than a theology of mystical contemplation already in possession of God. The biblical eschatology is transmitted but not really reflected upon, or where it is, there is a strong inclination to a doctrine of general reconciliation (see *Apocatastasis*). The "theology of history" as envisaged by St. Augustine is rather the theology of the eternal conflict of good and evil, not that of a genuine future and of a history of God himself. Hence too his theology of the immanent Trinity is kept apart from that of the Trinity of the economy.

There were three main themes in this

theology, two predominant in the East and one specifically Western: the Trinity and Christology, then the theology of the necessity of the grace of predestination, in which few out of many were chosen for salvation (see *Augustinianism, Pelagianism*).

Against Arianism, the doctrine of the Trinity upheld the consubstantiality of the Logos and the Pneuma with the Father. This was to stress the cosmic working of the power of God, and also a certain opposition to the hierarchical thinking of Hellenism (see *Arianism*). In Christology, Hellenistic terms were used *(physis, hypostasis)* to bring out the direct union of God with the world (in the hypostatic union of the Logos with the human "nature" of Jesus), and also the proper reality of the world (in the real, active humanity of Christ). This was the dialectic of Chalcedon — "neither confused nor divided" (see *Monophysitism, Monotheletism, Nestorianism*). St. Augustine's theology of grace brings out clearly the sovereignty of God — and hence gives the world a voluntaristic trait. But it also made the picture of man a chiaroscuro of election and reprobation, whose most extreme forms were only gradually softened in the course of the Middle Ages and the modern era.

2. *Medieval theology* (see *Aristotelianism* II, *Scholasticism*). In contrast with the theology of the Empire of patristic times, the theology of the Middle Ages breaks new ground, in the young nations of the West, from which patristic theology is seen as an established "authority". The *fides quaerens intellectum,* strongly optimistic as regards rational knowledge, launches a theology of its own with scientific preoccupations and techniques, and from St. Thomas Aquinas on, makes a clear distinction between theology and a philosophy autonomous to some extent. Theology is regarded explicitly as "scientific". The legacy of antiquity is present in the form of Platonism and of Aristotelianism, the latter in growing measure after its "baptism" (of fire) in the 13th century. There are clear differences between the schools, represented chiefly by the various religious orders (see *Augustinian School, Thomism, Franciscan Theology, Scotism, Nominalism,* etc.). But all are stamped strongly by a common mentality. There are "authorities" taken for granted in philosophy and theology. The Bible is a sort of textbook. It is the age of the Summas, aiming optimistically at a conceptual synthesis to be brought about by a

reason on whose powers scarcely a doubt was cast. The pessimism of Augustinianism was gradually eroded, and "nature" and the "world" were gradually recognized, at least in principle, as existing in their own "worldly" right. The anthropocentric revolution of the modern era was already being prepared for to some extent (see *Transcendental Theology*). But thought is directly concerned with the "object", and the "subject" is treated as one object among many others. Otherwise theology went beyond patristics in making all elements of the kerygma the object of reflection, though at different degrees of intensity. The doctrine of the Trinity is given speculative development beyond that of the Cappadocians and St. Augustine. Much attention was paid to angelology, original sin, sanctifying grace, justification, the hypostatic union and the sacraments. The history of salvation in general, soteriology and eschatology were brought into the system, but were still discussed in a pre-scientific language of imagery, while ecclesiology was developed rather in practice (see *Pope* I) and in canon law rather than in theology as such.

3. *Baroque Scholasticism* (see *Baroque* II and *Suarezianism*) was mostly a continuation of classical scholasticism, exploiting and overcoming the nominalism of the late Middle Ages. There were controversies with the theology of the Reformers, especially on justification, the sacraments and ecclesiology (see *Reformation, Calvinism*), but there was still much common ground in the theology of the schools: the Latin language, Suarezian-scholastic philosophy, efforts at system, Christology and trinitarian theology practically indistinguishable. The contrast between Catholic and Reformation theology was confined to the "categories" in which individual questions were debated, but did not penetrate to the "transcendental" presuppositions of which Luther was to some extent conscious — though not Protestant orthodoxy — as were the theological precursors of the "anthropological revolution" in the philosophy of the modern era. Controversies among Catholics were concerned with the recrudescence of an extreme form of Augustinianism in Baius and Jansenius (see *Baianism, Jansenism*).

The scientific interest in history awakened by the Renaissance produced a serious attempt at patrology, Church history and history of dogma. Theology and philosophy, on principle and in practice, were more clearly distinguished than in the Middle Ages, but remained very close.

Theology was slow to take up the controversy with "the modern age" as represented by the transcendental revolution (see *Cartesianism*) which turned attention to the subject, and by the Enlightenment, the beginning of rationalist criticism of religion, ideology and society. The debate was made more difficult by the new situation of the Church brought about by the French Revolution, and was slowed down by neo-scholasticism. Here theology justifiably defended itself against rationalism and modernism, claiming its rights as a genuine science of the faith. But it failed for the most part to enter into frank dialogue with the modern era, as the age of a transcendental philosophy and the beginnings of the "exact" sciences (see *Renaissance, Enlightenment, Rationalism, Modernism, Religion* I B, *Transcendental Philosophy*).

C. The Theology of the Future

1. The transition from Baroque scholasticism to the theology which is gradually emerging was made in neo-scholasticism, which overshadowed the efforts of the Tübingen school with its orientation to German Idealism (see *Neo-scholasticism, Tübingen School, Idealism*). The system of neo-scholasticism was mostly restorative in tendency, but it performed services on the level of the historical sciences of theology and Christian social doctrine which went far beyond Baroque scholasticism. In exegesis, Catholic theology is only now, slowly and painfully, catching up with Protestant studies.

The main efforts of neo-scholasticism in the 19th century were directed against fideism, traditionalism and ontologism, and in the beginning of the 20th century against modernism. It was a solid, ecclesiastical theology, but apart from exceptional figures like Newman, it was strongly restorative in tendency, with a diffident, defensive attitude to the intellectual trends of its own times. The new approaches of "mystery theology" and the *nouvelle théologie* remained on a modest scale. See *Fideism, Traditionalism, Ontologism, Sacraments* II, *Nouvelle Théologie*.

2. The new phase of theology begins with the end of neo-scholasticism. The Second Vatican Council can be taken as the watershed, though not widely recognized as such at the time. It is a theology which can no longer envisage the Church as a closed group within profane society. It sees itself as the scientific and rational reflection of faith in a Church which is in open dialogue, that is, one in which the outcome is not already determined by the ecclesiastical partner. It notes the irretrievable pluralism of philosophy, and hence reckons with a pluralism in theology itself. It feels obliged to a direct dialogue with modern sciences, which no longer see themselves as subordinate to and represented by philosophy. It includes the sociological sciences as well as history and the natural sciences in its debate. It sees that it must apply to exegesis all the methods used by modern (Protestant) critical exegesis and that it must take its findings into account. Though the faith and the kerygma of the Church contain a theological element in their self-expression, theology recognizes that it must bring out more clearly than before the difference between theological science and the confession of faith.

In its reflection on its own history, which is an intrinsic element of systematic theology because it is a theology of the history of salvation and revelation, theology sees that it has more to do than bring out the continuity of its history. It strives to see the configuration of this history in each of its epochs, none of which can be adequately reduced to the preceding or the following age, and it thus gains a direct relationship to each of these configurations in their individual uniqueness. Theology must therefore both justify, and mark the limits of, each of the great steps that it has taken (B. Welte). This is the only way in which it can profit by its history, apart from using it to be a testimony to the continuity of ecclesiastical tradition.

Theology today must be less an explicatory than "a reducing agent". There can be no question of a one-sided and discouraging stress on the formal authority of the magisterium — which remains unquestionable, but itself rests on foundations which are objectively and demonstrably prior to it, and which must be clearly regarded in the new light of each age. But the multiplicity of the individual propositions in which the faith of the Church is enunciated must be brought into relation with or reduced as far as may be to the central, original truth of the Christian faith, though this itself is historically mediated. (See the doctrine of Vatican II on the "hierarchia veritatum", *Unitatis Redintegratio,* art. 11.) Theology can therefore take on a systematic structure very different from that which has been customary in the last centuries. And it is an open question whether the traditional divisions of the theological disciplines will be maintained. When studying the formulas of the magisterium, theology will distinguish more clearly than hitherto between expressions on which the Church has justifiably but not irreformably ruled, and expressions which could not be otherwise without detriment to the reality of faith. Such theology will come back again and again to some "brief formula or formulas of the faith" in keeping with the insights of a given epoch, just as theology started with a similar formula, the Apostles' Creed. Theology will be more abstract because it will bear in mind the analogous nature of all theological propositions, and their orientation to the silent, adorable mystery. Hence its language will have less imagery and images. But it will also be an education and training for a "second spring" in which men will soberly make do with a theology which is forced to speak *in umbris et imaginibus*.

The world of man has ceased to be a numinous, sheltering and sovereign nature. It is no longer the object of the "speculative reason's" aesthetic and metaphysical contemplation. It has become the quarry from which man hews his own world according to his own creative plans, while learning at the same time to manipulate his own nature. It is the age of the practical reason, the age of a social dimension which is the only possible agent of such a creative thrust, with all its monstrous inherent dangers of titanic hybris and its component of sin. A theology which strives, as it must, to speak to such a race of men cannot but be the theology of an evolutionary world-view and a "political theology", which will also be a critique of society from a standpoint which is both within and without society.

This indication of two aspects of future theology does not of course mean that they are its only characteristics. The theology of the future will be characterized by a very considerable pluralism which will not be totally reducible to unity, but without detriment to the one confession of faith within the one Church. Under these circumstances, one need have no misgivings about the prospect of a theology which will be very "positivist" in its attitude. It will not be inspired by the mentality very widespread in the last hundred and fifty years, according to which systematic theology had reached such an unsurpassable peak that it could really do no more than look back on its past — much as at present philosophy has to a large extent abdicated in favour of research into its own past. This "positivist" theology will rather be very aware of the historical conditioning of even the newest theology, but will be somewhat sceptical as regards the hope of bettering it in the future. It will also be sceptical as regards, for instance, the effort to "sublimate" the present-day pluralism into a higher theological synthesis. It may therefore be foreseen that one of these theologies of the future will be characterized by such a positivist trait.

Under these circumstances it is also possible to foresee another type of theology, one in which the question of hermeneutics and the epistemology of theology in general will be in the foreground. It is true that theological hermeneutics cannot simply pretend to replace theology in general as the only true scientific theology. Nonetheless, a future theology may be very much preoccupied by the question of theological hermeneutics, just as linguistic philosophy is not the whole of philosophy but can be the starting-point and structural principle for philosophy in general. The future may also hold a counterpart to the technical rationality of today which is reflected in a theology of the practical reason and political theology with its social criticism. There may be a swing over to a theology of contemplation, proper to the "quiet in the land" (Ps 35:20), of initiation into a mystical experience, of a rightly understood "aesthetic". Transcendental theology, as an element in every theology which understands what it is doing, will again cut across these perhaps foreseeable theologies.

All this gives only a very formal outline of a theology to come. It is impossible to do more. But even such a forecast may be important if it helps to reinforce the hope and courage which can look forward to the future of theology without too many misgivings.

BIBLIOGRAPHY. See bibliographies on the articles referred to above and on *Theology* I; also: H. Hurter, *Nomenclator Literarius Theologiae Catholicae*, 6 vols. (3rd ed., 1903–13); E. Hocedez, *Histoire de la théologie au XIXe siècle*, 3 vols. (1947–52); E. Hirsch, *Geschichte der neueren evangelischen Theologie*, I–V (1949–54); G. Söhngen, *Katholische Theologie gestern und heute* (1964); B. Welte, *Auf der Spur des Ewigen* (1965), pp. 410–26; M. Grabmann, *Die Geschichte der katholischen Theologie seit dem Ausgang der Väterzeit* (2nd ed., 1966); K. Rahner, *Schriften zur Theologie*, VIII, pp. 13–149 (the contours of present and future theology); H. Zahrnt, *The Question of God* (1969) (20th century Protestantism).

Karl Rahner

THEORY AND PRACTICE

1. *Concept and problems.* The discussion of theory and practice is one of the primary themes of all philosophy. Since it examines the relation between idea and reality, word and deed, consciousness and being, concept and object, thought and action, purpose and history, the discussion of theory and practice could stand for philosophy itself. Where the relevance of theory to practice is denied in a radical scepticism or where they are merged in an undifferentiated identity, philosophy itself ceases to have any claims and its necessity disappears. Thought is left without an object. As in philosophy itself, the opinions on the relation of theory and practice can vary so widely that absolutely contradictory positions ensue.

But within this general framework there is a special aspect of the discussion which needs to be considered. In spite of variations in doctrine, practice is not identified as a rule with the world of objects. It is a summary way of indicating the individual and collective activity of man. But the very question as to whether such practice is the opposite of thought or whether they are allied in a way as yet to be determined, gives rise at once to controversy. A "pure theory" disdains all reduction to practice as a restriction upon the abstract logic 'of correct deduction or a belittling of the intrinsic value of its own non-utilitarian purpose, while theories concerned with empirical analysis, ethics, social philosophy, etc., often affirm the primacy of practice. Mention may finally be made of the general distaste for "fanciful speculation", which is partly due to unhappy experiences but also partly to resentment and to anti-intellectual emotions. In any case, the general view is that theory is unreal, futile and expendable.

In Christianity the relation between theory and practice likewise gives rise to many problems. As the gap between it and its origins grows, it becomes more and more difficult to relate the gospel to the life of faith, general norms to concrete imperatives, complicated theology to ordinary Christian action, preaching and everyday life. The problems cannot be solved by relegating them to the practical disciplines of theology and subordinating them to the basic systematical and historical treatises. This procedure involves a double danger. The practical disciplines may become casuistry and mere registration of facts, devoid of any connection with the major disciplines. And the latter tend to be distorted into independent historical and systematical theories without direct relevance to the present moment. The question of theory and practice can also be acute in the realm of criticism of religion, inasmuch as the actual, historical forms of Church life are assessed and criticized in terms of the self-understanding and origin of the Church, the gospel. The usual distinction between essence or reality and appearance is itself in need of justification. And the distinction likewise ordinarily made in spirituality and theology between the active and the contemplative life can now be scarcely maintained in the traditional form. The reasons for this are to be sought in the new understanding of science which has developed in the modern era. The concept now includes elements of biblical and Christian thought and their elaboration has not yet reached a point where they can be fully reconciled with the Graeco-scholastic tradition of Christian philosophy.

2. *The history of the problem.* As early as Herodotus, 5th century B.C., information (ἱστορεῖν) and examination (θεωρεῖν) are said to be the foundations of scientific history. In the natural philosophy of the Ionians, *theoria* designated the spiritual contemplation of abstract matters. In the religious realm, *theoria* originally seems to have meant a deputation sent by a town to some solemn feast. Later it meant contemplation in general, while the association with θεά, θεῖον is at least as early as Plato. Aristotle distinguishes between the βίος θεωρητικός and the βίος πρακτικός, the life devoted to intellectual contemplation and the life of ethical activity. A distinction is made between θεωρία, πρᾶξις and ποίησις. In *theoria,* contemplative thought has no other end and object but its own activity. In *praxis,* knowledge serves ethical action, in *poiesis* technical ability in the production of artefacts. The dualism of later Hellenism transformed the purely intellectual approach into an ascetical and contemplative way of life. *Theoria* became Gnosis.

The definition of theory in St. Thomas Aquinas is based on the universality of all speculative knowledge. The difference between theoretical and practical knowledge comes from the intention at work. God, being, etc., are the object of theory, while practical knowledge is concerned with ethics, politics and so on. The gap between theory and practice is more marked in nominalism. Here concept and consciousness have distanced themselves from their objects and anticipated some elements of modern systems of science, which construct their own axioms. And the isolated world of objects is left to empirical methods and inductive registration of facts. The thinking of the modern era thus took on an anti-Aristotelian, anti-contemplative character. The pure theory of mathematical knowledge goes hand in hand with an applied science looking only to the practicable and useful. "Tantum possumus, quantum scimus" (F. Bacon). Knowledge is power. Theory supplies principles which are to be tested and applied in practice.

Kant broke through this technological mode of thought, distinguishing the pure and the practical reason. Pure reason works out propositions and principles with methodical exactness. Practical reason, as reason in action, frees practice from the sphere of merely empirical registration of facts. By defining practice as the logic of action, Kant made practice subordinate to the rule of practical reason, instead of its being the mere extrinsic application of logically correct propositions to actions and objects. Hegel (Preface to Philosophy of Rights) saw practice as the historical manifestation of reason, its external existence. Reason and reality are identical. Theory cannot be an ideal surpassing practice, as in Plato, and it cannot be produced in the concrete by thought, as in Fichte. Since it is the mind of the world it only appears after the maturation of reality. Philosophy is "the times in thought". Idea and history, form and content, theory and practice are dialectically mediated moments of the one reality of the spirit.

The obviously questionable consequences in the field of politics and law — philosophy has not to find out what the State should be but how it can be recognized — were brought out and criticized by the Hegelians of the left. In the dialectical materialism developed above all by Karl Marx, the world is not just to be interpreted but to be brought in practice to conform to reason. Practice here is the totality of social relationships. An affirmative theory is nothing but "ideology", when put forward under the conditions under attack. Theory must be critical theory,

and as such aims at eliminating itself by a revolution in the present evil condition of society. No doubt thinking is determined by social existence, but theory and practice still contain historical elements which disrupt the present framework and can at last really reconcile the existing antagonisms. Revolution is then the historical identity of theory and practice. From the point of view of method, Marxism means that the relationship of theory and practice is brought as close as possible to a total identification. But it has also made it clear that for practical purposes philosophy must be completed by social psychology and the empirical, analytical, social sciences.

In Romanticism, life-philosophy and existential philosophy efforts are made to safeguard the concrete riches and manifestations of the life of the individual from the paralyzing grip of intellectualist abstractions and rationalistic thought. The relation of theory to practice is determined by the various ways in which life, spirit, soul, existence, etc., are envisaged. M. Heidegger criticizes the fixation of the object in modern theory. This is to be replaced by a fundamental ontology in which reason as the faculty of being is again given full rights. But the criteria for the functioning of reason in relation to being seem at times to be dangerously near to a mystical, Gnostic speculation.

The relationship of theory and practice is envisaged in different ways in the modern sciences. In the human sciences, certain methods of hermeneutics are taken to be valid in each case. Experimental sciences use hypotheses derived from standard propositions, and the hypotheses have then to be verified before they can be summed up as laws and brought together in a system, on the principle of scientific economy, and then formed into a coherent theory. Deductive theories are derived from principles prior to axioms and scientific theory.

3. *Systematical analysis and consequences.* The problems of scientific theory and the relationship of theory and practice as now discussed are already signalled in the last paragraph. In the natural sciences, the distinction between theoretical ("pure") and applied mathematics, physics, etc., has been proved valid, as may be seen from the way theory is established in such disciplines — either by logical deduction or by experimental methods. Outside the exact sciences, the

establishment of pure theory detached from practice appears problematical, as in the positivist or pragmatical theories of history, society, law or art. No matter how the theories are arrived at, they are hypothetical, and not only does the logical correctness of their various assertions and laws need to be demonstrated, but their verification or falsification depends on subjective experience. In fact, however, the criteria for these experiences are either purely quantitative, being established by a comparison of verdicts, on the analogy of the establishment of precedents in Anglo-Saxon law. Or they are based on the procedures developed by pragmatism (as in C. S. Peirce) or on a combination of both methods. The procedures are highly complicated, and their weakness lies in the lack of hermeneutical and dialectical reflection on the conditions of possibility of these experiences. In fact, the objectivity of such theory is no more than a flat tautology of practice. The result is a mere projection of realism, a reliance on mental images which has been rightly criticized as a fault shared equally by neo-scholasticism and the dogmatic forms of dialectical materialism. Practice is given a double in theory, theory and practice are merged in a changeless identity, reason and reality are once more the same thing, though now in an anti-Idealist version. This notion of theory and practice is based on the unavowed assumption that practice is to be identified with a definable regulative system mostly made up of constants and variables — a system in which the usefulness of the means, the functioning of relations and the norms of fact have the value of directives resulting from objective forces.

But these values are then erected into absolutes without any analysis of the historical and social transmission by which they are coloured. This can only mean a rejection on principle of philosophical hermeneutics. But the latter in turn, if taken alone, is equally inadequate, since the "hermeneutical circle" means that it is drawn into the dialectic of practice embodying theory and theory engendering practice.

The realization of the goal of a free, objectively assured unity of theory and practice depends on finding an exact method for combining philosophical hermeneutics and empirical analysis of practice. But the goal itself is subject to historical contingency, and this must be allowed for. In view of the multiplicity of methods now used in the establishment of theory, this formal determination must suffice. In other words, the problem of theory and practice can for the moment only be stated more sharply. It can hardly be solved peremptorily.

In theology and the Christian faith, in the distinction between contemplation and action, the same principle holds good. If the latter distinction is to be still rational, it cannot be fitted into a scheme somewhat like "leisure and work". One should not imagine that contemplation can attain an immediacy by virtue of which the general norms of theology will be compellingly transformed in concrete action. Since such direct contemplation dispenses with psychological and sociological reflection and the like, it is as open to the suspicion of ideology as a theology which leads to a mainly inward-looking, privately orientated understanding of the faith, or which has recourse in fundamental theology to a colourless believer, whose freedom is an abstraction since he is not affected by any given historical situation. Individual and society act and re-act upon each other. To hypostatize either of these factors means that the dialectic of theory and practice is neglected and theology is distorted into an ideology. The real discussion of the relation of theory and practice in theology is only beginning.

The dialogue between Church and world demanded by Vatican II is also to be envisaged in this context. Here the copula "and" suggests a separation which does not do justice either to the many Christian implications of present-day social and political practice, or to the many ways in which world history influences the Church and theology.

The same precautions are necessary when the relation of theology to the faith of Christians is analysed. Reflection on the relationship of theory and practice should aim at a hermeneutics which will use all apt scientific methods to enlarge the scope of existing principles and so approximate as closely as possible to the ideal of a free, objective identity of theory and practice.

See also *Religion* I, B, *Nominalism, Science* II, *Ideology, Revolution, Romanticism, Life-Philosophy, Existence* II, *Hermeneutics, Pragmatism, Marxism* II.

BIBLIOGRAPHY. W. Jaeger, *Aristotle: Fundamentals of the History of His Development* (2nd ed., 1948) (cf. on the intellectual virtues); J. and R. Maritain, *Liturgie et contemplation* (1959); K. R. Popper, *Logic of Scientific Discovery* (1959); H. Urs von Balthasar, *Verbum Caro*, I (1960); H.-G.

Gadamer, *Wahrheit und Methode* (1960); J.-P. Sartre, *Critique de la raison dialectique* (1960); J. Habermas, *Theorie und Praxis* (1963); id., *Erkenntnis und Interesse* (1968); H. Albert, ed., *Theorie und Realität* (1964); O. Pöggeler, "Hermeneutische und mantische Phänomenologie", *Philosophische Rundschau* 13 (1965), pp. 1ff.; J. Ritter, *Hegel und die französische Revolution* (1965); I. Bocheński, *Methods of Contemporary Thought* (1965); H. Blumenberg, *Die Legitimität der Neuzeit* (1966); J. Pieper, *Happiness and Contemplation* (1966); R. Carnap, *Logical Structure of the World and Pseudo-Problems of Philosophy* (1966); D. Henrich, ed., *Kant, Gentz, Rehberg: Über Theorie und Praxis* (1967); N. Lobkowicz, *Theory and Practice* (1967); J. Horkheimer, *Zur Kritik der instrumentellen Vernunft* (1967); id., *Kritische Theorie* (1968).

Werner Post

THOMISM

Thomism means normally the schools and systems of philosophy and theology which take the teaching or thought of St. Thomas Aquinas as their authoritative source. Here, however, we take Thomism as the doctrine of Aquinas himself, noting the main parts which are relevant to present-day discussion.

A. THE CHANGING AUTHORITY OF AQUINAS

1. Canon law speaks of the doctrine to be taught to candidates for the priesthood as follows: "In the study of systematic philosophy and theology and in the formation of candidates for the priesthood in these subjects, professors are to follow entirely the mind, doctrine and principles of the Angelic Doctor and to consider these principles as sacred" (can. 1366, para. 2; cf. 589, para. 1). When Vatican II speaks of the philosophical disciplines, in its Decree on Priestly Formation, it mentions no authorities and leaves the matter deliberately open, mentioning only "the perennially valid philosophical heritage" (*Optatam Totius,* art. 15). As regards the theological disciplines it simply speaks of an intellectual effort to be made in systematic, dogmatic theology *Sancto Thoma magistro* — a compromise which is meant to include the material importance of his doctrine as well as the exemplary character of his methods.

2. *Historical note.* There was at first no direct continuity with the great commentators on Aquinas in the 16th century (e.g.,

Cardinal Cajetan) when a neo-Thomism, primarily interested in philosophy, developed above all in Italy and Germany during the 18th and 19th centuries. This received ecclesiastical sanction from the encyclical *Aeterni Patris* (1879) of Leo XIII. In putting forward the "authority of St. Thomas", the Pope appealed in particular to the Council of Trent. This pronouncement of the magisterium led to more intensive historical work on the history of philosophy and theology in the Middle Ages. But another result was a non-historical textbook Thomism, which by the very fact was open to unconscious influences from the spirit of the times.

Side by side with the Thomistic "schools" and opposed by them to a great extent, there was the tradition of thought which tried to bring about a positive encounter between Aquinas and the thinking of the modern era: F. von Baader (*Thomas-Studium, c.* 1821) and J. E. von Kuhn (1806–87), who brought to light the ontological *a priori* (e.g., the *intellectus agens*) which was rejected by the Thomism of the schools; A. Rosmini (1797–1855); J. Maréchal (1878–1944) and the Thomists inspired by him, with a "dynamiste" approach especially in France, and a "transcendental" approach, especially in Germany.

B. AQUINAS IN THE HISTORY OF THOUGHT: CENTRAL QUESTIONS

1. *Philosophy and gospel.* St. Thomas lived during a renaissance, that of Roman law in the 12th and of Aristotelianism in the 13th century, which was accompanied by an "evangelical movement" seeking to revive the text and spirit of the gospel. He was more strongly systematic than his teacher, St. Albert the Great, as his thought moved between these poles. Furthermore, he disclosed to the West, especially in Christology, the tradition of the Greek Fathers. His achievement did not take the form of a timeless synthesis. It was a successful effort, never completed, but rather one on which he was still working to the end, to build up a theological structure with all the materials of his time, orientated to the subject-matter and spirit of tradition, pointing on without revolutionary overtones to a future which we are still not done with.

2. *The question of being and of God.* One of the most fateful pieces of translation ever made was the LXX's rendering of Exod 3:14 by "I am HE WHO IS". It identified the God of the

249

covenant who revealed himself in history with a basic term of Greek philosophy, changed from the neuter to the masculine. Thus it is an established fact for St. Thomas that "He who is" is the most suitable name for God (*Summa Theologica*, I, q. 13, a. 11). But he finds that this can be proved "by many arguments" ... "that God ... is his being" (*ibid.*, q. 3, a. 4), i.e., that his essence is to exist. The three proofs offered at this point are ontological expositions of the revealed names of God. He is the first (uncaused) cause, for which St. Thomas appeals (*Summa contra Gentiles*, I, 13) to Aristotle. He is pure actuality, which is St. Thomas's own notion of being. He is by his essence, and not by participation — which is a Platonic notion, re-interpreted and applied to being. But St. Thomas also transforms ontology into an "Exodus-metaphysic" (Gilson). Aristotle's world of movement becomes a world of beings, all of which have been produced as being (cf. *Summa contra Gentiles*, II, 6, 15). The Aristotelian *energeia*, orientated to the essence, is abandoned for being as act. The characteristic of the forms ("ideas") is projected upon being, interpreted as act.

3. *Creation as emancipation of the world.* The theological significance of this combination of the notion of God and of being is seen when the world is regarded as created. St. Thomas leaves the question of the temporal beginning of the world to faith and the positive statements of revelation, and concentrates on the relation of finite beings to the being who is being itself. The world, as a thing of movement and causes, is the manifestation of a world of beings in which God, the being who is, is directly, most intimately and perpetually present (*Summa Theologica*, I, q. 8; q. 104). God does not give the impulse to the world from outside (see *Deism*) but grounds by his presence in it the universal play of cause and effect (cf. *Summa contra Gentiles*, II, 21; III, 67 f.). He shows his greatness by giving things their being and their proper activity. "To diminish the perfection of the creature would be to diminish the perfection of God's causality" (*ibid.*, III, 69). St. Thomas is even more drastic in rejecting any type of *concursus* between God and the world, such as has been a drag on us since nominalism: "The one and the same effect is produced by the subordinate cause and by God, directly by both, though in a different way" (*ibid.*, III, 70). It is precisely

by being moved by God in this way that the subordinate causes receive their own proper character. "And just as he does not prevent the activities of natural causes being natural by moving them, so too when moving the voluntary causes he does not make their activity non-voluntary but rather brings it about in them" (*Summa Theologica*, I, q. 83, a. 1 ad 3). Even if the categories of principal and instrumental cause no longer seem apt models for describing the liberation conferred by God on man in action, there is another approach, also understood ontologically by St. Thomas, which reminds us of the relevance of his principle. Man as acting through will and reason is the representative of God's goodness in the world (*Summa contra Gentiles*, II, 46), the end and ruler of the world (*ibid.*, III, 22; see *God-World Relationship*).

4. *Laws of nature and history.* The lordship of man is that of reason over the "lower" realms within him and outside him. Man shares through his reason in the provident rule of God over the world. "Providence is the plan which underlies the ordination of things to their goal" (*Summa Theologica*, I, q. 22, a. 1). God rules the world by leading it to its goal (*ibid.*, I, q. 103, a. 1). The goal of the universe being a universal goal can be no other than the universal good, God (*ibid.*, I, q. 103, a. 2). When man, the bodily, spiritual centre of the world, has reached his goal, the world also reaches it. "God wills that man should have might in order to serve reason and that he should have reason because he was to be man: and he was to be man for the sake of the fulfilment of the world" (*In Ephesios*, 1, lectio 1, no. 12). Man as the creature endowed with reason "is under God's providence in the special sense of sharing in providence inasmuch as he is provident with regard to himself and other things" (*Summa Theologica*, I/II, q. 91, a. 2). This sharing of the rational creature in the "eternal law", i.e., in the reason of God (*ibid.*, q. 19, a. 4) is called the "natural law" (*ibid.*, q. 91, a. 2). Hence nature, as understood here, is not a rigid conceptual structure or a metaphysical register, but the nature of man as he plans and acts rationally (cf. *Summa contra Gentiles*, III, 78), that is, a nature which founds history. The historical dimension is disclosed by the hermeneutical consideration first carried through by the Protestant theologian U. Kühn: "The explanations of the law in general, of the

eternal, natural and human law, are given in view of the new law which is their real goal" (*Via Caritatis,* p. 229). But the "new law", the "law of the new covenant", is "above all the grace of the Holy Spirit which is imparted to those who believe in Christ" (*Summa Theologica,* I/II, q. 106, a. 1). There is an analogy with the "natural law", inasmuch as it is given in the most inward depths of man so that he does what is right from the depths of his freedom (*ibid.,* ad 2; cf. ad 1). This perspective is given its full content in the doctrine of the gifts of the Holy Spirit (I/II, q. 68). The man who is filled by the Spirit is amenable to the call and the action of God by virtue of his inmost disposition.

5. *History of salvation and contemplative wisdom.* The discussions of the law of the OT (I/II, qq. 98–105) and of the law of the NT (*ibid.,* qq. 106–108) form the closest approach to what we now understand by the theology of salvation-history. But they are divided by visible seams from other treatises. The *Summa Theologica* is a synthesis, successful but not fully carried out, between "the presentations of the doctrine of faith in the immediate and remote predecessors of St. Thomas, which in Abelard were quite non-historical, but were consistently in the framework of salvation-history in Hugh of St. Victor and Peter Comestor" (O. H. Pesch in *LTK,* X, col. 130). This effort at synthesis is possible, "because both the historical event and the intelligible meaning of this event are founded on the wisdom of God's action" (M. Seckler, *Heil in der Geschichte,* p. 35).

C. TRUTH OF THOUGHT AND OF REVELATION

1. *Propositional truth, ontological truth and the "truth" of the Fourth Gospel.* The effort to derive supratemporal intelligibility from the history of salvation derives from the effort, which can be traced in the West from the 2nd century, to expound the historical revelation of the prophets and Jesus Christ in terms of the Greek notion of truth (primarily Middle Platonism and neo-Platonism). The Middle Ages and hence St. Thomas inherited the ontological notion of truth for which St. Augustine was invoked: "The truth is that which (really) is." He also knew the Aristotelian approach to the truth of thought, as handed on through Boethius, St. Anselm of Canterbury and some scholastic writers, which was to predicate or deny of a thing

what it was or was not. Further, there was the notion of the "hierarchy" of the "true" in its many degrees, from the subsistent truth of God to the truth of human discourse, as propounded by St. Anselm in his widely read dialogue *De Veritate.* Then there were the efforts of William of Auxerre and his followers, to base faith on the First Truth. Finally there were the statements of the Fourth Gospel, as expounded by tradition in keeping with the given understanding of truth at each particular period. The saying of the Lord, "I am the way, the truth and the life" (Jn 14:6) was of particular importance here. The Aristotelian principle is given the function of a catalyst, as it were, by St. Thomas, though it was never solely predominant.

2. *Significance and limit of propositional truth.* The question of truth, as prepared by St. Anselm of Canterbury, and explicitly propounded by St. Albert the Great, may be said to have presented itself as follows to the contemporaries of St. Thomas. When we say that something is "true", has it this title simply because of the relation to the one truth which is in itself (God), or does it also merit the title in itself? St. Thomas answers: "It is the one truth, the divine, which makes all things true, being their efficient and exemplary origin. Nonetheless, there are many truths in created things, by virtue of which these are said to be true in themselves *(formaliter)*" (*Scriptum super Sententiis* 1, d. 19, 2 solutio). But within the realm of created things we say such propositions are true (in the sense of correct) as conforming to the things. Hence truth is a relation founded on the being of the thing and fulfilled in the judgment in which the being of the thing is understood. In the famous first *quaestio disputata* of the *De Veritate,* St. Thomas examines beings as such as to whether the fact that they *are* itself provides a relation by virtue of which they are to be called "true", and which explicates itself in terms of true propositions and true content (i.e., attained by the propositions). This basic relationship is concentrated in the "soul" which — itself a being — is open to all beings and thus places itself in a relation to itself in such a way that it reflects on itself as the place where all beings are collected (cf. along with *De Veritate,* 1, 1, *ibid.,* 10, 8).

The fundamental "truth" (transcendentally disclosed), the common nature or affinity of the being of beings and the being of the soul (or reason) is itself transcendentally grounded on the "First Truth" as the self-presentation of God (*De Veritate*, 1, 7; *Summa Theologica*, I, q. 16, a. 5). The being of all beings is the "reality" which as light makes beings present to reason (cf. *Super Librum de Causis*, prop. 6). The "active intellect" *(intellectus agens)* is the "participation in the uncreated light" (*Summa Theologica*, I, q. 84, a. 5), by virtue of which being is always present to man. Since this presence is voiced in the "principle of contradiction", it may be said that all "propositional truth . . . can be primarily reduced to the principle that affirmation and negation (of the same) cannot be true at the same time" (Avicenna) (*Scriptum super Sententiis* 1, d. 19, 5, 1 solutio).

Since the real site of intramundance truths is the intellect as it affirms or denies (*Summa Theologica*, I, q. 16, a. 2, etc.), they are to be understood in terms of the latter and not in terms of "eternal propositions" or "ideal truths". They should be termed finite, temporal (*Summa Theologica*, I, q. 16, a. 7, etc.), changeable (*ibid.*, q. 16, a. 8, etc.).

3. *The "First Truth" as foundation of faith.* For St. Thomas, the question of the "truth of faith" is not primarily that of the truth of the propositions in which faith is expressed. These have a mediating (communicatory) function, which will be hermeneutically discussed below (4). The fullest treatise on faith (*Summa Theologica*, II/II, qq. 1–16) begins by asking whether the First Truth is an object of faith (*ibid.*, q. 1, a. 1). This way of putting the question probably came into scholastic discussion through William of Auxerre. His formula became the "common" definition: "Faith is to assent to the First Truth for its own sake and beyond all [else]." This was probably to bring out the Godward-ness of faith as a theological virtue, and to distinguish it from the other theological virtues, hope and love. In a number of formulas, William describes the First Truth as light which beams the articles of faith into the soul and which streams forth from them. It is also the authority which demands obedience and provides full grounds for trust.

The question is posed by the fact that for the early scholastics of the classical age, the First Truth was not merely the beginning and end of faith but also, paradoxically, the medium of it. This "mediation" by the "First Truth" was meant to bring out the immediacy of dependence on God. For *medium, ratio credendi,* the ground of faith, could also be used.

In the *Commentary on the Sentences,* St. Thomas had already shifted the emphasis from the *ratio credendi,* the (subjective) foundation of faith, to the *ratio objecti,* the foundation of the objects of faith, primarily God himself, as the centre of belief (3, disp. 24, 1, 1 solutio). In *De Veritate,* 15, 8, he explains the meaning of the foundation of faith by means of the notion of testimony. God, who attests himself, and imparts in testimony a share of his truth, is the *medium* and *objectum* (*ibid.,* ad 9). The mediation takes place in the act of self-attestation, the object is that which is attested in the testification. In the *Summa Theologica,* II/II, q. 1, a. 1, St. Thomas transfers the relationship of *medium* and *objectum* wholly within the being of God. Inasmuch as the aspect "of the matter believed" is prior to that of "the person believing" (*Summa Theologica,* II/II, q. 1, a. 2), it points to the foundation of faith which is not opposed to man but provides the setting for the opposition of the believer and the believed. This foundation is the "First Truth", whose self-disclosure through the light of faith in man and through the historical mediations leads to the assent of faith (cf. *In Boethium de Trinitate,* 3, 1 ad 4).

4. *Hermeneutics of the coming of revelation.* In the bearers of revelation — the prophets, Jesus Christ, the apostles — God's self-communication becomes articulate speech (cf. *De Veritate,* 12; *Summa contra Gentiles,* III, 154; *Summa Theologica,* II/II, qq. 171 ff.). The word of revelation is concentrated in the Apostles' Creed (*Summa Theologica,* II/II, q. 1, a. 6 ff.) and its articles of faith. In medieval thought an "article" is a component, and also a principle of composition, in the indivisible totality which is mediated by speech as God communicates himself (*Summa Theologica,* II/II, q. 1, a. 6). Scripture contains both the content of these articles and many things which serve the *manifestatio,* the visible display of this content (*ibid.,* ad 1). Since "the truth of faith is scattered throughout Scripture, clothed in many different forms of expression and sometimes only obscurely present" (*ibid.,* q. 1, a. 9 ad 1), the Church's confession of faith is necessary (*ibid.,* ad 3). This must adhere fully to "the doctrine of Christ and the apostles", in which "the truth of faith is sufficiently propounded" (*ibid.,* q. 1, a. 10 ad 1). Through its mediation through Jesus Christ and the

apostles it is linked with the "First Truth". Through this mediation, which guarantees the identity and the content of the truth, each of the faithful shares in the First Truth itself. For "faith adheres to all the articles of faith by virtue of the one motive: for the sake of the First Truth, which is put before us in the Scriptures, which are rightly understood according to the norms of the teaching Church" (*ibid.*, q. 5, a. 3 ad 2). Thus we do not hear God's words, but as members of the Church we take part in a language-event brought about by God's action. In this event the First Truth reveals itself (*ibid.*), and the teaching authority of the Church is so closely linked with Scripture that it can expound the truth of faith contained in Scripture in terms of the discussions of a given period, for the good of the faithful (*ibid.*, q. 1, a. 10 ad 1). The Church is the "subject" of faith (i.e., believer) (*ibid.*, q. 1, a. 9 ad 3) and not an object of faith in the strict sense (*ibid.*, ad 5). The object of faith is the sanctification wrought in the Church through the Holy Spirit (*ibid.*, q. 1, a. 8).

5. *Theologia negativa and the dialectic of the "Three Ways"*. Within this salutary event, what is the value allotted by St. Thomas to the doctrines of faith (the propositions of theology) and their truth? His exposition of the "Yes" of faith is that it is an assent to propositions which are accepted as true (correct) without any fear of the opposite meeting the case (cf. *ibid.*, q. 1, a. 2–4; q. 2, a. 1). But he also affirms, with St. Augustine, that this assent remains *cogitatio,* i.e., questioning consideration, till faith is succeeded by the eternal vision. Further, the guide-line of all discourse about God, that is, of all theology, is that "we cannot know what God is, but only what he is not" (I, q. 3, prologue). And even this negative knowledge is only "something in the nature of knowledge" (*Summa contra Gentiles,* I, 14). But faith, using a way not that of reason, can penetrate through what is expressible and attain "to the reality", that is, to God (*Summa Theologica,* II/II, q. 1, a. 2 ad 2). Thus faith and the theology which expounds faith seem to be strangely poised between knowledge and ignorance. How precisely are they to be explained?

They represent the climax of the mediated and hence negative character of all knowledge. "We can designate a thing by name insofar as we can know its nature from its properties and effects. Since we can know the essence *(substantia)* of stone in its proper being through its nature [as it unfolds its essence there], knowing as we do [already] what a stone is, the word 'stone' designates the nature of the stone as it is in itself . . .

But we cannot know from the action of God the nature of God as it is in itself, so that we could know what it is. We can know it only by the way of eminence, causality and negation . . . This is the sense in which the word 'God' designates the divine nature. The word was introduced to signify something that is above all things, that is the source of all things and is different from all things as the wholly other *(remotum ab omnibus)*. This is what was meant by those who give God a name" (*Summa Theologica,* I, q. 13, a. 8 ad 2). Eminence, causality and negation are not three different approaches to God, any of which may be taken at choice. They are three moments of a dialectical process of knowledge. God, whose existence is known as the cause of all, is known at the same time as the wholly other, beyond all that is knowable. The only progress in this knowledge is a more and more precise negation (*Summa contra Gentiles,* I, 14). "Hence the supreme possibility of human knowledge of God is that man knows that he knows nothing of God, inasmuch as he knows that all we know of God is surpassed by that which God is" (*De Potentia,* 7, 5 ad 14).

D. The Understanding of Human Nature in the Tension of Theology and Philosophy

1. *The fulfilment of human existence (beatitudo) as the corner-stone of theology.* The supreme possibility of man in his earthly existence is to be open, in the dialectic of knowledge and ignorance, to the self-communication of God. The theology of St. Thomas, who is concerned only with God, takes man for its theme because man is "ordained to God as his origin and end" (*Summa Theologica,* I, q. 1, a. 7), because he is orientated to a fulfilment in which God gives himself in direct vision (*ibid.*, I, q. 12; I/II, q. 2, a. 8; q. 3, a. 8); because the incarnation of God is the ground of this union with God in vision; because this union with God is the only fully successful human existence (*Summa contra Gentiles,* III, 48 ff.).

Thus faith is concerned with the being of God in which our happiness will consist, and with the providence of God, by which he guides us to this happiness (*Summa Theologica*, II/II, q. 1, a. 7). Trusting in God's guidance, the movement of hope leads to the enjoyment of God, "since man cannot hope for less from him than himself" (*ibid.*, q. 17, a. 2). And "since there is really a fellowship of God and man, inasmuch as he communicates to us his happiness, this fellowship must (*sic*) give rise to friendship", which we call "caritas" (*ibid.*, q. 23, a. 1). The word friendship was uttered by Jesus Christ (*ibid.*, citing Jn 15:15), "who has shown us in himself the way of truth along which we can attain through the resurrection the happiness of eternal life" (*Summa Theologica*, III, prologue).

2. *Desiderium naturale as the basic situation.* St. Thomas investigates philosophical tradition as regards this definitive achievement of human existence. The theme of the Platonic *eros* in the form of the Augustinian longing for happiness, the Aristotelian and neo-Platonist longing to know and see, the ancient and medieval notion of a purposeful nature — all are combined in the keyword *desiderium naturale*. For St. Thomas, it is the innate desire of the finite spirit for everlasting being (*Summa Theologica*, I, q. 75, a. 6; *Summa contra Gentiles*, II, 55). It springs from the perception of "being as such" (*De Anima*, 14) and appears in the double form of the desire for happiness and for the vision of the First Truth (*Sententiis*, 4, disp. 49; *Summa contra Gentiles*, III, 25 ff. etc.). This "natural desire" is not to be assigned to any particular faculty of man. It is rather a basic situation of human existence, which is determined by the desirability of that which is-in-all, and always reaches out beyond the finite offer of fulfilment in each particular being. As an open "movement towards the future" (*De Spe*, 1, ad 6) it can take the form of resignation, despair or hope (cf. *Summa contra Gentiles*, III, 48; IV, 54).

3. *Hope as sketch-plan and as expectation of salvation.* Hope, if it is to be a responsible disposition, a virtue, can only exist where man, believing in God's self-communication in Christ, looks expectantly to God as the friend who not only makes possible the ultimate fulfilment which is impossible to man himself, but does so in such a way that it is given to man as his own possibility (*Summa Theologica*, II/II, q. 17). This hope of salvation, with its non-intellectual certainty, contains the confidence which Luther learned to look upon as the decisive criterion of faith. Like the fiducial faith of Luther, it is seen in the perspective of the individual, because it is only the individual who can accept his supreme possibility as a gift from the helper God. St. Thomas actually asks whether one can hope for another, and his answer is: "When union in love with the other is presupposed, one can hope and long for something for another as for oneself; and in this sense one can hope for eternal life for another insofar as one is united to him in love" (*Summa Theologica*, II/II, q. 17, a. 3). But it is in the line of St. Thomas's thought to say that we can insert the degrees of hope into the "We" which is constituted by the priority of the common good to that of the individual. For "the final goal of the many in society is not to live virtuously but to attain the beatific vision of God by a virtuous life" (*De Regimine Principum*, I, 15). The right is to be realized in common so that an order of peace may be attained in which men help each other to find the truth and impel each other to goodness (*Summa contra Gentiles*, III, 128). This order of peace prepares the "blissful fellowship which is called the 'heavenly Jerusalem'" (*De Caritate*, 2).

4. *Anthropology and theological eschatology.* The historical situation of St. Thomas is strikingly illustrated when anthropological interests come into conflict with theological tradition. The tension is noticeable, for instance, when an astonishing number of arguments are invoked to show that the full beatitude of man involves the body (I/II, q. 4, a. 6, arguments 1–6). On the theological level, the debate envisages the "Greeks" (cf. *Summa contra Gentiles*, IV, 91; *De Rationibus Fidei*, 3). But the tension is more marked between philosophical anthropology and theology. "Without the body the soul lacks its natural perfection" (*Summa Theologica*, I/II, q. 4, a. 6).

"The soul without the body is not man" (*ibid.*). The answers, which we do not find satisfactory, endeavour to show that the spiritual vision of God in his essence is the essential element of the blessed fulfilment, and that the being of man is fundamentally affected by this fulfilment (*ibid.*, ad 2). But this perfection is increased in extension by the resurrection (*ibid.*, ad 5). Man is only fulfilled when his glorified body serves the spirit in full harmony and gives it expression (*Summa Theologica*, I/II, q. 4, a. 6; cf. *Supplement*, 80 ff.; *Sententiis*, 4, disp. 44, 1, 2, q. 1).

5. *Individuated species or person?* Theological interests extend the conflict into philosophical anthropology itself. The body goes to make up perfection — but by virtue of its being material is in the nature of a limit. The individual man appears as a particular case of human being (cf. *Summa contra Gentiles,* I, 44; III, 65), though at the same time, like God and the angels, he is a person, "the independent individual being of a rational nature" (*Summa Theologica,* I, q. 29, a. 1 [citing Boethius]). The use of the word "person", introduced by the ancient Church in Christology and the theology of the Trinity, obliged theologians to take an analogous approach in working out the philosophical understanding of man. St. Thomas starts with freedom as "dominion of one's own act" (*Summa Theologica,* I, q. 29, a. 1) and concludes to the selfhood of the person (*ibid.,* a. 3 ad 1). Hence man as a person is not an individual case of a species but unique by definition (cf. *ibid.,* ad 1; *De Potentia,* 9, 2 ad 1). This principle, which contains in germ the history of the modern ontology of freedom, did not become in St. Thomas the foundation of his anthropology, but pointed nonetheless to consequences for the moral action of man. If, as our hermeneutical principle suggests, we understand the thought of St. Thomas as a process, we can think today along with the Thomas who points on to the modern era and lives by tradition, against the Thomas who was a prisoner of traditions partly imposed by authorities, and who could not fully and systematically attain the goal to which his thought impelled him.

See also *Aristotelianism* II, *Scholasticism.*

BIBLIOGRAPHY. *Works* (critical edition), Editio Leonina, 17 vols. to date (1882 ff.). CRITICAL EDITIONS OF INDIVIDUAL WORKS: *Super De Causis,* ed. by H. Saffrey (1954); *Super Boethii De Trinitate* (Decker, 2nd ed., 1955); — Best ordinary edition, *Opera Omnia,* 27 vols. to date (Marietti, Turin, 1948 ff.). ENGLISH TRANSLATIONS: *Summa Theologica,* by English Dominicans, Part I, 3 vols. (1911–12; revised ed., 5 vols., 1920–22); Part II, 9 vols. (1914–22); Part III and Supplement, 7 vols. (1913–22); Index (1925); reprint in 3 vols. (1947); *Summa Theologiae,* New Latin-English edition, ed. by T. Gilby (1964 ff.), 32 vols. so far, to be completed in about 65 vols.; *Summa contra Gentiles,* ed. by J. Rickaby (1905); by English Dominicans, 5 vols. (1924–29); *On the Power of God* by English Dominicans, 3 vols. (1932–34); G. Phelan and I. Eschmann, *On Kingship (De Regno, De Regimine Principum)* (1949); M. Fitzpatrick, *On Spiritual Creatures* (1949); R. Mulligan, *Truth (De Veritate,* qq. 1–9), 3 vols. (1952); L. Kendzierski, *On Charity* (1960); J. P. Rowan, *Commentary on the Metaphysics of Aristotle,* 2 vols. (1961); R. Blackwell, *Commentary on Aristotle's Physics* (1963); A. Maurer, *On the Division and Methods of the Sciences* (qq. 5, 6, of the commentary on *Boethius De Trinitate*) (3rd ed., 1963); C. L. Litzinger, *Commentary on the Nicomachean Ethics,* 2 vols. (1964); A. Maurer, *On Being and Essence* (new ed., 1968). INTRODUCTIONS: A.-D. Sertillanges, *La philosophie de S. Thomas* (1907); M.-D. Chenu, *Introduction à l'étude de S. Thomas* (1950); French Dominicans (collective work), *Initiation Théologique,* 4 vols. (1952–53); P. Grenet, *Le Thomisme* (1953); J. Pieper, *The Silence of S. Thomas* (1957); id., *Introduction to S. Thomas Aquinas* (1963); H.-F. Dondaine, D. Schlüter and O. H. Pesch, "Thomas von Aquin", *LTK,* X, cols. 119–34; O. H. Pesch, "Thomismus", *ibid.,* cols. 157–67; É. Gilson, *The Spirit of Thomism* (1964). BIOGRAPHIES: G. K. Chesterton, *St. Thomas Aquinas* (1933); A. Walz, *Thomas von Aquin* (1953). IMPORTANT PHILOSOPHICAL MONOGRAPHS: L. Oeing-Hanhoff, *Ens et unum convertuntur* (1953); W. Kluxen, *Philosophische Ethik bei Thomas von Aquin* (1964); K. Rahner, *Spirit in the World* (1968); id., *Hearers of the Word* (1968). MODERN THEOLOGICAL MONOGRAPHS: M. Seckler, *Instinkt und Glaubenswille nach Thomas von Aquin* (1961); id., *Das Heil in der Geschichte: Geschichtstheologisches Denken bei Thomas von Aquin* (1964); S. Pfürtner, *Luther und Thomas im Gespräch;* C.-F. Geffré, "Théologie naturelle et révélation dans la connaissance du Dieu Un", *Cahiers de l'actualité religieuse* (1962), pp. 297–317; U. Kühn, *Via Caritatis: Theologie des Gesetzes bei Thomas von Aquin* (1965); H. Vorster, *Freiheitsverständnis* (1965) (Aquinas and Luther); O. H. Pesch, *Theologie der Rechtfertigung* (1966) (Aquinas and Luther). ANTHROPOLOGY: J. Legrand, *L'univers et l'homme dans la philosophie de S. Thomas,* 2 vols. (1946); G. Siewerth, *Thomas von Aquin. Die menschliche Willensfreiheit* (1954); N. Hinske, *Thomas von Aquin: De Homine,* ed. by M. Landmann (1961); P. Engelhardt, ed., *Sein und Ethos* (1963); id., "Der Mensch und seine Zukunft", *Die Frage nach dem Menschen (Festschrift M. Müller)* (1966), pp. 352–74.

Paulus Engelhardt

THOUGHT-FORMS

The problems set by the "forms (or modes) of thought" have been treated under various names and from various viewpoints since the beginning of modern times. Differences in thought and styles of culture came to be consciously noted and analysed, and the experiences of the wars of religion led to human thought and knowledge being considered as something relative. This relativist view celebrated its greatest triumphs after the collapse of German Idealism into historicism in the 19th century. Comte speaks of various *stages* in man's view of the world and concept of science, Brentano of *phases* of philosophy, Kant announces the change in the *type of thought* with his critique, Trendelenburg constructs on the basis of fundamental logical concepts a typology of philosophical systems, Dilthey uses history to distinguish three *basic forms* of systems, Wölfflin demonstrates the presence of *categories* which determine styles in the history of art. Jaspers works out a psychology of general views of the world *(Weltanschauungen),* considering the various *techniques of thought,* Scheler seeks to determine in his sociology the main *kinds of knowledge;* Bocheński uses the term *methods of thought,* while Spranger speaks more comprehensively of *forms of life.*

The expression "thought-form" (form or mode of thought) was introduced into philosophical discussion by H. Leisegang. He understands by the term "the inwardly consistent sum of the rules of thought which results from an analysis of the writings of an individual and which appears likewise in other writers as the same structure". Its graphic presentation is the *Denkmodell* or paradigm of thought. Thus he investigates the circular form of thought as it appears from Heraclitus to St. Paul, and down to Hegel with his "circle of circles", and also the architectonic contrast to this organic type of thought, which is the "pyramid of thought", as in Aristotle, the Summas of the scholastics and Kant. The paradigm points in each case to a certain *Weltanschauung,* a general view of the universe, which is given its particular stamp by the dimension which predominates in the perspective. Hence thought-form means more precisely the sum of concepts and conceptual operations which are valid for the logical structure of a field of similar objects, and which then are transposed to other fields, to which they do not apply in the same way. Different fields of objects demand different types of logic. To investigate thought-forms it is therefore necessary to reduce the various systems to the precisely limited truth which they present (or start from), and also to work out their various logical structures, which should be fully enumerated and presented in a manual of logic.

A. Kandler takes up the expression and understands a thought-form as "the uniform structure of the rules" according to which a thinker "takes the individual tools of logic which he uses and applies them to form concrete assertions, as read in his works".

This definition is narrower than that of Leisegang. The latter takes a number of typical texts and uses "ideating abstraction" to try to give a general picture, while Kandler takes each text of an author and investigates relative frequencies: "The oftener a tool of formal logic occurs, the more characteristic it is as an expression of the thought-form."

In consequence of Heidegger's concept of the history of being and the fate of being, the term is used in J. B. Metz to treat of ontology and not the psychology of thought. It now means man's comprehensive understanding of being and of himself, the horizon that encompasses all events, and gives its essential nature to an epoch in the history of the spirit. And it is this general understanding which is determinative, no matter how great are the formal and material differences between the thinkers of the epoch in question — as for instance in Greek or modern thought. In this sense the thought-form can only be determined by the use of the hermeneutic circle: the discovery of the unspoken principle behind the statement — a principle ultimately beyond the range of speech — is only possible through investigation of the statements, but the statements can only be properly understood in the light of the principle. This sort of insight is outside the scope of the "objectivity" of Kandler's method, and it is also more "subjective" than Leisegang's ideation. It means that one must enter the mental horizon of another, without losing sight of or becoming fully and consciously aware of the special *a priori* of this understanding: it can only be "co-ascertained" in the very effort of understanding.

Here we can see at its clearest a principle which also holds good for the other views: that a thought-form is never merely a form and that it cannot be adequately distinguished from the content, difficult as it may be to establish definite laws for their co-relationship. This is just as impossible as it is to enumerate completely all forms of logic and thought. For both the forms of thought and the assertions themselves stem from the transcendental experience which the finite spirit has of beings and of itself. This experience takes place historically as an exercise of man's freedom and is therefore by the nature of things not fully open to inspection. What remains within sight is the very general structure of this experience, of the spirit and of beings. It has been set down in general logic, which, contrary to the tenets of psychologism and relativism, is the basis and framework of all its concrete data, where some fields of knowledge are more favoured than others and where expression, development, end and object vary, as well as presentation and interpretation. Groups of data take shape which may be investigated, related to one another and arranged according to type; possibilities of thought-forms as yet unrealized may suggest themselves; but a "full index" and complete systematization is on principle unattainable.

It is equally impossible to establish fixed laws for the origin, flowering and decline of the thought-forms of individuals or of epochs. A thought-form may develop new possibilities and a fuller life as freedom becomes more aware of itself and as stimulating contacts are made with other forms — though an encounter may be the impulse to withdrawal and ossification as well as to open-mindedness. "Classic" thought-forms are those which display a higher degree of universally valid truth and which can be taken over by later generations. But every thought-form is caught up in the dialectic of having to grasp and express the infinite truth in a finite way. If it claims to be an absolute, it becomes an ideology. But an ideology would be no less sceptical or relativist renunciation of truth. Every stride towards the truth, such as can be registered for instance in the validity of formal logic, enables us not merely to understand one thought-form from another, but also to judge the value of their various assertions, that is, to make the fundamental distinction between "not fully adequate" (which holds good in varying degrees in each case) and "false" — difficult though the decision may be in any given case. In his encounter with other thought-forms, man must become aware of his own, and recognize the validity and the limits of each, while seeing therein the absolute claim of truth, which calls him perpetually to new horizons.

See also *Language, Hermeneutics, Historicism, Relativism.*

BIBLIOGRAPHY. H. Leisegang, *Denkformen* (2nd ed., 1951); E. Cassierer, *Philosophy of Symbolic Forms,* 3 vols. (1953–57); W. Dilthey, *Essence of Philosophy* (1954); id., *Gesammelte Schriften,* IV (3rd ed., 1963), pp. 528–54; *ibid.,* VIII (3rd ed., 1962), pp. 73–118; A. Kandler, "Einleitung zur Untersuchung der theologischen Denkform des hl. Thomas von Aquin", *Miscellanea Francescana* 55 (1955), pp. 14–58; K. Jaspers, *Psychologie der Weltanschauungen* (4th ed., 1955); id., *Perennial Scope of Philosophy* (1968); M. Scheler, *Philosophical Perspectives* (1958); M. Heidegger, *Nietzsche,* II (1961); W. Waffenschmidt, *Denkformen und Denktechnik* (1961); J. Metz, *Christliche Anthropozentrik* (1962); H. Rombach, *Die Gegenwart der Philosophie* (1962); M. Müller, *Existenzphilosophie im geistigen Leben der Gegenwart* (3rd ed., 1964); I. M. Bocheński, *Methods of Contemporary Thought* (1965); H.-G. Gadamer, *Wahrheit und Methode* (2nd ed., 1965).

Jörg Splett

TIME

A. The Theological Dimension

1. The theological question as regards "time" must be posed in the context of the coming (or offer) of salvation, when man is summoned to decision, to accept salvation in fact, in his freedom. Hence the theological question does not start from a notion of time derived from the natural sciences. It is concerned with man's self-understanding as a being in need of and capable of salvation — an understanding which is prior to the view of man gained from science and technology.

Hence when theology inquires into time and the temporal, it asks what are the conditions of possibility for the history of freedom, and hence for the history of salvation, in mankind and in the individual. As Catholic theology understands the relationship between salvation and natural reality, between grace and nature, salvation-history and world history, the reality prior to and under grace is integrated into the total reality of salvation-history, but without losing its own structures. It is the *potentia oboedientialis* of which the supreme possibility is realized, remaining in a new form in the totality of salvation. Hence even in the deployment of salvation-history the concept of "natural" time remains, and since it is the time of man, it is an interpersonal, dialogal time. For it is impossible to "demythologize" time in such a way that the empirical "worldly" course of time would have no meaning at all in this history of salvation. Otherwise some dimensions of reality would have absolutely no meaning for salvation, or would be excluded. Salvation, justification, would not attain the realm where the world, time, the body, are found. But Christianity, the coming of salvation, aims at the salvation of man as he is in the concrete, in all his dimensions.

257

2. The Christian faith confesses that the world was created with a beginning in time, and rejects the notion of a "world existing from eternity" as heretical (*D* 428, 501–3, 1783). It confesses one irreversible history of salvation and perdition, and rejects the "eternal return of all things". It confesses the saving character of particular events of history and awaits the end of all history (see *Eschatology*). It assigns man a history, in freedom, which cannot be repeated at will and cannot be subjected to endless revision. History here appears as the production of the definitive in which the course of time is absorbed into its definitive harvest, which faith then calls "eternal life". Scripture uses the terms "the fullness of time" (see *Incarnation, Jesus Christ* I), "the hour" (the single, appointed opportunity bestowed on freedom with regard to salvation), the "once only" (ἐφάπαξ, the single event which, though only part of history, determines history irretrievably for ever). But faith also takes note of the external time which flows on, seeing it as the power which enslaves but which man is freed from by the grace of God in Christ. And faith knows of the time of salvation, in which man can act through grace in a way which remains valid for ever. The full act of faith includes as an inner element the virtue of hope, which takes him into an open future — which he still, however, awaits — a future which his independent planning can never master. Faith confesses the providence of God, by which he is not only Lord of time, but also guarantees an ultimate meaning of time for history. When speaking of the incarnation of the Logos, faith confesses that time becomes a predicate of the God who is immutable "in himself" and accepts and experiences his own real history "in the world". In the analysis of the history of revelation and the history of dogma, time and the reality of revelation are confronted with one another. The result is clear. Time is not just a determination of physical and material reality. It is also a determination of the spirit. Since the history of nature and the world is essentially determined by the history of freedom, it results clearly that the flow of time is not a power which enslaves man but a particular and deficient element of the personal, dialogal time of freedom.

3. In all the above statements, the notion of time is drawn from ordinary human experience. It is presupposed, but not further explained. But revelation does not eliminate the transcendental nature of man as it realizes and hence explicates itself, and it does not blot out this horizon. Hence theology, in its effort to give an account of itself, may have recourse to the perspectives of human selfhood as outlined by philosophy. But one must bear in mind in such a procedure that once revelation has reached its goal, there is a unity between the transcendental experience of self (in time) and man's eschatological experience of himself in and through Jesus Christ, as given in the history of revelation and salvation. But it is only this unity which enables "natural" reality to be displayed in all its dimensions. A merely transcendental explanation of man necessarily falls short. For it does not clearly contain the epochal, historical criterion of self-understanding. But the objectivating experience of time takes place on principle in the same dimension in which the history of revelation is deployed.

4. The statement of the Christian message cannot dispense with any of the various elements of the understanding of time — even though these again have a "history" in the self-understanding of man, in which they stand out with different degrees of clearness. Two elements in particular are theologically relevant.

a) One element is that of succession, movement, in the duration of the temporal. The succession is seen as objective, and its dimensions are considered in the perspective of the cosmos. This is the aspect under which the Greek, Western tradition apprehends "external" time. Time is extrapolated from the flow of the "Now" and becomes a quantifying, measuring, continuous and homogeneous field (*per se* empty). Every moment is of equal importance and each lives by the annulment of the previous. The movement of the world and hence of man takes place in this medium. Here man is exposed to time and made its slave, as though to a cosmic power. He does not himself form time, strictly speaking, either individually or collectively. The classical definition is given by Aristotle, where the formula derives from an objectivist view of physical reality: "numerus motus secundum prius et posterius" ("the enumeration of movement as encountered within the horizon of the earlier and the later") (*Physics,* IV, 11; 219 b; cf. Plato, *Timaeus,* 37, 10 f.). This then came to be dominant in the philosophy and theology of the Middle Ages, as in St. Albertus Magnus

(*Summa Theologica,* I, 21, 2) and St. Thomas Aquinas (*Summa Theologica,* I, q. 10, a. 1–6; *Contra Gentiles,* I, 15, 55; *In octo libros physicorum Aristotelis,* IV, 15–23). *This* concept of time was then transferred into the region of the subjective, as by Kant, for whom it was "a form of intuition given with the subjectivity", or by Hegel, for whom it was "negativity" (time as self-negation, as the presence of constant self-elimination, as the negative-in-itself, as the negation negating itself). But this introduced no essential change into the Greek notion of time.

b) What is primarily relevant in theology is, above all, as follows from what has been said, "internal", qualitative, time, which is seen as filled with content and measured in terms of man — time as event. It is formed by the free deployment of interpersonal presence. Time exists as the event in which the definitiveness of existence is freely brought about before God. This element of the time experienced by all men only becomes explicit in the specifically Christian understanding of existence. It is only when revelation-as-history colours fundamentally the (transcendental) understanding of existence that history is seen in its true light — in the light of revelation as event. This notion of time was first given speculative expression by St. Augustine, in his deduction of time from the self-interpretation of presence (existence) (*Confessions,* XI, 13–29). It was obscured in the philosophy of the Middle Ages and only comes to light again when man, the individual, is seen as a personal and non-interchangeable being (see *Person*), as the being whose essence it is to give itself its own reality and whose reality it is to have to find its own essence. This view is exemplified by Pascal, in Romanticism, in Schelling (with his philosophy of freedom, of the real positive act), in Kierkegaard and in M. Heidegger (who took from Dilthey and Yorck von Wartenburg the notion of man as a historical being, transferred it on to the ontological plane and expounded time in terms of history-of-being and the structural references of personal presence; see *History* I). Where theological anthropology speaks of man as "spirit" and "body", the difference and the unity of these two elements of the one time experienced by the multiplicity of men is also part of its statement. Hence when dogmatic theology speaks of time it cannot dispense with either element.

5. The ontologically prior and basic case of time and of its radical characteristics, as met with by man, is in his existence itself, in man's own action. Hence physical, objectivist, external time cannot be the starting-point for reaching the notion of time. Time, as the external measurement of time, remains extrinsic to existence in its temporality and its internal time. It hides the fact that measurement itself is possible only for a spiritual being which experiences what time is in the light of its own inner self-realization. The primordial notion of time must therefore be that it is the mode of becoming proper to finite freedom in bodily form: a coming from an unmastered beginning in a deliberate choice of one's own reality, and an arrival at the irrevocable unique completion of such an act. The oneness and distinction of these moments is the time of this existence. They are not therefore a pure succession of different elements. They form the *one* reality of time. The successiveness of experiences and the experience of this successiveness in time is not "explicable". They cannot be built into a synthesis composed of other elements, because the being and the experience of such would themselves be again under the sign of this temporality. But this existence, an internal time, brings on its eternity as it exposes itself to the otherness of an "external" world, to its history and hence to the time which characterizes this history. This derives at once from the nature of man, of which the notes are the unity and plurality of transcendence and the *a posteriori.* For this means that existence is part of the world and external time, in spite of the true beginning and the internal time which existence implies. And it also means that existence can be deployed in internal time only by taking over world-time, though the two elements of the one time of man cannot be considered identical. Man's internal time is always alienated from him in external time, and he nonetheless only finds his internal time in the external time of the world.

6. Where the internal time of experience has not yet been truly a matter of reflection, and is merely a propriety of the external time in which it is entirely absorbed, external time becomes an endless succession of self-contained units of time, the eternal return of the same, cyclic time (for the time of mythical thinking, see *Myth*). But since internal time must be understood as the unity of beginning and end before God, since it is a coming

forth from God and a return to him, the cyclic pattern of time remains justifiable and necessary, since the "transcendental" end and the "transcendental" beginning can only be thought of in the categories which embrace objects and can only be brought about in external time. But then again, since external time can only be thought of as a condition of possibility of the internal time of human existence, and since this existence has a true end, the fullness of time, the linear interpretation of external time is also the ultimate truth about this time. Hence the two proprieties of time, the cyclic and the linear, are theologically indispensable.

BIBLIOGRAPHY. M. Heidegger, *Sein und Zeit* (1927), E. T.: *Being and Time* (1962); id., "Zeit und Sein", *L'endurance de la pensée (Studies in honour of J. Beaufret)* (1968); E. Husserl, *Vorlesungen zur Phänomenologie des inneren Zeitbewusstseins* (1928), E. T.: *Phenomenology of Internal Time Consciousness,* ed. by M. Heidegger (1964); H. Wendland, *Geschichtsauslegung und Geschichtsbewusstsein im Neuen Testament* (1938); G. Delling, *Das Zeitverständnis des Neuen Testaments* (1940); L. Lavelle, *Du temps et de l'éternité* (1945); H. Marrou, *L'ambivalence du temps de l'histoire chez S. Augustin* (1950); O. Cullmann, *Christ and Time* (1951); J. Marsh, *The Fullness of Time* (1952); J.McIntyre, *The Christian Doctrine of History* (1957); A. Vögtle, *Zeit und Zeitüberlegenheit im biblischen Verständnis* (1961); J. Barr, *Biblical Words for Time* (1962); R. Wallis, *Le temps, quatrième dimension de l'esprit* (1966); K. Rahner, *Schriften zur Theologie,* IX (1969) (theology of time).

B. THE FUTURE AS THE FULLNESS OF TIME

1. Man is individually and socially a being who always keeps a step ahead of himself, so to speak. He makes himself what he is by planning his future and projecting himself into the future. But this future is never a fully fashioned plan. It is composed of single and different elements whose time runs out, and whose space is cramped. The projected future is finite and therefore comprised on principle within a further future of unknown possibilities. But even this finite sketch means that man expects the bits and pieces to fall into place and the surrounding void to be filled. The future must not therefore be considered just in the light of a sketch-plan, but in the light of a hope which sustains and surpasses all plans.

The future forms therefore a thematic unity with freedom, history, hope, progress, meaning and the end of man (see *Order* IV). It takes on a specific meaning in a philosophy and a theology where man, society and the world are not interpreted in the light of a static, unchanging essence, but where nothing is given except as a challenge and all reality is meaningful only in the light of what it yet must be.

2. The future cannot then be explained in terms of what is foreseen and on the way because man himself plans it and provides the technical means of realizing it. This sort of future would still be directly part of the present (in spite of its being itself beset by uncertainties). And the future cannot be explained in terms of evolution, because here it would be merely a prospective stage of something materially identical in structure with what is already given. It is instructive to note that these two forms of the reduction of the future to rationalized planning and material nature can be combined, and do in fact combine to stimulate each other in modern technology.

The future in the true sense — as Western thought has learned from the Jewish-Christian experience of history — is an advent, that which "comes" of its own accord, not an evolutionary derivative or a technical goal towards which we march in well-mapped stages. We have to deal with it as something that outbids all plans and normative development, something in fact which, while making such foresight possible, always makes it questionable and provisional. The future is the uncontrollable and incomprehensible which is not amenable to man's power. While it gives man his power, it ranges incalculably beyond it. Though the future comes imperiously to be in the realm which man designs and experiences as *his* future, it always remains his coming master, even where he represses or forgets the truth.

Nonetheless, the future is never completely detached from the past and the present. It is necessarily derivative, since it comes from the past and the present. For the present is always generating the past, and thus creating the past that will be. And this past gives rise to what will be the bearer and determinant of the future (see *Tradition*), because it comes as the ground of freedom, over which freedom never has total control and which freedom, never being entirely realized, does not find fully perspicuous. What the present lets go thus returns in the form of what is to come. It is the historical power which determines and takes in the present which is on its way. But this connection would be impossible if the present were not open to the future that is always still outstanding. For without this future there would be no past, not merely in the verbal analysis which shows that there can be a yesterday only because of today (which is or was its future), but in the real sense, that yesterday would lose all meaning and hence "reality" if today had no morrow. Past and present stem from the realm of futurity. All individual and social existence is ruled by the arrival of what is to come. The ambivalence of the past as that which is gone and that which is preserved is paralleled by the two modalities of the future: the future that is arriving and the future that is outstanding. It is true that freedom transforms the future into the present and decides it beforehand, but the future makes freedom what it is and challenges it to be. What comes absolutely to the individual is the end, death, and in such a way that the individual never knows the end as something over and done with. But since the end as such comprises the end of all present moments, the present is always absolutely determined by this end.

The acceptance of the future means taking it in the indissoluble and inexorable unity of its modes — as arriving and as outstanding. It must therefore be hope and openness. The acceptance of the past as a determinant of the future implies a positive attitude to the past. It is appropriated in a mood which is the only real basis of a critical view of it and allows for legitimate historical change in the individual and society — through contrition or revolution, as the case may be. These are ways of taking over the past in correct detachment from it. Where the element of the past in the future is denied, expectation becomes utopianism or absolute revolution, and the present loses all inner connection with the structure of the future. But again, where the past is regarded as the full and adequate ground of the future, conservatism and a wrong traditionalism ensue, since repressive fears have thrust the incalculable elements of the future out of sight (see *Contrition, Revolution*).

3. Since Christianity sees man, society and the world from the point of view of history of salvation, it rejects on principle the doctrine of a static essence. Man, society and the world, in the preaching of Christianity, are orientated to a history which so far from being doomed to the void, moves towards a future of fulfilment. This fulfilment has already been assigned to history, so that

history itself takes place within this (meaningful) future. Hence the message of Christianity can only be understood in the light of what it says of the future. Its interpretation of the past takes the form of a progressive unveiling of the approaching future. The meaning of the present for Christians is based on hopeful openness to the imminence of the absolute future which comes as a gift. This means that the essence of man, in Christian terms, may be defined as the possibility of attaining a future which has been definitively promised in the Spirit and the incarnation. But then the future is a state which is not encompassed by another, greater and still outstanding future which would diminish its significance. This dynamism towards the absolute future still outstanding has behind it a ground, norm and principle which reveal the horizon of the possible, and this principle is "the law of the beginning". But since the ultimate ground of the absolute fullness of reality and its last goal is God himself, who posits the beginning by making himself its goal, there is no realistic understanding of man, society and the world except in the light of the future. For the beginning is only fully disclosed there (see *Creation* III, IV).

4. Christianity as a religion and as a doctrine about the absolute future recognizes no future utopias within history. It proclaims that the life of the individual is decisive for salvation, and as regards humanity, it affirms that history has an end; see *Eschatology; Last Things*. It rejects as utopian ideology any view which erects into an absolute, beyond which there could be nothing and nothing could be expected, any future planned by man, to be achieved by the means over which he disposes in the world. Christianity imposes no ideal of the future for the intramundane history of man or society, but leaves it to man, and indeed makes it his duty, to plan the future properly (Vatican II, *Gaudium et Spes,* art. 5; Paul VI's encyclical, *Populorum Progressio*).

"Provided no utopian ideology dictates some intramundane future as the absolute goal, Christianity is not merely neutral with regard to all rational planning of the world's future, but positively favourable to such efforts. The purposeful, active, planned construction of the intramundane future, the liberation of man as far as possible from subjection to the forces of nature, the progressive socialization of man for the sake of the greatest possible deployment of individual liberty, are regarded by Christianity as a task imposed by the God-given nature of man. Man's duty lies here, and it is here that he fulfils his real religious task, the openness of freedom, in faith and hope, for the absolute future" (K. Rahner, p. 83). See *Political Theology, Theory and Practice*.

5. Efforts are now being made to supplement or even replace the traditional notions of transcendence (the supposedly localized images of "the above") by a new and decisively trenchant "paradigm", that of "the future". Such efforts have every right to criticize the classical images, but the new models also have their limitations, which must be definitely affirmed (see *Mystery, Transcendence*). Even if one allows on principle the priority of the dimension of futurity (so Heidegger, Bloch, Moltmann, Metz, etc., in their different ways), one must insist on the otherness, the always greater dissimilarity (discontinuity in continuity) of the "absolute future" of God's self-bestowal, as opposed to all human and worldly future. In the same way, tradition has always insisted on the difference between our present and the *nunc stans* of God. It is not true to say that in the past eternity and transcendence were only understood "spatially" without the necessary distinctions, in the light of the present. But once this question of principle has been stated, we may say that in fact the "future" is the best term for the OT and Christian experience of God. It implies the power of God within history which transcends history (cf. J. Moltmann).

BIBLIOGRAPHY. See bibliography on *Hope;* also: J. Mouroux, *The Mystery of Time* (1964); G. Sauter, *Zukunft und Verheissung* (1965); S. Unseld, ed., *Ernst Bloch zu ehren* (1965) (see especially essays by W. Pannenberg, J. B. Metz and J. Moltmann); E. Kellner, ed., *Christentum und Marxismus – Heute* (1966); J. Guitton, *Man and Time* (1966); H. Kimmerle, *Die Zukunftsbedeutung der Hoffnung* (1966); K. Rahner, *Schriften zur Theologie,* VI (1967), pp. 77–88 (Marxist utopia and Christian future); J. Moltmann, *Theology of Hope* (1967); J. Robinson and J. Cobb, eds., *Theology as History* (1967), especially pp. 197–220 (J. Cobb, "Past, Present and Future") and pp. 221–76 (W. Pannenberg, "Response to the Discussion"); J. B. Metz, *Theology of the World* (1968); M. Heidegger, *An Introduction to Sein und Zeit* (1968); M. Muckenhirn, *Future as the Presence of Shared Hope* (1968); E. L. Mascall, *Theology and the Future* (1968); J. Moltmann, "The Future as a New Paradigm of Transcendence", *Concurrence* 1, no. 4 (1969), pp. 334–45; E. L. Mascall, *Theology and the Future* (in preparation).

Adolf Darlap

TOLERANCE

A. Concept and Problems

This article does not deal with tolerance in the religious sense (see *Religious Freedom*) or with the juridical problems of tolerance in civil law or with the history of tolerance as it has in fact been. It is concerned with the problem of tolerance in social philosophy. For in spite of the claim to objectivity which every well-founded judgment must put forward, there is and has been a bewildering juxtaposition of claims to truth, which conflict with or exclude each other. The philosophical problem raised by tolerance has many aspects. Where theoretical differences take the form of a pluralism of world-views and systems of value, with competing claims in practical politics or in the social sphere, a fundamental problem of social philosophy arises. If the question is then asked as to the objective justification of social and political norms, with the further question of the possibility of the knowledge of truth and the problem of truth at various levels, a problem of the metaphysics of knowledge arises. If the historical origins and development of philosophical thought are considered, with all their many discords, it is a problem of philosophy in general and of the history of philosophy. The philosophical problem of tolerance may be formulated as the confrontation of truth and freedom, which takes the form, as a rule, of either dogmatism or relativism. There is no generally acknowledged definition of tolerance in the concrete, and the question is whether anything beyond a formal criterion does not run the risk of falling into dogmatism. On the other hand, the practical consequences are such that a merely formal definition proves to be an illusory solution, open to all sorts of abuse. For these reasons, the best method seems to be to give first a historical analysis, on the basis of which the motives and intentions of the champions of tolerance may be recognized, and then to try to draw various systematic conclusions.

B. History and Development

The term tolerance in the modern sense first appears about the end of the 16th century. But the notion itself is much older.

1. As long as there is a system of values universally acknowledged as binding, the problem of tolerance does not arise. Conflicts

arise only where there are ethnical or religious minorities, or in times of crisis or enlightenment, when earlier homogeneous structures break up. For this reason, nearly all programmes of enlightenment champion tolerance. This was done in a vague way by the ancient Sophists. Protagoras's "man is the measure of all things" was an implicit criticism of the traditional norms based on myth and religion, and hence raised the question of new principles of obligation. Gorgias doubted that there could be any demonstrable obligatory norms. Lycophron, after the break-down of traditional ethics, called for restrictions on the rights of the stronger. Antiphon, a contemporary of Socrates, took up again the contrast which had already been made between νόμος (custom) and φύσις (nature, necessity), to criticize purely traditional laws in favour of laws arrived at by mutual agreement. This is the first intimation of the notion of a "liberal" natural law.

In Critias, however, a radical rationalism led to totalitarian consequences. In his *Laws*, Book X, Plato demanded the death penalty for incorrigible atheists and adherents of strange religious cults, with an eye, no doubt, to certain followers of the Sophists. This open intolerance characterizes the radical solution of the problem in "closed" systems or world-views. It was put forward again and again in the course of history. Man can know the gods and hence the truth. The refusal of such knowledge and its consequences is equivalent to a surrender of the personality, and also endangers the fundamental consensus in the State which guarantees unity and survival. Truth is a *res sacra*. Men have to submit to this principle.

This relationship was first reversed by the Stoics. The *res sacra* was man, because he alone could know truth. Hence his principal virtues were *clementia, mansuetudo* and *humanitas*. Further, certain antinomies in knowledge suggested that the absolute claim of any given truth should not be overestimated. The ideal of the *sequi naturam* comes from a moral force intrinsic to man. Insofar as it is possible here to speak of the natural law, it is rather the consensus of all men than an authoritative deduction from first principles.

2. In the OT and NT, the problem of tolerance took concrete form primarily in the question of the relationship to other religions and to strangers (cf. G. Stählin, "ξένος", *TWNT,* V, pp. 1–36). On principle, the stranger was not regarded as an equal, and

was even considered an enemy, but in fact a sort of civil code existed for strangers in the Israelite State, and they enjoyed toleration; "for God loves the sojourner" (Deut 10:18). All peoples are under the power of God. Christians are to acknowledge heathen superiors. All men are created by God and bear his law in their hearts. Brotherliness, peace and hospitality are central virtues. Israel had practically no missions to the heathen. The Christian claim to absoluteness, which has often enough led to intolerance, is subordinated to the claim of freedom and love. Tolerance can also be seen in the fact that the biblical writings have adopted elements from non-Jewish or non-Christian religions. But the speculative problem of tolerance — how the absolute claim of truth and the legitimacy of divergent opinions can co-exist in practice and also be brought into a satisfactory synthesis — was not explicitly raised, much less answered.

3. Tolerance in the Roman Empire was mainly a question of religious freedom. The prevalent opinion was put as follows by Cicero: "Sua cuique civitati religio est, nostra nobis" (*Pro Flacco,* 28). The practice, from which the Oriental religions, Judaism and the mystery cults benefited, was due no doubt primarily to Roman political expediency, but goes back, especially in Cicero, to the philosophical principles of Stoicism in its scepticism with regard to the absolute claims of any world-view. But where Roman imperialism felt its legitimacy threatened by the universal claim of a religion, its tolerance came to an end, as the persecution of Christians shows. It is a classical example of the limit-case where tolerance is equivalent to the abolition of the prevailing system of political co-ordinates.

Though Christians then claimed both internal and external tolerance for themselves (Tertullian), they kept to these principles only partially after the Edict of Milan had met their claims (313). They admitted the theological maxim, "credere non potest nisi volens". But the Christian Emperors violated this principle in favour of religious unity as a basis of empire, and outlawed paganism, in spite of the fact that its representatives such as Libanius and Symmachus appealed for tolerance. Justinian forbade heretics to hold public office. The unbaptized were regarded as outlaws. Some theologians like St. Ambrose, Lactantius, St. Athanasius and St. Hilary suggested peaceful methods, while

263

some even recognized the good faith of pagans. But the Church soon left it to the civil power to impose penalties on pagans and heretics. In the case of the Donatists, St. Augustine also agreed that the laws should apply. A larger measure of tolerance came about only in the Arian Churches (Theodoric the Great). The problem of tolerance was complicated rather than solved by the unity of State and Church. Where the universal claim of a religion is supported by and supports the civil power, the best possible groundwork is laid for totalitarianism, that is, for intolerance.

4. In the Middle Ages too the unity of Empire and Church was predominant. A threat to the *sacerdotium* could only be seen as a threat to the *imperium*. The extrapolation of religious conflict into the political sphere seemed quite normal to medieval thought. But there were marked differences in the way in which heathens, Jews and heretics were treated. "Accipere fidem est voluntatis, sed tenere fidem iam acceptam est necessitatis" (St. Thomas Aquinas). The faith once accepted cannot be abandoned. Hence there was tolerance on principle for heathens and Jews, but not for heretics who called in question the legitimacy of *civitas* and *societas*. There were, however, constant outbreaks of persecution against Jews, and missions were at times forced upon heathens. The claim to absolute truth finally gave rise to the Inquisition. On the other hand, the distinction between error and the holder of error brought about a remarkable readiness to enter into discussion with the Aristotelian tradition of the Arabs and with Jewish and Greek philosophy.

This respect for other cultures and world-views took concrete form in a number of famous dialogues in which for the most part a Greek or Arab philosopher, a Jew and a Christian theologian debated the truth of religion (cf. Abelard, Ramon Lull, Roger Bacon, Dante, Nicholas of Cusa, etc.). But these discussions resemble later dialogues on tolerance only in their form, since they all ended with the proof that Christianity was the true and universal religion. The tolerance of these dialogues does not consist in their material results, but only in their form. Nonetheless, only the stronger arguments were supposed to be valid, which implies that the criterion for religious truth is its rational justification. And in contrast to the purely immanent procedures of prevailing theological argument, this represented important and far-reaching progress. The ground was laid for a rational discussion of tolerance, once theological premises had lost their binding character. As a speculative theory, this attitude appeared in Nominalism with its abandonment of the presumed unity of theology and philosophy, of God and the world, of subject and object. It became a factor of Church history at the Reformation, when various forms of Christianity put forward claims to absoluteness. In politics, it characterized the wars of religion and later edicts of tolerance.

5. The immediate effects of the Reformation were unfavourable to tolerance, in spite of the tolerant attitude urged by such leaders as Sebastian Franck, Melanchthon, Zwingli and Bucer. The old unity of *imperium* and *sacerdotium* was shattered. Its place was taken in Germany by the territorial principle of *cuius regio, eius religio*. Calvinism in particular developed many features hostile to tolerance, and the wars of religion added another. Nonetheless, the principle of freedom of conscience, which had been discussed in the Middle Ages, though there restricted in view of the indelible character of baptism, came to the fore again with the Reformation, while the philosophy of humanism helped to spread respect for the autonomy of man. The wars of religion, the Two-Kingdoms doctrine of Luther, the growth of nationalism and of independence in the States of the Empire led to the distinction between Church and State and inspired a number of edicts of toleration — not that they always guaranteed real tolerance, as may be seen from the "Act of Toleration", 1689, in England.

The methods of the natural sciences and the discovery of new cultures abroad likewise helped to make Christianity's claim appear less absolute. And the horrifying results of the wars of religion brought the moral aspect of humaneness to the fore. J. Bodin used the example of a real and artificial apple, which could not be distinguished from one another, to demonstrate the relativity of knowledge. F. Bacon put forward in his *Novum Organum* an anti-Aristotelian notion of science by which alone the distinction between idols and real ideas, superstition and faith, was to be possible. With intolerance prevailing in fact, thinkers took refuge in model utopias to show how a State based on reason could overcome confessional quarrels.

St. Thomas More depicted a State which pre-ferred the free exercise of religion to all compulsion in matters of faith and conscience. The criterion of the truth of a religion was its demonstrable rationality. The freedom of the individual was restricted only by the recognition of certain minimum religious demands, but T. Campanella in his *Civitas Solis* presented an extremely rationalistic picture of an all-powerful State where all demands for freedom would again be regu-lated strictly according to absolute principles. This programme of a high-minded dictator-ship anticipated features of the profane totalitarian States of the modern era, since the problem of tolerance was bypassed once more for the sake of a pseudo-religious principle of unity. F. Bacon, however, in his fragment, *Nova Atlantis,* anticipated some deistic notions. Religion appears as an attribute of reason and as a humanism. This tendency is even clearer in J. Toland, with his book *Christianity Not Mysterious* (1696): the truths of faith are all truths of reason and hence matter for debate. Hence the tendency which had already appeared in the Middle Ages, to subordinate religion to reason, came into play in the discussion of tolerance. It was a way of avoiding the dilemma of contradictory claims to absoluteness. And at the same time the dangerous principle was enunciated that freedom and truth should be regulated and determined in the name of a rationalistic system of unity (Campanella).

6. These two components characterized the problem of tolerance in the modern era. The apotheosis of reason meant that con-fessional controversies were dismissed as futile. In Hobbes's *Leviathan* the all-powerful State, the "natural kingdom of God", is completely in control of the religion as well as the freedom of the citizens. The State is the only mediator of God, whose will it determines in a certain way. Tolerance is reserved only for inward faith, but no public manifestations of the latter are allowed. This reduction of tolerance to the private, internal realm, with strict regulation of public free-dom, presupposes a difference between the mind of the individual and that of the all-powerful State, but cynically subordinates the problem of tolerance to a rigorous principle of order. Spinoza likewise grants the State the strict right to judge all actions, but his supreme norms are justice and love, since his aim is to guarantee freedom to all citizens, a freedom which in matters of

thought and judgment remains inviolable *(Tractatus Theologico-politicus)*. Respect for freedom of judgment is based on man's rational faculties, which necessarily grasp all being as the explication of God *(Deus sive natura)*. But then freedom is again subject to a determinism, and tolerance is possible only within a predetermined frame of reference.

John Locke urged separation of Church and State, saw the State as constituted by the common consent of the citizens and not on metaphysical grounds, and demanded the separation of executive and legislative pow-ers, with equal rights for all citizens. These principles made him the father of Liberalism and enabled him to be the first upholder of a theory of tolerance which avoided the conflict between rationalistic determinism and the absolute claims of a given world-view. The rights of man are inalienable. The task of the State is merely to safeguard the individual with his property and freedom. A distinction is made between civil law and divine law, though religion is still recognized as the source from which all that surpasses reason may be known. There is only one limit to tolerance: a danger threatening the State itself, as the guarantor of the freedom of the individuals *(A Letter concerning Tolera-tion)*. This may be all very well as a formal principle, but its application by Locke is highly questionable. Tolerance did not apply to Catholics and atheists, because the Pope was a foreign ruler and atheists did not recognize the moral foundation of the State, which was the status of revelation as the ultimate binding force which gave legitimacy to all laws. In spite of these misgivings, nearly all modern democratic constitutions are based on these liberalist theories of tolerance: the freedom of the individual and the separation of Church and State. In the 19th century, Locke's theories were taken up and developed by J. S. Mill.

The English Enlightenment was the great-est promoter of the notion of tolerance, though mostly at the expense of theology and of the binding force of the knowledge of truth (to which "common sense" was pre-ferred; see *Deism, Scepticism*). The French Enlightenment on the other hand took on strongly anti-clerical traits. The Encyclo-pédistes like Condillac, Lamettrie and Cabanis put forward a sensualistic materialism, which provided, in Scepticism or a mechanistic metaphysics, a very doubtful basis for the tolerance which was always in demand (Bayle, Montaigne, Voltaire). These theses came to be of great importance for tolerance because they paved the way for republican and democratic notions of the State. These political theories presupposed the enlightenment and maturity of the individual. This call for emancipation has remained, down to the present day, the fundamental element of the imperious demand for tolerance and the ground of its legitimacy. It went hand in hand with the demand for public freedom of speech.

The opposition between the denominations played an important role in Germany, where G. L. Lessing was one of the protagonists. In his *Education of the Race* he comprised "errors" among the elements of development. History was to bring about a reconciliation between reason and faith in a "Third Age of the World". Lessing's views were marked by Christian thinking and a certain sense of the historicity of knowledge. Critical reflection and the smoothing out of thesis and antithesis in German Idealism may be seen to some extent as the working out of Lessing's notion of tolerance, though the problems connected with it were never given any great attention in philosophy. But the dominant principles of Idealism, the autonomy of reason and will, include the suppositions which have been of abiding importance for the notion of tolerance. Independence, freedom, does not mean dispensing oneself from objectivity but consists precisely in finding its fulfilment in the truth.

C. ANALYTICAL SUMMARY

This brings us to the real problem. Since what tolerance aims at is truth, how can it be exercised at all if it means being patient with opposing views and therefore must renounce, at least to some extent, the effort to spread what seems to be the truth?

To define tolerance as mere patience is unsatisfactory. This is a relativist view of tolerance, and would be self-destructive. Politically, such formal tolerance is clearly untenable, since it would imply liberty for groups who would exploit this tolerance to set up power-groups who would themselves be intolerant. To avoid such formalism, one must consider the conditions under which an objective grasp of truth can be attained. For if truth is multi-dimensional, and cannot in the concrete be the monopoly of any group, it is possible to justify tolerance by the impossibility of attaining absolute truth. Here, of course, we are not speaking of the

functional notion of truth in the natural sciences. It is a matter of the notion of truth in the "practical sciences" whose task it is to determine social norms.

Dilthey (see *Historicism*) defined the truth valid for a given epoch as the expression of the way of life which it found meaningful. This meant that all claims to objectivity were whittled away and made relative to each epoch adduced in historical comparisons. For when "life" is the basis of all cultural norms, we are left with an irrational standpoint. Nonetheless, Dilthey's thesis points on to the "history and historicity" of truth, as propounded later in fundamental ontology (see *History* I), though here again the criteria for the valid exposition of truth, as being disclosing itself in history, remain problematic. Tautological solutions may be the only result of the analysis of practice undertaken by the philosophy of history.

To evade such ambiguities, philosophy of a positivist inspiration in its many branches reduces its claim to truth to formal logic and empirically verifiable analytical propositions. All other normative propositions are said to be scientifically incapable of demonstration. Hence objectivity is unattainable in the "practical" sciences, where pragmatical procedures should rather be aimed at. To proceed pragmatically (see *Pragmatism*) means that objectivity is replaced by the criterion of success, and hence that social norms are replaced by lines of conduct whose success can be checked. But since "success" is again a relative, subjective criterion, pragmatism cannot constitute an objective basis for the justification of tolerance. The "dialectical" social theories of Adorno, Horkheimer and Habermas insist that the individual is so conditioned by the system that he cannot see the flaws in the social code. Individual and society are so bereft of political sense that it is easy to perpetuate political and social forms which have become brittle and decayed. There are only vestigial traces of the public opinion which should hold a watching brief and criticize. And in fact criticism is genially absorbed by the "establishment" and exploited at once as a proof of its liberal views. Under such circumstances, formal tolerance is in fact repressive in character (Marcuse). Since the democratic urge is to a great extent domesticated by forces which actually function as coercive, objectivity becomes impossible. Then a false pluralism is appealed to, really a relativism, to avoid the charge of loss of objectivity. Since tolerance cannot be assured either by such relativistic pragmatism or by any dogmatic regulations, it remains for philosophy to develop a method by which the "practical sciences" can avoid this dilemma in defining tolerance.

Here it should be noted that the positivist method, and such claims as it has to objectivity, ignore the specific interests by which the "practical sciences" are guided. Their search is for a science of liberty. They strive to justify and further in present-day terms the emancipation of the human race which has taken place by virtue of historical imperatives. In spite of these terms of reference as a hermeneutical principle, there may well be differences in actual practice. Hence the principles underlying social practice must be upheld only hypothetically, that is, as propositions to be verified or falsified. Thus social and political life takes on the character of an experiment, based on a theory arrived at or tested empirically as well as speculatively (by dialectical interpretation) (see Theory and Practice). If such is the process of social and political life, the tolerance whose goal is social truth is provided with the best possible guarantees. The criteria by which it is justified are left open both to methodical and rational inspection and to the critical sense of public opinion. Tolerance is then in fact the outcome of traffic in communications all round. The purpose of tolerance is to protect minorities and to provide for a wide spectrum of freedom of opinion, while still aiming at least on principle at upholding truth and objectivity without dogmatic premises. It could be achieved in such a communicative society.

This notion of tolerance need not come into conflict in any way with tolerance as understood in theology. In any case, the machinery of tolerance is now under the control of the State, society and powerful social groups, while the Churches rather depend on tolerance than decide upon it. But even in theology and its understanding of truth, it is difficult — in spite of the obligatory character of fundamentals — to formulate concrete imperatives in a normative way, because the discovery of truth is a gradual process, mediated in many ways by historical factors, and always conditioned by contingency and concupiscence. The growing importance of hermeneutics emphasizes this fact. Creation itself must be treated with reserve in view of its eschatological destiny, and hence social practice is most in keeping with the theological understanding of the

world when it retains its experimental character. And social planning based on and justified by an interest in human emancipation does not contradict the principles of theology: especially as the finite ends and aims of social theory must grant the "eschatological reserve" its due rights, inasmuch as it is the question-mark over all plans.

See also (especially on the theological aspect) *Christianity* II, *Rights of Man, Revelation* I, *Religious Freedom, Political Theology, Theory and Practice*.

BIBLIOGRAPHY. H. van Loon, *The Story of Tolerance* (revised ed., 1940); T. W. Adorno and others, *Authoritarian Personality* (1950); H. Kelsen, *General Theory of Law and State* (1945); M. Horkheimer, *The Eclipse of Reason* (1947); J. Maritain, *Truth and Human Fellowship* (1957); H. Hamilton, *Free Order, National Goal, World Goal* (1963); K. Rahner, *The Dynamic Element in the Church* (1964); id., "Der Dialog in der pluralistischen Gesellschaft", in J. B. Metz and J. Splett, eds., *Weltverständnis im Glauben* (1965), pp. 287–97; K. Moore, *The Spirit of Tolerance* (1964); M. James, *The Tolerant Personality* (1964); S. Mandelbaum, *Social Setting of Intolerance* (1964); R. P. Wolff, B. Moore and H. Marcuse, *Critique of Pure Tolerance* (1965); J. Locke, *Second Treatise of Civil Liberty and Letter concerning Toleration*, (3rd ed. by J. Gough, 1966); J. Habermas, *Erkenntnis und Interesse* (1968).

Werner Post

TOTALITARIANISM

1. Totalitarianism is a term applied as a rule indifferently to all systems of total control of individual and social life by the State. It is therefore formally speaking a type of society in which the essential dialectical interplay of spontaneous interaction, and social conditions as a pre-established form of interaction, has ceased to be an equilibrium. A given form of social self-interpretation predominates exclusively and consistently and is rigidly institutionalized in fixed systems of administration, public order and the linguistic media of self-interpretation.

2. The usual pejorative sense of totalitarianism comes from a fundamentally liberal notion of society which projects its counterpart into the concept of the "totalitarian State". The ideal is the "free citizen", the creative spontaneity of the independent self-determining individual who enters into the free interplay of well-balanced forces which

267

are bound *a priori* to no fixed norms but constantly produce their own rules. He submits to certain legal restrictions of his sovereignty only where this is absolutely necessary. Against this background, totalitarianism appears as the reduction of all spontaneous self-development to a planned moment of a social process entirely organized by the State. No private realm is left for the direct creativity of the individual. Freedom is eliminated. This totalitarian image is primarily derived from the procedures of an irrational or abstractly rationalistic absolutism. Since its ideals, whether rigid or fantastic, are foreign to the social process and its intrinsic demands, it forces the individual into a dogmatic pattern which can only mean self-alienation for him and a total artificiality for society. The system can be maintained only by one form or other of terror. Hence in terms of liberalism, totalitarianism indicates the element of comprehensiveness in authoritarianism, i.e., in the denial and thwarting of personal choice and way of life by outside forces. And authoritarianism represents the "intensive" element of totalitarianism, i.e., the moulding of a society in terms of abstract, *a priori* concepts which embrace all aspects of life.

3. *Totalitarianism and total social integration.* Liberalism sees only two alternatives. On the one hand there is the creative spontaneity of the private individual. On the other hand there is totalitarianism, the inhuman subjection of the individual to a pre-established overall pattern. The "authoritarian" society which imposes alien, coercive institutions is implicitly identified with the "totalitarian" which aims at all-embracing institutions. But the contrast now appears highly problematical. Every viable society is "total". It incorporates all realms of life without exception into a consistent process of social self-reproduction, self-organization and self-interpretation, of which the State is only a partial expression. And such realms as are left untouched are expressly excluded, that is, benefit in turn from a definite, pre-established pattern.

Hence social mediation is *de facto* total. All self-realization is conditioned by intersubjective (linguistic) truths and patterns of conduct, as also by a combination of social values. Freedom cannot therefore be, as liberalism imagined, the isolation of the individual from society. For the concession of such a completely private sphere within the totality of social mediation — of which the State and its laws are only a specific moment — can only be an illusory distortion of the actual conditions of such "privacy" or a privilege contrary to social equality. Thus real freedom can no longer be sought merely in formal opposition to totalitarianism. It can be found only in the social mediation itself and in the acceptance of its *de facto* totality. Society as a whole should be such that it offers the individual adequate play and imposes on him no foreign commands, but only those which are his own will but socially mediated and hence become real. In other words, freedom lies originally not outside the social process, even the State and its laws, but finds itself and its objective reality in society.

Under these circumstances, totalitarianism no longer has a positive counterpart in the self-understanding of bourgeois liberalism, and the ordinary sense of totalitarianism needs to be decidedly modified. Totalitarianism is not merely (though it naturally includes this) the "extensive" aspect of authoritarianism in society. Where it is consciously pursued, it indicates in a particularly explicit form the totality of the social process as it reproduces itself comprehensively in technology, economics, bureaucracy, politics, speech and reflection. It sees its task clearly as the construction of the totally-integrated society which demands regard for individual and interpersonal freedom and spontaneity. In other words, the dangerous element of totalitarianism is not the comprehensive nature of social interests. Danger arises when society's interest in the individual is dictated by abstract premises and laws which do not stem from the dynamism of social equality but are justified by some extrinsic considerations and hence lead to authoritarian control and the resulting self-alienation of the individual and society.

Hence the alternative to totalitarianism in the pejorative sense cannot be the rejection of total social integration. It must be the elimination of all systems of rule which it would be the surrender of freedom to accept. It must be the effort to eliminate all self-alienation from the social context.

See also *Society, Freedom* I.

BIBLIOGRAPHY. H. Arendt, *The Origins of Totalitarianism* (1951); L. Talmon, *The Origins of Totalitarian Democracy* (1952); C. J. Friedrich, *Totalitarian Dictatorship and Autocracy* (1956);

V. Chalupa, *The Rise and Development of a Totalitarian State* (1959); K. R. Popper, *The Open Society and its Enemies,* 2 vols. (1962).

Konrad Hecker

TRADITION

God has revealed himself to man, and he has completed and perfected his salutary self-disclosure in the life and teaching of the incarnate Word, so that no new public revelation of God to man is possible till the parousia. In the encounter with Christ, in faith in his word and in allowing his grace to work, man receives his supernatural salvation. But how does the fullness of God's revelation reach the individual incorrupt and unmixed with error, so that the individual knows that he is really addressed and challenged by the word of God and not by one of the many claims of men?

The Christian answer to this question is: through the tradition of the Church. The word of God and his gifts of grace reach man through the preaching handed down in the Church. The mystery of Christ remains present in history because there is a fellowship of believers which in the vital process of life, doctrine and worship preserves the word of God, through the assistance of the Holy Spirit, through all the changes of history, and thus hands it on safely to all generations till the Lord comes in glory.

A. Tradition in Human History

What tradition means for human life in general may be most clearly illustrated from the exercise of human freedom. The spiritual nature of man, reaching out beyond any given concrete object of choice towards the Absolute — the transcendence of human freedom — is what makes possible all freedom of choice and also gives human freedom its religious seriousness. When man really acts freely, he always includes in his decision an attitude towards the Absolute, towards God. But this "experience" of the transcendence of freedom can never be grasped purely as such. It can only be experienced and known along with and through the given concrete object. But the bodily nature of human freedom means that though man reaches towards the definitive and the absolute in his self-determination, he can only do so by launching out towards "the other", towards the world. But this "other", through which the ex-

perience of transcendence in the free act is most truly to be grasped, and which makes the reality of freedom and the serious responsibility palpable, is the fellow-man. The self-realization of the person in freedom takes place primarily through intercourse with and conduct towards other persons. The You of the fellow-man is thus constitutive for each one's own freedom.

But the encounter with other men is always an encounter with history, with what has come about freely and outside the scope of the individual's power. The range of freedom within the scope of the individual is not merely — and not at all primarily — the area of permanently identical matter provided as it were by an abstract notion of nature. The free act of man is always co-determined by the history of others. In his intercourse with the persons around him, in his learning to speak, in his adoption of given thought-forms, in his manner of evaluating, judging and reacting, in his own self-understanding, man absorbs the history which is already living on in others. He takes over by necessity the thoughts, verdicts and values of others before him. But this means that man always lives by tradition. In his free growth towards definitive selfhood, man can only be and become himself as one who is inwardly stamped by tradition. It is only as stamped by tradition that he can adopt an attitude towards the world of men and things around him, accepting or rejecting the traditional. This determination of man's freedom by history will of course be experienced and recognized with different degrees of intensity at various epochs and at various stages of culture. Hence the attitude of the individual to tradition varies according to the period in which he lives. He either adopts it as "natural" and evidently acceptable, or he calls it in question, more or less radically, since he recognizes that it is the product of freedom and hence as not necessarily what it is. This gives rise to criticism of tradition, that is, the question as to what is of permanent value in the traditional, or what can and what must be changed in certain circumstances. The meaning and the problems of the natural law as the permanent norm of all criticism of tradition cannot be gone into here. But where a tradition has been established on the basis of a historical event, and where this historical event is also accorded permanent significance, the norm of a possible criticism of tradition must be primarily only the "return to the source", the investigation of what was originally experienced, done and meant.

B. THE CATHOLIC NOTION OF TRADITION

1. *Living tradition.* As a religion of revelation, Christianity is based on a historical event: the life, teaching and death of Jesus of Nazareth, and on his resurrection as known in the faith of the apostles. The apostles experienced the historical event "Jesus of Nazareth" as the saving event wrought by God for them, and knew at the same time that it was the definitive saving event for all mankind. Hence by the mandate of the Lord, they bore testimony to that event. The words and signs of the apostolic testimony form the permanent basis of all Christian tradition. But the witnesses know in faith that their testimony is not just the handing on of a past event in words and memory, as if it lived on only in the subjective remembrance and was active only as an "idea". It is the risen Lord himself and his Holy Spirit who in this testimony of the apostles' faith challenges man's freedom, offers his grace and bestows his life. One of the great achievements of Vatican II was to free the Catholic notion of tradition from the narrow limits to which it had been confined, chiefly in the post-Tridentine period. In the Dogmatic Constitution on Revelation, tradition does not appear primarily as a certain amount of matter, always the same, handed on in propositions and practices. The tradition of the Church is rather faith as lived: "The Church, in her teaching, life and worship, perpetuates and hands on to all generations all that she herself is, all that she believes" (*Verbum Dei,* art. 8).

In the comprehensive sense, therefore, tradition is not primarily a "something", an objectified datum. It is not exclusively, when taken in its full sense, either the transmission of the word of God in Scripture or the handing on of truths and forms of piety not committed to writing. It is the faith of the Church in action, which is more than its expression in propositions both because Christ works in this faith and because not all that is done in faith is adequately accessible to reflection and expression. For this reason too, the living faith of the Church is also the ultimate norm for criticism of tradition within the Church. Of this more will be said later. Here it is enough to note that tradition, in this sense, is not only prior in time to any crystallization of it in Scripture, but is also at the base of all faith. Just because in the profane realm man

encounters tradition and is formed by it in the re-living of history by others, so too the living tradition of the Christian faith is not something external and irrelevant to those who grow up or live in an area of Christian culture. Whether they like it or not, they always feel the impact of Christian tradition. Those who live in an area of Christian culture can only be themselves in contact with Christian tradition, in the acceptance or rejection of this living heritage.

2. *The content of tradition.* While it is true that the tradition of the Church is something more than the written word expressed in propositions or the word linked with the sign (see *Sacraments*), it is also true that the Christian faith must be capable of expression and definition. It must be possible to formulate the faith founded on a historical event in such a way that the event remains accessible to all ages, since the event itself cannot be repeated. That a community of believers should give expression to its faith in writing is in fact a universal phenomenon. And this is what happened in the early Church. In the 1st century, the "apostolic preaching" was committed to writing in the books of the NT. Nonetheless, Scripture is more than just the first of a series of books which go to make up written tradition, followed so to speak by other books of equal rank. Inasmuch as this written testimony to the faith of the primitive Church was willed by God as permanently normative for later times, it is directly inspired by God. Thus Scripture is the word of God, to which the sense of faith in the later Church is always bound, from whose salutary force it is nourished and impelled, by which it must always direct its steps. And the magisterium of the Church functions merely as hearer and servant of the tradition of the primitive Church, as inspired by God and committed to writing in Scripture.

But what of the post-biblical traditions of the Church, the truths of faith which were only formulated in later times, which as such cannot be found in the writings of the NT and are "merely" the relevant actualization of the Christian faith for a given period? What must be the attitude of the Catholic to the tradition of his Church? That there is and must be such a post-biblical tradition — and not merely within the Catholic Church — and that such a tradition can in certain circumstances be the criterion of membership of the Church, follows from the "historicity" of the Church itself. But is it true, as Protestant theology holds, that all post-biblical tradition must on principle always be open to revision, so that the one valid criterion of tradition can only be the verbal tenor of Scripture? The Reformers, as we know, with logical justification as it would seem, demanded a return to the sources, that is, to Scripture, in order to get rid of the dead weight which had been piled up on the Christian faith in the course of history.

The progress and growth of the Catholic notion of tradition, particularly from Trent to Vatican II, cannot be gone into here. But it is easy to understand that Catholic theology should have taken over the starting-point of the Reformers and have tried to justify its tradition by referring it to apostolic times, either by a scriptural proof (which was not perhaps always very happy) or by the notion of a "second source" of revelation, that of the oral tradition stemming from the apostles. Here the following points should be noted. It is true that the writings of the NT may be considered as a more or less accidental collection of the works of various authors. The book, by its very nature, does not claim to present the content of the faith of the primitive Church without omissions. It may be admitted without misgiving that the faith of the primitive Church was more extensive, in a certain fashion, than what was committed to writing in the books of the NT. Nonetheless, there is no compelling reason to assume that the writings of the NT, being the permanent and divinely-willed norm for all times in the Church of later days, do not contain materially all the essential truths of the Christian faith. Further, it is very difficult for the modern mind, with its alert sense of the historical, to imagine that such truths of faith, not committed to Scripture, should have been preserved without error throughout the ages, in spite of changes of culture and language. Here a too hasty recourse to the assistance of the Holy Spirit would be out of place. And the appeal to what the Church has "always" believed and "always" taught also seems to be questionable, for the same reasons. And there is a further question put by the Protestant Churches which Catholic theologians have to answer. While it is unthinkable that there should be no actualization of Scripture and the Christian faith for a given age which could not be revoked at another time — one need only think of the early Councils with their Christological and Trinitarian decrees — it is also not immediate-

ly evident that the Marian dogmas of recent times, which are constantly evoked in this connection, are permanently valid actualizations of Scripture. This poses a question for Catholics, which a priori they must answer in the negative, as to whether something "new" has not here been defined as revelation, though it stems only from post-apostolic times and hence is no more than a pious custom, venerable perhaps by reason of its antiquity.

The general answer must be as follows. There is on principle no formulation of the faith in post-apostolic times — which is what is in question here — which could not be formulated otherwise. This again does not mean that it does not matter what formula is chosen to give expression to a given reflection on the faith. But the true preaching of the faith always calls for a new assimilation and translation of the traditional faith as well as loyalty to revelation and its historical transmission. Such a "translation", if only because it must start from the experience of a given age and speak the language of the times, will perhaps use new terms to formulate the Catholic faith, while still dealing with a dogma which remains the same. Words change their meaning in the course of history. Their significance and connotations change according to the situation in which they are spoken and the hearers to whom they are addressed. This means that even a literal repetition of doctrines of the magisterium from past times is also basically a translation.

It should also be noted that dogmatically binding declarations of Church doctrine can only be obligatory where they are concerned with truths which have been revealed by God *for our salvation*. The whole ministry of the word, including that of the authentic magisterium, is *under* Scripture. And the books of Scripture only teach "faithfully, firmly and without error that truth which God wanted put into the sacred writings for the sake of our salvation" (*Dei Verbum*, art. 11). This is also true of the infallible utterances of the post-apostolic tradition of the Church. These must also be investigated with a view to discerning their historically-conditioned elements, to demarcate the *salutary* affirmation which they tried to make to the people of their times. Only when this has been done can the effort be made to translate the kernel thus singled out in the truth of faith, and to adapt it to the language of the day. To transplant inconsiderately the doctrinal utterances of the past into a later age may well be to falsify them.

And finally, it should also be noted that Vatican II used the term "hierarchy of truths" (*Unitatis Redintegratio,* art. 11), which has often been quoted since. Obviously, in the course of two thousand years of history, a believing community will have worked out religious practices and forms of piety which must always be open to critical investigation, inasmuch as they have not been "defined". But it is also understandable that even the tradition which is acknowledged as inalienable and as part of the substance of the Christian faith derives from given historical situations of the Church. If the notion of a hierarchy of truths is taken seriously, while it does not of course mean that a believer could deny this or that truth of faith which has been defined in the course of Church history, it does mean that he can admit with an easy conscience that a doctrine of faith in the Catholic Church, defined at a given time, in a given thought-form and for a given situation, may be for him, under certain circumstances, "too far away" from the central message of Christianity, so that in his practical religious life it may mean little or nothing to him. The Catholic Christian, even while acknowledging the permanent truth of a doctrine of faith which has once been defined, can assign many things to the realm of his implicit faith. Catholic theologians take it for granted that not all revealed truths are part of the knowledge of the faith necessary for salvation. And it seems to be equally evident that the truth of a doctrine of faith does not depend on whether an individual Christian recognizes it as an actualization of Scripture and the Christian faith which is significant for his actual life. This is all the more true, as the notion of the hierarchy of truths suggests, as regards the doctrines of faith (such as the Marian dogmas) which are not so immediately relevant to God's saving event in Christ — even if only because Christians of a later date do not or do not yet realize the salutary message contained for them in these truths.

Under these circumstances, it is impossible to see why there should not be, under the assistance of the Holy Spirit, so clearly promised for the whole Church in Scripture, progress and growth in the understanding of the matters and words of tradition (see *Dei Verbum,* art. 8). And it is impossible to see why this should not take the form of the Church as a whole (which is infallible, cf. *Lumen Gentium,* art. 12) recognizing that a given truth of faith is not only obligatory for its own time but for the whole time of the Church, and declaring it to be so. It is not true that such an estimation of tradition would expose the word of God to the arbitrariness of a human magisterium, such as that of the Pope. For nothing can be defined which has not been long believed by the Church and recognized as belonging to the substance of faith. A definition of the magisterium stemming merely from the piety of a Pope or a minority in the Church has never in fact been proclaimed, and indeed cannot be possible. And conversely, it is simply unthinkable that, say, the Christological declarations of the early Councils — which as such are not contained in Scripture — will ever be denied by believing Christians, or that slavery — tolerated as we know in NT times — will ever again be considered compatible with the Christian view of man.

Bearing in mind that faith in Jesus of Nazareth cannot in any case be given to man only in the dead letter of Scripture, but comes in the living faith and confession of believers, and that this is on principle the way in which God offers man his grace in history, we can see that confident faith in the promised assistance of the Holy Spirit, for the ultimate decisions and formulations of faith, is perfectly justified. It must then be recognized that it is quite possible for living faith to express itself in such a way that this expression is permanently acknowledged as revealed in Jesus Christ. This remains true even if one's own insights fall short in one way or another of the insight of a past time and can no longer take it in and retrace its route. Hence the Catholic Christian knows that his faith in the tradition of his Church does not leave him at the mercy of an arbitrary human magisterium, just as he is not at the mercy of the state of exegetical science at any given moment or of his own intellectual powers. He knows on the contrary that even in postbiblical times he remains — not indeed as an individual, but as sharing the fellowship of all who believe along with him — under the assistance of the Holy Spirit in the ultimate and decisive matters of faith. And he knows above all that his own faith would be robbed of the requisite moral seriousness if an item of faith once recognized by the whole Church as belonging to the substance of the faith and as such defined, could be abrogated tomorrow or at any future time and declared to be false or null. "Consequently, it is not from sacred Scripture alone that the Church draws her certainty about everything which has been revealed" (*Dei Verbum,* art. 9).

Tradition (or its content) in the strict sense, which has been the subject of discussion up to this, that is, the doctrines of faith defined in post-apostolic times by the Church and its magisterium, must be clearly distinguished from the broad stream of traditions which also took form in other ways in the course of Church history. As regards such tradition, which of its nature does not make the claim to be infallible or irreversible, the attitude of the Catholic Christian will be in general much as it is towards his profane historical heritage. He will not be short-sighted enough to surrender to the basically very stupid idea that he and his times have "at last" arrived at the true sense of faith and piety, and that everything traditional can be revised at any moment by anyone and thrown into a new mould. In matters of faith above all, which are to a great extent independent of scientific and technical progress, one must reckon with the possibility that in many ways earlier times had clearer insights and perhaps greater grace. In addition, an institutionalized society like the Church needs laws and precepts, if the fellowship is not to disintegrate into a multiplicity which could only destroy all bonds of union and hence the fellowship itself. But on the other hand all Christians, above all in times when the Church as well as mankind in general is so alert to the notion of historicity, must be always open-minded enough to call the traditional in question and to look for new forms and formulations of religious life, in keeping with their own times. This is a possibility for the Church (and indeed, if one takes seriously the importance of charisms in the Church of God, it can even be a moral duty), simply because many things, no matter how ancient and venerable, need not necessarily have been inspired and willed by the Spirit of God. And above all, something that was once correct for the Church in the changes of society and cultures need not be equally valid for all times. It is true that all reasonable Christians will be mindful of the limits of their own insights. It is true that they have to respect tradition or traditions even in non-defined utterances. It is true that they must pay attention to and weigh carefully all papal directives. Nonetheless, contradiction of such traditions does not mean division from the Church. It may even happen, as has already been said, that the individual Christian or a group of Christians will have to shake off a religious form or doctrine which has outlived its day, even if they have to go against the protest of the hierarchical Church. Such changes in the traditional heritage, in a Church which does not confine its annals to stories of triumph and which is also the Church of sinners, were brought about in the past for the most part only by charismatics. And there will be little change in this matter in the future, no doubt. That such men may then have to suffer from their Church even to the limit of their endurance is to be expected, since they are members of an institutionalized Church and must submit to certain precepts and disciplinary measures. But the hierarchical Church must be reminded of the duty it has to learn to listen to the Spirit of God and to acknowledge a legitimate pluralism in the Catholic Church.

See also *Church* III, *History* I, *Scripture and Tradition.*

BIBLIOGRAPHY. See bibliographies on *Dogma* II, *Scripture and Tradition, Magisterium, Freedom;* also: J. Ranft, *Der Ursprung des katholischen Traditionsprinzips* (1931); O. Müller, "Zum Begriff der Tradition", *Münchener Theologische Zeitschrift* 4 (1953), pp. 164–86 (on recent theology); O. Cullmann, *Tradition* (1954); H. Bacht, H. Fries and J. R. Geiselmann, *Die mündliche Überlieferung* (1957); E. Kinder, "Schrift und Tradition", in H. Asmussen and G. Stählin, eds., *Die Katholizität der Kirche* (1957), pp. 7–79; J. Pieper, *Über den Begriff der Tradition* (1958); H. Lennerz, "Scriptura sola?", *Gregorianum* 40 (1959), pp. 38–53; P. Lengsfeld, *Überlieferung* (1960) (modern Protestant and Catholic theology); H. Holstein, *La tradition dans l'Église* (1960); H. Beintker, *Die Evangelische Lehre von der Heiligen Schrift und der Tradition* (1961); G. Ebeling, "Tradition", *RGG,* VI, cols. 976–84; id., *Problem of Historicity in the Church and its Proclamation* (1967); id., *Word of God and Tradition* (1968); J. P. Mackey, *The Modern Theology of Tradition* (1962); id., *Tradition and Change in the Church* (1968); G. Scholem, "Tradition und Kommentar als religiöse Kategorien im Judentum", *Eranos* 31 (1962), pp. 19–48; R. Hanson, *Tradition in the Early Church* (1962); World Council of Churches, Faith and Order Commission, *Old and New in the Church: Study Report* (1962); K. Skydsgaard and L. Vischer, *Schrift und Tradition* (1963); Fourth World Conference on Faith and Order, *Faith and Order Findings* (1963); F. Lakner, "Zur Frage der Definibilität einer geoffenbarten Wahrheit", *ZKT* 85 (1963), pp. 322–38; Y. Congar, *Meaning of Tradition* (1964); id., *Tradition and Traditions in the Church* (1966); C. Journet, *Le message révélé* (1964); E. Ménard, *La Tradition* (1964) (on Aquinas); M. Thurian, *Visible Unity and Tradition* (1964); J. R. Geiselmann, *The Meaning of Tradition,* Quaestiones Disputatae 15 (1965); H. G. Gadamer, *Wahrheit und Methode* (2nd ed., 1965); K. Rahner and J. Ratzinger, *Revelation and*

Tradition, Quaestiones Disputatae 17 (1966); B. de Armellada, "La 'Tradition' en el Concilio Vaticano II", *Naturalezza y Gracia* 13 (1966), pp. 3–29; R. Latourelle, "La révélation et sa transmission selon la Constitution 'Dei Verbum'", *Gregorianum* 47 (1966), pp. 1–40; O. Semmelroth and M. Zerwick, *Vatikan II über das Wort Gottes* (1966); G. Biemer, *Newman on Tradition* (1967); R. Boeckler, *Der moderne römisch-katholische Traditionsbegriff* (1967); M. Thornton, *The Function of Tradition* (1968); H. von Campenhausen, *Tradition and Life in the Early Church* (1968); J. Ratzinger's commentary on the Dogmatic Constitution on Divine Revelation in H. Vorgrimler, ed., *Commentary on the Documents of Vatican II,* vol. III (1969), pp. 155–98.

Karl-Heinz Weger

TRADITIONALISM

Traditionalism is the doctrine according to which a primitive revelation was necessary for the human race, not only to acquire knowledge of the truths of the supernatural order, but even for the fundamental truths of the metaphysical, moral and religious order: the existence of God, the spirituality and immortality of the soul and the existence of a strictly obligatory moral law. This revelation comes down to us through tradition: whence the name of traditionalism given to the system which developed in France after the Revolution and in the first years of the 19th century. Joseph de Maistre (1753–1821) (cf. *Œuvres,* 13 vols. [1884–86]), Louis de Bonald (1754–1840) (cf. *Œuvres,* 15 vols. [1817–43]) and Félicité de Lamennais (1782–1854) (cf. *Essai sur l'indifférence en matière de religion,* 4 vols. [1817–23]) were the main representatives (cf. R.O.C. Maréchal, *Essai d'un système de philosophie catholique* [1906]).

Chateaubriand had shown that Christianity was useful: the traditionalists wanted to prove that it was absolutely indispensable for the moral and political order. According to de Bonald, thought is impossible without language, and words are necessary to establish the use of words. So it is essential that first of all someone should have spoken to man for man to be able to speak in his turn: this "someone" could only be God and his word is the primitive revelation from which all the indispensable truths originate. Such is the radical argumentation of this "émigré philosophy", as it has been called, reacting against the excesses of rationalistic individualism, the source of anarchy and incredulity: the social order rests on the moral order, whose foundation is God, known through the primitive revelation. The whole process of reasoning is revolutionary and extreme: it consists in establishing the existence in man of an intellectual life in society founded on language, then refusing its paternity to him and attributing it finally to God. And so in this way the equivocal notion of a primitive revelation is formed, a kind of amalgam in which all the truths declared to be both inaccessible and indispensable to man, whether they belong to the natural or supernatural orders, are found together in disordered confusion.

In the absence of any true philosophical and theological tradition, this undoubtedly attractive but dangerous traditionalism was adopted by the clergy, taking its lead from Lamennais according to whom Christianity could never be proved by any proof from human reason which is fallible by nature, and so rests on the authority of the *sensus communis* which recognizes it as the source of its traditional beliefs. Since the natural faith of the human race is the only source of certitude, the universal consent is that which proves the claim of the one true and revealed religion, whose authenticity is guaranteed by the following three characteristics: antiquity, perpetuity and universality. These are the essentials of Lamennais's traditionalism which enchanted the circle of disciples who gathered around the master, first of all at La Chesnaie, and then from 1823 to 1833 at Juilly. Combalot, de Coux, Gerbet, Guéranger, Lacordaire and Salinis became enthusiastic propagators of the new system which won over many seminaries and recruited fervent adherents amongst the junior clergy, before being attacked by Sulpicians and Jesuits, censured by the bishops and condemned by Gregory XVI in the encyclical *Singulari Nos* (1834). Even Lamennais's break with Catholicism did not stop the propagation of his philosophical and theological ideas, which Bonnetty's *Annales de philosophie chrétienne* continued to support till the First Vatican Council.

Parallel to this rigid form of traditionalism there developed a mitigated form according to which reason needs intellectual instruction to come to its full exercise. This was, under different forms, the position of R. P. Ventura de Raulica in Italy (1792–1861), of Ubaghs and Laforêt (*Les Dogmes catholiques* [1860]) in Belgium, where the traditionalism of the Louvain professors was mixed up with ontologism, and of Louis Bautain whose leaning towards fideism was allied to a sort of mystic intuitionism: man needed an external help to arouse the initial movements of his faculties, but, once contact with God was assured, with word and tradition being the usual means of attaining this, then the intelligence, once it had been activated in this way, had access to the certainties of the intelligible and supernatural world.

These different strands of traditionalism exercised a lasting influence through the whole of the 19th century, especially in the circles around Father Ventura in Italy, Mgr. Geissel in Germany, the University of Louvain in Belgium and the Abbé Bautain in France. Because many Catholics continued to find here a radical reply to the errors of rationalism, and in fact risked confusing the natural and supernatural order (so opening the way to scepticism), the First Vatican Council asserted unequivocally the power of reason to know God without being previously enlightened by a divine revelation. The Council appealed to Scripture and the patristic tradition: Dogmatic Constitution *De Fide Catholica,* 24 April 1870 (*D* 1781 to 1820). But it should be noted that the Council affirms the possibility and not the fact of such a natural knowledge of God independently of revelation, that it asserts the outstanding usefulness of such revelation for an exact knowledge and that it takes up no position on the question of whether some degree of formation is not presupposed for the full use of reason. An examination of the Council documents shows that Franzelin's draft proposal, reshaped by Bishop Martin of Paderborn with the help of P. Kleutgen, prompted repeated arguments in favour of moderate traditionalism, and that in their replies Mgr. Dechamps and Bishop Gasser clarified the meaning of the text: only extreme traditionalism was expressly condemned, it being nothing more than a form of fideism.

See also *Fideism, Ontologism, Revelation* III, *Tradition.*

BIBLIOGRAPHY. T. Combalot, *Éléments de philosophie catholique* (1833); A. de Riamborg, *L'École de Paris: Du rationalisme et de la tradition* (1834); E. Saisset, *Essais sur la philosophie et la religion au XIXième siècle* (1845); P. Chastel, *De la valeur de la raison humaine ou ce que peut la raison par elle seule* (1854); H. Maret, *Philosophie et religion* (1856); id., *Deux lettres à M. le Professeur Ubaghs* (1857); P.-L. Parisis, *Tradition et raison* (1858); J. Lupus, *Le Traditionalisme et le Rationalisme* (1858); M. Ferraz, *Histoire de la philosophie en France au XIXième siècle,* II (1880); H. Ricard, *L'École mennaisienne,* 4 vols. (2nd ed., 1895); J. Henry, *Le traditionalisme et l'ontologisme à l'Université de Louvain* (1922); H. Lennerz, *Natürliche Gotteserkenntnis* (1926); A. Michel in *DTC,* XV, cols. 1350ff.; J. R. Geiselmann, *Lebendiger Glaube aus geheiligter Überlieferung* (1942), pp. 30–119, 147–60, 508f.; id., *Die theologische Anthropologie J. A. Möhlers* (1955), pp. 1–20, 232–57, 345f.; E. Hocedez, *Histoire de la théologie au XIXième siècle,* I (1948), pp. 67–130; II (1952), pp. 69–112 (with bibliography); L. Foucher, *La philosophie catholique en France au XIXième siècle avant la renaissance thomiste et dans son rapport avec elle, 1800–1880* (1955); A. Franco, *Geschiedenis van het Traditionalisme aan de Universiteit van Leuven* (1955); F. X. Arnold, *Seelsorge aus der Mitte der Geschichte* (1958), pp. 112–51; R. Spaemann, *Der Ursprung der Soziologie aus dem Geist der Restauration* (1959); P. Poupard, *L'abbé Louis Bautain* (1961) (with bibliography); J.-R. Derré, *Lamennais* (1962); F. Brousse, *Lamennais et le christianisme universel* (1963); P. Grootens, "Was abbé Luis Bautain een fideïst?", *Bijdraagen* 25 (1964), pp. 29–63; W. G. Roe, *Lamennais and England* (1966); L. Le Guillou, *L'évolution de la pensée religieuse de Félicité Lamennais* (1966).

Paul Poupard

TRANSCENDENCE

A. The Horizon of the Classical Thinking on Transcendence

The notion of transcendence derives from experience. Beings present themselves in their distinction from one another and in their definite contrast with nothingness as "what" they are, but they are still — in themselves — incomprehensible, strange and obscure. The fluid multiplicity and the constant mobility of beings make the question of their basic origin and purpose more insistent. The answer can clearly be derived only from some being which is "unmoved" and which as the eternal exists of itself and for itself, "separate" and free, as the first and ultimate ground of all movement. This Greek line of thought attains a "First" which implies, in view of the perpetual mutability and temporality of phenomena, a transcendence towards a being which is the ground of the permanence in nature ("essence") and is therefore ultimately that which is permanent in itself ("divine"). When then the reverse course is followed ("descent"), and transcendence proves itself capable of justifying the *per se* enigmatic and hence "criticized" phenomena (in their existence and mode of being), it establishes itself as also the pre-existing "Beginning" of all things, their foundation and the source of their order.

This beginning, in terms of cosmogony, is represented as the first temporal event. More correctly, however, this origin is thought of as an "absolute" beginning, since if in succession initially, it would be itself perpetually submitted to other conditions and would presuppose a "prior". As pre-temporal and time-founding origin, transcendence is not itself a "given", but is thought of as "thought of thought", as pure act *(esse ipsum)*, as inexhaustible love, as eternal will and *hence* as non-temporal, eternal event and actuality. Western philosophy went more deeply into this fundamental relationship of transcendence, the "transition" from the "given" to its essence and from there to the first, supreme ground of all beings ("Being"), using the concepts of "Metaphysics", the "Absolute", the "Analogy of Being", "Act and Potency", "Participation", "Principle" and "Being" (see these articles). The demonstration of transcendence in the proofs for the existence of God (see *God* III) starts with the contingency of the world and uses the principles of causality and necessity to establish a natural theology (see *God* I, *Natural Theology*). Thinking in terms of transcendence uses the middle way of exemplarism to avoid the extremes of absolute identity (see *Identity-Philosophy*) and absolute difference (see *Dualism, God-World Relationship*). Transcendence is not a leap from a general idea to a "transcendent", indemonstrable reality, but takes place in the light of and by virtue of the primordial disclosure of the being of beings, which it refers to its "proper" nature — always there in a latent, non-explicated mode.

St. Thomas's notion of the *actus essendi* is one of the supreme achievements of thought here. Finite actuality of itself reflects through its exclusion of nothingness, its inner absoluteness and its pure "positiveness" the simple, absolute and unrelated ground. Through its *being,* it soars on principle into the divine uncreated life, which of itself fully eludes us in its own proper essence. The hidden ground of transcendence lies therefore in this "positiveness" of being, which pervades most profoundly all immanence and is nonetheless not simply absorbed there. Hence transcendence is both the far and the near, distance and intimacy. The difference within transcendence is as analogous as the unity. Precisely because it is as the absolutely Transcendent that God turns to the world in creation (and grace), he is the inmost principle, ground and goal of the creature. The

immanence of transcendence in the creature does not sequestrate the finite being but brings it more radically to its ultimate validity and consistency. The closeness of transcendence and the independence of the creature grow in the same, not inverse, proportion. (This is also true of transcendence as grace.) In the light of this truth, and presupposing the dynamism of the divine being and of the perpetually active creative power of God, evolution, immanent fulfilment and "life" can be understood — when contemplated "from below" — as self-transcendence, in which a being goes beyond itself to a grade of being essentially higher and thus rises above itself. This fundamental relationship is displayed most clearly in the nature of the human person. Since it is transcendence in its own proper nature ("immanence"), that is, (in a manifold sense) in the act of knowledge and of freedom, the person is radically incapable of having a merely immanent end and fulfilment. Transcendence, as act and fulfilment, is the only true "immanent" realization of personal knowing, willing and acting (cf. *L'action* of M. Blondel). Immanence and transcendence belong to each other and mediate each other, which shows both the necessity and the limitations of these concepts and their application.

Present-day thinking is perhaps more suggestive to a transcendence expounded anthropologically. In the disintegration of human existence there is latent *and* audible a fundamental "disquiet" (concern), in which man experiences the unattainability of what he strives to be, while knowing himself inexorably summoned to this unattainable goal. "L'homme passe infiniment l'homme" (Pascal). However, there are many ways of propounding the transcendence of man once it has dawned in this way.

B. Conceptual Clarification

Transcendence can form a barrier which throws man back on himself and limits him to his finiteness. But it can also be experienced as a "dialectical" limit, negatively separating and positively uniting, which is transcended in many ways: rational modes of knowledge, affective and mystical ecstasy, "union", faith, silence, concrete action, historical practice. And the "ascent" is mostly to another type of realm, differing in mode of being and degree of reality, related to what is transcended by such various links as opposition, coherence, intensification, paradox, reflection, dialectical pattern. The following formal distinctions are to be made. Transcendence (or transcendent) means: (i) the realm going beyond consciousness and independent of it: epistemological transcendence; (ii) the absolute, surpra-sensible "beyond", where knowledge of the idea (form) or essence (abstraction, intuition) and of its ultimate justification (deduction) rises above the multiplicity and mobility of phenomena and sensible experience, in a non-temporal, non-empirical ground: metaphysical transcendence; (iii) an opening out to the truth itself, to the absolute, indefeasible and incomprehensible horizon of human thought and will, which is either explicated metaphysically or theologically (see *God* I), or remains an open dimension or is totally reduced to the anthropocentric; (iv) the absolute otherness and freedom of God as regards the world, attained by the "desacralization" of the world, where God's inmost nature remains unknown to man and is best expressed in the categories of the holy and of mystery: theological transcendence; (v) the truly divine godhead of God, which is absolutely beyond the range of all human powers (see *Nature*), absolutely unattainable in spite of all connaturality (see *Potentia Oboedientialis; Order* IV) but discloses itself in free self-communication, where the incalculable gratuitousness of grace and the supernatural order brings the movement of human transcendence to its intrinsic limit and the moment of its transformation: strict theological transcendence.

Modern philosophy has formed concepts which break through these definitions in many ways. For Husserl, everything that makes its presence felt in the immanent sphere of the process of consciousness, and presents itself as an analysable element of the structure of consciousness, without being part of the pure "region of experience", is transcendent. For K. Jaspers, transcendent designates the hidden, all-embracing being (not simply identical with God), which is only bestowed in existentiell decision and declares itself only in the mysterious language of cipher. Transcendence is understood then in many different ways as the actual or habitual ascent to "being", again understood in many ways: as all-embracing world horizon, as temporality in general, as utopia, future, self-realization, progress. This sometimes takes the form of "transcending without transcendence" (E. Bloch) or that of a totally indeterminate, "empty" transcendence (see below). For a reformed Marxism of a humanist type, transcendence is the creative realization of the truly human in the individual and the social sense, a progressive and critical "transcendence" towards a non-alienated society. Transcendence can simply mean the element of self-criticism in any attempt to draw up a blue-print for a better world, which is recognized as not amenable to norms, or for an active re-moulding of the world which refuses to adapt to the existing one or lose itself there. Hence the concrete meaning of transcendence must be taken into consideration in each case.

In view of these variations, it is not enough to appeal to the "classical" and "clear" notion of transcendence. Formally, of course, this has a definite function: God's being is essentially distinct and different — not separate — from all that is in the world. But in the concrete, the classical notion of transcendence is multivalent, and is generally used indifferently: (i) to indicate the relationship by which beings are referred to "being"; (ii) to indicate the relationship of changeable beings to one higher which is at rest; (iii) to indicate the "supreme being" itself, which is also called "being". These relationships are part of the intrinsic structure of metaphysics. Their modifications and transformations reflect the historical changes in metaphysics and its present-day crisis.

C. THE INNER HISTORY OF THE NOTION OF TRANSCENDENCE

Transcendence was first propounded on the ground of the difference between thought and perception, and the critique of intramundane gods in Plato's doctrine of forms, in which the myths lost their spell-binding force. The separation of the changing world of appearances, the physical cosmos, from the "world" of forms which is its ground does not directly give rise to a two-world theory or a curtained-off world. The form is a "parousia", and its intenser, powerful being is the immanent "ground" of beings. Nonetheless, this fundamental difference is the framework of all mediation — "hypothesis", the ascent of *eros,* ethics, *paideia,* above all, the experience of beauty (see *Platonism*). The good, the "form of all forms", the source of all reality, is higher in dignity and power than the forms. It is "beyond being" (ἐπέκεινα τῆς οὐσίας), the uncaused that is prior to all, and can be known only with effort, in a sudden moment and by a few, in a "divine excess" (ὑπερβολή — transcendence). The form of the good is not expressly identified with "God", but has a religious significance and is in the realm of the divine. Transcendence appears as soaring beyond (μετ' ἐκεῖνα) the shadows "out to" (εἰς ταῦτα) the forms, which a dangerously ambiguous metaphor of Plato puts in a "higher than heavenly place".

The strongly cosmological colouring of Aristotelianism (cosmos — stars — Unmoved Mover), intended to eliminate the difficulties of Platonism, proved to be misleading, as it gave rise later to spatial notions of transcendence, which Plato's position rather tended to avoid (see *Aristotelianism* I). Later, contrary to Plato, the forms ("ideas") were transferred to the mind of God, the Demiurge, or the Logos, and emphasis was laid on the fact that the One, God, was outside all categories (which in Gnosticism went to the extreme of dualism), so that finally even thought, for instance, was not predicated of him. The dialectical ascent to this ultimate ground presupposes in the subject purification, simplicity and assimilation to God. It moves forward in a process of negation and is transposed into an explicitly analogous form of statement (through the *triplex via: positionis, negationis, eminentiae*). The ascent ends in the chiaroscuro of *docta ignorantia,* the wordless "touch", the consciousness of the disabilities of human thought, and (philosophical) "prayer". These represent the essential elements of classical transcendence. The possibility of attaining insight into the unknowability and ineffability of the primordial transcendence, which is not directly accessible, is based on the latent, image-like presence of transcendence in man prior to all reflection — the *illustratio animae, scintilla animae, apex mentis* or again, the *intellectus agens,* the *prima principia, esse commune,* the "voice of conscience", the dynamism of thought and will, the "I", the "Spirit", the understanding of "being". This mysterious centre and depth *in* the nature of man is what arouses him to his transcendent movement.

Along with other elements from neo-Platonism (self-communication of the Good, degrees of being in the universe, etc.) the transcendence of God in the patristic era (see *Hellenism and Christianity*) was chiefly defined by the additional notes of absolute authority, inviolable sovereignty, personality and lordship of history, as seen in the God of the Bible. The indifferent, unreflecting, impersonal "Oneness" which was the supreme act of self-transcending thought is transformed (with the help of Exod 3:14) into a personal God capable of self-utterance. However, the attributes of God, first considered in reference to history, were gradually transformed into absolute proprieties of his essence (e.g., omnipotence). Orthodox theology returned again and again to the formula of transcendence, adding a corresponding affirmation of immanence: "Omnia complet et omnia transcendit." In spite of the implicit rejection of all discourse about transcendence, it did not cease to be intelligible, the understanding of it being based on attaining the notions of divine freedom and creation. Along with this rather cosmological type of transcendence, Christian thinkers after St. Augustine recognize an "inner" transcendence, suggested by the neo-Platonic notion of reflux or return. The spirit has, not merely in its thought but in its being, a genuine relation to the Absolute. "Reflection" is the point of arousal for the transition of the soul, as it soars by degrees to its true ground. In St. Augustine, for instance, God is closer to the soul than the soul to itself (see *Augustinianism*).

Medieval thought succeeded again and again in bringing the latent tensions of this metaphysical basic structure of transcendence into a certain equilibrium, which was ultimately arrived at and maintained by the fundamental data of faith. But this meant that the structural antinomies of transcendence were concealed. Epicurus and Lucretius had already shown clearly that the peculiar ontic condition of transcendence was capable of swinging over into an indifferent and impotent transcendence, with the region of immanence governed as a consequence solely by its own laws (see *Deism*). The elements of voluntarism in the theology of the late Middle Ages and the Reformation gave radical effect to the notion of transcendence. God is not merely, by essence, the "wholly other". By his deliberate will, he withdraws from human thought into his incomprehensible hiddenness *(Deus absconditus),* a view which was in fact to isolate still more from its foundation the faith which was meant to be stimulated. These immanent tensions led almost to the self-dissolution of transcendence, a tendency reinforced from without by a mechanistic world-picture, Bacon's notion of "idols", (see *Ideology*), empiricism, rationalism, the Enlightenment and so on. The non-mediated distance of transcendence swung over into impotence. "Through the total removal of the divine to a sphere beyond and above a world paralysed by the loss of its principle of life", a false honour was paid to God and the empty world left to godless hands (Schelling).

German Idealism failed to achieve the desirable speculative integration, since its notion of the *absolute* mediation of the Spirit *to itself* served to eliminate the basic relationship of God's being both inward and over against. The critique of "reality" in transcendental Kantianism, the banishing of the Absolute into the immanence of consciousness (only "immanent transcendence" remaining), the merging of the God-who-is in the Spirit-that-thinks, the surrendering of God to history, the reduction of the notion of God to a function — that of being a concept for what is *a priori* inconceivable, and the immanent critique there of the traditional notion of God — all this left the predicates of classical transcendence in a profound ambiguity and meant the ruin of what was termed a "reified" transcendence. Transcendence now transforms itself into "re-scendence" (cf. "re-sidence") and appears there once more in a totally different form. It is the essential, relentless upward march ("transcendence") which is sited in the nature of man (the will to power, Marxist "practice"). The so-called self-dedication of man to the transcendent is stripped of its misleading objectivations and brought back downwards, as transcendence is reduced to sameness. At first, transcendence disappears in this "re-scendence". Religion has squandered on heaven the treasures of man and accepts in God what it refuses for itself. Transcendence is a substitute for the loss of the world. The supreme illumination of the Idea now becomes a will-o'-the-wisp, εἴδωλον, an idol, the "epiphenomenon" of social, practical relationships. Critical analysis unmasks these "imaginary" beings and duplicates as ideological reflections of the vital processes: the "superstructure" (see *Materialism, Marxism, Religion* I B). The identification of the Christian faith with such transcendence brings it under the same condemnation: "Christianity is the Platonism of the people."

Nonetheless, in spite of all polemics against transcendence, its formal structure (its functional position) is preserved in the new sketch-plans. It re-appears as the goals set for the immanent progress of the world, in natural evolution and self-fulfilment in work; as man's surpassing himself in the active process of creating world history; as utopia; as "something held open for a possible and as yet undecided future in this vacant space" (E. Bloch); as the non-final which is destiny; as the still unknown futurity; as the unsounded depths of man and so on. Transcendence can have so little content that it merely marks a tension in life which moves or provokes man to escape the banality of reality but no longer hints at arrival at a goal — the "empty" transcendence which has been signalled in Baudelaire, Rimbaud and Mallarmé (see H. Friedrich). Most of these transformations are Platonism in reverse, as is clearest in materialism, which Feuerbach presents by saying "being is sensible being". But when M. Heidegger, in the logic of the history of philosophy, interprets transcendence as "understanding of being", he opens up a new possibility: existence ("thereness") as the wide open place in whose brightness non-human beings (including the God) can show themselves. This understanding of being, transcendence, is the transcendental for all beings. It is not detached from existence, but it is not produced by it or hidden in the self-knowledge of the absolute Spirit. Inasmuch as Heidegger sees "transcendence" as event and hence as "historical" in a primordial sense (see *History* I), he abandons any metaphysical notion (and hence all discourse) of transcendence. In wide-ranging considerations of the "ontological difference" (see *Being* I, para. 1), which is discussed under various headings, there is a "return to the fundamental ground of metaphysics", that is, an authentic consideration of the essence and origin of all transcendence. The mode of thought thus arrived at, with its non-metaphysical structures, is displayed in the concept of the world in the later Heidegger. Transcendence now becomes the "destiny of being" (*Seinsgeschick* — "the apt sending of being"). The new possibilities of this way of understanding transcendence have neither been positively tested nor decided in the negative. A systematic and historical investigation of thinking on transcendence is one of the most important tasks of present-day philosophy and theology.

D. THE MODERN DISCUSSION

Present-day theology cannot afford to overlook the difficulties presented by the notion of transcendence. Even if it is historical and objective in rejecting as unjustified the negative characteristic of the traditional notion of transcendence, it cannot now think of an "Absolute" after the manner of a "Givenness". This means that notions of the beyond must be fully thought out. The history of the inner transformations of transcendence shows that even in the most imposing sketches of transcendence strong tensions are hidden, which are due to the structure of the thought. The result of this at present is a certain scepticism with regard to the application of the notion, though the matter has not been given much explicit attention. But the problem of transcendence cannot be evaded. A naive personalism fails to see the highly complicated structure of dialogal relationships, and does not deal with the problem of how the notion of person is to be applied to God in a meaningful way. It is impossible, on the other hand, to define the transcendent God solely, directly and without distinctions as personal responsibility in its unconditional nature, as the depths or grounds of our being, the source of our existence and the actuality of human love. The depths of being can appear to many as the absurd, as the painful limit of one's existence, as the drive to self-preservation and the will to be or be happy. The first thing to make clear is under what conditions the word "God" can be linked with the "depths of being" so as to disclose their meaning. A task as yet mostly neglected is the demarcation of the dimension "between" being, or the whole reality of the world, and the God whose essential realm must also be disclosed in the process as the holy and the divine. And it is also impossible to understand God merely as the answer to a question of meaning put exclusively in the transcendental sense, since such an answer ignores the question of the origin of human and non-human reality. Every new effort at interpretation must prove its value by being measured against the classical notion of transcendence, taken in its full meaning and in the light of all its functions in theology, with reference, for instance, to creation.

This demand must also be made with regard to a more recent approach, which conceives of the transcendence of God in the light of being as futurity and as "the power of the future". (This is done by means of a special interpretation of the OT promise which sees God as "He who comes"; and the categories used by E. Bloch are also invoked.) But this new approach seems to make God (or salvation) no more than a name for the summons to an endless, critical "transcending" into future history. If so, the real problem in the relationship of salvation and history ("the new earth") is implicitly solved, through a fluid notion of the future, more or less radically in the direction of immanence, with the word "eschatological" used in a way that is never made very clear (see *Political Theology*). In fact, the theological use of the notion of the future cannot be sustained without envisaging the whole range of the formal and material functions of the classical notion of transcendence. Every theology of the promise, of the future and of hope is confronted in fact with the same set of problems as are posed by the relationship of immanence in transcendence. To distinguish history totally from eschatological future brings about an apocalyptic negation of the world and its history. To make them coincide totally means ultimately a strictly permanent self-surpassing, which of itself is without a goal and hence is undoubtedly meaningless. (For it is anyway, even without a "Utopia", a "metaphysical" notion, in the sense of Heidegger, taking the place of transcendence.) The only meaningful approach seems to be (see J. Moltmann) to combine a transcendence superior to history with a historical process of transcendence, to note the critical differences but to believe that harmony is possible, to keep in view the qualitative difference when envisaging possible harmony. In this way a critique transcending all systems and an openness for a qualitatively new future can be combined with concrete steps towards a quantitatively new future *(ibid.)*.

When such positions are subjected to criticism, the problems which present themselves are seen no doubt as tasks which modern theology cannot evade. But the "solution" as so far presented contains no fewer difficulties than the classical notion of transcendence. This also tries to deal with the relationship between history and the supra-historical, between identity and difference. And by its very nature, it can only explain it as the coming-to-be of a fully developing transcendence. The mutation into another quality, which must also be presupposed here, can be understood theologically only as the "act of God" who is the "absolute future", in contrast to the future as "being", without limit. As the unrestricted fullness of reality, the mainspring of all dynamism of the future, it cannot be attained or surpassed by human experience or human efforts to change the world. A vision of the future concentrated only on changing the world must always find this theological affirmation "mythological". But futurity in the Christian sense is primarily "Advent", and it is there that it is radically new and "revolutionary".

The application of categories of futurity to the fundamental theological notions (God, salvation, etc.) does not perhaps depend on the actual use of the word "transcendence", but the validity of the application depends on how well it corresponds to the functions of the classical notion of transcendence in its ontological and hermeneutical bearings. But it is rather characteristic of modern theology that the two modes of thought ("transcendence" — "futurity") work in isolation and hence mostly reject each other. A similar problem arises in the "Death of God" theology. Insofar as "God" is really identified with the classical transcendence and above all with its inner history, deep questions undoubtedly arise. But these are not even seen in their proper depth, if the problem of transcendence is simply eliminated. Anthropological, Christological and uniquely eschatological "solutions" displace or bypass the really basic question. It is therefore clear that the notion of transcendence is indispensable from the theological point of view. But its actual usefulness in modern theological discussion depends entirely on whether it can be maintained fruitfully when confronted objectively and critically with the problem of history and the active effort to change the world. The legitimate variety of forms in which it can appear should not be lost sight of in the Christian faith, which is not identical with any given philosophy, world-view or world-picture. The term transcendence is not found in the Bible, though it definitely teaches "the thing signified" by the term.

It remains theologically relevant in all experience of transcendence — though in varying degrees — that finite man cannot himself bring about the fulfilment of his being, and cannot resolve the tension which this gives rise to. A precise analysis of his action and knowledge displays an absolutely necessary and relentless claim on this fulfilment, which proves, however, to be ultimately unattainable in spite of all his own efforts. This is when in the concrete man can hear, in the midst of the endless conflict between true and false transcendence (see *Superstition, Sin*) the invitation, full of promise, to open

his heart to the nameless presence of a grace and favour still perhaps undefined. This "heartfelt expectation of the unknown Messiah" (M. Blondel) is the provisional name for what a fully developed Christian faith calls grace. Since its mysterious ways are so manifold and incalculable, all the phenomena of human transcendence, even in the guise of symbol, are theologically interesting and significant.

See also *Symbol, Grace, Time* II.

BIBLIOGRAPHY. See bibliographies on *Absolute and Contingent, God* I–III, *God-World Relationship, Transcendental Philosophy, Secularization* (for "Death of God" theology); also: R. Roques, *L'univers dionysien* (1954); L. Richter, *Immanenz und Transzendenz im nachreformatorischen Gottesbild* (1955); C. de Moré-Pontgibaud, *Du fini à l'infini* (1957); *Recherches sur la tradition platonicienne* (Entretiens Hardt III [Vandœuvres-Genève] 1957); J. Vanneste, *Le mystère de Dieu* (1959) (on the Pseudo-Dionysius); *Les sources de Plotin* (Entretiens Hardt V) (1959); P. Henry, *The Christian Idea of God and its Development* (1961); H. Kuhn, *Das Sein und das Gute* (1962); E. Przywara, *Religionsphilosophische Schriften* (1962); B. Montagnes, *La doctrine de l'analogie de l'être d'après S. Thomas d'Aquin* (1963); H. Krämer, *Der Ursprung der Geistmetaphysik* (1963) (from Plato to Plotinus); K. H. Volkmann-Schluck, *Metaphysik und Geschichte* (1963); W. Bröcker, *Aristoteles* (3rd ed., 1964); E. von Ivanka, *Plato Christianus* (1964); G. Wolke, *Sein als Beziehung zum Absoluten nach Thomas von Aquin* (1964); H. Wolfson, *The Philosophy of the Church Fathers*, I (2nd ed., 1964); W. Beierwaltes, *Proklos* (1965); G. Sauter, *Zukunft und Verheissung* (1965); K. Flasch, ed., *Parusia (Festschrift H. J. Hirschberger)* (1965); H. Wagner, "Ist Metaphysik des Transzendenten möglich?" *Subjektivität und Metaphysik (Festschrift H. W. Cramer)* (1966), pp. 290–327; K. Kremer, *Die neuplatonische Seinsphilosophie und ihre Wirkung auf Thomas von Aquin* (1966); H. Friedrich, *Die Struktur der modernen Lyrik* (1967); H. Urs von Balthasar, *The God Question and Modern Man* (1967); K. Rahner, *Spirit in the World* (1968); id., *Schriften zur Theologie*, VIII, pp. 555–609; J. Moltmann, "The Future as a New Paradigm of Transcendence", *Concurrence* 1, no. 4 (1969), pp. 334–45.

Karl Lehmann

TRANSCENDENTAL PHILOSOPHY

1. *Introductory*. The consideration that philosophy, as knowledge of all reality in its principles, expresses itself through the medium of the concept, is of the very essence of philosophy and is as ancient as philosophical reflection itself. But the difference thus

posited between concept and reality, being and thought, is an implicit questioning of philosophy itself, which remains insignificant as long as the spontaneous idealism and optimism of thought and knowledge is not radically called in question. It is only in the light of certain spiritual experiences, which seem impervious to philosophy as a whole and confront it with the fundamental question of its own powers, that the problems contained in the distinction between concept and reality become explicit. Philosophy then becomes the question of its own possibility, and its function is to offer a critique of philosophy. That such experiences have gone hand in hand with philosophy from the start may be seen from the history of radical scepticism as well as from that of philosophical nominalism. Hence from the start philosophy was to some extent critical. But it could only become fundamentally critical when it produced of itself—stimulated by scepticism and nominalism—a counterpart to its own knowledge, which seemed by its very existence to demonstrate the impossibility of philosophy.

This antagonist was modern science with its basis of experiment and experience. Paradoxically, its challenge to philosophy was more radical than that of scepticism, because it offered positively verifiable knowledge in general, rejecting metaphysical knowledge in terms of pure concepts not verifiable by sensible experience. If philosophy was to maintain its claims, it had to rely radically on its own resources. It had to investigate its own possibility as well as the claim of science to be knowledge. It had to reflect critically on the foundations of knowledge as such.

The term "transcendental philosophy" was adopted to designate the investigation of the conditions of philosophical and scientific knowledge and has been used ever since with justice to describe every effort of radical re-thinking to give philosophy an absolute foundation and analyse its relationship to scientific knowledge in general and in particular. Thus the term "transcendental", in contrast to the usage of the scholastic Aristotelian tradition of the Middle Ages, received a new significance, which remained, however, formally akin to the old. It also served a new purpose. It no longer designates the realm of "notes" beyond the categories in which "being" presents its aspects (see *Transcendentals*) and their possibility of defining the nature of God (see *Transcendence,*

Absolute and Contingent). It now means the *a priori* conditions of knowledge, which precede all experience of objects and which are the primary constituents of all objects of knowledge and hence make knowledge possible. Criticism of philosophy itself and criticism of science with regard to the extent and limits of justifiable knowledge are therefore permanent characteristics of transcendental philosophy. Here the basic questionableness of purely conceptual thinking becomes permanently explicit and is given full value as essential at all stages of philosophy.

It follows that the central endeavour of all transcendental philosophy must be to return to the element which certifies and justifies all knowledge, and thence provide by deduction a critical explanation of concrete, scientific and philosophical knowledge. Hence the object of transcendental philosophy is neither being nor thought, neither the subject nor the object, but the actual unity of consciousness and being given in each act of knowing. Within the horizon of this "being-conscious" a twofold method of reduction and deduction is employed. There is the analysis of validity which reverses the process of universal doubt and gives the assurance of absolute truth as the source of all knowledge. And there is the constitutive synthesis and justification of the conditions of true knowledge as principles of reality. There is a "genetic" evidence of the absolute which goes beyond the merely factual and is at once insight into the intrinsic meaning and the "legitimacy" of the object of insight. When the absolute is thus displayed as at once absolute truth and veracity, such critical philosophy justifies its pure *a priori* concepts and principles as transcendental conditions of all knowing. As self-criticism of philosophy which has felt the weight of scepticism, it is a renewed, anti-dogmatic metaphysics whose basic character is incompatible with such common and one-sided designations as mere "theory of knowledge", "idealism" or "philosophy of subjectivity". Hence transcendental philosophy aims at being systematic knowledge of all reality through its principles, by providing a critical reflection on the transcendental conditions of the total reality of "being-conscious" as this reality presents itself in the act of knowing. As a critique of philosophy and science it is in a comprehensive sense a transcendental theory of knowledge.

2. *History.* This sketch of the problems of the validity and constitution of knowledge applies to all significant efforts in the history of philosophy which claimed to be transcendental reflection. Along with initial and disjointed efforts in all the great philosophical systems from Aristotle and Thomas Aquinas to Hegel, there were anticipations of transcendental reduction and deduction above all in the Platonic tradition, as for instance in Augustine, Anselm of Canterbury and Bonaventure. But the question of validity is put explicitly for the first time by Descartes in his effort to arrive analytically, passing through radical scepticism, at an absolute and unshakable foundation of knowledge in the absolute veracity and truth of God. This process of reduction is, however, only termed transcendental philosophy when the question of validity is linked with constitutive theory, that is, the basic structures of the object as such, in the philosophy of Immanuel Kant. His general statement of the problems in his three Critiques (critique of the pure reason, of the practical reason, of the judgment) has remained on the whole decisive ever since for all transcendental philosophy, both as critique of science and as self-justification of philosophy. Everything that has been put forward as transcendental philosophy since then has explicitly referred itself to Kant, though normally in a critical way.

Thus Johann Gottlieb Fichte's theory of science, as a system of the absolute and the absolute phenomenon, with its reconciliation of theoretical and practical wisdom in terms of the question of absolute truth (especially in the *Wissenschaftslehre* of 1804) is only intelligible in the light of Kant's approach. But Fichte's successors at Jena and Berlin, Schelling and Hegel, can hardly be seen as part of the history of transcendental philosophy, since they abandon the ground of transcendental criticism at various points of their approach. And indeed all further transcendental philosophy seems to be characterized by a growing eclecticism in its themes and obviously loses sight of the systematic and comprehensive framework as attained by Fichte. Neo-Kantianism, for instance, which is at once anti-speculative and anti-positivist, restricts the material object of the basic question of the conditions of validity in general to the findings of science. It has become at the hands of its practitioners (Cohen, Natorp at Marburg, Windelband, Rickert, Lask in south-west Germany) a critique of science in terms of theories of validity. The problem of the absolute, which Kant assigned ambiguously enough to the theory of the postulates of the practical reason, has here lost all its importance for the transcendental question, just as it also has in the transcendental phenomenology of Husserl. His constitutive theories aim, like the fundamental ontology and existentialism of the early Heidegger, at the self-justification of philosophy and a universal foundation for the sciences. But they also help to restrict the transcendental question more and more to the problem of the concrete subjectivity and terminate, though not without a breach of continuity, in the existential philosophy which, as developed in Jaspers and Sartre, has very few traits of the abstract and transcendental.

The transcendental discussion was taken up in scholasticism and neo-Thomism, having been launched by the pioneer work of Joseph Maréchal who made a functional comparison between the systems of Kant and Aquinas which served to reconcile transcendental philosophy and traditional metaphysics. But even here the full weight of the transcendental problem is hardly felt, as may be seen from the occurrence of the problem of the transition from the "dynamism" of the transcendental and reductive question to the "finalism" of a metaphysics of a pre-established reality. But the transcendental analysis of the judgment holds firmly to the validity theories of transcendental philosophy. Within this tradition a number of writers (K. Rahner, Siewerth, M. Müller, Lotz, Lonergan, Marc, Coreth) have exploited fruitfully the encounter between classical metaphysics and the claims of modern transcendental philosophy. Coreth's *Metaphysik* put forward an independent synthesis of phenomenology, fundamental ontology and classical ontology, according to the methods of transcendentalism. Recently Holz has sought to apply to the tradition of the school of Maréchal the neo-Kantian theories of validity, as fully elaborated by Hans Wagner.

Outside phenomenology and scholasticism there have also been fruitful efforts at transcendental philosophy. Wolfgang Cramer has followed up the objectivity theory of Hönigswald, while Hans Wagner's subtle system seeks to reconcile neo-Kantianism and phenomenology. The *Transcendentale Logik* of Hermann Krings links up with Fichte, Lask, Heidegger and neo-Thomism to show the connection between ontology and transcendental philosophy. Reinhard Lauth seeks to revive the full transcendental system of Fichte, though unmistakably critical in approach. In spite of all variations and defects there is fundamental agreement about the constitution and validity of knowledge, as presented in the judgment, whether the judgment actually contains a predicate or is prior to predication. A fully thought-out transcendental philosophy which would include Fichte and a critical appraisal of newer findings is, however, still wanting.

3. *Concept and task.* The common elements and the contrasts in the historical approach point to a strict concept of transcendental philosophy and to its decisive objective problem. It could then be described as a transcendental — "validity" — reflection which reaches from the structurally universal affirmation of consciousness (judgment, scientific knowledge and even simple registering of fact) to the unconditioned (the absolute, that which is "of itself", being, truth, goodness and even thought and understanding of being). It uses the factual evidence to remount to the genetic, while confronting and overcoming universal doubt. This reflection, in its reverse process, is the deductive, systematic constitution and legitimation of the initially hypothetical starting-point, of which the conditions of possibility have been analysed. And thus is provided the justification of concrete, scientific and philosophical knowledge, according to the precisely circumscribed possibilities at each level.

The problem of transcendental reflection is that beginning and end mutually determine each other. The perspective of the phenomena which constitute the starting-point is coloured by the anticipatory grasp of the ultimate and unconditioned ground, while conversely the interpretation of the absolute is qualitatively determined by the previous choice and interpretation of the phenomenal data. The problem which here looms up is that of the adequacy of the starting-point, which must be the object of critical reflection in transcendental philosophy, since its own comprehensiveness is a function of that of the initial approach. Such reflection is important for an adequate determination of the ultimate factor of justification, and also makes it possible to situate critically the historical and present-day forms of philosophy. It follows that it is insufficient

to interpret the unconditioned either as pure immanence (which would be to make an absolute of the idea) or as pure transcendence (which would be to make an absolute of the practical). It is also insufficient to reduce absolute truth to the mere functioning of a destiny which determines understanding (as in the "epochal" constitution of knowledge in the later Heidegger). And it would again be insufficient to make absolute truth merely function as the destructive force of negative dialectic which reduces all to untruth (as in the utopian constitution of knowledge in Adorno).

In all these cases the thinker's own act of knowing is left out of account. And consequently the unity of theory and practice which an adequate starting-point demands is envisaged only under one aspect, either that of mere theory or of mere practice. The danger of re-objectivating consciousness ("being-conscious") can probably be avoided only by an interpretation of the unconditioned which considers absolute truth as a sheer negativity for the concept but makes it manifest in positive functions (as mystery, "light"). As against a naively objectivating metaphysics in its many historical forms, and any absolute dialectic, positive or negative, the significance of transcendental philosophy is that it can maintain the historicity and finitude of the world, without having to give up its constitutive relationship to the hermeneutical ultimate of the good which is its positive meaning.

This positive affirmation is the ground of philosophy itself, and it is also the basis of the positive mode of knowledge which in the form of modern science inhibited all philosophy by its claims. Since the problematic element of science is not in its own nature, but in the importance attributed to it by man, it may not be considered on principle as the reflection of a depraved totality which must be swept away, of a non-original and artificially civilized world. Science now appears as a way for the realization of the good and hence as man's chance of self-affirmation and self-emancipation. This achievement shows the irreplaceable value of transcendental philosophy in this world of the sciences which ours will remain. Its task is to uphold critically the just metaphysical intention of man, by expounding the unconditioned which is posited in all knowing.

See also *Knowledge, Philosophy, Truth* I, *Existence* II, *Phenomenology, Science* I.

BIBLIOGRAPHY. H. Knittermeyer, *Der Terminus transzendental in seiner historischen Entwicklung bis zu Kant* (dissertation, Marburg, 1922); J. Maréchal, *Le point de départ de la métaphysique*, V (2nd ed., 1949); G. Morpugo Tagliabue, *La struttura del trascendentale* (1951); A. Marc, *La dialectique de l'affirmation* (1952); I. Mancini, "Il trascendentale come fondamento de l'atto metafisico", *Rivista di philosofia neoscolastica* 47 (1955), pp. 332–55; H. Wagner, *Philosophie und Reflexion* (1959); J. Kopper, *Transzendentales und dialektisches Denken* (1961); J. Manzana Martínez de Marañon, *Objektivität und Wahrheit* (1961); D. Henrich in *RGG*, VI, cols. 988f.; T. Seebohm, *Die Bedingungen der Möglichkeit der Transzendentalphilosophie* (1962); H. Krings, *Transzendentale Logik* (1964); K. Lehmann, "Metaphysik, Transzendentalphilosophie und Phänomenologie in den ersten Schriften Martin Heideggers", *Philosophisches Jahrbuch der Görres-Gesellschaft* 71 (1964), pp. 331–57; M. Müller, *Existenzphilosophie im geistigen Leben der Gegenwart* (3rd ed., 1964); M. Zahn, "Identité et synthèse dans la dernière philosophie de Kant et la théorie de la science de Fichte", *Archives de Philosophie* 27 (1964), pp. 163–85; M. Brelage, *Studien zur Transzendentalphilosophie* (1965); W. Cramer, *Grundlegung einer Theorie des Geistes* (2nd ed., 1965); R. Lauth, *Zur Idee der Transzendentalphilosophie* (1965); P. Schneider, *Die wissenschaftsbegründende Funktion der Transzendentalphilosophie* (1965); H. M. Baumgartner, "Über das Gottesverständnis der Transzendentalphilosophie", *Philosophisches Jahrbuch der Görres-Gesellschaft* 73 (1966), pp. 303–21; H. Holz, *Transzendentalphilosophie und Metaphysik* (1966); J. Habermas, *Erkenntnis und Interesse* (1968); E. Coreth, *Metaphysics* (1968); O. Muck, *The Transcendental Method* (1968).

Hans Michael Baumgartner

TRANSCENDENTALS

The inmost force which moves to philosophical thinking is being. Certain necessary notes of being recur in all beings as such, and are called transcendentals, because they reach out beyond the limited orders of individual beings or surpass all limits *(transcendere)*. These transcendentals are unity, truth, goodness, and also beauty. Here we discuss them historically and systematically.

1. *Historically.* For Plato, the forms or ideas constitute that which really is (ὄντως ὄν), in which the essence of being is fully and clearly manifested along with the notes mentioned above, in which earthly things partake at least in a fragmentary way. Aristotle examines expressly the notes of all beings as such: the one and the true in *Metaphysics,* X and VI, the good in the *Nicomachean Ethics,* I. Plotinus regards the supreme principle as the one and the good. From it proceeds the νοῦς which discriminates the forms in its thought, and hence is the true. The souls and all things partake of this in descending degrees. St. Augustine has illuminating formulas for the notes of being: "nihil autem est esse quam unum esse" (*De moribus Manichaeorum,* II, 6); "verum mihi videtur esse id, quod est" (*Soliloquium,* II, 5); "inquantum est quidquid, bonum est" (*De vera religione,* XI, 21). St. Albert the Great already offers some systematic discussion of the first three transcendentals. He adds reality *(res)* and particularity *(aliquid)*, the former being synonymous with being *(ens)*, the latter being comprehended within unity. Here the influence of Avicenna (Ibn Sina) may be felt, who held that to be and to be real were two different determinations, while he treated being and particularity as synonyms. St. Thomas Aquinas finds five transcendentals in all beings: reality, particularity, unity, truth and goodness (*De Veritate,* q. 1, a. 1); elsewhere he speaks only of the three main transcendentals (*De Veritate,* q. 21, a. 1, a. 3; *De Potentia,* q. 9, a. 7 ad 6). These catalogues do not include beauty; but it undoubtedly forms one of the transcendentals. In this Aquinas is in the line of Plato, Plotinus, St. Augustine and St. Albert the Great (*In De divinis nominibus,* cap. 4, lect. 5; *De Veritate,* q. 22, a. 1 ad 12; *Super Sententiis,* I, d. 31, q. 2, a. 1). The doctrine was later given systematic form by F. Suarez, who confined himself to the three main transcendentals (*Disputationes metaphysicae,* III, sect. 2, n. 3), while treating *res* and *aliquid* as did St. Albert the Great. The ensuing scholastic development followed the same lines, and its influence may be traced as far as the rationalist philosophy of the 18th century, as for instance in C. Wolff. The most prominent figure in this context is G. Leibniz, who conceived being as the monad, which was hence immediately determined as unity, truth *(perceptio)* and goodness *(appetitio)*. An echo of earlier thought is still to be heard in I. Kant, who accepts the three transcendentals at least as logical pre-conditions of all knowledge of things (*Critique of Pure Reason,* B. 113f.). G. Hegel returns by way of dialectic to the metaphysical depths of being, as may be seen from his *Logic.* F. Nietzsche affirms the identity of the transcendentals with their opposites, and thus arrives at his "Dionysiac" notion of becoming (*Wille zur Macht,* E. T.:

The Will to Power, ed. by O. Levy, London and Edinburgh [1909–10], nos. 12, 272, 298, 1005). In modern non-scholastic thought, N. Hartmann, for instance, ranges the essential notes of beings among the categories, which presupposes their restriction to the finite beings of the world. Finally, according to M. Heidegger, being is most intimately connected with truth above all; the one also shines through.

2. *Systematically.* The transcendentals are necessary notes of being, which explicates itself in them and displays itself most radically in them. Just as being never occurs without the transcendentals, so too each of them inevitably includes the others. Hence it follows that in the measure and in the manner that a being has being, it is characterized by unity, truth, goodness and beauty. Hence subsisting being implies the subsistence of the transcendentals. They are not mere synonyms of being, but the determinate expression of its content, which we first apprehend only in an indeterminate way. Hence the notion given in being and the various transcendentals is not quite the same: there is a conceptual distinction, founded on the varying content of each aspect. But the distinction is the smallest conceivable, as no division of content is possible: being and the transcendentals penetrate each other or are strictly and basically identical. On account of the distinction, the transition from being to the transcendentals forms a synthesis, which, however, on account of the indivisible basic identity is there *a priori* or implies a metaphysical necessity. This *a priori* synthesis, which is concerned with being itself, is of course essentially higher than that of Kant, which did not go beyond appearances.

As regards the individual transcendentals, all agree that they include unity, truth and goodness. When we also add beauty, we part company with those who insist that the beautiful is a matter of sensible contemplation. The two other notes mentioned by Aquinas with Avicenna do not appear to be independent transcendentals distinct from the others; reality *(res)* is contained in being as one of its components in unity and so too particularity *(aliquid)*. Duration and similarity are often included among the transcendentals; but they may be reduced to unity in or above time and to determinate agreement with regard to unity. Finally, order and totality are not, strictly speaking, transcendentals, because they imply multiplicity and hence are not applicable to God.

The transcendentals are found in an essential sequence. A being immediately implies unity. From this flow the true and the good, which imply determination, accessibility and conformity between each being and the act of knowing or willing. Further, since knowledge gives only an imperfect union between the spirit and being, while perfect union takes place only in willing or in love, the full expression of what begins in the true is found only in the good. Finally, beauty comprises at once unity, truth and goodness, in the fullness of their diversity and harmony. Thence flows the repose of contemplation and delight.

We may now indicate the grounds for affirming that the four notes of being are really transcendentals. The more a being has being, the more is it one, that is, self-contained and distinct from others. And vice versa, when a being loses its unity, it is also deprived of its being, so that it either ceases to exist or at least exists no longer as an unimpaired whole.

The explicit realizing of beings in concept and judgment is possible only because of the implicit concomitant realization of being. And since being embraces everything, the human spirit thereby attains everything without exception, because only nothingness is outside the range of being. But this means that everything is homogeneous, accessible, intelligible, that is to say, true, for the spirit.

In the same way, the will can only choose freely between limited goods as its material object, insofar as it is directed according to its formal object to universal being as the good, and hence finally to the unlimited good *(summum bonum in genere)*. Thus everything is homogeneous, accessible, appetible, that is to say, good, for the will or love. But if being and good are basically identical, badness and evil can only be the privation or lack of some perfection demanded by the natural tendencies.

Beauty, as the state of perfection and perfect harmony of unity, truth and goodness, constitutes a transcendental along with these three. This description holds good for what is perceptible by the senses and still more for what can be contemplated spiritually. We are moved by the radiance of beauty. But even the tedious and ugly contains a remnant of beauty, the complete extinction of which would be equivalent to the destruction of the being in question.

Ultimately, the transcendentals lead to God as the primordially one, true, good and beautiful.

See also *Being* I, *Unity*, *Truth* I, *Good*, *Art*, *Evil*, *Theodicy*, *Spirit*.

BIBLIOGRAPHY. G. Schulemann, *Die Lehre von den Transzendentalien in der scholastischen Philosophie* (1929); H. Kühle, "Die Lehre Alberts des Grossen von den Transzendentalien", *Philosophia Perennis*, I (1930), pp. 129–47; A. B. Wolter, *The Transcendentals and their Function in the Metaphysics of Duns Scotus* (1946); L. Lachance, *L'Être et ses propriétés* (1950); J. E. Twomey, *The General Notion of the Transcendentals in the Metaphysics of S. Thomas* (1958); J. Lotz, *Metaphysica operationis humanae* (2nd ed., 1961); id., *Ontologia* (1963); L. Elders, *Aristotle's Theory of the One* (1961); H. Kuhn, *Das Sein und das Gute* (1962).

Johannes Baptist Lotz

TRANSCENDENTAL THEOLOGY

1. *The approach to the concept*. The term "transcendental theology" was modelled on the analogy of transcendental philosophy to indicate a certain receptivity to the latter in Catholic thought (since Maréchal; see. O. Muck), with important influences on Catholic theology. This does not mean that transcendental theology is merely the application of a transcendental philosophy to theological subjects. The main thing is that a historical context is indicated in which a procedure always in use in theology, though perhaps not very explicitly, was clearly envisaged and given a special name. The principle of a transcendental theology is genuinely theological. Since theology deals with man's salvation (inasmuch as it consists of God's self-communication) and really with nothing else, its subject-matter is the perfect totality of man; man is the "subject" in the strict sense of the word and not a particular along with others. Hence salvation can be understood only as that of the subject as such (and so too all elements of salvation). To understand the reality or realities of salvation in this way is to grasp them transcendentally, that is, as related to the transcendental subject — which is such "by nature" and as so constituted is radicalized by grace. The fact that such a transcendental theology is clearly coloured (at least at first sight) by a recourse to transcendental philosophy does not deprive it of its genuinely theological character. For one

thing, the theological consideration of man's "nature" as the condition of the possibility of grace is part of theology, though a theology which looks like philosophy. Systematic theology can be called transcendental when it a) uses the instruments of transcendental philosophy and b) takes as its themes, more explicitly than before and not just in general (as in traditional fundamental theology), the *a priori* conditions in the believer for the knowledge of important truths of faith, using genuinely theological methods of investigation. It is applicable only where such a transcendental questioning is not impossible by the very nature of the object of knowledge.

2. *The problem*. The problem of the essence of a transcendental theology is therefore very like that of a transcendental philosophy. But there is also the special and authentically theological question, as to whether a transcendental enquiry into the conditions of possibility of knowledge in the subject himself can be envisaged with regard to an object of revelation and faith, i.e., with regard to the object in general and particular matters involved.

3. *The possibility of a transcendental theology*. a) It must first be noted that any *analysis fidei* (see *Faith*) implies some transcendental theology. This element then colours the whole of theology, on account of the nature of faith, outside of which there are no theological truths. For the analysis of faith asks how such an absolute assent to revelation, precisely as the word of *God*, is at all possible. When grace is then appealed to as the necessary condition for hearing the word of God as God's, a condition of possibility in the subject himself is examined and one which belongs strictly to theology. This is transcendental theology.

b) Theology has every reason to desire that transcendental philosophy should limit itself to its own proper sphere. If a transcendental philosophy were to claim absolutely to be the sole and non-derivative grounding of human existence, a "positive" religion of revelation, in a history of salvation embracing as such the existence of man and salvation as a totality, would be excluded from the start. This self-limitation, due to the recognition of the "historicity" of existence, which cannot be systematically categorized, and reflection on language and dialogal and hermeneutical experience, is an essential element in any correct transcendental philosophy. Otherwise philosophy falls victim to hybris and becomes a brutal effort to dissolve everything in its reflections. If this limitation were not imposed by philosophy itself, it would abandon its essential claim to enquire into everything and would be self-destructive. But this limitation of the transcendental self-understanding of man is also — on principle, and above all in the present situation of philosophy and theology — a task for fundamental theology. For to demonstrate the positive possibility of revelation and history of salvation, it must show that concrete history, not fully amenable to reflection, affects man in his primordial quality of subject, and hence can be a history of salvation and ruin. But if fundamental theology undertakes this task, it is already transcendental theology in the sense just mentioned. It is reflection on the fact that the created subject as such is intrinsically involved in history, the history precisely of its own true subjectivity. The self-communication of God in grace (by virtue of the universal salvific will of God) is undoubtedly a "transcendental" existential of man. But it has its proper being in the history of salvation and revelation (individual and collective) and this is the medium through which it is accomplished and comes to us. It is precisely the task of a transcendental theology to show that the metaphysical essence of a reality and its history (and hence grace as an existential and salvation-history) are not simply juxtaposed but condition each other (see *Salvation III A*).

Hence transcendental theology cannot and does not try to be the whole of theology, of which it is only one element. For theology, or more precisely faith, whose articulate elements and whose ultimate resistance to reflection theology reflects, must always speak of the historically concrete which is not amenable to deduction, and still show how this concrete history can really affect man in the ultimate ground of his existence and subjectivity. Without transcendental theology historical facts cannot be shown to be existentiell, that is, to affect man's salvation (see *Faith and History*). This is because the reality of such salvific events cannot be known simply *a posteriori*. If they are to address man as man, he must address himself to them with his whole being, that is, he must discover that he is by his very nature forced to turn to them. But if he approaches them with his whole being, his theology is transcendental. Reflection on the transcen-

dental orientation of man is not rendered impossible by the historical and unpredictable character of the saving events, their *a posteriori* nature, the fact that they are freely ordained by God. For what was first and most strictly ordained by God is the permanent supernatural existential of grace, the proffered self-communication of God, and hence a "transcendental" condition of man. And this free grace, as a transcendental determination of man, has its own proper history in what we call history of salvation and revelation, which cannot be and be grasped as such without this *a priori* possibility in man which is called grace, or the grace of faith.

4. *The transcendental theology of the fundamental dogmas of Christianity.* a) An important task is imposed at once on transcendental theology by the need to explain the true relationship of the world to God (see *God-World Relationship*). Only knowledge of God attained by a transcendental method prevents God being regarded as a part within the all, or a demiurge whose action on the world is merely "from without".

b) Little more needs to be said about the fundamental anthropological dogma that supernatural grace is the self-communication of God to man. For grace is not an element in some particular category of things which is superadded — even on the loftiest plane — to the nature of man. It is a determination of the transcendence of man's knowledge and freedom as such. And it is only in the light of this truth that the nature of grace as salvation, meaning supernatural salvation, is definitely disclosed.

c) If theology shows clearly that the "Trinity of the economy" and the "immanent" Trinity are identical, and that the latter is revealed through the former, the importance of a transcendental philosophy for theology becomes apparent, and such philosophy, when exercising this function, becomes a transcendental theology. For if the revelation of the mystery of God's self-communication is supposed, and it is seen that God is always the unoriginated and hence the permanently incomprehensible, even when imparting himself, a "transcendental" deduction demonstrates that this self-communication of God necessarily comes to man as transcendence and as history, in a unity and distinction of both elements. Then the revelation of God's self-communication is seen to contain implicitly what we call the economic and immanent Trinity of God (see *Trinity in Theology*).

d) This at once provides a starting-point for a Christology on the basis of a transcendental theology (see *Jesus Christ* III). Obviously, a transcendental theology as such cannot undertake to prove that Jesus of Nazareth is the Lord, the absolute bringer of salvation, the incarnation of the Word of God. This experience comes in history itself, not in an *a priori* theology of history. And a transcendental Christology need not proceed as if it had formed the Christian notion of the God-man independently of the historical experience of this God-man in the concrete figure of Jesus. The transcendental deduction of an "idea" is always subsequent reflection on a concrete experience. It is a reflection which notes explicitly the "necessary" in the factual. It is therefore justifiable and necessary, since it alone explicitly displays the essence of the concrete experience in its necessary essence, not just its factuality. Such a Christology may proceed "transcendentally" in various ways, though here it must be admitted that the word "transcendental" is used in a wider and somewhat indefinite sense, and that the word comprises all theological considerations which start from man as a being whose situation is transcendence, who reflects transcendentally on this his being.

Transcendental theology can make the "idea" of the God-man intelligible, as the climax, at least asymptotically and hypothetically, of the movement of the spirit, as its drive towards God continually carries it beyond itself. Such a Christology of the "Omega Point", as Teilhard de Chardin called it, need not overlook or minimize the truth that the Omega Point towards which the world moves in its spirit is what is theologically termed the kingdom of God as fully come in the vision of God, which is imparted to *every* spirit in its fulfilment. This is precisely what is explained by a transcendental understanding of the nature of man. The incarnation is not regarded in isolation as a singularly supreme stage of the self-transcendence of the world (which the divine self-communication sustains) and as something which is only "for our sake" subsequently. It is seen as the summit, a unique one indeed, of the heights of the self-communication of God to all spirit — the spirit which forms the heights of the historical, irreversible (eschatological) manifestation of the victorious self-communication of God to the world. The relationship (in terms of transcendental theology) between spirit (including grace) and history (including revelation-history) implies that history, the history of grace in the world, comes to a peak in the absolute bringer of salvation, who will be the God-man in the orthodox sense of the term. There is therefore a transcendental Christology which outlines theoretically the nature of the God-man, pointing on to the historical reality of the God-man in Jesus and instructed by this reality.

A Christology can also proceed "transcendentally", presupposing the unity of the economic and the immanent Trinity, by explaining why precisely the second person in God becomes man and why only he can. A full understanding of the nature of truth in transcendental terms, having regard to the primordial unity of objective and subjective truth, might argue as follows, not excluding but surpassing the classical Greek notion of truth. It must be the Logos, who is the personal fidelity of self-utterance displaying itself historically, who reveals the Father in the flesh and in doing so reveals the propriety of the Logos himself (cf. K. Rahner, *Theological Investigations*, IV [1966], pp. 77–104). Finally, a transcendental Christology must do with regard to Jesus Christ what all transcendental theology must do in keeping with its duty of self-limitation and self-denial. It must justify and encourage man not to seek his salvation in the "idea" but in history (as a unity of past, present and future), to encounter God in man and ultimately in the man in whom God definitively exists and historically appears in the world, that is to say, in Jesus Christ (see also *Virtue*).

BIBLIOGRAPHY. See bibliographies on *Theology, Theological Methodology, Transcendental Philosophy;* also: P. Rousselot, "Les yeux de la foi", *RSR* 1 (1910), pp. 241–59, 444–75, offprint with appendix "Sur le concept de foi scientifique" (1913); E. Simons, *Philosophie der Offenbarung: Auseinandersetzung mit K. Rahner* (1966); B. Welte, *Heilsverständnis* (1966); H. Bouillard, *The Logic of Faith* (1967); K. Rahner, *Schriften zur Theologie*, VIII, pp. 43–65, 66–87; id., *Hearers of the Word* (1968); O. Muck, *The Transcendental Method* (1968); E. Coreth, *Grundfragen der Hermeneutik* (1969); A. Gerken, *Offenbarung und Transzendenzerfahrung* (1969); W. Oelmüller, *Die unbefriedigte Aufklärung* (1969); H. Verweyen, *Ontologische Voraussetzungen des Glaubensaktes: Die transzendentale Frage nach der Möglichkeit von Offenbarung* (1969).

Karl Rahner

TRANSMIGRATION OF SOULS

In practice no clear distinction is made between the expressions metempsychosis, metensomatosis, palingenesis, re-incarnation and transmigration. Older writers (Plotinus and the Fathers) preferred to use metensomatosis. Palingenesis is a notion with a much broader connotation, in some sort of way presupposed by the more systematic ideas involved in that of metempsychosis.

Many cultures without written traditions (the so-called primitives) hold that the principle of life of a living being can pass into another after death, without having to remain in the same species. They have conceptions of transmigration which vary according to the nature and the function of the vital principles which reanimate a new individual, and also according to the correspondence between the principles of the individual life and the powers which rule the life of the cosmos. These powers are often seen as closely related to certain meteorological phenomena (the phases of the moon, the seasons). This cyclic conception of time dominates the mentality of agrarian communities, where, moreover, structures of a matriarchal type predominate, but is not unknown also in communities of hunters and shepherds. The very idea of "culture" implies that man has realized that to live he must follow nature, and that to follow it intelligently he must learn to precede it.

These were the basic ideas behind the working out of the initiation mysteries. Their purpose was to transmit the secret life to the rising generations under a sacramental form which nearly always signified "death and re-surrection". The initiate was introduced through the rite into the circle of the collective life of the clan. In this way he was "twice born", and already in this context we can speak of palingenesis. As a result, physical birth and death appeared in a different light. They were seen as events in the collective life of the clan, rather than as events in the life of the individual. It is very probable that it was against such a background that the idea emerged that the spark of life belonging to the clan which leaves the dead man must not be lost, and which is so well illustrated by the custom in certain tribes of their pregnant women thronging to the bedside of a dying person. In India, where re-incarnation plays such a great part in religious thought, very clear traces have been preserved of the importance in pre-historic times of an indeterminate group of "fathers" as a kind of collective reservoir of the vitality of the clan, although eventually fear overshadowed piety and, when new and more refined ideas about the soul prevailed, the revenants became in historical times terrifying and dangerous as well as wretched. All the same they have a particular place in the transmigratory cycle for which more recent systematic theories have no explanation.

A widely believed cosmo-biological myth has played a major part in firmly establishing the idea of palingenesis. According to this myth there is an identity of nature between the breath of the individual and the life that it supports and the breath that enlivens the whole universe and which itself is looked upon as a living being. The great cyclic stream of cosmic life thus embraces all the generations of mankind, according to a grandiose conception which allows of developments and applications in many directions. It can easily fit in with the idea of the power that moves the stars, in particular the moon and the sun. The moon, for example, can be compared to a shuttle which untiringly weaves the destiny of mortal men on the cosmic loom. As a result the sub-lunar world is subject to a different system or control to that of the celestial world which escapes these vicissitudes. Without it being possible to reconstruct in detail the interrelated developments of selenological mysticism and the ideas about transmigration, it cannot be doubted that they are bound up together. The moon was looked upon as the first of the dead, and it is apparent to all that even though dead it never ceases to be reborn. Further, the moon plays an essential part in the mystical complex of ideas relating to initiation. The same cosmic breath which animates the movements of the heavens presides over human life: "The air has woven the universe just as the breath has woven human life" (*Baṛhadâranyaka Upanishad*, 3, 7, 2). In neo-Platonism, Gnosticism, and the Hindu and Buddhist theosophies astro-biological ideas and re-incarnation are closely associated (*samsâra*, εἱμαρμένη).

The doctrine of re-incarnation takes on a new meaning when it is associated with the idea of retribution for moral acts. This came about (independently?) in India and in Greece. But while in Greece this idea remained the exclusive concern of small groups and the object of speculation among philosophers, for most of the religions and philosophies of Indian origin it became the common basis of their conception of the world, and then spread from India to the whole of eastern and south-east Asia. At the beginning the idea of retributive re-incarnation does not appear to have necessarily led to a pessimistic interpretation of life in this world, but very soon in India, even before Buddhism pursued the idea to its ultimate conclusions, the universe of beings swept along in the transmigratory wave *(samsâra)* came to be conceived in the spirit of the *vanitas vanitatum* of Ecclesiastes, a biblical book also strongly influenced by the cyclic periodicity of reality.

It must be further noted that both in religious Platonism and Gnosticism, as in the Stoicism of a Posidonius of Apamaea or in the Vedanta, metempsychosis is accompanied by a conception of the world which inclines to monism. This relationship is not just the result of chance, for it is clear that monism fits in better with the cyclic return of the fleeting appearances of the multiplicity of sensible forms, while the theistic and above all creationist theologies presuppose a notion of irreversible time *(Einmaligkeit)*. In these theologies the idea of palingenesis, when systematically expressed in theories about the after-life, leads more naturally to a belief in a resurrection of the dead at the end of time.

Neo-Pythagoreanism, Gnosticism and the Vedanta all share the conviction that an immortal principle of transcendent origin in relation to the world of the senses and their objects dwells in remains of a dead man. This principle, blessed by nature, for a time loses its bearings amidst the vicissitudes of mortal life through the ignorance and aberrations of the imagination and concupiscence. The long journey of the *âtman* through successive re-incarnations has nonetheless a positive significance, inasmuch as through this bitter experience the immortal principle, triumphing over its endless wanderings, finally achieves its true nature, which is foreign to the world of coming to be and passing away.

Between the materialistic monism of the Stoa, which held that the same events are necessarily reproduced in the same order in the course of successive cosmic periods, and the doctrine of the *karma,* according to which the situations arising in the course of each existence are completely determined by the fruit of moral acts performed in previous existences, intermediate solutions have been proposed, as for example by Origen. Without admitting the tenets of astral determinism or those of the *a posteriori* determinism of the law of *karma* (for he had to allow for the action of redemptive grace), Origen nonetheless explained the different conditions of rational beings at their birth in a particular cosmic period as being the consequence of acts performed in a previous existence. According to a schema that can also be found in the *Purânas,* Origen suggested the existence of successive worlds where the souls reappear in ever differing situations. Similar attempts to combine the principle of a just retribution for moral actions with the succession of cosmic periods, marked by catastrophes of a cathartic nature, had already been explored in the school of Plato, as well as in that of Pythagoras, and the Stoa took advantage of them. Probably for Origen, and certainly for a number of the Gnostic systems, including Manichaeism, the journey of souls capable of salvation does not go on indefinitely. At the end of a long process of purification they find an ultimate stability in a state of beatitude equal to that from which they fell at the beginning (see *Apocatastasis*).

Some Gnostic systems consider that for a soul to be ultimately freed from the flesh it is indispensable for it to have experienced all the possible situations in the world, and even that it should have in fact given in to all the kinds of temptation. This is the price it has to pay for its Gnosis being perfect, as the consciousness cannot achieve a realization of the nothingness of the world of generation until after each specific manifestation of the libido has been effectively nullified by the disgust that follows on satiety.

In the Orphic system, whose influence continued to be felt through neo-Pythagoreanism and Middle Platonism, the soul is buried in the body as in a tomb. In such a dualistic view of man it is natural to look on every new voluntary involvement of the spirit in the world of the flesh as the cause of new fetters chaining the soul down to the body. Only a punishment exactly proportionate to the fault can cancel out its effects. By contrast, it is all the more remarkable that Buddhism, although it explicitly refuses to recognize the existence of an immortal soul (the doctrine of the *anatta*), has in fact come to the same practical conclusions as Orphism as a result of its adoption of the pan-Indian conception of the *karma.*

The systems of retributive re-incarnation

must logically exclude every unwarranted intervention of the divinity in favour of his faithful. Nonetheless, wherever theistic ideas made their way, a parallel tendency developed to admit exceptions to the law of *karma,* as can be seen, for example, in the Indian sects such as the Bakti, who believe in avatars ("incarnations" of the divine).

The illumination which enables a Buddhist to live here below in *Nirvana* includes as one of its essential aspects the clear vision of all previous existences. This anamnesis in some sort of way thus fulfills the role of a psychoanalysis, at the end of which the libido binding him down to the law of *karma* finally withers away. In Hinduism and Gnosticism this illumination consists in a clear perception of the ontologically disengaged character of the true ego, a perception which at the same time dispels the illusion of the attribution of acts and their consequences to a particular individual subject. In this way of thought we can already discern the part played by metempsychosis in every gnostically inclined system, where it illustrates the necessary connection between the libido and palingenesis. This fact also inclines us to the opinion that the doctrines about transmigration result from a reflection on certain ascetical and mystical experiences in the course of which the consciousness finds itself transformed and transported on to planes of life which fall outside our normal experience, and which are more or less interrelated in ascending grades. Because of this it is possible to recognize the value of certain theosophical and anthroposophical ideas which have been instrumental in spreading the basic conceptions of the Eastern and Gnostic tradition throughout the West, as well as that of the psychotherapeutic investigations of the school of C. G. Jung which in their attempts to establish the ultimate structure of the soul have been based on the same traditions.

See also *Gnosis, Gnosticism, Manichaeism, Psychotherapy.*

BIBLIOGRAPHY. *HERE; Eranos Jahrbuch,* especially of 1939; — *RGG,* V, 1637–40; — C. de Prel, *Die monistische Seelenlehre* (1888); G. F. Moore, *Metempsychosis* (1914); R. Steiner, *Theosophy* (18th ed., 1920); E. Rohde, *Psyche: The Cult of Souls and Belief in Immortality among the Greeks* (1925, from 8th German ed.); E. R. Dodds, *The Elements of Theology of Proclus* (1933) (see Appendix II); H. von Glasenapp, *Unsterblichkeit und Erlösung in den indischen Religionen* (1938); J. Bidez, *Eos ou Platon et l'Orient* (1945); H. S. Long, *Study of the Doctrine of Metempsychosis in Greece from Pythagoras to Plato* (1948); H. Günther, *Das Seelenproblem im älteren Buddhism* (1949); F. Cumont, *Lux Perpetua* (1949); A. Festugière, *La révélation d'Hermès Trismégiste,* III (1953); J. Portman, *Ochêma* (1954); M. Nilsson, *Geschichte der griechischen Religion,* I (2nd ed., 1955); II (2nd ed., 1961); C. J. Bleecker, ed., *Anthropologie religieuse* (1955); N. David, *Immortalité et réincarnation* (1961) (China, Tibet, India); S. Brandon, *Man and His Destiny in the Great Religions* (1962); M. Eliade, *Rites and Symbols of Initiation: The Mysteries of Birth and Rebirth* (1963; former title: *Birth and Rebirth*); A. des Georges, *La réincarnation des âmes selon les traditions orientales et occidentales* (1966); W. K. C. Guthrie, *Orpheus and Greek Religion* (1966); C. J. Jung, *Psychology and Alchemy* (Collected Works, vol. XII) (2nd ed., 1968).

Étienne Cornélis

TRANSUBSTANTIATION

1. Transubstantiation is described by the Council of Trent as the change of the whole substance of bread *(totius substantiae panis)* into the body of Christ, and of the whole substance of wine *(totius substantiae vini)* into the blood of Christ, the species of bread and wine remaining unchanged (Session XIII, can. 2; *D* 884). This notion of transubstantiation is coloured by the branch of philosophy known as cosmology and is the result of a development which was not always consistent. Though the element of change *(metabolismus)* had been expressly stressed by St. Ambrose (see J. Geiselmann), the effect of the eucharistic change on the substance of bread and wine had presented no problem till Berengarius. The supporters of the metabolistic notion only tried to give it an ontological interpretation in the 11th century. The decisive influences here were Lanfranc of Bec (1005–89) and Guitmund of Aversa (d. before 1095). Their explanation of the eucharistic change as a change of substance is reflected in the *Jusjurandum Berengarii:* "substantialiter converti" (*D* 355). This was confirmed by the Fourth Council of Lateran in 1215, "transsubstantiatis pane in corpus, et vino in sanguinem" (*D* 430). The term *transsubstantiatio* seems to have been first used by Roland Bandinelli in the middle of the 12th century. (For the use of *transsubstantiatio* by the magisterium see H. Jorissen, p. 9, note 19; references to early scholasticism are taken from this work.)

It is important to note that all the scholastics of the 12th century regarded the logical relationship in the sentence between subject and predicate as the basis of the metaphysical relationship between subject and propriety. In particular, *materia* and *forma* were not yet understood in the sense in which the terms were used in classical scholasticism. The predominant view was that which was given its clearest form by Petrus Cantor and which continued to be strongly influential down to the middle of the 13th century. Petrus Cantor made a distinction between the form, which was the sum of the essential proprieties, and the substance, which was more or less the *hypostasis* or subject, and while fully indeterminate and without qualities was still determinable by the *forma*. (Subject and *materia* were identified at this period.) In keeping with this view, only the subject is changed in transubstantiation, while the essential properties remain unchanged and form the natural ground of inherence for the accidents (cf. H. Jorissen, pp. 95–110). As will later appear, the present-day efforts to go beyond the formulation of Trent is in keeping with the initial positions held in the 12th century, though the link is not always explicitly recognized or sought. It must be noted here that a notion of the eucharistic change which was current in the Church for over a hundred years should not be too hastily branded with the stigma of heresy.

Another line of thought which was to lead up to the classical doctrine of transubstantiation was laid down by Alan of Lille (de l'Isle) towards the end of the 12th century (cf. H. Jorissen, pp. 110–14). In contrast to Petrus Cantor, he understood the substance as the whole essence (matter along with form being the sum of all essential properties). According to Alan, the substance, understood as the whole essence, is changed, so that the existence of the accidents has to be explained by a miracle, or their objective reality must be denied. While Stephen Langton, Guido of Orchelles and William of Auvergne followed strictly in the steps of Alan, William of Auxerre already accepted the Aristotelian form as a single metaphysical principle. This position was taken to its logical conclusion by Alexander of Hales, who held that the change took place in the substance constituted by matter and form, while the accidents remained unchanged. For Alexander, therefore, transubstantiation is a positive action "by which an actual being, without being destroyed or annihilated, is changed according to its whole substance into another actual being"

(cf. H. Jorissen, p. 154). Classical scholasticism had nothing new to offer with regard to this notion. It was maintained at the Council of Constance against Wycliffe and was adopted into the definition of the Council of Trent. Speculative problems were dealt with in the light of the doctrine of transubstantiation which had been solidly established since the classical era of scholasticism. The following appeared to be the most important: Is the substance of bread annihilated or changed positively into the body of Christ in the eucharistic change? How is the body of Christ sited in a place under the consecrated species? How is the extension of the glorified body of Christ to be explained in the Eucharist?

2. As regards the question as to how the definition of Trent is to be understood hermeneutically, E. Schillebeeckx takes the standpoint that the Council wished to affirm nothing beyond the real presence (cf. E. Schillebeeckx, pp. 29 f.) and that the canon on transubstantiation was drawn up by the Council merely to safeguard the real presence against a symbolism or spiritualism which would so to speak volatilize it away. This seems a questionable stand, if one remembers that a group of theologians at the Council had been asked to discuss two propositions of Luther in which transubstantiation was rejected as Aristotelian and scholastic, and the theory of consubstantiation put forward. The canon of Trent on transubstantiation grew out of a dialectical demarcation against the doctrine of Luther (cf. E. Gutwenger, p. 260). Hence the Council went beyond the real presence to envisage the eucharistic change as such and to affirm it directly. To make room for a new interpretation, one cannot rely on forcing an affirmation about the real presence into the canon on transubstantiation.

To reach an understanding of the eucharistic presence which will be in accord with the modern era, the hermeneutical principle must be invoked according to which the philosophical context from which the formulation of a truth of faith is derived may be expendable and replaceable. This means that in a changed scientific and philosophical situation a truth of faith calls for new interpretations and formulations and hence must be grasped in a new light. The *tota substantia,* that is, the material substance composed of matter and form with its inherent accidents, is not in accord with

293

the world-picture presented by physics and philosophy at the present time. In detail, the following difficulties are now felt with regard to the definition of transubstantiation worked out on the basis of Aristotelian and scholastic cosmology:

a) The models used by modern physics give matter an atomic structure. The ultimate particles combine to form atoms which are grouped as molecules of various types. In certain combinations, the molecules form bread and wine as their end-results. Hence it cannot be said that the substance of bread or wine, composed of matter and form, is the ontologically prior reality from which in consequence the chemical properties result. Bread and wine are the last stage of a combination of atoms, molecules and forces. This is why in the twenties theologians had recourse to physics in the explanation of transubstantiation and transposed it to the level of the atom or molecule, which meant that the transubstantiation of a host contained an incalculable number of transubstantiations (historical survey with bibliography in J. Clark, pp. 24–51; see also E. Gutwenger, pp. 278–94, where there is an account of the last major discussion of the subject, between F. Selvaggi and C. Colombo). By the sixties, these efforts had to be considered a failure, because discussion of transubstantiation as a physical or cosmological process no longer seemed desirable.

b) The cosmological approach to transubstantiation presents the further difficulty that the survival of the accidents forms an unthinkable paradox. If one continues to maintain, along the lines suggested by the Councils of Constance and Trent, that the eucharistic accidents exist *sine subjecto,* there is extension but nothing that is extended, roundness but nothing that is round, hardness but nothing that is hard, weight without anything heavy, activity with nothing acting, passivity with nothing affected, etc.

c) The conventional notion of transubstantiation gives a far too impersonal impression. Aristotle took his categories and basic concepts mainly from the realm of the inorganic, which led in scholasticism to an objectified treatment of transubstantiation. At the present time, when existential philosophy and personalism are the order of the day, an effort is being made to see the eucharistic change in a different perspective. The idea is to emphasize the role of the glorified Lord who gives himself to his own as their spiritual food and desires to be one with them.

In view of the philosophical difficulties and the demands of personalism, the *nouvelle théologie* had sought to replace the notion of transubstantiation by that of transfinalization, but without explaining precisely whether a new terminology or a new interpretation was aimed at. If the bread receives a new ordination to an end, an ontological change must have taken place. The question is what is this change. Theologians from the Netherlands in particular have contributed to the fuller discussion of transubstantiation (C. Dupont, B. Möller, E. Schillebeeckx, P. Schoonenberg, L. Smits, I. Sonnen and others; see further L. van Hout, p. 173, note 2). They do not all take the same line. They presuppose the real presence. In the discussion of the process of its realization, L. Smits starts explicitly with the early scholasticism of the 12th century. Like other theologians, Smits makes much use of phenomenological approaches to throw light on the process of change, while Schillebeeckx treats it along the lines of ontology. They all agree in opting for a transfinalization or transignification of the consecrated bread and wine.

3. The more recent approaches suggest the following considerations. One has to remember that the words of institution indicate a change but do not give any guiding line for the interpretation of the actual process. As regards transubstantiation, it may then be said that substance, essence, meaning and purpose of the bread are identical. But the meaning of a thing can be changed without detriment to its matter. A house, for instance, consists of a certain arrangement of materials and has a clearly established nature and a clearly established purpose. If the house is demolished and the materials used for building a bridge, a change of nature or essence has intervened. Something completely different is there. The meaning has been changed, since a house is meant to be lived in and a bridge is used to cross a depression. But there has been no loss of material. In an analogous way, the meaning of the bread has been changed through the consecration. Something which formerly served profane use now becomes the dwelling-place and the symbol of Christ who is present and gives himself to his own. This means that an

ontological change has taken place in the bread.

In a general way, three classes of symbols may be distinguished. The first type are effects which actually point to their cause, like smoke and fire. The second type have by their very nature a certain potential signification, which needs, however, to be actualized by being determined and expressed, e.g., washing with water as a symbol of purification from sin. The third type of symbol do not by nature designate any given object either actually or potentially. They only become signs through human convention, like the colours of traffic lights. The bread should be included in the second type of symbols, since the fact that it is food makes it naturally apt to symbolize spiritual nourishment and union. But the consecrated bread possesses the further property of signifying that the Lord who offers himself as food is not just at a distance but is present in the bread. By virtue of this concentrated symbolism, the bread becomes the sacramental manifestation of the presence of Christ. Hence transubstantiation means a change of finality and being in the bread and wine, because they are raised to being symbols of Christ who is present there and invites men to spiritual union.

See also *Hylemorphism, Substance, Eucharist* I, *Sacrament, Symbol, Nouvelle Théologie.*

BIBLIOGRAPHY. See bibliography on *Eucharist* I; also: J. R. Geiselmann, *Die Eucharistielehre der Vorscholastik* (1926); J. T. Clark, "Physics, Philosophy, Transubstantiation, Theology", *TS* 12 (1951), pp. 24–51 (with bibliography); M. Schmaus, ed., *Aktuelle Fragen zur Eucharistie* (1960); E. Gutwenger, "Substanz und Akzidens in der Eucharistielehre", *ZKT* 83 (1961), pp. 260–94; H. Jorissen, *Die Entfaltung der Trans-substantiationslehre bis zum Beginn der Hochscholastik* (1965); L. van Hout, "Fragen zur Eucharistielehre in den Niederlanden", *Catholica* 20 (1966), pp. 179–99; K. Rahner, *Theological Investigations,* IV (1966), pp. 296–311; E. Schillebeeckx, *The Eucharist* (1968).

Engelbert Gutwenger

TRINITY, DIVINE

A. The Scriptural Doctrine of the Trinity

1. *The Old Testament.* Since revelation and salvation come in historical form, it cannot be expected that the Trinity of God should have been explicitly revealed in the OT. The OT as such is part of the revelation of God in word, though this word is essentially a moment and an interpretation of God's saving acts. Hence as long as God's self-communication in Jesus Christ was not yet an irreversible reality and the Spirit of God was not yet a triumphant eschatological manifestation but merely an offer, the revelation of the Trinity would have been word of a reality entirely outside the historical realm as such of man. Nonetheless, given the continuity of salvation-history and its permanent ground (see *Salvation* I, III), the OT is also important for the doctrine of the Trinity.

The OT doctrine of a word of God going forth in history while remaining the word of God even within the world, already contains a dynamic concept of revelation. This concept, in the progress of the history of revelation, was "bound" to lead to the concept of the self-communication of God which would imply the Trinity, since such self-communication cannot be reduced to the status of a human word "about" God, even as a mystery, but comes in faith in the word *of* God, sustained by God himself in grace. The personification of divine forces ordained to the world — the word, the wisdom, the spirit of God — which are distinct from God and are still not intermediate powers between God and the world, are formally and materially preludes to a doctrine of the Trinity in the NT.

2. *The New Testament.* a) There is no systematic doctrine of the "immanent" Trinity in the NT. The nearest to such a proposition is the baptismal formula of Mt 28:19, though it must be noted that modern exegesis does not count this saying among the *ipsissima verba* of Jesus. Along with the various separate statements about the Father, Son and Spirit and the relationship in each case to the other persons, it should be noted that in Jn and the NT letters the three terms have a marked tendency to occur in the same context. See for instance Eph 4:4ff., "One Spirit, one Lord, one God and Father"; 2 Cor 13:13, "The grace of the Lord Jesus Christ, the love of God, the fellowship of the Holy Spirit".

b) When the NT speaks simply of "God", it means the God who has been seen at work in the OT. He is the "Father", he has a Son and he gives his Spirit. "God" does not stand for the "triune Godhead". The statements about the Son and the Holy Spirit occur when the Son and the Spirit are spoken of in the context of salvation-history, but not within the framework of a systematic statement on the Trinity. While the NT authors cannot speak of Jesus as "God", since this would be, for them, to identify Jesus and the Father, they recognize the divinity of the Son. They do not look upon the Son as a cosmic power intermediate between God and the world. Where the Son appears as preexistent, he is clearly in the realm of the divine: Jn 1:1; Phil 2:6ff., etc. And they do not look on Jesus, who is for them simply "the Son", as a mere prophet. He is *the* absolute bringer of salvation. (The question of the self-understanding of Jesus in his pre-Easter life does not come up in this context. Here it is enough to note that even the pre-Easter Jesus of the Synoptics distinguishes himself from all others and claims prerogatives which belong only to Yahweh, whether or not he applied to himself the titles of majesty traditionally attributed to the Messiah.) Jesus is the presence of the Kingdom or Kingship of God (Mt 12:28; Lk 11:20), of judgment (Jn 12:31, 38; Mt 11:20–24, par.), of lordship over the Sabbath (Mk 2:23–28; 3:1–6), of the absolute situation of decision (Mk 13:9–13; 9:34–38; 10:17–27), of God in unthinkably close proximity (Jn 10:30–38), of the fullness of the Spirit (Lk 4:18). The pre-existence of the Son as God is then quite clear in John and Paul, and does not need to be discussed in detail here (see for instance Jn 1:1–18; Phil 2:5–11; see *Jesus Christ* I).

The NT authors also refuse to consider the Spirit as a cosmic or religious power intermediate between God and the world. He is simply the Spirit of God (Lk 4:18; Tit 3:5f.; 1 Cor 12:4, etc.) (see *Holy Spirit* I). Though they are thus the saving presence of God (the Father) himself, the Son and Spirit are not simply identical with him whom they reveal and whose radical closeness to men they are.

When one undertakes to distinguish the three "persons" from one another as depicted in Scripture, one should not start with some massive notion of person derived from modern thinking. Possibly they cannot be distinguished in the way which such a concept would demand. In St. Paul, for instance, it is difficult to distinguish the Spirit from the glorified Lord, or from God. But this is a far cry from proving that they are not distinguished in the same way in which the dogma of the Church speaks of them. The existence of some sort of distinction follows at once from the fact that the three words are not simply used interchangeably but occur beside one another in the same context. Further, the NT authors know that there is a certain relationship between the Son and the Father, and the Spirit and the Father (cf. Mt 11:27 par.; Jn 1:1; 8:38; 10:38; 1 Cor 2:10). The Father "sends" them (Jn 14:16, 26; 17:3; Gal 4:6) and gives the Spirit through the Son (Jn 15:26; 16:7). This shows of course very clearly how hesitant and groping the religious language of the NT authors is, when they try to speak of the unity and distinction of God as Father, Son and Holy Spirit. And the question remains as to where the basic primordial revelation is to be found, if — in relation to it — these statements of the NT are already to be envisaged as "theology" (though of course absolutely normative). It seems that the only possible answer to this question is that the concrete Jesus is the presence of God (the Father) for us and still is not the Father. And the difference is not merely due to the human created reality of Jesus. Otherwise his humanity would be only the livery in which God the Father was present, and nothing more. But the Spirit is just as definitely known as the *self*-donation of God (the Father), while at the same time the Spirit who is given reveals the incomprehensibility of God, the Father, the unoriginated, and so the distinction between the Spirit and God the Father. In the light of this experience of the Son and the Spirit, the NT authors, obeying an "instinct" which they feel no need to question, refuse to give a "rational" explanation by making the triad a matter of pure appearance and "aspects for us" of the one God. They also refuse to present the Son and the Spirit more intelligibly by treating them as mythological intermediaries or as a more strongly numinous human element — which would be fundamentally just as rationalistic.

c) But the NT authors also reflect explicitly on the one ground which underlies the essential identity and difference between the Father and the Son. The Son is the Father's own Son in contrast to the servants (Mk 12:1–12 parr.; Rom 8:3, 32; Heb 1, etc.). He is the eternal Word of the Father (Jn 1:1, 14; 1 Jn 1:1; Rev 19:13), the image (2 Cor 4:4; Col 1:15; Heb 1:3), the radiance of the glory of the Father (Heb 1:3). Such statements cannot be taken without more ado as referring to the life of the Trinity *ad intra*.

And they cannot be directly exploited in the sense of a "psychological" theology of the Trinity such as was put forward by St. Augustine. But in view of the basic principle of trinitarian theology (see *Trinity in Theology*), such primarily historical sayings, referring to the coming of salvation — the Son as the self-utterance of the Father to the world — already imply the "immanent" Trinity.

B. The History of the Doctrine of the Trinity

1. See *Modalism, Arianism, Cappadocian Fathers*.

2. See *Trinity in Theology*, D, *Incarnation, Jesus Christ* IV.

C. The Doctrine of the Magisterium

1. *The sources.* The important documents, along with the various creeds (Apostles' Creed, Nicene Creed, Athanasian Creed [*Quicumque*], Paul VI's Confession of Faith) are from the Council of Nicaea, 325 (*D* 54), the First Council of Constantinople, 381 (*D* 86), the Eleventh Council of Toledo, 675 (*D* 275–81), the Fourth Lateran Council, 1215 (*D* 428, 431 f.), the Second Council of Lyons 1274 (*D* 460) and the Council of Florence, 1439–45 (*D* 691, 703 f.).

2. *The doctrine (with some comments).* a) The Trinity is an absolute mystery (*D* 1795, 1915) which is not perspicuous to reason even after being revealed (on which see also *Collectio Lacensis*, VII, pp. 507 c, 525 bc). If there are any absolute mysteries in the Christian faith, that of the Trinity is undoubtedly the most fundamental. Why this should be so is not further explained in the doctrine of the magisterium and seems to be affirmed only for the pilgrim existence of man. Little explicit attention is given to why and how the mystery still remains meaningful for us and to its actual impact on the realities in which we encounter it, as distinct from its proposition as a truth of faith.

b) The one God exists in three persons, subsistences, hypostases (*D* 17, 19, 39, 48, 51, 58 ff., 79, 254, 275, 278–81, 428, 431, 461, 703 f., 993, 1919), who are the one divine nature (φύσις), essence (οὐσία), substance (as distinguished from subsistence) (*D* 17, 19, 39, 59, 78, 82, 86, 254, 275, 277 ff., 428, 431 f., 461, 703 f., 708, 993) and are equal, co-eternal and omnipotent (*D* 13, 19, 39, 54, 68–75, 254, 276 ff., 428, 461 ff., 703 f.).

There is no official definition of the terms *persona,* ὑπόστασις, *substantia,* οὐσία; and there is no explanation of the possible distinction between *persona* and *hypostasis*. The meaning of the terms is to be derived from the definition of the terms in scholastic theology; from the meaning of the terms in the dogmatic propositions themselves with their dialectical contrast between the terms (ὑπόστασις-οὐσία); from the fact that "essence" is the most readily understood here, meaning the divine being, the divinity, of the three in the absolute sameness of the divine essence. It is difficult to determine why a particular term was used in a given case. The more recent declarations of the magisterium have not taken into account later developments in the concept of person, but continue to use the term in the sense which the word received in the anti-Arian controversy and in Christology. When, however, the Holy Spirit is described as constituted by the "mutual" love of Father and Son, in spite of the fact that the procession of the Spirit is only one action and (from) one principle (*D* 691, 1084), this way of speaking may betray the influence of a modern notion of person.

c) These persons are also (really) distinct from one another (*D* 39, 281, 703 ff., 1655). The Father has no principle of origin (*D* 3, 19, 39, 275, 428, 703 f.). The Son is born of the substance of the Father (*D* 13, 19 f., 40, 48, 54, 69, 275 f., 281, 432, 703 f.) and only from the Father (*D* 40, 428, 703). The Spirit is not begotten (*D* 39, 277) but proceeds from the Father and the Son (*D* 15, 19, 39, 86, 277, 428, 460, 691, 703) as from one principle (*D* 460, 691, 704) in one single spiration (*D* 691). The *generatio* and the *spiratio* are distinguished. But they are at one in affirming that the divine essence is possessed by the Son and the Spirit as "communicated". They are distinct inasmuch as this communication is, as generation, from the Father alone, and as spiration from the Father and the Son (or the Father through the Son, *D* 460, 691) as one principle of communication in one (notional) act. How this "begetting" and "breathing" are further distinguished is not explained by the magisterium. The existence of such a distinction simply follows from the difference between the Son and the Spirit.

d) This is the foundation of the principle that there are really distinct relations in God (*D* 208, 278, 281, 296, 703) and proprieties (*D* 281, 296, 428), and hence also a virtual distinction between the essence of God and the divine persons constituted by relations (cf. *D* 17, 19, 523 f.). The distinction between the (absolute) essence of God and the relations which constitute the persons is meant to explain in terms of logic why a contradiction cannot at any rate be clearly proved to exist in saying that the divine essence is identically the same in the three divine· persons while these are relatively distinct from each other. That the distinction is based on the opposition of relations is suggested by the words Father and Son, in which an oppositional relationship is expressed. In the doctrine of the relations in the Trinity, which reached its peak with the axiom of the Council of Florence (going back to St. Anselm), the doctrine of the Cappadocian Fathers played a predominant role, especially that of Gregory of Nyssa, and affected the formulations of the magisterium more than did the psychological speculation of St. Augustine (but see *D* 296).

e) The "relative" persons in God are not really distinct from the essence of God (*D* 278, 296, 703) and hence do not form a quaternity (*D* 283, 431 f.). In God all is one, except where an opposition of relationship exists *(relationis oppositio)* (*D* 703). Each of the divine persons is fully in each other *(perichoresis, circumincessio, D* 704) and each of them is the one true God (*D* 279, 343, 420, 461).

f) The divine persons cannot be divided from one another in being (*D* 48, 281, 461) or in operation (*D* 19, 281, 428, 461) and form only one principle of action *ad extra* (*D* 254, 281, 428, 703). The activity of the three persons is one and the same and can be ascribed to any one of the persons only by appropriation (*DS* 3326). But here it must be noted that this axiom deals with the efficient causality of God (*D* 2290). It does not affect the truth that the Logos alone became man, or the theory of uncreated grace in which each of the three divine persons has his own special relation to men (in spite of *DS* 3331). Little attention has been given by the magisterium to the parallel doctrine of the "missions" of the Son and the Spirit by the Father (cf. *D* 277, 285, 794) in the economy of salvation.

D. Suggested Outline of a Systematic Doctrine of the Trinity

1. *The guiding principle as to matter and development*. a) The methodical principle is the identity of the Trinity of the economy of salvation and the immanent Trinity. The identity does not of course mean that one denies that the "economic" Trinity, one with the immanent Trinity, only exists by virtue of the free decree of God to communicate himself (supernaturally). But by virtue of this free decree, the gift in which God imparts himself to the world is precisely God as the triune God, and not something produced by him through efficient causality, something that represents him. And because he is the triune God, this "trinitarian character" also affects the gift and makes it triune. And conversely it is therefore also true that the trinitarian character of this divine self-communication, the economic Trinity, makes the immanent Trinity known, *quoad nos,* because they are the same. It follows that the two immanent processions in God correspond (in identity) with the two missions, and that the relationships to created realities constituted in formal (not efficient) causality by the missions as processions are not appropriations (procession of the Logos — hypostatic union; procession of the Spirit — divinizing sanctification of man). The relationships are proper to the person in each case. (The ordinary objection [cf. *Mysterium Salutis,* II, pp. 330–2], asking why the relation to the sanctified man proper to the Spirit is not a hypostatic union, cannot be dealt with here. But the objection presupposes something which is ultimately simply false, that the *hypostasis* of the Logos and that of the Spirit are of the same nature.)

b) The principle for the doctrine of the Trinity thus signalled can be confirmed by noting that the hypostatic union constitutes a case in which this general principle is verified. Then, as regards the doctrine of grace and of the vision of God as triune, for which as such the Trinity must be the ontological principle, the notion that the Spirit has a proper relationship to man in the state of grace is a theological opinion well supported by Scripture, (Greek) tradition and modern theology since Petavius. It is only when this principle is presupposed that the distinction between the order of creation and of grace, the natural and the supernatural, can be made clear. For the divine self-communication, which constitutes the supernatural order of salvation in contrast to the act of natural creation, cannot and should not be considered only as the communication of an abstract essence (a divine φύσις), but as the communication of God as he is, that is, as the triune God. For it is the triune God as such who "dwells" in the justified and who is contemplated in the beatific vision. Further, in keeping with the general nature of revelation as a unity of God's saving action and word, the revelation of the immanent Trinity can only be thought of as coming in the action of divine grace qua action, that is, by the immanent Trinity becoming the economic Trinity. If the Trinity as such is to be a revealed mystery of salvation, it must itself be revealed in the order of salvation. Finally, it must be affirmed that revelation, as it appears throughout the whole of the NT, never deals with the immanent Trinity alone or as communicated only in concepts and propositions. It tells of the Son and the Spirit being experienced in the salvation-history and the revelation-history of the individual and the collectivity. It only speaks of the Son and the Spirit of the Father insofar as God (the unoriginated Father) is close to us through the Son and the Spirit. The Trinity is revealed in such a presentation of salvation-history. This revelation is not just the presupposition of another concerning the immanent Trinity, but is already the revelation of the immanent Trinity. Otherwise it would only be a purely verbal communication about something that did not affect us, it would find in us no real point of contact and would only be a humiliating imposition on our knowledge. It should also be noted that an abstract hypostatic union in a "God-man", as we often say, and a purely sanctifying (created) grace could be revealed without this revelation of the Trinity. Hence there would be no need of revealing the Trinity as a proposition if it were not really there for us itself as such.

2. *The Trinity of the economy of salvation.*
a) *The economic Trinity as mystery.* If we now speak of the self-communication of God and try to understand the Trinity in the order of salvation and then also in its immanent nature in the light of this, it should be understood from the start that all statements containing or articulating the concept of self-communication remain within this self-communication qua mystery and are therefore not open to the charge of rationalistic speculation. For the self-communication in question is not only not deducible *a priori,* since it is a free act of God in fact. It is also by its essence a permanent mystery, since the possibility of God's being quasi-formal cause with regard to

a creature can never be positively understood. Further, the notion of self-communication which makes a systematic theology possible here, is itself derived from the statements of revelation, and thus does not eliminate the mystery of this message. All that can be systematically elaborated by virtue of this formal concept comes under this same heading.

b) *The unity of the self-communication of God in the two missions (of the Son and of the Spirit).* According to the Christian faith, God's turning to the world, even when the act of its creation is also presupposed as a free act, is a gratuitous grace (see *Nature and Grace*). But this does not prevent us from assuming that the divine self-communication to the world in the Spirit (grace) and the self-communication in the hypostatic union are one and the same free act, because these two communications are each the condition of the other. The hypostatic union is only rationally thinkable if it causes or implies the grace given to the world through the divine Spirit (or at least in the humanity of Christ, and then in all men, by reason of the social nature of his humanity). And conversely, the grace given to the world has its necessary historical manifestation and eschatological irreversibility in what we call the hypostatic union. Thus the two missions may be understood as inter-connected moments of the one self-communication of God to the world. And conversely, this free act is deployed in the divinization of the world in the Holy Spirit (taking the word for the moment in the general sense in which it is mostly used in Scripture, i.e., the creative, loving, sanctifying power of God which draws the world to God) — and in its historical and eschatological manifestation through the historical and definitive word of God ("word" here also being taken in the general sense, as in 2 Cor 1:19f.).

c) If this twofold self-communication of God is really *self*-communication, in contrast to creation, it must be attributed to God in himself, i.e., it must imply a quasi-formal causality into which God enters, and this must be a determination of God himself. (By reason of the freedom in which this quasi-formal causality with regard to the creature is brought about, it cannot be seen to be repugnant, any more than the creative act of God, which being identical with God's being exists necessarily and eternally, though free as regards the world.) This is the basis on which an understanding of the immanent Trinity is to be attained (see below, 3).

d) *The "essence" of the two missions.* If the two missions are intrinsically connected moments of the one self-communication of God, then on principle (cf. *Mysterium Salutis,* II, pp. 374 ff.), since the recipient of the self-communication is personal and historical, the notion could be analysed in such a way that a number of twin aspects would appear: origin — future, history — transcendence, offer — acceptance, knowledge — love. It could be shown that origin, history, offer and knowledge always correspond to future, transcendence, acceptance and love, and always form in each case a moment of this self-communication. Nonetheless, we begin here simply with the missions as they are known in the history of salvation.

The "essence" of the mission of the Spirit can be understood without any great difficulty (within the framework of the mystery). God imparts himself to the finite, needy, sinful creature. And this outgoing, without self-seeking or gain, taking a risk with others because one is great enough freely to be small among others, is precisely what is meant by love, in the sense of the NT *agape.* This is all the truer because God's self-communication aims at the innermost centre of the human person and is active there not only as the gift but as the power of the acceptance of the gift.

If one prescinds for the moment from the question of how the relationship between the love of God as proper to the essence and as forming the person can and must be distinguished, we are familiar with the "essence" of the mission. It is what traditional theology describes as the propriety of the third person in the "immanent" Trinity. In considering the mission of the Son, one must not simply begin with the notion of the Logos according to the Greek world of thought and then explain this mission as aiming at the revelation only of the truth of God, especially as this approach can attach the soteriological element to the mission only extrinsically and secondarily. It must be noted that truth in the full sense is the *lived* truth in which someone freely deploys his being for himself and for others, manifests himself historically as faithful and reliable and makes this state irrevocable. But this is precisely the mission of the Son in its essence, in which the aspects of revealer and saviour are united. It is the mission of the truth which is fidelity.

Under these circumstances we may rightly affirm that the divine self-communication has two basic modes, those of truth and of love. As truth, the self-communication takes place in history and is the offer of the free faithfulness of God. As love, it brings about acceptance and opens man's transcendence to the absolute future of God. Since the historical manifestation of God (the Father) as truth is only knowable in the horizon of transcendence towards the absolute future of God, and since the absolute future is manifested irrevocably as love by being promised in the concrete history of the faithful God (in the absolute bringer of salvation), these two aspects of the divine self-communication are neither disjoined nor joined merely by divine decree. Without being identical, they form together the one divine self-communication which explicates itself as truth in history, beginning and offer, and as love in transcendence, towards the absolute future, in acceptance.

3. *The "immanent" Trinity.* The transition from the Trinity of the economy of salvation to the immanent Trinity must be thought of along the lines indicated in D 1 and 2 c.

a) The Trinity *ad extra* and *ad intra* is identical, because one would not be speaking of a *self*-communication of God unless the two missions and the two persons thus there for us, in whom God comes to us, were "part" of God himself. If they were purely of the created realm, the communication of God's self would be absent. The missions are real "outgoings" *(processiones)* in God himself — the divine decree of self-communication being free, however.

b) The two processions are distinct, because they are the missions. The missions are of course distinct in their *terminus* in each case, and this difference is not simply that of the original missions *(missio principiative spectata)* as such (they terminate respectively in the human nature of Christ and the "created" grace of the justified, which are spatio-temporal entities). But the two moments of the one self-communication are also distinct on the divine side. They are moments of the self-communication of God which are related to each other in their difference. And this is also true of the processions.

c) These two processions, identical with the missions, can of course be considered as proper to God "in himself", being regarded as the "potentialities" of the twofold self-communication, i.e., still in the light of the economy of salvation. The Logos, Jn 1:1, is with God from eternity, and hence immanent, but is still considered as related to the world. (These "potentialities" are not of course entities in God which have to go through the stage of being actuated.) But since the processions, in their actual reality, have a free (contingent, so to speak) relation to the world, they must be proper to God not merely "in himself" but also "for himself". They must also have an "immanent" significance. It may therefore be affirmed that the real distinction between the two processions is constituted by a twofold immanent self-communication, inasmuch as the unoriginated God (the Father) is he who is expressed in the truth for himself (the Son) and he who is received and accepted in love for himself (the Spirit), and hence is he who can freely communicate himself *ad extra* in this twofold way.

d) The real distinction in God is constituted by a twofold communication of the Father, by which the Father communicates himself and through this self-communication, where he "utters" and "receives", posits his real distinction as regards the person "uttered" and "received". What is communicated, since it makes the communication really a self-communication of God, and does not eliminate the real distinction between God as communicating and communicated, can rightly be termed the divinity, and hence the "essence" of God is communicated.

e) The element importing a distinction which intervenes between the original self-communicator and the term expressed and received must be designated as relative (relational). This follows from the identity of the essence (substance, nature). This relational constitution must not be primarily regarded as a means of resolving an apparent logical contradiction in the Trinity. Its value in such a process would be very limited. Insofar as a relation is looked on as the least real of all realities, it loses value in explaining the Trinity, which is the most real of all realities. But the relation is as absolutely real as anything else that can be said of the Trinity. And apologetics for the "immanent" Trinity cannot proceed on the basis of the prejudice that a lifeless identity of an uncommunicated type is the most perfect mode of being of the absolute being, and then go on to eliminate the difficulty created by this prejudice by explaining that the distinction in God is "only" relative.

4. *The difficulties of the notion of person as applied to the Trinity.* a) It is so normal to speak of three persons in God, in our preaching and theology, that one has the feeling that there is absolutely no other way of expressing this mystery. But that this is incorrect follows at once from the fact that the NT does not use the term "person", and that it was only introduced gradually into ecclesiastical usage, while the Greeks rarely say πρόσωπον *(persona)* and mostly prefer ὑπόστασις *(hypostasis)*. In the contexts in question, all these statements mean the same thing, but not by virtue of their origin and history. And they have not *exactly* the same meaning, and did not retain such completely identical meaning in the further course of historical development. For while hypostasis, subsistence, as a concrete and as an abstract notion, can be predicated of any concrete being, and not merely of rational beings, *persona* always means the rational subsistent. And in the course of the history of the term, the situation of the consciousness of the spiritual subject as well as that of the ultimate concrete difference between one being and another has been modified. Spiritual subjectivity in consciousness and freedom is now not merely an essential note of the concrete subsistent if this is to be a person. In the modern notion of person, consciousness is intrinsically constitutive for the very existence of the person.

If this shift of meaning were applied to the doctrine of the Trinity, three divine persons would mean three consciousnesses, with three free wills. But this is wrong. Hence the classical formulation of the doctrine cannot and may not be adapted to this modern trend of thought. But the doctrinal statements of the magisterium cannot undo or change history. Hence the official terminology of the Church, which was regulated according to a contingent use of the word "person", is now constantly exposed to misunderstanding. The word "person", in view of its present-day use, is almost necessarily misunderstood in the formulation of the Trinity and hence generally explained by circumlocutions. But this should not really be necessary, since the accepted meaning of the words should explain the proposition, and the words used should not need to be corrected in the light of the proposition.

b) This does not imply that the formula "one God in three persons" should be eliminated. No individual preacher has the authority to do so, and the magisterium is hardly in a position at present to produce a better formula which could be made official, that is, universally intelligible, obligatory and obviously acceptable as obligatory. Nonetheless, the preacher must recognize the existence of the problem and try to meet it as well as he can. But this means that he must have a number of alternatives to draw on, so that he can give his explanations and avoid the classical formulation, without having to improvise at every moment.

c) The best way of dealing with the problem is of course to speak in the context of salvation-history, individual and collective, naming the Father, Son and Spirit and bearing in mind that the one God is spoken of throughout. But one could also, for instance, instead of speaking of three persons, speak of three distinct ways of being there (in the economy of salvation) and three different ways of subsistence (immanently) for the one God. The word "ways" could also be used to suggest that the persons are there as in relation to one another, this relationship, where one of opposition, constituting the difference in God (cf. *Mysterium Salutis,* II, pp. 389–92). Thus whenever the economy of salvation has to be propounded in formal terms, bringing out the unity of Father, Son and Spirit, the following formulations, offered merely as examples, could be used.

The one God subsists in three distinct ways. Father, Son and Spirit are distinct, qua oppositional, relations. Hence the three are not the "self-same", though they are "the same" (thing) (which is of course a subjectivity in the Godhead, free in our regard). The word "self", to avoid misunderstandings, should be reserved for a being in the ultimate concrete "individuality" in which it encounters another. Father, Son and Spirit are the one and the same God in the Godhead, in its different ways of subsistence. It is only with respect to the ways of subsistence that the number "three" can be applied to God, and here one must bear in mind that one is "adding up" a pure distinction within the numerical oneness of the essence, something that cannot be subsumed under the notion of a number of similar beings. God is "threefold" through his three ways of subsisting and being there. God qua subsisting in a given way (e.g., the Father) is another (not other) than God subsisting in another way. A way of subsisting is distinct from another by its relation of opposition, and is real by virtue of its identity with the divine being.

Hence "he who" subsists in such a way is truly God.

Such formulations of the Trinity tell exactly as much as those in which the word "person" is used. Possibly they sound just as abstract and formal. But without falling into modalism, they avoid misunderstandings in the sense of a tritheism such as could easily be evoked by the meaning now generally given to the term person.

5. *On the "psychological" approach to the doctrine.* a) The approach to the understanding of the Trinity which was put forward by St. Augustine and developed further by St. Thomas remains the classical explanation to the present day. It uses the pattern of the human mind — its knowledge and self-possession in the expression of the internal word and of love *(amor, voluntas)* — to illustrate the two immanent divine processions and so give some idea of the three persons in God. It is not the official doctrine of the Church, which offers at best only faint hints of it, and it is not the (direct) teaching of Scripture, which considers the Trinity only in terms of the economy of salvation. Hence the psychological interpretation of the Trinity is in no way normative. It is part of theology. But it can be considered legitimate, because there is a major theological tradition behind it, and also because the simplicity of God means that the three distinct ways of subsisting must have a necessary, intrinsic connection with the spiritual nature of God's being, a connection which is brought out in this doctrine. It appears all the more legitimate in the light of a metaphysical anthropology which demonstrates that there are only two fundamental acts of spiritual existence, knowledge and love. The obvious thing is to regard these basic acts as paralleled in the two divine processions.

b) However, the psychological interpretation of the Trinity fails to explain why God's self-possession in knowledge and love, a single act, as it were, flowing from the essence of the one God, should demand a *processio ad modum operati,* as *verbum* and as *amatum in amante,* given the absolute actuality and simplicity of God. Without such a procession there is no real triad of ways of subsistence.

c) Without prejudice to God's freedom, creation, self-sufficiency, etc., as *actus purus,* the relationship of God to the world (at least to the world as possible) could be viewed more positively than is generally done. This would mean that God's freedom with regard to the world would not have to be seen as a diminution or denial of his radical relationship to the world, but as its obvious and intrinsic mainspring. This would show still more clearly why the economic Trinity is the immanent Trinity (see *God-World Relationship*). God the Father's twofold power of expressing himself *ad extra* as Logos and Pneuma would then still remain a function of his "spiritual" nature, which is the permanent element in the psychological theory of the Trinity, but the psychological theory in this form would already be grasped as such as soon as the Trinity of the economy of salvation was considered.

BIBLIOGRAPHY. Among the textbooks of dogma and history of dogma see especially: 1. M. Jugie, *Theologia Dogmatica Christianorum Orientalium,* II (1926); M. Scheeben, *Mysteries of Christianity* (1946); E. Brunner, *Dogmatics,* I (1949); K. Barth, *Church Dogmatics,* I/1 (1957); P. Althaus, *Die christliche Wahrheit* (5th ed., 1959); M. Schmaus, *Katholische Dogmatik,* I (6th ed., 1960); D. Weber, *Grundlagen der Dogmatik,* I (3rd ed., 1964); B. Lonergan, *De Deo Trino,* I (2nd ed., 1964), II (3rd ed., 1964). — 2. R. Seeberg, *Lehrbuch der Dogmengeschichte,* 4 vols. (1895–98; reprint, 1953–54); W. Koehler, *Dogmengeschichte als Geschichte des christlichen Selbstbewusstseins,* 2 vols. (3rd ed., 1951); M. Schmaus and A. Grillmeier, eds., *Handbuch der Dogmengeschichte* (1951 ff.); L. Loofs, *Leitfaden zum Studium der Dogmengeschichte,* 2 vols. (5th ed., by K. Aland, 1951–53); A. von Harnack, *History of Dogma,* 7 vols. (reprint, 1958); A. Adam, *Lehrbuch der Dogmengeschichte,* I (1965). — 3. B. Piault, *What is the Trinity?* (1959); A. Wainwright, *The Trinity in the New Testament* (1962); H. Mühlen, *Der Heilige Geist als Person* (1963); id., *Una Mystica Persona* (1964); E. Jüngel, *Gottes Sein ist im Werden* (1965); K. Rahner, L. Scheffczyk, F. Schierse and R. Schulte in *Mysterium Salutis,* II, pp. 49–82, 85–129, 146–217, 317–97 (with bibliographies); L. Scheffczyk, *Der Eine und Dreifaltige Gott* (1968); K. Rahner, *The Trinity* (1970).

Karl Rahner

TRINITY IN THEOLOGY

A. INTRODUCTION TO THE STATE OF THE QUESTION

We are not enquiring here into the content of the doctrine of the Trinity and the problems which it raises, but the situation of the doctrine itself as such. Here the question arises both on principle and in terms of a given epoch.

1. On principle, one may ask where the treatise on the Trinity should fit into dogma. Its ordinary place, which it has occupied for a long time now, is in the dogmatic treatise *De Deo (Uno et Trino),* at the beginning of dogmatic theology, after the usual preambles. Here a further question arises. Should one follow St. Thomas, as has been customary, and simply put *De Deo Trino* after *De Deo Uno,* and so first round off the "essential" doctrine about God in an almost metaphysical treatise? Or should one combine the doctrine of the nature of God with that of God in three persons, as has been done once more recently by Schmaus, and so make the theology of the Trinity the basic structural principle of the whole treatise *De Deo?* In the most recent efforts of Protestant theology there is a tendency, partly inspired by the nature of this theology, and partly by the general principle of giving priority to hermeneutics and theological epistemology, to make a certain type of theology of the Trinity part of the prolegomena of systematic theology. This is meant as an indication of what discourse about God should be in general, based on the notion of the "economic" Trinity as the guiding line for all correct discourse about God.

It would also be possible to consider the theology of the Trinity as the climax and conclusion of all dogmatic theology, since it would bring God and his saving action together, presenting "theology" and the "economy of salvation" together as a single, final statement. If one takes up the Dutch *New Catechism,* one sees that an effort is already being made to do without a special treatise on the Trinity. It speaks of the Father, Son and Spirit as they occur in the statement of our relationship to God, but this threefold discourse about God is not then systematized and transposed into a discourse about God "in himself".

2. This may seem at first sight to be merely a question of arrangement. But it is, of course, basically a question about the precise meaning of the actual doctrine. It is also a question of the view to be taken of the development of the dogma in question, which has a history running from the NT with its unsystematic statements about Father, Son and Spirit in the economy of salvation, to the Athanasian Creed and the Council of Florence, with their doctrine of one divine nature in three persons. For since

then no important progress or changes have come in kerygmatic statement or religious practice.

3. Another point must be noted, since it makes itself insistently felt in the life of present-day Christians and Christian preachers. It is that the doctrine of the Trinity, in spite of its being so often extolled as the fundamental mystery of Christianity, plays a very modest role, if it occurs at all, in the actual life of Christians and in the teaching which they hear. There is no need to give detailed proof of this. Reference has already been made to the Dutch Catechism. The doctrine of the Trinity was of course in the mind of the Second Vatican Council, though referred to explicitly only in *Lumen Gentium* and *Unitatis Redintegratio* and hardly anywhere else. But it was never taken up as one of the basic themes, though it should be noted that a certain preference appeared for the Greek formulation of the Trinity in terms of the economy of salvation — "from the Father, through the Son, in the Holy Spirit". This may be taken as a tendency to speak more emphatically in terms of the economy of salvation when the Trinity is affirmed. Paul VI's confession of faith propounded the doctrine of the Trinity in such classical terms and perspectives that it could in fact hardly gain a new hearing for the doctrine in the present situation. The ultimate reason for this general lack of attention to the theology of the Trinity seems obvious. In an age of public and worldwide atheism, the question of God is urgently concerned with God's existence, not with his "inner" mystery. But a still deeper reason underlies this temper of the age. Since St. Augustine, the "immanent" Trinity has been so much to the fore in theological discussion of it, and the "economic" Trinity has been so obscured in Christology and *De Gratia* by the principle that all actions *ad extra* in God are common to all three persons or belong to God as one, that it is hard to see what Christian existence has to do with the Trinity in actual life. And then again, whenever faith in the Trinity is meaningfully evoked, it is as part of Christology, when we turn in faith to Jesus Christ as the definitive presence of God among us in salvation-history, or it is part of *De Gratia,* when we acknowledge the self-communication of God in the grace of the Spirit. But this is outside the framework of a systematic theology of the Trinity. And it is not reverent adoration of the Trinity as such.

B. Formal Principle for the Structure and Matter of the Theology of the Trinity

The questions raised under A above can only be answered when a formal principle has been worked out to comprise the matter and structure of the theology of the Trinity. This principle, taken in conjunction with other themes of faith and theology, should give clear directives for the procedures to be followed in the theology of the Trinity. Such a theme has been singled out in Mariology, for instance ("basic principle of Mariology"), but no such effort has been generally made in the theology of the Trinity. It is a matter, therefore, of taking the first hesitant steps. We propose, therefore, as the basic principle in question, for the organization of the matter and presentation, the identity of the immanent Trinity and of the Trinity of the economy of salvation. Our proposition would be that the economic Trinity is (already) the immanent Trinity, because the basic event of the whole economy of salvation is the self-communication of God to the world, and because all that God (the Father) is to us in Jesus Christ the Son and the Holy Spirit would not really be the *self*-communication of God, if the twofold missions were not intrinsic to him, as processions, bringing with them the distinction of the three persons. This principle need not be established and explained more fully here (see *Trinity, Divine*), but merely used to illustrate questions raised by the theology as such of the Trinity.

C. The Place of Trinitarian Theology in Dogmatics

With the above principle in mind, we may make the following affirmations.

1. No one would deny that trinitarian theology has an impact on theological epistemology and the hermeneutics of theological assertions, since, in the light of the basic principle of the theology of the Trinity, the Trinity is not just one object among others in the whole range of theological statements. For the whole economy of salvation has a trinitarian structure. And as an object of faith (which faith is itself a moment of the economy) the economy determines the concrete act of faith, which is not just an abstract assent on the basis of the formal authority of God, and gives the act of faith itself a trinitarian structure (deriving from

the object of faith and the grace of faith, which is none other than the trinitarian self-communication of God). But all this does not justify one in burying away the theology of the Trinity behind a theological epistemology or a hermeneutics. If this were a legitimate process, the basic principle enunciated above would oblige one to transpose the whole history of salvation and its theology into hermeneutics.

2. One consequence of the basic principle is that it is at least not obvious that a theology of the Trinity should be placed at the start of theology as a whole. The immanent Trinity is known in faith because the economic Trinity has been seen to be at work in the history of salvation. The economic Trinity is not merely the means of gaining knowledge of the immanent Trinity, but is the same thing. This cannot be said in the same sense of the doctrine *De Deo* in general, since the sense of dependence on God in which God is known comes at the start of all theological effort. This dependence on God came itself to be propounded in trinitarian terms in the course of the history of salvation and revelation. Dogmatic theology could parallel this historical process by beginning with an initial formal description of our relationship to God (as the permanent structural principle of history of salvation and revelation in general) and ending with an explicit treatise on the Trinity (as a summary of salvation-history which has come eschatologically to full self-explication). The Dutch Catechism makes some such effort at the end, though very briefly.

On the other hand, there is nothing in our basic principle which simply compels us to place the theology of the Trinity at the end. The *circumincessio* in which all the treatises of dogmatic theology are in the nature of things involved should not be lost sight of, especially as this *circumincessio* results directly from our basic principle. If the *Oikonomia* is really the whole of theology and likewise contains and reveals the immanent Trinity itself, the whole of dogmatic theology is trinitarian theology, which means that the theology of the Trinity is only really articulated by theology as a whole. But then there is nothing to prevent our putting a treatise *De Deo Trino* at the beginning, to give a rather formal preview of what comes up as the real trinitarian theology through the whole of what follows. But this initial treatise should not be an attempt to cover a

theme which can then be marked as read, but a preliminary orientation with regard to a theme which is still to be dealt with.

3. If the introductory treatise *De Deo Trino* is understood in this light, the present procedure may well be followed, which is to deal first with *De Deo Uno* and then take up *De Deo Trino*. For if the treatise *De Deo Uno* is to be real theology and not mere metaphysics, it cannot speak of the one God and his nature without speaking of the God of history and of a historical experience of him, of the God of a possible revelation and self-communication. Hence it is already orientated to the treatise *De Deo Trino,* which deals with such a God in salvation-history.

D. On the History of the Theology of the Trinity

1. In the NT, the theology of the Trinity, insofar as it is possible to speak of its existence there, is entirely orientated to the economy of salvation. God and the Father are synonyms. The Son and the Spirit are spoken of inasmuch as they come into the experience of faith as the actual presence of this God (the Father) in the history of salvation. Apart from this, the NT theology of the Trinity does no more than show the Son and the Spirit as being experienced as the absolute proximity of God himself, not as subordinate representatives of someone absent. There is also a certain tendency to co-ordinate the three names in the same context.

2. The main question in the period subsequent to that of the NT was of course the relationship of the Son to God (the Father), since the Spirit could be more readily accepted as a synonym for God. Hence statements about the Spirit appear rather as a consequence of Christological assertions. If we prescind from the theology of Judaeo-Christianity (and of the Ebionites), the basic trinitarian question in the patristic age is whether the Logos (and the Pneuma) should be considered in the light of the "hierarchical thinking" of Platonism and neo-Platonism and hence as a subordinate cosmic power other than the true God (see *Arianism*) or whether he was really God "consubstantial" with the Father, though not simply to be identified with him as in various types of modalism. Properly speaking, this makes the trinitarian theology of the Fathers a theology based from the start on the history of salva-

tion and soteriology. It says something about us, and defends the consubstantiality of the Logos and the Pneuma with God the Father on the ground that otherwise we should not be divinized in immediate relation to God himself. On these grounds the Greek way of thinking of the Trinity remains entirely orientated to man. The Father reveals himself through the Son and through him reaches man in the Holy Spirit. The Greeks distinguished *hypostasis* (which should not be taken as identical in meaning with *persona,* especially in the modern sense of the term person) from the nature (φύσις, οὐσία). The distinction served to bring out the truth that God (θεός, the Father himself) has come to us in his divinity through the Son and the Spirit, in real self-communication, while the trinitarian structure of our relationship with God as based on the economy of salvation remains unchanged. It remains historically definite (through the Son) and absolutely immediate (in the Spirit), contrary to modalism and Sabellianism, and again, contrary to Arianism, where the structure is a mediation serving not the establishment of immediacy but of a medium which only links inasmuch as it is the "between" which separates. Hence too Greek patristic theology was content to define the relation between the one nature and the three subsistents *(in se)* and the three ways of being there (for us) in terms of formal ontology, by understanding these as "relations". The concrete character of these "hypostases" is then deduced from their function in the history of salvation. In keeping with this approach, when grace is discussed, the relationship of each of the divine persons to the justified is not regarded merely as so many "appropriations" of the relationship of the one Godhead, now attached to each of the persons.

3. St. Augustine was the first to try to explain further the nature of the Trinity in the one Godhead without deriving the content from the way in which the three persons are there (for us) in the economy of salvation. He elaborated his "psychological" theology of the Trinity, using triads which we find in our spiritual processes, *memoria, intelligentia, voluntas, amor,* etc., to illustrate the immanent processions of the divine life. St. Augustine emphasizes that all God's activity *ad extra* is common to all three persons, since it proceeds from his one nature (*De Trinitate,* II, 17, 32) (and hence, for instance, the Father could have become

man if he had willed). The significance of the economy of salvation for the "immanent" Trinity is thereby much diminished, to say the least. St. Augustine's speculations do not start like the ancient and the Greek theology from the Father, but from the one divine *essentia,* for which the three persons are so to speak subsequent determinations including the Father. (In Baroque theology, this could lead to the question as to whether an absolute subsistence should not be attributed to God as well as the three relatives subsistences.) As an effort to show that God is also "immanently", in himself, what he displays in his actions in the economy of salvation, the psychological theory of St. Augustine had undoubtedly great importance, and it was also responsible for profound insights in existential anthropology. But it obscured the connection between the immanent and the economic Trinity, to the detriment of a vitally practical theology of the Trinity, a loss which is not fully compensated for by the lofty speculation on the immanent divine life.

4. Apart from the contribution of Boethius to the formal definition of the terminology applied to the Trinity, it may be said that scholasticism has been dominated down to the present day by the trinitarian theology of St. Augustine, whose influence was reinforced by that of St. Thomas Aquinas (with added elements of the Boethian terminology further elaborated mainly in the school of Gilbert of Poitiers). Another type of trinitarian theology, more on the line of the Greeks and also striving to apply to this theology as a whole a personal and psychological consideration of love, was given a strong impulse by Richard of St. Victor and was fully developed by Alexander of Hales and St. Bonaventure. But it did not succeed in establishing itself. Controversy with the Eastern Orthodox meant that the question of the procession of the Holy Spirit from the Son as well as the Father *(filioque)* (or through the Son) played a role in medieval Latin theology and was one of the preoccupations of the last Council to deal specifically with the doctrine of the Trinity, the Council of Florence, 1439–45 (*D* 691, 703 ff.). Another result of the development of dogma in the pronouncements of the magisterium which is of importance to modern theology is the fact that the principle of the oneness of the activity of God *ad extra* (*D* 703) refers to the efficient causality of God. Hence it cannot be applied without

more ado to "uncreated" grace. This cannot be subsumed under the concept of the efficient cause. And since it is the self-communication of God, it is the basic principle of the economy of salvation and the medium of the real revelation of the Trinity, since the Trinity cannot communicate itself as such *ad extra* to the world merely by conceptual communication. Close consideration of the precise official commentary on the ancient axiom by Pius XII would be a great help in applying consistently and courageously the principle enunciated as basic in B above, that is, in bringing out the aspect of the economy of salvation in the theology of the Trinity.

Not enough attention has been paid so far in the history of the theology of the Trinity to the divergent developments which the notion of person has undergone in the theology of the Trinity, where it has remained consistently the same, and in modern philosophy and general usage, where it has taken another line. This divergence constantly leads to misunderstandings when the theological proposition is put forward that the one God exists in three persons. It is almost inevitable that the word person in this proposition should now be taken in the modern sense, which is not that of a "way of subsistence" but of a "personal centre of action". This means that the theology of the Trinity would be infiltrated by a tritheism not easy to expose.

E. The Theology of the Trinity in Modern Preaching

The theology of the Trinity undoubtedly tries to bear on the central element of the Christian notion of God and so on the central element of Christian existence. The Trinity must therefore be preached and explained. There can be no doubt about this. But this does not mean that the theology of the Trinity, in the form which it took on during the first fifteen hundred years and which has scarcely been modified in the last five hundred, only needs to be "popularized" to some extent in order to be preached fruitfully today.

1. The preacher must first be convinced that when he speaks of three persons in God, his hearers will automatically import their notion of person into this proposition and either misunderstand it or right themselves only by taking evasive action, as it were,

taking refuge in "implicit faith" and the faith of the Church. This does not mean of course that the preacher must avoid completely the expression of "three persons" in God. This is a formula used by the magisterium, a rule of language which is to be respected and which it would be wrong not to allude to. But it would be equally dangerous to confine oneself to a stereotyped repetition of the formula, on the grounds that this is the briefest, clearest and most unambiguous way of stating what is meant. It is one's duty to bear in mind that the creeds with which the laity are most familiar do not contain the proposition about the one God in three persons and one nature, but confess the Father, the Son and the Spirit.

2. There is another consideration to be borne in mind as well as this difficulty arising from the changing connotations of the terms. The preacher who is justifiably cautious about using the formula of "three persons" should remember calmly that "three persons" is a way of subsuming under a sort of general denominator what distinguishes Father, Son and Spirit, not what unites them, as St. Thomas pointed out in the *Summa Theologica*, I, q. 30, a. 4 ad 4. In everything in which they agree they are absolutely one in the one identical substance (cf. *D* 703). A universalized notion of person applied three times over can only be used with extreme caution when speaking of the Trinity if the result is not to be more misunderstanding than insight. The subtle solution which points out that these are "transcendental" numbers which do not imply a "multitude" will be of little help to the ordinary Christian who is trying to avoid the mistakes to which he his liable. If the speaker actually uses the word three when talking of God, there is nothing to prevent him using other terms and concepts such as the classical "hypostases", "subsistents" or "ways of subsisting", "ways of being" (cf. *Mysterium Salutis,* II, pp. 364 ff., 385 ff., 389–93).

3. The general conclusion must be that the preacher will mainly speak of Father, Son and Spirit in whatever context of salvation-history and theology of grace they may occur. It is relatively easy to explain what the giving of God's Spirit in uncreated grace implies. If it is then made clear that in the gift God has given himself in a radical self-communication (Spirit), while still remaining the sovereign incomprehensible

God in his mystery, everything that needs to be said has really been said (apart from some possible distinctions of a secondary type). No further statement of the relation between Father and Spirit is needed in a kerygmatic theology of the Trinity. When Jesus Christ is proclaimed as simply and uniquely the Son, the Sonship in question may first be taken, without misgivings, as the absolutely unique situation of the man Jesus in the economy of salvation. It is in virtue of this situation that he is "the Son" in the synoptic gospels (Mk 12:6 parr.; Mt 11:27 par., etc.). As this concrete being, in and through his real humanity, he is the absolute and final word of God's fidelity (his "truth"), in which the Father addresses the world by a historical, irrevocable deed. In this way he is already *the* Son. But this sonship in the economy of salvation, as follows from the basic principle enunciated above under B, implies the expressibility of the Father which is eternally actual in God himself, and this forms a proper way of God's subsisting. In this sense (as for instance in Jn 17:5, 24) we can and must speak of the pre-existing Son, a truth which should not be overlooked and must be stated. But in view of what has been said, this Sonship may be explained, and has in fact already been explained, when this power of absolute self-utterance of the Father is understood as unshakable fidelity. When one affirms that Jesus is the faithful word of the Father, in which the Father definitively addresses *himself* to us, one has already affirmed the eternal "immanent" relationship between Father and Son, provided one understands that in Jesus the Father does in truth impart himself, and not something about himself, not something conceptual or real not identical with himself.

4. If this Trinity of the economy of salvation is preached in such a way that it can be consciously grasped as vital to religion and life, one may then speak of the Trinity in the usual terms of theology, as a summary of what is said otherwise, in which constant reference is made to the "economic" Trinity. This would correspond to a theology of the Trinity placed at the end of dogmatic theology as a general summary of the whole.

BIBLIOGRAPHY. See bibliography on *Trinity, Divine;* also: H. Geisser, *Die Trinitätslehre unter den Problemen und in den Prolegomena christlicher Theologie* (dissertation, Tübingen, 1962); G. Ebeling, "Existenz zwischen Gott und Gott", *Zeitschrift für Theologie und Kirche* 62 (1965), pp. 86–113; F. Bourassa, "Sur le traité de la Trinité", *Gregorianum* 47 (1966), pp. 234–85; K. Rahner, *Theological Investigations,* IV (1966), pp. 77–104; *A New Catechism: Catholic Faith for Adults* (1967) (Dutch Catechism); K. Rahner, "Der dreifaltige Gott als transzendenter Urgrund der Heilsgeschichte", *Mysterium Salutis,* II (1967), ch. V (with bibliography); H. Geisser, "Der Beitrag der Trinitätslehre zur Problematik des Redens von Gott", *Zeitschrift für Theologie und Kirche* 65 (1968), pp. 231–55.

Karl Rahner

TRUTH

I. Philosophical: A. Historical Survey. B. The Problem as it Appears Today. II. Truthfulness.

I. Philosophical

A. HISTORICAL SURVEY

1. *Old Testament.* Two main sources determined the development of the question of truth in the philosophy of the West. One was the OT, the other was Greek philosophy. The OT word for "truth" (אֶמֶת) really means to be firm, reliable, faithful. When Yahweh's *'emeth* is spoken of, it means the divine will to perpetuate his favour. Thus *'emeth* can be translated as fidelity. God's word is "truth" (2 Sam 7:28 — RSV, "thy words are true"; cf. Ps 119:160), cf. Ps 132:11, "The Lord swore to David a sure oath *('emeth)* from which he will not turn back", where the word means both sincerity and constancy. This fidelity of God means that he offers sure refuge (Pss 40:12; 54:7; 61:8, etc.). The faithfulness of God is affirmed in Deut 7:9; 32:4; Is 49:7 and Ps 31:6. When "truth" is affirmed of men, it means the loyalty of the people to God (Jos 24:14; 2 Kg 20:3; Is 38:3; Ps 26:3; 86:11). "To walk in the 'truth'" (1 Kg 2:4; 3:6; 2 Kg 20:3; Is 38:3; Ps 26:3; 86:11) and "to do the 'truth'" both mean to live a life of faithfulness to the law of God. Nonetheless, the OT also uses "truth" to signify the correspondence between assertion and reality, e.g., 3 Kg 10:6; 22:16. In the latest books of the OT, the Law is considered the "truth". "Practising the truth" (e.g., Tob 4:6; 13:6; Ecclus 27:9) is contrasted with serving the lie. It is the attitude of the man who observes the law of God.

2. *New Testament.* In the NT, "truth" (ἀλήθεια) has several meanings. It is the fidelity and reliability of God (Rom 3:1–7).

It is the quality of the genuine and obligatory which attaches to the gospel (Eph 4:21; Gal 2:5, 14; Rom 2:8; 2 Cor 4:2; Gal 5:7); the word of God (2 Cor 4:2; Gal 5:7); what can be known about God, i.e., evidently revealed by him (Rom 1:18); human sincerity (2 Cor 7:14; Phil 1:18; 1 Tim 2:7; 2 Jn 1). But it can also mean the authoritative doctrine, e.g., 1 Tim 6:5; 2 Tim 2:18; 3:8; 4:4; Tit 1:14, as Bultmann has noted. The preaching of the gospel is the word of truth (Eph 1:13; Col 1:5; 2 Cor 6:7, etc.). "To do the truth" (cf. Jn 3:21; 1 Jn 1:6) now means to fulfil the law of Christ (instead of the OT law), and to "walk in the truth" (2 Jn 4; 3 Jn 3f.) undergoes a parallel change of meaning. Jn combines a number of traditional meanings under the heading of "truth", but they are all referred to the reality revealed in Jesus. "Truth" is the reality of salvation which sets man free (Jn 8:32). "Truth" sanctifies (Jn 17:17ff.). Christ is the way, the truth and the life (Jn 14:6). The Paraclete, being the "Spirit of truth", continues the work of Christ. He gives testimony to Christ and glorifies him. The distinctive element in the NT is that both in Jn and Paul "truth" is the Christological truth.

3. *Antiquity.* The problem of truth is first explicitly considered in the didactic poem of Parmenides. There the goddess teaches the way of truth, which is contrasted with δόξα, opinion, the fallacious opinions of mortal men (Frg. I, 28ff.). To recognize that being is and that non-being is not is knowledge of the truth (Frg. 2 [4], 3ff.). Plato contrasts ordinary speech and opinion, which is liable to error (ψεῦδος), with the realm of truth. The myth of the cave (*Republic*, 7, 514ff.) describes the breakthrough of the human mind to truth. For Plato, this truth is the primordial self-manifestation of true being, the forms (see *Idea*). Truth is therefore considered as the coming out of concealment, an unveiling. The connection between the *logos* (reason), beings and truth is already affirmed. The *logos* "which affirms beings as they are, is true; but the mind which affirms them otherwise than they are is in error" (*Cratylus*, 385 b; cf. *Sophist*, 263 b). Aristotle investigates this connection in detail and reaches a definition of truth as judgment (*Metaphysics*, IX, 10; 1051b). Truth means the reference of the composition of concepts in the judgment to reality. In Middle Platonism, the forms were conceived of as exemplars in the mind of God. God is the truth beyond the ideas (Albinus, *Isagoge*, 10). Philo of Alexandria combined the Platonic myth of creation with the biblical account. The "ideas" are products of the divine mind which creates everything by its thought, which is also action. Plotinus, the founder of neo-Platonism, finds that the first origin can be defined only negatively. The *Nous* is the "second God", who contains the Platonic *mundus intelligibilis* (κόσμος νοητός) and hence is the ground of truth in its dialectic of mind-thinking and term of thought (*Enneads*, 5, 5). Truth is revealed to the contemplative soul by the presence of the *Nous* within it (5, 1, 3; 3, 4).

4. *Patristic and scholastic thought.* The "norm for the truth of beings", according to Clement of Alexandria, is God (*Protrepticus*, VI; *PG*, VIII, col. 173). This is the first attempt to combine Greek and NT thought. The great authorities here were Origen, the Cappadocian Fathers and the Pseudo-Dionysius among the Greeks, and St. Augustine among the Latins. St. Augustine combines the Johannine *Logos* with the neo-Platonist *Nous* (*Confessions*, VII, 9). The Son is the truth, since he is the Word who reveals the Father (*De Trinitate*, VII, 3). St. Augustine uses the *cogito* of the subject to justify truth as against scepticism (*Soliloquium*, II, 1, 2). He stresses the necessary nature of truth, which human reason does not create but discovers (*De Vera Religione*, 39, 72). In his *De Libero Arbitrio*, he describes the ascent to truth which determines the movement of thought. This truth is absolute, eternal and changeless (II, 15, 39). Illumination from God is required for the knowledge of the higher truth. Like Aristotle, Boethius refers truth to the judgment, because this is pronounced *secundum complexionem* (e.g., *In Categorias Aristotelis*, IV; *PL*, LXIV, col. 278; *De Interpretatione*, editio prima, ibid., col. 300). But his *De Consolatione Philosophiae* (IV, 4; V, 6) points to a Platonic conception. St. Anselm of Canterbury analyses the relation of logical to ontological truth. Logical truth is an effect of the *summa veritas*, mediated by created things (*De Veritate*, ch. 10). This means that the ontological connection is under the rule of truth as the *rectitudo sola mente perceptibilis* (ibid., ch. 11). Speech is recognized as having a fundamental kinship with truth (ibid., ch. 2). Hugh of St. Victor recognizes that truth has an intrinsic relation to the sciences (*In Hierarchiam Caelestem*, I, 1). The notion of a "double truth" is supposed to be typical of the Latin Averroists,

but was not in fact explicitly put forward in these circles.

In St. Thomas Aquinas, truth is the primordial opening out of being (*ens et verum convertuntur*), and also the function of the judgment (*adequatio intellectus et rei*, cf. *Contra Gentiles*, I, 59; *De Veritate*, I, 2). God is the first truth and the foundation of all truth. The transcendental truth (see *Transcendentals*) means that being has an intrinsic relation to spirit and hence to the spirit-soul, and also that spirit is ordained to (the grasp of) being (*De Veritate*, I, 1). St. Thomas combines the Aristotelian notion that the soul is "all things in a certain fashion" (see *Soul*) with the notion of the truth of things (cf. Aristotle, *The Soul*, 431 b, and *Metaphysics*, 993 b). The whole field of problems thus demarcated, where the influence of St. Augustine is also visible, is then placed in the perspective of the doctrine of being (see *Being*). St. Bonaventure's notion of truth is Augustinian. Duns Scotus recognizes an ontological and a logical truth.

When the medieval discussion of truth is considered, one should not forget the connection affirmed between truth and language. The connection was laid down by neo-Platonism and St. Augustine (see *Language*). Reflection on language is found in St. Anselm of Canterbury, especially in the *Monologion* and the *De Veritate*. Patristic and scholastic thought sees the foundation of this relationship in the Trinity, since Christ is the Word of the Father. Human utterance and trinitarian *expressio* are seen by St. Augustine and St. Thomas as related. In St. Thomas, the internal word is the revelation of the known in the knower (*Contra Gentiles*, IV, 11; *De Potentia*, 9, 5; *Summa Theologica*, I, q. 28, a. 4 ad 1). The word-event here appears as an approach to the resolution of the subject-object tension. The typical definition, probably stemming from William of Auxerre, of the relation between truth and faith takes the form: "Credere est assentire primae veritati propter se et super omnia." The First Truth is at once revelation of being and sure warranty, and hence can be *auctoritas*.

Classical medieval thought takes a new turn with William of Occam. The will of God replaces the truth of God in the centre of theological thought. The transcendentals are reduced to concepts. The problem of truth becomes more and more the problem of knowledge. Robert Holkot, a disciple of Occam, made a total distinction between philosophical and theological truth.

5. *The beginning of the modern era.* The tradition of "negative theology" going back to the Pseudo-Dionysius was taken up by Nicholas of Cusa, who held that God and his truth could not be known in their *aequalitas praecisa* ("exactly") (divine truth, for Nicholas, being identical with the incarnate *Verbum*). Nonetheless, divine truth remains the goal of all human knowledge, to which all its efforts must be directed. The truth is given to the intellect only in the form of *docta ignorantia* (*De Docta Ignorantia*, I, 3). In his highest speculative flights, Nicholas sees the unknowable divine truth reflected in the linguistic dialectic of the "Non-aliud". The contradiction between theological and philosophical truth, strongly emphasized by Luther, but modified by Melanchthon, Humanism and the Enlightenment, became a key problem of Protestant theology, brought out in particular by Kierkegaard and dominant down to Barth, Bultmann and Tillich.

In general, the problem of theological truth took on a new relevance through the Reformation. The word of God, regarded as the real authority, becomes the primordial truth. The word of God in preaching (Scripture in the act of self-exposition) is the source of the faith that justifies. Through Descartes, the logical and ontological problem of truth became the problem of certainty. The truth is what is seen clearly — the clear idea (*Meditationes*, III, 4). Nothing can be considered true which is not evident: this is the first methodical principle (*Discours de la méthode*, 2, 14). Descartes recognizes no ontological truth. But God is the guarantee of truth, since man cannot be the origin of his infinite idea. Occasionalism is tributary to Descartes. Malebranche's main work is called *Recherche de la Vérité*. All real knowledge of truth comes from contemplation of the divine ideas. In contrast to the nominalism of Hobbes, Leibniz deals with the logical problem of truth (*Works*, ed. by C. Gerhardt, VII, pp. 190 ff.). A permanent harmony between signs and objects is to be presupposed. The characteristics of Leibniz's notion of truth are that the original truth is anchored in God (*Théodicée*, II, para. 184) and that the truths of reason are linked with the principle of non-contradiction, which is considered fundamental (*Discours de métaphysique*, no. 13). This opened up an epistemological perspective of truth which has remained predominant in certain schools of thought down to the present day. Hobbes rejected all ontological truth: "Veritas enim in dicto, non in re consistit" (*Opera Philosophica*, I, 32). Spinoza also confined truth to the affirmation (*Opera*, I, 246f.). The notion of truth as the accord between a thing and its idea or definition is found in Clauberg (*Opera Philosophica*, II, 648), under the influence of Descartes. C. Wolff recognizes a transcendental truth but bases it on the first principles — non-contradiction and sufficient reason (*Philosophia Prima*, para. 498). In contrast to the scholastics, Wolff demanded a "distinct" concept of truth. This was a decisive step towards the reduction of metaphysics to logic, which was given even more emphatic expression by Wolff's disciple, Baumgarten (*Metaphysica*, paras. 89–93).

6. *From Kant to the present day.* In the "Copernican revolution" introduced by Kant into philosophy, truth was regarded as "agreement with the laws of the intellect" (*Critique of Pure Reason*, B, 350). The old definition of the *adaequatio* is thus reformulated in terms of transcendental philosophy. The empirical synthesis of experience attains truth inasmuch as it contains all that is necessary for the synthetic unity of experience (*ibid.*, B 197). The former ontological truth has become the basic synthesis of the transcendental apperception. A proposition in accord with the laws of thought and experience is objective. This view is also adopted by Fichte (*Werke*, 6, 19) but given a new orientation, inasmuch as the notion of the absolute I intervenes in the synthesis of the I and the Not-I, so that the problem of truth is seen basically as that of the interpretation of dialectical thought. When Schelling says that truth is the absolute identity of the subjective and the objective (*Werke*, VI, p. 497), the truth of the judgment has been referred back to its absolute foundation. This interpretation is given its fullest expression by Hegel, for whom truth is the all, the absolute concept, the absolute idea. Hegel undoubtedly affirms that truth is the agreement between notion and object, but he means by this only truth in the subjective intellect. A new approach to the problem of truth, which could be termed a modified Platonism, may be seen in Bolzano (truths in themselves) and Lotze (truths exist insofar as they are valid), a notion brought out by Husserl in his *Logische Untersuchungen* and characteristic of value-philosophy.

Hegel was attacked by Feuerbach, who maintained that the basic notion of truth was "life", which meant "man" (*Essence of Christianity*, Preface). Marx dismissed all discussion of the reality and otherwise of thought as mere scholasticism, unless it was based on *praxis*. It is in "practice" that man has to give proof of the truth of his thinking, that is, its reality and power, its relevance to life in this world (cf. *2nd Thesis on Feuerbach*). This was a rejection not only of Idealism but of the older forms of materialism. There is no such thing as truth as such. Truth comes to be through the orientation of our thought to practice. Theory is then the scientific generalization of practice, and practice as evolved in society is the criterion of truth (see *Theory and Practice*). The way to objective truth becomes a social process — when directed, as Lenin said, by Marxist theory. All other efforts lead only to confusion and deceit.

Hegel was also attacked by Kierkegaard. Here again truth is regarded as action, but now it is the action of the individual, and its basis is existence (see *Existence* I, II). Since human life contradicts faith, faith, which is "doing the truth", is a paradox. And this is why Christianity can never be understood in the light of "reason". Nietzsche also attacked Hegel and the metaphysicians in his effort to destroy the traditional notion of truth. What was once called truth is now known as an idol (*Werke*, XV, p. 105). Truth is the most debilitated type of knowledge (V, p. 149). The elimination of the world of truth has brought with it the elimination of the world of appearances (VIII, p. 82). Nietzsche calls for a truth which is still to be created and can be the source for identifying a process (XVI, p. 56). The will to truth is a form of the will to power. Jaspers dealt with the notion of truth in his extensive work, *Von der Wahrheit* (1947; cf. *Truth and Symbol* [1959]), distinguishing the truth of the realm which we ourselves are (conscience, presence, spirit, existence) and the truth of the realm which being itself is (world, transcendence). We speak of transcendence in a code to which no assignable meaning is adequate. Being cannot be separated from being true, being for us, and hence from communicability (see *Existence* II).

In Heidegger, truth, within the framework of the analysis of ek-sistence, is the opening out of ek-sistence, as concern and being-for-death, and is hence the historicity of being (see *History* I, *Being*). But the whole problem is dominated from the start by the question of being. And so truth is seen as the throwing open of being. And since this opening out brings with it a closing up, truth is primordially bound up with non-truth. Being displays itself to us as truth, as historicity and language. In Heidegger, therefore, in contrast to previous metaphysical and transcendental philosophy, truth is understood historically and as such determines this understanding of it (see *Existence* II).

All these trends — metaphysics, Marxism, existence-philosophy — are opposed by (linguistic or logical) positivism, which tries to apply consistently the principles of the older empiricism, with the help of formal logic (see *Logic*). Truth is dealt with in the context of meaning and verification. The protagonists here were the Vienna Circle, especially R. Carnap and L. Wittgenstein. Verification, as demanded by Carnap, is confirmation by empirical observation. Truth is verifiability. What is contradicted by facts is untrue. Metaphysical judgments are neither true nor false, they are meaningless. Even in the earlier Wittgenstein the boundary between the meaningful and the meaningless is the boundary between the experiential and the non-experiential. Any meaningful question can always be answered: there are no riddles (cf. *Tractatus*, 6, 5). Wittgenstein later criticized his earlier thinking and called in question important elements. In his later works, the meaning of a word is identified with its use in speech (*Philosophical Investigations*, 43). It is use which gives life to the sign (*ibid.*, 432). Meaning and purpose and hence too the problem of truth are referred to linguistic usage, the "language game".

B. THE PROBLEM AS IT APPEARS TODAY

The problem of truth now appears under two chief aspects. One school sees the problem in terms of hermeneutics, basing itself on Dilthey and Heidegger. This trend has also greatly influenced modern theology (Bultmann and his school). The other trend is represented by (logical) positivism, which recognizes truth only in the judgment and rejects entirely not only all metaphysics but even hermeneutical questioning, as a mere process of reflecting on self undertaken by the subject. It should be noted, however, that positivism is not implied in all logical examination of the problem of truth. The discussion of truth-functions and truth-values is a logical effort which does not imply any given ontology but does not exclude such interpretations.

The question of the historical, the non-historical or supra-historical nature of truth is now particularly acute in philosophy and in theology. The historicity of truth does not imply that it is merely relative. It rather involves reflection on the basic coming of truth, the event which makes possible the being of man. We think of this event as a primordial language by which we are addressed. This view is not confined within the limits of a personal-dialogal philosophy (truth as encounter), but considers in the light of language and in view of language how such encounter is made possible. This brings up the fundamental problem of being and speech.

Theologically, this would mean that revelation is the primordial coming of speech, addressed to men and answered by us as men. At the same time, once such a view is adopted, the ancient definitions of logical and ontological truth will be investigated anew in terms of the conditions of their possibility. The hermeneutical problem leads to a reappraisal of what "fact" really is and how the knowledge of such "fact" is to be characterized. We only know any event within given horizons. Hence all human knowledge of truth remains one-sided. The transcendence of reason enables us to follow up all the aspects which this "one-sidedness" suggests, but we cannot think of God and know him except in human ways. There is no human statement, therefore, which can be taken as definitive. For every statement is articulated within certain horizons which can no doubt signify the whole of what is meant but cannot explicate it completely. The disclosure of truth is always a dialogal process.

See also *Knowledge, Positivism, Meaning, Transcendence, Relativism*.

BIBLIOGRAPHY. F. Bradley, *Essays on Truth and Reality* (1914); P. Wilpert, "Das Problem der Wahrheitssicherung bei Thomas von Aquin", *Beiträge zur Geschichte der Philosophie des Mittelalters* 30, no. 3 (1931); id., "Zum aristotelischen Wahrheitsbegriff", *Philosophisches Jahrbuch der Görres-Gesellschaft* 53 (1940), pp. 3–16; H. Joachim, *The Nature of Truth* (2nd ed., 1939); B. Russell, *Inquiry into Meaning and Truth* (1940); C. Boyer, *L'idée de vérité dans la philosophie de St. Augustin* (2nd ed., 1940); M. Müller, *Sein und Geist* (1940); I. de la Potterie, "De sensu vocis 'emeth in V. T.", *Verbum Domini* 27 (1949), pp. 336–54; 28 (1950), pp. 29–47; J. Pieper, *Die Wahrheit der Dinge* (1951); P. Engelhardt, *Die Wahrheit in der Einheit und Entzweiung* (1953) (antiquity and Middle Ages); M. Heidegger, *Platons Lehre von der Wahrheit* (2nd ed., 1954); id., "Vom Wesen der Wahrheit", *Wegmarken* (1967), pp. 73–97; id., "Sein und

Zeit", *L'endurance de la pensée (Festschrift J. Beaufret)* (1968), pp. 16–68; F. Nötscher, "'Wahrheit' als theologischer Terminus in den Qumran-Texten", *Festschrift V. Christian* (1956), pp. 83–92; W. Stegmüller, *Das Wahrheitsproblem und die Idee der Semantik* (1957); K. Jaspers, *Philosophische Logik*, I: *Von der Wahrheit* (new ed., 1958); H. Schlier, "Meditationen über den johanneischen Begriff der Wahrheit", *Festschrift M. Heidegger* (1959), pp. 195–203; J. B. Lotz, "Aletheia und Orthotes", *Philosophisches Jahrbuch der Görres-Gesellschaft* 68 (1959), pp. 258–268; H.-G. Gadamer, *Wahrheit und Methode* (1960); W. Kamlah, "Der moderne Wahrheitsbegriff", *Festschrift G. Krüger* (1962), pp. 107–30; R. Schnackenburg, *Von der Wahrheit, die frei macht* (1964); id., *The Gospel according to St. John*, I (1968) (on 4:23 etc.); E. Brunner, *Truth as Encounter* (1964); G. Quell, R. Bultmann and G. Kittel, "ἀλήθεια", *TWNT*, I (1964), pp. 233–51; J. Möller, *Wahrheit und Geschichtlichkeit im philosophischen Denken* (1964); id., "Geschichtlichkeit und Ungeschichtlichkeit der Wahrheit", *Theologie im Wandel* (1967), pp. 15–40; W. Bretschneider, *Sein und Wahrheit* (1965) (with bibliography); L. Versényi, *Heidegger, Being and Truth* (1965); R. Lauth, *Die absolute Ungeschichtlichkeit der Wahrheit* (1966); G. Kung, *Ontology and the Logistic Analysis of Language* (1967).

Joseph Möller

II. Truthfulness

1. Any effort to analyse and co-ordinate the various approaches to truth in ethics is faced with the difficulty that the term "truth" is used on a variety of levels of meaning in philosophy and theology, the reason clearly being that man finds himself relying on truth and tied to it, while at the same time it is not something that he can control, since he is in the service of truth. A survey of the various ways in which truth has been understood also shows that the notion of truth depends to a great extent on changing epistemological foundations and suppositions and on decisions taken beforehand in the light of this or that world view (see *History* I). Such pre-existing mental horizons are inescapable, and hence the attitude to truth is always a reflection of its times to some extent and more or less one-sided.

Thus if truth is mainly taken as truth in the judgment, the ethics of truth will mainly be concerned with objective knowledge, to be made the norm of personal action and to be rendered faithfully. The ethics of truth will mainly take the form of an ethics orientated to the concrete action, accepting material responsibility.

But truth may be regarded primarily as ontological truth, the basic intelligibility of things, with God as the First Truth. Further, God is held to be knowable but incomprehensible, while man is understood as a being created in order to know and love God, who finds therefore his true self in being blessed by God and giving himself to God. The main task of an ethics of truth is then to remain as absolutely open as possible for the truth, in whatever guise man encounters it, and to follow out in action the known truth unconditionally. The ethics of truth will mainly take the form of an ethics of the disposition, insisting on the formal attitude.

2. To have a proper balance between an ethics emphasizing the exterior action and an ethics emphasizing the interior disposition, the following considerations should be noted.

As truth is disclosed to man, it impinges on his consciousness, which is coloured by a number of factors: his orientation to his social and biological milieu, his orientation to God which is channelled by the former, and grace. Hence an ethics of truth cannot do without reflection on one's personal consciousness and its implications. What will then be the formal and definitive criterium for the judgments, assessments and decisions of an ethics of truth? It must be the ordination of the agent to the truth as such. And the material and provisional criterium will be the acknowledged dependence on the world of men and things around one, and dependence on God channelled by these. This means that man must acknowledge his dependence on God, man and the world as he discovers the truth and regulates his life according to the truth which he has found. Thus the believing Catholic will take the doctrine of the Church as the criterium of the truth, to the degree in which it claims his adherence (see *Magisterium, Theological Notes*). Everyone has to guard against overestimating his own standing and the amount of truth in his own convictions. In addition, the connection between the ethics of truth and the surrounding world means that the laws of the objective order must be taken into account. As these are disclosed in the sciences, an ethics of truth would be one-sided if it did not acknowledge the importance of science for the knowledge of the truth.

In this sense, an ethics of truth consists formally of man's obligation to seek the truth and to act according to it, in whatever guise it appears. This truth which underlies and inspires the ethics of truth is not originally an objective or definable truth, but a value. This value is of itself independent of the subject, but can only be a subjective norm of action insofar as it is grasped. An ethics of truth then consists materially of man's dedication to truths actually known, insofar as they point beyond themselves to the non-objectivated truth itself. Hence propositional truths can determine the search for truth itself (and action in accordance with the truth) only insofar as they can be related to the all-illuminating but not perspicuous truth. Consequently the immediate norm for the ethics of truth and for the significance of the various propositions within this ethics is subject to constant change, since our actual knowledge of propositional truths is dependent on the subject and affected by the situation. But the definitive norm, the truth itself, is not subject to change. This means that the ethics of truth need not be relativistic, though it must take account of the fact that it is only ordained to absolute truth within the limits of various conditions. It can fail to attain the real truth and may be said to disfigure it to some extent at all times. But on the above principles, extremes may be avoided (see *Indifferentism, Integralism*).

3. To allow the ordination to the absolute truth to attain its full dynamism, it must also be remembered that the finding of the truth does not depend merely on love of the truth and knowledge of facts. It is also affected by the "doing of the truth", which for its part is demanded by the truth attained. Man's prejudices and pre-established convictions mean that his approach to truth is always one-sided, and that he represses unattractive aspects. By doing the truth, he corrects such prejudices and their consequent blind spots, as far as possible, and brings about the optimum disposition for bowing to and acting according to the truth. This is the only way of avoiding the mistake of erecting the truth so far attained into an absolute. The dynamism aiming at the truth as such is maintained. A barrier is set up to the fixation on pleasant truths which can do detriment to the truths summoning men to constant conversion.

On the other hand, the less one "does the truth", the harder is the access to the absolute truth. For partial truths are erected into absolutes when action is determined by criteria contrary to the absolute truth. Consequently, in the self-discovery of man

which is meant to serve the ethics of truth, such partial truths are given undue and indeed absolute importance. Man is thus deluded because he is wilful enough to let himself be guided exclusively by limited truths which he finds pleasant. He is guided by appearances and not by the total truth which he has apprehended — even though not comprehended — and which is binding on him.

Thus the optimum ordination to the truth itself is attained only when man gives propositional truths their proper coefficient, that is, when he subordinates them, by a responsible decision, to the truth itself, insofar as it makes itself known.

4. It is in the light of man's duty to be sincere in seeking the truth, bowing to it and acting in accordance with it that the duty of sincerity or truthfulness as between men must be defined. The problems which arise here are generally the main interest in discussion of the ethics of truth. The starting-point, as a rule, is the more or less considered conviction that in one's communications with one's fellowmen one must be sincere and truthful, at least in principle and as the normal thing.

The basis of the obligation of truthfulness is that without it reverence for the dignity of the person, social life and religion are impossible. The proper development of the human person in all its dimensions would be hindered if man were not truthful towards himself, his fellowmen and God.

On the other hand, there are personal spheres of intimacy which must be protected. There are secrets which must be kept, in the interest of individuals and for the sake of the common good. This means that the truth is not to be told to everyone who might like to know it or even perhaps try to extort it by unlawful means. Indeed, the demands of self-defence seem to suggest that one should deliberately deceive an opponent in certain circumstances, if, for instance, this were the only way of effectively safeguarding secrets. Thus it is not surprising that historically the main preoccupation of the ethics of truth has been devoted to the question of how deceit, lies, should be judged.

5. In rejecting ψεῦδος, which means both error and lie, the Greeks often used the argument that ignorance is an evil, while virtue consists of knowledge. In this view,

error is worse than a lie, since it involves more ignorance. But truth leads to the good. To miss this goal is the absolute evil, κακία, or malice, κακοφροσύνη. But a lie is permitted as a means to avert evil, and made a duty for doctors and statesmen (Socrates, Plato).

Aristotle recognizes that there can be no question of moral action except in deliberate acts. Hence he finds the distinction between conscious and unconscious falsehood essential. Only the deliberate lie is immoral. It is evil in itself, while truthfulness is good and praiseworthy. The reason is that truthfulness serves human intercourse, while lying undermines trustworthiness. But when the interests of the law or the nation are at stake, it may be well to say what is false, since truthfulness is merely a social virtue and does not take in the realm of justice. Hence it is not always intrinsically wrong to say what is false, since the supreme goal in the ethics of Aristotle is the happiness of the individual, which in turn is only attainable in the well-being of the State.

The Latins made a basic distinction between error and lie *(mendacium)*, transferring the attention from the objective phenomenon of the mistaken statement to the deliberately misleading statement. They were therefore more consistent than the Greeks in rejecting the lie. The condemnation of lying was perhaps given its most downright expression in Cicero, who held that the truly useful was inseparable from the moral. He condemned lying even when consideration of public welfare might seem to demand a lie (*De Officiis*, III, 14–32). The notion of fraudulent intent *(dolus malus)* came into legal usage from Rome.

6. In the ethics of the OT, the Israelite is to "walk in the truth" of God (Ps 86:11; cf. Ps 25:5; 26:3) or to "do what is true" (Tob 4:6; 13:6). This includes "doing the truth" with regard to the neighbour. The alternative is the spread of perjury and lying, murder and other crimes (cf. Hos 4:1f.). The eighth commandment (Exod 20:16; Deut 5:20) only seems to forbid lying which causes injury to the neighbour or the community. Nonetheless, lying is condemned in the OT in the sharpest terms (Lev 19:11; Prov 30:8; Ecclus 7:13; cf. Prov 6:16ff.; Ecclus 4:25).

According to the NT, Christ came into the world to bring the full truth and to bear witness to it (Jn 1:14; 8:40; 18:37). Sanctified through the truth and for the truth (Jn 17:17), we are to love it (1 Cor 13:6) and "do" it (Jn 3:21; 1 Jn 1:6), and it will set us free (Jn 8:32). For this, we must avoid lying and speak truthfully (Eph 4:25; cf. 1 Pet 2:1). We need not then even swear (Mt 5:34ff.), but we are still not to cast pearls before swine (Mt 7:6). We are to be guileless like doves, but still prudent as serpents (Mt 10:16). Thus there may well be times when an obscure form of words may be chosen (cf. Mt 13:10ff.). Lying, on the other hand, is explicitly stated to be the devil's work (Jn 8:44). It is a characteristic of the "old man" who is not yet redeemed (Col 3:9). The lake of fire and brimstone is the lot of "liars" (Rev 21:8; cf. 21:27; 22:15; 1 Tim 1:10).

7. *The role of the intention to deceive and of the nature of speech in the definition of lying.* The Christian analysis of lying was mainly inspired by the doctrine of St. Augustine, who was the first in the West to compose a special treatise on lying (*De Mendacio,* c. 395, and *Contra Mendacium ad Consentium,* c. 420). St. Augustine describes a lie as *falsa significatio cum voluntate fallendi* — a false statement with intent to deceive. It is not certain that he meant the "intent to deceive" to be essential to lying. He did not in fact mean to give a strict definition, as follows from the fact that he asks himself whether a lie only occurs where there is the intent to deceive. His personal opinion, at any rate, is that lying is intrinsically evil. But though his subjective opinion is fixed, he leaves the objective question open to a certain extent. This follows from the fact that he does not consider that the prohibition of lying is equally strong in all circumstances. The intent to deceive is what makes lying formally or morally wrong. The guilt therefore lies in the realm of the disordered relationship to another. Lying then can be forbidden in all circumstances only if this evil element in it, which is directed against the interlocutor, is present in all false statements. But this is something which St. Augustine shrinks from affirming.

In the early Middle Ages the conviction gradually prevailed that any false statement is *eo ipso* deceitful, so that the intent to deceive is always there when a deliberately false statement is made. The general definition of a lie is therefore *locutio contra mentem,* saying one thing and thinking another. St. Albert the Great was the first to come down firmly on the *indebita materia* as the essence of the lie, holding that it was a perversion of the nature and purpose of speech, which is essentially ordained to the truth, an end good in itself. Hence the lie is bad in itself. St. Thomas Aquinas also regarded the lie as something contrary to the nature of speech. His reason for saying that it is evil, i.e., contrary to love, is that it is essentially ordained to others. Apart from this relationship he finds that a false statement is not absolutely wrong and may be permitted in an emergency (II/II, q. 110, a. 3 ad 4).

8. *The emphasis on the formal aspect of lying*. With the coming of modern times and the paying of greater attention to the personal and individual, the problem of reconciling the prohibition of lying with the actual necessities of life was felt more keenly. Authors mainly influenced by the Augustinian or the Protestant tradition worked out a theory of the lie which stressed its social character exclusively. This purely formal approach led to a definition of the lie which was exclusively based on the notion of the right to the truth. Machiavelli held that all lies were permissible in a good cause. Luther held that the "officious" lie to help the neighbour and the emergency lie to defend one's own just interests were permissible, condemning only the lies which caused unjustifiable damage to the neighbour. The opinion which came to be most widely known was that of H. Grotius, who distinguished between the false statement *(falsiloquium)* and the lie. He defined the lie as the *sermo repugnans cum iure existente et manente illius quem alloqueris* — speech violating the actual and continuing right of the person addressed. The right which can be violated is the right to make up one's mind freely, without the hindrance of false information. According to Tanqueray, the only basis on which truthfulness is obligatory is in fact the right which each one has not to be deceived. At present there are many Protestants and writers on non-theological ethics who uphold similar theories, which allow lying under certain circumstances, when the interlocutor has no right to the truth or has forfeited it.

All theories based uniquely on the rights of the interlocutor disregard the fact that language is intrinsically ordained to communication. It is not just because of the speaker's attitude but because of the objective data that language is ordained to communication. Hence the duty of truthfulness must derive in the first place from the duty of the speaker and not from the rights of his interlocutor. But the theories in question are correct in affirming that language is essentially dialogal, so that its lawfulness is to some extent a function of the interlocutor. The purpose and hence the nature of any given statement cannot be determined purely objectively, without regard to the interlocutor.

9. *The emphasis on the material aspect of lying*. As regards Catholic authors, it may be said in general that they affirm the duty of truthfulness in the speaker, without asserting that it corresponds normally to the right to the truth in the hearer. The truth is a duty of charity in the speaker and not an obligation of justice. Hence St. Thomas makes truthfulness a potential part of justice, connected with it but not directly part of it.

Scholastic philosophers tried to grapple with the new questions posed from the end of the Middle Ages on, by looking for ways in which truth could be effectively concealed and secrets guarded, without involving a contradiction between what was thought and what was said. In other words, their efforts were based on a notion of the lie which mainly considered its material element. During the decline of scholasticism, the essential element in the lie came more and more to be regarded as the contradiction between the outward statement and the inner judgment. To soften or eliminate the contrast, it was suggested at first that ambiguous expressions could be used, and later, mental reservation or restriction. In the latter, the inner judgment is made to correspond with the outward statement by means of a mental correction. The two inner elements are only parts of the one whole. A distinction was then made between the negative and the positive law of truthfulness, the former forbidding the misuse of speech, and the latter demanding the telling of the truth. Like all positive law, the latter was held to oblige *semper non pro semper,* i.e., it was basically valid but had not to be put into practice at all times. Thus in the course of the 17th century the classical doctrine on lying was gradually abandoned by a large number of important theologians in all schools. In view of widespread criticism, the purely mental reservation was condemned by Innocent XI (*D* 1176 ff.).

The grave mistake of such purely individualistic approaches was that it concentrated on the immanent relationship between knowledge and statement in the speaker, neglecting entirely the more comprehensive relationship of the speaker to the hearer.

Nonetheless, the prohibition of lying continued to be based on the necessity of not misusing speech. But this was now considered as a natural faculty clearly ordained to communication. In keeping with the predominant notion of natural law this was said to mean that man ought not to act contrary to the nature of speech, but that he could use its laws to protect secrets. He could speak in such a way that the matters to be kept secret were not communicated. The chief method envisaged was the use of an unclear form of words (wide mental reservation) where the circumstances or the actual words used made it clear that the question was evaded. This in fact was not a mental but a verbal reservation, since at least on principle the expressions made it clear to the questioner that the desired information was being refused.

The disadvantage of this approach is that it does not provide an adequate safeguard for secrets in certain cases, especially where the speaker has little command of language. Further, it rejects all materially false statements as intrinsically bad, though they appear to be necessary to the security of the State in the operations of secret agents. It allows nonetheless that an opponent should be in fact deceived by unclear speech. Another point to be considered is that this approach is based on a notion of natural law which has now been to some extent abandoned. Man is no longer considered to be unconditionally subject to the laws of an order of things which can be defined purely objectively. Pushed to its ultimate logical conclusion, this approach would forbid even the least departure from the truth, even to defend oneself and others from grave injury where the truth is being extorted.

10. The difficulties arising from these rigoristic approaches and the reappraisal of natural law which was to some extent a consequence of these difficulties led a number of moralists in the 20th century to take another view of the matter. They permit the making of a false statement as an act of necessary self-defence in an emergency (so Vermeersch, Lindworsky, Ledrus, Laros, etc., using different arguments).

On the principle that the significance of speech, as an interchange between men, must be defined in terms of the hearer as well as the speaker, it must be admitted that under certain circumstances the significance of speech may be quite different for each of the two. If in this situation it is really to be of service to those involved, and not a means of injuring the personal dignity and just interests of one of the speakers, it may be right and necessary to use a false mode of statement, insofar as is necessary to ward off unjust aggression. Truthfulness is only right and rational insofar as it serves the purposes of communication between the speakers. But if it is exploited by one of the speakers to injure the other, human communication is actually impeded, on the level in keeping with human dignity. If the exploitation of the speaker by the questioner can only be avoided by the former's using a false form of words, this seems a necessary means for impeding misuse of speech. But this also means that the false statement becomes a lie as soon as it goes beyond the bounds of the necessary, since speech is then used to mislead the hearer in an unnecessary and an unjustifiable way. One is formally justified, therefore, in misleading another insofar as this provides effective defence of personal values against unjust aggression, the values in question being at least as valuable and as urgent as those materially injured by the misleading words.

Hence the definitive criterium for the moral evaluation of speech should not be its material ordination to communication, its intrinsic aptness for communication, since this is verified even in false statements. The criterium must be the actual significance of speech for the good of those taking part. But this significance depends to some extent on the interpersonal meaning given it in fact by the partners. Hence the moral significance of speech cannot on principle be determined independently of this interpersonal and concrete giving of meaning.

As to the moral gravity of lying, this must then be judged differently according to whether the fit development of the person against whom the lie is directed is hindered in its essence or merely in its completeness.

See also *Person* I, *Society* III.

BIBLIOGRAPHY. See bibliography on I above and the standard handbooks of moral theology; also: K. Häuser, *Die Lüge in der neueren Ethik* (1912); A. Vermeersch, "De mendacio et necessitatibus commercii humani", *Gregorianum* 1 (1920), pp. 11–40, 425–74; id., "Supplementum duarum priorum partium", *ibid.*, pp. 279–85;

O. Lippmann and P. Plaut, eds., *Die Lüge* (1927); E. Emmerich, *Wahrheit und Wahrhaftigkeit in der Philosophie Nietzsches* (1933); F. Manthey, *Die Sprachphilosophie des heiligen Thomas von Aquin* (1937); P. Wilpert, "Die Wahrhaftigkeit in der aristotelischen Ethik", *Philosophisches Jahrbuch der Görres-Gesellschaft* 53 (1940), pp. 324–38; M. Ledrus, "De mendacio", *Periodica* 32 (1943), pp. 5–58, 123–71; 33 (1944), pp. 5–60; 34 (1945), pp. 157–206; id., "Summarium de mendacio", *ibid.* 35 (1946), pp. 271–4; J. Dorszynski, *Catholic Teaching about the Morality of Falsehood* (1948); M. Laros, *Seid klug wie die Schlangen und einfältig wie die Tauben* (1951); W. Molinski, *Das Wesen der Lüge* (dissertation, Innsbruck, 1951); G. Müller, *Die Wahrhaftigkeitspflicht und die Problematik der Lüge* (1962) (with bibliography); J. Blank, "Der johanneische Wahrheitsbegriff", *Biblische Zeitschrift* 7 (1963), pp. 163–73; M. Klopfenstein, *Die Lüge nach dem Alten Testament* (1964); M. Brunec, "Mendacium — intrinsece malum — sed non absolute", *Salesianum* 26 (1964), pp. 608–82; G. Kalinowski, *Problème de la vérité en moral et en droit* (1967); K. Rahner, *Schriften zur Theologie,* VII, pp. 54–76 (intellectual honesty and Christian faith), pp. 223–51 (on truthfulness); H. Küng, *Wahrhaftigkeit* (1968).

Waldemar Molinski

TÜBINGEN SCHOOL

By the (Catholic) Tübingen School the group of theologians is meant who followed at Tübingen a common line of thought as against the Enlightenment, Romanticism and Idealism. They were disciples of J. S. Drey (and J. B. Hirscher) and their main aim was to show the intrinsic justification of the Christian faith in the various realms of theology. Though they gave their allegiance to the great tradition of the ancient Church and the Middle Ages, they had close contacts with the thought of Schleiermacher, Schelling and Hegel, and their discussion of contemporary thought was original and direct. The alternatives and the critique which they put forward were valid and genuine, as in J. B. Hirscher on scholasticism, F. A. Staudenmaier on Hegel, J. A. Möhler on L. Bautain and F. C. Baur, J. E. Kuhn on D. F. Strauss, or as in the controversy with Clemens and Schäzler on neo-scholasticism. Debate was the mainspring of their work, which remained to a great extent fragmentary, in spite of, or perhaps because of, the wide fields which it embraced. During the first half of the 19th century it represented classical theology on the Catholic side.

1. *The initial stages.* Like the Protestant school of theology at Tübingen — where C. G. Storr, of the older school, maintained an extreme supernaturalism, while F. C. Baur, of the younger school, put forward his *Tendenzkritik* and F. D. Strauss his myth-theory — the Catholic school had to face the basic question of modern critique of religion, as propounded explicitly since Lessing and Kant. It was the question of how a revelation given historically, known *a posteriori* — and still supernatural — could be decisive for the *a priori* subjectivity of human reason. The supernaturalist answer was to have recourse to the pure formal authority of God. Rationalism made a radical distinction between the immutable nature of man, essentially supra-historical, and the contingent changes of its historical manifestation. Idealism held that all religion was bound by the laws of its development to be absorbed in knowledge. But Drey and Staudenmaier, basing themselves on a primordial relationship between human reason and God, understood positive revelation as a necessary moment of (the self-development) of human history (see Drey, *Apologetik,* I; Staudenmaier, *Enzyklopädie*).

They argued that since history comprises in any case the whole of reality and is the vehicle of God's manifestation, it must disclose, by virtue of this very totality, the specific element which both unites and separates God and the world. Revelation communicates in the divine mode of history an absolute knowledge of itself (Staudenmaier, *Geist der göttlichen Offenbarung*). But this comes about of necessity. For the Tübingen School, development is an event which transcends pure nature as it originally is by virtue of creation. Development, directly brought about by God himself, has therefore a super-natural character (Drey, *op. cit.,* paras. 20–24). Nature and the supernatural are related, dialectically, like nature and the development of nature. Development is simply the corollary of grace and history is the real way to God. Revelation is history because history itself is revelation.

This thesis marked a definite break with German Idealism, since reason, grasping itself at its fundamental starting-point is thereby focused on the absolute *in* history itself. It follows that reason finds its absolute footing not in its intellectual quality but in faith and revelation. It has a necessary, intrinsic, dialectical relation to faith, which fulfils the function of "absolute knowledge" within the Idealistic systems.

These fundamental attitudes, in various transformations as circumstances demanded, were applied effectively to many problems. In the discussion of original justice man's likeness to God was seen in its ("supernatural") development as his becoming the image of God (Möhler, *Symbolism,* para. 2). In the discussion of knowledge of God, natural revelation and revealed faith could be distinguished, the certainty of the former being based on reflection, the latter providing an immediate certainty developing under a directly divine impulse (Möhler, "Sendschreiben an Bautain", *Theologische Quartalschrift* 17 [1835], pp. 421–53). The gratuitousness of grace appears as a participation in the divine nature made possible by God himself (Möhler, *Symbolik,* para. 1).

Pursuing the same line of thought, J. B. Hirscher regarded morality as the realization of the kingdom of God by the activity of man. The relationship between theology and philosophy is determined along the same lines. They coincide in the undifferentiated nature of the original state of justice. Philosophy only takes shape — first with the aid of the "mythological" tradition — as development takes its course (Drey, *Tagebücher*) and then becomes itself significant for the history of salvation (Staudenmaier, *Dogmatik,* III, pp. 92–93). Philosophy and theology are only adequately differentiated within the framework of revelation itself, inasmuch as the immediacy of divine communication alone sets reason free for its specific activity with an independent value (Staudenmaier, *Enzyklopädie* [2nd ed.], para. 118). Kuhn goes on to affirm, against traditionalism in particular, that the two disciplines are fundamentally independent. Their "higher unity — not identity — consists in the fact that reason is presupposed by revelation and its truth is recognized as the universal form of revealed truth, while revelation is seen as the fulfilment of reason and its truth is recognized as the concrete form of rational truth, without detriment to the independence of both realms of truth and their knowledge" (*Dogmatik,* I [2nd ed.], para. 16).

In a very different form, the same problem is then felt again in its acuteness in the theological realm itself, in the discussion of revelation and Church, dogma and development, identity and difference within Christianity in general. For there is a special problem posed apropos of Christian revelation itself — the divergence of knowledge and development. Drey sees the harmony between the Church and its origin in the uninterrupted perseverance of the original event ("the development of consciousness is simply the more intense repetition of the original act"), and attributes the articulate consciousness of the Church to controversy with heresy (as a dialectical process). But in the second edition of his *Dogmatik* Kuhn abandons the notion of "theological consciousness" and considers revelation itself, in faith, as being itself the principle of development of Church doctrine, by means of the (teaching) office instituted in the Church. Faith develops, of itself, dialectically. Christian dogma is the objective mind of the Christian consciousness (*Dogmatik,* I [2nd ed.], para. 9).

The Tübingen School undoubtedly reached its greatest heights with Kuhn. The whole vigour of this theology, its high quality demonstrated in so many specimens, its specific contribution to the solution of the fundamental dilemma of the new thinking on faith and hence its proper understanding of revelation were then to be developed along the classical lines in the framework of dogmatic theology. But — perhaps for this very reason — Kuhn in particular found himself in almost irreconcilable opposition to the neo-scholasticism which was gradually coming to the fore. Contrary to what has been affirmed since then, this was not due to the sharper emphasis placed on the "supernatural", but to the different anthropology, an essentially non-dialectical one. Schäzler, for instance, considered human nature, along the lines of the infra-human, as a "something" which was to be given an ontic, accidental "complement" in its extraordinary encounter with God. Hence its faculties could not have the role of mediation and dispose it for the reception of grace. Kuhn, however, regarded the personal element of nature, its self-possession in consciousness, as the natural principle of mediation of supernatural grace. When grace comes to man it impinges on his intrinsic structure, sets his freedom in motion and makes him "morally" better. Grace is a *perfectio* of his nature, and its essential transcendence can be described in terms of immanence (see, for instance, the doctrine of original sin or of the Trinity in the whole Tübingen School). Here the dynamic character of the supernatural appears in a personal version, and the fundamental affirmation does not change: without grace there can be no development of man towards God.

The Tübingen School is characterized by an essential unity of thought. In the very multiplicity of its theological blue-prints and the tensions of its own development — the great change in Drey being between his *Einleitung* and *Apologetik,* in Staudenmaier between the two editions of the *Enzyklopädie,* in Möhler between his *Einheit,* his *Anselm* (or *Athanasius*) and the 5th edition of his *Symbolik* — the Tübingen School is the classical representative of a dialectical theology within the framework of the Catholic mind. However, it never felt the need of a new eschatological orientation.

2. *Later developments.* There have been only a few followers of the Tübingen School in the strict sense. In Tübingen itself the main principles continued to be maintained — Kingdom-of-God theology, immediacy of the relationship to God, the notion of faith, Scripture and tradition in such theologians as P. Schanz, K. Adam and J. R. Geiselmann, the great historian of the school. The keen sense of historical problems was also to be seen in such authors as Hefele and Funk, there was the same proximity to Protestant theology and the indubitable influence in Germany. But at least in theological approaches, neo-scholasticism remained predominant. In the last twenty years of his life Kuhn published nothing at all, as a gesture. Nonetheless, the theology in question was not doomed to oblivion.

Its theory of revelation — "transformed into a practice" — became the formal starting-point for the basic principles of theological thought in a "post-metaphysical" society. It could be understood as a way of gaining access to the inner workings of this society and of disclosing the specific transcendence of Christianity in interpersonal action. The loss of the sense of history in present-day life also raises the question of a new orientation within theology itself. A reappraisal of dogmatic theology may be called for, since the present understanding of the Christian faith, though tested by Scripture and tradition, has been gained in the encounter with the modern world.

See also *Supernaturalism, Traditionalism, Idealism, Romanticism.*

BIBLIOGRAPHY. J. A. Möhler, *Symbolism* (1843); K. Werner, *Geschichte der katholischen Theologie* (2nd ed., 1889) (Trent onwards); J. R. Geiselmann, "Die Glaubenswissenschaft der katholischen Tübinger Schule", *Theologische Quartalschrift* 111 (1930), pp. 49–117 (on J. S. Drey); id., *Die lebendige Überlieferung als Norm des christlichen Glaubens* (1959); id., "Das Übernatürliche in der katholischen Tübinger Schule", *Theologische Quartalschrift* 143 (1963), pp. 422–33; id., *Die katholische Tübinger Schule — ihre theologische Eigenart* (1964); id., *Lebendiger Glaube aus geheiligter Überlieferung* (2nd ed., 1966) (Möhler and the Tübingen School); S. Lösch, *Die Anfänge der Tübinger Theologischen Quartalschrift* (1938); E. Hocedez, *Histoire de la théologie au XIXe siècle,* I (1949), pp. 231–51; II (1950), pp. 297–308; H. Lohmann, *Philosophie der Offenbarung bei J. S. von Drey* (dissertation, Freiburg, 1953); F. X. Arnold, *Seelsorge aus der Mitte der Heilsgeschichte* (1956); O. Chadwick, *From Bossuet to Newman: The Idea of Doctrinal Development* (1957); W. Ruf, *J. S. von Dreys System der Theologie* (dissertation, Freiburg, 1958) (on moral theology); A. Exeler, *Eine Frohbotschaft vom christlichen Leben* (1959) (on Hirscher's moral theology); A. Burkhardt, *Der Mensch – Gottes Bild und Gleichnis* (1962); P. Hünermann, *Trinitarische Anthropologie bei F. A. Staudenmaier* (1962); id., "Der Reflex des deutschen Idealismus in der Theologie der katholischen Tübinger Schule", *Philosophisches Jahrbuch der Görres-Gesellschaft* 73 (1965–66), pp. 48–74; B. Casper, "Der Systemgedanke der späten Tübinger Schule und in der deutschen Neuscholastik", *Philosophisches Jahrbuch der Görres-Gesellschaft* 72 (1964–65), pp. 161–79; J. Rief, *Reich Gottes und Gesellschaft nach D. S. Drey und J. B. Hirscher* (1965); B. Welte, *Auf der Spur des Ewigen* (1965), pp. 390–409; L. Scheffczyk, *Theologie in Aufbruch und Widerstreit* (1965); *Theologie im Wandel,* ed. by the Catholic Faculty of Theology at Tübingen (150-year *Festschrift,* 1817–1964) (1967); K. Friehlingsdorf, *Das Gottesverständnis J. B. Hirschers* (dissertation, Trier, 1968); K. Mattes, *Die Kontroverse zwischen J. von Kuhn und Constantin von Schäzler über das Verhältnis von Natur und Gnade* (1968); F. Schupp, *Die Evidenz der Geschichte* (dissertation, Innsbruck, 1968) (on Drey); E. Klinger, *Offenbarung im Horizont der Heilsgeschichte* (1969) (on OT in philosophy of revelation).

Elmar Klinger

U

UNBELIEF

1. *The notion and the discussion.* For the word "unbelief" (ἀπιστία, *incredulitas*) see, for example, Mt 13:58; Mk 9:24; Rom 3:3; 4:20; 11:20, 23; Heb 3:11, 19. Unbelief is the deliberate rejection of faith. It is presupposed that faith and unbelief (in the case of men capable of a decision) are not two possibilities among others, but that everyone either believes or refuses to believe and that there is no way of avoiding this choice. When the concept is so defined, the question at once arises as to whether (in the case of men who have come to the use of reason and freedom) there cannot be an absence of faith which does not need to feel itself a free negation of faith but feels that faith — known in others as a psychological phenomenon — is no longer a serious question. Are there men who simply and effortlessly find themselves a-religious and find no need to be anti-religious? It is unquestionable that the world-wide unbelief of the present-day (see *Atheism*), both in communist and in "Western" countries *tries* to understand itself in this way. It claims to be a completely neutral a-religious unbelief, and does not shrink from presenting itself in public as the normal attitude which is to be taken for granted in modern man. When we say "tries", we mean that such unbelievers imagine that both psychologically (existentielly) and socially faith offers no real alternative.

In other words, the question arises at the very beginning as to whether unbelief is ultimately a reaction to faith or a nonderivative phenomenon, which is only negative from the point of view of faith and can only be designated secondarily as unbelief.

This therefore is the basic problem: both faith and unbelief consider their positions as normal and universally obligatory, with no legitimate alternative. The reasons are of course different in each case. The believer's attitude is based on his faith in the word of God, the unbeliever's on the conviction that he has reached a point to which evolution will eventually bring all men, inexorably. But both have also to explain in terms of their own systems (without appealing to each other's) how it can be that believers and unbelievers exist who may not accuse each other *a priori* of stupidity or malice. And they must also explain why they can carry on a "dialogue" with each other, in spite of the "absoluteness" of their positions — why they are not reduced to mere co-existence on the biological and economic plane.

2. *Standard distinctions and further questions.* While heresy (cf. *CIC*, can. 1325) is the denial of individual revealed truths while the basic Christian faith remains *(nomen Christianum retentum)*, the state of unbelief is the habitual absence of any belief at all. As the disposition of the "infidel" *(infidelitas)*, this unbelief is usually said to take three forms. Negative infidelity is the inculpable lack of faith (cf. 1 Tim 1:13). Privative infidelity is the culpable lack of faith where the fault lies in indifference to religion in general. Positive infidelity is the direct, deliberate and culpable rejection of faith. As with sin in general, a distinction could be made between material and formal unbelief, the former being inculpable, the latter culpable. These distinctions, however, presuppose a notion of faith which envisages a conceptual, conscious articulation of the object of faith. Within these terms

321

of reference, there can certainly be an unbelief which is total (see *Atheism*) and still inculpable (cf. Vatican II, *Lumen Gentium,* art. 16; *Gaudium et Spes,* arts. 21 f.).

But there is another way of taking faith. It can be understood as the grace of faith and the accompanying illumination (not necessarily objectivated but still definite; see *Faith, Revelation*) which is offered to all men, according to the universal salvific will of God. In men who have come to the use of freedom, this can only exist as the free acceptance or the free refusal of faith. And in this context unbelief can only be culpable. But then it is also possible to affirm that such faith can be the possession of "those who, without blame on their part, have not yet arrived at an explicit knowledge of God, but who strive to live a good life, thanks to his grace" (*Lumen Gentium,* art. 16), that is, of "unbelievers" in the ordinary sense. In other words, in the ultimate depths of existence, under the perpetual offer of God's grace (see *Existence* III, B), there is no such thing as negative or material unbelief. Unbelief, at the level of conscious, conceptual objectivation, even in the form of atheism, even though "freely" chosen, is not necessarily the manifestation of an unbelief (in the ultimate depths of existence) which is culpable loss of the grace of faith. This may be illustrated by a possible parallel. The free profession of faith on the level of propositions and public confession is no certain proof of the existence of faith in the sense of the God-given decision for God, in a fundamental free act at the centre of the person. Even such a "work" of faith remains ambivalent.

Basing oneself on this notion of faith and unbelief, one could distinguish between existentiell (or "real") unbelief, which is always culpable, and notional unbelief, which can be culpable or inculpable. The standard theological distinctions would then refer primarily to notional (or "theoretical") unbelief. The classification would not of course mean that any given man could be definitely placed in one or other category as regards his relationship to God. Since all grace of faith is a grace of Christ, and since even men who apparently are acting only on the human level have a positive relationship to Christ, even though unconscious (cf. for instance Mt 25), faith in God and faith in Jesus Christ (or unbelief, on the various levels described above) may be treated alike, as in the language of St. John above all (e.g., 11:6). For the relationship to Christ is not just one object

of faith among others, but the "incarnational" definiteness of faith as such (in spite of Heb 11:6 and the whole theological question of what must be explicitly believed for salvation).

3. *On the theology of unbelief in general.* It should already be clear from what has been said above that there is really no theology of unbelief in any developed form. For even the simplest questions about the real nature of unbelief lead to difficulties not normally posed in theology and to theories which are not commonly held. As a rule, unbelief is simply regarded as a particularly grave case of sin. It is not clearly envisaged as the opposite of the faith which is the root and foundation of the right relationship to God (*D* 801). So too unbelief is described in merely negative terms, and faith appears simply as a sum of truths, that is, in its developed and articulate form, and unbelief is the denial of such propositions. The real nature of unbelief, the total deliberate decision, is left in obscurity. But it is ultimately a free choice by which man decides what his whole life will be, and hence either a blueprint for a life of total self-assertion with nothing on principle mysterious in it, or a defensive strategy of despair which allows of no wider a future than what man himself can create, for all its obvious insufficiency. Both forms of unbelief can be covered up and repressed, to re-appear as the sceptical, courageous (or apparently courageous) nonchalance of the man who has silently come to terms with the absurdity of existence. But of course this feat of every-day endurance is ambivalent, and can also be the reflection of faith. And there is no human power that can help anyone to pass a secure judgment as he reflects on his case (cf. *D* 805, 822 f.).

It must also be the task of a theology of unbelief to point out to believers the context of theory and practice within which an understanding of unbelief is possible. It cannot be simply an invader from a totally foreign world, if faith is to be the full understanding of human existence and the light in which all things can be judged (1 Cor 2:15). A theology of unbelief should not just throw light on its occurrence in the private individual's history of salvation or calamity. It must be able to treat it as a phenomenon of the collective history of salvation and of "the world". There is the "sin of the world" (Jn 1:19 etc.; see *Original Sin*), and likewise the "unbelief of the world", with its own history of development. It becomes more and more radical and presents itself more and more unconcernedly as the obvious and normal way of life. It does not merely deny the existence of God by an atheistic philosophy, but tries to establish a mental attitude in which the question of God can no longer occur. In the theology of history, the broad social phenomenon of atheistic unbelief and the accompanying process of secularization will appear possibly as a wrong reaction to a justifiable and basically Christian desacralization of the world, which allows God to appear as God and not as part of the world, in his inaccessible mystery.

4. *Unbelief in the believer*. Faith itself brings with it the possibility of unbelief. It is part of the pilgrim nature of man to be tempted to unbelief. This is because faith is essentially a free grace of God which can only come into play where the opposite is really possible. Further, the articulate expression of the original commitment of faith along the lines of truths of faith can only be analogous, and cannot possibly re-affirm in each proposition its dependence on the mystery — cannot indeed formulate expressly its primordial dependence. It is therefore exposed to the temptation of shedding the burden of such formulations by taking up a sceptical attitude or one of austere intellectual detachment (ἐποχή). Finally, there is concupiscence in the believer, which is not just a moral situation. It is also an intellectual factor, within and without, pluralist in character, not fully assimilated or indeed assimilable by the decision of faith. It furnishes ideas which come from unbelief and tend to unbelief (cf. *D* 792) and it makes the question of the individual's life insoluble: does it reflect concupiscence or the "works" of faith? Which of these are at the heart of existence? (See 1 Cor 4:4f.) If the Christian finds himself repeating the cry, "I believe, help my unbelief" (Mk 9:24), this is not a special case which should not really arise, but the normal situation of the believer, who is *simul fidelis et infidelis* as well as *simul justus et peccator*.

5. *Christian and preacher in face of modern unbelief*. This theme can of course be discussed only briefly here. At this moment of transition, as the Church of the masses becomes the Church of personally-committed believers, Christians must recognize that faith is not necessarily most at home in a situation where faith can also be identical with public opinion. The proper setting for faith is a situation in which the conventions of society do not relieve the believer of the burden of personal decision. And the preacher should not rely on such a conventional situation in his preaching. He must recognize that the message of the gospel must be presented otherwise today — in the light of a secularized world and in view of such a world, so that the secret unbelief of traditional Christians may be taken into account and catered for. If he speaks as though he were addressing the unbeliever of the present day, he will be saying something important for Christians.

Hence the theology by which the sermon is inspired must do justice to the modern mentality. The difference between a basic faith at the heart of existence and its conceptual articulation must not be lost sight of, though the value of the latter should not be underestimated, if only for the reason that faith and preaching are concerned with a salvation which came as a historical event. But preaching and propositional faith must be such that one can see their bond with the ultimate existentiell decisions (inspired by grace) which man's inescapable situation demands of him in one way or another. It is only because this bond is frequently left out of consideration that the impression is given that one only needs to be totally oblivious of explicit faith in order to be relieved even of deciding between faith and unbelief.

BIBLIOGRAPHY. H. de Lubac, *Drama of Atheistic Humanism* (1949); E. Borne, *Modern Atheism* (1961); A. Roper, *Die anonymen Christen* (1963); F. Jeanson, *La foi d'un incroyant* (1963); D. Jenkins, *Beyond Religion* (1964); B. Häring, "Unglaube und Naturrecht", *Theologie im Wandel (Festschrift der Tübinger Katholischen Theologischen Fakultät)* (1967), pp. 211–27; K. Rahner, "The Christian among Unbelieving Relations", *Theological Investigations*, III (1967), pp. 355–72; id., *Schriften zur Theologie* VI, pp. 262–76; VIII, pp. 187–212; G. Waldmann, *Christlicher Glauben und christliche Glaubenslosigkeit* (1968).

Karl Rahner

UNITY

1. *Concept and nature*. Unity is usually defined as the state by which a being is not divided in itself but divided from everything else *(indivisio in se et divisio a quolibet alio)*. Scholastic philosophy then distinguishes between *transcendental* unity, which is a property of being as such and *numerical* unity which is

limited to corporeal beings. The above definition, however, reflects certain presuppositions: it comes from the comparison of two or more *different* beings. To arrive at the full and original concept of unity (transcendental unity), we must go back further and consider unity as a concept as primordial as being itself. Unity, like being, is implicated and affirmed from the start in man's mental activity. As the analysis of this act shows, being explicates itself by means of an intrinsic plurality (see *Transcendentals*). This intrinsic plurality, as primordial as being itself, is not exclusively a feature of the finite. It indicates a perfection and is ascribable to all beings — as is readily recognized by Christian thought in the perspective of the mystery of the Trinity, the ultimate determinant of all Christian understanding of being. This (intrinsic) unity is not to be understood statically, in abstraction from the intrinsic plurality, nor as the posterior unification of the inner elements, but as an ontological ultimate. Unity is the coherence of an intrinsically plural being — a coherence achieved dialectically, i.e., by the mutual relationship of the elements.

Unity *ad extra,* by which a thing is differentiated from others, is to be unterstood in the light of this intrinsic unity. A true concept of unity demands that this distinction be understood dialectically: not as some abstract characteristic which isolates a being, but as pointer to the relationship whereby a being is all the more united in itself, and so distinguished from others, the more intimate its connection with them is.

2. *Analogy.* Unity is an intrinsically analogical feature of being. Hence the notion of unity is also analogical: it displays the various levels on which unity is realized. Unity takes a different form according to the varied dialectic of the intrinsic elements. The origin of all unity and its highest manner of being is the triune God, whose simplicity is not a lifeless identity but unity of and in diversity of persons (see *Trinity*). God has also a unity *ad extra.* He is distinct from the world (see *God-World Relationship*) but not separated from it. This distinctness points to his unique way of possessing being, in whose infinite fullness all created things participate in a finite way. Thus Christian thought attains a supremely nuanced understanding of the ancient problem of the unity of reality. All one-sided monistic and pluralistic views are subsumed and transformed in the profound Christian concept, whose full riches are revealed only to faith in the incarnation of God, and its accompanying theological reflection.

In the region of the finite, the unity of each being is characterized not merely by the primordial plurality which must be ascribed to all beings, including God, but also and essentially by the plurality of compositeness which is proper to the created being as such and involves imperfection: plurality of principles of being, of actual structure, of the various phases of self-realization, etc. This composite plurality must be understood in the last resort as "trace" and "reflection" of the primordial intra-trinitarian plurality. The intrinsic and extrinsic unity of created being must also be seen in the light of the multiplicity of created beings. Multiplicity necessarily presupposes a fundamental unity in being. But then the many existent beings comprise the most diverse kinds and degrees of unity. Apart from the unity of the concrete individual, account must be taken in particular of the unity of social groups and structures (see *Family, State*). Important above all in theology are the unity of the history of salvation, in which the multiplicity of religions is confronted with the absolute claim of Christianity (see *Christianity* II); the unity of the salvific action of Jesus Christ (see *Church, Church History*) and of its extension in history (see *Missions, Dogma* II, etc.). In all this, unity is not to be considered as an abstract determination independent of multiplicity, but as a positive dialectical relationship in which multiplicity in its various modes is always an intrinsic element of unity.

See also *Knowledge, Spirit, Being* I, *Identity-Philosophy.*

BIBLIOGRAPHY. F. M. Sladeczek, "Die spekulative Auffassung vom Wesen der Einheit in ihrer Auswirkung auf Philosophie und Theologie", *Scholastik* 25 (1950), pp. 391–468; L. Oeing-Hanhoff, *Ens et Unum Convertuntur* (1953); M. Heidegger, *Essays in Metaphysics: Identity and Difference* (1960); G. Siewerth, *Der Thomismus als Identitätssystem* (2nd ed., 1961); H. Volk, "Einheit als theologisches Problem", *Münchener Theologische Zeitschrift* 12 (1961), pp. 1–13; W. Kern, "Einheit-in-Mannigfaltigkeit", *Gott in Welt (Festgabe K. Rahner),* I (1964), pp. 207–239; E. Coreth, "Identität und Differenz", *ibid.,* pp. 158–87; K. Rahner, *Theological Investigations,* IV (1966), pp. 221–244; id., "Einheit", *LTK,* III, cols. 749 f.

Lourencino-Bruno Puntel

UNIVERSALS

The universal is what all have in common, the general denomination which fits all things or many things (i.e., all of a certain type or group).

1. *History of the problem: the controversy.* The existence of the universal or general is undeniable, and was not called in question even in the controversy on universals. For language uses the same word for several situations or to designate a multitude of particulars and it can only convey meaning on this supposition. The question is whether there is anything universal apart from the words, and it has been a constant problem in philosophy. In the form of the controversy on universals it dominated the epistemology of the Middle Ages (see *Knowledge*). The controversy took four main lines. a) Extreme nominalism held that the only universal was the name, the word. b) Conceptualism, often called moderate nominalism, held that there were universals in the mind, the general concepts, but that there was nothing corresponding to them in reality. c) Moderate realism held that what was meant by the general concept was to be found in things, though not as it was in the abstract and in general, but as a concrete particular. d) Extreme realism held that there was a structure of reality which corresponded exactly to the concept. Hence the universal was a distinct element of the particular, or could even exist independently of it. This last view was also known as Platonism.

Platonism does not here mean the whole philosophy of Plato or his school but the view taken of Plato in the controversy on universals, when he was counted among the extreme realists, his "forms" (see *Idea*) being assumed to be a realization of the universal prior to our thinking and outside the particular things. Strictly speaking, however, the forms were not existing universals but individual entities in a supra-temporal and non-material intelligible world (κόσμος νοητός), the only real world, the transitory things of the sensible world being only shadowy participations of these beings, whose true reality was the only explanation of the similarities and constant structures to be noted in the sensible world (see *Participation*). The universal first occurs as "second substance" in Aristotle, where it is derived by abstraction from the "first substance", or real beings. It is neither the essence of the particular nor an independent entity separate from the particular, like the form or idea of Plato (*Metaphysics,* VI, 13; 1038b). It is the element comprised in a concept which can be predicated of several things.

On the question of what had to correspond in reality to the predicate thus affirmed, opinions then differed. Some, like Porphyrius and Boethius, evaded the question as too difficult, while others took one or other of the four lines indicated above, though not necessarily fitting neatly into any given class. At the beginning of the medieval controversy the main debate was between the protagonists of the extreme positions, while later the two moderate opinions were the main interest.

Through the writings of St. Anselm of Canterbury (1033–1109), the extreme realist position was influenced by St. Augustine and his neo-Platonism, according to which the essences of created things are in the mind of God as exemplars or *rationes aeternae.* They are in created things as the *rationes seminales* which determine their development, and are known to man by virtue of an illumination given in his contemplation of the *rationes aeternae.* This laid the groundwork for the medieval distinction of universals "ante rem", "in re" and "post rem", while it also heralded the tendency to identify them in extreme realism.

John Scotus Erigena (9th century) was wholly within this tradition when he defined the universal (essence) as a substance which subsists in particulars in the manner in which it is known by us. But the most radical formulation of this view was given by William of Champeaux (d. 1122), who first taught that there was only one single essence, "man", for instance, identical in all particulars of a given type, these being only accidentally different from each other. When it was objected, as for instance by Abelard, that this view led to pantheism, like the doctrine of Erigena, William gave up the identity of the essence throughout, maintaining merely that the essence was the same in each particular (i.e., indistinguishable).

The contrary position, equally extreme, was maintained at the same period by William's opponent Roscellinus of Compiègne (according to *his* opponents, e.g., St. Anselm of Canterbury). The common essence was now treated merely as a *flatus vocis,* an empty word. Roscellinus has therefore been looked on as the founder of medieval nominalism. Abelard, a disciple of Roscellinus and also of William, put forward an intermediate position, which became the prevailing view in classical scholasticism in the form of the moderate realism into which it was elaborated, e.g., by St. Thomas Aquinas. According to Aquinas, following Aristotle, the universal is that which can be asserted of a multitude of things. It has its being *ante rem* in the mind of God, but has no other being *in re* than that of the particular and only becomes a universal *in mente* and *post rem* by the operation of the *intellectus agens,* in abstraction.

The notion of "abstraction" provided an accepted compromise for a long time, but the solution was by no means definitive. This is clear from the resumption of the debate some time afterwards and its persistence down to the present day. Duns Scotus (d. 1308) suggested a *distinctio formalis ex natura rei* in things, corresponding to the conceptual distinctions. This brought him close to extreme realism, while William of Occam (d. 1349) was closer to a moderate conceptualism. These two main lines have been continued in the philosophy of the modern era. Empiricists and positivists, from Hobbes and the English empiricists down to the neopositivism of the Vienna Circle and analytical philosophy (see *Science* II) have nearly always inclined to nominalism, since their whole attention was concentrated on the concrete particular. Rationalism and Idealism, however, rather tended to look on the universal as the true reality. Those who, like Kant, on the other hand, explain the universal in terms of the structure of the intellect do not fit into this schema. But the phenomenologists who assume an "ideal being" for essences, independent of thought, and the modern mathematicians and logicians who assume a similar existence for abstract entities (such as sets and groups and propositions) may well be considered as extreme realists. And present-day linguistic philosophy which tries to reduce the meaning of words or propositions merely to their usage may well be considered nominalists.

This sketch of the historical problem shows that the task of finding the proper balance between the two trends described above remains a perpetual problem. Those who are mainly preoccupied with the individual empirical sciences will be rather tempted to take up a nominalist position, while those engaged in the *a priori* universal sciences will find extreme realism a greater danger.

2. *On the solution of the problem.* Both the tendency to extreme realism and to nominalism fail to note the true nature of the universal, the reason being that both are orientated to the particular merely in the guise of a "thing". Hence the ultra-realists take the concept to be a thing realized in a multitude of things, while the nominalists oppose the individual word to the multitude of individual things, but leave it without any relationship to them. In the universal, as Aristotle saw, a relation is affirmed between the one and the many, as when we use one word to designate several particulars, the word "man", for instance, applying to all individual men. If we used a special word for each particular in each different situation, language would be as little capable of conveying meaning as if the relation of the linguistic element to things or cases remained purely arbitrary — that is, as if we could indicate no possible basis in the objects for attaching such labels to them. It is therefore necessary and sufficient for the validity of a universal term, that is, for its meaningful use, that there should be some individual basis in each case — the non-individual does not exist — which makes it possible to apply this concept to the case by virtue of a human consensus.

See also *Nominalism, Platonism, Neo-Platonism, Rationalism, Positivism.*

BIBLIOGRAPHY. M. Carré, *Realists and Nominalists* (1946); H. Veatch, *Realism and Nominalism Revisited* (1954); I. M. Bochenski, A. Church and N. Goodman, *The Problem of Universals: A Symposium, Notre Dame* (1956); W. Stegmüller, "Das Universalienproblem einst und jetzt", *Archiv für Philosophie* 6 (1956), pp. 192–225; 7 (1957), pp. 45–81; J. Schobinger, *Vom Sein der Universalien* (1958); R. Hönigswald, *Abstraktion und Analyse* (1961); G. Küng, *Ontologie und logistische Analyse der Sprache* (1963); J. Eyde, *Die Objektivität des Allgemeinen* (1965); F. Suarez, *Disputation VI: On Formal and Universal Unity,* translated by J. Ross (1965); P. Butschvarov, *Resemblance and Identity* (1966); J. Möller, "The Problem of Universals", *International Philosophical Quarterly* 6 (1966), pp. 557–73; R. I. Aaron, *The Theory of Universals* (2nd ed., 1967).

Albert Keller

UTILITARIANISM

1. *Concept.* Utilitarianism, from the Latin *utile,* expedient, is the name given to the theory of ethics which judges the moral value of an action by its contribution to

"the greatest happiness of the greatest number". Its opposite is the ethics which regards an action as good because it belongs to a definite class of actions, i.e., as valuable in itself and not only by reason of its consequences. Insofar as utilitarianism maintains that the only self-justifying value which man can strive for is pleasure (Greek ἡδονή), it may be termed hedonism. But it is not necessarily egoism, since other creatures' pleasure is also aimed at. The two maximums suggested in the utilitarian formula are only conceivable if the various pleasures which are felt by a given subject differ only quantitatively, and if the various subjects also differ only numerically.

Under these circumstances, the upholders of utilitarianism hope on principle to be able to calculate the correct action in each case from an analysis of the situation — the "calculus of pleasure".

2. Since utilitarianism was mostly developed in Great Britain, its origins must probably be sought in the pragmatical and empirical attitudes of Anglo-Saxon thinking. The first use of the slogan of utilitarianism, "the greatest happiness of all", appears in the *De Legibus Naturae* of Bishop Cumberland (1672). To bring this about is seen as God's supreme commandment to man. The influence of David Hume (*Treatise on Human Nature,* 3 vols. [1740]) led the way to the full statement of utilitarianism in Jeremy Bentham. Bentham (*A Fragment on Government* [1776]; *Introduction to the Principles of Morals and Legislation* [1789]), who was mainly interested in political and legal reforms, found the formula a universal criterion for judging the value of laws. He tried to improve this instrument by investigating the measurability of pleasure and by applying it to the administration of the country. He had little interest in providing the principle with a fuller theoretical justification. His friend and disciple James Mill (*A Fragment on Mackintosh* [1835]) and Mill's son, John Stuart Mill (*Utilitarianism* [1861]) developed utilitarianism further, it having meanwhile become the predominant moral philosophy in the English drawing-room and in the practical field of political economy. J. S. Mill popularized the word "utilitarianism", but introduced certain notions into his system which basically rendered utilitarianism impossible. He made qualitative distinctions between "higher" and "lower" pleasures, and recognized non-pleasurable values such as virtue and knowledge, which were nonetheless desirable in themselves. The last important upholder of utilitarianism was Henry Sidgwick (*Method of Ethics* [1874]). Sidgwick tried to show that there was no fundamental contradiction between the fact that each one strives only for his own happiness, and the moral law, that he ought also to strive for the happiness of others. But his effort brought him to abandon the empirical basis which is proper to utilitarianism. Today the great days of utilitarianism seem to have passed away, though practical utilitarianism survives in the form of the welfare State.

3. *Types.* One must first distinguish between utilitarianism, as the mere effort to describe systematically the ethical convictions of man ("descriptive utilitarianism") and utilitarianism as a theory put forward to justify ethical convictions ("normative utilitarianism"). The success of the former is called in question even among the upholders of utilitarianism. The latter can again be understood in two ways, either as "act-utilitarianism" or "rule-utilitarianism". The former says that an individual action is morally good if it promotes the general happiness. The latter says that an action is good if it is done in accordance with a rule whose regular result is a maximum of possible happiness. Since it can happen that in particular cases action according to rules regularly useful can bring about harm, rule-utilitarianism is obviously subordinate and secondary to act-utilitarianism. And in fact most of the upholders of utilitarianism considered it only in the form of act-utilitarianism.

4. The verdict on utilitarianism must be a criticism of its anthropological presuppositions, of its definition of morality and of the practicability of its methods.

a) The notion that pleasure is the only self-justifying value degrades man to the status of an impersonal seeker of pleasure. If more than the pleasure of the individual seeker is meant, the doctrine is without justification. If it means only one's own pleasure, it is egoism, and has to postulate a necessary harmony between egoistic pursuit of pleasure and general happiness or well-being. And then immorality is only lack of ability to use properly the calculus of pleasure.

b) Concern for one's own (or others')

pleasure is not always good in itself, but only when this pleasure is itself morally justifiable, i.e., when it remains within the finality intrinsic to the being of man.

c) No methods of measurement can be indicated by which any given pleasure could be clearly determined by an appropriate coefficient of pleasure-units. The quantification of pleasure is only possible within very narrow limits. It breaks down in face of the qualitative difference between various joys and differences of taste. And the other element of the maxim, the "greatest number", also escapes clear definition. Should only the living be counted, or should the unborn be included (for how long?), since their number depends to some extent on the regulation of births? Must animals perhaps be included, as Bentham thought, in the "greatest number" of sensitive beings? Hence utilitarianism, as an objective and empirical method of determining the moral good, in the light of social utility, must be said to fail.

See also *Ethics, Good, Morality.*

BIBLIOGRAPHY. L. Stephen, *The English Utilitarians,* 3 vols. (1900); E. Albee, *A History of English Utilitarianism* (1901; 2nd impression, 1957); G. Myrdal, *The Political Element in the Development of Economic Theory* (1953); J. Plamenatz, *The English Utilitarians* (2nd ed., 1958); J. J. C. Smart, s. v., *Encyclopedia of Philosophy* (1967) (with bibliography).

Gerd Haeffner

UTOPIA

1. *The notion.* a) The term "Utopia" comes from the title of St. Thomas More's novel of the ideal State (1516; Greek, οὐ τόπος, No-place) and designates the partly satirical and partly programmatical sketches of State and society which form a fairly common literary genre. There are "positive" Utopias which build on existing conditions to open up the widest possible perspectives on the ideals which have been planned or longed for. Others are deliberately negative, displaying the possible abuses of the achievements of modern civilization in terms of a terrifying future. Both types are constructed to some extent on the basis of real conditions.

b) But the notion of utopia is also used for a philosophical, socio-ethical and theological set of values. In Ernst Bloch, for instance, Utopia is the wealth of present potentialities of which we are still unconscious and of which little has yet been realized in the world. Utopia is the "reality of the incomplete" which is a basic ontological determination of the real, displayed in the categories of "tendency" and "novelty". It is also a pointer to man's way of being, since he is always a step ahead of himself in the utopian dream-world of his self-engendered future. In this view, utopia is the first step in human self-fulfilment, the "principle of hope" is the great human factor. But this "transcendence without the transcendent" is achieved at the cost of utopian completeness and utopianism becomes evolution.

c) The notion of Utopia becomes utopianism when the fulfilment of the future is sought within history. This ultimately breaks down on the anti-utopia of death, where man's whole being is called in question. Utopianism necessarily ends in disappointment, a disappointment which may be called a metaphysical one. The future of history must be qualitatively new (see *Eschatology*). The future must transcend the experiment of history itself. All Utopias within the framework of history ("horizontal") are contingent on the "eschatological reserve", the total otherness of the absolute future of God — which is also the total alteration and reversal of all alienations, including death.

2. *History.* The Utopias of human dreams, one of the oldest forms of wishful thinking, have given rise to a wide literature. Plato's *Republic* is the early Utopia in the classical form of an ideal State and a critique of statecraft. In Stoicism, as in Zeno's *Republic,* the ideal city-state of Plato is extended to take in the whole world. It is based on philanthropy and freedom, men are citizens of the world, their country has no national bounds. The campaigns of Alexander enlarged the geographical horizons and helped to illustrate the Hellenistic Utopias. Distant regions were peopled with dream-cities, idyllic islands and wonderlands: as in the epics, "travels" and romances of such writers as Iambulos *(Islands of the Sun),* Hecataeus *(The Land of Egypt)* and Euhemerus *(The Sacred Inscription, c.* 300 B.C.).

Something comparable to the sharp critique of social conditions in these Utopias may also be found in the Bible. The preaching of the classical prophets, with their appeal to the ancient revealed law as affecting public life and not just the pious individual, was preoccupied with social criticism (Amos 2:5–7; 5:2, 24; Is 5:7; 54:11, 14, etc.). And there were also idyllic pictures of the future: "They shall beat swords into ploughshares, and their spears into pruning hooks; nation shall not lift up sword against nation, neither shall they learn war any more" (Is 2:4; Mic 4:3). Israel's Utopia is a new Canaan, a new Zion with a new temple (Ezek 40–48).

The beatitudes in the Sermon on the Mount (Mt 5:1–12 par.) proclaim eschatological justice for the deprived, the oppressed and the afflicted. According to Mt 11:28, Jesus invites the weary and the heavily burdened to come to him for relief. But, as E. Bloch says, the point of the social utopias is to paint a picture of a happy city where the weary are at rest and so on. The biblical view of history, with its hope of the Last Things dawning in Jesus Christ, readily inspires a utopian vision. The time between dawn and denouement is coloured by the light from the eschatological fulfilment. In the *De Civitate Dei,* St. Augustine expresses this hope in terms of a philosophy of history. The "city of God", currently hidden in the Church though not coinciding with it, is locked in an ancient struggle with the "city of the devil". The "city of God" is not really completely established and has within it the seeds of a Utopia: the Thousand Year Reign and then the fulfilment in the perfect Reign of Christ, in the heavenly Sabbath (see *Millenarianism*). This notion of the struggle between the spiritual and the worldly kingdoms brought the notion of the millennium into Christian views of history. The "ecclesiastical Utopia" lay ahead of historical reality. This utopianism found the institutional Church too narrow and found outlets in various religious and social movements of the Middle Ages: the Catharists, the Spirituals and most sucessfully of all in the social utopia of Joachim of Fiore. Then at the beginning of the modern era there were the Hussites, the Anabaptists, the Rosicrucians, the Independents (English Congregationalists), Thomas Münzer and so on. A "spiritual utopianism" often tried to counteract the secularization of the Church by the revival of an ideal primitive Christianity. The *Rei publicae christianopolitanae descriptio* of J. V. Andreae (1610) was an outline of an ecclesiastical Utopia.

With the Renaissance and the early stages of the Enlightenment writing on Utopia reached one of its highpoints. St. Thomas More's vision of social freedom gave the name to the genre: *De optimo rei publicae statu sive de nova insula Utopia* (1516). This was followed by such works as T. Campanella's *Civitas Solis* (1602), the just society with total conformism, F. Bacon's *Nova Atlantis* (1627), the first Utopia along the lines of industrialism and science, J. Harrington's *Commonwealth of Oceana* (1656), with a constitution based on natural law. The Utopias of the Enlightenment were mainly aimed at criticizing the absolutist State, e.g., F. de Fénelon's *Aventures de Télémaque* (the model prince).

In the 19th century, the sense of social responsibility was the mainspring of such writing. Social difficulties were to be solved with the help of industrialization and highly-efficient organization. See for instance J. G. Fichte, *Der geschlossene Handelsstaat* (1800), the self-contained mercantile state, socially organized according to the law of reason, C. Fourier, *Le nouveau monde industriel* (1829), E. Cabet, *Voyage en Icarie* (1839), sketch of State socialism, H. de St. Simon, *Réorganisation de la société européenne* (1814) and *Nouveau christianisme* (1825), R. Owen, *The Book of the New Moral World* (1836), guild socialism, W. Weitling, *Die Menschheit wie sie ist und wie sie sein sollte* (1838), "mankind as it is and as it ought to be", universal community of goods, E. Bellamy, *Looking Backward* (1888), W. Morris, *News from Nowhere* (1891).

Most of the Utopias written before about 1900 were full of faith in progress and the general improvement of the world. But along with the utopian science-fiction of the 20th century, the negative type came to the fore. The future is seen as fatally menaced by a technological Frankenstein, the dangers of mass indoctrination and depersonalization and the atomic bomb, and becomes the spectre of an inferno, depicted cynically or pessimistically or in terms of the absurd. In A. Huxley's *Brave New World* (1932) the individual is eliminated in favour of a push-button society. G. Orwell's *Nineteen Eighty-four* conjures up a Stalinism in full control in a technological dictatorship. But the first great modern anti-Utopia was *We* by the Russian Communist Y. Zamyatin (*c.* 1920; definitive E. T., 1960 and 1969).

E. Bloch's life-work, *Das Prinzip Hoffnung* (2 vols., 1959), written over the years 1938–49, seeks to counteract the nihilism of the negative utopias by the concept of "the concrete process of Utopia", which is opposed to any methodical planning of a brave new world.

3. *Utopia and theology.* a) The variables of the literary Utopias, with their constantly changing projections, each reflecting some historical contingency, may be contrasted with the constant in the Utopian mind and will of man. The fact that he is consciously and deliberately always a step ahead of himself and always projecting himself into the future — or rather, always open for the coming of the absolute future — is a sign of his self-transcendence and an ontological constituent of his being (see *Time,* B). Man is a "Utopian being" (Ortega y Gasset), "not self-contained" (E. Bloch), "with his centre of gravity outside himself" (H. Plessner). He is in his natural element when he is prescinding from the limits of his environment and creatively planning his history.

b) The history of man cannot be simply reduced to his past. It is an event which is taking place and still outstanding, with the emphasis on the category of the future. But this shape of things to come must be seen in the perspective of its antecedents, if it is not to be distorted by utopianism and permanent revolution.

c) For a clear view of and a proper attitude towards Utopian thinking, the important thing is to note how the future projected by man is envisaged. Is it a future in the categories of the present, supposed to be within the range of planned production and remaining within the framework of a further future merely as yet undefined? Or is it the "absolute", free and supreme future of God, which is the mainspring of all thrust into the future?

d) The whole future must be recognized as under the ".eschatological reserve of God" (J. B. Metz). It is not just the result of historical strivings. But then it can be seen as reconciliation and novelty.

e) In God's self-communication in Jesus Christ (see *Incarnation*) God became man's absolute future. History became prophecy, pointing beyond each given moment to the eschaton, the new world. (This is the qualitative difference between history and eschatology.) The Kingdom of God has come close (the historical dimension) and still remains beyond history as the eternal fulfilment of all that is left unfulfilled in history (the supra-historical dimension). In any case, it is only as the new thing that makes all things new, as the future from Christ, that the Kingdom is reconciliation and salvation, what Tillich calls the "vertical Utopia". It cannot be reduced to the horizontal dimension of human plans, but it is the guide and driving force of human action as it works its way in the world to this eschaton.

f) The "new world" which has dawned in Jesus Christ does not merely loom on the horizon of the future, so to speak. It is the world of history as it comes to be through responsible Christian action. The Utopian purpose of Christians must be crystallized in the constant transformation of profane structures which ring hollow. It cannot be a resigned detachment, but must be a constantly renewed effort to stamp historical reality with the truth of the eschatological promises — freedom, peace, justice and reconciliation. The Church itself must prove to be an institution for creative criticism of society, of ideologies, of institutions. One of the basic hermeneutical problems of theology is to analyse the relationship between the understanding of the faith and social practice (see *Political Theology*) — where the necessity of avoiding the "privatizing" trend of theology must be noted. The Christian Utopia brings to light a new dimension. All shaping of the future through personal effort, re-construction of society and manipulation of the material world must be an effort to reach out towards the fundamental totality (see *Absolute and Contingent*), since man is not just a free agent, but always remains the receptive as well as active "quintessence of the whole" (K. Rahner). The delimitation of Utopia, which also opens out its new frontiers, is formed by eschatology, its future and also its transcendence.

BIBLIOGRAPHY. *Ideal Commonwealths: More's Utopia, Bacon's New Atlantis, Campanella's City of the Sun, Harrington's Oceana* (1901); E. Bloch, *Geist der Utopie* (1918); id., *Der utopische Staat,* ed. by K. Heinisch (1960) (with bibliography); L. Mumford, *The Story of Utopias* (1922); J. O. Hertzler, *The History of Utopian Thought* (1923); R. Ruyer, *L'Utopie et les utopistes* (1950); K. Mannheim, *Ideology and Utopia* (1958); J. Ortega y Gasset, *Man and Crisis* (1958); id., *Meditations on Quixote* (1961); R. Gerber, *Utopian Fantasy* (1955); H. Schulte-Herbrüggen, *Utopie und Anti-Utopie* (1960); K. Thieme, *Biblische Religion heute* (1960); F. Polak, *Images of the Future* (1961); P. Ludz in *RGG,* VI, cols. 1217–220 (with bibliography); T. Molnar, *Utopia, the Perennial Heresy* (1967); W. Nelson, ed., *Twentieth-Century Interpretations of Utopia* (1968).

Karl Woschitz

V

VALUE

1. *The notion of value.* In contemporary philosophy, value is defined as: that which is, or makes something, desirable, attractive, worthy of approval, admiration, etc.; that which inspires feelings, judgments or attitudes of esteem, commendation; that which is useful in view of certain ends. Value cannot, it seems, be completely identified with the "good" of classical (and scholastic) philosophy, whether taken materially *(bonum)* or formally *(bonitas)*. On the one hand, it always implies a relationship to man (or to the spiritual subject in general), while the good, in Aristotle for instance, is the correlative of the tendency, the teleological orientation, which reigns throughout the whole of nature. This is because it implies, apparently, a judgment which evaluates: it enters on the scene, one may say, when the good is recognized. (There is no moral value till I recognize, perhaps in spite of myself, that "the law is good"; something useful or necessary only has value when, for instance, its rarity attracts attention to it.)

On the other hand, contemporary philosophies of value are very far from seeing in it an abstract notion derived from concrete goods. They are rather inclined to regard these as embodiments and realizations of value. Finally, values are often regarded as having a twofold polarity, so that the ugly, the bad, the false, appear as "negative values". Here, however, others prefer to speak of "anti-values", keeping the word "value" for the positive pole only.

2. *The philosophy of values. General outlines.* The contemporary philosophy of values

cannot therefore be reduced to the classical treatment of goodness as a "transcendental" attribute of being or to the discussion of moral good. We are now concerned with a systematic study of the universe of values, not from the point of view of being, but in itself, or again, from the point of view of the evaluating subject (the individual, the society, the transcendental subject). In this sense, the term "axiology" is also used (from the Greek ἄξιος : that which is worthy, merits). In the strict sense of the term, the philosophy of values is distinguished from the simple "science of values" by its tendency to concentrate exclusively on the point of view of value, which is considered superior to being or as constitutive of real being. In a word, metaphysics is subordinated or reduced to axiology. Values are sometimes considered as entirely separate from being, indeed, as the opposite of being; so much so, that they cannot be realized without perishing.

Various problems are discussed in the philosophy of values: their nature, their relation to being, their priority or dependence with regard to the value-judgment, to the tendencies or feelings of the subject, individual or social, their classification, their hierarchy (hierarchy of different classes of values and hierarchy within each class); the various relationships between them, their combinations and reciprocal influences; their origin in conscience and in history; their evolution, their decline and the laws of such processes. The problem of the hierarchy and classification of values is particularly difficult, and many different systems have been proposed. The best and simplest seems to be based on the relationship to the spiritual subject: values are ranked according to whether they are concerned with it more or less directly. Thus there are infrahuman values, valid for man, but not in what makes him man: hedonist and biological values (pleasure, health — though some refuse to recognize real values in these, especially in pleasure); there are inframoral human values: economic, still linked to material needs, and spiritual (intellectual, aesthetic and so on); moral values, and above these again, though closely linked to them, religious values. In each of these orders, one must further distinguish the values of subject and object.

3. *History.* The philosophy of values is a recent development, generally taken to have been initiated by Hermann Lotze (1817–81). But there have been more or less notable anticipations of it throughout the history of philosophy. (i) First, of course, came the Platonic exaltation of the Good which is "out beyond essence". The truest form of knowledge is that which grasps beings from the point of view of finality and beauty, that is, of value. (ii) In St. Thomas, there are the different modes of the attribution of being and goodness, either *simpliciter* or *secundum quid* (*Summa Theologica,* I, q. 5, a. 1 ad 1), and above all, the doctrine of the degrees of perfection or of the "nobility" of beings. (In St. Thomas, the notion of perfection links ontology and axiology.) (iii) In Malebranche, there is the distinction between the *rapports de grandeur* and *rapports de perfection.* (iv) There are the two last Critiques of Kant, and the whole philosophy of the *Sollen* ("what ought to be") in Fichte, where reality is subordinated to value, as in Platonism.

We may also note that before the philosophy of values took shape, two types of value had already been studied very profoundly: moral values, since antiquity, and economic values, especially in the 18th and 19th centuries.

There are various reasons for the development of the philosophy of values in the second half of the 19th century: (i) Distrust of speculation, arising from the development of criticism and the conflict of systems, which encouraged many thinkers, like Socrates long ago, to abandon reality as it is in itself, to envisage things in their relationship to the subject — their important and interesting aspects. (ii) A reaction against the objectivism of science, which eliminated the subject and recognized no value but the truth (or the "verifiable"). The philosophy of

values re-asserts the right of the subject to take an interest in its own point of view. (iii) The tragic character of contemporary history, which calls in question, very peremptorily, the meaning and value of existence. Man feels his values threatened and contested, and hence takes a keener interest in them. This tendency is reinforced by the changes due to technical progress, because the new style of life thus introduced renders certain traditional values problematical. (iv) The development of economic sciences where the problem of value occupies a large place, and gave rise, in the 19th century, to widely famous theories which attracted the attention of philosophers to the problem of values in general. (v) We must note finally the influence of Nietzsche, with his fierce criticism of accepted values. Nietzsche is one of those who have been most influential in shifting the interest of contemporary thought in the direction of value (identified with life). To a more modest degree, pragmatism worked in the same direction: to judge truth by usefulness is to substitute the axiological point of view for the intellectualist. Phenomenology, finally, furnished a method which, when applied to the data of axiological thinking, made it possible to describe it more precisely.

4. *Principal types.* Several tendencies may be distinguished in the philosophy of values (understood in the wider sense). (i) Idealist, "transcendentalist", neo-Kantian (Rickert, Windelband) or neo-Fichtean (Münsterberg): value is a category, an ideal, a transcendental norm, an estimative consciousness in general. (ii) The psychological interpretation: value is founded on the tendencies and desires of the subject (C. von Ehrenfels, Ribot, Müller-Freienfels). (iii) The sociological interpretation: the centre of reference here is society: values are social phenomena and must be examined along with other social phenomena. It is in fact the evaluations which are studied, rather than the values (Durkheim, Bouglé, Lévy-Bruhl). Marxism evidently tends in this direction: the ways of evaluating a society are a function of its economic and social substructure. It contains, however, a humanist aspect which seems to surmount this relativism: man is the true source of value — cf. the theory of economic value—and a classless humanity, prefigured by the proletariat, seems to be for the Marxist the criterion of an authentic scale of values. (iv) The existentialist (Sartre)

and "libertarian" (Polin) interpretation: values are created by freedom, which is itself the supreme value. There is no absolute, objective norm. (v) At the other extreme, there is the phenomenologist, Platonizing interpretation, which attributes to values a sort of independent subsistence *(Ansichsein)*, different from that of categorized essences inasmuch as it is not the object of an intellectual but of an emotional intuition (M. Scheler, N. Hartmann). This is really a metaphysic of values. (vi) The same holds good for the spiritualist interpretation, which refers values to the activity of the spirit, and through it to the Absolute, to God. Values are a manifestation of the Absolute. God is the identity of being and value (L. Lavelle, R. Le Senne, D. von Hildebrand). We omit those who hold that value judgments simply express a subjective emotion or a commandment, without giving them meaning. This is the position of certain neo-positivists, like A. J. Ayer. Such theories are the negation of all philosophy of values.

5. There is no reason to quarrel with the contemporary notion of value or with its being chosen as the centre of interest. The philosophy of values has led to an exploration of the world of the spirit in a new dimension, and we owe it several precious analyses. The difference has been demonstrated, for instance, between the values (or pseudo-values) of hedonism and values properly speaking, in their way of presenting themselves. Studies have been made of the means by which values are apprehended, of the role of conflict and preference in their perception. The study of moral value, in the framework of a general theory of values, enables us both to understand it better and have a better grasp of its originality.

The great danger is to forget or to deny that value is founded upon being, is in being and of being, under pain of being nothing. Every affirmation of value is an explication of a primordial affirmation of being. This is what has been well brought out by Lavelle, for instance. This is no doubt the reason of Heidegger's distrust of the philosophy of value, which he sees as a consequence of the obscurity cast upon being. Yet the affirmation of value cannot be simply reduced to the affirmation of being. It adds to it, as St. Thomas says of goodness, the notion of perfection, which has no meaning unless being appears as intrinsically ordered, orientated, given an end and endowed with life, so to speak, from within, by the *actus essendi*. We believe that only a metaphysic revolving round the concept of the act of being (of the Thomist *esse*) will enable us to link up the metaphysic of the good (or of value) with that of being, axiology with ontology.

See also *Good, Nature* I, *Person* II, *Metaphysics, Morality* I, *Pragmatism*.

BIBLIOGRAPHY. W. Windelband, *History of Philosophy,* 2 vols. (1901; reprint, 1958); H. Rickert, *System der Philosophie* (1921); id., *Science and History: A Critique of Positivist Epistemology* (1962); C. Bouglé, *Leçons de sociologie sur l'évolution des valeurs* (1929); J. B. Lotz, "Sein und Wert", *ZKT* 57 (1933), pp. 557–613; R. Le Senne, *Obstacle et valeur* (1934); O. Kraus, *Die Werttheorien* (1937); R. Ruyer, *La philosophie des valeurs* (1941); id., *Le monde des valeurs* (1948); R. Polin, *La création des valeurs* (1944); J. Hessen, *Wertlehre* (1948); M. Reding, *Metaphysik der sittlichen Werte* (1949); P. Romano, *Ontologia del valore* (1949); L. Lavelle, *Traité des valeurs,* 2 vols. (1950–55); *Il problema del valore (Atti del XII Convegno di Gallarate, 1956)* (1957); W. Ehrlich, *Hauptprobleme der Wertphilosophie* (1959); E. Albert and C. Kluckhohn, *Selected Bibliography on Values, Ethics and Esthetics in the Behavioral Sciences and Philosophy* (1959); J. Bjelke, *Zur Begründung der Werterkenntnis* (1962); A. Stern, *Philosophy of History and the Problem of Values* (1962); W. Oates, *Aristotle and the Problem of Value* (1963); R. Maliandi, *Wertobjectivität und Realitätserfahrung* (1966); F. Battaglia, *Heidegger e la filosofia dei valori* (1967); R. Hartmann, *Structure of Value* (1967); K. Baier and N. Rescher, *Values and the Future* (1968).

Joseph de Finance

VIRGINITY

To make a correct evaluation of the evangelical counsel of virginity, it is well to start with the specification of man through his sexual nature. Because of this sexual nature he can achieve a full realization of his being as a person only if his attitude to sex is an open one, in the sense that he places it at the service of an ordered self-love, love of neighbour and love of God. If he does this, he exercises the virtue of chastity. Now this sexual specification of man, calling for a free personal decision and therefore for further specification, can be such that he can in all reason decide upon full sexual abstinence. That is the situation when one is incapable of marriage, or when one has not in the concrete the possibility of marriage. Again, specification can be such that a particular person achieves the best possible development if he decides to marry. Finally, it is also possible that a person in the face of a capability as well as a possibility of marriage, freely foregoes all use of the sex faculty. According as each person makes a free choice in his own way about his sexual life, there is in each case a specific form of chastity or unchastity. Virginity is a specific form of chastity of this kind by which a person opts for permanent abstinence from sexual activity. One speaks always then of following the evangelical counsel of virginity in the narrower sense when one is not "naturally" obliged to complete continence, when therefore perfect continence is chosen as the "concrete *bonum melius et possibile*" (cf. St. Thomas Aquinas, *Summa Theologica,* II/II, q. 152, a. 1).

Virginity in the theological sense is, besides this, basically an eschatological ideal which holds for all mankind equally, but not for all in the same way. Jesus expresses it in his own way when he says: "At the resurrection men and women do not marry; no, they are like the angels in heaven" (Mt 22:30; Mk 12:25; cf. Lk 20:34–36). In this sense in Rev 14:4 the followers of Christ appear simply as virgins. Thus in the last analysis the limitless love of God, of neighbour and of self in the next life, is in its direct vision called virginal, and the attainment of this eschatological virginity is regarded as a desirable goal for all. At the same time the expression and the translation into act of this love through human sexuality is characterized as provisional and ambivalent. Man indeed (as the more recent anthropology has shown), is characterized through and through by his sexuality, but he is not simply identical with his sexual nature. Man should therefore fully accept his sexuality, but he does not need to activate it directly without sublimation. This non-activation coupled with sublimation can, for those called to it, be a help to the actualization of greater love and an expression of it. Because of the subordinate significance of sex from the eschatological point of view, man should not lose himself in it; "Those who have wives should live as though they had none" (1 Cor 7:29).

Thus both the voluntarily and involuntarily unmarried as well as the married are all equally oriented, each in his own way, to eschatological virginity which, though not yet finally realized, yet is already realized to the extent that they are chaste, each according to his own situation. This means that man shares in eschatological virginity because of his sexuality in the measure in which he is chaste according to his state in life. Every form of chastity according to one's state in life is a sharing in eschatological virginity, yet each in its own specific manner, and each relates in a dialectical tension to the other forms. Since each form presents a particular aspect of eschatological virginity and expresses it in sign, this aspect must also be reflected by the other form of chaste love but not equivalently presented and signified. Thus Christian marriage is a sign of the relationship between Christ and his Church which is brought to direct realization in the following of the counsel of virginity. On the other hand, marriage portrays the intimacy of eschatological virginity in a way that the life according to the evangelical counsel cannot do. Similarly, the continence which is borne of necessity expresses the humble character of eschatological virginity better than virginity of the counsel, which in turn brings out better the magnanimity of eschatological love. Everyone of these forms of chastity is dependent on the others, since none of them represents or expresses fully the eschatological virginity in which, however, they all share and to which they have their orientation. Yet one can say that chastity according to the evangelical counsel is its most perfect form, since it expresses and represents most perfectly the eschatological significance of chastity (cf. *Summa Theologica,* II/II, q. 152, a. 3–5; *D* 980 and Vatican II, *Lumen Gentium,* art. 42: "This total continence embraced on behalf of the kingdom of heaven has always been held in particular honour by the Church as being a sign of charity and stimulus towards it, as well as a unique fountain of spiritual fertility in the world").

Jesus recommends virginity to those who are capable of it for the sake of the kingdom of heaven (Mt 19:10ff.; Lk 18:29ff.). He distinguishes such a voluntary renunciation of marriage from incapacity for marriage from birth and from incapacity which is humanly induced, and characterizes this virginity as the incapacity for marriage which is the fruit of zeal for the kingdom of God. It should be freely accepted by those called to it, that is, the evangelical counsel is directed to those who are so captivated by the definitive onset of the kingdom of God in Christ that this world, including human sex, appears in its provisional nature and in its ambivalence, and, as a consequence of this, in an entirely new light. Hence all they now think of is how to please the Lord (1 Cor 7:32–35). The evangelical counsel of virginity is thus not directed to all, but only to those who experience a call of grace to it.

Similarly Paul, who himself was not married, in 1 Cor 7 recommends virginity as better than marriage which is nevertheless not sinful. He justifies his advice with the possibility of serving Christ better in this way, especially in view of the proximate end of time.

The other NT books also show a high reverence for virginity (Acts 21:9) but protect marriage from being undervalued (1 Tim 4:3). The Pastoral Letters do not demand celibacy for those taking up an official position, but only in the case where one holding office loses his partner (1 Tim 3:2, 12; Tit 1:6; 1 Tim 5:9).

As a consequence, Christian theology has always esteemed virginity highly and regarded it as a protest against the excessive valuation of the world and of sex, and this to such a degree that it put virginity beside martyrdom in its significance for the Church. Trent expressly defined that the state of virginity is a higher and holier state than that of matrimony (*D* 980).

This appreciation of virginity, however, has been partly responsible for the not infrequent failure of theology to resist the tendency to relegate sexuality and marriage to the second place in a two-tiered morality. This temptation has been all the more real for theology because at its most basic and radical it has an ambivalent relationship to sex as to the world in general, convinced as it is of their infirm and vulnerable nature. This is quite clear from the counsel to practise virginity for the sake of the kingdom of God. But it must at the same time be recognized that the argumentation of the NT as of theology for the justification of virginity lays the chief emphasis on its charismatic character. For this reason virginity is specifically interpreted as a particularly appropriate symbolic representation of the priesthood of Christ or as a typological expression of the bridal love of the Church for Christ. Thus virginity is seen as the expression of the sanctifying role of the priest, to continue as *alter Christus* the *generatio spiritualis,* which man derives from Christ as the second Adam (1 Cor 4:15; Gal 4:19).

It should cause the priest, because of his universal pastoral love, to sacrifice the very intimate love and self-giving in marriage and the family, in favour of a less intimate but more universal self-dedication in love to the flock entrusted to him. Such dedication is endangered by worldly commitments (see *Celibacy*).

Whereas in the priest's motivation to virginity the aspect of love of neighbour comes more to the fore, in the virginity which is a type of the Church, greater emphasis is laid on the aspect of the love of the spouse for God. Virginity, to give itself to God who gives himself to us in Christ (see *Eucharist* I), transcends the world with its functionalization, and sex, the significance of which is seen in the last analysis to be merely relative.

Virginity so regarded is an attempt to free oneself as far as may be from earthly ties and to set up a standard for the neighbour, who is tempted to lose himself to the world and especially to sex. Love of neighbour must be transcended to the love of God, perfect human fulfilment is possible only in this dialogue with God which rises superior to the neighbour. Man is still on pilgrimage to him, yet on this journey, God, although hidden, already comes to meet him.

The evangelical counsel of virginity is consequently misunderstood if, in a type of two-tiered morality, continence is regarded in principle, not only in the individual case, as of higher value than well-ordered sexual activity, and consequently the latter as of less value in principle. Such is the case when continence is demanded as a means to liberation or purification from diabolical influences or for attaining power over these influences because a dualistic concept of man (see *Dualism*) considers the spirit as good and the body as evil. Sexual activity is then seen as rendering impure and as a result continence is demanded. The same tendency is seen in the Stoic theory of the passions (see *Stoicism*), according to which the actualization of sex is diametrically opposed to the cardinal virtue of ἀταραξία, imperturbable self-control. Sexual activity in this view, because of its lack of control, endangers the powers of the soul, whereas continence leads to higher wisdom. Insufficient too is the justification of continence taken from ethical intellectualism, according to which the sexual act is regarded as of less value because of the *iactura mentis,* thus, e.g., in Aristotle. Not far removed from this is the egocentric view that family and sexual activity are a barrier to individual perfection, since they are a distraction (even St. Jerome justifies celibacy with the argument that it preserves one from the inconveniences and difficulties of family life). Related to this view too is the notion that he who possesses the love of God must renounce human love. Dedication to God is held to exclude self-giving dedication to man. Thus, for example, in various mystery and sacerdotal cults, continence is regarded as a necessary pre-condition for certain religious functions, especially at ritual ceremonies. In this connection the notion crops up that continence (in a magical way) has power to put one in contact with the Omnipotent (especially in Indian religions) and leads to ecstatic union with God (ἱερὸς γάμος). In the OT too continence is required during the sacred ministry (Exod 19:15; 1 Sam 21:4; Zech 7:3). Frequently, however, in pagan philosophy chastity, virginity and marriage are regarded as adiaphora, as being morally indifferent between virtue and sin.

On the other hand, for the true evaluation of the significance of virginity all over-valuation in principle of well-ordered sexual activity, as opposed to continence, is to be rejected (D 2336). Such misinterpretation of continence obtains in the case where it is regarded as desirable only for those who are still unmarried, when, namely, extra-marital chastity is regarded as meaningful only as a preparation and protection for marriage, so that the unmarried is held in principle to be inferior to the married. This notion is widespread in non-Christian religions, e.g., in Islam and in Amida-Buddhism. This concept prevails also in the OT where the pre-marital chastity of girls is valued and demanded (Gen 34:7, 31; Exod 22:15f.; Deut 22:14–19, 28f.; Lev 21:13f.; cf. 21:7; Ezek 44:22; 2 Sam 13:20; Deut 22:20f.). But to remain unmarried (Is 4:1), and even to be childless (Gen 30:23; 1 Sam 1:6, 11, 15; Is 49:21), is regarded as a disgrace. To die before marriage is a disaster (Jg 11:37f.), to which in times of emergency even polygamy is preferable (Is 4:1). In early Judaism these notions undergo a change. In circles close to the Essenes even abstention from marriage is held to an extent in honour.

Our point of view requires that in preaching justification for the value of virginity must abstain from all devaluation in principle of sexuality and of marriage and that the charismatic character of virginity must be stressed. (Motives such as "domination over the body", "full possession of the spiritual self", etc., are not specifically Christian.) Pastoral care should stress that only those markedly capable of love are suited to a life of virginity and can credibly present it in its character as witness. Only thus can one do justice to the natural significance of *eros* and *sexus,* which should unfold in the life of virginity in *philia* and *agape,* especially since abstention from marriage can, without love, easily turn to hardness, eccentricity, etc. In spite of the important connection between personal vitality and the experience of the gift of human love, one should not go so far as to regard only the strong and sound personalities as suited to a life of virginity, since charismatic capability and natural temperament are not the same thing. This imposes on the Church authorities a serious responsibility to advise and accept a commitment to a life of virginity only from those who are prudently judged to be really suited to it. The juridical obligation to a life according to the counsel which is not a matter of general obligation (see *Law* II) is from this point of view questionable, above all if the charismatic power of loving is absent or extinguished. This can easily lead to serious psychosomatic disturbances. Care must further be taken that the capability of young unmarried people of growing in love must be encouraged and they must also be given the human love they need. On the other hand, preaching would be just as defective if it gave way to the tendency to over-value sexuality and marriage, for it is precisely the counsel to virginity that should make clear their basically relative significance.

See also *Evangelical Counsels, Vow, Celibacy* (with bibliographies), *Sex* I, *Marriage* I, *Martyrdom.*

BIBLIOGRAPHY. E. von Dobschütz, *Christian Life in the Primitive Church* (1904); J. Fischer, *Ehe und Jungfräulichkeit im Neuen Testament* (1919); J. Dillesberger, *Wer es fassen kann* (1932); A. D. Nock, "Eunuchs in Ancient Religion", *Archiv für Religionswissenschaft* 23 (1925), pp. 25–33; J. Möhler, *Der ungeteilte Dienst* (1938); T. Camelot, *Virgines Christi* (1944) (in French); D. von Hildebrand, *In Defence of Purity* (1950); W. Schöllgen, *Anima* 7 (1952), pp. 194–201; A. Löhr, *ibid.,* pp. 207–20; L. M. Weber, *ibid.,* pp. 220–7; W. Umbricht, *ibid.,* pp. 227–35; A. Willwoll, R. Gutzwiller, J. Zürcher, J. Miller and L. Hunkeler, *ibid.,* pp. 235–57, 262–7; *Mystique et Continence* (Collective work, Bruges, 1952); F. Bourassa, *La virginité chrétienne* (1953); O. Nemecek, *Die Wertschätzung der Jungfräulichkeit* (1953); Pius XII, *Sacra Virginitas* (encyclical); *AAS* 46 (1954), pp. 175 ff.; G. Delling, "παρθένος", *TWNT,* V, pp. 824–35; J.-M. Perrin, *La virginité chrétienne* (1955); G. Novello, *La virginità nel laicato* (1955); R.

Guardini, *Ehe und Jungfräulichkeit* (1956); id., *Virtues* (1967); J. Blinzler, "εἰσὶν εὐνοῦχοι", *Zeitschrift für die neutestamentliche Wissenschaft* 48 (1957), pp. 67–99; J. I. O'Connor, *American Ecclesiastical Review* 140 (1959), pp. 17–26; H. Fichtner, *Erfüllung der Ehelosigkeit* (1959); J. Fuchs, *De castitate et ordine sexuali* (1959), pp. 21–29; J. Ziegler, *Die Modifizierung der Tugend der Jungfräulichkeit unter dem Einfluß der antiken Philosophie* (dissertation, Würzburg, 1959); id., *Antike Enthaltung und christliche Jungfräulichkeit* (*ibid.,* 1959); W. Bertrams, *Der Zölibat des Priesters* (1960); H. Doms, *Dieses Geheimnis ist gross* (1960), pp. 20–41; A. Gajary, *Die dogmatischen und aszetischen Grundlagen der Jungfräulichkeit* (1960); L. Hödl, "Die lex continentiae", *ZKT* 83 (1961), pp. 325–44; M. Thurian, *Consecration of the Layman* (1963); W. Pesch, "Paulus über die Ehelosigkeit", *Ordenskorrespondenz* 6 (1965), pp. 279–91; L. M. Weber, *On Marriage, Sex and Virginity* (1966); J. Guitton, *Feminine Fulfilment* (1967); id., *Human Love* (1967).

Waldemar Molinski

VIRTUE

I. Acquired and Infused Virtues. II. Love as the Key Virtue: A. Methodical Preliminaries. B. Love in General. C. God's Love for Man. D. Justification by Love in Theology. E. Love of God and Love of Neighbour: Unity and Difference.

I. Acquired and Infused Virtues

1. *Introduction and general concept.* Virtue in the widest sense is any perfectly developed capacity of man's spiritual soul, or the development itself. There can therefore be virtue, for example, in the domain of cognition: intellectual virtues. In the narrower sense, virtue is the power (ability, skill, facility) to realize moral good, and especially to do it joyfully and perseveringly even against inner and outer obstacles and at the cost of sacrifices. The contrary of this habitual ability and readiness (over and above the mere capacity) is vice. According to origin, nature, goal (and mode of acquisition), distinctions are drawn between natural and supernatural ("infused") virtues. The natural virtues are rooted in the corporeal-spiritual nature of man, concern the ability and readiness of man's natural powers and are developed by correct and constant practice in accordance with the nature of those powers and their acts. They are therefore acquired virtues and have a corresponding component in the corporeal-psychological substratum of man, in instinctive drives, associations, etc. They perfect human character, concern the moral formation of its corporeal-spiritual individ-

uality and are the necessary, habitual defence against concupiscence and domination by instinctive drives. According to the ancient standard classification, the most important basic and comprehensive natural virtues, which of course by grace and the infused virtues can be supernaturally directed towards God himself and the direct possession of God, are the cardinal virtues, prudence, justice, fortitude and temperance. The endeavour is made with greater or less success by means of various logical classifications to reduce to these four virtues the innumerable ways of objectively and subjectively appropriate moral action in relation to the whole of reality.

We speak of supernatural, infused virtues, i.e., virtues bestowed by God in justification, as the dynamism of sanctifying grace. This is because by man's supernatural vocation and by supernatural grace as God's self-communication, the whole personal, spiritual life of man is directed in knowledge and freedom (love) towards direct, eternal sharing in the life of the triune God, and this goal has to be reached by the free acceptance of God's self-communication. Consequently grace renders man's spiritual faculties capable of this acceptance (which is one but manifold). This happens in such a way that these acts also correspond as regards the subject performing them, to the acceptance of divine self-communication. They must therefore also have God himself as their ground. These virtues orientate the religious moral being and action of man even in this life towards a direct sharing in the life of the triune God. They thus confer the possibility of directing one's life freely to that goal in a way that is proportionate to its nature, and to attaining it as truly one's own. Such supernatural virtues are therefore very closely connected with the supernatural sanctifying grace of justification of which they are simply the living dynamism. They are only distinguished from the grace which divinizes man's very being as its dynamic extension into his faculties, analogous to the way in which man's faculties are distinguished from his substance. They are a number of ordered ways (of increasing degrees of intensity) in which man can concretely and freely accept the proffered grace of justification, and in which that grace, when accepted, takes roots and is distributed as it were through man's manifold nature.

The supernatural infused virtues, therefore, which do not belong to man's essence but

337

are bestowed by God as a loving favour in his free self-communication, are not really like the natural, acquired virtues, the habitual ability to use a permanent capacity, but are the very capacity for salutary action itself, the capacity to share even now in the life and glory *(doxa)* of God and to shape one's life as a history of the coming of eternal life in time. The infused virtues as such do not therefore necessarily imply any special facility in salutary action, even though they are bestowed in conjunction with justification and although they involve a real dynamism for the development of the divine life in us. Habitual ability and facility in such a supernatural life has to be acquired, in the same way as with natural virtues.

It must not be overlooked either, that these supernatural virtues stand in a similar relation to the natural capacities (and their *habitus* and virtues) as supernatural grace does to man's spiritual nature. That grace is not a second nature superimposed on natural nature; it is the opening out of the natural spiritual essential ground of man towards the immediate possession of God, the teleological orientation of man's natural spiritual nature towards the life of God. The supernatural virtues are therefore not virtues side by side with the spiritual faculty or side by side with the natural virtues. They are the orientation of precisely those faculties and their natural virtues towards the life of God. As the whole man is to be brought to salvation by the whole activity of his life, it is really self-evident that grace and the dynamism of its virtues should direct the whole life of man towards God and that accordingly there are as many supernatural virtues for the branches and growth of the one root of supernatural life, as there are natural virtues. An actually Christian ethics in the concrete does not therefore need to be very much concerned about the distinction between natural and supernatural virtues. In the actually existing order of God's universal salvific will, the natural virtues have in fact a supernatural goal and the supernatural virtues are accomplished and manifested in what we have to experience and carry out as natural virtues in the sober, empirical and harsh reality of everyday life. If one asks what supernatural virtues are, it can be said very simply and in slightly "demythologized" terms, that they are the willing, well-practised and genuine (not merely half-hearted or hypocritical) decency of an honest, courageous, loving man,

inasmuch as these human things by God's action are much more than human, because in them in faith, hope and love the eternal life is at work in which man possesses the life of God himself.

2. *The three fundamental supernatural virtues, the "theological virtues".* From what has been said of the virtues in general, it follows that the real function of the supernatural, infused virtues is to orientate the whole religious ethical life (which itself expresses the spiritual nature of man) towards the immediate possession of God. Scripture and tradition accordingly speak of a triad of such fundamental supernatural virtues which are specified by their being the basic modes of increasing acceptance of the divine self-communication by grace and of directing man's spiritual, personal life towards the trinitarian God of eternal life by a sharing in God's life itself. They have God himself as formal object by the fact that God in uncreated grace himself is the ground of the "capacity" and its act, and is both immediate object and co-principle of the act of faith, hope, love. This triad is already found in the NT (1 Cor 13:13; 1 Thess 1:3; 5:8; Eph 1:15–18; Col 1:4f.; Heb 10:22–24). The Council of Trent declared the three theological virtues to be "infused" with the grace of justification (*D* 800), without seeking to determine the exact relation between sanctifying grace and infused charity (e.g., are they identical or not?). At all events the infused virtues (not love, but) faith and hope can remain even when sanctifying grace is lost (*D* 808, 838). It is disputed whether they can be acquired, as *habitus,* even *before* justification, by actual faith and hope. They are called theological virtues (in contradistinction to infused or acquired moral virtues) because their formal object is not a finite moral personal value (veracity, moral worth of honouring God, etc.), but God himself, as he makes himself the life of man by his self-communication. They are to be regarded as *habitus* (*D* 821), as a lasting capacity for a life directed to God.

These three theological virtues do not come into action only when it is a question of actions expressly related to the God who has revealed himself. They crown the whole moral life of the justified person and direct it towards eternal life as its goal, when a human being in a fundamental decision which is the basis of, and contributes to determine, all particular acts, hears God's promise of himself, hopes in the absolute future and in love of God's love and glory entrusts himself wholly to God. To that extent it is really more a question of terminology than of substance whether or not there are infused moral virtues in addition to the theological virtues (as is generally taught: *D* 483; *Catechismus Romanus,* II, 2, 50). At all events the activity of the justified person in the power of the Holy Spirit is accomplished not only in explicitly religious acts but in the whole activity of moral life, as, for example, where the neighbour is loved in an act of the theological virtue of love of God. "Theological virtues" is the rather portentous name for the experience of the accepted grace of God, which is, ultimately, God himself. Wherever man unconditionally (with unconditional responsibility, in love, in hope, etc.) accepts his transcendence over everything finite and under his command, a transcendence which is truly set free by God's grace for God himself and his incomprehensible mystery, he experiences, though perhaps in a very implicit and anonymous way, impossible to objectivate the attraction of the divine Spirit towards God himself, his cry of Abba-Father in inexpressible sighs (Rom 8:16f., 23, 26), the life of the divine virtues.

See also *Good, Nature* I, *Grace* I, II, *Justification, Faith* II, *Hope, Charity, Habitus, Transcendence, Virtue* II.

BIBLIOGRAPHY. GENERAL: J. Stelzenberger, *Die Beziehungen der frühchristlichen Sittenlehre zur Ethik der Stoa* (1933); W. Wittmann, *Die Ethik des heiligen Thomas von Aquin* (1933), pp. 217–317; C. Spicq, *Revue Biblique* 53 (1946), pp. 36–46; O. Bollnow, *Wesen und Wandel der Tugenden* (1958); J. Pieper, *Prudence, the First Cardinal Virtue* (1959); id., *The Four Cardinal Virtues* (1965); R. Schnackenburg, *The Moral Teaching of the New Testament* (1965); R. Guardini, *Virtues* (1967); see also the general works, A. Landgraf, *Dogmengeschichte,* I/1 (1952), pp. 161–83; O. Lottin, *Morale fondamentale* (1954); id., *Psychologie et Morale aux XII*ᵉ *et XIII*ᵉ *siècles,* 4 vols. (1942–54), III, pp. 97–535; IV, pp. 27–92; B. Häring, *Law of Christ,* I (1961); *DTC,* XV, cols. 2730–99; *Ephemerides Theologicae Lovanienses* 40 (1964), pp. 135ff. SPECIAL: N. Heinrichs, *Die Bedeutung der Missionstheologie* (1954) (Western and Chinese notions of virtues); P. Cirsis, *Ennoblement of Pagan Virtues* (1955); G. Bullet, *Vertus morales infuses . . . selon S. Thomas d'Aquin* (1958); R. Hofmann, *Moraltheologische Erkenntnis und Methodenlehre* (1963); J. Alfaro, *Fides, Spes, Caritas* (1963).

Karl Rahner

II. Love as the Key Virtue

A. METHODICAL PRELIMINARIES

1. Love is here understood in such a way that it can be predicated of the relationship of God to man, of the relationship of man to God and of men among themselves (on which last aspect see also *Charity* II). Such a use of the word means that its scope is so enlarged and at the same time so manifold that it can only with difficulty escape being reduced to a sort of barely intelligible code-word.

2. The word "love" takes in so much in Christianity that it can no longer denote only a particular element somewhere within, so to speak, our world of experience. It has to mean the whole of experience, in the mode proper to it, if it is to be capable of goodness and perfection. (And here again, goodness and perfection must be thought of as love, if the notion of such fulfilment is not to degenerate into a rigid formalism.) It follows at once that such love cannot be defined by elements outside itself or from which it can be "composed", as though of parts. It can only be described, not defined.

3. Since love is a mysterious key-word for the (true) whole of man — for it means the whole man as he is drawn away from himself into the incomprehensible mystery of God — its content is determined by all that makes him man, and hence by his historicity (see *History* I). Love has a history, which means more than its recurring again and again in time. It takes on in its exercise, and in reflection on its acts (in the theory of its practice), constantly changing forms and aspects and shifts of emphasis in each concrete moment of its commitment. As a result, love may be, and in fact has been, simply one of the key-words by which men have sought to express the totality of historical existence (see *Existence* I). Hence "love", being a word which aims at summing up the whole of a human existence and not just this or that process within it, is found in one way or another in all religions (cf. T. Ohm). It takes a very central place as early as Deuteronomy (Deut 6:4f., etc.) but only becomes the real key-word and absolutely central theme in the NT, while the subsequent history of theology can hardly be said to have maintained it clearly in this role. So it still remains objectively possible to envisage this basic relation of the whole man to God and his fellows under another aspect and hence

to describe it by means of another key-word. Obvious competitors, from the Bible and the history of theology, are faith or hope. But others are conceivable. Since the transcendentals *(unum, verum, bonum)* are related to each other in a unity and difference which form together an ultimate, any of these words, if thought out in full, will merge into the others and can thus be used as a key-word, though none of them says quite the same thing. The historical background — and kerygmatic discretion — suggest that the interchangeability of the permanently diverging elements of such key-words of human experience should be borne in mind. Kerygmatically, the word "love" should not be harped upon too much. Nonetheless, it remains the great NT word for what God is and for what man ought to be, and must always remain central in the preaching of the Christian message.

4. The methodological question becomes still more acute when the attribution of love to God extends to the affirmation that God *is* love, that love is his "essence" ("Deus formaliter est caritas", according to Duns Scotus.) One can of course explain what one means by saying that God is love (see C below). But then one has to remember that love then merges into the absolute mystery of God's being, and hence becomes incomprehensible to us, so that the affirmation — particularly as regards love for *us* — can only be a radical act of faith and hope. The love of God for us is not simply an experience to be taken for granted. It is hoped for, in faith, "against hope" (Rom 4:18).

B. Love in General

1. *Classical definitions.* We cannot here attempt to trace the history of the concept of love in philosophy and theology. Much less can we attempt here a phenomenology of love as it is known by men in their interpersonal experiences, with all their different stages of bodily and mental development (the relationship of mother and child, sexual love in the strict sense, etc.; see *Marriage, Sex*). We confine ourselves to certain themes of philosophy and theology which seem to suggest ways of rounding out and differentiating the notion. It will not always be possible to make a neat distinction between the various approaches in question, and the history of the various "definitions" must be omitted. Our main interest will be to bring out the problematic element which remains consistently throughout.

a) *Love as amor benevolentiae and amor concupiscentiae — "selfless" and "desirous" love.* If love is the total act in which one person achieves the fully correct relationship to another (see *Human Act*) by "acknowledging" and accepting the other in his total personal excellence and dignity, two aspects of this relationship appear at once. There is the relationship of the one who loves to the other, and the converse relationship which is also grasped and accepted in the giving of love.

The subject, through the transcendence and freedom in which it can grasp the substantial selfhood of the other and thus be truly its own self (i.e., attain "happiness"), acknowledges and accepts the other in its independence, dignity and irreplaceable otherness. It recognizes the other as truly and validly existing "in itself". It wills the other subject as the permanently other. But at the same time the subject grasps and affirms the significance of the other for itself (the loving subject) and refers it to itself. Hence *amor benevolentiae* and *amor concupiscentiae* are not in mutual conflict. They are aspects of the same love, which are based on the transcendence of the subject which is capable of affirming and willing the other. One is ordained not merely to know but also to will the personal reality of the other qua other, and this is precisely what one grasps as significant for oneself.

This truth does not mean that there cannot be shifts of emphasis acting and reacting on these elements of the one love. One result of this is that traditional theology has rather insisted on the opposition between *amor benevolentiae* and *amor concupiscentiae,* so much so that the two acts could appear to be separable. But then the *amor benevolentiae* could be reduced to an uninterested willingness to let the other be, or was regarded — as by Spinoza — as merely the mechanism by which "objective" acknowledgment was brought about *(amor intellectualis Dei).* The *amor concupiscentiae* then becomes "self-centred" and part of the theological virtue of hope rather than of charity (the *amor benevolentiae,* as the response to God's self-communication, the grace which inspires this response). But in spite of all possible shifts of accent as between the two aspects, it is to be noted that the most "selfless", self-forgetful ("ek-static") love, being the most radical commitment, is "passionate" in the most sublime sense. Otherwise it would not achieve the fullness of its being. It is therefore by its nature the affirmation of, the happiness of, the being of the subject itself. And an *amor concupiscentiae* which tried to make the other merely a means to its own happiness would not be love at all but a selfish effort to satisfy a particular desire. And this would mean that the subject itself failed to attain its own real being. (In the light of these considerations, the whole debate about attrition and contrition would need a radical reappraisal; see *Contrition*.)

b) *Eros — agape*. This distinction, worked out by A. Nygren, means that *eros* (in the Greek interpretation of love) is the love of desire and "passion". Fascinated and carried away by the actual excellence and beauty of the "You", the object of aesthetic contemplation and love, it tries to draw the beloved to itself as its own happiness. *Agape,* however (in the biblical sense), is the love of God which bends down to the sinful and worthless, the love that gives without receiving, that lavishes itself foolishly and is the sole reason why man becomes worthy of this love. And it is only by pure grace that man is enabled finally to participate in this divine *agape* and display it towards God and his fellowman.

This distinction is correct and (religiously) important, inasmuch as only God's love can be really absolutely creative. Created love is always a response to an actual excellence (which is ultimately God's primal love). The radical conversion to the fellowman and to God is inspired by God's radical love of us which is there in his self-communication. But the distinction cannot be used simply to distinguish pagan and Christian love or to designate types of love which are mutually exclusive. For over and beyond the word of revelation in the OT and the NT there is the self-communication of God which is coextensive with all history (by virtue of the universal salvific will), and this offers all men the possibility of *agape* towards God and their fellowmen which only grave sin can exclude. "Natural" *eros* (see *Nature and Grace*) is at once a *potentia oboedientialis* for such *agape,* since, if it does not culpably forfeit its own nature, it wills the other *as* the other and not just its own happiness. (For when this happiness is rightly understood and fully perfected, it consists of "selfless" love of the other.) Hence all human love, even "spiritual" love, which flows from "bodily" man, has also an "erotic" foundation which it

need not be ashamed of and which comes to its fulfilment in the very fulfilment of this personal love (see *Resurrection* II, *Potentia Oboedientialis*).

c) *Love of self — love of others*. Can one love oneself, as seems to be assumed by Scripture, Mt 22:39, or is all self-affirmation, no matter how transcendentally necessary, essentially "egoistic", the inevitable sinfulness of man, the inextinguishable reflex of original sin, and hence the opposite of love? Scholastic theology in general rightly affirms that love — even as *virtus caritatis theologicae infusae* — can and ought to refer the subject to itself, making this love a "duty". The assumption is that such self-affirmation is not simply surrender to the instinctive drives of the "struggle for existence", but is based on objective recognition of the value and dignity of the subject within reality as a whole and in relation to God. This God-given excellence is not loved simply because it is one's own, but because it *is* and is of value. This is of course not to deny that in actual fact the *amor sui* (in St. Augustine's sense) is not constantly perverted into egoism (as *contemptus Dei*). In view of this fundamentally affirmative answer to our question, it must also be affirmed that God loves himself. This does not make him an egoist, for he affirms his infinite "objective" perfection, and does so precisely inasmuch as it is the *bonum diffusivum sui,* the "selfless love" which is his essence (cf. 1 Jn 4:7–10). These considerations are important for a proper understanding of the biblical and ecclesiastical doctrine of the glory of God.

d) *Thomist and Scotist interpretations*. The debate between these schools on the nature of love may be understood and theoretically solved on the basis of the foregoing. Scotism regards love as the "ecstatic" outgoing of the lover from himself. He forgets himself to take a "centrifugal" attitude towards what is no longer seen in terms of himself, what is not *his* good. He loves God for what he is in himself and not for what he is for us. He would still love God if, *per impossibile,* he were to damn the lover. Thomism sees in love the natural inclination by which the subject seeks its good, which in the case of man, in contrast to the infra-human creature, can only "satisfy" when infinite. Hence love of God and a rightly understood self-love, which does not culpably fall short of man's nature, are two aspects of the same love in which man finds himself when he loses himself in the love of God. The Thomist view is correct in terms of existential ontology. But from the point of view of phenomenology, and in view of the seriousness of life's decisions, in view of the difficulty man has in finding himself in his sin-ridden history, Scotism is right in pointing out that he must make an effort which is apparently almost suicidal if he is to attain his true being. He must break out of his finite categories and his sinful egoism, in faith and hope, inspired by a love which must be bestowed on him by the selfless agape of God.

e) In the history of the discussion, several other aspects of love have been brought out, which can only be exemplified here by a small, random selection. Up to the present, we have considered love only as addressed to a personal, spiritual subject, basing ourselves on the correct assumption that love in the strict sense can only exist in these terms. It remains true, however, that love is often mentioned in connection with other objects. If what is meant is some positive good will and correct attitude, and if the distinction between this and true interpersonal love is not lost sight of, in theory or practice, there is no objection to such a use of the term, e.g., when speaking of "love" of animals. It is even possible that such love of seemingly impersonal things may really be addressed to the God who is hidden and present and really loved himself there, provided that such things are not wrongly loved when their nature is mistaken and idolized. There is a right and a wrong sense in which men may speak of an *amor fati* or a "cosmic" love or be, like Keats, "in love with easeful Death". Hence love can be interpreted in the light of other basic human experiences, e.g., as actual fellowship, as friendship, as selfless service, as adoration (in love of God).

f) In the historical debate on the nature of love, a problem which is basically the same has constantly come up — that of the relationship between knowledge and will (which reappears at a different stage in the three divisions of man's spiritual faculties in modern, non-metaphysical thinking). In "Greek" intellectualism, the will seems little else than the dynamism and mechanism of knowledge (will to truth, love of truth). And then love is just the connatural happiness of the possession of the good — which is truth. Conversely, knowledge can appear as the mere pre-condition (light) of love. Neither view does justice to the unity of truth and goodness (and hence of intellect and will), which a profounder view sees

persisting even in their mutual irreducibility. Love is not merely a prelude to and by-product of Gnosis, as there was a tendency to hold in Greek patristics. And knowledge is not merely the presupposition of love. The "dualism", the unity but not total identity of the two acts is seen to be irreducible in the doctrine of the two "processions" in the Trinity.

But then the problem arises once more as to why the whole of Christian existence can simply be characterized as love, as is done in tradition. In the light of this question-mark, one is forced to say that love only represents the ultimate key-word of Christian existence insofar as it makes this existence fully sound and complete (like the *ordo* in the trinitarian processions). But then it is truly the key-word. Nonetheless, this does not mean that the knowledge which comes "earlier" in the transcendental structure of man's spirit is to be assigned a merely instrumental function, or that love is to be understood as merely the bliss of possessing the truth.

2. *Further characteristics.* Since there can be no question of giving a "definition" of love, what has been said under B, 1, above, may be taken as a general description of love. A few remarks are now added to call attention to some points which are perhaps less explicitly treated in scholastic theology than the matter given in B, 1.

a) The dualism of *essentia* and *esse,* of idea and reality (in the sense of *existentia* in Scholasticism), has always been recognized, and has always remained an impenetrable enigma. They are unintelligible except in constant relationship to one another, but neither can be reduced to the other or understood as a mere moment of the other. One can follow St. Thomas, and take *esse* to be prior to *essentia* (ideal being), so that the real is not just the there-ness of an ideal quiddity, adding nothing, as far as one can see, to the "eternal truth". But this does not really get rid of the continuing dualism. It has to be accepted as an inescapable fundamental reality, in spite of all the considerations that must be offered on the matter, and above all on the many changes in the relationship of the two elements and the unity which they form without being flatly identical. But the notion of love is particularly relevant when this mysterious element in the make-up of all beings is considered. If idea becomes reality and reality takes on the light of the ideal and attains the essence accepted by it (an acceptance necessary if reality is not to waste away in darkness); if reality is also accepted in its "factualness" (and God himself, being free, is "factual" in his aseity, which cannot be reduced to an "eternal idea") — then love is at work, i.e., the will, which does not shrink from accomplishing this. Love is reality's harmony with itself in the positive non-identity of *essentia* and *esse,* which implies an element of the *de facto* — though the latter is only true of God in an analogous way.

b) *Love as offer and response.* The point to be made here is perhaps best approached by repeating the ancient question as to whether one can love if one is not loved by the beloved. If the answer is in the affirmative, it must be remembered that such unrequited love can always be inspired by the hope of a future return of love, no matter how unforeseeable. (In fact, since St. Augustine, traditional theology has explained the possibility of love of enemies on this ground and affirmed that the damned cannot be loved.) Hence the principle must be maintained that love is dialogal. Otherwise the interpenetration of *eros* and *agape,* of selfless and "desirous" love (see A, 1, above), would be unintelligible. One cannot truly, validly and responsibly commit oneself to another (i.e., love) unless the other accepts fundamentally and definitively this radical gift of self (i.e., unless he loves too). But here we must anticipate what will be said under E below on the unity of love of God and of the neighbour. Wherever love is offered to another, the loving God is always partner in the dialogue (though mostly in a non-explicit way). This means that it is always rational to open the dialogue of love, though it does not mean that every such offer of love among men will be answered by a similar love, one that is perhaps desired only selfishly. But the appeal of love is always such that an answer from the other part must be given. Love is dialogal. And hence love of God is always in the nature of a response to the *agape* of God, which is an unfathomable grace. Responsive love is nonetheless free and marvellous, in the eyes of him who offers love. For by its nature love does not move with the stringent certainty of deductive truths. Its realm is that of the freely factual, actual reality. Love is always grace and true grace is love.

c) *Love and hope.* In spite of the doctrine of the three theological virtues, it seems hard to fit hope, and its relationship to love, into the schemata used to describe love above. The schemata in question were always twofold: knowledge and will, *essentia* and *esse,* the two trinitarian processions and so on. One could simply say that hope was love under the aspect of *amor concupiscentiae* as long as such love was still not in possession of its good *(bonum arduum)* but did not need to despair of attaining it. But this is certainly to do less than justice to the relationship of hope and love. Since love is dialogal, it always depends on the possible answer of the other (or if given, on its freely remaining so) and hence on the incalculable. There is therefore an element of hope in all aspects of love, not just in "desirous" love. Even when love is perfected, hope remains (1 Cor 13:13) (on the function of hope as mediator between faith and love, see K. Rahner, *Schriften zur Theologie,* VIII, pp. 561–79). See also *Hope.*

C. GOD'S LOVE FOR MAN

1. As regards the truth and meaning of the affirmation that God loves man, in *agape,* the major elements are dealt with under other headings; see *Creation, Grace, Providence, Salvation* I, IV, *Revelation* II. The biblical and ecclesiastical commentaries on this proposition may be supposed from these articles. Ultimately, God's *agape* consists in his giving himself in love to the world in the spiritual creature. Through his self-communication he makes himself the inmost mystery of his creation, and its history and its fulfilment. He is not just Lord and Guardian, while creation itself remains "outside" God. This love is the cause of there being others than itself, but it holds these differences together in their relationship to its own oneness, which is God. It contains (analogously) an element of "jealousy" ("desire") because the self-sufficient God willed in a free act of love to need a world which is his own history because of his self-communication in grace and the incarnation. It is dialogal ("bridal"; see *Covenant*), because it is the foundation and principle of man's love for God, since by grace man can love God in a divine way, just as he can utter the word *of God* in human words (see *Faith, Revelation* I). In this way man's loving Yes to God is from God. This explains why the notion of "Father" is only partially adequate to express the love of God for man. "Son" must be understood in the sense in which Jesus knew himself to

be Son and us as sons by participation. It is only the radical intimacy of self-communication in grace and the incarnation that eliminates the overtones of the external and paternalistic which may be heard in the "Fatherliness" of God. This love can appear as the sovereign law which demands the humbly obedient love of the "servant". But then all the elements which go to make up the relationship of law and gospel must be considered (see *Law and Gospel*).

2. It is difficult to preach today that God loves man, that by his self-communication he is love itself for him. This situation must be seen clearly and soberly. It has become clearer — though it was "always" recognized — that God is not part of the world, that he is not to be found as a particular reality within the realm of our experience. His "distance", his inexpressibility, the radical mysteriousness of his being, is the epochal hall-mark imposed on our existence. It is not so easy to realize as is sometimes supposed in unthinking pious talk that this God can love us, with a personal relationship to each individual which offers shelter to each. The atheism which appears as "silence about that of which one cannot clearly speak", as well as the atheism of tragic despair at the horrors of human existence, are now challenges which consistently menace even the faith of Christian theists in the love of God, in a loving God. We cannot now speak of God's love for us as though we were addressing men who have repressed all their experiences of the absurd and are so comfortably well-balanced that they find it very instructive to be told that the world is on the whole very well ordered and governed by a God of love. There must be a deep solidarity with a world in torment before one dares speak of the love of God. And then all merely "philosophical" analysis will naturally fall away. To speak of the love of God will be to testify to it in deeds and words, to appeal to men for an ultimate decision in faith and love, where no stringent assurance can be provided. After Auschwitz, it has been said, there is nothing for it but to be an atheist. But it has also been said that in face of the dead of Auschwitz we have to believe in God and hope in his love, since there is no justification for them otherwise and they are betrayed by their own absurdity. In any case, it has to be clearly affirmed that the happiness of posterity — always hoped and planned for in the world and just as con-

stantly crashing to ruin — does not justify the miseries of the past and present. We must not flinch from asserting the hard truth that the love of God is just as much of a mystery as God himself. Cursing the darkness of the world does not make it any brighter. To bear the predestined impotence of our faith in God's love is not the same as to refuse culpably to believe in that love, though frustration and unbelief may not be very far apart. And to love others truly, in deed and will, without self-deception, to do so as an absolutely sacred duty, is fundamentally to believe in God and his love for man, even perhaps unknown to oneself.

D. Justification by Love in Theology

1. *Scripture*. Love of God in the OT and the NT is not described by such words as ἔρως or στοργή. The word φιλία is rare. Instead, the word ἀγάπη is used, with the corresponding verb. The word was introduced into literary and religious usage by the LXX, and given a new content. *Agape* means the love of God for us, and also love of the neighbour, of enemies and of God (in Jn, though also in St. Paul, e.g., 1 Cor 8:3). Our main interest here will be the justifying love of man for God and his neighbour (on the unity of which, see below). This is an act which integrates the whole of man's existence ("with the whole heart" etc.) (Mk 12:20 parr., citing Deut 6:4f.). It is inspired by the Spirit of God (see *Grace*), it is the fruit of the Spirit (Rom 15:30; Gal 5:22; Col 1:8; 2 Tim 1:7). It is the realm of existence within which man should remain (Eph 5:2; 1 Jn 4:16). There one is justified (Rom 13:9f.; 1 Jn 4:16; Gal 5:6; 1 Cor 13:13; Mt 22:36–40; Lk 10:25–28).

2. *Church teaching*. The decisive declarations of the extraordinary magisterium with regard to love were made in connection with the doctrine of justification in the sixth session of the Council of Trent. The fundamental statement is that justification is inseparable from the infused virtue of love (*D* 800, 821) and that the process of justification freely entered upon by the adult only comes to its climax and its fullness in an act of charity (love) (*D* 800f., 819, 889). (This remains true even if one supposes that the grace of justification can be "infused" in the sacrament by reason of mere attrition and only later become actual in an act of

charity [love] — though this is necessary, *D* 1101, 1155 ff., 1289.) Hence in ecclesiastical terminology faith and hope, in spite of their intrinsic tendency to perfect themselves in love (see *Religious Act*) are acts whose specific nature does not imply the full union of man with God in grace (*D* 801, 819, 839, 1525), while this union is rightly and fully expressed by the word "love". The question as to whether charity is infused in infants at baptism, left open earlier (*D* 410, 483), was decided in the affirmative by Trent (*D* 799 f. along with 791 f.), though without denying that the free acceptance of the grace of justification by the adult, through an act of charity, marks the possession of grace. Unlike faith, the infused virtue of love is lost by any mortal sin (*D* 808, 837 f.). No exact description of this love is given. It is distinguished from "natural" love of God, which is thereby treated as theoretically possible (*D* 1034, 1036), and from imperfect and initial (salutary) forms of love of God (*D* 798, 889, 1146). Trent suggests that it can be considered as "friendship" with God (*D* 799, 803). The relationship between love of God and love of the neighbour is not defined precisely. It seems to be a "free opinion" in theology that the two modes of love have exactly the same formal object (Patres S.J. in Hispania, *Sacrae Theologiae Summa*, III, no. 240). The general doctrine of the magisterium on the supernatural virtues, on salutary acts, loss of grace, growth in grace and experience of grace also applies, of course, to the *habitus* and act of this virtue. While the magisterium treats love as the sum total of Christian life which embraces and integrates all else, it resolutely rejects the notion that this excludes all differences in moral and salutary acts. A relative pluralism remains. There are positively salutary acts which are not simply acts of love (*D* 915, 898, 817 f., 798), and the justified, being finite creatures still on pilgrimage and hence unable fully to integrate themselves, can still rightly act from motives other than that of love (*D* 508, 1327 f., 1349, 1394–1408, 1297).

E. Love of God and Love of Neighbour: Unity and Difference

1. This question needs special consideration today. With atheism a social phenomenon, there is a strong temptation to treat God and the love of God merely as a code-word for the inviolable status of man and love of the neighbour, to "demythologize" prayer by treating it as mental dialogue with man and so on. This situation obliges Christians to profess unwaveringly their faith in God. God is not only the "absoluteness" of man. And they must also profess their love of God, which remains the "first commandment" (Mt 22:38). They are also bound to try to reach a real understanding of the true unity of love of God and love of the neighbour, which does not mean that one term can be substituted indifferently for the other. But it is a unity which solves from within the problem of atheistical love of the neighbour, since a love of the neighbour which is truly absolute includes at once a (non-articulated) theism and an implicit love of God. This is in fact why the love of God must be made an explicit theme, since it is the hidden and sublime mystery of human existence.

2. This unity is affirmed by Scripture and tradition. The two commandments (love of God and of the neighbour) are alike. There is nothing in the law and the prophets which does not depend on them (Mt 22:39 f.; Lk 10:28; Mk 12:31). So much so, that St. Paul can simply say that to love the neighbour is to fulfil *the* law (Rom 13:8, 10; Gal 5:14). In Mt, when Jesus speaks of judgment in his eschatological warnings, the only measure mentioned by which man is to be judged is love of the neighbour, and the nature of the final rebellion against God is indicated by saying that the charity of many will grow cold (Mt 25:34–46; 24:12). Love of the neighbour is the royal law (Jas 2:8) and the definitive form of Christian life (1 Cor 12:31–13:13).

The Johannine writings provide the first conscious effort to justify the radical importance thus allotted to love of the neighbour, which might otherwise appear as a pious exaggeration, just as it was later toned down in Christian exhortation, which explained love of the neighbour as a particular element of the Christian obligation, without which, however, in spite of its difficulty, salvation cannot be attained. According to St. John, we are loved by God (Jn 14:21) and by Christ in order that we should love one another (Jn 13:34). This love is the new commandment of Christ (Jn 13:34), his own specific commandment (Jn 15:12), the commandment which he lays upon us (Jn 15:17). For St. John the consequence is that God, who *is* love (1 Jn 4:16), has loved us not in order that we should love him in return but in order that we should love one another (1 Jn 4:7, 11). For we do not see God. He cannot be attained truly alone in an inward mystical Gnosis which would enable him to be really loved in this way (1 Jn 4:12). It is only the "God in us" of mutual love that we can love (1 Jn 4:12), so much so that it is really true, and for St. John an absolutely stringent argument (though one that we do not normally find evident) that "he who does not love his brother whom he has seen, cannot love God whom he has not seen" (1 Jn 4:20).

Traditional theology has resolutely maintained at least that the infused virtue of union with God, the theological *virtus caritatis in Deum,* is also the virtue by which the neighbour is loved. This is all the more striking because tradition admits the existence of other theological and moral virtues distinct from love, and it would not have been difficult to describe love of the neighbour as a special and subordinate virtue. It must be admitted, however, that much remains obscure as regards the unity in question, as proposed in Scripture and tradition. This results in a constant tendency to think of love of the neighbour merely in terms of a duty entailed by the love of God, of which it would also be the touchstone and guarantee.

3. Nonetheless, it should still be maintained that there is a genuine unity, of a radical nature, between the two modes of love. (The presupposition is always that of the self-communication of God in grace to men, the object of love of the neighbour. Merely "philosophical" grounds are not invoked.)

We must bear in mind the following points. A distinction must be made between an explicit, propositional affirmation and an affirmation (bearing on a reality not clearly envisaged) which is virtually there in an act referred explicitly to another object (see *Atheism, Transcendence, Revelation, Human Act, Religious Act*). Then we must recall that all metaphysical knowledge is mediated by historical, intramundane experience, in the light of which alone access is at all possible to the understanding of transcendental realities. Further, the encounter with the neighbour in love must be recognized not as one experience among others, but as the central act of human existence which integrates the whole personal content of experience. Finally, any absolute, (positive)

moral decision must be recognized as implicit theism and "anonymous Christianity". Under these circumstances, it can be affirmed on principle that the act by which the neighbour is loved *is* really the primal (though still non-explicit) act by which God is loved. That God must also be loved in explicit, conscious terms is not thereby excluded — on the contrary. For if there is an implicit reference to God in every moral act, and hence primarily in the love of the neighbour, it must become explicit in man's words and life, since this Godwardness is the ultimate source and force of this central experience of the world (love of the neighbour). Love of God and of the neighbour each live by the other, because they are ultimately one *(inconfuse, indivise)*. Love of God as a deliberate response to the structure of existence is only real when it is love of the neighbour; and the ultimate mystery of love of the neighbour only comes fully into play, its absoluteness and the possibility of this absoluteness – with regard to finite and sinful men — when it surpasses itself to be love of God.

4. The history of salvation shows that the climax and the ultimate guarantee of the unity of love of God and of the neighbour is our love of Jesus Christ, in whom God and man are united (see *Incarnation*). Speaking as the Son of man, he declares that he is the mysterious partner who is included in all active love for men (Mt 25:34–40), so that the unity of the love which embraces him and the fellowman is decisive for the destiny of each man, even where this unity is not recognized (Mt 25:37ff.). This is better understood when one recalls that genuine love for man opens out on love of all, and that dialogal, responsorial love for a finite and sinful man, untrustworthy therefore and possibly hostile, is an implicit affirmation of the God-man, present or hoped-for, as its ground and guarantee. This is how it has the absoluteness which is due to it as an act done by divine grace. Jesus therefore demands explicitly that his disciples should love him (Jn 8:42; 14:15, 21, 23, 28), so that the love of the Father for the Son may embrace those who love the Son (Jn 14:21, 23; 17:23, 26) and that these may "abide in his love" (Jn 15:9f.; 1 Jn 4:7), the all-embracing love which takes in God, the God-man and man, who are all both subjects and objects of this one love.

See also *Charity* I.

BIBLIOGRAPHY. See bibliography on *Charity* I; also: J. Klein, *Die Caritaslehre des Johannes Duns Scotus* (1926); N. Glueck, "Das Wort hesed im alttestamentlichen Sprachgebrauch", *Beiheft zur ZAW* 47 (1927); H. Arendt, *Der Liebesbegriff bei Augustinus* (1929); J. Moffat, *Love in the New Testament* (1929); H. Preisker, *Die urchristliche Botschaft von der Gottesliebe* (1930) (comparative religion); J. Ziegler, *Die Liebe Gottes bei den Propheten* (1930); G. Combès, *La charité d'après St. Augustin* (1934); W. Schlatter, *Die Liebe Gottes* (1935) (biblical); F. Weinrich, *Die Liebe im Buddhismus und Christentum* (1935); R. Frieling, *Die göttliche Liebe im Johannes-Evangelium* (1936); M. D. Philippe, *Le rôle de l'amitié dans la vie chrétienne selon St. Thomas d'Aquin* (1938); id., *Mystère de l'amitié divine* (1949); E. Walter, *Glaube, Hoffnung und Liebe im Neuen Testament* (1940); F. Prat and others, "Charité", *DSAM*, IX, cols. 507–691; H. Riesenfeld, *Étude bibliographique sur la notion biblique d'ΑΓΑΠΗ* (1941); M. Lottin, *Psychologie et Morale aux XIIᵉ et XIIIᵉ siècles*, 4 vols. (1942–54); C. E. Raven, *Jesus and the Gospel of Love* (1942); E. L. Allen, *A Christology of Love* (1944); Z. Alszeghy, *Grundformen der Liebe* (1946) (Bonaventure); J. Burnaby, *Amor Dei* (in English) (1947); E. Mersch, *Morale et Corps Mystique* (1949); T. Ohm, *Die Liebe zu Gott in den nicht-christlichen Religionen* (1950); H. Asmussen, *Das Geheimnis der Liebe* (1952); J. Gaer, *Love in the New Testament* (1952); L.-B. Geiger, *Le problème de l'amour chez St. Thomas d'Aquin* (1952); A. Pépin, *La charité envers Dieu* (1953); F. Buck, *Die Liebe Gottes beim Propheten Osee* (1953); F. Ross, *Meaning of Love in Hinduism and Buddhism* (1953); L. Moraldi, *Dio è amore* (1954); E. Reisner, *Glaube, Hoffnung, Liebe: Eine Philosophie der christlichen Tugenden* (1954); M. Scheler, *Nature of Sympathy* (1954); id., *Liebe und Erkenntnis* (1955); D. Barsotti, *La rivelazione del amore* (1955); F. X. Durwell, *La charité selon les synoptiques et St. Paul* (1955); A. Malet, *Personne et amour dans la théologie trinitaire de St. Thomas d'Aquin* (1956); C. van Ouwerkerk, *Caritas et Ratio* (1956) (in Dutch); H. Schlüter and others, *Gottesliebe und Weltverantwortung* (1956); R. Völkl, *Die Selbstliebe in der heiligen Schrift und bei Thomas von Aquin* (1956); H. Braun, *Spätjüdisch-häretischer und frühchristlicher Radikalismus,* 2 vols. (1957); P. Delhay, "La charité reine des vertus", *Supplément Vie Spirituelle* 41 (1957), pp. 135–70; M. Nédoncelle, *Vers une spiritualité de l'amour et de la personne* (1957); R. Spiazzi, *Teologia della carità* (1957); F. Varillon, *Fénelon et l'amour pur* (1957); C. Wiéner, *Recherches sur l'amour pour Dieu dans l'Ancien Testament* (1957); H. Christmann, *Thomas von Aquin als Theologe der Liebe* (1958); K. Barth, *Church Dogmatics,* IV/2 (1958), para. 68; R. Grosche, "Verkündigung und christliche Liebe: Et intra et extra", *Theologische Aufsätze* (1958), pp. 64–73; C. Massabki, *Le Christ rencontre les deux amours* (1958); J. Rausch, *Agape and Amicitia: A Comparison between St. Paul and St. Thomas* (1958); C. Spicq, "La philanthropie hellénistique", *Studia Theologica* 12 (1958), pp. 169–91; S. Kierkegaard, *Either/Or,* 2 vols. (1959); H. Vogel, "Die Krisis der Liebe . . .", *Evangelische Theologie* 19 (1959), pp. 314–30; P. Watson, *The Concept of Grace* (1959); M. Busti, *Il primato della carità* (1960); M. Huftier, *La charité dans l'enseignement de St. Augustin* (1960); J. Perrin, *Le mystère de la charité* (1960); T. Ohm, W. Zimmerli, N. Dahl and R. Mehl, in *RGG,* IV, cols. 361–9; A. Royo Marin, *Teología de la caridad* (1960); E. Przywara, *Demut, Geduld, Liebe* (1960); id., *Schriften,* I (1962), pp. 323–77; R. Romaniuk, *L'amour du Père et du Fils dans la sotériologie de St. Paul* (1961); J. McIntyre, *On the Love of God* (1962); L. Richard, *Dieu est l'amour* (1962); J. Alfaro, *Fides, spes, caritas: Adnotationes in tractatum "De virtutibus theologicis",* 3 vols. (1963); C. S. Lewis, *The Four Loves* (1963); P. Helwig, *Liebe und Feindschaft* (1964); K. Rahner, "The 'Commandment' of Love in relation to the Other Commandments", *Theological Investigations,* V (1966), pp. 439–59; VI (1969); J. Ratzinger, *Open Circle: The Meaning of Christian Brotherhood* (1966); W. Heinen, *Liebe als sittliche Grundkraft und ihre Fehlformen* (3rd ed., 1968); H. Urs von Balthasar, *Love Alone* (1968).

Karl Rahner

VISIONS

The free self-donation of God implies a revelation of his personal mystery. Within man's consciousness it cannot be comprehended by any sort of introversion; it cannot be "seen" in the sense of ontologism, but only co-experienced (in the acts of the theological virtues). And yet such a non-objective co-experience of the divine light and speech in the Christian who knows how to discern it is basically already a *visio* and *auditio* (see *Revelation, Ontologism, Virtues* I).

The basic elements of this experience can then be deepened through the "light of infused contemplation" and pass over to mystical perception. Under this special influence another "curtain" falls away (cf. St. John of the Cross, *Living Flame of Love,* IV, 7) and the illumination and speech of God becomes less indirect.

The usual mystical elements of vision and audition generally remain in their simple form, beyond thought, images, or words. Yet this simple state can simultaneously be expressed in the conceptual and perceptual sphere, in ideas, images, and words. In a perceptible vision, "the picture that is shown to the soul is the momentary form of grace, its visible evidence which is, so to speak, tangible for the inner senses. At the same time, however, the grace of the divine union itself penetrates the soul with so strong and yet so tender an inspiration that in comparison the image can only seem like the accidental accompaniment of the grace. God himself takes possession of the inmost centre of the soul. He penetrates both the soul and the image that he has put before the soul . . . He instructs the soul in a similar way concerning the mystical sense of what the soul sees. And it is he whom the soul loves in what it sees; it is he himself whom the soul perceives therein" (Lucie Christine, *Journal spirituel,* 30 January 1887). It is similar in the case of audition: "the soul perceives the words as though in its deepest centre; it perceives them, but it does not form them. And the words cleave to the presence of the Lord and are one with him" (*ibid.,* 25 September 1882).

The occasion of the intellectual, imaginative, or verbal translation of the simple basic experience of the divine mysteries can either be the individual psychophysical capacities of the subject himself which are projected unconsciously into his way of thinking and perceiving; or the occasion can be a special intervention of God which is outside any normal concrete psychophysical laws (although its effect on the person is psychophysical and subjectively conditioned, according to his religious education, age, and aesthetic development). In this last case one speaks, in the religious sphere, of a "genuine" vision or audition.

The genuineness of such experiences cannot be established simply on the grounds of the piety or sincerity of the subject; these are no proof against error with regard to visions. Even saints have been deceived. When the Church recognizes the holiness of a person, it pronounces no judgment on the genuineness of the visions the saint may have had. In the decree which affirmed the heroic virtue of Gemma Galgani, it is expressly said that "this decree is not to be taken as a judgment upon the nature of the exceptional charisms exercised by this servant of God"; to which the clause is added: "so too in other cases of this kind" (*AAS* 24 [1932], p. 57). Health, both of body and soul, is also no unequivocal criterium for "genuine" visions. Psychogenic projection of the simple basic experience into the faculties of the mind and senses can occur in those who are completely normal. Also, such projections cannot in themselves be called a symptom of "illness". The truth is rather that the psychic process cannot be adequately scrutinized and it thus remains ambiguous. Even the good effects that such a vision might have, a deepening of the religious feeling of the subject which begins with the experience and endures, is no unambigous criterium. For purely psychogenic visions can also have such beneficent effects and be considered as proceeding "from the good Spirit". For an observer the one criterium of genuineness in the case of visions is that which establishes the genuineness in a formal way, a miracle (in the determination of which the existence of genuine telepathy etc. must be reckoned with; see *Psychology* IV). As miracles are seldom ascertainable, one must be satisfied with a greater or lesser probability in distinguishing genuine from psychogenic visions.

A vision that has been taken to be genuine can naturally only be granted a *fides humana,* insofar as the evidence of a vision is able to support such faith. Especially with "prophetic" visions which make assertions concerning future events strict evidence is to be demanded. If an ecclesiastical forum judges certain visions to be worthy of credibility, but the reasons for such credibility seem to one to be too weak to support it, then one can inwardly consider that judgment as erroneous and can make one's private opinion known, with all due respect for ecclesiastical authority (Benedict XIV). The believer, however, must avoid the basic scepticism, which, if radically carried through, would deny the very possibility of a historical revelation of God and thereby also deny Christianity as a supernatural, historical, and revealed religion. It is somewhat easier, after what has just been said, to judge the genuineness of a vision in the absence of any underlying experience of God and especially in the absence of moral probity on the part of the believer concerned.

While these intelligible and perceptible elements of a vision or audition are only an expression of that non-objective illumination and speech of God which can be experienced by any Christian, it is an experience which is essentially bound to the revelatory word of Christ. This is the reason why tradition within the sphere of visions must be measured against and interpreted by the revelation of Christ in the Church, and why it must yield to that visible continuation of the revelation and words of Christ in the sacraments and the word of the Church. In St. John of the Cross the heavenly Father says: "I have already told you everything in my Word, which is my Son. I have then nothing else and nothing better to answer or to reveal to you . . . In him is all that I have spoken, all that I can answer, all that I can give you to understand, all that I can reveal" (*Ascent of Mount Carmel,* II, 22, 5–6).

Yet it would be a mistake to consider that visions were therefore superfluous. They can in the first place be the occasion of a more vital experience of the reality of the Christian mystery for the subject involved, and they can also fulfil a function within the Church. Though in their content they could only correspond to that which is known already in faith and theology, nevertheless they can express an imperative demand of the will of God for the actions of the Church in a given historical situation in which that will could not be unequivocally ascertained by the application of the general principles of dogma or moral or by an analysis of the given situation.

See also *Mysticism* I, II C, *Revelation* IV.

BIBLIOGRAPHY. Benedict XIV, *De Servorum Dei Beatificatione et Beatorum Canonisatione,* III (1737), especially chs. 50–53; Gabriele di S. Maria Maddalena, *Visioni e rivelazioni nella vita spirituale* (1941); J. de Guibert, *Leçons de théologie spirituelle,* I (1946), ch. 24; W. Keilbach, V. Maag and A. Strobel in *RGG,* VI, cols. 1408–12; K. Rahner, *Visions and Prophecies* (1963); K. V. Truhlar, *Christuserfahrung* (1964); id., *Antinomiae vitae spiritualis* (in German) (4th ed., 1965); id., *Structura theologica vitae spiritualis* (3rd ed., 1966); id., *Teilhard und Solowjew: Dichtung und religiöse Erfahrung* (1966).

Karl Vladimir Truhlar

VOLUNTARISM

Voluntarism is the doctrine which accords the will precedence over reason. It takes various forms, according to whether the will is regarded as spontaneity, freedom, love, act or drive, and according to the starting-point of the enquiry — theological, ontological or anthropological.

1. Theological voluntarism, which generally occurs in connection with a voluntarist theory of knowledge, dissociates the will of God from any fixed order — of being, nature or knowledge — which would be previous to the act of God's will. Any such (apparent) dependence is said to run counter to the freedom and sovereign transcendence of the divine person. This type of voluntarism stems from Christian impulses: the desire to maintain that creation was a free act and that redemption was accomplished through love. Theologians also felt that certain texts of the OT, such as those dealing with polygamy, the despoiling of the Egyptians and so on, could only be explained by voluntarism. But its fundamental principles remain tributary to a metaphysics of essence which really contradicts voluntarism; or else it tries to rid itself of such principles, and then it falls into agnosticism or becomes a voluntarist metaphysics. Theological voluntarism, of which the foundations were laid by Scotus, leads in the nominalism of Occam — which influenced Luther and through him Protestant theology, especially of the dialectical type — to the assertion that the moral good is positively determined by the arbitrary will of God. According to Descartes, even truth depends on the free act of God's omnipotence as first cause.

The will of God is in fact in no way determined by anything really distinct from him. But it is not lawless or formally arbitrary. It is the lucid and loving fullness of being of God, whose self-knowledge, identical with his self-affirmation, includes at once the structure and truth of what is possible on the finite plane (the *possibilia*). Since the creation and the consummation of the finite are one and the same thing in God's plan, the very nature of man is a concrete expression of the personal call of God to moral good. If the moral good were merely a matter of positive law, God would be contradicting the decree of his own will, as laid down in creation.

2. Metaphysical voluntarism, such as that upheld by Böhme and Schelling or Schopenhauer and Nietzsche, sees the ultimate principle of reality as an opaque, non-spiritual and instinctive will, which is either in dualistic opposition to the spirit — or the idea, or the good — or forms the sole structure of reality. Behind this type of voluntarism lies the violent effort to eliminate a notion of being too one-sidedly orientated to knowledge (see *Intellectualism*). But this purpose cannot be carried out by introducing a non-spiritual component from the will into an already one-sided notion of being, or by a radical rejection of the spiritual structure of reality. We must return to the authentic understanding of being which will allow us to see the lucidity of being as the active freedom in which it takes possession of itself: and the striving of instinct as a limited and defective form of the latter.

3. Psychological voluntarism emphasizes the predominance of the will — or desire,

instinct or act — in human life and consciousness. According to its strict form (Wundt) all psychic processes are to be understood on the analogy of acts of desire and will. But the will alone does not constitute the essence of the person. It does so only along with knowledge, which does not actively determine its own perceptions. And the person, being in the body and in the world, can only "come to itself" by the exercise of a plurality of psycho-physical functions distinct from the will. In the same way, the blessedness of heaven does not lie solely in the will, but consists of the interpenetration of receptive vision and the love which gives itself.

4. *Epistemological voluntarism*. In certain theories of knowledge, a decisive function is ascribed to the will (or to love, or feelings) either in the assent to an acquired piece of knowledge (Descartes, Fichte) or in the very process of arriving at truth (so in various forms Kant, Jacobi, Scheler; pragmatism and conventionalism; some schools of existentialism). The assent to the known truth is a fully personal act of the spirit as a unity; the will as an individual faculty only becomes decisive in this act when the truth is not clearly evident of itself (free certainty, faith). If the will takes over the role of intellect in the finding of the truth, by trying to determine the truth independently, truth is perverted into a postulate or convention without contact with reality (see *Irrationalism*). The will, however, has the power of choosing between the objects set before it by knowledge. And in certain domains, access to the truth can be had only by an active interest in the object, absolute dedication to truth, sympathetic love, moral purity, an open-minded inclination. The decisive objects of knowledge — knowledge of values and of persons, ethical and religious truths, knowledge of one's own vocation — concern the essence of the person so profoundly that even when known and acted upon, their truth can be grasped only by the kernel of the person. But in the inmost depths of the person, knowledge and will are still so united as to be almost indistinguishable: knowledge, love and self-determination can take place only as a unity. The more the object of knowledge is exterior, the more the act of knowledge is differentiated from that of the will; and then the will plays a lesser role in the disclosure of truth, and the necessity of

confronting the object with the whole human person is less urgent.

See also *Will, Knowledge, Truth* I, *Nominalism*.

BIBLIOGRAPHY. R. Knauer, *Der Voluntarismus* (1907); J. Auer, *Die menschliche Willensfreiheit bei Thomas von Aquin und Johannes Duns Skotus* (1938); id. in *LTK*, X, cols. 870 ff. (with bibliography); A. Bellieri, *Dal naturalismo al neo-voluntarismo* (1940); A. Forest, "Le réalisme de la volonté", *Revue Thomiste* 46 (1946), pp. 457–76; *DTC*, XV, cols. 3309–22; R. Crippa, "L'intellettualismo agostiniano e le correnti esigenzionalistico-volontaristiche della filosofia contemporanea", *S. Agostino e le grandi correnti della filosofia contemporanea* (1956), pp. 77–95.

Klaus Riesenhuber

VOW

1. Vows are a phenomenon frequently met with in the history of religion. They are pronounced in the form of a promise to the divinity, usually in order to win favour or to secure a return of gifts, but also for reasons of moral purification, of gratitude and appreciation, or of dedication to God. Moral theology accordingly describes a vow as an act of divine homage by which man freely binds himself to the performance of a good work not of general obligation, which is better than its concrete opposite: *bonum possibile et melius*. The validity of a vow demands therefore a corresponding capability of moral responsibility; one has also to make a prudent judgment, however, as to whether a particular vow really serves its purpose; also one should beware of the hasty taking of vows. The prophets long ago warned against abuses (Mal 1:14; Jer 44:25; cf. Deut 23:19). Jesus also sharply condemns the taking of vows with the purpose of evading responsibility for providing for one's parents (Mk 7:9–13; cf. Mt 5:33f.). Nevertheless vows have found a fruitful soil in the Judaeo-Christian understanding of the covenant with God. They are highly thought of (Ps 61:6; Lk 1:15) and conscientiously kept (2 Sam 15:8f.; Acts 18:18; cf. 1 Cor 8:13).

2. The purpose of the vow is a special consecration to God of a man himself, or of individual acts or particular gifts, so that in a certain sense by means of the vows he freely places himself or what is his at the service of God in a way not universally demanded by the law of God. This occurs in a radical fashion in the case of the vow to

live according to the evangelical counsels, through which one consecrates one's whole life in a special way entirely to God and erects a barrier against the great obstacles on the road to holiness — concupiscence of the eyes, concupiscence of the flesh, pride of life. It is furthermore the aim of the vow to protect oneself by means of this self-imposed obligation against inconstancy in the dedication to God once it has been freely made.

3. The obligatory nature of the vow once taken arises primarily from its character as an act of divine worship, which has become fully possible for the Christian by reason of his baptism and his universal or even special priesthood. The gravity of the obligation depends objectively on the person's will to dedicate himself, as well as on the significance of the thing vowed, while subjectively it depends on the capabilities of the one who is vowing and above all on his moral accountability. Since the vow is in a sense a self-imposed law, the extent of the obligation is to be estimated according to the same rules and dictates of prudence as in the case of law. In the case of a private vow, the person can himself decide for himself whether its fulfilment is, in view of the circumstances, possible or impossible, helpful or injurious, required or forbidden. But since for the correct judgment of the nature of a vow a considerable moral and religious maturity is called for, it is earnestly recommended that one should take counsel of an experienced spiritual guide. Moreover, man is, even in his entirely personal religious actions, involved in social relationships. He who has dominative, not merely domestic power over someone, can, in the measure in which he has disposal over the will of the person entrusted to him, abrogate his vow (*CIC*, can. 1312, § 1; cf. Num 30:4–17). The obligation of vows concerning material objects transfers to the heirs (*CIC*, can. 1310, § 2).

Furthermore, the Church in its capacity as the divinely instituted medium of salvation claims the right to regulate the vows of the faithful, in the sense that it has the power to decide about the scope of a personal vow. In the interest of the salvation of the individual or of the common good of the Church — not therefore arbitrarily — vows can be suitably dispensed or commuted (already in Lev 27, we find commutation dealt with). The Church is all the more justified in officially regulating the nature of vows inasmuch as a) Christian vows are related to divine worship (the dedication of one's person or possessions to God) and are therefore an actualization of the universal priesthood of the faithful and as b) the power of religious binding and loosing is committed to the Church on earth (see *Ecclesiastical Authority*).

Thus the scope of the vows of the faithful is determined by canon law (especially can. 1307–15). According to these canons, the validity of a vow demands, among other things, freedom from external coercion. Solemn vows render one incapable of owning property and of marriage, and are more difficult to dissolve than simple vows which merely render marriage and the acquisition of property unlawful. The decision about the validity and scope of public vows is reserved on principle to the Holy See. Dispensation from private vows can in general be given for appropriate reasons by the Ordinaries, but only with the permission of the Holy See in the case of those over 18 years of age who make private vows of perfect and perpetual chastity or of entering an order with solemn vows.

From all this it is clear that vows of the faithful must be seen in the dynamic relationship between office and charism and they must be judged from this standpoint, that is to say, because of the religious character of a vow, referred to the Church as an act of divine worship, it demands by its very nature to be subject to canonical regulation. This, however, means that the person taking a vow binds himself before God from the start according to the rule and interpretations of canon law. This is expressed in Vatican II, *Lumen Gentium:* "This consecration gains in perfection, since by virtue of firmer and steadier bonds it serves as a better symbol of the unbreakable link between Christ and his Spouse, the Church" (art. 44). Thus he who takes solemn vows thereby enters a closer bond of consecration than the person taking simple vows. Precisely because of this the Church authorities have the grave obligation of regulating vows through canon law with such human prudence and sincere reverence for God that the salvation of the individual member of the faithful as well as the common good of the Church will be thereby really furthered. The canonical regulations about vows must therefore be also subordinated to pastoral purposes. To meet these properly, man's weakness, which will be countered by

God's grace alone, must be taken entirely seriously and, in reliance on the power of the liberating grace of God, be given brotherly and, as needed, fatherly support.

If this pastoral purpose of canon law is neglected, there is a great danger that the law will make the relationship to God more difficult instead of easier, since the fulfilment of a vow can be objectively willed by God only to the extent that it actually contributes to the perfection of the person.

Since, furthermore, what is merely of counsel (by its very nature in the case of a vow) has an objectively different bearing on perfection to what is obligatory, whether under pain of grave or venial sin, vows must not only be subjectively free, but also be judged differently by the Church authorities to which the charism is related in its own specific way.

4. Such a relation of the personal charism to the official Church is present in a special way in the case of the vows of a religious order. Through them an effective charism is institutionalized in the Church in such a way that through being taken over by a community a) its continued effect is secured and strengthened (see *Religious Orders, Secular Institutes*).

Then, the institutionalization of life according to the counsels in the orders, with its eschatological orientation, means b) that the eschatological structure of the Church is given a concrete symbol and exemplar (see *Sacrament, Sacramentals, Liturgy* I), while life according to the counsels is institutionally secured and protected. Finally, in this way c) the charism is placed consciously at the service of authority in the Church and tested and directed by it. Religious vows always have, therefore, as their aim a voluntary dedication, offering one's entire life for service to God at the disposal of the Church. This dedication is thus joined to a definitive charismatic mission so that the member of the religious order is ready within this framework to be disposed of by the Church authorities to the full extent of his entire personal life. It follows that the function of the religious vows is to be judged directly from the charismatic aims of the order and indirectly from the purpose of the order within the Church on the way to God, that is, from its bearing on salvation.

See also *Evangelical Counsels, Law* I, II.

BIBLIOGRAPHY. See bibliographies on *Evangelical Counsels, Poverty* I, *Obedience, Virginity;* also: RECENT DOCUMENTS OF THE MAGISTERIUM: Vatican II, Dogmatic Constitution on the Church, *Lumen Gentium,* ch. VI; Decree on the Appropriate Renewal of the Religious Life, *Perfectae Caritatis.* See H. Vorgrimler, ed., *Commentary on the Documents of Vatican II,* I (1967), II (1968). STUDIES: G. Gold, *Gelübde nach Bibel und Talmud* (1926); A. Wendel, *Das israelitisch-jüdische Gelübde* (1932); J. Zürcher, ed., *Die Gelübde im Ordensleben* (1956); P. Séjourné, "Vœu, vœux de religion", *DTC,* XV, cols. 3182–281; B. Häring, *Law of Christ,* II (1963); J. Gerhartz, *"Insuper promitto". Die feierlichen Sondergelübde katholischer Orden* (1966).

Waldemar Molinski

W

WAR

An attempt at a theological examination of war must deal in turn with the phenomenon of war, the problem of the right to make war (*jus ad bellum*) and the conduct of hostilities (*jus in bello*).

1. *The phenomenon of war*. Basically, apart from its specific manifestations, war may be defined as armed and sanguinary conflict between organized groups. The arms may make themselves felt by mere intimidation, before they are actually used. Such intimidation indeed plays a dominant role in the confrontation of great powers in our day, because the use of nuclear arms would threaten all belligerents with utter catastrophe (the strategy of the deterrent). Besides arms which are designed to destroy living bodies and material goods, there are psychological techniques that directly attack the human mind. Whether the "cold war" and the "war of nerves" are really war is a question which needs further discussion. War is international, civil, or revolutionary, according as the adversaries are different States, or sections of one population.

International war is armed conflict between States, desired by at least one of the belligerents and undertaken in a national interest. The latest technical devices do not necessarily displace earlier ones. In the age of the atomic bomb the bayonet is far from outmoded. The fact that atomic wars may break out does not mean that conventional (or classic) wars are now impossible. Even though world conflict threatens, certain wars may still remain limited ones. For all its variety, modern war logically becomes totalitarian (total war). Any country which

embarks on it must face the total mobilization of its resources: economic, demographic and psychological. Thus conflict becomes extremely violent, and the most elementary moral standards are commonly disregarded. Losses of men and material reach astronomical proportions: more than fifty-five million persons died during the Second World War. The figure would be much higher had the most recent means of destruction been used. A thermo-nuclear conflict could cause three hundred million deaths in a matter of hours. Chemical and bacteriological weapons would also wreak great havoc.

Civil war and revolutionary war are alike fratricidal, and rely heavily on psychological weapons. Civil wars have been so numerous, so cruel, and so disastrous that they have largely shaped the course of human history. When caused by social or ideological antagonism they have been most terrible of all. The prehistory of revolutionary war goes back to Sun Tze. After reaching a decisive stage with the French Revolution, it was taken in hand by the great Communist leaders. These, in order to gain their revolutionary ends, had recourse to no less revolutionary means, showing a preference for the techniques of subversive war: organization (mobilizing populations through the system of parallel hierarchies); propaganda (using every means to mould public opinion, particularly myths and brain-washing); agitation (terrorism and military intervention); the ideal of the five stages whereby a handful of resolute men advance from underground conspiracy to control of the population and final victory.

2. *The problem of the right to wage war (jus ad bellum)*. Disregarding those whose

353

cowardice or selfishness makes them feel that any injustice must be endured for the sake of physical survival, we shall observe that two diametrically opposite attitudes may be taken towards the chameleon-like phenomenon of war: either *every* war which seems to serve one's interests is legitimate, or *no* war is legitimate (absolute pacifism). The first attitude, that the end justifies the means, is that of the Machiavellians of every age, that of European "international law" before the time of the League of Nations and that of dictatorships and totalitarian States, Leftist or Rightist. If not in theory, then in practice all who take this view accept the dictum of Clausewitz that war is "simply a continuation of politics by other means". By contrast, absolute pacifism objects to all wars, even those of justifiable self-defence, holding that bloodshed is always wrong and that violence may only be resisted by non-violent means. Christian pacifists base their position on the Ten Commandments and the gospel.

Traditional Catholic doctrine accepts neither of these views. It repudiates the doctrine of "power politics", which it regards as a criminal aberration condemned alike by natural law and by the gospel. Because of the spiritual nature of man and the fact that all of his race are brothers, human conflicts — of whatever sort — must be settled by essentially reasonable and peaceful means: hence the basic rule of international law that all differences between nations must be resolved peacefully. Peace is an elemental duty for all. Are we, then, to become absolute pacifists? Theologians think not, because absolute pacifism ignores the fact of human nature as it actually exists, wounded by sin. Unscrupulous statesmen do exist who drag their peoples into criminal adventures. Experience shows that often violence and injustice can only be stopped by violent means. Do not justice and charity towards others demand that we resist crime so far as we are able? Thus, despite its intrinsic unreasonableness and its horrors, war may become legitimate if there is no other means of remedying injustice.

Four conditions must be fulfilled (the theory of the just cause): one side must persist in committing an injustice (legitimate self-defence); all peaceful means of settling the dispute must have been exhausted; there must be a due proportion between the gravity of the injustice and the damage which the war would do (principle of the lesser

evil); and there must be a reasonable hope of success. War can only be a desperate remedy in a desperate situation, used in order to spare humanity a still greater evil when all essentially reasonable and peaceful means have proved ineffective, for only in these circumstances can war acquire the necessary (though accidental) rationality. Unjust war is a monstrous crime.

Even in modern conditions the foregoing principles retain their relevance, despite the vast changes we have witnessed in the phenomenon of war. Violence remains a terrible reality of our age — the oppression of conscience, social injustice, racialism, militarism — and when it grows to monstrous proportions, must we not understand why the oppressed revolt? And has a State not a right to defend its existence? Most theologians hold that war may still be legitimate in order to resist an attack on the basic personal rights of a great many human beings, or on the existence of a State. Obviously, the rule of the lesser evil must still be observed. Even in a just cause, it cannot be lawful to unleash a general nuclear war, which would inevitably cause hundreds of millions of deaths, reduce the whole world to a ghastly chaos, and gravely prejudice the genetic future of the human race. That would be madness. Instead, we should have to rely on spiritual resistance, an alternative too long ignored, whose astonishing fruitfulness has been demonstrated by Gandhi and multitudes of Christians in totalitarian countries. The soundest deterrent is a community of human beings who are brave and intelligent, accustomed to thinking for themselves and acting according to the dictates of their conscience.

The very excesses of modern war compel us to avoid it by every means in our power. A spirit of universal solidarity and brotherhood must be cultivated. Enemies though they were for centuries, is war now thinkable between Great Britain and France, or between France and Germany? Yet allowance must be made for States ruled by criminals. Peace can only be maintained if — apart from finding a solution to the other enormous problems facing mankind — an effective world government is set up which is able to lay down the law even to the most powerful States. Once that is done, war will have ceased to be rational in any respect, even accidentally; for justice will be accessible to all. Such military operations as the world government undertakes will simply be police action on an international scale, to keep the peace.

3. *Conduct of hostilities (jus in bello)*. Though war of its own nature is something savage, Christianity was able in some degree to humanize conflicts among the nations of Europe. But when weapons of mass destruction were invented, when nationalist ideologies exacerbated the opposing sides and totalitarianism had firmly established itself, war once more became thoroughly brutal and far more devastating than in the past, thanks to technical progress. Total war logically leads to unlimited violence. Victory being essential, it is said, the surest means to that end must be used: "Necessity knows no law."

To one who would behave as a human being, let alone as a Christian, this algebra of violence is unacceptable. In time of war no less than in time of peace, the absolute values basic to natural law must be respected. The following principles always hold good (in civil or revolutionary wars as well as in international ones): respect for human life (no human life to be sacrificed unless in lawful self-defence); respect for the person (ruling out all inhumane treatment, especially torture); immunity for the civilian population (in principle, the distinction between combatants and non-combatants must be preserved, and only military objectives may be attacked); all intrinsically evil acts are forbidden (assassination, rape, torture, treason, defamation, etc.). The right of legitimate self-defence exists, but it is limited by reason and the above conditions. These rules have been admirably elaborated and confirmed by various international conventions (the Hague Convention of 18 October 1907; the Treaty of Washington, 6 February 1922; the Geneva Protocol, 17 June 1925; the Geneva Conventions, 12 August 1949, etc.). Such of their provisions as form part of natural law (and the majority do) are binding on belligerents even if they have not signed such treaties.

Nuclear weapons present special problems. Not only are their immediate effects dreadful (appalling destruction by heat and blast, poisoning on an enormous scale by the initial radiation of alpha, beta, and gamma rays); their residual radiation is unforeseeable — no one knows where or when delayed fall-out may occur, causing grave biological damage (notably leukemia and bone cancer). Theoretically there might be cases where such weapons could be used subject to the general rules that govern the conduct of hostilities (bombing a squadron in mid-ocean, for example, or guided-missile sites far from centres of population). But even limited operations of this kind are on a dangerous path. Repeated explosion of tactical nuclear weapons can add up to a radioactivity as deadly as that of megaton bombs, and of course might well lead to full-scale nuclear warfare. Many think it an illusion to suppose that States with a full panoply of nuclear arms would conduct a limited atomic war. As John XXIII said: "It is becoming humanly impossible to regard war, in this atomic age, as a suitable means of re-establishing justice when some right has been violated" (*Pacem in Terris,* no. 127). The banning of nuclear arms by international convention is an urgent necessity.

Vatican II dealt at great length with the theme of modern warfare in the Pastoral Constitution on the Church in the Modern World *(Gaudium et Spes)*. It not merely condemned atrocities in war (art. 79), total war (art. 80) and the armaments race (art. 81), but also demanded an absolute condemnation of war and called for world-wide action to prevent it (art. 82). The Council recommended the setting up of an international organization for the safeguarding of peace, whose main duty would be to eliminate the causes of war (arts. 83–90). These demands were underlined by Paul VI in his many efforts for peace and above all by the directives of the encyclical *Progressio Populorum.*

See also *Revolution, Resistance, Necessity* II.

BIBLIOGRAPHY. A. Vanderpol, *La doctrine scolastique du droit de guerre* (1919); R. Regout, *La doctrine de la guerre juste* (1935); Q. Wright, *A Study of War,* 2 vols. (1942); B. de Solages, *Théologie de la guerre juste* (1947); A. J. Toynbee, *Civilisation on Trial* (1948); L. Delbez, *La notion de guerre* (1953); L. Kotzsch, *The Concept of War in Contemporary History and International Law* (1956); K. Mannheim, *Man and Society in an Age of Reconstruction* (1959); F. F. Clair, *The Ultimate Defence* (1959); R. W. Tucker, *The Just War* (1960); R. Bainton, *Christian Attitudes towards War and Peace* (1960); W. K. Hancock, *Four Studies of War and Peace in this Century* (1961); H. Standke, *Der Krieg im Völkerrecht* (1961); P. Ramsey, *War and the Christian Conscience* (1961); R. Coste, *Le problème du droit de guerre dans la pensée de Pie XII* (1962); id., *Mars ou Jésus? La conscience chrétienne juge la guerre* (1963); id., *Les communautés politiques* (1967); id., *Évangile et politique* (1968); B. Russell, *Has Man a Future?* (1962); J. Lasserre, *War and the Gospel* (1962); W. Stein, ed., *Nuclear Weapons* (1962);

J. C. Bennet, ed., *Nuclear Weapons and the Conflict of Conscience* (1962); M.-D. Chenu, "L'évolution de la théologie de la guerre", *La parole de Dieu*, II (1964), pp. 571–92; J. G. Lawler, *Nuclear War: The Ethic, Rhetoric, the Reality: A Catholic Assessment* (1965); J. Tooke, *The Just War in Aquinas and Grotius* (1965).

René Coste

WILL

1. *Terminology.* There is no generally accepted definition of what precisely the "will" means. The various definitions put forward in the course of history diverge from each other in many respects. An analysis of the present-day understanding of the term shows that it can have many different meanings according to the context in which it is used. The main usages are as follows.

a) Will as volition, the act of willing (the scholastic *actus voluntatis qua appetitus rationalis, intellectivus*). Examples of the use of the word in this sense are texts which speak of the will as the act of choosing, striving, purposeful desire, responsible self-determination, resolve, etc.

b) Will as faculty, power, tendency or disposition with regard to the acts of the will such as were mentioned under a). The problems which arise when the word is used in this (controversial) sense suggest that sharper definition is needed in many cases. This can be approached by using concrete examples to show how far the concept is applicable even in cases of diminished responsibility, e.g., in the state of sleep, hypnosis or intoxication, in the early phases of psychological development, in pathological loss of will-power (aboulia).

c) Will as the subject capable of acts of volition (see *Person, Spirit, Soul;* cf. the ego, the self, the transcendental ego), either in the form of mere capability of willing without the actual exercise of the will, or in the mode of actual volition. Examples of such use of the term may be seen in phrases like "voluntas vult, movet . . ." But it is not the power or the faculty or even the act of will that is capable of willing, but only the person or subject.

d) Will as the content of the will or what is willed, in such phrases as "to do the will of the legislator".

e) Will as the disposition to implement what has been resolved. Since there is so much variation and vagueness in the use of the term, it is better to define what is meant by "will" by means of phrases including a verb like "to will". But even here usage can vary. The "will to power" in Nietzsche, for instance, uses the term in a wider sense than that of modern psychology. However, the variations here are mainly concerned with marginal elements of the content of volition. As regards its "kernel", "willing something in the strict sense", there is a relatively wide consensus, which has been confirmed by the experimental investigations of modern psychology.

2. *Psychology and anthropology of willing.* When man wills something, he seems to exist in a specially active way and to be determined by the personal ego itself. It might then be said that willing is an act which proceeds from the reality which each man knows as "I myself", the I-centre.

In contrast to other modes of existence, when man wills he does not find himself under alien domination but as master of himself. He is not pinned down or directed by others, but self-constitutive and self-directed. He has not to do something, but can, may or ought to do it. In other words, he is determinant, not subject to determination. He brings about something which is not exclusively determined by factors outside the volition of the "I" (as in purely mechanical processes) but is at least in one component due to the "factor" in man which is capable of responsible disposition of self. Acts of the will make it possible for man to add a "plus of determination" to the fields of activity imposed upon him (e.g., psychophysical organism, material surroundings). He can influence and help to shape the world and human existence in a way which he finds personally desirable and in keeping with the goals which he has set himself.

Psychologically, the act of the will is characterized by a sense of personal initiative and activity, which points to a fundamental difference between willing and other psychical experiences. Drives and inhibitions can be sensed, even against my will. Since drives which give rise to inclinations, compulsions, attractions, etc., can be called centripetal, heading for the centre of the person, the act of willing can be called centrifugal. It flows outwards rather than inwards and is determined by the person himself. Instinctive impulses can arise whether I want them or not, but this is not true of acts of the will.

The subject who wills is of a personal nature, and not just by virtue of an element merely integrated into the totality of the person, but by virtue of the personal principle itself in man (see *Spirit*). Hence a fundamental assertion may be made which holds good for all controversies on the problems of the will. It is that one cannot assume *a priori* that the same laws will hold good in all respects as are valid for mere things, non-personal objects. Caution is necessary when, for instance, the findings of natural science based on the observation of non-personal objects are used to prop up theses which affect the nature and possibilities of human life.

In the matter of the relationship between will and knowledge, a number of aspects must be borne in mind: the fact that human life is a whole, a unity (see *Person*); the elements of knowledge which defy subjective arbitrariness, the "objectivity" of knowable reality (see *Truth, Knowledge*); the fundamental function of knowledge with regard to willing *(nihil volitum nisi praecognitum);* and the many ways in which the will can influence the intellect. Here factors subject to the influence of the will play a role not merely in the creation of the conditions for the attainment of knowledge (by the nature of the questions, the direction of the search, inward openness, intellectual honesty, etc.), but also in the interpretation, assessment and application of knowledge.

On the role of the will in specifically scientific thought, interesting perspectives have been opened up by the analysis of the basic problems of natural science and metaphysics in recent years, examples of which may be found in R. Carnap, K. Popper and W. Stegmüller. Light has been thrown on the radical problems and limitations of human claims to knowledge, on the difficulty of finding "absolutely" certain foundations and on the basic role of personal assumptions and decisions. There are, for instance, the attitudes adopted to basic questions of epistemology, in the acceptance or otherwise of principles of thought, evidences, axioms, empirical bases and so on. Consequences ensue which do not just lead to absurdities (see *Scepticism*) but rather to emphasis on the element of freedom and hence of responsibility. Questions are laid bare whose solution cannot be given by stringent proofs. Nonetheless, and in spite of positivistic polemics, an answer is possible and indeed meaningful, because sufficiently probable, fruitful, credible and so on. The answer may contain hypothetical components — though here the justifiable elements of the critical philosophy of Kant, of modern empiricism, of Wittgenstein and so on must be taken into account — but the answer is still sufficiently well motivated in practice to be humanly feasible and responsible.

As regards the controversy between the upholders of determinism and indeterminism, the ambiguousness and vagueness of some central concepts should be noted. There is therefore need of a prior linguistic analysis and a clarification of terminology. When this is done, many apparent contradictions disappear at once.

Determinism is correct in assuming that the will does not go into action without sufficient reason (see *Causality*). It is wrong in assuming that this excludes freedom. But indeterminism is correct in assuming that acts of the will are not determined in the way large-scale physical processes or pre-personal psychic movements are determined. It is wrong in assuming that acts of the will take place without a reason and uninfluenced by components which restrict the freedom of the will. The act of the will likewise has a cause, or better, an author, but this is to be sought in the "I" which can will, and make itself a cause (see *Spirit, Transcendence*). Freedom is therefore not random action or action without a cause, but the possibility of responsible self-determination, when the cause is the self. In this sense, man is not free by being released from his impulses, but by being able to act and be as he himself wills.

The will therefore has motives. And since "motive" is a term used in a variety of senses, it is here understood as the reason by which one is moved to make an act of the will. The motives in question very often exist on many levels. They are complex, and not fully and adequately recognized by the person who acts. In contrast to the intentional content of the will, which can only be made the goal when the agent is conscious of it *(nihil volitum nisi praecognitum),* motivating factors can also be influential when they are unconscious. Depth psychology and psychotherapy provide very valuable bases for the understanding of such unconscious factors. The empirical findings of such approaches show how important the unconscious is for the motivation of acts and attitudes of the will.

Among the factors which constitute the realm of motivation we may signal the fundamental desire for self-fulfilment, love and happiness; the sense of what ought to be, stirrings of conscience and grasp of values; structures of unconscious drives and inhibitions; the urges of self-preservation, aggression and se⁀ ⌐ity; appetites and aversions, inclinations and repulsions, tensions set up by all sorts of needs. Under certain conditions, these are to a great extent outside the scope of the free will. Nonetheless, it is often possible to decide, within certain limits, which of the motivations may be allowed to guide the act of the will and which resolutions will be taken in consequence. Normally, when one feels oneself urged in a certain direction, one retains a number of possibilities of reaction and of further action, differing in value — even though one is not free to control the sense of being urged. Under certain circumstances, I can decide whether I will ("voluntarily") give in to the drive, resist it or sublimate it, and again, how I do so — reasonably or unreasonably, aiming at higher or lower values, using means destructive of or helpful to life. Which of the possibilities open to me I do in fact will to choose is not ultimately decided by a factor outside the control of the will, such as a drive, but by the "I" which is personally master, which can itself decide and resolve on the basis of motives and in accordance with motives. I decide in accordance with motives which I myself accept and choose to decide by (see the discussion of the *option fondamentale,* the basic decision; note the possibility of a dialectical relationship in which one can confront motivations, pronounce on their values, respond deliberately, etc.).

The metaphor of "conflicting motives" among which one motive emerges as victor can be misleading, if one does not remember that the "I" with its power of willing can intervene in this conflict and determine actively which of the motives in question is to be the "victor", that is, is to be authoritative and normative for the decisions to be made by the "I". For instance, in conflicts between "duty and inclination", I may allow myself to be led by motives corresponding to the inclination or by motives corresponding to the duty; so too in conflicts between reason and passion, egoism and desire for solidarity, hatred and love and so on.

Motivating factors may impel, urge, incline, dispose, stimulate to certain acts of the will. They cannot compel. Motives do not make free acts impossible but meaningful, since they provide reasons for them. They do not determine, in the sense of excluding freedom, but motivate, by giving the "I" a reason for its self-determination — a reason for *willing* something.

There are certainly situations in which one may be driven irresistibly to certain modes of behaviour: by neurotic compulsions, psychoses, addictions, "possession", hypnosis and so on. But we justifiably feel that these are not "normal cases". It is "normal" for man that his freedom should be restricted, but not excluded, by the predestined psychophysical context into which the "I" of the will is integrated (instinctive drives, milieu, etc.). The limits of freedom are different in each individual and vary according to age, character, stage of spiritual development.

The question of the origin of the motivating factors at work in man, like the question of the origin of the existence and the will-power of the person exposed to them, leads to matters which in spite of all that can be said and surmised on the point go beyond the realm of scientific knowledge. It leads finally to the mystery of the ground of human existence itself.

3. *Theological discussion.* On the theological themes involved, see *Contrition, Decision, Faith, Freedom, Grace and Freedom, Hope, Human Act, Nature and Grace, Original Sin, Sin.*

In problems of moral theology, the fundamental solutions depend on the ability to distinguish voluntary from involuntary components of life and action. The type and degree of control, e.g., the extent to which actions can be influenced, guided, attempted and avoided, is the direct coefficient of freedom, responsibility, accountability or otherwise, guilt and so on. It is instructive to compare the modern theological interpretation of concupiscence with the findings of physiology and psychology on vital functions and forms of experience which are wholly or in part outside the control of the personal will (cf. the causes and effects in the workings of nerves and glands, involuntary fantasies, feelings, moods, needs, emotions, drives, inclinations, repulsions, etc.).

In practical pastoral effort, the importance of the will in the matter of the meaning of life and man's salvation poses the question of how effective formation of the will is possible. Since the formation of the will is the formation of an adequate, consistent set of motives, many ways are available (see *Psychology, Education* I, III, *Health* II, *Psychotherapy, Pastoral Theology*). The most effective methods are those which help not only to know how one ought to be and act but also how one can begin to love what ought to be — that which is good here and now.

BIBLIOGRAPHY. See bibliography on *Freedom;* also: A. Schopenhauer, *World as Will and Idea,* 3 vols. (1883); J. MacVannell, *Hegel's Doctrine of the Will* (1896); A. Pfänder, *Phänomenologie des Wollens* (1900), E.T.: *Phenomenology of Willing* (1967); T. Lipps, *Vom Fühlen, Wollen und Denken* (2nd ed., 1907); H. Reiner, *Freiheit, Wollen und Aktivität* (1927); J. Lindworsky, *Training of the Will* (1929); G. W. Allport, *Personality* (1949); id., *Pattern and Growth in Personality* (1961); V. Frankl, *Der unbewusste Gott* (2nd ed., 1949); T. V. Moore, *The Driving Forces of Human Nature and their Adjustment* (1950); G. Heyer, *Organismus der Seele* (3rd ed., 1951); W. Keller, *Psychologie und Philosophie des Wollens* (1954); J. Nuttin, *Psychoanalysis and Personality* (1954); J.-P. Sartre, *Being and Nothingness* (1957); L. Wittgenstein, *Philosophical Investigations* (2nd ed., 1958); R. Guardini, *Freedom, Grace and Destiny* (1962); K. Jaspers, *General Psychopathology* (1962); J. de Finance, *Essai sur l'agir humain* (1962); V. Bourke, *Will in Western Thought* (1964); P. Ricœur, *De l'interprétation, Essai sur Freud* (1965); id., *Freedom and Nature: The Voluntary and the Involuntary* (1966); B. Schüller, *Gesetz und Freiheit* (1966); E. Straus and R. Griffith, eds., *Phenomenology of Will and Action* (1968).

Peter Rohner

WISDOM

1. *Preliminary definition.* The correlative terms of truth and wisdom have long been seen as the goal of effort in knowledge. Truth suggests primarily the spontaneity and the methodical accuracy of the act of knowledge, while wisdom suggests on the contrary the sovereign dominion of the longed-for coming of truth. But each of the concepts so strongly suggests the other that they can be defined in terms of each other, so that some pre-understanding of them may be arrived at. Wisdom is the truth beyond the effort of thought, which can still not be attained without it, while truth is wisdom under the aspect of being arrived at. More simply, it may be said that wisdom is truth bestowed and truth is wisdom won.

2. *History of the notion.* a) *The non-biblical notion.* The notion that wisdom is essentially not within the range of man's powers has been brought out in different ways. In theology, wisdom has been assigned to the sphere of transcendence. In anthropology, the sage was idealized as man striving for self-fulfilment by the pursuit of wisdom. In epistemology, the sciences were subordinated to philosophy, understood since Plato as the love of wisdom. These are the essential characteristics of wisdom in non-biblical thought.

(i) Hence the High Gods of the ancient Oriental religions always include a figure distinguished by superior knowledge, of which the oldest known trace is found in the Sumerian *gish-char,* the divine plan of creation. In Babylonian mythology the sea is the place of wisdom, and Ea its Lord (like Ahura Mazda in early Iranian religion). In Egypt, where a copious wisdom literature developed (e.g., the "Instruction of Ani", the "Instruction of Amen-em-Opet"), the notion of wisdom was embodied primarily in the myth of Isis and Osiris. Within the sphere of influence of these lofty forms another notion of wisdom is to be found, of Canaanite and Aramaean origin, which may be regarded as the prototype of the "lower Sophia", some of whose traits, especially its erotic nature and its link with the motif of descent, influenced the biblical and post-biblical notion of wisdom. In the Greek pantheon, Athene is the purest embodiment of wisdom. It may be deduced from her epithet of ἐργάνη that she originally implied skilful handicraft. But the myth of her birth from the brain of Zeus shows that she was early understood as φρόνησις, insight or prudence. While the Celts revered Lug and Dagda as gods of skill and wisdom, the ancient German religion recognized wisdom only as the quintessence of skilful human planning, the blessing of the sage who could await the hour.

(ii) In philosophical thought, however, the empirical element in the notion of wisdom was predominant. Wisdom appears here primarily as the fruit of patient reflection on experience. It is insight into the order of nature and history so well-developed that it can be the rule of life. Thus for Heraclitus, anticipating Stoic thought, wisdom consists in a way of life modelled on the Logos, the law of nature which pervades and governs all things (Fragment 112). For Plato it is the harmony of intellect and will (*Laws,* 689 d) based on self-knowledge (*Charmides,* 164 d).

But this practical wisdom only takes on its full contours in the Stoic programme of life. According to Chrysippus, the sage is beyond all illusions. He cannot be deceived (*Dialectica*), he is irrevocably pledged to the

359

law and finds there total freedom *(Ethica)*. For Seneca, the wise man is wholly self-sufficient, as sublimely aloof as the godhead from the demands and vicissitudes of life *(De Constantia Sapientis,* 5, 1; 8, 2). Cicero sees the sage as the peak of human development, more kingly than Tarquin, more lordly than Sulla, richer than Crassus, subject neither to his own or others' whims and hence truly happy *(De Finibus,* III, 75).

(iii) Parallel to this line of thinking there was a notion of philosophy in which speculative or theoretical knowledge was predominant, and where philosophy was regarded as the attainment of wisdom. Wisdom is the supreme and purest science (Plato, *Philebus,* 58 d), a goal worthy of every effort *(Parmenides,* 135 d), since it is wisdom that turns the soul to the contemplation of being *(Republic,* 521 c). According to Posidonius, wisdom brings knowledge of things human and divine (cf. Seneca, *Epistola,* 89, 5).

b) *The biblical notion of wisdom.* (i) *In the Old Testament.* On the whole, the notion went through much the same development as outside the Bible, though in the reverse direction. According to the original use of the word (חָכְמָה), the basic notion was that of experience and skill gained in active contact with men and things. Hence in the earlier books, especially Proverbs, wisdom is the fruit of experience, and its origin in practical realities is reflected by the form it takes — maxims often couched in paradoxical terms and strung together without much logical sequence (von Rad). Wisdom can therefore be taught (with the help of explanations drawing on a variety of sources, since the wisdom literature of Israel was heavily dependent on Edomite, Egyptian and Babylonian precursors). But it was more easily to be attained from the contemplation of models like Joseph and Solomon. For this reason, OT wisdom made increasing use of metaphors to explain and bring home its message. Then, especially in the post-exilic period, the element of revelation and divine gift came to the fore. Wisdom is the medium through which, in meditative reflection, one gains understanding of oneself *(Ecclesiastes),* of the world (Wis 7:15–21) and of history (Wis 10:1–19:22). It then becomes a principle spontaneously inspiring thought and effort (Wis 7:1–14); in Prov 1:5 it takes the form of a κυβέρνησις, skilful guidance ("intelligens gubernacula possidebit", Vg; "the man of understanding acquire[s] skill, *RSV*). It

finally becomes a hypostasis or personification endowed with divine insight and power (Prov 8:22–31; Ecclus 24:1–29; Wis 7:22–30). This conception was both an answer to the challenge of Greek *philosophia* and a preparation for the NT concepts of wisdom.

(ii) *In the New Testament.* Wisdom also occurs in the NT as a human quality or faculty. But the main interest is the specifically theological aspect, prompted apparently by the contrast brought out by St. Paul between the wisdom of the world which is blind to the things of God, and the "wisdom of God" (1 Cor 1:18–30) which is communicated by the preaching of the cross. In consequence, the NT mainly concentrates on the relationship of wisdom to Christ, who in the synoptics appears in the role of wisdom (Mt 11:19 par.; 12:42 par.; Lk 11:49) or speaks in terms drawn from the wisdom literature (cf. Mt 11:28, with Ecclus 24:19 ff.), and who is formally identified with divine wisdom by St. Paul (1 Cor 1:30). Christian instruction therefore becomes "sapiential", wisdom-teaching (1 Cor 2:6) and preaching is the announcement of the manifold wisdom of God (Eph 3:10), for which the spirit of wisdom and revelation enlightens the eyes of the heart (cf. Eph 1:17 f.).

c) *Post-biblical tradition.* (i) *Patristic and scholastic.* Gnostic speculation, reflecting ancient Oriental notions, divided wisdom into a "higher" and a "lower" Sophia (in a dualistic sense, as in the system of Valentinus). It also made wisdom once more a mythical figure (as in the various systems of emanations, cf. the *Sophia Jesu Christi,* the *Pistis Sophia,* the *Books of Jeû).* The notion was therefore taken up only hesitatingly at first by the Fathers (Justin, *Apologia,* I, 6, 13, 60 f.: the wisdom of God; St. Irenaeus, *Demonstratio,* I, 4–10: the Spirit of God as wisdom; Clement of Alexandria, *Stromata,* V, 1, 6, 3: the Logos as the wisdom of God made manifest; Origen, *Contra Celsum,* III, 41; *In Matthaeum,* XIV, 2, 7; *in Romanos,* I, 1: Christ as the all-embracing Idea of God, the αὐτοσοφία; Athanasius, *Contra Arianos,* I, 16; II, 37, 81: Christ as the true wisdom which has come to man). But it then became one of the guide-lines of patristic thought (Cayré), mainly under the influence of neo-Platonism. The Augustinian notion was important for the further development. Following a line of thought suggested by Origen and the Cappadocian Fathers, St.

Augustine identified wisdom with the divine "mundus archetypus" (*De Civitate Dei,* XI, 10, 3) and underlined its Christological character (*De Doctrina Christiana,* I, 11, 11). He also emphasized its function in the theory of knowledge (as in his explanation of his vision at Ostia, *Confessiones,* IX, 10, 24 f., and in *De Libero Arbitrio,* II, 27, 41 ff.), while maintaining the unity of the two aspects (*Confessiones,* XII, 15, 20). Along the same lines, St. Thomas Aquinas defined wisdom as "quaedam participatio divinae sapientiae" (*Summa Theologica,* II/II, q. 23, a. 1 ad 1), which is the directive principle of all knowledge (I, q. 1, a. 6 ad 1) and therefore leads to a comprehensive understanding of beings in the light of their ultimate causes (I/II, q. 57, a. 2 ad 1) and to a well-ordered mode of action ("sapientis est ordinare"). According to St. Bonaventure, it is a principle of mystical knowledge (*Itinerarium Mentis in Deum,* 4, 8; 5, 3) which makes it possible to go beyond creaturely analogies and know God through himself (*III Sententiarum,* disp. 35, q. 3 ad 3). In the Logosmysticism of Meister Eckhardt, wisdom is the formal ground of the knowledge of God and the "birth" of God in the soul. In Henry Suso, wisdom characterizes the dialogue set up by the *Unio mystica.* The mystical interpretation then found its most important spokesman in Nicholas of Cusa, who affirmed the oneness of wisdom ("simplicissima forma", *De Sapientia,* I, fol. 77) but true to his doctrine of participation ("omnia in omnibus") saw it at work on all levels of spiritual being and hence as the principle and goal of all spiritual activity (*De Venerabili Sapientia,* c. 2, 201) (cf. *De Pace Fidei,* c. 4, fol. 115).

(ii) *The modern era.* The history of interpretation in the modern era is mainly characterized by theosophical accretions, as above all in Böhme (wisdom as the mystery of God manifesting itself in all creatures), Swedenborg (wisdom as the sun of the spiritual world) and Oetinger (wisdom as the self-communication of God in creation and of creation to God). Something similar is heard in Schelling (wisdom as the archetype of things and the basis of the mind's notions), Novalis (wisdom as the eternal "priestess of hearts") and Soloviev (wisdom as the vision of universal unity; cf. Claudel, *Ode* 2). All these approaches share a universalism based on the function of wisdom, which they use to display no doubt certain overriding connections but also (as in the case of Frank-Duquesne and Teilhard de Chardin) to ignore some vital differences and inviolable limits. One may hear echoes, however, of the ancient empiricist and epistemological notion of wisdom when Kant defines wisdom as a practical "Idea" bearing on the necessary unity of all possible goals (*Critique of Pure Reason,* 1, B, section 2), and when he defines science as a methodically assured training in wisdom (*Critique of Practical Reason,* Conclusion). The Stoic notion seems to be taken up again and deepened when Peter Wust relates wisdom to the *insecuritas* of the Christian situation.

3. *General theory of wisdom.* If one now tries to integrate the notion of wisdom in a general survey, one must start with the mutual relationship of wisdom and truth, as suggested at the beginning, and see how it stands to the historical development. Taking as basis a notion of wisdom which is in the mean between the empirical and the theological interpretations (though neither are denied), one notices that in contrast to the constant threat posed by appearance and illusion to truth, there is no negative counterpart to wisdom. "Foolishness" (in the biblical sense) only means that wisdom has not yet come. It is not the formal negation of wisdom. Compared therefore with truth, wisdom has reached a definitive position, having passed the critical limit of where it could be confused with its opposite. This is confirmed by the function it has in all its variants — that of being an unshakable safeguard within the realm which it embraces. And the variants in turn may be explained as so many efforts to indicate the sufficient reason of this assurance, experienced as evidence and protection, and at the limit even as a mystical rapture. In the empiricist view, the ground is the sum total of personal and traditional experience. In the epistemological approach, it is the ever increasing certainty of the philosophical knowledge bearing on the ultimate grounds of being. In theology, it is the communication with the divine knowledge and being, a communication mediated by wisdom. Naturally, the theological interpretation constantly gives rise to efforts to give concrete form to this mediation. In the Pseudo-Dionysius, wisdom is a passive experience of the divine (*De Divinis Nominibus,* 7, 1: παθεῖν τὰ θεῖα). In Wust, there is a "wisdom of faith" (already outlined in St. Thomas), where faith is the "risk inspired by wisdom"

which overcomes "insecurity" (*Ungewissheit und Wagnis*, XV). To the same context we may attach the visionary presence of wisdom personified (from Athene guiding Ulysses to the visions of Sophia in Böhme and Soloviev), as also the biblical identification of wisdom with Christ. In the latter case, however, the function of wisdom is not exhausted by the safeguard it offers. It is the principle of knowledge as well as of certainty. But the wisdom identified with Christ and so based on the historical existence of an individual is a noetic principle inasmuch as the identification elevates the individual existence of Christ to the rank of the absolutely universal.

This means that all inadmissible generalizations are avoided when the life of one single man is taken as the visible representation of the totality of being and history, and these are explained in the light of that one figure (K. Barth, R. Guardini, H. Urs von Balthasar). This is the ancient recapitulation theory of St. Irenaeus. The problem of how wisdom is its own light is solved by the truth that Christ "was made wisdom for us" (cf. 1 Cor 1:30). But Christ proves himself wisdom by lightening the darkness of all beings by his own way of existing, even when reason seeking the truth fails — in the question of the meaning of each life and of history.

This is the reason why the category of the personal was so fully worked out in the wisdom speculation of the Alexandrian and Cappadocian theologians, and why the most important attempts at a theology of history in patristic and scholastic thought came from enlightened students of wisdom such as St. Augustine, Joachim of Fiore and St. Bonaventure. In this line of thought, wisdom is superior to truth both in certainty and in importance, while truth is merely a stage destined to be absorbed in the greater riches of wisdom. The achievement of such a goal now seems to be more urgent than ever, now that the sciences are being encapsulated into so many different specialities and thus becoming more and more alienated from each other. But with the trend towards abstraction growing stronger than ever, especially in the quantified thinking of the natural sciences and the schematic operations of technology, the present time seems to be threatened most acutely by the "decline of wisdom" (G. Marcel). The threat must be countered all the more vigorously by considered attention to the wisdom in which the opposition between abstract and concrete, universal and particular, idea and reality is both established and comprehended.

See also *Knowledge, Truth* I, *Transcendence, Philosophy, Old Testament Books* III.

BIBLIOGRAPHY. E. van Steenberghe, "Nicolas (24) de Cusa", *DTC*, XI/1 (1931), cols. 601–12; F. K. Ballaine, *Relations between Wisdom and Science* (1936); R. Remsberg, *Wisdom and Science at Port-Royal and the Oratory* (1940); B. Schultze, "Der gegenwärtige Streit um die Sophia, die göttliche Weisheit, in der Orthodoxie", *Stimmen der Zeit* 70 (1940), pp. 318–24; J. Maritain, *Science and Wisdom* (1940); W. Jaeger, *Aristotle: Fundamentals of the History of His Development* (2nd ed., 1948); J. M. Clark, *The Great German Mystics* (1949), pp. 7–35 (Eckhardt), pp. 54–74 (Suso); id., *The Little Book of Eternal Wisdom, etc.* (by Suso), translation, introduction and notes (1953); *Les sciences et la sagesse: Actes du 5e Congrès des sociétés de philosophie de langue française, Bordeaux* (1950); O. Lacombe, ed., *Sagesse* (1951); É. Gilson, *Wisdom and Love in St. Thomas Aquinas* (1951); P. Rotte, "Niccolà Cusano", *Enciclopedia cattolica*, VIII (1952), cols. 1819–22; E. Biser, "Was ist Weisheit?", *Wissenschaft und Weisheit* 15 (1952), pp. 51–58, 98–108; R. Jolivet, *De Rosmini à Lachelier*, with A. Rosmini's *L'idée de la Sagesse* (1953); G. Marcel, *Le déclin de la sagesse* (1954); F. Cayré, *La contemplation augustinienne* (1954); J. Vialatoux, *L'intention philosophique* (2nd ed., 1954); M. Kevin O'Hara, *Connotations of Wisdom according to St. Thomas Aquinas* (1956); E. Rice, *Renaissance Idea of Wisdom* (1958); M. D'Arcy, *Meeting of Love and Knowledge, Perennial Wisdom* (1958); J. Ratzinger, *Die Geschichtstheologie des heiligen Bonaventura* (1959); G. von Rad, *Old Testament Theology*, I (1962), pp. 411–53; H. Schmidt, "Wesen und Geschichte der Weisheit", supplement to *ZAW* 101 (1966); R. Murphy, "The Interpretation of Old Testament Wisdom Literature", *Interpretation* 23 (1969), pp. 289–301.

Eugen Biser

WORD OF GOD

A. Biblical

The primal human sense of the importance of the word can already be seen among the primitive peoples, where the word has magical powers and can be used to put compulsion on the gods. But there is another perspective, in which the word appears as the power of a godhead, which explains its presence in the theogonies of ancient Egypt and the cosmogonies of Babylon (creation epic). But here too the word is supposed to have magical power, raised to its highest coefficient in the primal godhead.

In the OT, the word of God is given special theological significance in the Priestly writings (e.g., the account of creation, Gen 1:1–2:4b), though the noun-form, "the word of God", is not used in the account of creation. The power and wisdom of the creator is revealed as he speaks. The saving function of the word of God is also brought out. The notion of the word of God as both creative and salutary was underlined by the fact that the conservation of the world and the historical path of Israel were attributed to the power of the word of God (e.g., Ps 147:15, 18f.).

But it was in the prophetical writings that the word of God was given its really central place, just as it was in these writings that the theological development of the notion was rooted. The character of the word appears in the vocation narratives, where the decisive element is always the transmission of the word of Yahweh (cf. Is 6:1ff.; Jer 1:9f.; Ezek 2:8f.; Hos 1:1f.; Joel 1:1; Jon 1:1; Mich 1:1; etc.). The transmission of the word is such as to show its absolute power. Hence, in the mouth of the prophet, its function is not merely to convey truths such as the prediction of the future. The word communicated by the prophet is charged with power and moulds history (1 Kg 17:1). As the proclamation of the primal word of Yahweh, the prophetic saying is the means by which the divine decrees are put into force — the will of God to judge, but also to give new life (Ezek 37:1ff.) and to set up a new covenant (Jer 31:31ff.; Is 54:10). In the Deuteronomic history, the word, as well as being illuminating event, is also seen from an aspect which opens up greater scope for propositional articulation. A single precept (Deut 15:15) or the whole law (Deut 30:14) can be called the word of God. The word of God given objectivated form in the law is also seen as having salutary character: it is the word which "gives . . . life" (Ps 119:50). Towards the Christian era, the Torah appears as an unfailing source of life for the individual as for the people. In all its forms, the word of God has a "dialogal", responsorial character, which presupposes that the receiver hears it as he ought (Deut 6:4; Is 7:13; Jer 22:2), that is, turning to God with his whole heart and soul.

In the NT, the word of God retains the meaning given it in OT prophetism. Thus the whole revelation attested in the OT can be called the word of God (Mt 1:22; 2:15; Mk 12:26; Rom 15:10). But the word of God is given a special character by being linked to the person of Jesus and the Christ-event. On the lips of Jesus, the word of God is the good news of the saving event which is taking place (Lk 5:1; 8:11, 21) and it has as such an especially powerful character (Mt 7:28f.). The words of Jesus bring about the events of salvation (cf. Lk 24:44) and show, above all in the miracles, a coincidence between word of God and striking deed (cf. Mt 8:8). A certain coincidence between the word of God and the person of Christ is indicated in the synoptics in the assertion that those who are ashamed of the words of Jesus are ashamed of the Lord himself (Mk 8:38; Lk 9:26). St. Paul goes still further in this direction when he speaks of Christ as the Yes and Amen in which all the divine promises are fulfilled (2 Cor 1:20). Similarly, the Letter to the Hebrews explains that the word of God has been finally and completely uttered in the person of the Son (Heb 1:1f.).

The firmest identification of the word of God and the person of Christ is found in the writings of St. John, where Christ is the word of God coming from the realm of pre-existence (Jn 1:1f.) which appeared in the flesh (Jn 1:14) and which represents the definitive power of salvation in the world, since it is the life of God (1 Jn 1:1). An important element of the NT concept is that the word incarnate in Christ persists in the Church and remains present in it. Thus the apostles, the ministers of the word by the call of Christ (Lk 1:2), see themselves not as the conveyors of a doctrine but as heralds of the salvation come in Christ and of the mystery of God revealed in him. This salvation, and hence Christ himself, is present in the word of the apostles. Hence the "word of God" or "word of the Lord" (Acts 13:46f.; 1 Cor 14:36; Phil 1:14; Col 3:16), which builds up the Church as it is preached by the apostles, is not merely a message coming from the Lord, but the word in which Christ himself imparts himself to men. Hence St. Paul can declare succinctly: "We preach . . . Jesus Christ as Lord" (2 Cor 4:5). But how can Christ himself speak in the words of the apostles? According to the NT, it is because the Holy Spirit, in whom Christ discloses himself after his departure (cf. 2 Cor 3:17), gives human words the spiritual dynamism which makes this representation possible.

As presence of the salvific Christ-event,

the preaching of the word of God must be a permanent divine institution in the Church. Hence even in the lifetime of the apostles there are fellow-workers in the field of the gospel, to whom the service of the word of God is committed (Acts 8:4ff.; 1 Cor 16:10; 2 Cor 1:19; 1 Tim 4:12f.; 2 Tim 4:2; Tit 2:1). This service is not confined to oral preaching. It soon takes the form of fixing this preaching in writing. It is a specific trait of the apostles that they claim the same authority for their letters as for their preaching (2 Thess 2:2, 15; 3:14; 2 Cor 10:11f.; 1 Tim 3:14f.). Their letters are also a "word of exhortation" (Heb 13:22; 1 Pet 5:12) in which the grace of God is at work. Hence the synoptics can identify their record of the coming of salvation in Christ with the gospel, that is, with God's revelation of salvation in Christ (Mk 1:1; 14:9; Mt 24:14; 26:13). The conviction was early formed in the Church that the fixation of the apostolic testimony to Christ in certain writings was an expression of the living gospel of Christ and hence the word of God in the words of men.

B. History of Theology

For the ancient Church the words of the apostles, committed to writing, were the word of God which was to be preserved inviolate (Rev 19:9; 21:5; 22:8). In the letter of the Roman bishop, Clement, to the Church of Corinth (c. A.D. 96) both the OT (13, 3; 40, 1; 53, 1) and the words of Jesus transmitted in writing (13:1; 46, 7) are designated as the word of God which brings about faith and builds up the Church (48, 5).

St. Ignatius of Antioch uses a metaphor which was to be echoed again and again. He sees the Scriptures as the flesh and blood of the incarnate Logos. In the (pseudonymous) second letter of Clement, the most ancient Christian sermon, the notion of the word of God as saving is extended to take in the ecclesiastical preaching, which is called a saving power (15, 1), and in which God brings about "joy" for the obedient and "damnation" for the disobedient (15, 5). The *Didache* also affirms that the Lord is present where his glory is preached (4, 1). In Origen, Scripture, understood incarnationally (in connection with inspiration), is the "one complete body of the Logos" (*Homily on Jeremiah,* Fragment 2), while Church preaching is also the word of God

(*De Principiis,* III, 1, 1). In Scripture reading, prayer and preaching the "manna of the divine word" is distributed to believers (*Homily on Exodus,* XI, 3). These views continued to be held in Greek theology, where St. Basil the Great, for instance, calls Church preaching "the morning and evening meal" of the faithful (*In Hexaemeron,* Homily VIII, 8). St. John Chrysostom speaks of Scripture as the medicine of the soul (Homily *In Lazarum,* 3, 1) and of preaching as a liturgical sacrifice (Sermon *Cum Presbyter,* 1). Side by side with this notion of preaching as a salutary act, there is a sacramental theology of worship, though no explanation of how they are linked is given.

In the theology of the West, St. Augustine represents the convergence of thinking on the word of God. At times neo-Platonist influence can be noted in a strongly transcendent notion of the word of God (cf. *Enarrationes in Ps* 44, 5), but thanks to his realistic understanding of the incarnation, St. Augustine sees there an "inverbation" and considers the word of God as a permanent saving power. Thus Scripture is the handwriting of God, in which the word of God lives for us. The preaching of the word, which goes back to the apostles, is linked with the Church, where the "word-event" goes on, efficacious for salvation, as appears from its various designations: the "wholesome food" (*Tractatus in Joannem,* VII, no. 24), the "divine banquet" (*ibid.,* no. 2), the "bread of angels" (*ibid.,* XIII, no. 4) and the "voice of the Spirit" (*ibid.,* XII, no. 5). This explains how St. Augustine can equate word and sacrament, as may be seen from the affirmation that we are "born in the Spirit through the word and the sacrament" (*ibid.,* XII, no. 5). With his dialectic of "foris" and "intra", St. Augustine opens up new depths in the theology of the word, as may be seen above all from his notion of Christ as the inward teacher, who is also the decisive force in the preaching. A number of considerations put forward by St. Augustine on the philosophy of language and the theory of knowledge, especially with regard to the "inner word", seem to deprive the spoken word of some of its significance. But the incarnational element is maintained, in the sense that the outward word of preaching is a necessary help for fallen man in the mediation of salvation.

In the early Middle Ages, Scripture and preaching — the latter mainly commentary on Scripture — remained efficacious means of salvation, so that Alcuin (d. 804) could say that the preacher generates, through his words, new sons for the King of Heaven, just as through the administration of the sacraments (*In Canticum,* c. 6). But in the interiorized spirituality of monasticism, the process of salvation was mainly seen as an inner, spiritual event, which led to the accent being shifted from the outward word and its preacher to the inward, mystical action of God and his grace. In the same way, interest in Scripture is centred less on the actual words than on a spiritual and mystical interpretation of them. One of the main questions left unanswered was how preaching in the biblical sense could be understood as an efficacious means of salvation.

St. Thomas Aquinas answers the question by a comparison between natural procreation and preaching. In the latter, the communication of the divine word brings about the transmission of the life of grace (*In Epistulam ad Titum*). Here the preaching of the word of God takes on a didactic character. The growing interest in the sacraments and the grasp of their objective efficacy also obscured the salutary function of preaching and reduced the function of the word in the Church to the creation of a disposition. This did not lead, however, to any disregard of Scripture as the word of God or of the preaching which expounded Scripture. According to St. Bonaventure, the word of Scripture is a divine seed which brings about rebirth in man (*In Lucam,* ch. 8, no. 17). The preacher too utters "God's precious, pure and melodious word" (*Prothema primum*) and thus becomes the "mouth of God" (*In Lucam,* ch. 10).

Along with this realistic conception of God's activity in the word, spiritualistic trends were also at work in the Middle Ages which made everything depend on the inner enlightenment and neglected the word of Scripture (the Beguines). But they were not enough to deprive the word of its incarnational and kerygmatic significance. Word and (eucharistic) sacrament come very close together in Thomas à Kempis, when he speaks of the table of the holy altar and of the table of the divine law which contains the holy doctrine and gives instruction in the true faith (*Imitation of Christ,* IV, 11). The unity of word and sacrament which was here signalled was dissolved by Wycliffe, with whom the *sola scriptura* principle makes its appearance, subordinating the sacraments to the preach-

ing of the word of God. The Council of Trent attributed also to tradition the normative character of the word of God by citing the Nicene Creed and speaking of it as the "sword of the spirit of the word of God" (Session III). The Reformation led to new developments in the understanding of the word of God (see D below).

C. THEOLOGICAL SURVEY

Theological investigation of the word of God must rely on a previous philosophical elucidation of language and human speech, since the word of God always comes as word of man, so that the natural speech of man is the medium of the word of God. This preliminary examination shows that human language has a rational, aesthetic and dynamic function which provides the prerequisites for the coming of the word of God as divine truth, divine deed and self-dedication of God. It can also be shown that man the hearer can receive the transcendent, supernatural word of God. The possibility is based on the responsive character of man's person with regard to God. But for the actual hearing of the supernatural word, the recipient needs the faith and grace which make the assimilation of the word of God transcendentally possible. This does not lessen the importance of the external word of God, coming in history and in human terms, since it is only by this that the subjective, *a priori* power to hear is actuated. This historical word has a history which came to a climax in Jesus Christ, the "Word made flesh", and which leads to various developments of the word in the Church. To signal the various forms of the word of God is a special task of systematic theology. It begins with Scripture, which according to the Catholic view not only contains but actually is the word of God. But here it should be noted that the "literary" character of the biblical documents is only a stepping-stone on the way to a new life of the word in the preaching, in which the original life of the word of God spoken by the apostles is again brought into action.

In spite of its being the word of God, a character essentially based on its inspiration, Scripture is not simply identical with the word of God. It also has the character of human testimony, that of the apostles and the primitive Church, to the revelation which has come. It is the word of God inasmuch as it is the human answer in faith to this word. But the answer is not merely the self-understanding and self-expression of the believer. The answer rather takes up the word coming from God and gives testimony to it by giving it expression.

Further, when understood as testimony to the word of God, Scripture is not identical with revelation. It rather points to revelation, but not after the manner of an empty sign. It acts in a quasi-sacramental way, presenting and actualizing what has been attested.

Understood in this way, the word of God is never at the disposition of human words and never completely rendered by them. So the Church itself, when applying and explaining Scripture, finds itself always in front of the word of God as something greater than itself and something to which it is subject. Scripture may therefore be understood as the prolongation of the word of revelation which came in Christ, and hence as word of God in the incarnational sense. Nonetheless, the "divine" element in it is not to be brought down to the level of something static which could be considered as a type of "thing".

The word of God becomes fully and actually itself only in the preaching of the Church. This is confirmed by the truth of experience that the scriptural words as such are not the essence of the preaching, but the scriptural word which is preached (i.e., the scriptural statement). The Catholic understanding of preaching may therefore be expressed in the formula which was earlier claimed most readily by the Churches of the Reformation: *Praedicatio verbi divini est verbum divinum*. Here theology must strive to show in detail how the word of God today can still come in its full reality through a human preacher. First, the preacher must be called and sent by Christ or through the Church which continues his work. For "how can men preach unless they are sent?" (Rom 10:15.) This mission binds human will and action so closely to God that preaching is essentially a ministry or service commanded and made possible by God. But this bond does not explain how the human words of the preacher really give expression to the word of God according to its meaning.

This is only guaranteed when the preaching reflects revelation and its normative attestation in Scripture. Hence the scriptural nature of preaching is the decisive criterion of the content, showing that the divine self-utterance takes place in the human discourse of the preacher. This does not imply a mere parrotting of the words of Scripture (biblicism). It is the attestation, with the help of the Spirit, of this divine word or message, which can speak to the hearer in his particular situation when the preacher starts from a given text and makes it relevant in new words. As a salutary event, the preaching of the word of God comes close to the sacraments. The relationship between word and sacrament must be defined in such a way that there is no superfluous doubling of the salutary act, while at the same time neither must appear as deficient compared with the other.

Various explanations of the relationship are given in Catholic theology. Preaching is the "foreword" to the most highly "condensed" word, that of the sacrament (H. Schlier). Or the correlation can be described as the unity of word and action (G. Söhngen), or as the co-ordination of offer and reality of salvation (V. Warnach). From another point of view, the sacrament is understood as the closest form of union with Christ (M. Schmaus) or as the supreme realization of the efficacious word, in the radical commitment of the Church (K. Rahner). Finally, the relationship may also be understood as a twofold movement, from God to man (the word) and from man to God (the sacrament) (O. Semmelroth). It is always maintained that word and sacrament are not disparate things but interlocking phases of the one process of salvation.

D. PROTESTANT THEOLOGY

In the Churches of the Reformation the word of God has always been a central concept both for faith and theology, though understood in many different ways down to the present day. According to Luther's Christological explanation of the word of God in the gospel and in the preaching, the saving event is present in the word, but only for those who possess the Spirit of God, and only in the form of the actual preaching. In contrast to the stress here laid on the *extra nos* and the incarnational structure of the word of God, there is a certain spiritualization of the word in Zwingli and Calvin. Stress is laid on the divine action, which is of an inward nature, without the medium of the word. When the principles of "Scripture alone" and verbal inspiration came to the fore, ancient Protestant orthodoxy was led to identify Scripture and the word of God and to affirm the *efficacia Verbi divini etiam ante et extra usum,* which brought with it the view that the word of God was a set of doctrines. The supernaturalistic concept of the word of God (see *Supernaturalism*) held by ancient Protestantism was attacked by theologians under the influence of the Enlightenment, and also by Schleiermacher, inspired by his religious subjectivism. This paved the way for a loss of understanding for the word of God which was particularly clear in W. Herrmann, who reduced revelation in the strict sense to the inward experiences of Jesus. It was left to dialectical theology to win a hearing for the theological understanding of the word of God.

In the theology of K. Barth, the word of God has three forms, revelation, Bible, preaching. The non-identity of Scripture and the word of God is stressed. Thus Scripture and preaching have to become the word of God anew at each moment, in an "actualist" sense. This actualism or new creation at each moment is still further emphasized by R. Bultmann, for whom the word of God is an existentialist and eschatological address, with no real content, but only leading man to a new self-understanding. This reduction of the word of God to its formal element ("formalization") is corrected by E. Brunner, who sees in the word of God the self-disclosure of God to mankind. This includes God's making known the truth about himself. Similarly, G. Ebeling regards the word-event as God's self-presentation, which illuminates the situation of man's existence and opens up to him the "future" (salvation).

This breakthrough to a high theological and anthropological estimation of the word of God is abandoned by P. Tillich, who sees the word of God as a symbol for the mystery of the divine ground of being, which possesses the character of "Logos". W. Pannenberg takes a resolute stand against a word-of-God theology, since he looks for revelation outside the word of God and sees universal history as revelatory in its effect.

Whenever the relationship of word and sacrament is discussed in Protestant theology, a lower value is often assigned to the sacraments. Their role is simply to bring out clearly the character of act in the word (P. Althaus). Or they are simply clearer ways of giving the message (K. Barth). Or they are considered simply on the psychological plane, as a way of visualizing the mystery of the divine presence in the word (H. Stephan).

See also *Dialectical Theology, Inspiration, Prophetism, Protestantism* I, *Revelation* I, II, *Sacraments* I.

BIBLIOGRAPHY. F. Gogarten, "Das Wort und die Frage nach der Kirche", *Zwischen den Zeiten* 4 (1926); E. Thurneysen, *Das Wort Gottes und die Kirche* (1927); K. Barth, "Das Wort in der Theologie von Schleiermacher bis Ritschl", *Gesammelte Vorträge*, II (1928); id., *Church Dogmatics*, I: *The Doctrine of the Word of God*, 1 (1949), 2 (1956); id., with E. Thurneysen, *Revolutionary Theology in the Making* (1964); E. Brunner, *The Word and the World* (1931); id., *The Word of God and Modern Man* (1965); F. Schmidt, *Der Primat des Wortes in der evangelischen Kirche* (1931); F. Häussermann, "Wortempfang und Symbol in der alttestamentlichen Prophetie", supplement to *ZAW* 58 (1932); H. Bornkamm, *Das Wort Gottes bei Luther* (1933); R. Bultmann, *Jesus and the Word* (1934); id., *Essays Philosophical and Theological* (1955); id., *Existence and Faith* (1961); L. Dürr, *Die Wertung des göttlichen Wortes im Alten Testament und alten Orient* (1938); R. Asting, *Die Verkündigung des Wortes Gottes im Urchristentum* (1939); E. Eilers, *Gottes Wort: Eine Theologie der Predigt nach Bonaventura* (1941); H. Ringgren, *Word and Wisdom* (1947); R. Wallace, *Calvin's Doctrine of the Word and Sacrament* (1953); J. Crehan, "Verbum dei incarnatum et verbum dei scripturae", *JTS,* new series 6 (1955), pp. 87–90; R. M. Grant, *The Letter and the Spirit* (1957); Z. Alszeghy, "Die Theologie des Wortes Gottes bei den mittelalterlichen Theologen", *Gregorianum* 39 (1958); H. Noack, *Sprache und Offenbarung* (1960); A. Brandenburg, *Gericht und Evangelium: Zur Worttheologie des jungen Luther* (1960); S. Mowinckel, *The Old Testament as Word of God* (1960); L. Bouyer, *Word, Church and Sacraments in Protestantism and Catholicism* (1961); G. Auzou, *La parole de Dieu* (3rd ed., 1962); P. Ackroyd, "The Vitality of the Word of God in the Old Testament", *Annual of the Swedish Theological Institute* 1 (1962), pp. 7–23; R. Guardini, *The Word of God* (1962); H. Schlier, *Wort Gottes* (2nd ed., 1962); H. Volk, *Zur Theologie des Wortes Gottes* (1962); G. Söhngen, *Analogie und Metapher: Kleine Philosophie und Theologie der Sprache* (1962); G. Ebeling, *Word and Faith* (1963); id., *God and Word* (1967); id., *The Word of God and Tradition* (1968); L.-M. Dewailly, "Course et gloire de la Parole", *Revue Biblique* 71 (1964), pp. 25–41; H. Urs von Balthasar, *Word and Revelation* (1964); M. Schmaus, *Wahrheit als Heilsbegegnung* (1964); G. von Rad, *Old Testament Theology,* II (1965), pp. 91–94; P. Bormann, *Die Heilswirksamkeit der Verkündigung nach dem Apostel Paulus* (1965); H. Ott, *Theology and Preaching* (1965); O. Semmelroth, *The Preaching Word* (1965); G. Wingren, *The Living Word* (1965); K. Rahner and J. Ratzinger, *Revelation and Tradition,* Quaestiones Disputatae 17 (1966); K. Rahner, *Theological Investigations,* IV (1966), pp. 253–86; L. Scheffczyck, *Von der Heilsmacht des Wortes* (1966); F. Schnitzler, *Zur Theologie der Verkündigung in den Predigten des heiligen*

Augustinus (1968); F. Sobotta, *Die Heilswirksamkeit der Predigt in der theologischen Diskussion der Gegenwart* (1968); M. Schoch, *Verbi Divini Mysterium* (1968); A. Malet, *Thought of Rudolf Bultmann* (1969).

Leo Scheffczyk

WORK

The person who considers the development of Christian thought as a synthetic whole cannot fail to notice an essential trait which escapes purely theoretical and scholarly analysis. This is the fact that in Christianity kerygmatic revival and the attention to earthly realities, a new impetus to the gospel message and the involvement of the Christian in a constructively evolving society go hand in hand. This combination is in direct contradiction to the current but facile separation of the apostolic ministry from doctrinal speculation. In fact, it is the paradox of the gospel, which has been realized down the centuries, that the Word of God, which of its very nature is both transcendent and gratuitous, finds expression in an incarnation by being immanent in the very course of history. We have here one of the laws which constitute the economy of salvation.

If we wish to situate and define theologically this human reality which we call work, our first impulse should not be to consider it from the point of view of its moral conditions, sound or harmful, but rather to view it as an earthly reality which has an obediential potency to the impact of the gospel. We shall thus align ourselves with the realistic approach of the history of salvation where the distinction between nature and grace does not so separate profane work from the mystery of Christ, which is accomplished through a recapitulation of the whole of creation, that the former becomes mere matter for merit.

At the moment we are passing through one of those periods in the history of Christianity when the evangelical awakening includes an earthly involvement in the progress of the world. It is true that excess and distortion threaten their healthy cohesion, either by too naturalistic an interpretation of the economy of salvation, which confuses it with human progress, or, on the contrary, by a lack of appreciation of the eschatological dimensions of earthly enterprises. Thus, behind the current controversies, the relationship between nature and grace is once more in question, this time in historical terms, as the problem of the coming of the Kingdom of God and of the construction of the world. The theology of work is at the very heart of this problem. That is why, after long neglect, this reality occupies a place henceforward in contemporary theology.

It would therefore be a mistake to see the theological study of work as a passing whim, provoked by the impact of industrial civilization on a disconcerted Christian community. It is true that the individual and collective transformation of the condition of man has taken a particular form of Christian conservatism by surprise, a conservatism which has remained closely though unconsciously allied to an artisan society and an agrarian economy. But at this conjuncture it is not enough to modify practical behaviour. What is required is a deeper understanding of the divine plan which will enable us to determine the relationship between man and the cosmos in what was formerly referred to as "divine government". It was in this way that anthropology found its place in the tract on creation in the Summas of the Middle Ages.

Consequently, one can foresee that a purely historical study of the ancient texts of the Scriptures and of the Fathers as a *locus theologicus* will not suffice. In fact, the simple way of life of the craftsman did not permit man to gauge his capacity for transforming the material world, nor his role in the march of history. An immutable nature in an unchanged universe, man only perceived in a summary way his orientation to society and his historical dimension. Hence classical philosophy, from the Greeks to the 18th century, upholds a static conception of man. And Christian catechesis long considered work merely from the point of view of its psychological and moral consequences.

However, if re-read as the highly relevant word of God, these laconic texts engender a deep appreciation of the religious value of man's activity, not only for his subjective perfection, but in the work itself. These texts are not only principles from which conclusions and applications may be drawn; they are charged with a religious meaning which ferments in each new situation. Living tradition enables the ancient Scripture to throw light on the destiny and the functions of man as he becomes more conscious of them under the impulse of a new civilization. "Fill the earth and subdue it; have dominion over the fish of the sea and over the birds of the air and over every living thing that moves upon the earth." This poetic and naturalistic proclamation of Genesis (1:28) now takes in magnificently the cosmic powers and techniques of a humanity which is discovering and exploiting the laws of nature. These laws of providence are communicated to man's intelligence which is thereby associated in the work of creation. This co-operation gives its full dimension to the doctrine of the *imago Dei* of the Greek Fathers. We are therefore justified in seeking in these ancient texts, composed for a primitive society, a religious and Christian understanding of scientific and industrial humanity in the 20th century. This task is not restricted to theoretical theology; catechetical instruction and especially adult catechesis has the pressing duty of integrating the economic and social content of civilization into a doctrine of work.

It is in this perspective that the OT must be read, with due allowance for its archaic basis. Its vocabulary is already significant. Two terms are used: *melakha,* denoting God's creative work and defining his presence in history as carrying out the plan drawn up on the first day; *avoda,* which means the work of a slave or servitude including the slavery imposed by Nebuchadnezar. But the words overlap, and work has the paradoxical connotations of inexorable constraint and joyful expansiveness, unremitting compulsion and liberating self-fulfilment. And many languages bring out the contrast between labour which is tiresome, slavish, deadly, and work which is exalting, perfecting, sacred.

In this way, in keeping with the conditions of time and place, according to the temperament of the sacred writers, the books of the OT provide the most disparate judgments on man's work. It is impossible to give an abstract classification of these teachings; it is better, in keeping with the rules of sound biblical theology, to point to the various social settings in which they evolved: the transition from nomadic to town life, legislation on slavery, the description of the great building enterprises of the kings, the adjurations of the prophets in favour of the poor and oppressed, the encouraging or sceptical maxims of the sages. Almost any conclusion can be drawn from these texts; in fact, Judaeo-Christian thought throughout the ages reveals the relativity of the conclusions and prescriptions that theologians, catechists and teachers have drawn from them. Thus, for

centuries the statements of the Book of Proverbs or of Ecclesiasticus (especially 38:24–34) have nourished a form of theological reflection which did not go beyond a prosaic moral code made up of modest courage, disillusioned honesty, earthly foresight, mediocre ambition and practical wisdom.

The inspiration for a theology of work is to be found in the wide perspectives of the economy willed by God and realized in nature and history rather than in these detached elements connected with practical utility. Moreover, it is here that the contrast with myths of pagan cosmogonies is most in evidence. God himself "works" by bringing his work into being. The first chapter of Genesis has been and still is the epic symbolism and imagery which inspire all theology of work. From this creation the free and sovereign power passes into the conduct of peoples and individuals; the anthropomorphic images make intelligible for us the co-operation of this supreme power with the freedom of the creature whom the Creator has associated with his work at the centre of the visible universe. God, who plants the vine and gathers in the harvest, is like an energetic worker subject to fatigue and failure; he is like a woman "in labour". Once his work is completed he takes his rest; for rest is the delightful state in which all activity finds its completion. But for man, this ideal is never attained: work which should be a joyful, spontaneous activity is, in fact, difficult and painful and has the character of a punishment. Nature refuses to obey man; the primitive relationship between them has been distorted. The earth is no longer a marvellous garden whose cultivation brings happiness. The theology of original sin draws inspiration from this fact.

This doctrine of divine government loses nothing through the coming of the New Covenant; but the fact that the Word of God has become man to incorporate man in the divine life, transforms both the relationship of man to nature and the end of history. Human undertakings are both exalted and devalued: exalted because Christ recapitulates in man the whole of reality and with it the values which have been established through man's relationship with the world. Now all creation enters in some way, through the glorification of the sons of God, into the economy of salvation. But man's undertakings are also devalued because total salvation is achieved outside of history. The

Kingdom of God belongs to an order other than the construction of the world. The pericope Rom 8:18–22 gives a cosmic setting to the evangelical preaching on renunciation, suffering, and poverty as means of liberation, and as conditions of fraternal charity while awaiting the return of Christ. There will be new heavens and a new earth (cf. 1 Pet 3:13); the resurrection of the body contributes to this mysterious transformation.

Christians are caught in the inner ambiguity of this mystery. The expectation of the Parousia leads the Thessalonians so to undervalue earthly tasks that they fall into idleness. Without going to this extreme, the interpretation of Scripture and pastoral preaching lay down a continuous line of spiritual doctrine according to which heaven is the homeland and the earth a place of exile. There is a general belief, supported by apocalyptic themes, that the passage from the world to final beatitude at the end of time will be marked by a violent rupture. The world is only a temporary scaffolding, the earth with its works will be utterly consumed (cf. 2 Pet 3:10).

Throughout the whole of Christian antiquity, simple catechetical instruction and spiritual doctrine did not develop an organic doctrine co-ordinating the elements scattered throughout the Scriptures. For lack of such a doctrine, which social conditions did not demand, the current way of thinking was preoccupied with a form of morality more conscious of the dangers of luxury and riches than of the possible benefits of the production of goods. The simple subsistence economy of these centuries did not give rise to a different perspective. There was nothing there to bring to light other demands of the gospel. The efficacity of the gospel, evoked by a sense of brotherhood rather than by objective reflection, bore on the dignity of work, no matter how lowly, in contrast to the contempt in which it was held by the philosophers of antiquity. Although the dissolution of the institution of slavery was slow, the Christian spirit penetrated deeply into its structures, as it was later to do in the case of feudal serfdom. The monastic state ratified, both socially and institutionally, this evolution. The example of Christ, of his life of labour and his modest trade mystically nourished this rehabilitation. The theme of Christ the artisan expressed a new feeling for the reality of the incarnation and at the same time conferred on the hard life of the worker an evangelical value beyond its

moral worth. Henceforward in the Church, at each economic upheaval, the theme of the workshop of Nazareth and of the hidden life of Christ was to be taken up again, right into the 20th century. But this image has a certain ambiguity because it leaves in the background the double perspective of the Word-Creator (St. John) and the recapitulating Christ (St. Paul).

The doctors of the Middle Ages sought to lay the foundations for a theology of work, not directly in a study of the Scriptures, but in a philosophy of nature. This led them to affirm the ontological and epistemological reality of secondary causes and consequently of human activity, within the framework of a providence at once transcendent and immanent. The school of Chartres (12th century), the reading of the neo-Platonists and of Aristotle, together with some borrowings from the Greek Fathers were the determining elements in a new understanding of man in his relationship to nature. Man is a "microcosm" and, therefore, in the divine plan, can no longer be considered — as the Gregorian tradition would have it — as a substitute for the fallen angels, whose place he is intended to fill. The technical advances of the 12th and 13th centuries, the growth of market economy, the conquest of communal liberties, combined to engender, together with the spirit of initiative, not only the human problems of corporative organization, but also a more or less explicit consciousness of man's role in the construction of a City whose terrestrial significance is not diminished by eternal hopes. Theologians began to ask the question: Is a man's trade not part of his vocation? While the monks were content to take the life of the angels as their model, the new Mendicant Orders strove to become the native counsellors of the city confraternities where evangelical fraternity found a favourable soil in the relationships of work or even in the communal assemblies.

With the Renaissance the pace quickened in the exploration of nature, the knowledge of man, economic expansion and above all the extraordinary growth of the sciences. Great religious fervour was not lacking to sanctify the new man. But theology, both scholarly and popular, remained alien to this new vision of the world. In order to produce a theology of work it would have been necessary to formulate first a theology of science whose rational autonomy would have been recognized without detriment to its divine origin. Christians were destined to suffer from this divorce right into the 20th century. Science and technology are producing a "civilization of work" outside the light of faith. An evangelical and apostolic reaction has forced Christians to formulate the problem, to welcome this earthly conjuncture, to grasp the relevance of the ancient word of God.

Summary though it may be, this review of biblical and traditional thought shows how disappointing they are as a basis for a "theology of work". Because they are closely linked to their economic context, to different categories of thought and to the conditions of their place and time, these texts can only provide norms when they are considered on the higher level of God's design which, taken together, they reveal, and with reference to a philosophy of nature which it was not their task to provide. In other words, they will only shed light if attention is paid to the evolution of events, to the development of societies and civilizations and to the rationalization of knowledge and conduct, in short, to a philosophy of terrestrial realities. It would be erroneous to envisage a "spiritualist", abstract and timeless theology which would not integrate into its structure a rational investigation of the nature and history of man in terms of the Christian and terrestrial experience of man. Such is the *locus theologicus* of our reflections.

According to the principles already enunciated by the Greek Fathers and by the masters of the Middle Ages, and amplified by the new sense of extraordinary technical progress, the first fact to be established is the dynamic relationship of man to nature as opposed to the static juxtaposition of an absolute subject and an immobile and indifferent universe. Because he is a nature within nature, man's nature and perfection cannot be defined independently of this nature, even while he dominates it. In the encounter of man with nature, work is his proper activity, the original condition of man, the embodiment of his being. But man cannot be wholly defined by work alone because by his work he imposes his will on nature and thus dominates it. Work is an "outpouring of the spirit" (Proudhon). While the animal is one with nature and cannot reflect on it, man differs from nature, not only by his thought, but even by his activity. If he is subject to its laws, he still sits in judgment on them and is by that very fact autonomous and free. His perfection consists in exercising this freedom

and autonomy, in becoming something other than what he is by nature. In virtue of this capacity, man produces in nature a world which bears his hall-mark and not just that of natural forces. Hence, by becoming conscious of his work, man becomes conscious of himself. In this relationship of free creation he perfects himself, he becomes civilized. A "civilization of work" is built on the very nature of man. Work is not merely a technical instrument; it is a human value. There is a humanism of work.

Work, therefore, not only perfects the worker but transforms things. In the objective reality of the world thus constructed it is a *perfectio operis*. The duality is essential. It was lost sight of by a theology so preoccupied with the *perfectio operantis* that it has unconsciously neutralized the objective content of work. In the new technological era which we are entering the objectivity of work becomes more intense and more manifest, since the machine, by replacing the hand-tool, makes possible a form of production more and more independent of the personal intentions, activities and projects of the worker.

This twofold and unique power of man resides in τέχνη (skill, dexterity, "artistry"), a virtue which fits man to act in accordance with his nature, matter and spirit in a single substantial form. An idealist anthropology, though it is apparently favourable to a spiritual life, is incapable of giving a human and Christian sense to temporal commitments, except as external or provisional conditions. The ancient analysis of *ars et natura* must be amplified to accommodate an *ars* which places nature definitely under the control of reason. Technique is rationalization, which introduces a capacity for beauty into its utilitarian goals. Moreover, work is not only labour (in the sense of the Latin — "toil"). It is also "practice": *praxis*. This means that it is not merely ordained to the satisfaction of economic needs, but also to the betterment of human existence.

The religious depth of the phenomena is here revealed: man, by the accomplishment of the task of building the world, participates in God's creative work. God did not create a finished universe to which man was then brought in like an angelic spirit to heterogeneous matter, or like a foreign spectator in a countryside, at once alluring and overwhelming. God has called man to be his co-worker in the progressive organization of a universe in which he is to be the image of God, the demiurge and the conscience. He is

371

the image of God precisely and primarily in virtue of the fact that, associated with the Creator, he is thereby the master and builder of nature. No matter how worthy the spiritual act by which the good Christian offers to God his work and his day, it is still insufficient, both for the sanctification of the individual and for the building up of the Kingdom of God.

It is urgent, in order to pass sound judgment on this Christian situation and its apostolic structure, to note here that the more conscious man becomes of his ascendancy over nature, the more clearly he perceives that he is a cause. Therefore, in this autonomy and freedom of action, he frees his relationship to God from a numinous quality which, up to now, proceeded from his feeling of helplessness in the face of an unknown and terrifying nature. The civilization of work is a profane one. But it is this that makes it capable of being intensely religious, since it is his autonomy as second cause that makes man the *imago Dei*. It is necessary to leave behind all forms of religious immaturity and to cease to treat this "profanation" with suspicion. The theology of work implies a theology of the laity. The advent of industrial society is leading to a transformation of the mission of the Church. The rather facile theme of the "consecration of the world" will be suitably modified. It is a wonderful situation. Never before has the confrontation of man with nature provoked such a living consciousness of the biblical revelation of creation both in scholarly theology and in the lucid spirituality of elementary catechesis.

Through the technological domination of the cosmos and its actual procedures, a second dimension of human nature is revealed: work creates new systems of solidarity in keeping with the mechanical transformation of the world. These solidarities in the production and distribution of goods are purely material and rather crude at the outset, but through the multiple relationships to which they give rise, they become gradually humanized. Man, who is by nature social, becomes more social, not only through exchange and voluntary contracts, but through the interweaving of his activities into a social fabric. Numerous problems arise as a result; on the level of structures, of groups and classes, on the level of social justice and of collective morality. But from the outset, through the upgrading of work, the realm of "the neighbour" emerges with

new and unforeseen dimensions. One's neighbour, whom the letter of the gospel and social practice left, so to speak, at the artisan stage, now extends, under the impulse of the astounding growth in production and in the means of communication, by the standardization of the language of science and technological civilization, from group to group, from continent to continent to embrace the whole world. Catechesis must undertake the difficult task of providing moral guidance for the world of business and of politics. But it is even more important that it become the architect of the universal spread of the gospel of fraternal charity.

It is obvious that we thereby transcend the limits of a charity directed solely towards our immediate neighbour, of a charity exercised between individuals, to arrive at a love which perceives and embraces every human being despite the anonymity of institutions, despite the depersonalization of human functions, despite the rigidity of technological society. As Pius XI stated as far back as 1927 (in an address to the Catholic Federation of Universities), charity must become "political", that is to say, it must effectively reach one's fellowman through the common good of the city, especially in that major sector of the modern city which is the world of work.

We may add that by this socialization of man's work the community of men weaves its own history, a history in which technical progress strongly conditions collective consciousness but where such conditioned liberties are the sole factors of real progress. The theology of work implies a theology of history.

Finally, this participation in the construction of the world and this socialization of fraternal charity through the forward march of humanity are fulfilled in the mystery of the incarnation. Christ recapitulates the whole of reality in his mystical body. It is this which provides the real meaning and the keystone for a theology of work. For this recapitulation embraces not only men, but, as the Greek Fathers stated, following the exact sense of Rom 8, the whole of creation. It is precisely through man who co-operates in creation and who is the vehicle of history that all creation enters into the economy of salvation. "For the creation waits with eager longing for the revealing of the sons of God . . . We know that the whole of creation has been groaning in travail together until now" (Rom 8:18–22). In the light of this faith, all that goes to make up the current theology of work, all the establishment of arts and crafts as a part of man, as a part of the universe, as a part of the community, are thereby raised to the dignity of a divine hymn of praise, offering and liberation, which are the three characters of the sacrifice accomplished through Christ's paschal act.

This "Christological continuity" allows the natural laws of worldly enterprise to work. The autonomy of technical, economic and sociological problems does not allow the Christian to succumb to the myth of an economic theocracy of which he himself would be the administrator. Nonetheless, zeal for progress is directed by a messianism which, in spite of its eschatological scope, does not lose touch with the appeal of earthly realities, which are so clearly proclaimed in the texts of the two Testaments. The target of the gospel message and the test of its efficacity are the reign of justice and love in the community of man.

See also *Creation, Progress, Nature and Grace, Reign of God, Industrialism, Profession, Theory and Practice, Secularization.*

BIBLIOGRAPHY. G. Thils, *Théologie des réalités terrestres* (1946); E. Welty, *Vom Sinn und Wert der menschlichen Arbeit* (1946) (on Aquinas); J. Vuillemin, *L'être et le travail* (1949) (psychology and sociology); J. H. Oldham, *Work in Modern Society* (1949); A. van Bienen, *De zedelijke waardering van de arbeid in het industrialisme* (1951); A. Battaglia, "Filosofia del lavoro", *Rivista di filosofia neoscolastica* 45 (1953), pp. 57–74; A. Richardson, *Biblical Doctrine of Work* (1953); J. Todoli, *Filosofia del trabajo* (1954); J. Lacroix, *Personne et amour* (1955), ch. V; J. Vialatou, *Signification humaine du travail* (1955); J. David, "Theologie der irdischen Wirklichkeiten", *Fragen der Theologie heute* (1958), pp. 549–67; A. de Bovis, *L'enfant et son avenir professionnel: Perspectives théologiques* (1959); R. C. Kwant, *Philosophy of Labor* (1960); C. Dawson, *Historic Reality of Christian Culture* (1960); J. Höffner, *Industrielle Revolution und religiöse Krise* (1961); S. Hopkinson, *God at Work: The Working World and the Kingdom of God* (1962); P. Naville, *Vers l'automatisme social?* (1963); K. Brockmöller, *Industriekultur und Religion* (1964); P. Schoonenberg, *God's World in the Making* (1964); M.-D. Chenu, *Theology of Work* (1965); E. G. Kaiser, *Theology of Work* (1966); D. Clark, *Work and the Human Spirit* (1967).

Marie-Dominique Chenu

WORKS

1. "Works" came into theology from St. Paul, who condemned the notion of justification through the "works" of the law and saw justification coming to man from the free, merciful grace of God, which is had in faith. Works (of the law) and faith are contrasted (Rom 3:20, 27f.; 4:2, 6; 9:12, 32; 11:6; Gal 2:16; 3:2, 10; Eph 2:9; 2 Tim 1:9; Tit 3:5), as mutually exclusive.

There can be no doubt, of course, that in the NT the word "work" (ἔργον) does not necessarily have the meaning which was sometimes given it by St. Paul. It can mean the obedient fulfilment of the law of God, and there are "good works" which merit eternal life (Acts 9:36; Rom 2:6ff.; 13:3; 1 Cor 12:13; 2 Cor 9:8; Gal 3:28; Eph 2:10; Phil 1:6; Col 1:10; Jas 1:25; 1 Pet 1:17; 2:12; 2 Pet 1:10, etc.). In view of this simple fact, it is obviously insufficient to say that there are two different ways of using the word "work" — in the sense of man's independent effort which allows him to justify himself before God, without having to be justified by God himself in free grace, and in the sense of something done in the grace of God, something freely given by God, etc. — which must simply be noted.

The real point is that the reality designated by the word "work" is itself ambivalent, and that it is this that gives rise to the ambiguity of the word. The difference in the usage has continued. In Protestant theology, "works" have remained the opposite of the faith which justifies, while in Catholic usage ("good works") they have a positive value for salvation (*D* 809f., 842). It is not our intention here to expound the Pauline theology of justification by faith alone without works. What is needed is a theological concept of works which will automatically integrate this Pauline doctrine according to its due sense and its limitations, while also giving the proper place to a "justice of works". The task is all the more urgent at present, since there is a justifiable suspicion of all that seems merely private "inwardness" and an "ethics of the disposition" (under the heading of which faith is ranged). The general feeling is that concrete work and deeds (with their social relevance) are more salutary.

2. It must first be noted that the contrast between works and disposition (or attitude, "mind") is extremely imprecise, misleading and problematical in terms of a metaphysical anthropology. For what is usually meant by disposition is, like "works" and "deeds", an occurrence in the psycho-physical realm of man. On principle, it is just as open to manipulation (on the genetic, medical,

psychological and social levels) as the "outward actions" (the *actus externi* of moral theology), and offers no certain and clearly discernible criterion of man's relationship to God. Otherwise man could "judge" at least his own case, that is, have conscious certainty of his standing before God, which is denied him in principle (*D* 802, 822f.). The essential difference is not between works and disposition in the superficial sense of these words, but between the primal act of freedom and the incarnation of this free act in a "work", through which the free subject objectivates itself, displays itself and thus alone can be conscious of itself. The "external" or "internal" character of this work (in the ordinary sense used in moral theology) is a secondary matter, though important from the point of view of social relationships. Every act contains therefore the duality of the primal subject in its free decision and the conscious (intentional, articulated) object of freedom, with its objectivation ("work"), part of which is the "inner" element (psychological, considered motivation, etc.).

The elements of this duality stand in the relationship of mutual causality to each other, but they are not identical. The first element is the "transcendental", the other the "predicamental" or categorized. The first cannot be exhaustively grasped in thought and cannot be fully comprised and "objectivated" by a subsequent reflection. Its primary manifestation, with which, however, it does not fully coincide, is the "work" in which precisely the primal free act takes shape, and at once sees and loses sight of itself. The "work" (the objectivation in terms of categories, external or internal to the body-soul complex) is of its nature ambivalent, ambiguous, because all that is objectivated in it could also exist without springing from the primal free decision. The medium in which it takes root and spreads is also that of others' freedom, a medium to some extent necessarily determined by the structures given it by others' freedom, including sin (see *Original Sin, Concupiscence*). The "work" always contains foreign elements, which cannot be adequately distinguished from one's own. It is never the pure and unmistakable manifestation of the primal freedom, which, while it can never exist without it, cannot be clearly deciphered there (see *Human Act*).

3. Given man's bodily and dialogal nature in the world, the works of his free acts, in which he disposes of himself, must always take place in "objectivations", where alone the inner "disposition" (better, the primal free act) can genuinely go into action. In the ontology of existence and hence as an ethical principle it may be affirmed that the disposition only becomes (and is) genuine inasmuch as it goes into action in the "otherness" of the work, which is its real symbol (i.e., symbolic reality) and manifestation. Hence no genuine disposition can actually exist, there can be no true interior "mind", except in attention to the objective task, the "work", the "achievement". This is clear above all from the fact that there is no love of God and the neighbour, the quintessence of morality, except in a genuine attention to God and the neighbour in which the mentality of self-seeking is excluded and in which the neighbour and God through the neighbour — given the unity of love of God and neighbour — are really attained in the corporeal deed.

Nonetheless, this "work" (as such, in its objectivation in terms of categories, where it can be reflected on and inspected) is not the "deed" which God who sees the heart really demands. What he demands is the deed springing from freedom, which can never be fully analysed, where man does not do this work or that but gives himself to God — by accepting God's self-communication in grace (which alone makes the acceptance possible and actual). The difference between the primal (transcendental) free act and the (predicamental) work prevents man "judging" himself (consciously and articulately) (cf. *D* 802, 805, 823). The work itself remains ambivalent. Inasmuch as it is in the dimension of objects (internal or external) and can be there taken cognizance of, it is something that could exist and *so* exist even without the free inner act; and it is something that could in principle be given another function, either as the expression of another disposition or as an element of another (bad) work.

4. In the present dispensation of divinizing grace through the self-communication of God, a positive, salutary "good work" can only take place (in the manner determined by the difference between the primal free act and its objectivating work) as acceptance of God's self-communication, that is, as faith which is active in love of God and of man (including the stages of commitment which this acceptance can exist in: "fides informis, fides caritate formata", *D* 808, 811ff., 817,

819, etc.). But on these terms, the work as such fulfils the commandments of God and Christ (Jn 14:15, 21), is the necessary manifestation of faith (Jas 2:14–26) and meritorious (see *Merit*), because it is a concrete form of the divinely-sustained life which is dynamically ordained to eternal life as its fulfilment (Mt 5:16; Rom 2:6f.; 2 Cor 9:8; Col 1:10, etc.; *D* 804, 809f., 828ff., 835, 836, 842).

But because of the permanent difference between the primal free act under grace — such as faith — and work, the work can be done without faith. It can be a way of man's defending and justifying himself before God, an achievement of his own supposed to free man from having to accept salvation as God's free grace, supposed to win him the right to a bliss which he can demand of God. It can be a work through which not even one's own act, in essence and existence, is accepted as it could and should be, as the gift of God (through his elevating and efficacious grace), but is posited merely as one's own.

This is the sort of work which St. Paul excludes as the pernicious opposite of faith and its gift of salvation. One must note, however, the situation in which St. Paul has to preach his message of man's receiving his salvation, God, through the one mediator Christ. He has to challenge men who saw themselves in a positive relationship to God by virtue of the ancient covenant and the fulfilment of its law. He can tell them that they do not in fact fulfil this law at all and hence that they need the grace of God to forgive their sins. This is his first line of approach (Rom 2–3). But in view of the obvious objection that Jews (and pagans) do produce works which are pleasing to God (as St. Paul himself says elsewhere), he has to say that these works by which the law is fulfilled are not salutary, because they are not done with Christ and through his Spirit in explicit faith. He cannot yet see clearly — though hints are there — that there can be works of faith, in the Spirit, which are not explicitly referred to Christ. The situation is different today. We must now preach the virtue of the selfless deed, done for the individual, in the context of the community, and use it to disclose to men the depths of their own — God-given — deed where it is faith and love in hope, brought about by the Spirit of God in Christ as his own work. We must try to explain how any one who does the works of mercy does them to the Son of man (Mt 25), whether he knows it or not;

and also show that it is blessedness to know this explicitly.

See also *New Testament Theology* II, *Faith* II, *Revelation* II, *Law* I, *Symbol*.

BIBLIOGRAPHY. See bibliographies on *Justification, Grace* I, II; also: H. Graffmann, "Das Gericht nach den Werken im Matthäusevangelium", *Theologische Aufsätze (Festschrift K. Barth)* (1936), pp. 124–36; M. Lackmann, *Sola fide: Eine exegetische Studie über Jak 2* (1949); W. C. van Unnik, "The Teaching of Good Works in 1 Peter", *New Testament Studies* 1 (1954), pp. 92–110; J. Jeremias, "Paul and James", *Expository Times* 66 (1954–55), cols. 368–71; E. Lohse, "Glaube und Werke", *Zeitschrift für die Neutestamentliche Wissenschaft* 48 (1957), pp. 1–22; G. Bertram, "ἔργον", *TWNT*, II, pp. 635–55; F. Hauck, "θησαυρός", *ibid.*, III, pp. 136ff.; "καρπός", pp. 614ff.; M. Dibelius and H. Greeven, *Der Brief des Jakobus* (11th ed., 1964) (see on Jas 2:14–26); F. Mussner, *Der Jakobusbrief* (1964), pp. 12–23, 127–57 (with bibliography); R. Walker, "Allein aus Werken (Jak 2:14–26)", *Zeitschrift für Theologie und Kirche* 61 (1964), pp. 155–92; R. Schnackenburg, *The Moral Teaching of the New Testament* (1965); id., *Christian Existence in the New Testament* (1968).

Karl Rahner

WORLD

The "world" is one of the central notions of philosophy and theology, both of which tell of "God and the world". This article will discuss the various formal notions of the world, the various ways in which it can be understood, in the light of linguistic, historical and conceptual data. For other aspects, see *World Picture, God-World Relationship, Church and World*.

A. Linguistic Usage

The English word "world" (cf. Old English *woruld*) is probably from *wer*, man, and the root of *old*. It meant age or life of man. Its present meaning reflects the Church Latin *saeculum*. It can mean human society, as in such phrases as "cutting oneself off from the world", or a realm of human life, as in such phrases as the bourgeois world, the scientific world, the New World. Those who can deal skilfully with their milieu are "worldly-wise". But the realm of human life takes in the whole earth, so there are "world kingdoms", "world languages", "world powers", etc. Since the earth is part of the heavenly bodies, the whole structure is then called the "world", sometimes as the creation of God. In such phrases as the "world of ideas", the word is used loosely to indicate simply a group or class or unity. In philosophy and theology, the basic meaning is, more or less, the total reality within which we are comprised. This basic meaning varies according to the context, but above all according to the correlative or opposite notion, e.g., as in the phrases "God and the world", "consciousness and the external world", "spiritual and worldly", etc.

B. THE CHANGING UNDERSTANDING OF THE WORLD

The manner in which thinking men have brought to mind and expressed the total reality around them has been profoundly "historical" (see *History* I). This is not just a matter of the various meanings or values attributed to the world. It is true of the formal aspect under which the totality is always envisaged, as in mythical narratives, philosophical outlines or under the guise of (apparently) scientific world-pictures. Since the historical forms under which the world has been understood remain to some extent open to us, and since the articulateness of our notion of the world depends on some grasp of the notions that have been provided, it is necessary to survey the changes that have come over the notion of the world.

1. *Greek thought.* The Greek word for world is κόσμος, which meant originally "order", both the formal characteristic and the actually well-arranged object skilfully composed of parts. It was applied especially to good order among men, e.g., the established order and constitution of the State. Ladies' adornments were also included — coiffure etc. The application of the term to the world or universe — first made in philosophy and then becoming general under Stoic influence — thus appears as highly significant. The Greeks regarded the world as something intrinsically well-ordered and beautiful. This sense was still lively in late classical times, so that the development of a neutral sense for the word, implying no value-judgment, was a slow process. It should be noted that the world was described by a concept taken from human affairs, and that then the order of human life, individual or social, was often considered as patterned on the order of the world. The notion of the macrocosm and the microcosm, which occurs

as early as Anaximander (Fragment 2), is therefore implied to some extent in the genesis of the Greek concept of the world itself.

Anaximander compared the laws according to which things come and go to the constitution of the State. And Plato described the All as a cosmos in which "heaven and earth, gods and men" are joined together by friendship in unity (*Gorgias* 507e–508a). However, the praise of the beautiful structure of the universe is diluted by the notion that the sensible world is only the image of a true world accessible to the spirit (cf. the combination of the two themes in the *Timaeus,* 92c). Aristotle also regarded the world as a cosmos. The principle of all things, nature (φύσις), is the skill (ἐντελέχεια) which is at work there, of which the world is unconscious. The guarantee and prototype of the universal heavenly order is God, who exists in the bliss of full self-consciousness, and whose perfect and perpetual immutability is imitated by all sensible things, most notably by the stars in their perpetual revolutions, then by men (*Physics,* VIII). Hence the most important and the fundamental science is not anthropo-logy but cosmo-logy (cf. *Nicomachean Ethics,* VI, 7). The Greek notion of the divineness of the world reached a last peak in the Stoa. Here God is the all-pervading reason (logos) (the world-soul). His providence is the law of the universe.

But it was at this moment when "cosmic piety" was at its height that a mentality appeared which denied the world all value in comparison with a radically different "other world". This was Gnosis, a way of voicing man's experience of the impotence of the spirit in face of the laws of nature, in face of the injustice of world history, in face of the body with its imperious drives and its doom of sickness and death — a reaction to be repeated in all later forms of such "Manichaeism". Salvation is no longer sought in the sheltering unity of the cosmos and the blessed contemplation of its beauty, but in flight from the body and the sensible world into that other world, whose counterpart in the world is the experience of the lofty acme of the soul. Introspection opens up new realms of experience, and eagerness to explore the objective sensible reality almost vanishes.

2. *Jewish and Christian revelation.* The Israelites had a notion of the world which was essentially different from that of the

Greeks. The world is not the ultimate divine space, which embraces gods and men but is itself perpetually threatened by the chaos of matter. It is a non-divine though perfectly good work (Gen 1:31) of the God beyond the world, whose fidelity guarantees the consistency of the world's course (Gen 8:22). Its creation is the first of the saving deeds of the God of the covenant, which go from the election of Noah and Abraham to the covenant with Israel on Mount Sinai and the conquest of the land (according to the view of the Priestly writing in Gen 1). In Israel therefore faith in creation is not merely later than faith in Yahweh as helper, from the literary point of view (apart from a few old documents such as Gen 14:19). Even when it appears, it is mostly in a supporting role, when Israel is summoned to praise Yahweh for some saving deed or to have faith in the saving power of Yahweh in some particular situation (cf. Is 42:5f., 43:1; 44:24–28; 54:5; Pss 74; 89:10ff.). This original setting of creation in the framework of the history of salvation was later combined with a view in which the world itself was directly regarded when the creative power of Yahweh was hymned or his wisdom admired in the order and government of the world. This was probably under Canaanite (e.g., Ps 8; 19:1–7; 104) and Egyptian influence, working through the wisdom literature. The strictly cosmological concepts of the OT, like those of the NT, remained within the framework generally accepted in the Near East. Israel did not live by them, any more than they formed the content of the message of God's drawing nigh in Jesus.

The NT understanding of the world is determined in the light of Jesus being the Christ: the world — primarily the world of man, but with roots going deep down into the "cosmic" — is always the good but fallen creation. It is the realm of the evil one, but it is already fundamentally redeemed and headed for definitive salvation. Hence the ambivalence of the NT notion of the world, which plays a large role in St. Paul (κόσμος or αἰών) and in St. John (κόσμος only), is not accidental, but is intrinsic to the history of salvation. The world is created in Christ and hence good (Jn 1:10). But through sin, since Adam, it has turned more and more away from God, so that the world can rightly connote enmity to God and the doom of corruption. The crucifixion of its Lord is at once the climax, the disclosure and the defeat of all its wickedness. He came from

another realm (Jn 17:14; 18:36) into this world to be its light (Jn 1:9; 12:46), to save it (Jn 3:17; 6:51). To bring out the novelty and incisiveness of the situation created by Jesus, the NT authors make free use of the notion of the present, corrupt aeon as contrasted with the coming aeon in Jewish apocalyptic. This may be due to some extent to the expectation of the end which was dominant in early days and to the persecutions to which the primitive Church was subject. But the NT nowhere urges Christians to flight from this world, though they are warned to use things "as though they were not" dealing with them, and there is no programme for a better life in the world.

3. *The synthesis between Christian and Greek attitudes.* In both Greek and Christian thought there were positive and negative attitudes to the world, with a mixture of motives in each case. The conflict thus set up was one of the central themes in late antiquity and the Middle Ages, with the solution of St. Augustine predominant, which was to affirm that the beauty and order of the world appeared in contrasts *(Enarratio in Ps 148)*. He took a higher view of the world than the ancients had done, since their admiration had been confined to the structure and order of the world, whose matter was the source of all deficiency and evil, while for St. Augustine the material world was also created by the good God and hence was itself good (e.g., *Enchiridion* 23). And he also took very seriously the anthropology implied in the Christian faith. The essence of man is not so much to fit into and be a tiny reflection of the whole order of the world as to be a person in face of God. The significance of the cosmos for man's well-being is reduced. It is not there that man finds the satisfaction of his needs. Man's heart can never rest until it rests in God, his supreme good (*Confessiones,* I, 1, 1). God and the soul — the rest does not matter (*Soliloquia,* I, 2, 7). The great marvel is not that something abides in the chaotic flow (Plato, *Theaetetus,* 155 d), but the unfathomable soul (*Confessiones,* XIII, 13, 14). The whole of reality is divided up from the perspective of the soul: there is the world which is external (*Confessiones,* X, 6, 9), there is that which is in the soul and there is that which is both above the soul and within its depths, God — a division which is still reflected in the three ideas of reason in Kant. The fellowship of the cosmos is divided into two communities, the city of God and the

city of the earth. The unity of the ideal world order becomes a duality, since there are two possible choices there.

St. Augustine's synthesis, perhaps under a reverse causation from the Manichaeism against which it was drawn up, remained in essentials the model for the whole of the Middle Ages. Its spiritualism left its mark on St. Bonaventure's symbolic interpretation of the world in terms of its source and goal (*Itinerarium mentis in Deum*), as it did on the late medieval *Imitation of Christ* with its flight from the world. But other notions were also at work. The rediscovery of Aristotle in the 12th century revived interest in the objective investigations of natural science. With the spiritual origin of all material reality assured, science could hope to use mathematical methods to describe and explain the natural processes, an attempt previously held to be useless on account of the lower degree of being underlying them. Now nature became the open book of God's creation. The Christian faith which made man lord of the world also enabled him to abandon the geocentric system which Stoicism had used as a metaphor for man's metaphysical place in nature (Blumenberg). For an immortal soul called by God to salvation is no less a pilgrim in a geocentric than in a heliocentric or completely uncentred world picture. A number of reasons — the over-literal interpretation of the Bible, force of habit, a perhaps not unjustifiable fear of the world's losing its solidity if man were to be anchored in the transcendent without reference to his bodily nature — made it impossible for many Christians to recognize that it was their faith which had opened up the new perspective. This mistake led to the trial of Galileo and to a growing alienation of modern science and philosophy from the Christian self-understanding of the Church.

This was the context of the concept of the world which was dominated by 17th-century mechanics and explained by Descartes, Locke, etc. It was a vast machine regulated by the laws of physics, explored by the mind which rejected the illusions of the senses, but still threatening to overwhelm its admirers. The materialism of the 18th century thought that man himself might be a sort of machine — as Descartes had already accepted as regards the human body. The world mechanism had to be proved to be a construction of the human mind and thus placed within its power if freedom and morality were to be preserved. This was the achievement of Kant. He explained the nature of the Newtonian world — though only of the world at this level, which explains the strictly limited character of his contribution to the notion of the "world". The world is now the "Idea" or quintessence of all phenomena, not a possible object of knowledge. Any effort to form and justify propositions about the world as a totality becomes involved in inner contradiction (the antinomies). The antinomies force reason back upon itself, and it discovers that its concepts are valid only for objects of possible experience. The world as a totality is never experienced but remains an ideal assigned to the strivings of knowledge. Thus the concept of the world is without content. It is entirely absorbed in its function, which is to be the ideal horizon of the most perfect possible knowledge and the critique of all imperfect knowledge.

The formal structure of the phenomena of nature in the sense of Kant is provided by the principles of Newtonian physics. For Kant, the world is the quintessence of all these phenomena. Kant saw correctly that the world as he had conceived it was on an entirely different plane, in cognition, from a phenomenon in nature, that it could not therefore be grasped like the latter in terms of categories but could only be envisaged as an "Idea". The totality was not a matter of objective knowledge but only of methodical reflection.

But are all the problems suggested by the word "world" completely solved by considering it merely as the ideal horizon which man sets before his knowledge? This would mean that man's understanding of the world was at once decided dogmatically with no scope for real questioning. For Kant, the world in itself only means the objectivated counterpart and source of sensible impressions in our knowledge. The known world has no other meaning than that given it by man. The world has little meaning for the real being of man, his moral nature. The question of the proper, intrinsic meaning of the world is not asked.

But Nietzsche was passionately interested in it. With the significance of the world whittled away, as he saw it, by Christian and Platonic philosophy, his effort was to restore to it its ontological validity by eliminating man from the special place which he claimed there for his spiritual nature. Nietzsche therefore set out to expose the illusions which engendered this sense of election — the transcendent God, the notions of truth and freedom — since they concealed the true nature of man and the world, the will to power. When man has lost all the values by which he could orientate himself, and finds himself in the situation of absolute nihilism, his true homeland appears: the blind, meaningless chaos of natural events, which asserts itself in the eternal cycle, the perpetual Today which is devoid of history. In his *amor fati,* where man wills himself as part of this world, man renounces his "eccentric" standpoint with regard to the world. His renunciation of his spiritual character deprives all types of nihilism of their possible basis.

In phenomenology, however, an effort was made to maintain the independence both of man and the world. Important pointers were already there in Hegel. Though his notion of absolute knowledge ultimately deprived the world once more of its true reality, his notion of universal mediation was of great importance for the philosophy of the world. There is no immediacy which is not mediated, just as there is no mediation which does not suppose a profounder immediacy. Our knowledge of the world comes from all our previous experiences. But these *are* experiences and thus were possible only by encounter with an organized world. Thus both the totality of our experiences and the world of experience have at once a subjective and an objective character.

E. Husserl, trying to get down to "the real business", first took up the pure life of the "I" or the consciousness, which provides the various possibilities of the modes of phenomenal existence. Later he became more and more convinced that this conscious life can be understood only within the horizon of our concrete "living-world". The "world" was therefore both something constituted in consciousness and the ground underlying all constructions. Heidegger took the matter further in his *Sein und Zeit* (1927; E. T.: *Being and Time* [1962]). Here he sees all grasp of meaning, all understanding of things, as presupposing a horizon of pre-understanding, a non-thematically grasped total frame of reference, which is no other than the world. But in itself the world is nothing. It is rather the ground of all that is "in itself", being the sketch-plan of his possibilities as projected by man in his understanding of being. Man and world are two poles of the same phenomenon. Man is essentially "being-in-the-world", the world is an existential (see *Existence* II, 4; III, A). But the view taken in *Sein und Zeit* laid undue stress on the pole constituted by man, which led Heidegger later to explain the world as much as man in terms of the sovereign truth of being as it lights up and throws shadows. The world is the realm of the historical play of light, in which beings as such become manifest, in which man can be man. The world in all its dimensions is the product of the divine and human, the bright and the dark, as they combine with and pull against each other. It is language: the space-time of articulated meaning, through which being addresses itself in its fateful coming, and where man is to prepare a place for being by his skilful response to it.

C. SYSTEMATIC CONSIDERATIONS

Man always of course considered the world as the setting of his life — as may be seen from the linguistic history of "world" and of "cosmos". But it is only today that he is beginning to understand the world explicitly in terms of himself, as the "world of man". The world is no longer primarily the reliable ground of meaning. To a great extent it only receives meaning inasmuch as it is laid bare and exploited in the service of human life. This understanding of the world is due to the sense of freedom brought by Christianity and the growing power of man over nature through technology.

Hence the meaning of the world, as the totality of the real, is disclosed to man, whose being is being-in-the-world. The human world is slanted towards the life of man and all its needs. It is within the framework, no matter how variable, of what man must and can be that the facts of the world present themselves. It is the world of man, that is, of a bodily existent whose nature is determined by biological, psychological and similar factors. At the same time it is always my world and our world, thrown open to my understanding by the medium of language. Indeed, for the most part I do not know it directly, but only through the reports and interpretations of others. It is a world which is continually showing new aspects and hiding others, as our limited perspectives shift historically and as our work re-moulds it. It is a world in which we find ourselves faced with inherited possibilities and burdens, by which and in spite of which we have to live. It is a world always open to new discoveries; a world whose meaning we try, consciously or unconsciously, to read, in a religious sense or in some similar way.

This world which is part of man, so to speak, and which in spite of being open to extension and re-shaping at his hands is still always the pre-existent horizon of his life, is the primary form in which we encounter the world as the totality of the real. Hence the world-for-me (or for-us) is prior to any world-in-itself of which definitive knowledge may be attained. Any *given* world "in itself" is the product of an objectivating sketch-plan. The world pictures of science in particular have the character of such sketch-plans. But they are not drawn up in the hope of attaining some satisfying, formative knowledge of the inner structures of the cosmos. Science aims merely at enabling man to assert himself against the superior might of the cosmos, at ridding it of its terrifying strangeness and at domesticating it. The very method of scientific knowledge, the reduction of phenomena to processes which can be repeated by us at will, shows that its purpose is to incorporate natural processes into the realm of technological mastery.

Thus the world of nature is becoming more and more the world of culture, "natural history" more and more a man-made story. Man no longer lives by the world of nature, which is hardly visible any longer except as the material of our planning and the setting of our recreation. But a new sort of nature is making its appearance: our man-made technical culture, which is at least as much of a threat as untamed nature was to primitive man.

With man in danger of suffocating under his own works and with the dwindling away — at least apparently — of objective values ("nihilism"), man is looking for a meaning for his life in this world which this world of lost enchantments cannot furnish. This secularized world resists all efforts at re-sacralization. Hence meaning is not to be sought in the technological world or in the spontaneous realm of nature. In the former we find only a mirror of ourselves, while the meaning of life must be something *given*. A re-integration in the latter, such as Nietzsche demanded, breaks down at man's indomitable sense of freedom. But if one refuses to confine the meaning of life to the struggle against nature and the establishment of a humane society — an attitude which, to say the least, excludes tranquillity — the ultimate goal of our existence must be sought in the ground which makes both our freedom and self-subsistent nature possible: in the free and liberating presence of God to us. The world as creation, that is, seen and accepted as a gift, has a meaning which it has not to wait to be given by man. But the meaning is only fully there when man has understood and implemented it. And this meaning does not render man's freedom superfluous, but gives it illumination and direction. God, whom we are allowed to call our Father, has given us this world as our heritage not only in part but in full (cf. Rom 8:15ff.). The world is not part of God but reposes in its own non-divine, wholly worldly solidity. It belongs fully to us because we also belong to ourselves, that is, because we are free and corporeal beings.

There are therefore three possible ways of understanding the world. We can underestimate God's generous love and be afraid of the world, like the Manichees, and only half dare to accept the world (as our task and our joy). Or in order to be sovereign lords of the world, we can "put to death" the giver in the background, who is supposed to be basically envious of our possessions. These first two positions share the same false premise: that God is not love but small-minded envy, a premise which may often be in fact a projection of crabbed avarice. The truth is once more in the mean: to accept the gift bestowed without reserve as sons who are free, in thankfulness, responsibility and tranquillity.

See also *Order* I, *Gnosis, Creation* I, *Aeon, Manichaeism, Materialism, Phenomenology, Language, Technology, Meaning.*

BIBLIOGRAPHY. LINGUISTIC: H. Sasse, "αἰών", *TWNT,* I, pp. 197–209; id., "κόσμος", III, pp. 867–95; W. Kranz, "Kosmos", *Archiv für Begriffsgeschichte,* II (1955–57); G. Stadtmüller, "Saeculum", *Saeculum* 2 (1951), pp. 152–6. HISTORICAL: P. Duhem, *Le système du monde: Histoire des doctrines cosmologiques de Platon à Copernic,* I–X (1913–59); K. Reinhardt, *Kosmos und Sympathie* (1926); F. M. Cornford, *Plato's Cosmology* (1937); E. Sauer, *Die religiöse Wertung der Welt in Bonaventuras "Itinerarium Mentis in Deum"* (1937); R. Allers, "Microcosmus", *Traditio* 2 (1944), pp. 319ff.; L. Spitzer, "Classical and Christian Ideas of World Harmony", *Traditio* 2 (1944), pp. 409ff.; 3 (1945), pp. 307ff.; W. Jaeger, *The Theology of the Early Greek Philosophers* (1947); É. Gilson, *Dante the Philosopher* (1948); A.-J. Festugière, *La révélation d'Hermès Trismégiste,* II (1950); R. Bultmann, *Theology of the New Testament,* 2 vols. (1952, 1955), paras. 3, 10, 26, 42, 44; M. Eliade, *The Myth of the Eternal Return* (2nd ed., 1954); G. von Rad, *Old Testament Theology,* 2 vols. (1962–65) (see under

"Creation", "Cosmology", "Cosmos", "World", in index); H. Jonas, *Gnosis und Spätantiker Geist,* I (3rd ed., 1964); H. Blumenberg, *Die kopernikanische Wende* (1965); K. Löwith, *Der Weltbegriff der neuzeitlichen Philosophie* (2nd ed., 1968); H. Flender, "Das Verständnis der Welt bei Paulus, Markus und Lukas", *Kerygma und Dogma* 14 (1969), pp. 1–27. SYSTEMATIC: E. Husserl, *Erfahrung und Urteil* (1939) (and see bibliography on *Phenomenology*); M. Heidegger, *Existence and Being* (1950); id., *What is a Thing?* (1968); E. Biemel, *Le concept du monde chez Heidegger* (1950); N. Hartmann, *New Ways in Ontology* (1953); W. Dilthey, *The Essence of Philosophy* (1954); L. Wittgenstein, *Philosophical Investigations* (German text with English translation by G. Anscombe) (2nd ed., 1958); P. Teilhard de Chardin, *The Phenomenon of Man* (1959); M. Merleau-Ponty, *Phenomenology of Perception* (1962); H. Urs von Balthasar, *Herrlichkeit,* I ff. (1961 ff.); R. Carnap, *The Logical Structure of the World* and *Pseudoproblems in Philosophy* (1966); W. Gallie, *Peirce and Pragmatism* (2nd ed., 1966); J. Splett, *Sakrament der Wirklichkeit* (1968).

Gerd Haeffner

WORLD HISTORY

In the Western interpretation of history, doubts were cast on the unity of world history and its possible existence as a knowable object only when the meaning given history by the economy of salvation ceased to be believed. It became a problem even where the biblical revelation was preserved, as soon as universal world history was detached from its links with the history of salvation.

A. HISTORY OF THE PROBLEM

The process began with humanism and took place on several levels. Humanist history emancipated itself from the biblical chronicle to concentrate on political history and on regional detail. This led to the taking-up of a "worldly" view-point, but not to a secular "world history", since this was for the moment still left to theological surveys. But in Reformation theology the medieval identification of salvation history and world history was abandoned, Philipp Melanchthon using the distinction between the "Two Kingdoms" to make a distinction between *historia sacra* and *historia profana*. This did not mean, however, that profane history was left without all links with salvation history. Theologians strove hard, in the 17th century, particularly in the interest of the missions, to harmonize biblical with Chinese chronology or the discovery of new peoples with universal descent from Adam and Eve. The

situation changed when the "divine history", still in a privileged position in J. Bodin's *Methodus ad Facilem Historiarum Cognitionem* (1566) and for long after, became the object of historical criticism. Here Voltaire was typical. His *Essai sur les mœurs et l'esprit des nations* (1756) challenged the notion of Israel's special place in the economy of salvation by comparing the historical reality of the little Jewish State with the great empires of the ancient East, and by affirming that divine providence was equally concerned with all the peoples of the earth. This was an attack on J.-B. Bossuet's *Discours sur l'histoire universelle* (1681), which had once more presented world history as salvation history in the Augustinian sense.

From then on, constant efforts have been made to read "universal history" on the level of world history itself — a field hitherto given its contours by the divine interventions in the economy of salvation. G. Vico's *Scienza Nuova* (1744) was one such attempt. The key to the understanding of world history was that history, unlike nature, was the production of man, working according to the eternal plans of divine providence. The task of a "rational theology" was to discover the workings of providence in "historical facts". The notion of world history as a theodicy is also found in G. W. Leibniz (1646–1716), though in contrast to the "cyclic" theory of Vico he saw the nations and civilizations moving onwards to one comprehensive fulfilment. The notion of a general development in which mankind would find its true self was made the key to world history as presented by 18th-century writers. G. E. Lessing's *Erziehung des Menschengeschlechtes* ("Education of the Human Race") (1780) saw the progressive translation of revealed truths into truths of reason as the divine plan working throughout world history. Condorcet saw the progress of the human spirit as the goal of world history (*Progrès de l'esprit humain* [1794]). J. G. Herder, in his search for the "genetic spirit" of each people, sought to justify the history-writing of each nation (as distinct from universal history), but still regarded all peoples as sharers in the one world-soul and heading for a common intramundane final destiny (*Ideen zur Philosophie der Geschichte der Menschheit* [1785–92], E. T.: *Outlines of a Philosophy of the History of Man* [1800]). Man is the supreme degree of creation on earth, but also the link between two overlapping systems of creation.

These basically like-minded efforts of the Enlightenment were summed up and surpassed by G. W. F. Hegel in his *Philosophie der Weltgeschicht* ("Philosophy of World History") (1822–23). Christians have a key to world-history in divine providence, but it can now be understood as a gradual ascent, embodied in the great nations of history, the "moments" of the process whereby the one universal spirit finds itself in its higher whole. L. von Ranke, while refusing to treat any particular history as a mere "moment", still saw the tradition of the West as a panorama reflecting all history. But historians of the later 19th century abandoned the universal perspective to devote themselves to the power politics of the national State, with a positivist approach which dismissed all questions as to the unity and meaning of history as metaphysical or theological speculation.

At the same time, knowledge of world history was being expanded to take in vast new regions, with the study of prehistory, ethnology, and the ancient East, while the historical sections of the systematic sciences, e.g., comparative religion, history of law, economic and social history, also played their part. The traditional restriction of history to Europe, and here mainly to political history, now seemed to be justified in its self-imposed limitations. It was left to writers who were not technically historians to try to exploit all these findings in the interest of world history. Some continued the philosophical approach of the 18th century (e.g., P. von Lasaulx, K. Jaspers). Others sought to establish a typology of cultures (e.g., K. Lamprecht, Alfred Weber, Max Weber) (under the influence of A. Comte's division of cultures into theological, metaphysical and scientific [positivist], a law of movement already suggested by Vico). Others examined patterns of civilization, with a closer attention to their historical manifestations. Spengler's verdict was: a six-thousand-year long accident befalling the accident man within the accident life.

The habit of centring history on Europe had been criticized as early as the Enlightenment, but had persisted in the fashion of treating history as progress with one's own day as the summit. The most radical criticism was perhaps that of O. Spengler, in his *Decline of the West*, 2 vols. (E. T., 1926–28). Criticism of the idea of making Europe the goal of history continued. The historical world was treated as many-centred, as in A. Toynbee. But no attempt was made to see world history as the history of mankind. The Middle Ages had identified it with the history of salvation, the Enlightenment had first used the unifying notion of human progress and then simply treated it as the *de facto* world domination of Europe, with colonialism and imperialism as the climax of all civilization. None of these approaches is possible in the present situation, where economic, social, political and cultural interdependence means that there is something like "One World" with one world history. Apart from some idealizing sketches, the notion of the unity and purposefulness of world history, so highly cherished by the Enlightenment, now survives only in historical materialism (see *Marxism* III), on the level, however, of a social ideology.

B. BASIC PROBLEMS

It is the actual interdependence of cultures and realms of human activity in the 20th century which poses once more the question of world history. As the bibliography below shows, there are collective works which attempt an answer. But the real question is generally avoided, either by being passed from author to author, or by the traditional concentration on Europe. Efforts to go beyond the juxtaposition of all the elements are rare. It remains therefore to ask: 1. What is the unity of history? 2. What is the movement impelling this history? 3. What does it open out to — in other words, what is the meaning of this history in its unified movement? But the old problem is more acute than ever. The very existence of the problem seems to be challenged by the simple factualness of the world-wide happening. The facts suggest no direct meaning for world history and seem to resist all effort to give them meaning. The problem is at its obscurest, as well as at its most urgent, with the destiny of all States and nations actually involving the destiny of mankind.

1. *The unity of history as world history.* The concrete unity of mankind could only be envisaged as a historical problem when the Christian reading of its salvation-history had given way to a more profane attitude. Salvation-history is in itself universal. But the unity had been lost sight of when the original totality of "Jews and Christians" was replaced by a division between Christians and "barbarians", the latter to be evangelized by their lords and masters. The deistic uni-

versalism of the Enlightenment was no great improvement. And the idea of unity in world history was in fact only effective in Western thought as long as the history of salvation pointed the way. In the 19th century history became merely profane facts, and the number of new horizons opened up never succeeded in forming one world horizon. It is impossible to return now to the ancient unquestioning identification of salvation-history and world history. If the latter is a unity, the question now is: What are the immanent factors which determine human unity?

If these factors are only there where they present themselves in a word-wide context, world history must be said to have begun in the age of discovery and all the preceding centuries must be relegated to "prehistory". The difficulty cannot be solved by synoptic chronological charts. These could give an illusion of unity, where there was no real historical inter-connection. And in fact the chronological guide-line only exists since the 15th century. It is of course possible to trace the spread of culture-circles from truly prehistoric times. And there were in fact interchanges between advanced but practically isolated civilizations. But they were only marginally felt, and their significance only discovered by modern research. They prove at best that the whole earth is the field of a more or less interwoven history, but not the unity of world history.

The unity is rather to be sought in the fact that man always understands his world as the "One World". On the mythic level, one single couple is regarded as the parents of the human race. Great empires understand themselves as world empires. Symbolism bears on the world and humanity. Independent innovations have an underlying unity. The spread of the early culture-circles is very like a natural process but it takes place in historical exchanges which reveal basic forms of world history. The unity of history is reflected in the fact that it is thought of as global and not in terms of "histories", just as myth, a special type of historical experience, is always a single all-embracing explanation.

This universal bearing is to be sought in the history of all peoples as they existed individually. But the age of discovery still marks a definite epoch in world history, the age of enlightenment. There is thus an inevitable *de facto* alignment with Europe, but the wider and more basic universalism

remains, a pointer perhaps to new alignments with the history of salvation.

2. *The one movement of world history.* Can a consistent movement be traced in world history, bringing humanity progressively to what its essence or fundamental dispositions imply?

In the Christian history of salvation, the world had only "yet a little while", to be filled out by the preaching of a salvation. The end was already basically arrived at. And hence the new could be accepted only when justified by the old. The Roman Empire was seen as the last of the Kingdoms prophesied in Dan 7, a sort of appendix to a history of salvation already closed. A really new thrust in world history and in salvation history was envisaged only by the speculation of the 12th and 13th centuries, as for instance in Joachim de Fiore's kingdom of peace and love which was to come with the Age of the Holy Spirit. The unity of world history was thus placed in its goal as well as in its origin and in the promise already fulfilled. These notions coincided in fact with the break-up of ancient culture in the early Middle Ages and the coming of a new dynamism which was to give birth to "Europe" (see *Occident*).

In the 18th century this type of theology of history reappeared in the guise of a theological introduction to the philosophical notion of progress. Without the idea of progress neither the movement of world history inspired by Europe nor the notion of world history as a unity can be conceivable. The notion was never put forward uncritically by its great representatives, though it did not escape scientific and philosophical criticism when presented, as so often, rather heavy-handedly. Its unassailable position is now clearer than ever, since the ancient notion of cyclic history reappeared in the modern era, assuming laws which confused nature and history more bewilderingly than any impact of evolutionism on the notion of progress, and losing sight of the unity of mankind by envisaging a movement outside the ambit of civilization. The notion of progress took the place of the theological category of promise — in spite of critical deformations and historicist atomizing.

The catastrophes of the 20th century seem to make the notion of progress absurd. But the challenge to understand and thus master world history remains, all the more urgent since the catastrophes were extensive, and since technology survived them to offer even more radical threats. If man is not to be swept away by the torrent, he must make the moral and intellectual effort to swim against it, that is, to re-assert the ideal of progress. But how is this to be done?

A critical survey of the notion of progress must strictly distinguish nature from history and world history from the economy of salvation and then ask how progress is verified in fact and in historical consciousness as consistent self-discovery. It presupposes that one can discover a human tradition to take up the running after the breakdown of the individual cultures. It presupposes that the cultures have a universal coefficient. It presupposes that man is becoming the conscious agent of universal history as it moves forward in the concrete, and finding here the full measure of his being. If all this can be verified, the unity of world history is the way in which mankind finds its true being, through all the ups and downs of a movement which never ceases to thrust forward. History may repeat itself, produce the same blessings and the same evils, the same self-understanding and the same incomprehensions, but it is not entirely exhausted in such repetition. Mankind summons up its strength to greater effort, of which we now experience a peak. With the disappearance of the old boundaries between "Greek" and "barbarian" a new quality has developed, a new contact with humanity as such, where mistakes cannot be rectified by substituting one culture for another. Man moves towards lordship of the world, but it is a forward movement, and one which is part of the universal movement of mankind towards unity. This may be seen as the counterpart of the "gathering" of the peoples in salvation-history, though it must not be confused with it. Obviously, the two movements have not the same form.

3. *The openness of world history.* In the economy of salvation, the promises both set a goal and left things open: the Son of man comes to judgment, but no one knows the day and the hour. When a process immanent to history was substituted for the promise, a dilemma was posed. The goal was determined, but individual cultures could have real meaning only in terms of an open history, not by virtue of the meaning of universal history. The dilemma seemed to be resolved in the 20th century in favour of the absolute meaning of historical particularities. The only defenders of the perfectibility of history were the representatives of historical materialism. But then they were joined by the upholders of the "One World" ideologies, who held that man could not afford to risk new frontiers — the *openness* of history. The *necessary* One World now seemed also feasible, with the new means available. Thus the Enlightenment's faith in progress, which responded after all to a transhistorical element, and saw perfectibility in the *future,* that is, in strictly *historical* expectation, gave way to the assumption of a non-historical perfectibility, i.e., where nothing really new or unforeseeable is awaited, but a programme already settled is carried out according to plan.

But if the unified movement of world history has indeed produced the One World — as seems fairly clear — has not history arrived at its goal? There may be some loose links to be tied up, but in what direction can it go "further"? In historical materialism, the question of the end-stage is answered by affirming that the dialectical process continues, but that the universal communist society will no longer need its historical stimulus, class contradictions. In the West, this static stage is dreaded as tedium, to be catered for by proper "leisure", or by the full freedom to be human, when man is freed from hunger, war and all similar distress by the political and economic organization of world society. The transhistorical moment seems within reach of history, with variations according to whether the outlook is that of historical materialism or that of the "West".

This time of peace and security could be explained in terms of salvation-history as the epoch of Antichrist. But if the difference between salvation-history and world history is maintained on the objective level, it may be noted that all optimistic or pessimistic prognostications are based on the course of world history as it has been up to the present. They miss the point of the break with the past which the present represents — a greater stride forward having been taken than that from the primitive cultures of the food-gatherers and hunters to sedentary agriculture and the advanced civilizations. Just as the primitive hunters could not imagine a Roman Empire, so too it is impossible to imagine what comes next, now that world history seems to be at its goal. It is one of the most striking novelties of the present day that the course of past history can be explained in terms of its "end" as never before. Nonetheless, the future remains open, with its possible blessings and disasters. We can recognize the unity of world history as the progress of humanity to its conscious unity. But what the future holds for this unity, whether it is to display its riches or to collapse once more in catastrophe and be forgotten, whether it is to bring out clearly the contours of humanity or reduce it to a faceless mass, is as unknowable as the beginning of world history, which we can only guess at from fragments. History as a whole remains open. But the coming of the One World reveals the meaning of world history, though only in its provisional manifestation. But however the full and final meaning may be explicated, the end can never annul this essential purpose. One may wonder whether this provisional achievement is not the precursor of the promise of the history of salvation. But the answer to this question is buried in the mystery of this economy and of human freedom.

See also *History, Historicism, Salvation* III A, *Enlightenment, Progress.*

BIBLIOGRAPHY. RECENT PRESENTATIONS: H. Berr, *La synthèse en histoire* (1911; 2nd ed., 1953); id., *L'histoire traditionelle et la synthèse historique* (1921); E. Cavaignac, ed., *Histoire du monde* (1922 f.); *The Cambridge Ancient History*, 12 vols. (1923–39; revised ed. in course of publication by fascicles); *The Cambridge Medieval History*, 8 vols. (1911–36); *The New Cambridge Modern History*, 14 vols. (1957 ff.; 10 vols. so far); L. Halphen and P. Sagnac, eds., *Peuples et civilisations: Histoire générale*, 20 vols. (1926 ff.); A. J. Toynbee, *A Study of History*, 12 vols. (1934–61); abridged ed. of vols. 1–10 by D. C. Somervell in 2 vols.: I (1947), II (1957); F. Valjavec, ed., *Historia Mundi*, 10 vols. (1952–61). STUDIES: G. W. F. Hegel, *Lectures on the Philosophy of History* (1832), E. T. by J. Sibree (1956); P. E. von Lasaulx, *Neuer Versuch . . . einer Philosophie der Geschichte* (1856); E. Troeltsch, *Der Historismus und seine Probleme* (1922); id., *Der Historismus und seine Überwindung* (1924); O. Spengler, *The Decline of the West*, 2 vols. (1926–28); H. P. Adams, *Life and Writings of Giambattista Vico* (1935); J. Thyssen, *Geschichte der Geschichtsphilosophie* (1936); J. Burckhardt, *Reflections on History* (1943); R. G. Collingwood, *The Idea of History* (1946); id., *Essays in the Philosophy of History*, ed. by W. Debbins (1965); A. Weber, *Farewell to European History, or the Conquest of Nihilism* (1947); K. Löwith, *Meaning in History* (1949); H. Butterfield, *Christianity and History* (1949); G. P. Gooch, *History and Historians in the Nineteenth Century* (1952); H. Freyer, *Weltgeschichte Europas* (2nd ed., 1954); O. Köhler, "Was ist 'Welt' in der Geschichte?", *Saeculum* 6 (1955), pp. 1–9; id., "Versuch, Kategorien der Weltgeschichte zu bestimmen", *ibid.* 9 (1958), pp. 446–57; C. Dawson, *Dynamics of World History* (1959); M. C. D'Arcy, *Meaning and Matter of History* (1959); K. R. Popper, *Poverty of Historicism* (1966); K. Jaspers, *Origin and Goal of History* (1968); K. Rahner, *Theological Investigations,* VI (1968) (on pluralist society); H. Butterfield, *Man on his Past: The Study of the History of Historical Scholarship* (1969).

Oskar Köhler

WORLD PICTURE

A world picture is a set of statements about reality into which all immediate data are fitted. A world picture only really functions if all that is encountered can at least on principle be assigned a place in it. Further, since it can fit all realities into its system, a world picture makes reality intelligible, even if no explicit explanation is articulated.

World pictures use for instance causality, to divide things into cause and effect, and evolutionary processes which show against the background of causality the combination of phenomena into earlier and later, into coming to be and passing away, both as regards individuals and the whole.

Sometimes they have been exclusively mythical, as in some sketch-plans of the Ionian philosophers. Sometimes they are more or less rationalized, even to the stage where philosophical outlines using strictly critical methods arrange phenomena and experiences in order of relevance — here of course being influenced by the starting-point of the world picture in question.

A world picture is a survey of the whole, and here of course the problems begin. If, as the ancients said, the whole is greater than the sum of its parts, no world picture can be established on the basis of experience alone, since experience never presents anything but the particular. Only the individual is known from direct contact with reality, not the totality. The totality is only constituted by an act of the mind which brings together the particular items and makes a whole or unity of them. This seems to lead towards the position of Kant, who held that knowledge is always intellectual knowledge. But it does not follow from the fact that the intellect constitutes the unity and therefore goes beyond direct experience that there is no unity of being apart from this constitutive act. However the philosophical relevance of the principle of the whole and the parts is to be defined, no world picture and no philosophical sketch-plan of the world in history has ever been simply the totting-up of direct particular experiences and individual insights into reality. The process has always been to draw up a schema and to maintain either that its relationships are evident from the start or that it is verified by the application to reality.

Another inescapable problem is that the experiences to be integrated into any world picture are always growing in number. This enlargement of reality is a general phenomenon in the history of mankind. Scientific knowledge increases, while historical experiences such as the usefulness of certain types of State or economic systems, affecting human society in general, constantly change their courses. The question then is whether new scientific findings and historical insights can still be fitted into the existing world picture. In the realm of history, world pictures or philosophical sketch-plans of the world are brought face to face with reality. It may be possible to construct here and now a sketch-plan of the world on the basis of actual experiences in science and history. But there is no guarantee that new experiences of reality which may come in the future will fit into such a sketch-plan. Hence any world picture must of necessity remain provisional, because man's experience of reality is not static but is subject to perpetual development.

It follows that all world pictures and philosophical sketches are inevitably conditioned to some extent by their times. The accumulation of knowledge and experience means that they become totally or partly historical relics, depending on how far they can hold their own against the inevitable advances. This is why we have the problem of successive world pictures coming and going. Scientists have made this a reproach to philosophy, using it as an argument that such mental efforts are futile. Even among philosophers there are strong tendencies to reject all world pictures, on the ground that they are on principle outside the reach of human knowledge. The tendency is particularly strong in present-day existence-philosophy.

Nonetheless, the point made by W. Dilthey must be noted — that even the breakdown of world pictures in the confrontation with historical reality represents an enrichment of experience which would have been impossible without them (see *Life-Philosophy*).

The failure does not merely signal the fact that a wrong road was taken. It also represents realms of reality where the way is barred to the intellect or where it is side-tracked into impasses.

The classical representative of a fully thought out world picture is the geocentric system of the Middle Ages. Here, against the religious and metaphysical background of biblical and Christian thought, the immediate data of reality are incorporated and explained. It is not just the sum total of individual experiences. It is based on a system of theological propositions which are understood as revelation (see *Scholasticism*). It was the positing of this system as a theory of knowledge that made the geocentric world picture of the Middle Ages a view of the whole which was more than the mere addition of particulars.

It is generally admitted that the geocentric world picture is false — not so much because of the theological system on which it is founded as because of its incompatibility with natural science. As far as the scientific point of view is in question, the geocentric world view has merely historical interest, now that science has progressed beyond it. But this is not true of the underlying experiences, e.g., the possibility of explaining astronomical phenomena on a geocentric basis, an approach which is still significant (in terms of the relativity of movement). But then the geocentric element in the self-understanding implied by the world picture in question does not simply mean the central geometrical position of the earth in the universe. It also implies the question of the central position of man in all reality. And here the last word has not yet been spoken. For in the present state of our knowledge, we cannot say what is the role of life in the universe as a whole, or whether life may not still develop elsewhere into a spirit-charged phenomenon. All that has been said on the subject up to the present, and often taken for granted, is at any rate in the light of science no more than speculation or wishful thinking. We do not know the role which the unique phenomenon man has to play in the whole, and this is only another way of saying that a given world picture, even when it has become a thing of the past, need not necessarily have forfeited its philosophical and historical interest.

When world pictures sink to the level of historical relics, this is not a proof of some sort of relativity of truth. World pictures become outdated, not because they are false, but mainly because new experiences present themselves in the course of history which do not fit into the existing world pictures. Kant's outline succeeded in being comprehensive because it set up a system of categories by which all knowledge must be *a priori* directed, and because the basic phenomena of space and time were posited as the form of intuition for the external and internal senses. The question is posed as to how any knowledge is at all possible. But this question makes it possible to subsume under it all known objects. Anything that is known can be considered within the framework of the established system of categories. The resulting sketch-plan is consistent. But the question is whether it was confirmed by history. Had Kant known, for instance, of the existence of non-Euclidian geometry, which only came to light seventy years later, he would probably have enunciated much of his system differently. Nonetheless, Kant's question remains, and no philosophy or science can ignore it.

World pictures and plans take two forms, though the distinction cannot always be followed out in detail. In one type, the basic affirmation or system is laid down critically and methodically, as in the sketch-plan of Kant. Above all there is an effort, explicit or implicit, to arrive at a sure starting-point. This is true of the Thomistic system (with its Aristotelian bases), if one prescinds from its theological elements which are in fact kept strictly apart, as theology, in the system itself. Every effort is made to establish the basic conceptions by which the real is comprehended (see *Act and Potency, Analogy of Being, Transcendentals*).

Such world pictures are open systems, that is, they take as their basis a limited system of propositions, but they have the advantage of being able to integrate new experiences and to trade-in outdated opinions, without having to stultify themselves. This means in general that they can never sink to the status of relics and that they always have a relevance, an extrapolated continuity of thought such as is usually ascribed only to the special sciences. We may also include here Descartes's sketch-plan, with its starting-point of *cogito, ergo sum*.

The other type of world picture is represented, for instance, by the Idealism which followed Kant. Here the fundamental principle is reached by intuition and then applied to all experiences of reality. The dialectical principle laid down by Hegel is an outstanding example. These are not open systems, since they are compelled from the outset to fit all that they encounter into the fundamental principle which they have formulated. Kant's table of categories, on the other hand, can be changed without changing the fundamental point of view. So too the doctrine of act and potency, the principle that the real must first be possible, is under no such compulsions. The application of the dialectical principle to history, for instance, is undoubtedly fruitful. But is it meaningful to explain the plus and minus of mathematics or the north and south poles of the magnetic field as instances of dialectics? In other words, the application of the dialectical principle to the whole realm of scientific knowledge is more than questionable.

The sketch-plan of Teilhard de Chardin, as expounded in his *Phénomène Humain,* is of the same type. It lays down at the outset the concept of the inward and the outward aspect of things, which act upon each other in harmony to produce the whole riches of reality through evolution. Teilhard's sketch-plan, as a world picture, is of particular interest, because the mainspring is not so much the effort to explain phenomena as the tendency to arrange them in the sequence of earlier and later, which is one of the essential constituents of a world picture. The difficulty with Teilhard's system is that proof is needed of the existence of such an inward aspect (in each electron, atomic nucleus, etc.).

A historical parallel to the succession of world pictures in philosophy may now be seen in the mathematical sciences as applied to cosmology. Efforts are made to find a basic mathematical formula into which the phenomena of the universe can be fitted. Einstein's special and general theory of relativity, Lemaître's theory of the expanding universe, the steady state theory — these are milestones along the way, which represent a dialogue of the intellect with reality in mathematical terms, corresponding to the succession of philosophical sketch-plans. Hence all the factors which affect the philosophical approach reappear in cosmology — becoming outdated, limitation of starting-points, new experiences, etc. There are far-reaching analogies here which can throw light on the whole effort of human thought and on the mutual understanding of philosophy and science.

See also *Myth, Being* I, *Reality, Existence* II, *Life, Person* II A, *Dialectics.*

BIBLIOGRAPHY. A. Eddington, *The Expanding Universe* (1933); A. N. Whitehead, *Adventures of Ideas* (1933); id., *Modes of Thought* (1938); id., *Science and Philosophy* (1947); C. F. von Weizsäcker, *History of Nature* (1949); H. Sihler, *Das Weltbild der Naturwissenschaft* (1953); W. Dilthey, *Essence of Philosophy* (1954); F. Tschirch, *Weltbild, Denkform und Sprachgestalt* (1954); E. Schrödinger, *Expanding Universes* (1956); A. Auer and B. Thum, *Weltbild und Metaphysik* (1958); H. Precht, *Das wissenschaftliche Weltbild und seine Grenzen* (1960); E. Tillyard, *Elizabethan World Picture* (1961); R. Money-Kyrle, *Man's Picture of the World* (1961); L. Foley, *Cosmology: Philosophical and Scientific* (1962); M. Heidegger, "Das Zeitalter der Weltbilder", *Holzwege* (3rd ed., 1963), pp. 69–104; P. Heelan, *Quantum Mechanics and Objectivity* (1966); A. Pfeiffer, *Dialogues on Fundamental Questions of Science and Philosophy* (1967).

Joseph Meurers

WORLD, VIEWS OF THE

The German term *Weltanschauung* ("world-view"), which has been widely used in English, has been taken in many ways. Wilhelm Dilthey, one of the main representatives of "life-philosophy", compares a *Weltanschauung* with a lyrical poem and its context: It is a "setting, a series of feelings, and hence frequently a desire, drive and activity" ("Die Typen der Weltanschauungen", *Weltanschauung*, ed. by M. Frischeisen-Köhler [1911], p. 12). Thus a world-view includes a world-picture and becomes an "evaluation of life" and an "understanding of the world", and finally, the "dominant conscious attitude", a "comprehensive plan of life", a "supreme rule of action".

There are a bewildering number of such "life-engendered" world-views. Dilthey reduces them to three types. Naturalism has a sensualist theory of knowledge, a materialist metaphysics and a hedonist code of morals. The Idealism of freedom starts from the consciousness in its theory of knowledge, and develops a metaphysics of the supra-sensible, while acknowledging that the world-picture is conditional. Objective Idealism sees the parts along with the whole. Here reality has two aspects. Externally, it is a sensible object. To personal experience, it is an extensive vital context. Its ethics is contemplative and deterministic. Dilthey had no criterion to test these contrasting products of life for their validity, and so was exposed to the danger of slipping into a general relativism of world-views.

The relativism of science with regard to world-views was reinforced by critical scepticism as regards values and the allied ideal of freedom as regards values. This ambience was exploited by National-Socialism to develop its "Myth of the Twentieth Century". The world-view, according to Krieck and Rosenberg, determines the supreme value which gives meaning to life. Values are not a matter of knowledge but of faith, and faith depends on race, people, "blood and soil" *(Blut und Boden)*. The value of the world-view depends on the value of the race and the maintenance of its purity. Science must take its directives from the world-view. History, biology, physics and even mathematics are conditioned by race (cf. J. de Vries, "Wissenschaft, Weltanschauung, Wahrheit", *Stimmen der Zeit* [1937], pp. 93–105).

H. Rickert describes the average world-view as the view taken of "the purpose or meaning of human existence in the world, which can, and indeed must, determine the practical behaviour of those who hold such a view" (*Grundprobleme der Philosophie* [1934], p. 2). Rickert's neo-Kantianism prevented his holding any scientifically established truths about God and concrete moral values. Hence a world-view can only express subjective and relatively limited views of the ground of reality. Its "world" is a small one. The realm of science is even smaller, but its view-points are more comprehensive and hence linked up with a larger world. There can be no scientific world-view, according to Rickert, but there can be a scientific doctrine of world-views, which can apply scientific standards to them. While Dilthey's life-philosophy left him helpless in face of the phenomenon of manifold and contradictory world-views, Rickert could point out that his doctrine enabled him to refute naturalism as scientifically untenable (p. 230).

In limiting or contesting the validity of any world-view, modern neo-positivism goes further than neo-Kantianism. It tries to show that the various world-views are merely systems which extrapolate upon all reality individual or social phenomena.

Like Rickert, Max Weber held that value-judgments could not be established scientifically or philosophically and hence that the scientist had to renounce value-judgments in his work. The danger of hastily or abusively established values in the social sciences led him to underestimate the danger of arbitrary values in handling social and political problems (cf. Marianne Weber, *Max Weber: Ein Lebensbild* [1926], pp. 328 ff.).

Rickert's attitude is understandable but questionable, timorous and arrogant at once. K. Jaspers criticized it as follows: "Man is not a being who knows everything and can be his independent self when adopting this or that form of world-view. If he is serious, he is necessarily within a given world-view, which gives him his perspective on everything and which for him is the only true one. He cannot look beyond it, because it is never complete. And no one can survey it from outside, because it only really exists when it self-consciously develops from its own origin. Hence world-views are never considered for what they are, when one is living within them. A plurality of world-views would not really be a world-view" (*Philosophie,* I [1932], p. 242). Since Jaspers, like Rickert, is mainly inspired by Kant, he also finds the scientific justification of a world-view problematic. "Faith is the kernel of a world-view" (*ibid.,* p. 246).

Like Jaspers, Scheler recognized the justification and necessity of a world-view, but did so in the light of a systematic philosophy of the concrete, whose task was to criticize world-views and establish a doctrine dealing with them. Scheler defined a world-view as "the organic and historical way in which large, closely-knit groups look upon and evaluate the world, the soul and life. In this sense each man, each profession, each class, each state of life and each nation has 'its' world-view, just as each person has his language, whether or not the holder of a world-view has succeeded more or less in making it the object of conscious and articulate judgment" (*Schriften zur Soziologie und Weltanschauungslehre,* I [1923], p. VI). Scheler considered that the theory of world-views could be practical at high school or secondary level. It was a "pre-condition" for the coming of philosophy, but should not replace metaphysics (*Versuche einer Soziologie des Wissens* [1924], p. 72).

J. Hessen's verdict on the analysis of world-views is like that of Scheler. Metaphysics and theory of values are the foundations, where the world-view takes in God, the spirit and history. Metaphysics, the scientific consideration of being, is not enough to found a world-view. "The ontological consideration must be completed and deepened by the study of values (axiology)" (*Wertphilosophie* [1937], pp. 10 f.; cf. *Lehrbuch der Philosophie,* 3 vols. [1950], pp. 272–351).

In contrast to such readiness to discuss world-views as parts of philosophy as a whole, Alois Müller insists that the two matters are totally different. Two questions can be put as regards the world. What is its structure? And, what is its meaning? Philosophy deals with the structure, a world-view with the meaning. Philosophy is a matter of understanding, a world-view a matter of practical proof. Philosophy is an affair of individuals, a world-view is held by a society. Philosophy as a science is always fragmentary, but a world-view is a complete whole, which can be expanded but does not radically change. "Philosophy and world-views are not just like different countries, they are in completely different spheres" ("Die Philosophie im katholischen Kulturkreis", *Archiv der Philosophie* 1 [1947], p. 136).

Like Scheler and Hessen, the Thomist P. M. de Munnynck affirms that rational philosophy must be the norm of any world-view. There is a spontaneous world-view which is exposed to many hazards. Rational philosophy cannot answer all questions definitely and not all its proofs are conclusive. Thus round the bony structure of a rational philosophy a world-view forms on the periphery, a zone of convictions which have some connection with the perspicuous truths of the philosophy in question but cannot simply be deduced from them ("Philosophie und Weltanschauung", *Divus Thomas* 14 [1936]).

In contrast to the previous views, present-day Marxism identifies science, world-view and philosophy. There are of course many individual sciences along with philosophy. But while the sciences investigate "the special laws of various parts of nature or society", dialectical materialism studies "the general laws which are valid for all things and for all decisions" (*Wissenschaftliche Weltanschauung,* I: *Dialektischer Materialismus,* by G. Klaus, A. Kosing and G. Redlow, 1; *Der dialektische Materialismus — die Weltanschauung des Sozialismus* [1959], p. 14). In this sense, dialectical materialism is "the scientific doctrine of the universal in the world" (p. 21). It is the basis of all individual sciences, the natural sciences and political economy, and it is the guide "of the proletariat as it struggles for its liberation" (p. 22).

Everyone needs a world-view for his thinking, feeling and will, and it may be conscious or unconscious. "The unconscious, naive world-view is not buttressed by science and made part of a theoretical system. It is a rudimentary and partly emotional view of the world as a whole, of its origin and nature, of the meaning of life and many other fundamental questions" (p. 13). The naive world-view is materialistic. Conscious world-views include fatalism, religion and Idealism, which in contrast to the true, scientific and materialistic are all erroneous.

Insofar as a world-view rests on an unconditional, unjustifiable philosophical faith, which calls in question and explains in its own way all the rest, while excluding revelation, or is based on the deliberate denial of God, it is in contradiction to theological faith, man's personal relation to God and the resulting acceptance of revealed truths. Theological faith is compatible with many different types of philosophical world-views, sceptic, dogmatic, rational or mystical, realist or Idealist, so long as they can be open to revelation. The contents of faith are open to many types of philosophy (and vice-versa), which means that in the present pluralism of world-views and critical approaches to them, faith has, if not absolute freedom, a wide range of choice among world-views.

See also *Marxism, World-Picture.*

BIBLIOGRAPHY. F. Klimke, *Die Hauptprobleme der Weltanschauung* (1910); K. Jaspers, *Psychologie der Weltanschauungen* (1919; 4th ed., 1954); P. Ernst, *Die Weltanschauung und ihre Problematik* (1930); M. Heidegger, *Holzwege* (1950); W. Dilthey, *The Philosophy of Existence: Introduction to Weltanschauungslehre* (E. T., 1960); W. Weischedel, *Philosophische Grenzgänge* (1967); W. Weymann-Weyhe, *Revolution im christlichen Denken* (1967).

Marcel Reding

WORSHIP

1. *Term and concept.* This article is an endeavour to explain the notion of worship, not to give an account of its various forms.

In a world of industrialization and technology, there could be a temptation to dismiss worship as outmoded, because unproductive. Kant held that worship was a form of fanaticism and superstition. L. Feuerbach and K. Marx then made a still more radical attack on worship. According to Feuerbach, "God" is a personification of human wishes and satisfactions in a non-human form which has been erected into an absolute. If man is not to dissipate his energies and lose himself, he must devote himself to his fellow-men and not to this figure of fantasy.

Man's only God is man. The friend of God must become the friend of man, the believer must become a thinker, the supplicant a worker. Feuerbach's idea was not to eliminate worship but to give it a "horizontal" direction. Marx substitutes for God, whom he considers a human invention, a society freed from the bonds of private property and the State. This society is to be paid the reverence which the masses once paid to God in the days when they created religion as a euphoric opium for their distress. The attitude which came to the fore in such theses still influences many theories and practices of the present day. It falls within the prophetic perspective which characterizes the Revelation of St. John. The 13th chapter contrasts the "worship of God" and the "worship of the world" under the imagery of the two beasts.

All these notions ignore the specifically religious element of worship, as demonstrated by the modern philosophy of religion (R. Otto, M. Scheler, H. Scholz, B. Welte and others).

The question of worship is intimately connected with the question of man. If man is to be seen merely in the dimension of the economic and political, merely as *homo faber* or as *animal sociale et politicum,* worship must be condemned as a useless waste of time or indeed as a harmful preoccupation. But if real transcendence is the fundamental existential of human life, worship must be regarded as an essential act, without which a whole realm of human life would remain atrophied. In this perspective worship is a process in man's self-realization. It presupposes God's turning to man in grace and blessing, so that he makes himself accessible to man. Since worship can only be a response to God's word, it has the character of a salutary encounter of man with God.

In view of the significance of worship for the whole nature of man, one can readily understand that it is as old as mankind itself. It has never been entirely wanting, either in the religions of nature or in the higher religions, though it has taken on a wide diversity of forms. One can deduce the nature of worship from the historical phenomena. The decisive element is the reverent homage paid to God or to the divine by means of outward signs, and the hope of life and salvation which goes with such homage. In Christianity, worship was given a special and unique quality through Jesus Christ ("worship as a Christological function").

Much attention has been paid to the question as to whether worship is always offered by a group or whether it can also be the act of the individual. Most theologians and historians of religion incline to the former view. But one can hardly deny that the individual can also perform cultic acts. But such individual worship, like the whole life of the individual, is inspired and stamped by the social setting.

2. *On the theology of worship.* Worship, the cultus, plays a central role in the Bible, beginning with the OT. There is no particular word for cultus in the OT, but there are a number of words connected with service (work) which are used very instructively in this connection. The cultic activities of the patriarchs are now for the most part buried in obscurity, but from the time of Moses on, worship was characterized by the prohibition of images, and the introduction of the sacred tent and the ark of the covenant. It consisted mainly of sacrifice (burnt offerings and cereal offerings). In the time of the monarchy, the cultus received an impetus with far-reaching effects, when David brought the ark of the covenant to Jerusalem, thus making Jerusalem the central shrine. Solomon built the temple and Hezekiah made Jerusalem the one place where the worship of Israel could be offered. The Canaanite environment was very influential. It was from here that the notion of the liturgical feast came into Israel. But the feasts were transformed in the light of the faith of Israel: they were memorial celebrations of the saving deeds of God. The people of God was created by its worship and renewed again and again as the worshipping people. Worship received a considerable expansion, which was again to have far-reaching consequences, in the Babylonian captivity. Since sacrifice could not be offered, worship took the form of prayer and preaching. In the Qumran community, the only worship offered was the "liturgy of the word". With the destruction of Jerusalem in A.D. 70 sacrificial worship came to an end throughout the whole of Judaism.

The NT writings express the conviction that Christ's work included the fulfilment of all that was aimed at by the OT worship. He is the representative of all mankind and therefore *the* offerer of worship in the full sense. God himself, the Logos of the Father, is present in Christ — salvation has entered human history, in the form of a person. The man Jesus has dedicated himself to God without reserve, in the name of all and in favour of all. He is described in Scripture by a number of cultic formulae. He is the temple (Jn 2:19), the holy one of God (Mk 1:24), the high priest (Heb 2:17), the one mediator (Heb 8:6; 9:15; 12:24; 1 Tim 2:5), the minister in the sanctuary (Heb 8:2). By virtue of what he was and what he willed to be, his whole life was an act of worship, fully open to the will of the Father. His obedience was at its most intense at his death on the cross, when he submitted himself to the grace of the judgment of God as representative of sinful man. This made his death an act of expiation through which men were reconciled with God. He died as a sacrificial offering (Eph 5:2; Heb 7:27, etc.), as a sacrificial lamb (Jn 1:29, 36; 1 Pet 1:19; Rev 5:6, 12; 13:8). Further, the NT writings make Christ himself proclaim his death as a means of salvation (Mt 26:26ff.; Mk 14:22ff.; Lk 22:19f.), the sacrifice of the covenant with the new, "true" people of God. Its efficacity is revealed in the resurrection. According to the synoptics (see *Eucharist* I), the sacrifice was anticipated by Jesus among his apostles in the form of a meal, before it was enacted historically. At this cultic anticipation of his death, he gave a command which was of supreme importance — that his disciples should celebrate the memory of his death in the form of a meal, till he came again. He himself remains, in his glorified state, the agent of salvation for the community formed by him and around him as its head, being present in the Holy Spirit whom he has sent.

When the new people of God assembles to celebrate his memory in the Holy Spirit ("worship as a pneumatological function"), it looks back to Good Friday and Easter Sunday and upwards to the exalted Lord, while he, the "minister of the sanctuary", acting through his "mystical body", the Church, makes the past so truly present that his flesh and blood, present in the signs of the bread and wine, have the saving power of Good Friday. The whole people of God can thus enter into that process of salvation and dedicate itself in and through Christ, its Lord, to the Father. In this central act, the people of God becomes more and more truly what it is: the body of Christ. This is how it attains its fullness. At the same time, the participants in this sacrifice, which takes place in the form of a fraternal repast, are joined more and more closely in fraternal union. The celebration of the Eucharist is the vital centre which leaves its mark on all the activity of the Church. For everything that is done in the Church for the furtherance of its ends is determined by the saving death of Christ, though all is not in the nature of sacrifice. The Church is the universal sacrament in which the salvation of Christ remains active and efficacious. Hence all the actions of the Church are cultic in character. This is true both of its preaching of the word and its use of the sacramental signs.

The worship of the Church is always offered by the whole people of God, even when only a small group takes part in the act of worship. It has an official character — being *cultus publicus* in contrast to *cultus privatus,* non-official worship. The individual can only fully benefit by its saving power when he joins in the cultic act with his own personal faith. Salutary participation includes love of God and of the neighbour. St. Augustine lays so much stress on the fraternal unity of all worshippers that he makes it an essential element of all celebration of the Eucharist. He says that the sacrifice on the altar of stone is meaningless if it is not accompanied by the sacrifice on the altar of the heart. Real participation in the eucharistic worship proves its fruitfulness in the works of mercy, in the effort to re-shape the world in a way more worthy of man, so that the whole Christian life has the character of worship, while worship is sterile when it is not prolonged in everyday life, when divine service does not become service of others. Worship and morality are inseparable.

The Church offers its worship till the end of time, so that all the generations of men may partake in the saving act of Christ and so be able to attain salvation. The Church will cease to exist in its sacramental form when Christ comes again at the end to complete his work, when he makes it the full blissful dialogue between man and God and between man and man, leading to an exchange growing deeper and broader for all eternity. The Church in its worship also necessarily looks forward to its future perfection ("the eschatological function of worship"), which is present under the veil of signs since the death and resurrection of Christ (see also *Religion* I).

BIBLIOGRAPHY. R. Will, *Le culte,* 3 vols. (1925–35); E. Underhill, *Worship* (1936); E. Dublanchy in *DTC,* IX, cols. 2339–474; see also XIII, cols. 2312–76, XIV, cols. 870–978; E. Jombert, *Dictionnaire de Droit Canonique,* IV, cols. 861–83; S. Mowinckel, *Religion og Kultus* (1950); J. Pieper, *Leisure the Basis of Culture* (1952); A. Kirchgässner, *Die mächtigen Zeichen: Ursprung, Formen und Gesetze des Kultus* (1959); M. Schmaus and K. Forster, *Der Kultus und der heutige Mensch* (1961); E. Lohmeyer, *The Lord of the Temple* (1962); B. Welte, *Auf der Spur des Ewigen* (1965); id., *Heilsverständnis* (1966); H.-J. Kraus, *Worship in Israel* (1966); H. H. Rowley, *Worship in Ancient Israel* (1967); J. F. White, *The Worldliness of Worship* (1968).

Michael Schmaus

Z

ZIONISM

1. *Historical.* Zionism has had three aspects. The first was the "practical Zionism" occasioned by pogroms in Russia, 1881 on, and also inspired by the writings of L. Pinsker (*Auto-Emancipation* [1882; E. T., 1891]), head of the movement of the Hoveve Zion, the "Lovers of Zion". Funds were raised by Western Jews, institutionalized as the Palestinian Office, Jaffa, 1908, and it brought some 60,000 Jews to Palestine, then a province of the Turkish Empire, by 1914. The second aspect was "political Zionism", crystallized in yearly (1897 ff.) and then two-yearly (1901 ff.) Zionist congresses. The programme was the "creation for the Jewish people of a publicly recognized, legally secured home in Palestine" (Basle, 1897). The leader was T. Herzl, whose *Judenstaat* (1896; E. T.: *The Jewish State*) rejected assimilation as impracticable because of the anti-Semitism of the West. From 1914 on, under C. Weizmann and N. Sokolow, the base was London. Its great early successes were the Balfour Declaration of November 1917 ("His Majesty's Government view with favour the establishment in Palestine of a national home for the Jewish people"), and its insertion into the mandate over Palestine given in July 1922 by the League of Nations to Great Britain.

Herzl was not strictly "Zionist" at first. When the Turkish Government refused his larger demands, he was ready to accept the highlands of Uganda offered by Britain in 1903. British interest in Zionism was as old as Lord Shaftesbury (1801–85), and was based on the fundamentalist Bible-reading which dominated Victorian England. This was not an irrelevant factor, even in the Balfour Declaration. And the same view proved — to the surprise of Zionists who had been casting round for possible settlements in Morocco and Argentine — to be the dominant conviction of the Jews, to whom emigration appealed as the only refuge from discrimination or worse. By 1935, when the number of Jews in Palestine had risen to 300,000, the third or religious aspect was fully apparent, the conviction that the reality of Jewish religion and life could not be adequately affirmed, except when at least a substantial part of the Jewish people possessed the ancient land of Palestine.

2. *Religious Zionism.* With the prevalence of this "religious" Zionism, the State of Israel, founded in May 1948, was given a "theological" connotation. The "historical" right of the Jewish people to Palestine, re-conquered in the "War of Liberation", recognized by the United Nations Organization (November 1947), was now seen by many hitherto non-religious Jews and many Christians as divinely confirmed by the Lord of Armies. It was the "election of which the Scriptures tell, which the Haggadah interprets, of which the voices of the Exile sing . . . the true picture of the Eternal drawn with the strokes of history" (M. Buber, p. 146). The entry into the land where alone "the Jewish people can exist, work and be holy" (*ibid.,* p. 147), after so many years of longing and suffering, climaxed by the killing of six million Jews in the Nazi persecution, was seen as a fulfilment of the ancient, unabrogated covenant. More, it was proclaimed as an eschatological and messianic event, the inauguration by the

"servant Israel" of the kingdom of God. "Israel needs a land of its own to build up the kingdom of God on earth", writes Buber. "Through him (the servant Israel) redeemed Zion becomes the centre of the redeemed world" ... "The people of Israel is called upon to be the herald and pioneer of the redeemed world." What the Bible offers and what is now realized is "a Zionocentric view of cosmic proportions" (Buber, *ibid.*, pp. 35ff.). Thus religious Zionism can be the affirmation of Judaism as the one absolute religion of mankind, with a sort of "hypostatic" union with Zion.

3. *The present situation.* Zionism, which had begun as the search for the solution of the material problem of refuge from persecution (T. Herzl), as the search for a land where the Jewish people could cease to be a ghost and become a nation (L. Pinsker), as the search for a centre of culture and spirituality radiating to a vast diaspora (A. Ginsberg [Ahad Ha°am]), seems now to have stabilized as an expression of the "mystery of Israel" in its most realistic terms. "Zion is to be defended against every kind of spiritualistic evaporation of the concept" (Buber, p. 137). Hence Zionists are not disturbed by criticism from within Judaism, such as that of the "American Council of Judaism", founded in 1943 to oppose Zionism, which has parallels elsewhere. "Our central proposition is that to be a Jew one need have no rights in the State of Israel. A Jew does not have to be a Zionist ... A religion cannot be allied with a State without having its spiritual integrity destroyed. Zionism's claim that every Jew has rights in and obligations to Israel" cannot be admitted (Rabbi Elmer Berger). To such criticism Buber replies: "Judaism is fundamentally national, and all the efforts of the 'Reformers' to separate the Jewish religion from its national element only ruined both the nationalism and the religion" (*ibid.*, p. 268).

Zionism, therefore, is much more than the effort — now successful — "to eliminate the basic abnormality of Jewish existence, its ubiquitous minority status" (cf. *New Catholic Encyclopedia* [1967], XIV, p. 1122a). It is the theological proposition, which must now be an element in dialogue between Christians and Jews, that the Israeli State, unknown perhaps to its political representatives or even the majority of its population, is the intrinsic consequence of the persistence

of the Jewish people with a special place in the history of salvation. Christians who speak of the "mystery of Israel" (cf., for example, *Traduction œcuménique de la Bible, Épître aux Romains* [1967], p. 84, note on Rom 11:13), acknowledging thereby Judaism as a national "revealed" religion, are on the way to granting that religion what it claims as the minimum for existence as a nation — a land of its own. This would not, of course, prejudice the ultimate settlement of the continuing conflict with the dispossessed Arabs, of whom a million or more are now displaced persons by reason of the foundation and expansion of the Israeli State. But even when, as one may hope, the Arabs are compensated, re-settled and perhaps resigned, the question of the "Zionist" State will remain for Catholic theology. It may even be a matter with practical consequences, since it may seem to demand of Christians a respect for the State of Israel such as Catholics once gave to the Papal States. As a *sine qua non* of Judaism, Zionism may claim the allegiance of all who see in the "mystery of Israel, a strange and awe-inspiring character" (cf. H. Urs von Balthasar, pp. 27f.).

4. *Christian critique.* For a Christian, the question turns on whether after the coming of Christ, the religion of Judaism, i.e., the Jewish people as religious, still has a special, divinely-appointed character, and what this entails. To Christians, Christ is the end of the law (Rom 10:4) and hence the end of the promise of the land, not the retractation of the promise, but its fulfilment in Christ, in the very concrete reality of the new creation of the risen Christ, in whom "all the promises of God find their Yes" (2 Cor 1:20). Thus if Judaism and its hope of the land really survive as a divinely constituted mystery, they can only do so insofar as they tend, like the law and the prophets, to faith in Christ. "The answer will have to reduce both land and temple to the body of the Word of God, which in the living man Jesus Christ becomes the principle of unity ... alive and free, not a material thing ... and also dying and rising again" (von Balthasar, p. 81). The same author continues: "It is the dynamic conception of faith which makes the Zionist notion of the sacramental principle of Israel so questionable from a theological point of view and throws doubt on the absolute correspondence between the people of Israel and the land of Palestine. It is surely clear that it is no longer valid from a

Christian point of view, and it does not require the Crusades as a counter-proof to confirm the fact. Jerusalem in the post-Christian era cannot be looked upon even as a secondary centre of significance. Nor is it clear that it provides a theme of vital interest to the people of Israel themselves. The fact that the Temple was destroyed is relevant insofar as it is a genuine eschatological symbol, but once the centre, the sanctuary, has ceased, the Land can no longer have any biblical significance" (von Balthasar, p. 106).

This last argument is not convincing. And Buber argues that priesthood, kingship and law can be sifted out from the "statement" of the OT, while the people and its land remain. But even on this hypothesis, the historical and the biblical argument must not be confused. What is arguably the historical or practical minimum for a people? No one knows. The British Commonwealth kept only the Crown as the symbol of unity. Historical demands can always change. What seems immediately the *sine qua non* of Judaism is not a land or State, but simply its sacred books of the Bible.

5. *The "mystery of Israel"*. A permanent attachment to the "law, the prophets and the writings" may be quite sufficient to found the "mystery of Israel" insofar as it exists. Through these books, read even "with the veil upon the heart" (2 Cor 3:15), the Jewish people has a theological significance not proper, say, to Islam, and one which gives them a special affinity to the "true Israel", the Church, the people of God and the body of Christ. There is an intrinsic urge to Christ in the OT.

But this again should not be misunderstood. Christ is the significance of the OT, but not its logical conclusion, as if from the OT, with sufficient goodwill and insight, the Christian kerygma could be deduced. The OT needs to be completed by and integrated into the words and works of Christ before it can yield its secret. His resurrection is the key to the OT. The *latens Christus* of the OT only becomes patent in the preaching of the gospel.

But the "mystery of Israel" needs to be looked at more closely. For St. Paul, it is above all the "mystery, that a hardening has come upon part of Israel, until the full number of the gentiles come in, and so all Israel will be saved . . . As regards the gospel they are enemies of God, for your sake; but as regards election, they are beloved for the sake of their forefathers. For the gifts and the call of God are irrevocable" (Rom 11:25 ff.; cited by Vatican II, Declaration on Non-Christian Religions, art. 4). The mystery is the hardening of Israel (cf. Mk 4:11 f.), an "hour" which came and went. To none of the NT writers except Paul does the persistence of an "Israel according to the flesh" pose a problem. Elsewhere, the people (as a people) is simply, when hardened, rejected for its rejection of Christ, the kingdom of God taken from it and given to another people (cf. W. Trilling, *Das wahre Israel* [1962], especially pp. 34, 47, 65, 67 ff., 70). As a specific people, it is eliminated from the history of salvation, though of course it still has to be preached to, as the disciples "teach all nations" (Mt 28:20; cf. Trilling, pp. 12 f.).

But the position of Paul is strange and complicated. Many Pauline texts affirm that all national traits are now irrelevant (Rom 10:12; Gal 3:28; Col 3:11 — there is no longer Jew or Greek). But the Letter to the Romans, wrestling not with human justification but with the problem of the faithfulness of God to his promises, keeps "Israel according to the flesh" specifically in the picture. Logically Paul had rebutted the charge of God's being faithless or unjust, by proving that the promises had always been to faith and not to a people as such (Rom 1–8). He then reinforced his argument by proving in Rom 9–11 (especially 11:7) that the promises were in any case to a Remnant only, and that the Remnant, the elect, the Jews believing in Christ, had in fact obtained the promises.

This is a complete theology, which coincides fundamentally with the rest of the NT. But then Paul affirms that the faithfulness of God *also* means that *all* Israel will be saved (Rom 11:25). This peculiar tension in the thought of Paul must be explained by his "imminent eschatology". The gathering in of the twelve tribes of Israel was part of the world-picture of apocalyptic, and as such formed part of Paul's eschatological outlook (cf. "mystery", Rom 11:25; 1 Cor 15:51). But once cosmic pictures such as 1 Thess 4:15 ff. and 1 Cor 15:51 ff. have lost their direct relevance, the rest of the eschatological "apparatus" may also be considered expendable, and hence too the conversion of "all Israel". This to Paul was still an immediate hope, but was long abandoned when Mt and Jn were written (cf. Trilling, pp. 68f.). With this, the "mystery of Israel", as an ethnic religion, ceases to be of significance, except, as has been said, insofar as Jewish tradition is faithful to the reading of the OT. And hence too Zionism as a theological proposition lacks interest. (No judgment is implied on "political" Zionism.)

6. *Conclusion.* This is the Christian critique of Zionism. The Jewish critique, based on faith as propounded in the OT, must be that the prophecies cannot be limited and petrified in anything so precise as Zion and a land. This would be to commit God to a historicist (or "fundamentalist") realization of his call, to force certain means on him, to deprive the future of its real futurity, history of its real historicity. That the promises could leave Israel facing a blank, an unthinkable future to be awaited only from God as an incalculable grace, was already proclaimed by Amos (8:2 etc.; cf. H. W. Wolff, *Amos* [*Biblischer Kommentar, Altes Testament* XIV, 6, fasc. 1] [1967], pp. 124f.). And Micah, who saw the future of Jerusalem only as "Zion shall be ploughed as a field, Jerusalem shall become a heap of ruins", held out no other hope except what was implicit in the presence of God in history. There is no authentic reading of the OT except in such an openness of hope. When Christian theology refuses to accept Zionism as a prophetic element, it is not because it does not see God's call as going out irrevocably to the Jewish people, but because the "oracles of God" (the OT, Rom 3:2) promise them Christ, nothing more and nothing less.

See also *Judaism, Judaism and Christianity, People of God, Secularization* I.

BIBLIOGRAPHY. M. Hess, *Rom und Jerusalem* (1862), E.T.: *Rome and Jerusalem* (1918); George Eliot, *Daniel Deronda* (1876); L. Pinsker, *Auto-Emancipation* (1882; E.T., 1891); T. Herzl, *Der Judenstaat* (1896), E.T.: *The Jewish State;* A. Ginzberg (Ahad Ha῾am), "Slavery or Freedom", *Selected Essays* (1912); id., *Ten Essays in Judaism and Zionism* (1922); id., *Essays, Letters, Memoirs* (1946); N. Sokolow, *History of Zionism, 1600–1918,* 2 vols. (1919); A. Ruppin, *The Jews in the Modern World* (1934); H. M. Stationery Office, *Reports of the Palestine Commissions* (July 1937); *ibid.* (October 1938); *Report of the Anglo-U.S. Commission of Inquiry* (March 1946); *Issues,* published by the American Council for Judaism, New York (quarterly, 1944ff.); E. Berger, *The Jewish Dilemma* (1946); C. Weizmann, *Trial and Error* (new ed., 1950); M. Buber, *Israel and Palestine: The History of an Idea* (1950); M. Freedman, *A Minority in Britain: Social Studies of the Anglo-Jewish Community* (1955); L. Stein, *The Balfour Declaration* (1961); H. Urs von Balthasar, *Martin Buber and Christianity* (1961); N. Mandel, "Turks, Arabs and Jewish Immigration into Palestine", *St. Anthony's Papers* 17 (1965), pp. 77–108; J.-P. Sartre, ed., *Le conflit israëlo-arabe. Dossier* (Jewish and Arab contributors) (1967).

Kevin Smyth

GENERAL INDEX

and

LIST OF CONTRIBUTORS

GENERAL INDEX

to volumes I–VI

Entries in italics denote titles of articles in the encyclopedia. Roman numerals indicate volume numbers. The letters "a" and "b" after page numbers refer to the left-hand and right-hand columns respectively.

LIST OF CONTRIBUTORS
to volumes I–VI

AHLBRECHT, ANSGAR: Ecumenism VI B

ALBERIGO, GIUSEPPE: (with Piergiorgio Camaiani) Reform II D

ALFARO, JUAN: Faith II, III, IV, Nature I B, II, III

ALONSO-SCHÖKEL, LUIS: Inspiration, Old Testament Theology

ALSZEGHY, ZOLTAN: Scholasticism II A

ANTON, HUBERT: Reform II A

ARANGUREN, JOSÉ LUIS: Ethics

ARNALDICH, LUIS: Old Testament Books II

AUBERT, ROGER: Modernism

AUDINET, JACQUES: Catechesis

AUER, JOHANN: Grace II A

BALIĆ, CARLO: Scotism

BAUM, GREGORY: Baptism II

BAUMGARTNER, HANS MICHAEL: Life-Philosophy ("Bergsonism"), Transcendental Philosophy

BECK, HANS-GEORG: Byzantine Empire

BECK, HEINRICH: Collectivism II, Education V

BEIERWALTES, WERNER: Neo-Platonism

BEINERT, WOLFGANG: Bishop II

BENDER, HANS: Psychology IV

BENDER, LUDWIG: Ecclesiastical Law IV

BENZO, MIGUEL: (with Ernst Niermann) Laity II

BERGER, KLAUS: Apostolic Church I, Bible I A 2, Bishop I, Freedom I, Grace I, Justice I, Law I, Lord's Prayer, Parousia I, Salvation III A 1

BETTENCOURT, ESTÉVÃO: Charisms, Millenarianism

BETZ, JOHANNES: Eucharist I

BEYER, JEAN: Secular Institutes

BISER, EUGEN: Wisdom

BLEISTEIN, ROMAN: Collectivism I, Environment, Leisure I, II

BLINZLER, JOSEF: Passion of Christ

BOEHM, LAETITIA: Crusades

BÖKMANN, JOHANNES: Moral Psychology

BORST, ARNO: Catharists

BOUESSÉ, HUMBERT: God, Glory of

BOUILLARD, HENRI: Dialectical Theology

BREUNING, WILHELM: Apostolic Succession, Communion of Saints

BROSSEDER, JOHANNES: Ecumenism IV B

BROX, NORBERT: Apologists, Apostolic Fathers, Church Orders

BRÖKER, WERNER: Life I

BULST, WERNER: Resurrection I C 1

CAMAIANI, PIERGIORGIO: (with Giuseppe Alberigo) Reform II D

CAMELOT, PIERRE-THOMAS: Creeds

CARPENTIER, RENÉ: Charity I, Evangelical Counsels

CAZELLES, HENRI: Commandments, the Ten, Covenant, Old Testament Books I

CHENU, MARIE-DOMINIQUE: Work

COGNET, LOUIS: Mysticism II E

COHEN, ARTHUR A.: Judaism IV

CONZEMIUS, VICTOR: Ecumenism II, Modern Church History, Old Catholic Church, Quietism, Reform I, Schism II

CORNÉLIS, ÉTIENNE: Transmigration of Souls

CORNÉLIS, HUMBERT: Afterlife

COSTE, RENÉ: War

CROUZEL, HENRI: Apocatastasis, Biblical Exegesis III, Origenism

DANIÉLOU, JEAN: Apostolic Church II, Judaeo-Christianity

419

LIST OF CONTRIBUTORS

Darlap, Adolf: Creation III, IV, Devil I, Eternity I, Faith and History, (with Jörg Splett) History I, Mercy, Religion III B, Salvation III A 2, Society II, Time

David, Jakob: Marriage III

Deblaere, Albert: Mysticism II B

Deissler, Alfons: Old Testament Books V

Delaruelle, Étienne: Gallicanism

Delcourt, Jacques: Ecclesiastical Regions

De Letter, Prudent: Anointing of the Sick

De Vooght, Paul: Hussism

Didier, Jean-Charles: Illness I

Díez-Alegría, José Maria: Justice II, Law III, Rights of Man, Society III

Donohue, John W.: Education III

Du Buit, Michel: Biblical Geography

Dumont, Christophe: Schism I

Duncker, Petrus Gerard: Biblical Exegesis II A

Dupont, Jacques: New Testament Books III, Sermon on the Mount

Dürig, Walter: Burial

Dvornik, Francis: Schism III

Eckert, Willehad Paul: Antisemitism, Ecumenism V

Eder, Gernot: Matter, Science III

Edwards-Errázuriz, Anibal: Mysticism II D

Engelhardt, Paulus: Thomism

Engels, Odilo: Council II, Religious Orders

Ernst, Cornelius: Theological Methodology I

Fabri, Enrique: Docetism

Fasbender, Johannes: Superstition III

Fetscher, Iring: Communism

Feuillet, André: Eschatologism, Metanoia

Finance, Joseph de: Eternity II, Value

Finsterhölzl, Johann: (with Heinrich Fries) Infallibility, Theological Notes

Fischer, Heribert: Mysticism I

Franco, Ricardo: Justification

Frangipane, Domenico: Old Testament Books III

Frank, Suso: Patrology II

Fransen, Piet: Confirmation, Orders and Ordination

Franzen, August: Church History, Communion under Both Kinds

Fries, Heinrich: Faith and Knowledge, Fundamental Theology, (with Johann Finsterhölzl) Infallibility, Myth, Revelation III

Füglister, Notker: Passover

Gabel, Émile: Communications Media

García Villoslada, Ricardo: Avignon Exile

Gieraths, Paul-Gundolf: Mysticism II C

Giers, Joachim: Social Philosophy, Social Sciences

Glazik, Josef: Missions IV

Gómez Caffarena, José: God III, Suarezianism

González, Ireneo: Positivism II

Gordon, Ignazio: Curia I

Görres, Albert: Psychoanalysis

Gössmann, Elisabeth: Scholasticism II C

Graef, Hilda: Mysticism II A

Granero, Jesús María: Spirituality III B

Grelot, Pierre: Apocalyptic, Messiah

Grillmeier, Aloys: Jesus Christ III, Monophysitism, Monotheletism, Nestorianism

Gross, Heinrich: Creation II

Gründel, Johannes: Natural Law I, Sex I, II, III

Gründler, Johannes: Sects, Christian

Guillet, Jacques: Biblical Historiography

Gumpel, Peter: Limbo

Gutwenger, Engelbert: Transubstantiation

Guzzetti, Giovanni-Battista: Apostasy

Haardt, Robert: Gnosis, Gnosticism, Mandaeism, Manichaeism

Haeffner, Gerd: Infinity, Monism, Subjectivism, Utilitarianism, World

Haensli, Ernst: Preaching I, II

Haible, Eberhard: Theological Methodology II

Halder, Alois: Art I, Idealism, Knowledge, Metaphysics, (with Max Müller) Person I, Reality, (with Max Müller) Science I, Technology

Häring, Bernhard: Morality I, Moral Theology I, III

Hasenhüttl, Gotthold: Ecumenism IV A

Hasler, August B.: Ecumenism I

Hättich, Manfred: Pluralism, Politics

Häussling, Angelus: Breviary, Liturgy II, III

Hecker, Konrad: Humanism I, Jansenism, Liberalism and Liberal Theology, Rationalism, Renaissance, Revolution and Restoration I, II, Society I, Totalitarianism

Heggelbacher, Othmar: Censorship of Books

Heinemann, Heribert: Heresy I

Heinzmann, Richard: Scholasticism II B

Hemmerle, Klaus: Being II, Enthusiasm, Evil, Holy II, III, Power

Henrici, Peter: Apologetics II, Immanentism

Henry, Paul: Hellenism and Christianity

Hermann, Ingo: Bible IV, Biblical Movement

Heydte, Friedrich August, Freiherr von der: International Law

Hofmann, Rudolf: Conscience, Morality III

Hostie, Raymond: Illness II A, Psychology III

Houtart, François: (with Ernst Niermann) Parish I, II

Huerga, Alvaro: Humility

Hünermann, Peter: History II, Reign of God

Iparraguirre, Ignacio: Spirituality III D 1

Javierre, Antonio: Apostle

Jedin, Hubert: Conciliarism

Johann, Robert O.: Positivism I

Jubany, Narciso: Deacon

Jungmann, Josef Andreas: Eucharist II, Liturgical Movement, Liturgy I, IV

Kasper, Walter: Christianity II, History III, Law and Gospel

KEILBACH, WILHELM: Religion II D

KELLER, ALBERT: Ontologism, Ontology, Order I, Secularization I, Universals

KEMPF, FRIEDRICH: Reform II C

KERBER, WALTER: Profession

KERN, WALTER: Absolute and Contingent, Cartesianism, Deism, Dialectics, Dogmatism, God-World Relationship, Identity-Philosophy, Necessity I, (with Jörg Splett) Theodicy

KERSTIENS, FERDINAND: Hope

KINDER, ERNST: Lutheran Churches

KIPPER, BALDUINO: Biblical Chronology

KLINGER, ELMAR: Modalism, Purgatory, Soul, Tübingen School

KLOPPENBURG, BONAVENTURA: Superstition I

KLOSTERMANN, FERDINAND: Laity III

KLÜBER, FRANZ: Property

KÖHLER, OSKAR: Absolutism, Occident, Romanticism, World History

KORNFELD, WALTER: Old Testament Ethics

KRENN, KURT: Kantianism

KÜNG, HANS: Council I

LACHENSCHMID, ROBERT: Hell II

LAKNER, FRANZ: Salvation IV B

LANCZKOWSKI, GÜNTER: Religion II A, B, C

LAY, RUPERT: Natural Law II

LECLERCQ, JEAN: Reform II B

LÉCUYER, JOSEPH: Bishop III, Episcopalism

LEDERER, JOSEF: Ecclesiastical Finances

LEEMING, BERNARD: Anglican Communion

LEFEBVRE, CHARLES: Ecclesiastical Tribunals

LE GUILLOU, MARIE-JOSEPH: Church I, II

LEHMANN, KARL: Experience, Hermeneutics, Phenomenology, Transcendence

LENTNER, LEOPOLD: Education IV

LÉON-DUFOUR, XAVIER: New Testament Books I

LOBKOWICZ, NIKOLAUS: Marxism III

LOHFF, WENZEL: Pietism, Protestantism III

LÖHRER, MAGNUS: Sacramentals

LÓPEZ IBOR, JUAN JOSÉ: Illness II B

LORTZ, JOSEPH: Reformation

LOTZ, JOHANNES BAPTIST: Being I, Essence, Reflection, Substance, Transcendentals

LUTZ, HEINRICH: French Revolution

LYONNET, STANISLAS: Form Criticism II

MAASS, FERDINAND: Josephinism

MAIER, HANS: Historicism

MAISCH, INGRID: (with Anton Vögtle) Jesus Christ I, Salvation II

MARALDO, JOHN CHARLES: Baptists, Methodist Churches, Syncretism

MARCIC, RENÉ: Law IV

MARCUS, WOLFGANG: Arianism

MARLÉ, RENÉ: Demythologization I, II

MARTIN, NORBERT: (with Wigand Siebel) Sociology

MASSON, JOSEPH: Missions I

MAY, GEORG: Ecclesiastical Law I

MAYR, FRANZ KARL: Causality, Existence III A, Language

MEINHOLD, PETER: Presbyterian Churches, Protestantism, I, IV

MELLOR, ALEC: Freemasonry

METZ, JOHANN BAPTIST: Apologetics I, Miracle I, Political Theology, Religious Act

MEURERS, JOSEPH: World Picture

MICHL, JOHANNES: Apocrypha

MIKAT, PAUL: Church and State

MOLINARI, PAOLO: Saints III

MOLINSKI, WALDEMAR: Authority, Birth Control, Charity II, Commandments of the Church, Despair, Equity, Human Act, Indifferentism, Integralism, Law II, Life II, Marriage I, II, Merit, Necessity II, Obedience, Punishment (Capital), Responsibility, Scandal, Situation Ethics, Temptation, Truth II, Virginity, Vow

MÖLLER, B.: Leisure III

MÖLLER, JOSEPH: Person II A, Truth I

MONDEN, LOUIS: Miracle II

MÖRSDORF, KLAUS: Bishop IV, Cardinal, Clergy, Diocese, Ecclesiastical Authority, Ecclesiastical Law III, Ecclesiastical Office I, Forum, Hierarchy, Jurisdiction, Mass Stipend

MOUROUX, JEAN: Religious Experience

MUCK, OTTO: Science II, Scholasticism II E

MÜHLBAUER, REINHOLD: Education II

MÜLLER, MAX: Aristotelianism I, Education I, Freedom II, (with Alois Halder) Person I, (with Alois Halder) Science I

MÜLLER, KARLHEINZ: Qumran

MUÑOZ IGLESIAS, SALVADOR: Biblical Exegesis II B

MURPHY, EDWARD L.: Missions V

MUSSNER, FRANZ: New Testament Books II, V, VII, New Testament Theology III

NAUROIS, LOUIS DE: Ecclesiastical Penalties

NELL-BREUNING, OSWALD VON: Economic Ethics I, Social Movements, I, II, III, IV

NEUENZEIT, PAUL: Canon of Scripture

NEUHÄUSLER, ENGELBERT: New Testament Books IX

NEUNHEUSER, BURKHARD: Baptism I, Sacraments II

NIERMANN, ERNST: Indifference, Laity I, (with Miguel Benzo) II, (with François Houtart) Parish I, II, Priest, Providence, Relics, Saints II, Secularization II, Spiritualism, Spirituality III D 2, Supernaturalism

NORMAN, FRIEDRICH: Alexandrian School of Theology, Antiochene School of Theology, Cappadocian Fathers

OBERTI, ELISA: Art II

OELMÜLLER, WILLI: Religion I C

O'FARRELL, FRANCIS: (with Jörg Splett) Relation

OSTER, HENRI: Sunday

OVERHAGE, PAUL: Evolution I

PAREJA, FELIX M.: Islam

PESCH, RUDOLF: Antichrist, Form Criticism I, Jesus Christ II, Man (Anthropology) II

LIST OF CONTRIBUTORS

PIETSCH, MAX: Economic Ethics II, Industrialism

POST, WERNER: Anthropomorphism II, Ideology, Marxism I, Persecutions, Religion I B, Scepticism, Society IV, Theory and Practice, Tolerance

POUPARD, PAUL: Fideism, Traditionalism

POZO, CANDIDO: Dogma II

PRADO, JUAN: New Testament Books VIII

PÜNDER, MARIANNE: Social Movements V

PUNTEL, LOURENCINO BRUNO: (with Jörg Splett) Analogy of Being, Nihilism, Participation, Spirit, Unity

QUASTEN, JOHANNES: Patrology I

QUILES, ISMAEL: Pantheism

RAAB, HERIBERT: Enlightenment

RAHNER, KARL: Angel I, II, Atheism, Beatific Vision, Bible I B, Christianity I, Church III, IV, Church and World, Contrition, Conversion, Death, Devil II, Disposition, Dogma I, III, IV, Ecumenism III, Eschatology, Evolution II, Existence III B, Faith I, Freedom III, Grace II B, III, Grace and Freedom, Hell I, Heresy II, Incarnation, Indulgences, Jesus Christ IV, Last Things, Magisterium, Man (Anthropology) III, Missions II, Monogenism, Mystery, Order III, IV, Original Sin, Parousia II, Penance I, II, People of God, Person II C, Philosophy and Theology, Potentia Oboedientialis, Predestination II, Prophetism, Resurrection I A, C 2, D, Revelation I, II, IV, Salvation I, III B, C, IV A, C, Scripture and Tradition, Sin II, States of Man (Theological), Theologumenon, Theology I, II, Transcendental Theology, Trinity (Divine), Trinity in Theology, Unbelief, Virtue I, II, Works

RATZINGER, JOSEPH: Ascension of Christ, Resurrection II B

REDING, MARCEL: Materialism, World (Views of the)

REINDEL, KURT: Invasions (Barbarian), Middle Ages II A

REINER, HANS: Morality II

REISCH, ERICH: Charity III

RICHARDS, HUBERT J.: Biblical Commission

RICHTER, VLADIMIR: Natural Philosophy

RICKEN, FRIEDO: Platonism, Pre-Socratics, Stoicism

RIESENHUBER, KLAUS: Irrationalism, Natural Theology, Voluntarism

RINGEL, ERWIN: Psychology II, Psychotherapy

ROBLEDA, OLIS: Dispensation, Privilege

ROHNER, PETER: Will

ROLDÁN, ALEJANDRO: Religious Feeling

ROMMEN, HEINRICH A.: State

RONDET, HENRI: Nouvelle Théologie, Pelagianism, Predestination I

RUSSELL, JOHN: Entelechy

SALAVERRI, JOAQUÍN: Encyclicals

SAND, ALEXANDER: Person II B

SAURAS, EMILIO: Church V

SAUSER, EKKART: Archaeology II, Patrology III, Pilgrimage, Saints IV

SCHADE, HERBERT: Images

SCHAEFER, HANS: Health I

SCHAEFFLER, RICHARD: Philosophy I, II

SCHAUERTE, HEINRICH: Religious Customs

SCHEFFCZYK, LEO: Analogy of Faith, Concupiscence, Eucharist III, God I, Sacrifice II, Word of God

SCHEIT, HERBERT: Hylemorphism

SCHELKLE, KARL HERMANN: New Testament Theology II, New Testament Books IV, VI

SCHERER, ROBERT: Culture

SCHIFFERS, NORBERT: Religion I A

SCHIWY, GÜNTHER: Structuralism

SCHLETTE, ANTONIA RUTH: Race

SCHLETTE, HEINZ ROBERT: Colonialism, Empiricism, Individualism, Missions III, Monotheism, Nominalism, Religion III A, Religious Freedom

SCHMAUS, MICHAEL: Holy Spirit I, II, Mariology I, II, III, Pope I, Worship

SCHMID, JOSEPH: Biblical Exegesis I, Resurrection II A

SCHMITT, JOSEPH: Resurrection I B

SCHNACKENBURG, RUDOLF: New Testament Ethics

SCHNITH, KARL: Middle Ages I, III

SCHÖLLGEN, WERNER: Pastoral Medicine, Resistance

SCHOONBROOD, CLEMENS: Pragmatism

SCHOONENBERG, PIET: Sin I

SCHREINER, JOSEF: Bible I A 1

SCHREUDER, OSMUND: Religion II E

SCHULTE, RAPHAEL: Sacraments I

SCHULTZE, BERNHARD: Eastern Churches, Russian Religious Philosophy

SCHURR, VIKTOR: Pastoral Ministry

SCHUSTER, HEINZ: Pastoral Theology

SCHWAIGER, GEORG: Baroque I, Pope II

SCHWANK, BENEDIKT: Archaeology I, Old Testament History

SCHWEMMER, OSWALD: Act and Potency, Habitus, Logic

SEMMELROTH, OTTO: Ecclesiastical Office II, Martyrdom, Mediatorship, Sacrifice I, III

SIEBEL, WIGAND: (with Norbert Martin) Sociology

SILLEM, EDWARD: God, Attributes of

SIMONS, EBERHARD: Augustinianism, Dualism, Existence I, God II, Kerygma, Personalism, Sacred Times and Places, Scholasticism I, Spirituality III A

SMULDERS, PIETER: Baianism, Creation I, Order II

SMYTH, KEVIN: Bible II, Curia II, Zionism

SPECHT, RAINER: Baroque II

SPLETT, JÖRG: Agnosticism, (with Lourencino Bruno Puntel) Analogy of Being, Anthropomorphism I, Aristotelianism II, Body, Categories, Concept, Consciousness, Decision, Existence II, Good, (with Adolf Darlap) History I, Holy I, Humanism II, Idea, Immortality, Man (Anthropology) I, Meaning, Nature I A, Play,

Principle, Progress, (with Francis O'Farrell) Relation, Relativism, Saints I, Superstition II, Symbol, (with Walter Kern) Theodicy, Thought-Forms

SPRINGER, ROBERT H.: Taxation, Morality of
STAKEMEIER, EDUARD: Ecumenism VI A
STICKLER, ALFONS M.: Ecclesiastical Law II
STOCKMEIER, PETER: Constantinian Era, Early Church
SUAREZ-MURIAS, EDWARD L.: Health II
SUDBRACK, JOSEF: Prayer, Spirituality I, II, III C

TERÁN-DUTARI, JULIO: Peace
THOMA, CLEMENS: Judaism I, II, III, Judaism and Christianity
TOURNAY, RAYMOND J.: Old Testament Books IV
TRILLHAAS, WOLFGANG: Moral Theology II
TRUHLAR, KARL VLADIMIR: Discernment of Spirits, Holiness, Possession (Diabolical), Visions
TÜCHLE, HERMANN: Inquisition I, Investiture Controversy, Middle Ages II B, States of the Church (Papal States)

VAN STEENBERGHEN, FERNAND: Intellectualism

VERHEY, SIGISMUND: Poverty I, II
VERRA, VALERIO: Spinozism
VILLIGER, JOHANN BAPTIST: Schism IV
VÖGTLE, ANTON: Aeons, Bible III, (with Ingrid Maisch) Jesus Christ I, New Testament Theology I
VRIES, WILHELM DE: Patriarchate

WEBER, LEONHARD M.: Celibacy
WEGER, KARL-HEINZ: Tradition
WEIER, REINHOLD: Scholasticism II D
WEIGEL, GUSTAVE: Americanism
WETTER, FRIEDRICH: Franciscan Theology
WETTER, GUSTAV A.: Marxism II
WITTE, JOHANNES: Calvinism
WOLF, ERIK: Protestantism II
WOSCHITZ, KARL: Utopia
WULF, FRIEDRICH: Asceticism, Spirituality III E

ZALBA, MARCELLINO: Fasting
ZELLINGER, EDUARD: Psychology I
ZUMKELLER, ADOLAR: Augustinian School of Theology
ZWETSLOOT, HUGO J.: Inquisition II